THE LIBRARIANS'
GLOSSARY

of terms used in librarianship
and the book crafts

AND REFERENCE BOOK

THE LIBRARIANS' GLOSSARY

of terms used in librarianship
and the book crafts

AND REFERENCE BOOK

Leonard Montague Harrod

FELLOW OF THE LIBRARY ASSOCIATION

ANDRE DEUTSCH

A GRAFTON BOOK

THIS 3RD (REVISED) EDITION
FIRST PUBLISHED IN 1971 BY
ANDRE DEUTSCH LIMITED
105 GREAT RUSSELL STREET
LONDON WCI
COPYRIGHT © 1971 BY L. M. HARROD
ALL RIGHTS RESERVED
PRINTED IN GREAT BRITAIN
BY EBENEZER BAYLIS AND SON LTD
THE TRINITY PRESS
WORCESTER AND LONDON
ISBN 233 96013 9

The Librarians' Glossary was originally published
in 1938 and the 2nd (revised) edition in 1959 by
Grafton & Co.

Contents

Preface to First Edition

The need for an adequate glossary of terms used in librarianship has been felt by students of library work and by librarians in the performance of their duties for a long time. This work is an attempt to meet that need. It is primarily a glossary of *library* terms, but includes such subjects as printing, paper-making, publishing, binding, and illustrating, with which a librarian must be familiar, not only for the satisfactory performance of his professional duties, but also to meet the requirements of the Library Association's examinations. These other subjects have, therefore, been included, but only partially, because complete glossaries of these subsidiary subjects would not only be of immense size and beyond the purse of the average library assistant, but would be duplicating material which can be found in other books. The terms associated with these subjects have, therefore, been selected with the needs of the examination student and the practising librarian in mind.

This work has been compiled primarily for the use of students of librarianship who have always needed such a book at hand during their studies, and was intended to be of more immediate value for those preparing for the new Library Association syllabus, which included a section on terminology. The postponement of the adoption of this syllabus for a couple of years will not make the need for the book any the less.

It is anticipated that not only will the book be useful to public, university, county and school librarians, but that it will also find a place on the open shelves in reference libraries.

In certain subjects connected with librarianship, terms are used with different meanings by different people. In some cases it has been possible to give several definitions, in others the more usual definition and the one generally accepted has been used.

The classified lists of terms at the end of the book have been provided as a check-list for students, but they will also be useful as a reminder when trying to remember a term which is temporarily evasive.

I am indebted to my former Chief, W. C. Berwick Sayers, to my former colleague, Henry A. Sharp, and to Kenneth G. Hunt, for their valuable suggestions made when looking through the Classification, Cataloguing and Bibliography sections, respectively. Mr. Sharp has, in addition, permitted me to use the definitions which form an appendix to his *Cataloguing*. I am indebted also to Miss Helen M. Briggs for compiling the definitions of the terms used in palæography and archives.

I am grateful to the following publishers for permission to use definitions from certain books published by them: R. R. Bowker & Co. (Holden's *Bookman's Glossary*); G. E. Stechert & Co. (Hitchler's *Cataloguing for Small Libraries*); Spalding and Hodge, Ltd. (*Paper Terminology*); Allen and Unwin, Ltd. (Knight's *Business Man's Guide to Printing*); The Library Association (*A. A. Code*); United Typothetæ of America (*Dictionary of Graphic Arts Terms*); Grafton & Co. (Coutts and Stephen's *Library Bookbinding*, *Library Economics*).

Preface to Second Edition

Not until one compares the Library Association's examination papers of 1938 with those of 1956, or makes a systematic review of post-war library literature, does one realize the enormous progress that has taken place in the field of librarianship during this period.

When the first edition of the *Glossary* became out of print it was obvious that it would be unsatisfactory to reprint it. Complete revision was necessary, not only because of the development of the theory of librarianship and of library techniques, but also because of changes in the constitution and activities which library and bibliographical organizations have undergone.

The purpose and coverage of this edition of the *Glossary* are still the same but the scope has been very slightly widened to include some terms which, though not strictly limited to librarianship and the book crafts, are frequently met with by librarians in the course of their daily work. To find a satisfactory, or comprehensive definition of such is sometimes not easy.

This edition contains about 1,200 (75%) more entries than the first edition.

I am again grateful to friends for assistance with terms on certain subjects, and should like to express my great appreciation to the following for definitions of a few terms in fields in which they are specialists: Mr. W. Turner Berry for elucidating some printing terms; Mr. P. McGrath for definitions concerning British Government publications; Mr. B. Palmer for definitions of some terms used by Ranganathan; and Mr. F. A. Sharr for clarification of terms concerning county library work.

Singapore, November, 1958.

Preface to Third Edition

The second edition quickly went out of print but rather than re-print it, the publisher agreed that owing to the enormous development which had taken place since this edition had been prepared in the traditional field of librarianship and the new fields of knowledge which librarians have nowadays to be concerned with it, would be preferable once again to revise the work completely.

The extent of revision required was so great that it took much more time than was anticipated. The whole field covered has been gone over again to make the work more complete, and new subjects have been included.

In order that the book should be even more useful than in the past a number of headings are now included which do not lend themselves to 'definition'.

It was also found desirable to give more information than was necessary for a definition, and in many cases a 'definition' in the limited sense of the word either could not be used or would be totally inadequate. It is for these reasons that the title has been extended.

Librarianship has developed enormously in the last ten years, not only in its traditional areas, but has had to absorb new areas involving completely new techniques and the uses of equipment which has been developed to enable more work to be achieved with the minimum of extra manpower. This expansion is continuing. The whole field of librarianship and information services is now so wide that some areas are quite foreign to others, and in many cases specialization has become so great that one librarian or information officer is completely unfamiliar with the work and terminology of another.

Writings in English, wherever they originated, have been examined, and special attention has been given to American organizations, ideas and terminology as these are less familiar to English librarians.

This work could not have been revised without the assistance of numerous specialists, former colleagues at the School of librarianship, North-Western Polytechnic (especially John Morris with help on historical bookbinding and book-decoration terms), librarians of special and public libraries, and the secretaries of professional and learned societies all over the world, all of whom have readily given information on which definitions have been based. Their help is greatly appreciated.

A number of definitions in print have been included. I am grateful to Dr. Erhard Ühlein for permission to reproduce those marked (*Concepts . . .*) from his *Concepts of reprography*; to IBM United Kingdom Limited for those marked (*IBM*) from their *Reference manual*; to the late H. R. Verry for those marked (*Verry*) from his *Document copying and reproduction processes*, and to the Editor of the *Library Association Record* for those marked (*County libraries*) which appeared in the issue of that publication for August 1960.

June 1970

Acronyms and Abbreviations
in general use

Abbreviations other than of organizations are in the main sequence of definitions. Entries will usually be found in the main sequence under acronyms and sometimes under unpronounceable abbreviations, where these are easily remembered; where a full name appears to be more familiar, or more appropriate, entry is made under it. Entries in this list with a * do not have an entry in the main sequence; they are included here solely for the purposes of identification.

AACOBS   Australian Advisory Council on Bibliographical Sources.
AACR   Anglo-American Cataloguing Rules.*
AAL   Association of Assistant Librarians.
AALL   American Association of Law Libraries.
AALS   Association of American Library Schools.
AASL   American Association of School Librarians.
ABLS   Association of British Library Schools.
ABTAPL Association of British Theological and Philosophical Libraries.
ACM   Association for Computing Machinery.
ACRL   Association of College and Research Libraries.
ACT   Advisory Council on Technology.
ADBPA   Association pour le Développement des Bibliothèques Publiques en Afrique. *See entry under* ASSOCIATION FOR THE DEVELOPMENT OF PUBLIC LIBRARIES IN AFRICA.
ADI   American Documentation Institute.
AFIPS   American Federation of Information Processing Societies.
AHIL   Association of Hospital and Institution Libraries.
AID   Association Internationale des Documentalists et Techniciens de l'Information. *See entry under* International Association of Documentalists and Information Officers.
AIDBA   Association Internationale pour le Développement des Bibliothèques en Afrique. *See entry under* INTERNATIONAL ASSOCIATION FOR THE DEVELOPMENT OF LIBRARIES IN AFRICA.
AIInfSc   Associate of the Institute of Information Scientists.
AIL   Association of International Libraries.
AJL   Association of Jewish Libraries.

ALA   American Library Association, and Associate of the (British) Library Association.

ALAA   Associate of the Library Association of Australia.*

ALCL   Association of London Chief Librarians.

ALJH   Association of Libraries of Judaica and Hebraica in Europe.

ALTA   American Library Trustee Association.

AMCL   Association of Metropolitan Chief Librarians.

AMLS   Master of Arts in Library Science.*

AMMLA   American Merchant Marine Library Association.

ANRT   Association Nationale de la Recherche Technique.

APLA   Authors' and Publishers' Lending Right Association Committee. *See entry under* PUBLIC LENDING RIGHT.

ARC   Agricultural Research Council.

ARL   Association of Research Libraries.

ASA   American Standards Association. *See entry under* American National Standards Institute, Inc.

ASD   Adult Services Division of the American Library Association.

ASD   Association Suisse de Documentation.

ASFEC   The Arab States Fundamental Education Centre.

ASIS   American Society for Information Science.

ASL   American Association of State Libraries.

ASTIA   Armed Services Technical Information Agency; now the Defense Documentation Center.

ATALA   Association pour l'Etude et de la Linguistique Appliquée.

ATLA   American Theological Library Association.

BASc   Bachelor of Applied Science.*

BASIC   Biological Abstracts Subjects In Context.

B.BIBL   Bachelier en Bibliotheconomie et en Bibliographie.

BC   Borough Council.

BLSc   Bachelor of Library Science.*

BHI   British Humanities Index.

BIB   Biennale of Illustrations Bratislava.

BIOSIS   Bio-Sciences Information Service of Biological Abstracts.

BIRS   British Institute of Recorded Sound Ltd.

BM   British Museum.

BML   British Museum Library.

BN   Bibliothèque Nationale.

BNB   British National Bibliography.

BNBC   British National Book Centre.

BPBIRA   British Paper and Board Industry Research Association.

BRA   British Records Association.

BSA   Bibliographical Society of America.

BScB   Bachelier ès Science Bibliothéconomie.*

BSI   British Standards Institution. *See entry under* STANDARDS.

BSIB   British Society for International Bibliography.

BTI   British Technology Index.

BUCOP   British Union Catalogue of Periodicals.

CAB   Commonwealth Agricultural Bureaux.

CALL   Canadian Association of Law Libraries.

*CBI   Cumulative Book Index.**

CC   County Council.

CCC   Central Classification Committee of the FID.

CDCR   Center for Documentation and Communication Research.

CEDI   European Documentation and Information Centre.

CEN   Comité Européen de Coordination des Normes. *See entry under European Committee for Co-ordination of Standards.*

CERN   European Organization for Nuclear Research.

CETIS   Centre Européen pour le Traitement de l'Information Scientifique. *See entry under* CETIS.

CFSTI   Clearinghouse for Federal Scientific and Technical Information.

CIA   Conseil International des Archives. *See entry under* INTERNATIONAL COUNCIL ON ARCHIVES.

CIB   Conseil Internationale du Batiment pour la Recherche, l'Etude et la Documentation. International Council for Building Research, Studies and Documentation.

CICRIS   Co-operative Industrial and Commercial Reference and Information Service. *See entry under* CICRIS.

CIDB   International Council for Building Documentation. *See entry under* INTERNATIONAL COUNCIL FOR BUILDING RESEARCH STUDIES AND DOCUMENTATION.

CIDESA   The International Centre for African Social and Economic Documentation. *See entry under* CIDESA.

CLA   Canadian Library Association – L'Association Canadienne des Bibliothèques. The form CLA–ACB is also used.*

CLA   Catholic Library Association.

CLR   Council on Library Resources, Inc.

CML   Central Music Library.

CMR   Committee on Manpower Resources for Science and Technology.

CNLA   Council of National Library Associations.

CNRS   Centre National de la Recherche Scientifique et Technique. *See entry under* CNRS.

CPL   Council of Planning Librarians.

CRG   Classification Research Group.
CRIS   Command Retrieval Information System.
CRL   Center for Research Libraries.
CROSS   Computerized Rearrangement of Special Subjects.
CRSG   Classification Research Study Group.
CSD   Children's Services Division of the American Library Association.
CSIRO   Commonwealth Scientific and Research Organization.
CSL   Circle of State Librarians.
CSLA   Church and Synagogue Library Association.
CSP   Council for Scientific Policy.
CTFE   Colleges of Technology and Further Education Sub-Section of the University and Research Section of the Library Association.
DC   Decimal Classification.
DDC   Defense Documentation Center. Dewey Decimal Classification.
DLSEF   Division of Library Services and Educational Facilities, U.S. Office of Education.*
DOCA   Section Documentation Automatique (Automatic Documentation Section). A working party of CETIS (*q.v.*).
DRC   Defence Research Committee.*
DSIR   Department of Scientific and Industrial Research.
EALA   East African Library Association.
EDUCOM   Interuniversity Communications Council.
EFLA   Educational Film Library Association.
ERIC   Educational Resources Reading Center. *See entry under* ERIC.
ESEA   Elementary and Secondary Education Act.*
ETC   European Translations Centre.
FIAB   Fédération Internationale des Associations de Bibliothécaires. *See entry under* INTERNATIONAL FEDERATION OF LIBRARY ASSOCIATIONS.
FID   Fédération Internationale de Documentation. *See entries under* INTERNATIONAL FEDERATION FOR DOCUMENTATION, AND UNIVERSAL DECIMAL CLASSIFICATION.
FIInfSc   Fellow of the Institute of Information Scientists.*
FIP   Fédération Internationale des Phonothèque. *See entry under* INTERNATIONAL FEDERATION OF RECORD LIBRARIES.
FIT   Fédération Internationale des Traducteurs. *See entry under* INTERNATIONAL FEDERATION OF TRANSLATORS.
FLA   Fellow of the Library Association.*
FLAA   Fellow of the Library Association of Australia.*
FLAI   Fellow of the Library Association of Ireland.*
FLIC   Film Library Information Council.

FLIP   Film Library Instantaneous Presentation.

FNZLA   Fellow of the New Zealand Library Association.*

FSALA   Fellow of the South African Library Association.*

HADIS   Huddersfield and District Information Service. *See entry under* HADIS.

HALDIS   Halifax and District Information Service. *See entry under* HALDIS.

HATRICS   Hampshire Technical Research Industrial and Commercial Service. *See entry under* HATRICS.

HERTIS   Hertfordshire County Council Technical Information Service. *See entry under* HERTIS.

HILC   Hampshire Inter-Library Center.

HMSO   Her Majesty's Stationery Office. *See entry under* PARLIAMENTARY PUBLICATIONS.

HULTIS   Hull Technical Interloan Scheme. *See entry under* HULTIS.

IAALD   International Association of Agricultural Librarians and Documentalists.

IABLA   Inter-American Bibliographical and Library Association.

IALL   International Association of Law Libraries.

IAMCR   International Association for Mass Communication Research.

IAML   International Association of Music Librarians.

IASLIC   Indian Association of Special Libraries and Information Centres.

IATL   International Association of Theological Libraries.

IATUL   International Association of Technological University Libraries.

IBBD   Instituto Brasileño de Bibliografía e Documentaçao. Brazilian Institute of Bibliography and Documentation.

IBBY   International Board on Books for Young People.*

IBFD   International Bureau of Fiscal Documentation.

IC   Implementation Committee.*

ICA   International Council on Archives.

ICC   International Children's Centre.

ICCP   International Conference on Cataloguing Principles.

ICOM   International Council of Museums.

ICLS   Irish Central Library for Students.

ICRSC   International Council for Research in the Sociology of Co-operation.

ICSI   International Conference on Scientific Information.

ICSSD   International Committee for Social Sciences Documentation.

ICSU   International Council of Scientific Unions.

IDC   International Documentation Centre.

IEC   International Electrotechnical Commission.*

IFA   International Fiscal Association.*

IFD   International Federation for Documentation.

IFIP   International Federation for Information Processing.

IFLA   International Federation of Library Associations.

IGO   Inter-governmental Organizations.

ILAS   Inter-related Logic-Accumulating Scanner.

IMS   International Musicological Society.

INTREX   Information Transfer Exchange.

IPA   International Publishers Association.

IR   Information retrieval.

IRA   International Reading Association.

IRO   International Relations Office (of the American Library Association).*

IRT   Institute of Reprographic Technology.

ISA   International Federation of National Standardizing Associations. *See entry under* INTERNATIONAL ORGANIZATION FOR STANDARDIZATION.

ISAD   Information Science and Automation Division (of the American Library Association).

ISBN   International standard book number. *See entry under* Standard Book Number.

ISLIC   Israel Society of Special Libraries and Information Centres.*

ISO   International Organization for Standardization.

ITU   International Telecommunications Union.*

IYL   International Youth Library.

JFR   Joint Fiction Reserve

JLA   Jewish Librarians Association.

KC   The Kyle Classification. *See entry under* CLASSIFICATION FOR SOCIAL SCIENCES.

L of C   Library of Congress.

LA   Library Association. Library automation.

LAA   Library Association of Australia.

LACAP   Latin American Cooperative Acquisitions Project. *See entry under* LACAP.

LAD   Library Administration Division of the American Library Association.

LADSIRLAC   Liverpool and District Scientific, Industrial and Research Advisory Council. *See entry under* LADSIRLAC.

LAI   Library Association of Ireland.

LASER   London & South Eastern Library Region.

LC   Library of Congress.

LCLA   Lutheran Church Library Association.

LED   Library Education Division (of the ALA).

LINOSCO   Libraries of North Staffordshire in Co-operation. *See entry under* LINOSCO.

LIST   Library Information Service for Teesside. *See entry under* LIST.

LPRC   Library Publications Relations Council.

LSA   Library Science Abstracts.

LTP   Library Technology Program. (*Formerly* Library Technology Project.)

LULOP   London Union List of Periodicals.

MAinLS   Master of Arts in Library Science.*

MAGB   Microfilm Association of Great Britain.

MALS   Master of Arts in Library Science.*

MARLF   Middle Atlantic Regional Library Federation. *See entry under* MARLF.

MBSJC   Metropolitan Boroughs Standing Joint Committee. *See entry under* ASSOCIATION OF METROPOLITAN CHIEF LIBRARIANS.

MILC   Midwest Inter-Library Center. *See entry under* CENTER FOR RESEARCH LIBRARIES.

MISLIC   Mid-Staffordshire Libraries in Co-operation. *See entry under* MISLIC.

MLA   Medical Library Association. Music Library Association.

MRC   Medical Research Council.

MSC   Metropolitan Special Collection. *See entry under* ASSOCIATION OF METROPOLITAN CHIEF LIBRARIANS.

MSinLS   Master of Science in Library Science.*

MSLS   Master of Science in Library Science.*

MSLSc   Master of Science in Library Science.*

NACL   National Advisory Commission on Libraries.

NAL   National Agricultural Library.

NALGO   National and Local Government Officers Association.*

NANTIS   Nottingham and Nottinghamshire Technical Information Service. *See entry under* NANTIS.

NAS – NRC   National Academy of Sciences – National Research Council.

NBL   National Book League.

NBN   National Book Number.

NBS   National Bureau of Standards.

NCL   National Central Library.

NCRLC   National Committee on Regional Library Co-operation.

NEDL   New England Deposit Library.

NELL North East Lancashire Libraries. *See entry under* NELL.

NELTAS North East Lancashire Technical Advisory Services. *See entry under* NELTAS.

NFSAIS National Federation of Science Abstracting and Indexing Services.

NGO Non-governmental Organizations.*

NIDER The Netherlands Institute of Documentation and Filing (Nederlands Instituut voor Documentatie en Registratuur).

NJFR National Joint Fiction Reserve. *See entry under* JOINT FICTION RESERVE.

NLA National Libraries Authority.

NLB National Library for the Blind.

NLL National Lending Library for Science and Technology.

NLLST National Lending Library for Science and Technology.

NMA National Microfilm Association.

NPAC National Program for Acquisitions and Cataloguing.

NRCD National Reprographic Centre for Documentation.

NRLSI National Reference Library of Science and Invention.

NLM National Library of Medicine.

NTBL Nuffield Talking Book Library for the Blind.

NUCMC National Union Catalog of Manuscript Collections.

NVBF Scandinavian Association of Scientific Librarians.*

OFR Office for Recruitment (ALA).*

OLE Office for Library Education (ALA).*

ONULP Ontario New Universities Library Project. *See entry under* ONULP.

ORD Office for Research and Development (ALA).

OS Ordnance Survey.

OST Office for Science and Technology.*

OSTI Office for Scientific and Technical Information.

PANSDOC The Pakistan National Scientific and Technical Documentation Centre.

PATRA The Printing, Packaging and Allied Trades Research Association.

PIRA Printing Industry Research Association.

PLA Private Libraries Association. Public Library Association.

PLR Public lending right.

PNLA Pacific Northwest Library Association.*

RDC Rural District Council.

RSD Reference Services Division of the American Library Association.

RSIS Reference, Special and Information Section of the Library Association.

RTSD Resources and Technical Services of the American Library Association.

SAA Society of American Archivists.

SAALIC Swindon Area Association of Libraries for Industry and Commerce.

SALALM Seminars on the Acquisition of Latin American Library Materials. *See entry under* SALALM.

SBN Standard Book Number.

SCANDOC Scandinavian Documentation Center. *See entry under* SCANDOC.

SCEL Standing Committee on Education in Librarianship.*

SCI-TECH Science-Technology Division of the Special Libraries Association.

SCL Scottish Central Library.

SCOLLUL Standing Conference of Librarians of Libraries of the University of London. *See entry under* SCOLLUL.

SCOLMA Standing Conference on Library Materials on Africa. *See entry under* SCOLMA.

SCONUL Standing Conference of National and University Libraries. *See entry under* SCONUL.

SCOTAPLL Standing Conference on Theological and Philosophical Libraries in London. *See entry under* SCOTAPLL.

SDI Selective dissemination of information.

SINTO Sheffield Interchange Organisation. *See entry under* SINTO.

SLA School Library Association. Scottish Library Association. Special Libraries Association.

SLIC Selective Listing In Combination. *See entry under* SLIC INDEX.

SM Master of Science.*

SMCCL Society of Municipal and County Chief Librarians.*

TALIC Tyneside Association of Libraries for Industry and Commerce. *See entry under* TALIC.

TTS Teletypesetting.

UCC Universal Copyright Convention.

UDC University Decimal Classification. Urban District Council.

UNESCO United Nations Educational, Scientific and Cultural Organization. *See entry under* UNESCO.

USASI United States of America Standards Institute.

USBE United States Book Exchange. *See entry under* USBE.

USGPO United States Government Printing Office.*

USIA United States Information Agency.

USIS United States Information Service.

VINITI   Vsesoyuznyi Institut Nauchnoi Tekhnicheskoi Informatsii (All-Union Institute of Scientific and Technical Information). *See entry under* VINITI.

VOLS   Voluntary Overseas Libraries Service.

WALIC   Wiltshire Association of Libraries of Industry and Commerce.

WANDPETLS   Wandsworth Public, Educational and Technical Library Services.

YASD   Young Adult Services Division of the American Library Association.

YEWTIC   Yorkshire (East and West Ridings) Technical Information Centre.

Glossary

The word-by-word method is used.

Hyphenated words are arranged as if separate words if the part preceding the hyphen has a separate meaning; in cases where words with hyphens are sometimes spelt as one word without the hyphen, the practice has been to arrange these as one word.

Abbreviations consisting of letters separated by points, and unpronouceable acronyms whether so punctuated or not, are arranged at the beginning of each letter sequence. Those consisting of two or more letters, and pronounceable acronyms, are arranged as if whole words in their normal place in the letter sequence.

36-LINE BIBLE. Printed in Latin anonymously at Bamberg c. 1460, probably by Heinrich Keffer. It has 882 printed leaves, two columns to a page, 36 lines in each column, and is usually bound in three volumes.

42-LINE BIBLE. *See* MAZARIN BIBLE.

48-LINE BIBLE. The Bible printed by Johann Fust and Peter Schöffer at Mainz on 14th August 1462. The type, a medium gothic of humanistic design, was probably cut specially for this work in which it first appears. Many copies were printed on vellum.

A4 SIZE. A European standard size of paper, 210 × 297 mm ($8\frac{1}{4}$ × $11\frac{11}{16}$ inches). *See also* DIN, PAPER SIZES.

A5 SIZE. A European standard size of paper, 148 × 210 mm ($5\frac{13}{16}$ × $8\frac{1}{4}$ inches). *See also* DIN, PAPER SIZES.

A7 LIBRARY CARD. Standard size card of 74 × 105 mm ($2\frac{7}{8}$ × $4\frac{1}{8}$ inches), eight of which can be cut from a DIN A4 sheet of 210 × 297 mm ($8\frac{1}{4}$ × $11\frac{11}{16}$ inches). Also called 'A7 size card'. *See also* CARD, DIN, PAPER SIZES, STANDARD SIZE CARD.

AACOBS. Acronym for the AUSTRALIAN ADVISORY COUNCIL ON BIBLIOGRAPHICAL SERVICES (*q.v.*).

A.B.C.   Abridged building classification for architects, builders and civil engineers. See INTERNATIONAL COUNCIL FOR BUILDING RESEARCH, STUDIES AND DOCUMENTATION.

ABTAPL.   Abbreviation for Association of British Theological and Philosophical Libraries. Founded in October 1956 on the recommendation of the International Association of Theological Libraries to promote the interests of libraries, scholars and librarians in these fields and to foster co-operation between them. One of its main objects is to make the bibliographical resources of constituent members as widely known as possible. Publishes *Bulletin* (irreg.). *See also* SCOTAPLL.

A.C.S.   (*Pl.* A.Cs.S.) (autograph card signed).   A card wholly in the handwriting of the signer.

A.D.S. (autograph document signed).   A document entirely in the handwriting of the signer.

A.L.   *See* A.L.S.

A.L.S. (autograph letter signed).   A letter entirely in the handwriting of the signer. If unsigned it is referred to by the letters 'A.L.'; if written by someone else but signed, by 'L.S.'; if typed and signed by hand, by 'T.L.S.'.

A.Ms.S. (*Pl.* A.Mss.S.) (autograph manuscript signed).   A manuscript wholly in the handwriting of the signer.

ANRT   Acronym for Association Nationale de la Recherche Technique. A French association which is particularly concerned with problems of technical information.

A.N.S. (*Pl.* A.Ns.S.) (autograph note signed).   A note wholly in the handwriting of the signer.

AP   Abbreviation for AUTHOR'S PROOF (*q.v.*).

ASD   Acronym for Association Suisse de Documentation. The Swiss Association for Documentation; it was formed in 1939 after having been in existence as a study group since 1930. Publishes *Kleine Mitteilungen/Petites Communications* (irr.).

A.T.S.   Abbreviation for Animal Tub-sized. *See* TUB-SIZING.

ABBREVIATED CARD.   A catalogue card which gives an abbreviated entry.

ABBREVIATED CATALOGUE ENTRY.   A catalogue entry (title, subject, translator, etc.) which does not give as much information as the main entry card. *See also* ADDED ENTRY.

ABERRANT COPY.   One in which binding or machining errors, and not merely defects, occur, and the correct state of which can be recognized.

ABRIDGED DECIMAL CLASSIFICATION.   An abridgement of

Dewey's *Decimal Classification* intended for use in small and slowly growing libraries.

ABRIDGED EDITION. An edition in which the author's text is reduced in length, or which summarizes the original text of a work. *See also* EXPURGATED EDITION.

ABRIDGEMENT. *Synonymous with* EPITOME (*q.v.*).

ABSOLUTE LOCATION. *See* FIXED LOCATION.

ABSOLUTE SIZE. *See* EXACT SIZE.

ABSORBENCY. The ability of paper to absorb printing ink. This quality varies widely between different papers.

ABSORBENT PAPER. Paper having the quality of absorbing and retaining ink or other liquid.

ABSTRACT. 1. A form of current bibliography in which sometimes books, but mainly contributions to periodicals, are summarized: they are accompanied by adequate bibliographical descriptions to enable the publications or articles to be traced, and are frequently arranged in classified order. They may be in the language of the original or be translated into English or some other language. Periodicals which contain only abstracts are known as journals of abstracts or abstract journals. Abstracts may be *indicative*, mainly directing to the original, *informative*, giving much information about the original, summarizing the principal arguments and giving the principal data, or *evaluative*, when they comment on the worth of the original. A *general* abstract is one which covers all essential points in an article, and is provided where the interests of readers are varied and known to the abstractor only in general terms. A *selective* abstract contains a condensation of such parts of an article known to be pertinent to the needs of the clientele and are prepared by a librarian (a) for the executives, research workers and specialists within his organization or those normally making use of his library services, (b) in response to a request for a literature search, or (c) to keep the staff of the organization or users of the services informed of developments in their field as revealed in the daily or periodical press, documents or reports. An *author* abstract is one written by the author of the original article. A *comprehensive abstracting service* endeavours to abstract every publication and article appearing in its subject field, whereas a *selective abstracting service* selects for abstracting only those publications and articles which it considers are likely to be of use to a specific class of reader. 2. The individual entry. 3. In documentary literature, three types of abstracts are found, (a) *traditional abstract*, a literary-style statement of the essential qualities of a work such as a book or periodical, and which may be descriptive or informative; (b) an *extract* from the original which is intended to provide its important subject matter; (c) a *telegraphic abstract*, a detailed index composed of (i) significant words selected from the document, (ii) code symbols called 'role indicators' which supply a context for the selected words, and (iii) punctuation symbols which separate and group the words and role indicators in various units as does conventional punctuation. An *auto-abstract* is an extract made by a machine. 4. (*n.*) An epitome or summary of a document. An abstract may be locative, illative, indicative or informative. A *locative abstract* (used solely in a few legal libraries) specifies the place where the original document may be found. An *illative abstract* (used solely in a few legal libraries) specifies the general nature of the material in the document. An *informative abstract* includes and specifies all pertinent material in the original document, summarizing all relevant arguments, data and conclusions. An *indicative abstract* points out what is in the original document, but usually does not include any of the material; from this the user determines whether or not to consult the original. 5. Printers' type, the design of the face of which is based on mechanical drawing, with more or less straight edges and lines of uniform thickness, having no serifs (sans-serif) or square serifs of the same weight as the letter (block-serif). Futura, Lydian and Optima are examples of sans-serif, and Beton, Cairo, Karnak and Memphis of block-serif. *See also* SYNOPSIS, TYPE FACE.

ABSTRACT BULLETIN.   A publication, produced by any duplication, printing, or other means, which consists of abstracts. Also called 'Abstract journal'.

ABSTRACT JOURNAL.   *See* ABSTRACT.

ABSTRACTING SERVICE.   The preparation of abstracts, usually in a limited field, by an individual, an industrial organization for restricted use, or a commercial organization; the abstracts being published and supplied regularly to subscribers. Also the organization producing the abstracts. Such services may be either comprehensive or selective.

ABSTRACTION.   The mental process of dividing and grouping which is involved in classifying.

ACADEMIC LIBRARIES.   Those of universities, university colleges, and all other institutions forming part of, or associated with, institutions of higher education.

ACANTHUS.   An ornament, representing two acanthus leaves pointing different ways, used in tooling book-bindings.

ACCESS.   1. In information retrieval (i) a device or method whereby a document may be found; (ii) permission and opportunity to use a document (*IBM*); (iii) the approach to any means of storing information, e.g. index, bibliography, catalogue, electronic computer.

ACCESSION. To enter in an ACCESSIONS REGISTER (*q.v.*) particulars of each book in the order of its acquisition.

ACCESSION BOOK. *See* ACCESSIONS REGISTER.

ACCESSION CARD. *See* ACCESSIONS REGISTER.

ACCESSION DATE. The date on which a publication is entered in the ACCESSIONS REGISTER (*q.v.*).

ACCESSION DEPARTMENT. *See* CATALOGUING DEPARTMENT.

ACCESSION NUMBER. The number given a book from the ACCESSIONS REGISTER (*q.v.*). It may also be a number given to an article in a periodical, or other document, which is indexed by the Uniterm Concept Co-ordination System. *See also* UNITERM CONCEPT CO-ORDINATION INDEXING.

ACCESSION ORDER. The arrangement of books on the shelves according to the order of their addition to a class; a numerical and chronological, as distinguished from a classified, arrangement.

ACCESSION PART OF THE CRITICISM NUMBER. *See* ASSOCIATED BOOK.

ACCESSION RECORD. *See* ACCESSIONS REGISTER.

ACCESSION SLIP. *See* PROCESS SLIP.

ACCESSION STAMP. A rubber stamp which is impressed on the back of a title-page; when the information is written in the appropriate panels of which the stamp is comprised, it gives much information concerning the records, and processing, of the individual book.

ACCESSIONS. A group term indicating additions to the stock of a library.

ACCESSIONS CATALOGUE. *Synonymous with* ACCESSIONS REGISTER (*q.v.*).

ACCESSIONS LIST. *See* ACCESSIONS REGISTER.

ACCESSIONS REGISTER. The chief record of the books added to a library. Books are numbered progressively as they are added to stock and entered in the register. It may be in book form or on cards, and may give a condensed description of the acquisition and history of each book from its reception to its withdrawal. Materials other than books which are added permanently to stock and of which records should be kept are similarly recorded. Not to be confused with ACQUISITION RECORD (*q.v.*).

ACCESSIONS SECTION. A section of a cataloguing or processing department which is concerned with accessioning library materials.

ACCIDENT. *See* PREDICABLES, FIVE.

ACHROMATIC LENS. One which is corrected for black and white photography.

ACID BLAST. The spraying of half-tone and zinc plates with acid as part of the etching process. This results in a sharper image.

ACID-FREE PAPER. In principle, paper which contains no free acid or having a pH value (when determined by the standard method) of 7 or more. Commercial practice permits a limited amount of acid under this designation. *See also* pH VALUE.

ACID RESIST. An acid-proof protective coating which is applied to metal plates before etching.

ACQUISITION. The processes of acquiring, or the department concerned with acquiring, books for a library. *See also* FARMINGTON PLAN, SCANDIA PLAN.

ACQUISITION DEPARTMENT. The department of a library concerned with the ordering of books and possibly their cataloguing and processing also. Often other functions such as obtaining books by exchange or gift, administration of serials and binding are undertaken. One in which ACQUISITION WORK (*q.v.*) is performed (American). *See also* CATALOGUING DEPARTMENT, ORDER DEPARTMENT, TECHNICAL SERVICES DEPARTMENT.

ACQUISITION RECORD. A record of all books and other material added or in process of being added; it is usually kept in alphabetical order. It may be (1) in two parts consisting of (a) a file of orders completed and of orders outstanding, and (b) a register of periodicals – including government publications – received, or (2) separate files for each of these records. If a DEAD FILE (*q.v.*) is kept this would also be considered a part of the acquisitions record (American).

ACQUISITION WORK. The work of book selection, ordering, obtaining by gift or exchange, serials control, and rebinding (American).

ACQUISITIONS OFFICER. An assistant who undertakes the duties necessary for acquiring new books for a library.

ACROGRAPHY. A method of producing relief surfaces on metal or stone by means of tracing with chalk, for making electrotype or stereotype plates.

ACRONYM. A word formed from the initial letter or letters of each of the successive parts of the name of an organization, group or term, e.g. Neddy (National Economic Development Council), UNESCO (United Nations Educational Scientific and Cultural Organization), Asfec (The Arab States Fundamental Education Centre), FLIP (Film Library Instantaneous Presentation), YEWTIC (Yorkshire (East and West Ridings) Technical Information Centre).

ACROPHONY. In pictographic writing, the principle that the value of each consonant is the value of the first letter of its name, as the *b* of *beth*, the *g* of *gimel*, and the *d* of *daleth*.

ACTING EDITION. An edition of a play which gives directions concerning exits, entrances, properties, etc. It is intended for actors and is often published in a limp cover, usually of paper.

ACTS. *See* PUBLIC LIBRARIES ACTS.

ACTUAL ARRANGEMENT. *See* IDEAL ARRANGEMENT.

Ad loc. Abbreviation for *ad locum* (*Lat.* 'At the place cited').

ADAPTATION. 1. A book that has been re-written or edited, wholly or in part, for a particular purpose such as for reading by children when the original was intended for adults, or a novel adapted for dramatic presentation. Not to be confused with an abridgement or EPITOME (*q.v.*). 2. A work re-written or presented in another intellectual form to serve a different purpose from the original version, or converted into a different literary form (IFLA).

ADAPTER. One who adapts a literary work by simplifying the text, omitting passages, or changing its form, e.g. novel into play.

ADD-TO-CARDS WORK. Data which is to be added to cards already in a catalogue. Elements which are subject to change, such as a statement of holdings, are usually entered in pencil. This work is usually performed by clerical assistants.

ADDAMS AWARD, JANE. Awarded annually by the Jane Addams Peace Association and the Women's International League for Peace and Freedom to the children's book of the year best combining literary merit, themes of brotherhood, and creative solutions to problems.

ADDED COPIES. Duplicate copies of titles already in stock. Not to be confused with ADDED EDITION (*q.v.*).

ADDED EDITION. A different edition from the one already in the library.

ADDED ENTRY. 1. A secondary catalogue entry, i.e. any other than the MAIN ENTRY (*q.v.*). Where printed cards are used, it is a duplicate of the main entry, with the addition of a heading for subject, title, editor, series, or translator. When printed cards are not used, the added entry is formed from the main entry by the omission of all or part of the imprint and collation, and sometimes of sub-titles, and the addition of an appropriate heading. It must not be confused with a CROSS REFERENCE (*q.v.*). Added entries may be made for editor, translator, title, subjects, series, illustrator, translator, etc., and in the case of music, for arranger, librettist, title, medium, form, etc. additionally. *See also* GENERAL SECONDARY. 2. The heading chosen for an added entry.

ADDED TITLE ENTRY. An entry, not being a main entry, made under the title for books with distinctive titles or in cases where title entries would be an advantage, such as anonymous works.

ADDED TITLE-PAGE. A title-page additional to the one from which a main entry for a catalogue entry is made. It may precede or follow the one chosen and may be more general, such as a series title-page, or may be equally general, as a title-page in another language, and placed either at the beginning or end of a book.

ADDENDUM (*Pl.* ADDENDA). 1. Matter included in a book after the text has been set. It is printed separately and is inserted at the beginning or end of the text; it is less extensive than a SUPPLEMENT (*q.v.*). 2. A slip added to a printed book. *See also* CORRIGENDA. *Synonymous with* APPENDIX.

ADDITION. (*Classification*) The simple extension of an existing ARRAY (*q.v.*), either by interpolation or extrapolation.

ADDITION. (*Noun.*) A book or other item that has been obtained for addition to the stock of the library. This term is sometimes used to refer to such items before they have been accessioned; this is, strictly, incorrect. *See also* ADDITIONS, LIST OF.

ADDITIONS, LIST OF. A list of recent books added to a library's stock. It may be in alphabetical, classified, or accession order.

ADDRESS. 1. A label, name or number which designates a register, a location, or a device in a computer where information is stored. 2. That part of an instruction in a computer programme which specifies the register, location or device upon which the operation is to be performed (*IBM*).

ADEQUATE DESCRIPTION, PRINCIPLE OF. The provision of enough information in a catalogue entry to enable a reader to make a right choice of books. *See also* CATALOGUING, PRINCIPLES OF.

ADJUSTABLE CLASSIFICATION. A scheme of classification designed by James Duff Brown in 1897. It was of little value, as the provision for new subjects was by leaving blank certain numbers in the notation. It was superseded by his SUBJECT CLASSIFICATION (*q.v.*).

ADJUSTABLE PERIODICALS LISTS. A list, consisting of the titles of periodicals typed or printed on small strips of card which are kept in position by xylonite strips attached to a wooden backing and framed, or in a visible index.

ADJUSTABLE SHELF. A shelf whose position may be adjusted to accommodate books of varying heights. *See also* 'LUNDIA' SHELVING, TONKS FITTINGS.

ADJUSTABLE SHELVING. Shelves which may be raised or lowered at will. Shelving which enables this to be done while the books are still on them are the most useful in libraries. STORAGE SHELVING (*q.v.*), requiring the use of nuts and bolts, is not normally used because of the inconvenience of adjusting the shelves, which go into slots cut in the ends of the shelves as the latter are pushed into position. Although most modern shelving restricts adjustability to one inch there are some kinds which make closer intervals of adjustment possible. The most convenient form of adjustable steel shelving to operate, and which also gives unrestricted adjustability, is the bracket type where the position of the shelves can be altered by moving a small spring lever built into the bracket. Wooden shelving is rendered adjustable by using Tonks fittings consisting of slotted strips inserted in the shelf uprights, into the slots of which studs are placed to support the shelves, by resting shelves on wooden pegs inserted in holes in the uprights, or by using the Lundia shelving which consists of thin metal rods with turned ends which are inserted into holes in the uprights and the grooved ends of the shelves sliding over the projecting part of the rods. *See also* BRACKET SHELVING, CANTILEVER SHELVING, SLOTTED SHELVING.

ADMINISTRATIVE BOARD. *Synonymous with* ADMINISTRATIVE COUNCIL (*q.v.*).

ADMINISTRATIVE COUNCIL. A committee of the officers and faculty of an American college whose function is largely legislative and policy-making. It is appointed and elected by the president and faculty, and is usually advisory to the president in administrative matters, but it may exercise considerable authority in its own right. Also called 'Administrative board', 'Prudential committee'.

ADMINISTRATIVE OFFICE ASSISTANT. In American libraries, a person, such as a business manager or secretary to the Chief Librarian or Director, who performs work of a specialized nature but does not require to have a library training.

ADOLESCENT LIBRARY. One which is provided for the use of adolescents, usually as a bridge between the children's department and the adult department of a public library.

ADOPTION OF THE PUBLIC LIBRARIES ACTS. The decision of the local authority to take the necessary administrative and legal steps to provide library facilities as permitted by law.

ADULT DEPARTMENT. The department of a library which provides books for the use of adults.

ADULT SERVICES DIVISION. A Division of the American Library Association, having been established in 1957 as the Adult Education

Division. It is concerned with those library services designed to provide continuing educational, recreational, and cultural development for adults in all types of library. Abbreviated ASD. Publishes *Newsletter – Adult Services Division* (q.), *Library Services to Labor* (2 p.a.), both free to membs.

ADVANCE COPY (SHEET). A copy of a book, usually bound, but sometimes in sheets, to serve as a proof of the binder's work, for review, notice, advertising or other purposes.

ADVERTISEMENT FILE. A file of advertisements, usually arranged by the name of firm or of product. Such files are most often maintained in a firm's library or advertising agency.

ADVISER, READERS'. *See* READERS' ADVISER.

ADVISORY COUNCIL. *See* LIBRARY ADVISORY COUNCIL.

ADVISORY COUNCIL ON SCIENTIFIC POLICY. The 1949–50 annual report of this body recommended a central library service for scientific literature, possibly based on the Science Library; this resulted in DSIR being elected responsible for the scheme in 1956, and the eventual formation of the NATIONAL LENDING LIBRARY FOR SCIENCE AND TECHNOLOGY (*q.v.*).

ADVISORY COUNCIL ON TECHNOLOGY. This Council was set up in November 1964 to advise the Minister of Technology on the application of Science to British Industry. Abbreviated ACT.

ADVOCATES' LIBRARY, EDINBURGH. *See* NATIONAL LIBRARY OF SCOTLAND.

AERIAL MAP. A map made from one or more photographs taken from above the surface of the earth.

AEROGRAPH. An instrument, used for blowing, by means of compressed air, a fine spray of liquid colour on to a lithograph stone or drawing, or when re-touching photographs.

AFFILIATED LIBRARY. One which is part of a library system, but has its own board of management and is not administered as part of the system.

AFNOR. Acronym for Association Française de Normalisation, the French equivalent of the BRITISH STANDARDS INSTITUTION (*q.v.*).

AGAINST THE GRAIN. Said of paper which has been folded at right angles to the direction in which the fibres tend to lie. In a well-printed book the back fold of the paper is never 'against the grain'; the grain direction should run from head to tail in the finished book in order that the pages will lie flat when the book is opened. *See also* CROSS DIRECTION, GRAIN DIRECTION, WITH THE GRAIN.

AGATE. (*Binding*) A bloodstone or agate used in hand binding to burnish gold or coloured edges. (*Printing*) Used to denote $5\frac{1}{2}$ point type.

AGATE LINE. An American standard of measurements for the depth of columns of advertising space in a newspaper. Fourteen agate lines make one column inch.

AGENT. In the U.S.A., an individual or firm acting as a middleman between librarian and publisher in the acquisition of material. An agent is commonly used in connection with periodical subscriptions, back numbers of periodicals, and foreign publications. *See also* LITERARY AGENT.

AGRICULTURAL RESEARCH COUNCIL. Created by Royal Charter in 1931; it consists of from fifteen to eighteen members of whom four or five are Government scientists and officials, the remainder being independent scientists or farmers. It is responsible to the Secretary of State for Education and Science for the organization and development of agricultural research and for research on food other than fish. It has under its control nine research stations and fifteen research units in the charge of distinguished university scientists. It also gives financial support to fourteen independent agricultural research institutes, and makes grants to universities and other bodies for special investigations, and awards research fellowships and post-graduate studentships for training in research in agriculture and veterinary science. Abbreviated ARC.

AIGLONNE. Trademark of a microfilm processor made by the Andre Debrie Corporation.

AIR BRUSH. *Synonymous with* AEROGRAPH (*q.v.*).

AIR-DRIED. Hand-made, or good machine-made, paper, or brown paper which is hung over lines and dried slowly in air at a uniform temperature, as distinct from paper which is machine-dried in heat.

AISLE. The passageway between two parallel bookcases.

AJOURÉ BINDING. A style of binding practised in the last third of the fifteenth century at Venice. It was in the traditional Eastern manner with arabesques, gilding, and cut-out leather, over a coloured background.

ALASKA SEAL. Sheepskin or cowhide made to imitate sealskin.

ALBEMARLE REPORT. *The youth service in England and Wales*, 1960. Known as the Albemarle Report from the fact that the Countess of Albemarle was chairman of the committee which had been set up in November 1958 by the Minister of Education to enquire into the youth service.

ALBERTYPE. A process of making pictures with a gelatine-covered plate, the printing being a variety of photogravure (*United Typothetae*).

2

ALBION PRESS. Invented in 1823 by R. W. Cope of London; it was an improvement on the STANHOPE PRESS (*q.v.*) and enabled sufficient pressure for printing to be achieved with a single pull on the spindle bar. It was simple in construction, durable, cheap, and easy to work. Its American counterpart was the Washington Press, and its German one, the Hagar Press. The Albion and COLUMBIAN (*q.v.*) presses were used commercially well into the twentieth century; several British private presses used the Albion.

ALBUM. A book of envelopes or jackets for holding gramophone records, usually with a decorative cover and sometimes with descriptive notes.

ALBUM. A book of blank leaves in which literary extracts, quotations, poems, drawings, photographs, autographs, newspaper cuttings, stamps, etc. are written, inserted or fixed.

ALBUM LETTER (NUMBER). A serial letter or number allocated by the producers to an album of gramophone records.

ALBUM TITLE. The title appearing on the cover or the inside of a gramophone record album. It is sometimes based on the original title of the composition but is often a title assigned by the producing company and differing from the title appearing on the record itself.

ALBUMEN PROCESS. The most commonly used sensitizer for coating photo offset plates (*Verry*).

ALCOPHOTO. A photo-mechanical process for making zinc, aluminium or other litho plates which has been developed in England. It has standardized the deep-etching process for all kinds of plates.

ALCOVE. A recess formed by placing two presses at right angles to a wall, and touching it at one end. Also called a CELL (*q.v.*).

ALCOVE MARK. In an old library, the mark used to indicate in which alcove any particular book may be found. Books in such libraries are arranged according to location and not classification. *See also* FIXED LOCATION.

ALDINE (ITALIAN) STYLE. (*Printing*) Ornaments of solid face without any shading whatever, used by Aldus and other early Italian printers. The ornaments are Arabic in character, and are suitable for early printed books. (*Binding*) Late fifteenth and early sixteenth century Venetian bindings in brown or red morocco which were carried out for Aldus Manutius. They had the title, or the author's name in a simple panel in the middle of the front cover of a book so that it could be seen when the book lay on a shelf or table. Early examples were decorated in blind with an outer frame and a central device. It is assumed that as Aldus was the leading printer in Venice he would supervise the binding of his books which was done by the Greek binders he employed.

ALDINE LEAVES. Small binders' stamps bearing a leaf and stem design; used on books bound for ALDUS (*q.v.*) *c.* 1510.

ALDINE PRESS. The Italian press which achieved fame for introducing italic type in 1501. The Press was founded by Aldus Pius Manutius. *See also* ALDUS, ITALIC.

ALDUS. An Italian publishing firm founded at Venice in 1495 by Teobaldo Manucci (Aldus Pius Manutius; Aldo Manuzio) 1450–1515. Aldus specialized in small-size editions of Greek and Latin classics which were published between 1494 and 1515, and the first ITALIC (*q.v.*) type, which was cut for Aldus by Griffi, was first used for a small format edition of the classics. Aldus's printer's device of anchor and dolphin has frequently been used by other printers, e.g. William Pickering for the Chiswick Press in the late nineteenth century. Between 1515 and 1533 the press was managed by his brothers-in-law, the Asolani, during which time the work of the press deteriorated. In 1533 his youngest son Paulius Manutius (1512–74) took over the press and concentrated on Latin classics.

ALFA. An alternative name for esparto grass. *See* ESPARTO.

ALGOL. Acronym for Algorithmic Language, an international algebraic, procedure-oriented language which is similar in concept and content to FORTRAN (*q.v.*).

ALGORITHMIC CODE. One that has rules for converting source (i.e. common language) words into code equivalents.

ALGRAPHY. The process of printing from aluminium plates by lithographic and offset printing. Also called 'Aluminography'.

ALIGNMENT. 1. The exact correspondence in a straight line of the top and bottom of the letters and characters in a fount. 2. The arrangement of type in straight lines. 3. The setting of lines of type so that the ends appear even at the margins.

ALL ALONG. The method of sewing by hand the sections (usually on cords or tapes) of a book, when the thread goes 'all along' or from KETTLE STITCH (*q.v.*) to kettle stitch of each section. Also used to describe machine book-sewing when each section is sewn with the full number of stitches. *See also* TWO SHEETS ON.

ALL-OVER STYLE. The style of book decoration which covers the whole of the side of a binding, as distinct from a corner, centre or border design, whether made up of a single motif, different motifs, or a repeated motif.

ALL PUBLISHED. Used in a catalogue entry and in other connotations, concerning a work, the publication of which has been started but is not completed. Also relates to all the issues of a periodical, publication of which has ceased. *See also* CEASED PUBLICATION.

ALL-PURPOSE LINOTYPE. A machine similar to the LUDLOW (*q.v.*) in that the matrices are hand-set in a special stick. Matrices from Intertype, Linotype and Ludlow machines may be used. The casting mechanism of the machine is similar to that of the ordinary Linotype machine except that the slugs are ejected into a water-cooled compartment before being dropped into a galley. Blanks and ornaments, etc., can be cast as well as type. The machine is made by the American Linotype Company.

ALL RIGHTS RESERVED. A phrase placed in a book usually on the back of the title-page, signifying that the copyright is reserved, and that proceedings may be taken against any person doing anything which infringes that copyright.

'ALL THROUGH'. *Synonymous with* 'Letter by Letter' alphabetization. *See* ALPHABETIZATION.

ALL-UNION INSTITUTE OF SCIENTIFIC AND TECHNICAL INFORMATION. *See* VINITI.

ALLOCATE, TO. The process of deciding into which department or library of a library system books and other material shall be allocated.

ALLOCATION. The act of allocating books. *See also* ALLOCATE, TO.

ALLONYM. A false name, especially the name of some person assumed by an author to conceal identity or gain credit; an alias; a pseudonym.

ALLUSION BOOK. A collection of contemporary allusions to a famous writer.

ALMANAC(K). A publication, usually an annual, containing a variety of useful facts of a miscellaneous nature, and statistical information. It was originally a projection of the coming year by days, months, holidays, etc.

ALPHABET LENGTH. (*Printing*) The length, usually stated in points, of the twenty-six letters of the alphabet. The relative compactness of a type face is determined by the comparison of alphabet lengths. The alphabet length in points, divided into 341, gives the number of 'characters per pica'. *See also* TYPE FACE.

ALPHABET MARK. A mark, such as the CUTTER AUTHOR MARK (*q.v.*), which is incorporated in the call number of a book to enable alphabetic order to be maintained on the shelves without the use of abnormally long symbols.

ALPHABETIC SUBJECT CATALOGUE. One arranged alphabetically by subjects, usually without subdivisions.

ALPHABETIC WRITING.   The third, and final, stage in the development of writing, in which a single symbol was used to represent a single distinctive sound feature in the spoken language, rather than ideas or syllables.
See also PHONETIC WRITING, PICTOGRAPHY.

ALPHABETICAL ARRANGEMENT.   The systematic arrangement of entries in a catalogue, index, bibliography or other list of items, or of books on the shelves of a library in alphabetical order of authors, subjects, titles or other distinguishing characteristics.

ALPHABETICAL CATALOGUE.   One in which the author, title, and/or subject entries are arranged alphabetically.

ALPHABETICAL COLLATERAL SEARCH.   An examination of entries under headings alphabetically adjacent to, or near to, the headings covered in a HIERARCHICAL SEARCH (*q.v.*). *See also* SUBSTITUTION GENERIC, SYSTEMATIC COLLATERAL SEARCH.

ALPHABETICAL DEVICE.   One of the principles used in the Colon Classification for determining the sequence of subjects. It is used only when no better systematic order is apparent, e.g. to proper names, trade names, etc.

ALPHABETICO-CLASSED CATALOGUE.   An alphabetical subject catalogue, in which entries are not made under specific subjects, as in the dictionary form, but under broad subjects arranged alphabetically, and each sub-divided alphabetically by subject to cite more specific sub-divisions. Author and title entries may be included in the same alphabet under the appropriate subject headings.

ALPHABETICO-DIRECT CATALOGUE.   One in which 'direct' headings, i.e. consisting of natural language and the natural form of phrases, as 'stamp collecting', 'subject cataloguing', are used, the headings being arranged in alphabetical order. *Synonymous with* ALPHABETICO-SPECIFIC CATALOGUE (*q.v.*).

ALPHABETICO-SPECIFIC CATALOGUE.   *Synonymous with* ALPHABETICO-DIRECT CATALOGUE (*q.v.*).

ALPHABETICO-SPECIFIC SUBJECT CATALOGUE.   One in which alphabetically arranged headings state precisely the subject of the literary unit indexed, whether it is a whole document or only a portion such as a chapter, section or paragraph of it. Also called 'Dictionary index'. *See also* BASIC ANALYSIS, COLLATERAL REFERENCE, DOWNWARD REFERENCE, QUALIFIED LIST, UPWARD REFERENCE.

ALPHABETIZATION.   Arranging a list of words, names, or phrases according to the letters of the alphabet. In the main there are two methods in use: 1, 'word by word,' or 'nothing before something'; 2, 'letter by letter' strictly according to the letters irrespective of their division into words, or of punctuation. This may also be called the 'solid' method. In 1969 the British Standards Institution issued a Standard (no. 1749) on *Alphabetical arrangement* in which it recommends the 'word by word' or 'nothing-before-something' method (which is used in this book) whereby items which have the same first or second words are arranged in the alphabetical order of the subsequent word, e.g.

> Black Acts
> Black Book
> Black Earth
> Blackberry
> Blackburn

If the 'letter-by-letter' or 'follow-through' method were used these words would be arranged

> Black Acts
> Blackberry
> Blackburn
> Black Earth

The British Standard also recommends that when words are joined by a hyphen they shall be arranged as separate words, the hyphens being treated as spaces for filing purposes, e.g.

> Switch   Pre-impregnated
> Switch-plug   Precipitation
> Switch starter   Prefabrication
> Switchboard   Pressure

Apostrophes are similarly treated. Hyphenated proper names, proper names containing apostrophes, and words incorporating hyphenated prefixes all come under this ruling, e.g.

> Jack, E. and L., Ltd.
> Jack's Café
> Jack, T.
> Jacks, A. B.
> Jacks-Bateson, M. L.

This Standard was first issued in 1951.

ALPHABETOLOGY. The study of the development of ALPHABETIC WRITING (*q.v.*).

ALPHAMERIC. *Synonymous with* ALPHANUMERIC (*q.v.*). *See also* ALPHA-NUMERICAL INDEXING.

ALPHANUMERIC. A contraction of 'alphabetic-numeric'; characters which may be letters of the alphabet, or numerals, or their symbols. *See also* ALPHA-NUMERICAL INDEXING.

ALPHA-NUMERICAL INDEXING. An indexing scheme which uses a combination of the alphabet and numbers, broad subjects being listed in alphabetical order and the subdivisions under them being given numbers. No attention need be paid to the first letter of the first word, and there may or may not be a hierarchical significance. The documents are identified with the number and filed according to it.

ALTERATIONS. (*Printing*) Changes made in a PROOF (*q.v.*).

ALTERNATIVE LOCATIONS. Bliss considers that one of the principles of classification is to provide alternative locations for certain studies or sciences regarded from different points of view or preferred in other allocations.

ALTERNATIVE TITLE. 1. A secondary title following the words 'or', 'a' or 'an'. More commonly known as the SUB-TITLE (*q.v.*). 2. One of several titles, which in particular circumstances (e.g. in multi-language publications with titles in the languages of the text) could be used as the MAIN TITLE (*q.v.*).

ALUMINIUM PLATES. Extremely flexible plates used in OFFSET PRINTING (*q.v.*).

ALUMINOGRAPHY. *Synonymous with* ALGRAPHY (*q.v.*).

AMBIGUOUS TITLE. One which is so vague that it may be misunderstood. In a catalogue, amplification may be made in brackets immediately following the title, or in a note.

AMBROGAL PRINTING. An offset printing process invented by Ambrosius Galetzka; it is reminiscent of American aquatone printing. Sheets of celluloid are prepared for lithographic printing. *See also* AQUATONE.

AMERICAN ASSOCIATION OF LAW LIBRARIES. Established 1906. Aims 'to promote librarianship, to develop and increase the usefulness of law libraries, to cultivate the science of law librarianship and to foster a spirit of co-operation among members of the profession'. Abbreviated AALL. Publishes *Law Library journal* (q.), *Index to legal periodicals* (m. and cum.), *Index to foreign legal periodicals* (q., 4th. q. cum.), *Current publications* (9 a year), *Law libraries in the U.S. and Canada* (bi. an.), *AALL publication series*.

AMERICAN ASSOCIATION OF SCHOOL LIBRARIANS. A Division of the American Library Association since 1 January 1951 and a Department of the National Education Association since June 1960; founded in 1951, it is concerned with the improvement and extension

of library services in elementary and secondary schools. Abbreviated
AASL. Publishes *School libraries* (irreg. to membs. only).

AMERICAN ASSOCIATION OF STATE LIBRARIES. A Division
of the American Library Association, since 1 January 1957, when the
State Library Agencies Division and the National Association of State
Libraries merged. It is a society of professional librarians, and is
responsible for the functions of the ALA appertaining to all library
services performed on a provincial, state or territorial level, including
the Commonwealth of Puerto Rico. Abbreviated ASL. Publishes
President's Newsletter (2 p.a., free to membs.).

AMERICAN BRAILLE. An obsolete variation of BRAILLE (*q.v.*).

AMERICAN DOCUMENTATION INSTITUTE. *See* AMERICAN
SOCIETY FOR INFORMATION SCIENCE.

AMERICAN FEDERATION OF INFORMATION PROCESSING
SOCIETIES. Founded in the U.S.A. in 1961 to serve as a national
voice for the computing field; to advance knowledge of the information processing sciences. Formerly the National Joint Computer
Committee. There are two membership classifications: member
societies – those constituent societies whose primary interest is in
computers and information processing as determined by the Board
of Directors of AFIPS, and affiliated societies – those societies which,
although they are not primarily concerned with computers and
information processing, do have a major interest in this field.
Abbreviated AFIPS.

AMERICAN FINISH. *See* PAPER FINISHES.

AMERICAN LIBRARY ASSOCIATION. Founded 1876 'to promote
library service and librarianship'. The Association caters for special
needs through fourteen divisions as follows, each division acting for
the Association within its field of responsibility: *Type-of-library* divisions concerned with all activities that affect their types of library,
American Association of School Librarians, American Association of
State Libraries, Association of College and Research Libraries, Association of Hospital and Institution Libraries, Public Library Association; *Type-of-activity* divisions concerned with the functional,
technical, and resource fields which are related to their designated
interests, Adult Services Division, American Library Trustee Association, Children's Services Division, Information Science and Automation Division, Library Administration Division, Library Education
Division, Reference Services Division, Resources and Technical
Services Division, Young Adult Services Division. Brief entries appear
under each division name. Abbreviated ALA. Publishes *ALA Bulletin*

(*Amercian Librarian* from January 1970—11 times a year to membs.),
Membership directory (a.), *Proceedings* (a. to membs.); *The Booklist and
Subscription Books Bulletin* (23 p.a.); a number of periodicals are pub-
lished by divisions, departments and 'round tables'. *See also* DIVISION.

AMERICAN LIBRARY TRUSTEE ASSOCIATION. A Division of
the Library Association since 1 September 1961; founded in 1890 to
study and encourage the development of libraries in all types of community and all types of library services in the U.S.A. and Canada; to
study the library programmes of the several states and of Canada, and
to disseminate the information gained from such study; to strengthen
state trustee organizations. Abbreviated ALTA. Publishes *The Public
Library Trustee* (4 p.a., free to membs.).

AMERICAN MERCHANT MARINE LIBRARY ASSOCIATION.
Founded in 1921 to maintain a library for the free use of the officers
and crews of American ocean-going vessels of passenger, freight,
tramp and tanker fleets, Great Lakes fleets, Coast Guard personnel and
other members of the armed forces, lighthouses, lightships, etc. More
than a million volumes are in circulation in American ships; eleven
shore libraries are maintained. Collects books and other materials on
nautical subjects for reference and research. Abbreviated AMMLA.

AMERICAN NATIONAL STANDARDS INSTITUTE, INC. The
U.S.A. organization for issuing recommendations as to the production,
distribution and consumption of goods and services; it is the American
equivalent to the BRITISH STANDARDS INSTITUTION (*q.v.*) and is the
United States member of the INTERNATIONAL ORGANIZATION FOR
STANDARDIZATION (*q.v.*). Standards issued by the Institute are known
as American National Standards. From 1918, when it was founded,
until 1966 it was known as the American Standards Association
(ASA) and from then until October 1969 as the United States of
America Standards Institute (USASI) its Standards being known as
U.S.A. Standards. *See also* INTERNATIONAL STANDARDS.

AMERICAN RUSSIA. Cowhide used for bookbinding.

AMERICAN SOCIETY FOR INFORMATION SCIENCE. Founded
in 1937 to undertake the 'discussion, publication and critical analysis
of work dealing with the theory, practice, research and development
of all elements involved in the communication of recorded specialized
information'. Known as the American Documentation Institute (ADI)
until 1967. This professional association is now 'organized for
scientific, literary and educational purposes and dedicated to the
creation, organization, dissemination and application of knowledge
concerning information and its transfer'. Abbreviated ASIS. Publishes

Journal of the American Society for Information Science (q.), *Information Science Abstracts* (formerly *Documentation Abstracts*) in conjunction with the Chemical Literature Division of the American Chemical Society and the SLA (q.), *Annual Review of Information Science and Technology*, Papers and proceedings of ASIS annual meetings, *ASIS Newsletter* (bi-monthly).

AMERICAN THEOLOGICAL LIBRARY ASSOCIATION. Founded 1947 to bring its members into closer working relations with each other and with the American Association of Theological Schools; to study the distinctive problems of theological seminary libraries; to increase the professional competence of the membership; and to improve the library service to theological education. Abbreviated ATLA. Publishes *Proceedings* (a.), *Newsletter* (q. to membs.).

AMERICANA. Material relating to the Americas, whether printed about or in, the Americans, or written by Americans or not.

AMMONIA PROCESS. (*Reprography*) A two-component diazo process in which both the diazo and the coupler are on the base. Development is achieved by neutralizing the acidic stabilizers by evaporating aqueous ammonia. *See also* DIAZO.

AMPERSAND. The abbreviation, sign or character for the word 'and', thus: &. Also called 'Short and'.

-ANA (often with the euphonic *i* added: IANA). A suffix to names of persons or places, denoting a collection of books, anecdotes, literary gossip, or other facts or pieces of information, e.g. Americana, Johnsoniana, Lincolniana.

ANAGRAM. A transposition of the letters of a word or sentence resulting in some new word or sentence.

ANALECTS. A collection of literary fragments, gleanings or other miscellaneous written passages.

ANALET. A 'small analysis' or statement of the (*classification*) steps taken to analyse a complex subject.

ANALYSIS. (*Cataloguing*) A book is said to be 'analysed' when any part of it is recorded separately in a catalogue by means of an ANALYICAL ENTRY (*q.v.*). (*Classification*) Breaking down a subject into its facets. *See* FACET.

ANALYTIC. *See* ANALYTICAL ENTRY.

ANALYTICAL BIBLIOGRAPHY. The kind of bibliography which determines facts and data concerning a publication by examining the signatures, catchwords, cancels and watermarks, and making a record in an approved form of the results. Also called 'critical' or 'historical bibliography'.

ANALYTICAL BOOKLET. A booklet of descriptive or bibliographical notes accompanying a gramophone record album or an individual record. *See also* LAID IN.

ANALYTICAL CATALOGUING. The branch of cataloguing which is concerned with making analytical entries. *See* ANALYTICAL ENTRY.

ANALYTICAL ENTRY. An entry in a catalogue for part of a book, periodical or other publication, article or contribution of separate authorship in a collection (volume of essays, festschrift, serial, volume of musical compositions, etc.). The entry includes a reference to the work containing it. The entry is supplementary to the comprehensive, or MAIN ENTRY (*q.v.*), for the whole work. Such entries, called 'Analytics', may be made under authors, subjects or titles. In special libraries they are often made for significant paragraphs, sections, tables, etc., and occasionally for particular facts or figures, in addition to parts or chapters of books, units of a series and of a collection.

ANALYTICAL INDEX. 1. An index in which the entries are not arranged in one straightforward alphabetical sequence, but the subject of the work is divided into a number of main headings and these in turn are sub-divided as necessary, each sequence of entries being arranged alphabetically. The abstracts (or papers) included in the volume to be indexed are then classified according to these main headings and so placed in their appropriate places in the analytical index. 2. An alphabetical subject index to information in articles of broader connotation than the subject index headings, as in an encyclopaedia. 3. A classified index to material under specific subjects, as in a reference book. (*ALA Gloss.*)

ANALYTICAL METHOD. In classification, the breaking down of a specific subject into constituent elements according to a given formula, these elements then being reassembled in a pre-determined order designed to give the most useful arrangement.

ANALYTICO-SYNTHETIC CLASSIFICATION. A scheme which gives the classifier the maximum autonomy in constructing numbers for new specific subjects not enumerated in the schedules. Ranganathan's *Colon Classification* was the first scheme of this kind. A FACETED CLASSIFICATION (*q.v.*).

ANASTATIC PRINTING. A process or method of obtaining facsimile impressions of any printed design or engraving by transferring it to a plate of zinc, which, on being subjected to the action of an acid, is etched or eaten away, with the exception of the parts covered with ink. These parts are left in relief and can be printed from readily.

ANASTATIC REPRINT. An unaltered reprint made in the mid-nineteenth century, especially in France, by making an inked offset of the type on metal plates which were etched in relief.

AND OTHERS. When there are more than three joint authors, collaborators, etc., a catalogue entry is made only under the first to be mentioned followed by *and others*.

ANDERSEN AWARD, HANS CHRISTIAN. In full, the International Hans Christian Andersen Youth Book Award. First awarded in 1956 (to Eleanor Farjeon for *The little book room*), it is now awarded in recognition of the work of a living author in the field of children's literature. The Award takes the form of a medal and is made every two years by the International Board on Books for Young People, Munich. Diplomas are also awarded to an Honour List of fifteen writers of good books.

ANEPIGRAPHON. A publication whose title-page is missing.

ANGLE BRACKETS. *See* BRACKETS.

ANGLO-AMERICAN CODE. The cataloguing code devised by the Library Association and the American Library Association, and published in 1908. It consists of definitions, 174 substantive rules (with variations where the two committees could not agree, and where some recognized authority such as the Library of Congress differed from the rule recommended) appendices of abbreviations, transliterations, and sample catalogue cards illustrating the rules. In 1949 the American Library Association published the *ALA Cataloguing Rules for Author and Title Entries* which incorporated the Library of Congress rules printed as 'supplementary rules' in the 1908 edition and ignored the English variations of certain rules which appeared in this edition. Considerable clarification took place, and better, and more numerous, examples were given. Committees of the ALA and of the LA met concurrently to prepare revised codes, and close co-operation was maintained by the exchange of minutes and working papers; later members of each committee met the other committees. The result was the publication in 1966 of the *Anglo-American cataloguing rules: North American text* and in 1967 of the *British text*. These rules are based on the Paris Principles which were adopted by the International Conference on Cataloguing Principles held in 1961. Some of the rules differ materially in the two texts. Manuscripts, incunabula, maps, music, motion pictures, filmstrips, phonorecords, pictures, designs and other two-dimensional representations are all provided for.

ANGSTROM. A unit of measurement, equal to one ten-millionth of a millimetre, used to express the length of light waves. In colorimetry, the millimicron (ten angstrom units) is used more frequently.

ANGULAR MARKS. *See* BRACKETS.

ANHYDROUS. Water-free. Normally used with reference to chemical salts and solvents. (*Verry.*)

ANIMAL TUB-SIZED. *See* TUB-SIZING.

ANIMALS IN FOLIAGE PANEL. A panel in a book-binding decoration which is divided vertically into two, each half containing curving foliage with an animal within each curve. It is the characteristic Netherlands design.

ANNAL. An entry in a record of events in their chronological order year by year.

ANNALISTIC ARRANGEMENT. A bibliography of an author's writings arranged in order of publication.

ANNALS. A record of events arranged in chronological order.

ANNOTATE. To make an annotation.

ANNOTATING. The act of preparing an ANNOTATION (*q.v.*).

ANNOTATED. Said of a catalogue or bibliography entry which has been provided with an ANNOTATION (*q.v.*).

ANNOTATION. A note added to an entry in a catalogue, reading list or bibliography, to elucidate, evaluate or describe the subject and contents of a book; it sometimes gives particulars of the author. The term originally embraced notes of all kinds which followed the collation, but modern practice provides bibliographical notes as the fifth part of a MAIN ENTRY (*q.v.*) and the annotation as the sixth and final part.

ANNUAL. A serial publication issued once a year. *See also* BI-ANNUAL, YEAR BOOK.

ANONYM. 1. An anonymous publication. 2. An anonymous person or writer. 3. A pseudonym.

ANONYMOUS. A publication is said to be anonymous when the author's name does not appear anywhere in it, either on the title-page or cover, or in the preface, introduction or foreword. According to some authorities, if the authorship can be traced in catalogues or bibliographies it may be considered not to be anonymous.

ANONYMOUS CLASSIC. A work of unknown or doubtful authorship, commonly designated by title, which may have appeared in the course of time in many editions, versions, and/or translations.

ANONYMOUS ENTRY. An entry in a catalogue for a book the author of which is not mentioned on the title-page.

ANOPISTHOGRAPHIC BLOCK BOOK. One that is printed on only one side of the paper.

ANOPISTHOGRAPHIC PRINTING. The manner of printing early

block books, using writing ink and printing on only one side of the leaf. *See also* BLOCK BOOK, OPISTHOGRAPHIC.

ANSAPHONE. Trade name for a telephone answering machine which records on a tape telephone messages when a line is engaged or the staff not in attendance. Somewhat similar machines are RECORDACALL and TEL-STOR (*qq.v.*). In libraries they are intended mainly to deal with the renewal of books after the library has closed but they will, of course, record all messages.

ANTE-DATED. A book which bears a date of publication which is earlier than the actual date. The opposite of 'Post-dated'.

ANTERIOR NUMERAL CLASSES. The first group of the main classes of Bliss's *Bibliographic Classification*. They are bibliothetic in character and conform to the generalia classes of other schemes. Three of the nine divisions accommodate general works (2 bibliography, 6 periodicals, 7 miscellanea); the remainder provide for special collections of books which for some reason it is preferred to shelve apart from the main collection. *See also* SYSTEMATIC AUXILIARY SCHEDULES.

ANTERIORIZING DIGIT. (*Classification*) The digit which, when added to a class number, causes the resulting class number to have precedence over the number to which it was added. For example the *a* in the class number X*a* is the anteriorizing digit. Also called 'Anteriorizing common isolates'. *See also* ANTERIORIZING VALUE.

ANTERIORIZING VALUE. (*Classification*) Said to be possessed by a digit which, when added to a class number (and which is then said to be the 'host class number'), causes the resulting class number to have precedence over the host number. For example, in the Colon classification, class numbers containing lower case roman letters, or arrows, have precedence over class numbers without them, as: X*a* precedes X, B63*a* precedes B63, L23: 45*a* precedes L23: 45, N ← M precedes N.

ANTHOLOGY. A collection of choice extracts, usually of poetry, or on one subject, from the writings of one author, or various authors, and having a common characteristic such as subject matter or literary form.

ANTIPHONARY. A liturgical book intended for use in a choir. Generically it includes antiphons and antiphonal chants sung at Mass and at the canonical Hours, but now refers only to the sung portions of the BREVIARY (*q.v.*).

ANTIQUA. A German name for Roman types. A small book hand based on the Caroline minuscule, called *lettera rotonda* or *lettre ronde* (round letter) in Italy and France. Type based on this writing is now known as Roman, and is the usual kind of type (as distinct from *italic*) used for book work.

ANTIQUARIAN BOOKSELLER. One who deals with very old books, many of which may have had several owners, and which are rare enough to command higher prices than ordinary second-hand books.

ANTIQUE. (*Paper*) The name given to printing papers made from esparto grass. They usually have a rough surface, and the poorer qualities are called *featherweight*, so loosely woven that 75 per cent of the bulk is air space. The term originally referred to machine-made paper made in imitation of hand-made paper. Antique papers have a matt or dull finish and are neither calendered nor coated. They are suitable for printing type and line engravings, but not for half-tones, and are used for most books without blocks. (*Binding*) Designates blind tooling. *See* TOOLING.

ANTIQUE FINISH. (*Paper*) A rough surface, suggestive of old hand-made printing paper. Generally used to indicate an 'unfinished' paper, i.e. one not calendered, and usually of the FEATHERWEIGHT PAPER (*q.v.*) class.

ANTIQUE GOLD EDGES. *See* GILT EDGES.

ANTIQUE LAID. Originally, paper made on moulds of which the chain wires were laced or sewn direct to the wooden ribs or supports of the mould, and so causing the pulp to lie thicker along each side of every chain line in the sheet of paper. Now, any rough-surfaced laid paper. *See also* MOULD.

ANTIQUE TOOLING. A form of blind tooling.

ANTONYM. A word having the opposite meaning of another. The opposite of synonym.

ANTONYMOUS CATCHWORDS. Headings used in an index, which are exactly opposite in meaning.

APERTURE. The area of the hole available for light rays of an axial beam traversing the lens of a camera, or reproducer, to form an image on the sensitized film behind the lens. The lens is equipped with a diaphragm or stop which restricts the area to control the brilliance of the image (the larger the aperture, the more light passes through, and the greater the exposure) and to control the depth of field of the lens (the smaller the aperture, the greater the depth of field). The size of the aperture is indicated by its f- number, i.e. the ratio of the diameter of the opening to the focal length of the lens; a low f- number indicates a large aperture.

APERTURE CARD. A card with one or more openings (the number depending on the amount of space required for identifying stored document images) into each of which is mounted a 'frame' cut from a strip of microfilm. The identification on the card can consist of

written information, punched holes, or characters on film. Also called
IMAGE CARD, PEEPHOLE CARD (q.v.).

APOCALYPSE OF ST. JOHN. See BLOCK BOOKS.

APOCONYM.   A name changed by the cutting off or elision of letters or
syllables.

APOCRYPHAL.   Of unknown authorship or doubtful authenticity.

APOGRAPH.   A copy of an original manuscript.

APOSTIL (APOSTILLE).   An annotation, or marginal note (archaic).

app.   Abbreviation for APPENDIX (q.v.).

APPARATUS CRITICUS.   The sources of information and the existence of manuscripts, letters and other material used by an author, and
enumerated by him in footnotes, marginalia and commentary in support of his text, and thus associated with the preparation of the
definitive edition of a work. Includes particularly, information concerning variant readings, doubtful texts and obscurities.

APPENDIX.   Matter which comes at the end of the text of a book and
contains notes which are too long for footnotes, tables of statistics, or
other items for which there is no room in the body of the book, or
which, from the nature of the information, is more suitably placed at
the end of the text.

APPLICATION BLANK.   *Synonymous with* APPLICATION FORM (q.v.).

APPLICATION FORM (VOUCHER).   The form, usually a card size
5 × 3 inches, on which persons wishing to join the children's or adult
lending libraries, or to obtain books for use in (or away from) a reference library, make their application. In many libraries, applicants for
lending library tickets have to obtain the signature of a ratepayer as
guarantor, but more often as recommender. In some libraries,
applicants whose names appear in the current list of electors are permitted to borrow without obtaining the signature of another person
but the practice is increasing of not requiring *any* counter-signature
as verification of the applicant.

APPLIED BIBLIOGRAPHY.   *Synonymous with* HISTORICAL BIBLIO-
GRAPHY (q.v.).

APPRAISAL.   An estimate of the value of a book as a contribution to a
subject.

APPROACH TERM.   The word which a catalogue-user seeks in a
catalogue, in anticipation that it will lead him to a statement in SUB-
JECT HEADING LANGUAGE (q.v.) of a required compound subject.

AQUATINT.   1. A process of etching on copper or steel plates by means
of nitric acid, producing an effect resembling a fine drawing in water
colours, sepia or India ink. It is used to render tonal effects rather than

lines. Now supplanted commercially by lithography. 2. A print made by this method.

AQUATONE. A photographic printing process which is similar to collotype, but is used with offset presses.

ARAB STATES CENTRE FOR FUNCTIONAL LITERACY. *See* ARAB STATES TRAINING CENTRE FOR EDUCATION FOR COMMUNITY DEVELOPMENT.

ARAB STATES TRAINING CENTRE FOR EDUCATION FOR COMMUNITY DEVELOPMENT. Established late in 1952 as the Arab States Fundamental Education Centre (ASFEC) – a regional project for the whole of the Arab states. It was subsequently named the Arab States Centre for Functional Literacy, the name being again changed to the present one in 1969. It is sponsored mainly by UNESCO, although it derives part of its finances from the host government, the United Arab Republic. Its main purposes are: (a) training fundamental education workers from the Arab states; (b) conducting research in topics related to socio-economic development; (c) producing prototype materials in such fields as literacy teaching, health education, agriculture extension, home economics with a view to calling the attention of the participating governments to the importance of such materials. Since 1953 batches of students have been accepted from most of the Arab states for courses in varying subjects and for different periods.

ARABESQUE. A species of decoration consisting of interlaced lines and convoluted curves arranged in more or less geometrical patterns; so-called because it was brought to its highest perfection by Arabian or kindred artists. Also applied to a fanciful mixture of animals, birds, and insects, and of plants, fruit and foliage, involved and twisted; but pure arabesque has in it no representation of living forms, as this is forbidden by the Koran.

ARABIC FIGURES. The numerical characters 1, 2, 3, etc., as distinct from roman numerals I, II, III, etc., so called from having been introduced into European from Arab use: they have been used for foliation since the last quarter of the fifteenth century. Arabic numerals first appeared in European MSS. in the twelfth century, although the Arabs probably brought them from India in the eighth century. Arabic is used for numbering the text pages of books. 'Old Style' numerals are as follows 1, 2, 3, 4, 5, 6, 7, 8, 9, 0 and have ascenders and decenders, although tabular work makes it desirable to have 'lining figures' (1, 2, 3, 4, 5, 6, 7, 8, 9, 0) as an alternative. These are also known as 'Modern'. It is the presence or absence of ascenders and descenders which indicates whether the figures are 'Old Style' or 'Modern'. This distinction applies to italic as well as to roman: Old Style – *1, 2, 3, 4, 5, 6, 7, 8, 9, 0*. Modern – *1, 2, 3, 4, 5, 6, 7, 8, 9, 0*. *See also* FOLIATION, HANGING FIGURES, LINING FIGURES, PAGINATION, ROMAN NUMERALS.

ARBITRARY CODE. *Synonymous with* TABULATED CODE (*q.v.*).

ARC LAMP. A powerful source of artificial light obtained from an incandescent arc of light formed between two electrodes.

ARCHBISHOP PARKER'S BIBLE. *See* BISHOPS' BIBLE.

ARCHETYPAL NOVEL. Commonly used to describe the earliest romances, tales and works of fiction; the fore-runner of the modern novel.

ARCHITECTURAL BINDING. A sixteenth-century style of book cover decoration which consisted of columns supporting an arch under which was a panel to contain the title. The contents of the books so decorated seldom related to architecture.

ARCHIVAL QUALITY. (*Reprography*) The degree to which a processed film or print will retain its characteristics without loss of quality over an indefinite period of storage under controlled conditions.

ARCHIVES.   1. Public records or historical documents kept in a recognized repository. 2. Documents which formed part of an official transaction and were preserved for official reference; these include documents specially made for, and those included in, an official transaction (*Jenkinson*). 3. The repository itself. 4. Colloquially a collection of old books or documents. 5. Written documents, or annexures to them, compiled for the purposes of, or used during, a public or private business transaction of which they themselves form a part; and which are preserved by the persons concerned with the transaction, or their successors, in their own custody for their own use. Similarly, any records of the activities of societies or groups. *See also* RECORDS.

ARCHIVIST. A person who has the care of archives, and also makes them available under proper safeguards to historians and researchers.

AREA (*County Libraries*) A part of the County Library area, not as extensive as a region, served by a number of branches and/or centres, and forming a library unit for administrative purposes. It will normally comprise two or more county districts or parishes.

AREA HEADQUARTERS (*County Libraries*) The premises from which the Libraries in an Area are administered, which may or may not be a library to which the public has access.

AREA LIBRARIAN. One who is in charge of a compact and limited portion of a county library area, and responsible for a small number of branches and other service points in that area.

AREA OF SERVICE. A term applied to a geographical area to the residents of which a public library provides a free service, and from which (or on behalf of which) the library receives an income.

AREA SEARCH. Examination of a large group of documents to segregate those documents pertaining to a general class, category or topic. Screening (*IBM*).

ARISTO PAPER. A photographic copying paper, the colloid being gelatine.

ARISTRONYM. A title of nobility converted into, or used as, a surname.

ARITHMETICAL NOTATION. *Synonymous with* INTEGRAL NOTATION (*q.v.*).

ARM. The projecting, or unclosed, horizontal or upward-sloping stroke of a type letter.

ARMARIA. Used in the first centuries of the Christian era to indicate cupboards for keeping books.

ARMARIAN. A worker in a monastic library whose duty it was to prevent the books under his charge from being injured by insects, to look after bindings, and keep a correct catalogue. He presided over a SCRIPTORIUM (*q.v.*) and supplied the scribes with parchment, pens, ink, knives, awls and rulers. Also called an 'Armarius'.

ARMARIUM. A wardrobe, or cupboard, possibly a separate piece of furniture in which scrolls, or subsequently books, were kept. Closed armaria apparently developed in Imperial times and survived in monastic libraries until the Renaissance or later.

ARMARIUS. *See* ARMARIAN.

ARMED SERVICES TECHNICAL INFORMATION AGENCY. A United States governmental organization, now known as the DEFENSE DOCUMENTATION CENTER (*q.v.*). Abbreviated ASTIA.

ARMENIAN BOLE. A bright-red clay which is used as a colouring material and also to dust on to the edges of books before gilding to act as a base for the gold, to which it gives a greater depth and lustre. It is obtained mainly from Bohemia, Italy and Silesia.

ARMING PRESS. A hand blocking press used now only for short runs but originally for impressing armorial bearings.

ARMORIAL BINDING. One decorated with the arms or other device of royalty or nobility. Generally applied to bindings earlier than the mid-nineteenth century.

ARMS BLOCK. An engraved brass block or a binder's ZINCO 2 (*q.v*) made by a line-block maker and used in an arming or blocking press to impress a coat of arms on leather bindings.

ARRANGEMENT.   The adaptation of a whole musical work, or an integral part of a musical work, to a medium of performance other than that for which it was originally written, e.g. the casting of a song as a piano piece, or of an orchestral overture as an organ piece. Sometimes also, a simplification or amplification, when the musical structure and the medium of performance remain the same.

ARRANGER.   One who transcribes a whole musical work, or a part of a work, for a medium of performance other than that intended by the composer. The arrangement may be a simplification or amplification, the medium of performance and the musical structure remaining the same.

ARRAY.   1. In classification, the series of co-ordinate sub-divisions which are obtained by dividing a class or a division according to a single characteristic: e.g. Literature divided according to characteristic *Form* gives the array Poetry, Drama, Novel, Essay. Each co-ordinate division in an array should exclude all of the others, and the whole array should be exhaustive of the contents of the class. The order of the divisions in an array should be that deemed most helpful to users. 2. A set of co-ordinate terms (i.e. terms subordinate to the same genus). Also used in information retrieval for a sequence of headings in a file (Taube) and as a set of search terms (Bernier). An ordinal arrangement of informational materials (*IBM*). 3. A set of mutually exclusive co-ordinate subclasses totally exhaustive of a class, derived by its division according to some one characteristic (*IBM*).

ARRESTER.   (*Classification*) The second curve; used in the Colon Classification to enclose the Subject Device Number. The first, or opening, curve is called the 'Starter'. *See also* BRACKETS, CIRCULAR BRACKETS, CURVES.

ARS MEMORANDI.   *See* BLOCK BOOKS.

ARS MORIENDI.   A mediaeval block book setting forth by means of pictures and text the art of dying becomingly.

ART.   The name given to papers coated on one or both sides after the paper is made by brushing on China clay, sulphate of barium, or sulphate of lime and alumina (the last for the 'satin-white' finish) and afterwards polished. In *imitation art* the paper is 'loaded' (i.e. the China clay is mixed in with the fibre) not 'coated'. *Matt art* is unglazed coated paper with a smooth, soft, egg-shell finish.

ART CANVAS.   A cloth for bookbinding, also known as *light-weight buckram*.

ART PAPER. *See* ART.

ART PARCHMENT. *See* VELLUM PARCHMENT.

ART VELLUM. 1. A brand name for a lightweight book cloth. 2. A fabric used for classes of works which do not require a very strong cloth.

ART WORK. A term covering all forms of illustrative matter (line drawings, photographs, paintings, diagrams, hand lettering, etc.) used in a printed publication to distinguish it from type-set matter. In America the term is used to distinguish any material prepared by hand as camera copy.

ARTIFICIAL CHARACTERISTIC. *See* CHARACTERISTIC OF A CLASSIFICATION.

ARTIFICIAL CLASSIFICATION. One in which some accidental thing is adopted as the 'difference'. *See* PREDICABLES, FIVE. Classification by analogy, i.e. by external or accidental likeness, unlikeness, or apparent purpose. *See* CHARACTERISTIC OF A CLASSIFICATION.

ARTISTIC MANUSCRIPT. A record or document produced by hand, and decorated or illustrated in such a way as to achieve distinction as a work of artistic merit. Illuminated manuscripts are the most important examples. *See also* LITERARY MANUSCRIPT.

ARTISTIC MAP. One made by an artist rather than by a cartographer; such maps consequently appeal to the eye and are often not correct cartographically. They are used as illustrations, endpapers, and for advertisement.

ARTIST'S PROOF. A proof of an engraving or etching, usually with the signature of the artist in pencil, and sometimes with a small sketch, known as a remarque, in the margin. Used as a model or sample. Also called 'Remarque Proof'.

ARTOTYPE. A photo-engraved picture made by one of the gelatine processes (*United Typothetae*).

ARTYPE. Type letters which are printed on acetate sheets gummed on the back. Those required are cut out of the sheet and pressed in the required position to form 'copy' which is photographed for printing by the offset process.

ARUNDEL PSALTER. Two Psalters bound together, and each illuminated in a distinct style. The first, containing many miniature-filled initials was probably done by an early fourteenth-century court artist. The second is typical of the East Anglian School and is probably earlier. It has full-page scenes from the Passion and a large number of allegorical scenes. It is in the British Museum.

AS ISSUED. Indicates that a book offered for sale secondhand is in its original format.

AS NEW. Used in secondhand booksellers' catalogues to indicate that the physical condition of a book offered for sale is 'almost indistinguishable from the condition of newness'.

ASCENDER. The vertical ascending stem of lower-case letters such as b, d, k, etc.; that part which extends above the X-HEIGHT (*q.v.*). *See also* DESCENDER.

ASCENDER LINE. (*Printing*) The imaginary line which runs along the top of ascenders. This will be above the CAP LINE (*q.v.*) in the case of types the capitals of which are lower than the ascenders. *See also* ASCENDER, BASE LINE, CAP LINE, MEAN LINE.

ASCETONYM. The name of a saint used as a proper name.

ASFEC. *See* ARAB STATES TRAINING CENTRE FOR EDUCATION FOR COMMUNITY DEVELOPMENT.

ASHENDENE PRESS. One of the most distinguished British private presses. It was founded in 1895 by C. H. St. John Hornby, a partner in the firm of W. H. Smith & Son, and undertook fine printing at the instance of Sydney Cockerell in 1900.

ASLIB. Founded 1926 as the Association of Special Libraries and Information Bureaux. Merged with the British Society for International Bibliography in 1939. Aims 'to facilitate the co-ordination of any systematic use of sources of knowledge and information in all public affairs and in industry and commerce and in all the arts and sciences'. It has geographical branches and subject groups to which members may belong, provides an information service, maintains an index of translations into English of articles on scientific and technical subjects, keeps a register of translators, provides training courses and organizes conferences and meetings. Publishes *Aslib proceedings* (m.), *Aslib Book list* (m.), *Index to theses* (a.), *Journal of documentation* (q.).

ASPECT CARD. A record used in an ASPECT SYSTEM (*q.v.*) of recording information for retrieval. A separate card is used for one subject or point of view and entered on it are the numbers or other identification symbols of each document which has this quality. The number is entered on as many cards as are necessary to record every aspect of the document.

ASPECT SYSTEM. A method of indexing which assumes that a DISCRETE RECORD (*q.v.*) represents a single subject (or aspect) and contains, in searchable form, information as to which documents in a file have this subject in common. *See also* DISCRETE RECORD, TERM ENTRY.

ASSOCIATE LIBRARIAN. American term for a deputy librarian.

ASSOCIATED BOOK. As used in connexion with the Colon Classification, a book which is written about another book, as e.g. a criticism of, or reply to, it. The book which is the subject of the criticism or reply is called a 'Host book'. The BOOK NUMBER (*q.v.*) of an Associated Book should consist of that of the Host Book followed by ':g'. The number so added is called the 'Criticism number'. Where there is more than one Associated Book of the same Host Book, a digit, 1, 2, etc., representing each additional Associated Book, may be added to the Book Number and so becomes part of it. The number added in this way may be called the 'Accession part of the Criticism number'.

ASSOCIATION. *See* LINKS.

ASSOCIATION BOOK. One having an autograph inscription or notes by the author, or which was in any way intimately connected with a prominent person who may have owned or presented it, or which had belonged to someone connected with its contents. Evidence in or on the book of the association is essential. If there is no signature or presentation inscription there should be a bookplate, or binding stamp, or marginal or other notes to indicate the association.

ASSOCIATION COPY. *Synonymous with* ASSOCIATION BOOK.

ASSOCIATION FOR COMPUTING MACHINERY. Founded in the U.S.A. in 1947 to advance the science, design, development, construction and application of modern machinery for performing operations in mathematics, logics, statistics, and kindred fields. Abbreviated ACM. Publishes *Communications* (m.), *Journal* (q.), *Computing Reviews* (bi-monthly).

ASSOCIATION FOR THE DEVELOPMENT OF PUBLIC LIBRARIES IN AFRICA. Founded at Dakar, 13th September 1957 and renamed the INTERNATIONAL ASSOCIATION FOR THE DEVELOPMENT OF LIBRARIES IN AFRICA (AIDBA) (*q.v.*) in 1960. Abbreviated ADBPA.

ASSOCIATION INTERNATIONALE DES DOCUMENTALISTS ET TECHNICIENS DE L'INFORMATION. *See* INTERNATIONAL ASSOCIATION OF DOCUMENTALISTS AND INFORMATION OFFICERS.

ASSOCIATION LIBRARY. A library in Canada which is financed by the members of an association and staffed by volunteers. So named to distinguish such libraries from rate-supported or free public libraries.

ASSOCIATION NATIONALE DE LA RECHERCHE TECHNIQUE. *See* ANRT.

ASSOCIATION OF ACADEMIC LIBRARIANS. Founded in Germany in 1900 'to safeguard the professional interests of the German Librarians, to stimulate interrelations among them and among the academic libraries, and to promote the academic library system'. It was re-established on 28th April 1948.

ASSOCIATION OF AMERICAN LIBRARY SCHOOLS. Founded 1915 to advance education for librarianship. Abbreviated AALS. Publishes *Journal of education for librarianship* (q.).

ASSOCIATION OF ASSISTANT LIBRARIANS. A Group of the Library Association; it caters for members of a particular status rather than, as in the case of other groups, for those engaged in a particular branch of librarianship. It is organized in Divisions which operate at local level. Originally known as the Library Assistants' Association, it was formed on 3rd July 1895 at a meeting convened by Mr. W. W. Fortune; the name was changed to the Association of Assistant Librarians in June 1922. It was an independent association until 1st January 1930 when it became a Section of the Library Association. Abbreviated AAL.

ASSOCIATION OF BRITISH LIBRARY SCHOOLS. Founded 1962 to further the work of the full-time schools of librarianship by affording heads of such schools, lecturers who are not heads, and some representatives of the library and professional organizations opportunities of meeting to discuss education in librarianship. Much of the work of the Association is carried out by an Executive Committee. Abbreviated ABLS.

ASSOCIATION OF BRITISH THEOLOGICAL AND PHILOSOPHICAL LIBRARIES. *See* ABTAPL.

ASSOCIATION OF COLLEGE AND RESEARCH LIBRARIES. A Division of the American Library Association since 1938; founded in 1889 to represent and promote 'libraries of higher education (institutions supporting formal education above the secondary school level), independent research libraries, and specialized libraries'. Has five sections. Abbreviated ACRL. Publishes *College and Research Libraries* (6 issues p.a. membs. only); *ACRL News* (11 p.a.); *Choice: books for college libraries* (11 issues p.a.).

ASSOCIATION OF CO-OPERATIVE LIBRARY ORGANIZATIONS. Formed during the meeting of the American Library Association held in June 1969 to provide a channel for the exchange of information on co-operative measures.

ASSOCIATION OF HOSPITAL AND INSTITUTION LIBRARIES. A Division of the American Library Association since June 1956 by amalgamating the former Division of Hospital Libraries and the Institution Libraries Committee; founded in 1944. Represents libraries which serve the recreational, educational, rehabilitative and therapeutic needs of patients, inmates and residents of hospitals and institutions, and libraries which serve the needs of the various professional staffs in hospitals and institutions, and of students and faculty of affiliated training schools and colleges, by providing material for their clinical, research, educational, public health and recreational programmes. Abbreviated AHIL. Publishes *AHIL Quarterly* (q. to membs.).

ASSOCIATION OF INTERNATIONAL LIBRARIES. Founded in September 1963 at the Sofia meeting of the International Federation of Library Associations, of which it is a Section Aims: to facilitate co-operation between international libraries. Membership is open to (a) individuals capable of promoting co-operation between international libraries, (b) libraries of international organizations, in particular the libraries of inter-governmental organizations, (c) all other libraries whose international character is recognized by the Executive Committee. It is financed by members' dues. Abbreviated AIL.

ASSOCIATION OF JEWISH LIBRARIES. Formed in June 1966 by the amalgamation of the Jewish Librarians Association and the Jewish Library Association 'to promote and improve library services and professional standards in all Jewish libraries; to serve as a centre of dissemination of Jewish library information and guidance; to encourage the establishment of Jewish libraries; to promote publication of literature which will be of assistance to Jewish librarianship; to encourage people to enter the field of librarianship. Abbreviated AJL. An American association.

ASSOCIATION OF LIBRARIES OF JUDAICA AND HEBRAICA IN EUROPE. Founded in Paris, 28th April 1955, to facilitate the use of literature on Judaica and Hebraica in European libraries; to create a catalogue of such literature in Europe; to give bibliographical and other help to affiliated libraries and others. Has an information bureau and arranges training courses in Jewish librarianship. Abbreviated ALJH.

ASSOCIATION OF LONDON CHIEF LIBRARIANS. The organization which was formed in succession to the ASSOCIATION OF METROPOLITAN CHIEF LIBRARIANS (*q.v.*) when the boroughs of greater London were reconstituted as from 1st April 1965. The London Boroughs now total thirty-two: the City of London is in addition and was not altered. Abbreviated ALCL.

ASSOCIATION OF METROPOLITAN CHIEF LIBRARIANS. An advisory body to the Metropolitan Boroughs Standing Joint Committee (MBSJC) which was composed of representatives of the Metropolitan Borough Councils and the Corporation of the City of London until 31st March 1965. It consisted of the respective chief librarians who met regularly to consider mutual library problems, advised on library developments in the area and managed the LONDON UNION CATALOGUE (*q.v.*). It has been responsible for, amongst other matters, organizing interavailability of tickets, standardizing some Library materials and routines, setting up the Metropolitan Special Collection (MSC) and the Metropolitan Joint Fiction Reserve (JFR) which includes play-reading sets. Abbreviated AMCL. This body continued the work of the Committee of Metropolitan Chief Librarians formed in 1934, and was so named on the adoption of a formal constitution early in 1945. It ceased to function after 1st April 1965 when the reorganization of the London boroughs became effective. *See also* ASSOCIATION OF LONDON CHIEF LIBRARIANS.

ASSOCIATION OF RESEARCH LIBRARIES. Founded 1931 to develop and increase by co-operative effort, 'the resources and usefulness of the research collections in American libraries'. It supervises the work of the FARMINGTON PLAN (*q.v.*). Publishes *Minutes* (semi-a.). Abbreviated ARL.

ASSOCIATION OF THE LIBRARIES OF INTERNATIONAL ORGANIZATIONS. *See* INTERNATIONAL FEDERATION OF LIBRARY ASSOCIATIONS.

ASSOCIATION POUR L'ETUDE ET DE LA LINGUISTIQUE APPLIQUÉE. *See* ATALA.

ASSOCIATION SUISSE DE DOCUMENTATION. *See* ASD.

ASTERISK (*). The first and frequently most used reference mark for footnotes, technically known as a 'Star.' *See also* REFERENCE MARKS.

ASTERISM. 1. A group of asterisks, as in a triangle, $*_*^*$ or $_*^{*}{}_*$, drawing attention to a following remark, passage or paragraph. 2. The use of a number of asterisks instead of a proper name, as Mr. T******; a form of pseudonym.

ASTIA. *See* DEFENSE DOCUMENTATION CENTER.

ASTRONOMICAL MAP. One showing the stars. Also called a 'Star map'.

ASYNDETIC. Without cross-references. The reverse of syndetic. *See also* SYNDETIC CATALOGUE.

ATALA. Acronym for Association pour l'Etude et de la Linguistique Appliquée. Founded in 1959 to act as a focus for experimental and research work in progress on the mechanization of information.

ATLAS. A volume of maps, with or without descriptive letterpress. It may be issued to supplement or accompany a text, or be published independently. Also, a volume of plates, engravings, etc., illustrating any subject; a large size of drawing paper measuring $26\frac{1}{2} \times 34$ inches;

a large folio volume, resembling a volume of maps, sometimes called 'Atlas folio'. The word 'atlas' was first used in the title of the first collection of maps – Gerardus Mercator's *Atlas sive cosmographicae meditationes de fabrica mundi*, Düsseldorf, [1585]–1595, which was composed in three parts in 1585, 1590 and 1594, and issued after his death by his son Rumold Mercator in 1595.

ATLAS FOLIO. The largest size folio. About 25 inches by 16 inches. *See also* ELEPHANT FOLIO.

ATLAS SIZE. A large square folio book, size about 25 × 16 inches.

ATTACHING. (*Binding*) The process of attaching the boards to the sewn sections after rounding and backing. The attaching joint is a strip of tough paper pasted to the outside of the end leaf to serve as a connecting link with the boards. Not to be confused with CASING (*q.v.*).

ATTENTION NOTE. A note, sometimes combined with a ROUTING SLIP (*q.v.*), attached to a periodical in order to draw the attention of users to specific articles or items of information in which they may be interested. It is individual with respect to items to which attention is drawn and the individual addressed.

ATTRIBUTE. In co-ordinate indexing, a characteristic mentioned as subject-matter. *See also* CHARACTERISTICS OF A CLASSIFICATION.

ATTRIBUTED AUTHOR. The person to whom a book is attributed, because of doubt as to the authorship. *See also* SUPPOSED AUTHOR.

AUDIO CHARGING. A form of Transaction Charging in which the loan serial number, and the essential details of the book and of the reader are spoken into a microphope and recorded on a tape or disc. When all the Transaction Cards representing returned books have been sorted into serial number order, any missing ones represent overdue books. The appropriate parts of the record are played back, and the details, recorded in respect of the missing cards, entered on overdue notices. *See also* CHARGING METHODS, TRANSACTION CARD CHARGING.

AUDIO-VISUAL AIDS. Material such as gramophone records, tape recordings and various VISUAL AIDS (*q.v.*) used as an adjunct to teaching.

AUDIO-VISUAL AREA. An area within a library building, or serving as an adjunct to a library, which is equipped with apparatus for screening or listening, and for storing materials used in connexion with the apparatus.

AUDIO-VISUAL MATERIALS. Non-book materials such as gramophone records, tapes, slides, transparencies, films and filmstrips which require apparatus to render them usable.

AUDIT. Checking accounts for accuracy and to see that expenditure is authorized by the appropriate authority. The Local Government Act, 1933, sect. 219, provides that in England and Wales the following accounts shall be subject to audit by a district auditor:

(a) the accounts of every county council, metropolitan borough council, urban district council, parish council and of every parish meeting not having a council;

(b) the accounts of any committee of any such council or parish meeting;

(c) the accounts of any joint committee appointed by combined authorities of which one or more of whose accounts are subject to district audit.

The accounts of boroughs may be audited by borough auditors or district auditors or by a PROFESSIONAL AUDITOR (*q.v.*) (in which case the above-mentioned provision of borough auditors does not apply), or by the district auditor. Auditing is undertaken by borough auditors unless the council resolves to adopt the systems of district, or of professional, audit. The system of borough auditors is little used except as a tradition in a few boroughs. In Scotland, accounts of county and town councils are audited by an auditor appointed by the Secretary of State. In Ireland, library accounts must be audited in the same way as the other accounts of a local authority. *See also* DISTRICT AUDIT, MUNICIPAL AUDIT.

AURIANNE AWARD. Established in 1956 by the Executive Board of the American Library Association, and made under the will of Miss Augustine Aurianne. Awarded annually 'to an author for a book published in the preceding year but one, which is considered the best book of the year on animal life which helps to develop a humane attitude in the young'. The Award is of $200 cash and a certificate designed by Valenti Angelo; it is administered by the Children's Services Division, and the selection of the book to receive the award is made by the Aurianne Award Committee of this Division. The first award was made in 1958 to John and Jean George for *Dipper of Copper Creek*.

AUSTRALIAN ADVISORY COUNCIL ON BIBLIOGRAPHICAL SERVICES. Founded in April 1956 to plan and recommend to appropriate authorities measures for the development and co-ordination of Australian bibliographical resources and to co-operate with the International Advisory Committee on Bibliography. Represented on it are the governing bodies and principal librarians of the Commonwealth National Library, State libraries and library boards, the universities, the Commonwealth Scientific and Industrial Research Organization and the Library Association of Australia. The Council's secretariat is the AUSTRALIAN BIBLIOGRAPHICAL CENTRE (*q.v.*). Abbreviated AACOBS.

AUSTRALIAN BIBLIOGRAPHICAL CENTRE. The Centre, which was established in 1956, is administratively part of the National Library of Australia; it is financed by the Commonwealth Government and undertakes projects for the AUSTRALIAN ADVISORY COUNCIL ON BIBLIOGRAPHICAL SERVICES (*q.v.*) or arranges for them to be undertaken by other bodies as recommended by the Council. It serves as the recognized centre in Australia for international enquiries and for other requests not met elsewhere for bibliographical information.

AUSTRIAN SOCIETY FOR DOCUMENTATION AND BIBLIO-GRAPHY. *See* Oesterreichische Zeitschrift für Buch-und Bibliothekswesen, Dokumentation und Bibliographie.

AUTHOR. The person, persons, or corporate body, responsible for the writing or compilation of a book or other publication not a periodical. Usually to be distinguished from an editor, translator, compiler, etc., although, failing any alternative, these may be regarded as authors for purposes of cataloguing. In a wider sense, an artist, a composer of a musical work, and a photographer are authors to whom would be attributed work which they had created.

AUTHOR ABSTRACT. *See* ABSTRACT.

AUTHOR AFFILIATION. The organizations with which an author is affiliated, as indicated on the title-page, or in a periodical article or proceedings, and appearing after the author's name in a library catalogue.

AUTHOR ANALYTIC. *See* ANALYTICAL ENTRY.

AUTHOR AUTHORITY LIST. *See* NAME AUTHORITY FILE.

AUTHOR BIBLIOGRAPHY. One listing books, articles, or other contributions to knowledge by, or by and about, a particular author. It may include biographies and criticisms of his work as well as works by him.

AUTHOR CARD. A catalogue card bearing an author entry; usually the main entry card. *See also* MAIN ENTRY.

AUTHOR CATALOGUE. A catalogue of author entries arranged alphabetically under authors' names; it usually includes entries under editors, translators, composite authors, corporate bodies, first words of titles, or any other words or names used as headings for the main entries.

AUTHOR ENTRY. A catalogue entry under the name of the person or body responsible for the writing, or compilation, of a published work. Failing one or more real names, the author entry may have to be made under a pseudonym, initials, or some other heading. For music, it is generally an added entry under the name of the author of the text accompanying a musical work, e.g. librettist, or author whose work served as the basis or inspiration for a musical work, the main entry being made under the composer's name. It is usually the MAIN ENTRY (*q.v.*).

AUTHOR HEADING. The heading under which an author entry is made.

AUTHOR INDENTION. *Synonymous with* FIRST INDENTION (*q.v.*).

AUTHOR INDEX. An index of authors' names.

AUTHOR MARK. Symbols (letters, figures, or other signs) used to represent authors and so individualise books having the same class, subject, or shelf number, in order to simplify the arrangement of books and catalogue entries. *See also* BOOK NUMBER, CUTTER AUTHOR MARKS, MERRILL ALPHABETING NUMBERS.

AUTHOR NUMBER. *Synonymous with* AUTHOR MARK (*q.v.*).

AUTHOR ORDER. Said of books, or of entries relating to books, which are arranged in alphabetical order of authors' names.

AUTHOR-PUBLISHER. The writer of a work who is his own publisher.

AUTHOR STATEMENT. That part of a catalogue entry which mentions the author when transcribing the title. It is usually omitted unless it contributes data which is essential in some way to the entry, e.g. it would be given for joint authors, as by R. H. Mottram, John Easton *and* Eric Partridge.

AUTHOR STYLE. The usual combination of black capitals and lower-case letters which is used for author headings in a catalogue. *See also* SUBJECT STYLE.

AUTHOR TABLE. A printed list used in assigning author numbers, e.g. the CUTTER AUTHOR MARKS (*q.v.*), or the CUTTER-SANBORN THREE-FIGURE TABLE (*q.v.*).

AUTHOR-TITLE ADDED ENTRY. An added entry which involves two elements, placed in a TRACING (*q.v.*) and also at the top of a secondary entry. It would be given for the author's name followed by the title of a book when an adaptation, supplement, etc., is involved, or in a subject heading for a commentary on an individual work.

AUTHOR-TITLE INDEX. One which has entries under authors' names and under titles, either in one or in two alphabetical sequences.

AUTHORITATIVE EDITION. *See* DEFINITIVE EDITION.

AUTHORITIES. *See* PRIMARY SOURCES, SECONDARY SOURCES.

AUTHORITY CARD. 1. A card which gives the form selected for a heading in a catalogue. If a personal name is used as a heading, references to sources and records of variant forms are given; if a corporate name, sources, brief history and any changes of name are given. 2. A card which bears the classification number given by the classifiers to a subject, and also the subject index headings for entries made out for it. Where chain indexing is undertaken, a separate entry would be made for each step taken in determining the number. *See also* AUTHORITY LIST, CHAIN INDEXING, NAME AUTHORITY FILE, SUBJECT AUTHORITY FILE. 3. In acquisition work, a term sometimes used to denote a request, requisition or recommendation card, so named because it bears the signature or authority for an acquisition transaction.

AUTHORITY ENTRY. An entry for a society or institution, giving such particulars as the date of founding, date of incorporation, changes of name, and affiliation or union with other societies.

AUTHORITY FILE. *Synonymous with* AUTHORITY LIST (*q.v.*).

AUTHORITY LIST. 1. A list of all personal and corporate names, names of anonymous classics and sacred books, the titles of anonymous books and the headings for series cards, which are used as headings in the catalogue; sometimes references are given to books in which each name and its variants were found, and in the case of corporate entries, sources, a brief history and particulars as to changes of name. The entries are made when a heading is first decided upon. It gives the cataloguer a record in the forms used in the public catalogues. If the list is kept on cards, one entry to a card, each card is known as an 'authority card'. 2. A list in classified order of classification symbols or numbers which have been allocated to books, with their corresponding index entries. Also called 'Authority file'. *See also* AUTHORITY CARD, CHAIN INDEXING, NAME AUTHORITY FILE, SUBJECT AUTHORITY FILE.

AUTHORIZED EDITION. An edition issued with the consent of the author, or of his representative to whom he may have delegated his rights and privileges.

AUTHOR'S AGENT. *See* LITERARY AGENT.

AUTHOR'S ALTERATIONS. *Synonymous with* AUTHOR'S CORRECTIONS (*q.v.*).

AUTHORS' AND PUBLISHERS' LENDING RIGHT ASSOCIATION COMMITTEE (APLA). *See* PUBLIC LENDING RIGHT.

AUTHOR'S BINDING. A superior binding used on a few copies of a book as presentation copies from the author.

AUTHOR'S COPIES.   The complimentary copies of a book, usually six in number, presented on publication to its author by the publisher.

AUTHOR'S CORRECTIONS.   Deviations from the original copy, as distinct from corrections by the author of printer's errors marked on a printer's proof. *See also* AUTHOR'S REVISE.

AUTHOR'S EDITION.   1. The collected or complete edition of an author's works, uniformly bound, and indicating on the title-page that it is the complete works of the author. 2. An edition the publication of which has been authorized by the author. *See also* DEFINITIVE EDITION.

AUTHOR'S PROOF.   The clean proof sent to an author after the compositor's errors have been corrected. Abbreviated: AP

AUTHOR'S REVISE.   A proof bearing the author's or editor's corrections as distinct from one corrected by the printer.

AUTHOR'S RIGHTS.   Those secured to an author under a copyright act.

AUTO-ABSTRACT.   1. (*Noun*) The resulting product of a machine preparing an extract consisting of complete sentences from a document which is so abstracted. *See also* ABSTRACT 3 (b). 2. (*Verb*) To select an assemblage of keywords from a document, commonly by an automatic or machine method, in order to form an abstract of the document (*IBM*).

AUTO-ABSTRACTING.   The art of abstracting automatically by machine.

AUTO-BIAS DEVICE.   The linking, when determining notation in the Colon Classification, of two foci within the same facet by the use of a hyphen. *See also* FACET, FOCUS.

AUTOBIOGRAPHY.   The life of a person written by himself.

AUTO-ENCODE.   To select keywords from a document, by a machine method, in order to develop search patterns for information retrieval (*IBM*).

AUTO-ENCODING.   The process of producing either auto-abstracts or automatically generated index entries on the basis of word frequency.

AUTOGRAPH.   A person's signature. In the book trade, a description of cards, documents, letters, manuscripts, etc., written or signed with the writer's own hand.

AUTOGRAPHED EDITION.   An edition of a work, copies of which are signed by the author. *See also* LIMITED EDITION.

AUTOGRAPHY.   1. The author's own handwriting. 2. Reproductions of the form or outline of anything by an impression from the thing itself. 3. A lithographic process of reproducing writing, drawing, etc., in facsimile. 4. That branch of diplomatics which is concerned with autographs.

AUTO-LITHOGRAPHY. A lithographic method in which the artist draws in reverse directly on to the stone or other medium.

AUTOMATIC ABSTRACTING. The selection by machine of words and phrases from a document for quotation in order to describe its content. *See also* AUTOMATIC INDEXING.

AUTOMATIC INDEXING. 1. The selection of keywords from a document by a machine method in order to develop index entries. 2. The use of machines to extract and assign index terms without human intervention once programmes or procedural rules have been established. *See also* AUTOMATIC ABSTRACTING, MECHANIZED INDEXING.

AUTOMATIC ROUTING. *See* ROUTING.

AUTOMATIC SELECTION. *Synonymous with* MECHANICAL SELECTION (*q.v.*).

AUTONYM. The real name of an author.

AUTOPOSITIVE. Trade name for a Kodak direct positive copying process and for certain types of film which yield a direct positive image. *See also* DIRECT POSITIVE PROCESS.

AUTOPOSITIVE PAPER. Trade name for a type of SILVER HALIDE PAPER (*q.v.*) which gives a positive image without the necessity for first making a negative when making copies by a Lensless Process. *See also* LENSLESS COPYING.

AUTOTYPE. To make a copy by a carbon process.

AUTOTYPY. The process of making copies by the carbon process.

AUTOTYPE REPRODUCTION. One reproduced by the autotype process, which is a variety of the collotype process, in which the plate is coated with a light-sensitive resin instead of a gelatine.

AUXILIARIES. *See* UNIVERSAL DECIMAL CLASSIFICATION.

AUXILIARY NUMBER. One placed after the class number in order to group the books by some method, such as alphabetically or chronologically. The OLIN BOOK NUMBER (*q.v.*) and CUTTER AUTHOR MARKS (*q.v.*) are auxiliary numbers.

AUXILIARY PUBLICATION. The process of making data available by means of specially ordered microfilm or photocopies. Auxiliary publication usually presupposes that the materials have not been published before, although it is sometimes applied to publication of microcard copies of out-of-print books (*IBM*).

AUXILIARY SCHEDULES AND TABLES. Tables of sub-divisions which are appended to schedules of all schemes of classification. They

3

consist of items of relationship, time, locality, etc. and then symbols of the different items can be added to book classification numbers. Broadly, they fall into three groups: those which (a) are common and can be used with the same meaning throughout the classification, e.g., the common subdivisions of Dewey's Decimal Classification; (b) are common to, and may only be applied to, certain subjects, e.g. the Systematic and Auxiliary Schedules of Bliss's Bibliographic Classification; (c) can be applied in only one place as in most of the Library of Congress Classification Schedules. *See also* SYSTEMATIC AUXILIARY SCHEDULES.

AUXILIARY SYNDESIS.   The accessory apparatus – e.g. cross reference – which is used to supplement indexing sequence so as to reveal other relations (*IBM*).

AUXILIARY TABLES.   In the Universal Decimal Classification tables of secondary aspects of subjects which may be applied to primary aspects to qualify them, and are distinguished by a special symbol, or 'facet indicator'. For a synopsis of auxiliaries, *see* UNIVERSAL DECIMAL CLASSIFICATION.

AVERAGE SLOPE MAP.   One which indicates the average steepness of land slopes.

AZOFLEX.   Trade name for an Ilford process for making translucent masters on a reflex foil from which copies are made by the diazo, or dyeline, process. Another method is to allow carbon to be transferred to a translucent paper which is then used as a master. Known in Holland, where it was originally introduced, as Océ. *See also* DIAZOTYPE PROCESS.

AZURE TOOLING.   (*Bookbinding*) Tooling in which horizontal lines are shown close together.

AZURED TOOL.   A bookbinder's tool with close parallel lines running diagonally across its surface. Derived from the use of thin horizontal lines used in heraldry to indicate blue.

B.BIBL.   Bachelier en Bibliotheconomie et en Bibliographie. A degree in librarianship awarded in Canada.

b.f.   Abbreviation for BOLD FACE type.

BSIB.   *See* BRITISH SOCIETY FOR INTERNATIONAL BIBLIOGRAPHY.

BACK.   1. The 'back' or inside margins of pages. 2. *Synonymous with* SPINE (*q.v.*). 3. The surface of a piece of movable type parallel to the BELLY (*q.v.*).

BACK BOARD.   The piece of millboard or strawboard which is used for the back cover of a book.

BACK CORNERING. (*Binding*) The cutting off of a small portion of the inner corners of the boards near the headcaps in order to improve their setting.

BACK COVER. *Synonymous with* REVERSE COVER (*q.v.*).

BACK FILE. The file or 'back numbers' (i.e. those preceding the current issue) of a periodical.

BACK FOLD. *See* BOLT.

BACK ISSUE. *Synonymous with* BACK NUMBER (*q.v.*).

BACK LINING. A piece of material (paper, cloth, calf skin) glued to the back sections of a book after sewing, before securing the cover.

BACK LIST. The titles which a publisher keeps in print because of continuous demand.

BACK MARGIN. The margin of a printed page which is nearest the fold of the section. Also called: 'Gutter', 'Gutter margin', 'Inner margin', 'Inside margin'.

BACK MARK. A small oblong block or number printed in such a position on the sheet that when the sheets of a book are folded and placed together for casing, the oblongs or numbers will follow each other in a slanting and/or numerical sequence down the spine and thus show if any section has been duplicated, misplaced or omitted. Also called 'Collating mark', 'Quad mark'. *See also* BLACK STEP.

BACK MATTER. Matter which is published at the end of the text, e.g. addenda, appendix, author's notes, bibliography, glossary, index, reference matter. Also called 'End-matter,' 'Subsidiaries.' *See also* PRELIMINARIES.

BACK NUMBER. An issue of a periodical which precedes the current number.

BACK ORDER. An uncompleted order which is held back for future delivery.

BACK PAGE. The verso, even-numbered, side of a leaf of a book or sheet of printed paper or manuscript. The back of a page.

BACK-PROJECTION READER. A reader in which an enlargement of a microform image is projected on to the back of a translucent screen for reading from the front by transmitted light.

BACK TITLE. The title which is placed on the spine, or back, of a book. *See also* BINDER'S TITLE, COVER TITLE.

BACK-UP. To print the second side of a sheet after the first has been printed.

BACKBONE. *Synonymous with* SPINE (*q.v.*).

BACKED. 1. A damaged leaf of a book, whether text or plate, which has been 'laid down' on, or pasted on, to paper, gauze or linen. 2. The spine of a book which is covered with a different material to the sides, as 'marbled boards backed with leather'. 3. The spine of a book which has been recovered with a different material to the original, a 're-backed' one having been re-covered with similar material to the original.

BACKING.   The bookbinding operation whereby the sewn sections of a book, after glueing, are placed securely between backing boards after ROUNDING (*q.v.*), and hammered to splay them outwards from the centre of the book. It adds permanence to the rounding, and forms an abutment, or ridge, into which to fit the boards: the ridge so formed is called a 'joint'. This operation is carried out in Britain and America after ROUNDING (*q.v.*): in most Western European countries Rounding only is done. *See also* FLAT BACK, ROUND BACK.

BACKING BOARDS.   (*Binding*) Boards used when backing and form-ing the groove or joint. They are made of very hard wood and some-times faced with iron. The edge intended to form the groove is thicker than that which goes towards the fore-edge, so that when placed on either side of the book in the lying press the power of the press is directed towards the back.

BACKING MACHINE.   A machine for backing books, generally used for publishers' binding and cheap work.

BACKING UP.   *See* PERFECTING.

BACKLESS BINDING.   A volume which is bound in such a way that the spine is flat or concave, covered with paper and gilt, and probably tooled, so as to look like the fore-edge which is itself finished in a similar manner.

BACKLINING.   The material, usually paper, pasted on the inside of the SPINE (*q.v.*) of a book.

BACKS.   The back margins of pages, i.e. those nearest the fold of the section. *See also* BACK.

BACKSLIDE.   The block which is placed behind the cards in a catalogue drawer, and is moved backwards and forwards according to the quan-tity of cards in the drawer to prevent them from falling out of an upright position. It is usually made with its front sloping back at the top to permit of easy consultation.

BACKSTRIP.   *Synonymous with* SPINE (*q.v.*).

BACONIAN CLASSIFICATION.   The scheme propounded by Francis Bacon in his *Advancement of Learning* (1605), which more than any other philosophical scheme of thought, or classification of knowledge, has had the greatest influence on library classification. It was based on the three faculties, Memory, Imagination, and Reason, and these produced the three main headings, History, Poetry and Philosophy. The scheme was used for the arrangement of books, and its inversion is the basis of Dewey's *Decimal Classification*.

BAD COPY. 'Copy' which is difficult to read. This reduces the speed, and increases the cost, of typesetting. *See also* COPY I.

BAD LETTER. *Synonymous with* DAMAGED LETTER (*q.v.*).

BAILIFF. 1. Official under a sheriff mainly concerned with serving writs and making arrests. 2. Manorial official, usually next in rank to the Steward, and standing in a similar relationship to him as (1) to the sheriff.

BAKER REPORT. The Report of the Working Party appointed by the Minister of Education in March 1961, *Inter-Library Co-operation in England and Wales*, 1962. Mr. E. B. H. Baker was Chairman of the Working Party. *See also* BOURDILLON REPORT.

BALL. *See* INK BALL.

BALL. In typography, the finishing element at the top of the strokes of the type letter *a* and *c*.

BANDS. The cords or strings whereon the sheets of a book are sewed. With FLEXIBLE SEWING (*q.v.*), the bands appear upon the back. When books are sewn so as to embed the cord in the back, or in modern books sewn on tapes, the appearance of raised bands is sometimes produced by narrow strips of leather or cardboard glued across the back before the volume is covered. The space between the bands is called 'between bands'.

BALOPTICON. An instrument for projecting opaque materials; originally a trade name. Usually now called an OPAQUE PROJECTOR (*q.v.*).

BANK LETTER. A bulletin or other periodical publication issued by a bank primarily to give information on current industrial, business and financial conditions in general.

BANNED. Prohibited from sale by ecclesiastical or secular authority.

BAR. The horizontal stroke of letters; e.g. A, H and e.

BARRIER. 1. The fixture placed beside a staff enclosure to form a passage through which readers must pass to have their books charged or discharged. *See* CHARGE. 2. A fixed or movable structure placed to keep the public within bounds or to prevent access to a department or part of the building.

BARYTA PAPER. A form of metallic paper, consisting of a suitable body paper coated with barium sulphate; marks can be made on this with a metal point or stylus. It is used in some types of automatic recording apparatus and also for text impressions on photo-composing machines.

BASAN SKIN.   Sheepskin tanned with the bark of oak or larch.

BASE LINE.   (*Printing*) The lowest limit of the body of a piece of type; the imaginary line on which the bases of capitals rest. *See also* CAP LINE, MEAN LINE.

BASE OF A NOTATION.   (*Classification*) The series of symbols used. Their number is the length of base, or its first dimension. In the Dewey *Decimal Classification* it is ten – the ten arabic numerals, in Bliss's *Bibliographic Classification* it is thirty-five – the twenty-six letters of the English arabic combined with the nine arabic numerals.

BASE OF TYPE.   The feet, or lowest part, on which the base of a capital letter rests.

BASE PAPER.   *Synonymous with* BODY PAPER (*q.v.*).

BASE STOCK.   The material, such as plastic, paper or cloth, used as a carrier for a photosensitive emulsion.

BASIC.   Abbreviation for Biological Abstracts Subjects In Context, a computor-composed subject index to *Biological Abstracts* in which keywords in the titles are arranged in alphabetical sequence and printed out mechanically. It is issued as a separate publication every two weeks.

BASIC ANALYSIS.   The citation in upward hierarchical order of the constituent elements of a composite subject. It is the first stage in converting a classification symbol into a verbal subject heading for an alphabetico-specific subject catalogue. The second stage is producing the QUALIFIED LIST (*q.v.*).

BASIC CLASS.   (*Classification*) *Synonymous with* MAIN CLASS (*q.v.*).

BASIC STOCK.   Standard books which it may be considered should form the basis of a well-balanced and authoritative book stock.

BASIC WEIGHT.   (*Paper*) The substance of paper is expressed as the weight of a given superficial area, the units most commonly used being either pounds per ream or grammes per square metre. For example '20 × 30 inches 36 lb 480s' means that if the paper were cut into sheets measuring 20 × 30 inches, then 480 sheets would weigh 36 lb.

BASIL.   A thin sheepskin not suitable for library bookbinding. It is mostly used for binding account books.

BASKERVILLE.   A type face named after John Baskerville (1706–75) of Birmingham, famous printer and type-founder who was printer of Bibles and prayer books to the University of Cambridge 1758–68. His folio Bible of 1763 was his masterpiece. The type is a modification of Caslon. For a specimen alphabet, *see* TRANSITIONAL, TYPE FACE.

BAS-RELIEF PRINTING.   *Synonymous with* EMBOSSING (*q.v.*).

BASSO CONTINUO. Italian for continued bass, or FIGURED BASS (*q.v.*).

BASTARD TITLE. *Synonymous with* HALF TITLE (*q.v.*).

BASTARD TYPE. Type having the face larger or smaller than the size proper to the body, as a nonpareil face on a brevier body, or 10 point face on 12 point body (as this book), used to give the appearance of being leaded. *See also* GOTHIC TYPE.

BASTARDA. *See* GOTHIC TYPE.

BATCH PROCESSING. A technique by which items to be processed in a data processing machine must be collected into groups prior to their processing; contrasted to in-line processing (*IBM*).

BATCHELDER AWARD, MILDRED L. Awarded, for the first time in 1968, to an American publisher for a book considered to be the most outstanding of those originally published in a foreign language in a foreign country, and subsequently published in the United States during the calendar year preceding the appointment of the Mildred L. Batchelder Award Committee which is appointed annually. This Committee nominates from three to five books, and the final choice made by the membership of the Children's Services Division. The Award was first made to Alfred A. Knopf, Inc., publisher of the American edition of Eric Kästner's *The little man.*

BATTELLE MEMORIAL INSTITUTE. Formed in 1929 under the will of Gordon Battelle as a memorial to the Battelle family who were among the first settlers in Ohio and were prominent in developing the Ohio iron and steel industry. The Institute contracts with industry and government by providing the physical plant, equipment and personnel for the conduct of research, the results of which are utilized to encourage progress in science and in other ways benefit the public welfare.

BATTEN CARDS. Those, used in the Batten retrieval system, which represent the presence or absence of each document by a hole or no-hole in a specific position on the record card. *See also* PEEK-A-BOO.

BATTEN SYSTEM. A method of indexing, invented by W. E. Batten, utilizing the co-ordination of single attributes to identify specific documents. Sometimes called the 'peek-a-boo' system because of its method of comparing holes in cards by superimposing cards and checking the coincidence of holes (*IBM*).

BATTERED. Type matter or electros when accidentally injured, or so worn that they give defective impressions, are said to be battered.

BATTERED LETTER. *Synonymous with* DAMAGED LETTER (*q.v.*).

BATTLEDORE. *See* HORN BOOK.

BAY. A U-shaped arrangement of shelving.

BAY GUIDE.   A guide to the subjects of the books shelved in a BAY (*q.v.*).

BAY PSALM BOOK.   *The whole Book of Psalmes faithfully translated into English metre;* the first book printed in Cambridge, Mass., in what is now the U.S.A., in 1640 by Stephen Day, on the first press introduced into English-speaking America in 1638.

BEARD.   That part of the shoulder of a piece of movable type that slopes down from the 'face', or bottom of the printing surface of the letter to the front of the 'body', but more particularly that portion sloping from the bottom serifs of the face to the 'belly'. It consists of the BEVEL (*q.v.*) and the SHOULDER (*q.v.*).

BEARERS.   (*Printing*) Type-high strips of metal placed around pages of type when locked in formes from which electrotype plates are to be made. They appear as black borders on proofs. *See also* FORME.

BEATER.   *Synonymous with* BREAKER (*q.v.*).

BED.   The flat steel table of a printing machine or press on which the *forme* of type is placed for printing. When the forme has been secured, it is described as having been 'put to bed'. *See also* CHASE.

BEDFORD BINDINGS.   Bindings by Francis Bedford (1799–1883) an Englishman who succeeded to the business of Charles Lewis. He was the greatest English binder of his time, but his work has little artistic merit and little originality. He attained good results by imitating early Venetian work, with twisted or Saracenic ornament, as well as the later Veneto-Lyonese style, practised in England in Queen Elizabeth's time.

BELLES LETTRES.   Polite literature, or works of literary art showing grace and imagination, as poetry, drama, criticism, fiction and essays. From the French; literally 'beautiful letters'.

BELLOWS PRESS.   A small flat-bed platen press used for jobbing work, e.g. envelopes, broadsides, cards, hand bills, etc. The presses manufactured by the Adana Company, and often used by amateurs, are of this kind.

BELLY.   The front of the part of a piece of movable type called the body.

BEMBO.   A Roman type face cut originally by Francesco Griffi for Aldus and first used by him in Cardinal Pietro Bembo's *Aetna*, 1495–6. It was the model followed by GARAMOND (*q.v.*) and was re-cut by the Monotype Corporation in 1929. It is regarded by many as the most beautiful of the old-face designs; the modern 'Monotype' Bembo is one of the best book types available. It is relatively condensed, a good space saver, and having long ascenders, is legible and pleasant even when set solid. For a specimen, see TYPE FACE.

BEN DAY PROCESS. A process invented by Ben Day to produce shaded tints or mottled effects by transferring various inked designs in relief on a gelatine film to the metal plate which is later etched.

BENCH PRESS. A small press, resting on a work bench and used by bookbinders to press cased books. *See also* STANDING PRESS.

BENEVENTAN HANDWRITING. A beautiful minuscule hand-writing used in Southern Italy and Dalmatia which survived a number of national varieties developed from the Italian semi-cursive minu-scule, itself a descendant of the Roman cursive. *See also* CURSIVE, HANDWRITING.

BERGHOEFFER SYSTEM. A filing system first used by Prof. Dr. Christian W. Berghoeffer who compiled the Frankfurter Sammel-katalog in 1891. It has been accepted as workable by the Committee for Union Catalogues of the International Federation of Library Associations.

BERKSHIRE LIBRARIES GROUP. Arrangements were begun in 1965 whereby Berkshire libraries were willing to lend books and periodicals to one another, and also exchange information. There are no set standards for membership of the Group, but applications must be approved by the management committee. There is no formal head-quarters; the County Librarian acts as secretary.

BERNE CONVENTION. In full, Berne Convention for the Protection of Literary and Artistic Works. *See* BERNE COPYRIGHT UNION.

BERNE COPYRIGHT UNION. An International Convention was first held at Berne in 1886. Representatives of nine countries met, drew up, signed and ratified the Convention, known as the 'Berne Convention,' for protecting effectively, and in as uniform a manner as possible, the rights of authors over their literary and artistic works. Originally signed on 9th September 1886 and 'completed' in Paris on 4th May 1896, it was revised in Berlin on 13th November 1908, 'completed' at Berne on 20th March 1914, revised at Rome on 2nd June 1928 and finally revised at Brussels on 26th June 1948. Member countries agree to protect without formalities both the unpublished works of nationals of other member countries and also all works first published in Con-vention countries. The United Kingdom has been a signatory from the beginning but the U.S.A. has not been able to accede to it because of the provisions of its domestic laws. A British copyright owner could only secure copyright protection in the U.S.A. by having his works not only registered but set up in type there, whereas American copyright owners could, by publishing their works in the U.S.A. and also in a Berne Convention country, obtain complete protection. This anomaly has been removed by the U.S. signing the Universal Copyright Convention which came into force there on 16th September 1955. Whereas the protection given by the 'Brussels Convention' of 26th June 1948 is for the author's life and fifty years after his death, under the 'Universal Convention' the period is twenty-five years after death. *See also* COPYRIGHT, INTERNATIONAL.

BESPEAKING BOOKS.   *See* RESERVED BOOK.

BEST BOOKS.   A group of books considered to be the most authoritative on a subject or group of subjects.

BEST SELLER.   A book which is so popular that unusually large numbers are sold.

BETA PHI MU AWARD.   Donated by the Beta Phi Mu, an American national honorary library science fraternity, to a library school faculty member or anyone making an outstanding contribution to education for librarianship. The Award was established in 1954, and became an official ALA award in 1956; it is administered by the Library Education Division of the ALA and made annually. Only persons nominated by an ALA member are considered. The Award is of $50 cash and a citation of achievement. The first recipient was Rudolph H. Gjelsness in 1954. The Award is not to be confused with the Beta Phi Mu Good Teaching Award, which has been given annually since 1959 to a library school instructor for excellence in teaching; this award is administered by the Beta Phi Mu Fraternity.

BETWEEN BANDS.   *See* BANDS.

BEVEL.   The part of the shoulder of a piece of movable type immediately sloping down from the 'face'. The distance from the face to the bottom of the bevel is known as the 'depth of strike'. Also called 'Neck'.

BEVELLED BOARDS.   Heavy boards with bevelled edges principally used for large books in imitation of antique work.

BI-ANNUAL.   A publication which is issued twice a year. This word is sometimes used synonymously with *Biennial* which strictly means 'published every two years'. To avoid misunderstanding, the terms 'Half-yearly' or 'Twice a year' are tending to be used instead of Bi-annual. *See also* Bi-monthly.

BIAS PHASE.   1. In classification, where one topic is described (usually in a relatively elementary manner) for the benefit of those working in, or concerned with, another field, a document is classified under the topic introduced, not under the persons for whom it is written, e.g. anatomy for speech therapists would go under anatomy, not speech therapists. 2. The treatment of a subject generally and fairly completely, if concisely, from the point of view of a class of users whose primary interest is in another subject. It is one of Ranganathan's three chief 'phase relations,' the other two being INFLUENCE PHASE and TOOL PHASE (*qq.v.*).

BIBELOT. An unusually small book, valuable as a curiosity because of its format or rarity. Also called 'Dwarf book,' 'Thumb book'.

BIBLE. *See* BISHOPS' BIBLE, COMPLUTENSIAN POLYGLOT, 40-LINE BIBLE, GENEVA BIBLE, MAZARIN BIBLE, POLYGLOT, 36-LINE BIBLE, VINEGAR BIBLE, VULGATE.

BIBLE PAPER. A very thin tough opaque paper used for Bibles or other lengthy books which are required to have little bulk. It is made from new cotton or linen rags. Often erroneously referred to as INDIA PAPER (*q.v.*). Also called 'Bible printing'. *See also* CAMBRIDGE INDIA PAPER, OXFORD INDIA PAPER.

BIBLE PRINTING. *See* BIBLE PAPER.

BIBLIA PAUPERUM. A type of mediaeval picture book of scriptural subjects, with descriptive vernacular text. Very popular among clergy and laity in continental countries before the Reformation. Many manuscript copies are preserved in different languages. It was one of the first books printed in the Netherlands and Germany, originally from blocks and then from type. It was reprinted several times in later years, most recently in 1884, with a preface by Dean Stanley.

BIBLIO. The bibliographical note and/or imprint which is placed on the back of the title-page. *See also* PRELIMINARIES.

BIBLIOCLASM. The destruction of books, or of the Bible.

BIBLIOCLAST. A destroyer of books.

BIBLIOGENESIS. The production of books.

BIBLIOGNOST. One versed in knowledge about books and in bibliography.

BIBLIOGONY. The production of books.

BIBLIOGRAPH. A bibliographer.

BIBLIOGRAPHEE. A person concerning whom a bibliography has been made.

BIBLIOGRAPHER. 1. A person who is able to describe the physical characteristics of books by recognized methods. 2. One able to prepare bibliographies by recognized principles.

BIBLIOGRAPHIC. *Synonymous with* BIBLIOGRAPHICAL (*q.v.*).

BIBLIOGRAPHIC CENTRE. An organization, often a department of a library, which maintains a collection of Reference books from which it is possible to give information concerning the availability of books. In the U.S.A., some of these centres, with financial assistance from LIBRARY SERVICES ACT (*q.v.*) funds, are providing general reference information services. Also, a centre which acts as a depository for books and an agency for organizing book exchanges.

BIBLIOGRAPHIC CLASSIFICATION. A scholarly and detailed scheme devised by H. E. Bliss and first applied in the College of the City of New York where the author was librarian in 1902. In addition to normal sub-division there are Systematic Auxiliary Schedules which are used on similar lines to Dewey's common sub-divisions: these provide for sub-division by form, geography, language, historical period, and of the philology of any language, of an author's works, etc. Apart from these schedules and the Anterior Numerical Classes, the notation is alphabetical, and although not extending beyond four letters, tends to be complete. *See also* BLISS CLASSIFICATION ASSOCIATION. It is usually referred to as the Bliss Classification. The Bliss Classification Working Party operates in England and has prepared *The Abridged Bliss Classification; the Bibliographic Classification of Henry Evelyn Bliss revised for school libraries* which was published by the School Library Association in 1967. *See also* BLISS CLASSIFICATION ASSOCIATION.

BIBLIOGRAPHIC INDEX. A subject index to current bibliographies, whether published separately as books, or pamphlets, or bibliographies appearing in books and pamphlets, or as periodical articles. Published semi-annually, with annual and three-year cumulations, by the H. W. Wilson Company.

BIBLIOGRAPHIC INDEX. 1. A systematic list of writings or publications (e.g. of books or periodical articles) with or without annotations. 2. An index of publications or articles which contains no material descriptive of their contents other than bibliographical references. Also called 'Bibliographical index'.

BIBLIOGRAPHIC INFORMATION. Details concerning a publication which are sufficient to identify it for the purpose of ordering. They may include the following: author, title, publisher, place of publication, edition, series note, number of volumes, parts and/or supplements, and price; editor, translator or illustrator may also be necessary in the case of certain books. Sometimes called 'trade information'.

BIBLIOGRAPHIC ITEM. An article in a periodical, a technical report, a patent, a monograph, or a chapter in a symposium, which is capable of being given a separate bibliographical entry in a catalogue or bibliography. *Also called* 'Bibliographical item'.

BIBLIOGRAPHIC PROCESSING. *See* PROCESSING.

BIBLIOGRAPHIC VOLUME. A unit of publication distinguishable

from other units by having its own title-page, half title, cover title, or portfolio title. If a periodical, all the parts which comprise the publisher's volume. *Also called* 'Bibliographical volume'.

BIBLIOGRAPHICAL. Of, or relating to, or dealing with, bibliography.

BIBLIOGRAPHICAL CENTRE. A place where bibliographies and catalogues of libraries, and those issued by publishers, are assembled, and information on books is given. They are usually associated with book-lending agencies, co-operative book stores, or national libraries, and may or may not be intimately connected with the lending of books. In the U.S.A. they also serve as bureaux organizing the inter-lending of books between libraries.

BIBLIOGRAPHICAL CLASSIFICATION. One designed for the classification of books and other literary material, and for the entries in bibliographies and catalogues. *See also* KNOWLEDGE CLASSIFICATION.

BIBLIOGRAPHICAL DESCRIPTION. The description of a published work of literary or musical composition, giving particulars of authorship, of others who have contributed to the presentation of the text (editor, translator, illustrator, arranger, etc.), title, edition, date, particulars of publication (place and name of publisher and possibly of printer), format, etc. In the case of music it may relate to a single gramophone record or to an album of the same, as well as to printed music, and is concerned only with the publication as a 'record'; its physical representation, not its musical content. Not to be confused with MUSICAL DESCRIPTION (*q.v.*).

BIBLIOGRAPHICAL INDEX. *Synonymous with* BIBLIOGRAPHIC INDEX (*q.v.*).

BIBLIOGRAPHICAL ITEM. *Synonymous with* BIBLIOGRAPHIC ITEM (*q.v.*).

BIBLIOGRAPHICAL NOTE. 1. A note, often a footnote, containing a reference to one or more books or periodical articles, etc., as sources for the work. 2. A note in a catalogue or in a bibliography relating to the bibliographical history of, or describing, a book. 3. A note, often a footnote or annotation, in a catalogue, mentioning a bibliography contained in a book.

BIBLIOGRAPHICAL SERVICE. The facilities, procedures and devices which are employed to produce a bibliography consisting of a continuing series of publications, or bibliographical information as requested.

BIBLIOGRAPHICAL SOCIETY. The leading bibliographical society in the United Kingdom. It was founded in 1892. Publishes *The Library* (q.).

BIBLIOGRAPHICAL SOCIETY OF AMERICA.   The leading bibliographical society in America. It was founded in 1904 to promote
bibliographical research and to issue bibliographical publications.
Abbreviated BSA. Publishes *Papers* (q. to memb.).

BIBLIOGRAPHICAL SOCIETY OF CANADA. Founded in May
1946 to (a) promote bibliographical publication, (b) encourage the
preservation of printed works and manuscripts, and extend knowledge
of them, particularly those relating to Canada, and (c) facilitate the
exchange of bibliographical information. Membership is open to
individuals and to institutions. Publishes *Papers* (a.).

BIBLIOGRAPHICAL SOCIETY OF THE UNIVERSITY OF
VIRGINIA.   Founded in 1950, this Society represents the most
advanced school of thought in modern bibliography.

BIBLIOGRAPHICAL TOOL.   A publication, such as a list of books,
which is used by a bibliographer in the course of his work.

BIBLIOGRAPHICAL UNIT.   A document (*Fr.* ouvrage) [*see* DOCU-
MENT 2] which is an independent unit and described in a separate
main entry in a catalogue (*IFLA*).

BIBLIOGRAPHICAL VOLUME.   *Synonymous with* BIBLIOGRAPHIC
VOLUME (*q.v.*).

BIBLIOGRAPHING.   The action of consulting bibliographies.

BIBLIOGRAPHIZE.   To make a bibliography concerning some person
and/or his writings, or of some subject.

BIBLIOGRAPHY.   The terminology of bibliography is complicated,
largely because different terms have been used by different people for
the same kind of bibliography, partly because a bibliography can be
constructed in such a way that different kinds of bibliographical
description or arrangement can contribute to its make-up. Bibliographies can be arranged in two main groups: 1. *Critical bibliographies*
(describing the physical appearance of books) and 2. *Systematic* or
Enumerative bibliographies, the history of books, MSS and other
publications arranged in some logical order giving author, title, date
and place of publication, publisher, details, of edition, pagination,
series and literary contents. The following definitions have been
obtained from a variety of sources: 1. A list of books, and sometimes of other material such as periodical articles and illustrations,
written by one author, or on one subject, or printed by one printer,
or in one place, or during one period: the literature of a subject.
Bibliographies may be (*a*) complete; (*b*) general or universal,
i.e. attempting to include books published in every country and
age, and on all subjects; (*c*) national, i.e. those printed or published

in a specific country; (d) select, usually 'best books', or books, suited to a special purpose; (e) special, i.e. limited to one author or subject; (f) trade, compiled primarily to facilitate the sale or purchase of books. 2. The art or science of correctly describing books (their literary contents, or their physical make-up); loosely, the science of books, which Van Hoesen and Walter consider can be divided in four parts. These are: *Historical*, dealing with the history of book production and including the description of books as physical objects (also called 'Critical' or 'Analytical' bibliography); *Bibliothecal*, concerned with the collection, preservation, and organization of books in libraries; *Enumerative*, listing all kinds of books and periodical articles by an author or about a subject, with annotations enumerating their contents; *Practical*, dealing with the methods of work of student and author in compiling bibliographies. 3. The preparation of lists of books, the study of lists of literature; the lists themselves are generally called bibliographies, and their use is termed bibliographing (*Schneider*). 4. The art of recording books. The science of the making of books and of their extant record (*Esdaile*). 5. A list of books arranged according to some permanent principle. (*Besterman*). 6. An annotated catalogue of documents (*IBM*). 7. The process of compiling catalogues or lists (*IBM*). 8. The technique of compiling systematically descriptive lists of manuscripts or published records of different kinds which are not in the possession of one library or owner. *See also* BIO-BIBLIOGRAPHY, CARTOBIBLIOGRAPHY. Conrad Gesner (1516–65), also known as Konrad von Gesner, a Swiss naturalist, compiled a series of bibliographies which were the earliest systematic books about books and are the beginnings of modern bibliography. His *Bibliotheca universalis*, Zurich, 1545–9, contained the titles of all the books then known in Latin, Greek and Hebrew, with summaries and criticisms of each.

BIBLIOGRAPHY NOTE. *Synonymous with* BIBLIOGRAPHICAL NOTE (*q.v.*).

BIBLIOGRAPHY OF BIBLIOGRAPHIES. An extensive list of bibliographies.

BIBLIOKLEPTOMANIAC. A book-thief who is regarded as insane.

BIBLIOLATER. One who exercises BIBLIOLATRY (*q.v.*); one who has excessive admiration or reverence for books. Also called a 'Bibliolatrist'.

BIBLIOLATROUS. Given to, or characterized by, BIBLIOLATRY (*q.v.*).

BIBLIOLATRY. Book-worship.

BIBLIOLOGICAL. Pertaining to bibliology.

BIBLIOLOGIST. One versed in bibliology.

BIBLIOLOGY. The scientific description of books, dealing with their construction from the beginnings to the present day, including paper and other materials, typography, illustration and binding. Also called 'Analytical', 'Critical', 'Descriptive' or 'Historical' bibliography. *See also* Bibliography.

BIBLIOMANCY. Divination by books, generally by verses of the Bible.

BIBLIOMANE. An indiscriminate collector of books.

BIBLIOMANIA. A mania for collecting and possessing books. Also called 'Bibliomanianism', 'Bibliomanism'.

BIBLIOMANIAC. One affected with a mania for collecting books, particularly old or rare editions. Also called 'Bibliomanist'.

BIBLIOMANIST. A BIBLIOMANIAC (*q.v.*).

BIBLIOPEGIC. Relating to the binding of books.

BIBLIOPEGIST. A bookbinder.

BIBLIOPEGISTIC. Of, relating to, or befitting, a bookbinder. Also called 'BIBLIOPEGISTICAL'.

BIBLIOPEGY. The art of bookbinding.

BIBLIOPHAGIC. Of, or pertaining to, a BIBLIOPHAGIST (*q.v.*).

BIBLIOPHAGIST. One who 'devours' books.

BIBLIOPHEGUS. The name used in early Christian times for a bookbinder.

BIBLIOPHILE. A lover of books who knows how to discriminate between good and bad editions. Also called 'Bibliophilist'.

BIBLIOPHILE BINDING. A special binding such as might be used by a bibliophile.

BIBLIOPHILE EDITION. A specially printed and bound edition of a book which is published for sale to bibliophiles. *See also* FINE PAPER COPY.

BIBLIOPHILIC. Of, or pertaining to, a BIBLIOPHILE (*q.v.*).

BIBLIOPHILISM. The love of books.

BIBLIOPHILIST. *Synonymous with* BIBLIOPHILE (*q.v.*).

BIBLIOPHILOUS. Addicted to BIBLIOPHILY (*q.v.*).

BIBLIOPHILY. A love of books; a taste for books.

BIBLIOPHOBIA. A dislike, or dread, of books; an aversion to books.

BIBLIOPOESY. The making of books.

BIBLIOPOLAR. Of, or belonging to, booksellers. Also called 'Bibliopolic', 'Bibliopolical'.

BIBLIOPOLE. One who deals in books, especially rare or curious ones.

BIBLIOPOLISM. The principles, or trade, of bookselling.

BIBLIOPOLIST. A bookseller.

BIBLIOPOLISTIC. Of, pertaining to, or befitting, a bookseller.

BIBLIOPOLY. The selling of books. Also called 'Bibliopolery'.

BIBLIOPSYCHOLOGY. The study of books, readers and authors and their mutual relationships. It was formulated by Nicholas Rubakin in his Institute of Bibliopsychology in Switzerland, 1916–46.

BIBLIOSOPH. One who knows, or knows about, books.

BIBLIOSOPHIST. A BIBLIOPHILE (q.v.).

BIBLIOTAPH. One who keeps his books under lock and key. Also called 'Bibliotaphist'.

BIBLIOTAPHIC. Of, or belonging to, a bibliotaph.

BIBLIOTEKSTJANST. The Swedish library supply agency (a company since 1960) which developed from a central selling agency founded in 1936 by the Swedish Library Association (Sveriges Allmauna Biblioteksforening). It publishes lists of recommended new publications and binds them when ordered by public and school libraries, supplying them through local booksellers. It also publishes indexes of newspapers and periodicals, publications including book lists and library guides on behalf of the Swedish Library Association, schedules of the Swedish Classification scheme, and printed catalogue cards. Other activities are designing and manufacturing furniture and giving advice on library planning.

BIBLIOTHEC. Belonging to a library or librarian. A librarian.

BIBLIOTHECA. 1. A library. 2. A bibliographer's catalogue.

BIBLIOTHECAL. Belonging to a library.

BIBLIOTHECAL CLASSIFICATION. A classification scheme for the arrangement of books on the shelves of a library.

BIBLIOTHECAL SCHEMES. See BIBLIOGRAPHICAL CLASSIFICATION.

BIBLIOTHECAR. A librarian. See also BIBLIOTHECARIAN.

BIBLIOTHECARIAN. 1. A librarian. 2. Of, or belonging to, a library, or a librarian.

BIBLIOTHECARY. 1. A librarian. 2. A library. 3. Of, or belonging to, a library.

BIBLIOTHÈQUE NATIONALE. The oldest of the European national libraries; it has existed in Paris since the fourteenth century, although in its early days as the personal library of the sovereigns. It possesses over 6,000,000, volumes of printed books, 5,000,000 prints and 175,000 mss. It is the French legal deposit library. Abbreviated BN.

BIBLIOTHERAPIST. A person skilled in BIBLIOTHERAPY (q.v.).

BIBLIOTHERAPY. The use of selected reading and related materials for therapeutic purposes in physical medicine and in mental health. As an aspect of hospital and institution librarianship it requires an acquaintance with a wide range of literature and a knowledge of the techniques of group leadership and individual guidance.

BIBLIOTHETIC. Pertaining to, or based on, the placing or arrangement of books.

BIBLIO-TRAIN. A railway coach fitted up as a mobile library.

BIENNIAL. *See* Bi-ANNUAL.

BIENNALE OF ILLUSTRATIONS BRATISLAVA. An international demonstration of children's book illustrations which, with the co-operation of the Unesco national commissions, seeks to develop this art-form by creating a suitable environment for their evaluation. The Grand Prix BIB (value Kcs 20,000=US 1250 approx.) and many other prizes are awarded on the recommendation of an international jury. The first BIB was held in Bratislava, Czechoslovakia, in September 1967, and the first recipient of the Grand Prix BIB was Yasuo Segawa of Japan for his illustrations for *Taro and the bamboo shoot* by Masako Matsuno.

BIFURCATE CLASSIFICATION. 1. A classification branching in pairs, positive and negative, such as the Tree of Porphyry. Also called classification by dichotomy. 2. The bifurcate division of a genus by a single significant difference into a species and a residuum, which may or may not be disregarded in further division.

BIFURCATION. A method of subdivision in classification whereby every class is divided into two only, a positive and a negative group. Also called 'Dichotomy'.

BILL. 1. A written complaint at law. 2. A draft of a proposed law introduced in a legislative body. 3. A North American term for an account of money owing for goods supplied or services rendered. *See also* INVOICE.

BILL BOOK. A book in which invoices or bills (accounts) are entered as received. The entries are usually arranged alphabetically under the suppliers' names (American).

BILL OF MIDDLESEX. A precept having the same force as a writ, but with the formal opening omitted.

BILL OF TYPE. 1. A complete assortment of any fount of type. 2. The plan or ratio by which founts of type are made up by type founders in order to provide the correct proportion of each letter or character, as ascertained by experience as to probable requirements. Also called 'Fount Scheme', 'Scheme'.

BI-MONTHLY. A serial publication issued in alternate months.

BINARY. (*Information retrieval*) 1. A number system using only two symbols, the digits one and zero. 2. A number system where quantities are represented in base 2 rather than base 10.

BINARY NUMBER SYSTEM. A system, used in many electronic computers and in information theory, which has only one digit, I, and a zero. Thus the first ten whole numbers of this system, together with their decimal equivalents, which consist of nine digits and a zero, in parentheses, are: 0(0), 1(1), 10(2), 11(3), 100(4), 101(5), 110(6), 111(7), 1000(8), 1001(9), 1010(10).

BIND, TO. To assemble and fasten securely printed or manuscript SHEETS (*q.v.*) within a cover which may be made of wood or board covered with leather or cloth, plastic, stiff card (board) or paper. *See* also BOARDS 1, SHEETS.

BIND IN. To fasten supplementary material securely into a bound book.

BINDER. 1. A person who binds books. 2. A case, or detachable cover, for filling magazines, pamphlets, etc. usually on wires or cords, one for each publication.

BINDER'S BLOCK. *See* BINDER'S BRASS.

BINDER'S BOARD. *See* MILLBOARD, STRAWBOARD.

BINDER'S BRASS. A design, or letters of the alphabet, cut in brass and used by a bookbinder's finisher in lettering book covers. When a BLOCK (*q.v.* –2) is used it is called a 'Binder's block'. *See also* ARMS BLOCK, ZINCO.

BINDER'S DIES. (*Binding*) Lettering or designs cut in brass and used for decorating book covers by stamping or embossing them. Also called 'Panel stamps'.

BINDER'S TICKET. A small engraved or printed label, usually fixed to the top outside corner of one of the front end papers between about 1750 and 1825, and giving the name of the binder. These tickets were superseded by the binder's name stamped in gilt, ink, or blind, on one of the inside boards, usually on the extreme lower edge: this is called a 'name pallet'.

BINDER'S TITLE. The title lettered on the back of a book when re-bound, to distinguish it from the publisher's title on the cover or title-page. *See also* BACK TITLE, COVER TITLE.

BINDER'S WASTE. Printed sheets which are surplus to a bookbinder's needs and which are sometimes used in bookbinding for lining purposes.

BINDERY. A place in which books are bound or re-bound.

BINDING. 1. The cover of a volume. 2. The finished work resulting from the processes involved in binding a book. 3. Colloquially, a number of books in a library which are waiting to be re-bound, or those which have been re-bound. *See also* BOOKBINDING.

BINDING BOOK. A book in which are entered particulars of books sent to a binder for re-binding. It may vary in information given, from a title list to full binding instructions.

BINDING CLOTH. *See* BOOK CLOTH.

BINDING COPY. A book which is so worn as to need rebinding.

BINDING DEPARTMENT. The department of a library or printing establishment in which books are bound or re-bound.

BINDING EDGE. A back edge of a volume, or the folded edge of a section; the edge opposite the FORE-EDGE (*q.v.*). *See also* RIDGE.

BINDING FROM SHEETS. Purchasing books in unfolded sheets and having them bound by the library binder.

BINDING RECORD. A record of books sent to the binder. This may consist of the book-cards, a duplicate of the binding slips, or a special record such as that kept in a BINDING BOOK (*q.v.*).

BINDING SLIP (SHEET). The form on which instructions for binding are written for the binders' guidance. A slip relates to one book only and is usually inserted in a book before it leaves the library and remains in it throughout all the binding processes.

BINDING VARIATIONS. The bindings of books, which, although published in the same edition, vary in colour or type of book cloth, tooling, etc. This may arise through a number of manufacturing causes, especially if the whole of an edition is not bound at the same time, or through storage under unsatisfactory conditions, e.g. dampness.

BINOMIAL. (*Classification*) A name which consists of two, and occasionally three, terms.

BIOBIBLIOGRAPHY. A bibliography which contains brief biographical details about the authors.

BIOGRAPHEE. A person who is the subject of biography.

BIOGRAPHEE ENTRY. The entry in a catalogue (dictionary, name, or subject) under the name of the BIOGRAPHEE (*q.v.*); the subject entry for a biography.

BIOGRAPHER. A person who writes a biography of another.

BIOGRAPHICAL DICTIONARY. A collection of lives of people arranged in alphabetical order.

BIOGRAPHY. 1. A written account of a person's life. 2. The branch of literature concerned with the lives of people.

BIOGRAPHY FILE. A file of records on standard size cards, or of cuttings, giving information about individuals. Also called a 'Who's who' file.

BIOSIS. Abbreviation for Bio-Sciences Information Service of Biological Abstracts, the organization responsible for publishing (1) the fortnightly *Biological Abstracts* with its four computer-composed indexes (a) BASIC (*q.v.*), (b) CROSS (*q.v.*), (c) *Author Index* and (d) *Bio-systematic Index*; (2) BASIC – separate publication; (3) subject sections of *Biological Abstracts* on microcards; (4) *Biological Abstracts* on microfilm; (5) *Bio-Research Titles* (m.) which reports titles not abstracted in *BA*; (6) unpublished information service on cards.

BIRMINGHAM AND DISTRICT LIBRARY ASSOCIATION. An autonomous Association which became the Birmingham and District Branch of the Library Association on 1st April 1929.

BIRMINGHAM AND DISTRICT PERIODICALS INTERCHANGE SCHEME. An organization for the interloan of periodicals. It has been operating since 1953, and is centred on the Technical Library, Ratcliff Place, Birmingham, 1, but the holdings of this Department are not available for loan.

BIRMINGHAM NOTATION. *See* GKD NOTATION.

BIRMINGHAM PUBLIC LIBRARIES WORKS LIBRARIES LOAN SCHEME. Industrial libraries which are properly constituted and under the care of a designated librarian may become members and so borrow material for short periods from the Birmingham Reference Library. The Scheme has been in operation since 1958 and is organized from the Technical Library, Ratcliff Place, Birmingham 1.

BIRTH AND DEATH DATE. The years of birth, and possibly of death, given in personal name entries in catalogues.

BISCOE TIME NUMBERS (BISCOE DATE TABLE). A table (designed by W. S. Biscoe) which allocates letters to year periods in order to arrange books in chronological, rather than alphabetical, order both on the shelves and in the catalogue. The full table is as follows:

A	B.C.	J	1830–1839	S	1920–1929
B	0–999	K	1840–1849	T	1930–1939
C	1000–1499	L	1850–1859	U	1940–1949
D	1500–1599	M	1860–1869	V	1950–1959
E	1600–1699	N	1870–1879	W	1960–1969
F	1700–1799	O	1880–1889	X	1970–1979
G	1800–1809	P	1890–1899	Y	1980–1989
H	1810–1819	Q	1900–1909	Z	1990–1999
I	1820–1829	R	1910–1919		

Examples of use: a book published in 1676 would be lettered E76, a book published in 1916 would be lettered R6.

BISHOPS' BIBLE. A Bible printed [1568] in London by Richard Jugge, senior Queen's Printer to Elizabeth I. Sometimes called 'Archbishop Parker's Bible'.

BISHOP'S RULES. A set of rules for abbreviating periodical titles: (1) if the journal title consists of a single word, the first four letters are taken; (2) if of two words, the first two letters of each word; (3) if of three words, the first letter of each of the first two words and the first two letters of the last word; (4) if of more than four words, usually the first letter of each of the first four words. *See also* CODEN.

BIT. A contraction of 'binary digit'. The smallest unit of information; a zero or a one; a 'yes' or 'no'.

BITE. The term given to the action of acid eating into metal in the process of block making or plate engraving.

BI-WEEKLY. *Synonymous with* FORTNIGHTLY (*q.v.*) and 'Semi-monthly'.

BLACK. A mark made unintentionally on a sheet of paper by a lead, space or piece of furniture which has risen. Also called 'Work up'.

BLACK FACE. *Synonymous with* BOLD FACE (*q.v.*).

'BLACK' HEADINGS. Headings, other than subject headings, in a dictionary catalogue. The term has its origin in the fact that it was the practice in many libraries to use red for the subject headings and black for all the others.

BLACK LETTER. A term used to indicate old English, text, or church type, which was based on the writing in mediaeval manuscripts. *Synonymous with* GOTHIC TYPE (*q.v.*).

BLACK-LIST. A list of readers who have lost books and not paid for them, or owe fines, and of guarantors who have not fulfilled their obligations in respect of readers they have guaranteed.

BLACK STEP. A rule about 6 points thick and up to 24 points long printed between the first and last pages of a section so as to show on the spine of the section when folded. In the first forme it is positioned opposite the top line of text, and about 24 points lower in each successive forme, so that when all the sections of a book have been gathered and placed together a diagonal line is seen across the spine. Any error in gathering is immediately apparent. Also called 'Back mark', 'Collating mark' (*qqv.*), 'Quad mark'.

BLANK. An unprinted page which is part of a SIGNATURE (*q.v.*) and is consequently recorded when making a bibliographical description of a book in the form 'bl.' following the unprinted signature or page number in [ ].

BLANK BOOK. A bound book consisting of blank leaves only; used for notes, records, accounts, etc.

BLANK COVER. The cover of a bound book which is devoid of lettering or ornamentation.

BLANK LEAVES. The unprinted leaves to be found at each end of a book. If these are conjugate with printed leaves they should be included in a bibliographical description of the book, but if only binder's fly-leaves, ignored.

BLANK PAGE. A page of a book on which nothing has been printed.

BLANKET. 1. The packing used on the impression cylinder of a printing machine; it may consist of cloth, rubber or paper. 2. The resilient rubber sheet attached to a cylinder on to which the image to be printed is transferred, or offset, from the inked lithographic plate, and then offset on to the paper.

BLANKET CYLINDER. *See* OFFSET PRINTING.

BLANKING. (*Binding*) An impression made on the cloth cover of a book with a heated brass stamp as a base for lettering or decorative stamping.

BLEACH. The process of whitening pulp or cellulose, usually with a solution of chlorine.

BLEACHED KRAFT. A white paper made from bleached sulphate wood pulp and used for a variety of purposes when strength is required, e.g. as a body paper for coating. *See also* KRAFT PAPER.

BLED. A book the letterpress or plates of which have been cut into by the binder is said to have been 'bled'. *See also* CROPPED.

BLEED. 1. To trim printed matter so close that the text or plates are cut into. *See also* CROPPED, CUT, TRIMMED, UNCUT. 2. In the diazotype process of reproduction, the dye image which has run or spread.

BLIND. Lettering on a book or other article without using gold leaf or colour.

BLIND-BLOCKED. Lettering on book covers not inked or gilt, only embossed or impressed.

BLIND EMBOSSING. Raising paper in a pattern, or in the shape of letters, by means of dies but not using ink on the raised (i.e. embossed) parts. *See also* EMBOSSING.

BLIND INDEX. A form of indexing equipment in which the headings on cards or slips cannot be seen until those immediately in front are turned over. The opposite of VISIBLE INDEX (*q.v.*).

BLIND P.   The paragraph mark ¶. *See also* PARAGRAPH MARK, REFERENCE MARKS.

BLIND PAGE.   An unnumbered, and usually blank, page which is included in the overall pagination. These usually occur in the PRELIMINARIES (*q.v.*).

BLIND REFERENCE.   A reference in an index to a catchword which does not occur in the index, or a reference in a catalogue or bibliography to a heading under which no entry will be found.

BLIND STAMPING.   Embossing lettering or a design on to book covers, whether by hand or in a press, without using gold leaf or colour. Also called 'Antique', 'Blind blocking' and 'Blind tooling'.

BLIND TOOLING.   *See* TOOLING.

BLINDED-IN.   A design which is impressed on a book cover with heated tools but not coloured or gilt.

BLISS' BIBLIOGRAPHIC CLASSIFICATION.   *See* BIBLIOGRAPHIC CLASSIFICATION.

BLISS CLASSIFICATION ASSOCIATION.   Formed in May 1967 to replace the former British Committee for the Bliss Classification consequent upon the receipt of the copyright of the BC from the H. W. Wilson Company. Publishes *BC Bulletin* (a.).

BLOCK.   1. To print with a solid shading at the bottom or sides, as a second impression in a different colour and in a projecting position. 2. In bookbinding, to emboss or letter book covers with a block or frame containing the entire device, and at one operation, as distinguished from die stamping. 3. A large stamp without a handle used in a blocking press by bookbinders for impressing a design on a book cover. 4. A type-high piece of wood or metal, either with or without a design, from which an impression can be made. A general term which includes line-blocks, half-tones, electros, etc. 5. To secure a plate to its proper position for printing. 6. A piece of wood or metal on which a stereotype, electrotype or other plate is mounted to make it type high. 7. A piece of hard wood used by engravers. 8. The core of a roller on a lithographing press. 9. In photography, to paint over a part of a negative to prevent or modify its printing. 10. A stop in a catalogue drawer. *See also* BACKSLIDE.

BLOCK BOOKS.   Those printed from engraved blocks of wood. Block books originated in the Netherlands and in Germany after about 1410; most are dateable from 1460 to 1480. They were printed on one side of the leaf in a thin brownish ink. Generally they may be divided into three groups; 1. those which have pictures and words descriptive of the pictures engraved at the foot of the picture or in cartouches proceeding from the mouths of the principal figures; 2, those which have pictures on one page and a full page of explanatory text opposite, or form distinct and separate units on the same page; 3, those with xylographic text only. The *Biblia pauperum* and *Apocalypse of St. John* are well-known examples of Group 1; *Ars memorandi*, *Ars moriendi* and *Speculum humanae salvationis* of Group 2; and the *Donatus de Octobus Partibus Orationis* of Group 3. Block books continued to be printed well into the sixteenth century and several of the later ones were printed on a press with printer's ink, in such instances often on both sides of the paper. Those printed on one side only of the paper are called 'anopisthographic'. Books printed from engraved wood blocks, are called 'xylographic' books. *See also* OPISTHROGRAPHIC, WOOD BLOCK, WOODCUT, XYLOGRAPHY.

BLOCK CALENDAR. A calendar with small pieces of paper bearing the date, one for each day, and pasted in a pile to form a block, the top one being torn off daily.

BLOCK INDEXING. 1. A system of indexing wherein 'blocks' of materials are collected, each block being small enough to permit easy manual search of the group contained therein. (*IBM*) 2. A system for separation of information on microfilm into groups or 'blocks' identified by readily distinguishable numbers to facilitate reference.

BLOCK PRINTING. Making an illustration, or printing a design on paper or material, from wood or metal blocks with the design in relief.

BLOCK-PULL. A proof of an illustration or text engraved on a block as distinct from type.

BLOCKING. The impressing of a gold leaf, metal foil, or other graphic medium into the book-cover by means of a stamp having a raised surface. The term is also applied to the impressing of type, blocks, etc., without any intervening media, this operation being known as 'blind-stamping'.

BLOCKING FOIL. A paper foil coated with gold, white metal or coloured pigment which is transferred to the leather or cloth cover of a book by means of a heated die used in a blocking press. The process using these materials is known as 'foil blocking'.

BLOCKING OUT. (*Reprography*) The use of opaque, or indian, ink to paint part of a negative to prevent areas from printing.

BLOCKING PRESS. A press using heated blocks to impress, or stamp, lettering, designs, etc., on the book covers and cases. In machine bookbinding, ribbons of blocking foil of varying widths are used; these contain their own glair or adhesive. The press is also used for blind or ink blocking, no heat being necessary for the latter process.

BLOTTING PAPER.   Absorbent paper made from specially prepared rags, and unsized.

BLOW UP.   1. A photograph, jacket, book review, specimen page of a book, etc., greatly enlarged for exhibition or advertising purposes. *See also* GIANT BOOK. 2. In documentary reproduction a copy having a larger scale than the original; an enlargement or PROJECTION PRINT (*q.v.*).

BLUE BOOK.   A more lengthy official publication of similar character to a WHITE PAPER (*q.v.*), printed with a blue paper cover. (The traditional blue cover is now used principally for Select Committee Reports and for certain Accounts and Papers presented to Parliament under statute). The French colour is yellow; German, white; Italian, green. *See also* GREEN PAPER, PARLIAMENTARY PUBLICATIONS, WHITE PAPER.

BLUE-LINE PRINT.   1. A positive print made by the DIAZOTYPE PROCESS (*q.v.*). 2. A blue-print with blue lines on a white field, made by printing from a negative master.

BLUE PRINT PROCESS.   A method of reproducing documents whereby a sheet of paper, which has been treated with a preparation mainly consisting of ferro prussiate, together with the document are exposed to powerful arc lamps. The paper is then developed by placing it in running water. A blue and white negative results and this can be used to produce a blue and white positive. Only single-sided documents which are perfect (having no creases or alterations) are suitable for reproduction by this process.

BLUEPRINT.   A blue on white, or white on blue, print submitted by a blockmaker as a rough proof before blocks are supplied. Also, a print produced by the BLUEPRINT PROCESS (*q.v.*).

BLURB.   The publisher's description and recommendation of a book, usually found on the front flap of a book jacket. *See also* PUFF.

BOARD LABEL.   The label pasted on the inside of the front board of a library book to show ownership, and usually bearing a few of the more important rules. Also called a 'Book plate' or 'Book label.'

BOARD OF DIRECTORS.   *Synonymous with* BOARD OF LIBRARY TRUSTEES (*q.v.*).

BOARD OF LIBRARY TRUSTEES.   The committee responsible for the control of an American library system. Also known as 'Library Board,' 'Board of Directors,' 'Library Trustees' and occasionally, 'Library Commission.'

BOARD PAPER.   *Synonymous with* PASTE-DOWN (*q.v.*).

BOARDS.   1. The sheets of millboard, pasteboard or strawboard used for bookcovers. When covered with paper, a book so bound is said to be

bound in 'paper boards,' when covered with cloth, in 'cloth boards.'
2. So named because wood was used originally. 3. A general term
which includes pulp, index, paste, ivory and other forms of card used
for printing. *See also* BRISTOL BOARD, IVORY BOARD. 4. The pieces of
wooden board used by a binder to grip a book when pressing, cutting,
backing, burnishing, etc.

BOAR'S HEAD PRESS. A private printing press founded in 1931 by
Christopher Sandford who afterwards acquired the GOLDEN COCKEREL
PRESS (*q.v.*).

BODONI. An early MODERN FACE roman type designed in 1790 by
Giambattista Bodoni (1740–1813) of Parma, the most celebrated
printer of his day. It was re-cut for contemporary printing in 1921.
Characteristics are mathematically vertical stress, long ascenders and
descenders, fine straight-line serifs, and thin hair lines. For a specimen
alphabet, *see* TYPE FACE.

BODY. (*Printing*) 1. The measurement (or thickness) from back to front
of a type letter, slug, rule, lead, etc. 2. The part of a piece of movable
type from the foot to the flat surface at the upper end, above which is
the 'SHOULDER' (*q.v.*) and from which the moulded letter rises. It
comprises the 'BELLY,' 'BACK,' 'FEET,' 'SIDES,' 'PIN-MARK,' 'NICK'
and 'GROOVES' (*qq.v.*). Also called the 'Shank' or 'Stem.' (*Paper*). The
apparent weight of a sheet of paper.

BODY MATTER. (*Printing*) The text, as distinct from display matter,
or illustrations.

BODY OF THE BOOK (WORK). The main part of the book, commencing at the first page of the text and including any illustrations or
foot-notes which may accompany it, and excluding any preliminary
or appended matter.

BODY OF THE ENTRY. The part of a catalogue entry which
describes a publication. It usually follows a heading (thus beginning
with the title) and excludes any annotation.

BODY PAPER, or BOARD. The foundation for art, chromo, coated,
blue print, gummed, photographic and other papers which are made
by coating or treating with a composition of any kind. Also called
'base' or 'raw' paper.

BODY SIZE. *See* TYPE SIZE.

BODY TYPE. Type, of 14 point or less, used for the main body of a
composition, as distinguished from the display type used in headings,
etc. It also includes sizes of type up to 24 point which may be used in
book work. Display type may begin at 18 point.

BOILER. The part of paper-making machinery in which the raw

material is boiled in water before it goes into the BREAKER (*q.v.*). Also called 'Kier.' *See also* DIGESTER.

BOLD FACE.   Heavy-faced type, also called 'Full face' and 'Black face.' **This is bold face,** and is indicated in a MS. by wavy underlining 〜〜〜〜〜〜. Bold face is usually used to give emphasis to certain words, and for headings. In machine setting, bold characters can normally be set or tapped in the same line as the roman and italic. Most FOUNTS (*q.v.*) have a bold face based on the same design as the medium weight as well as the roman and italic. Bold face developed from the CLARENDON (*q.v.*) face which has only slight contrast in the up and down strokes and was used, with other type faces, for emphasis. Clarendon grew out of the Antique face cut by Vincent Figgins prior to 1815 believed to be the earliest of the designs now generally known as Egyptian. It is peculiar in giving equal emphasis to the up and down strokes and serifs. *See also* EGYPTIAN, TYPE FACE.

BOLE.   (*Printing*) To reduce the height of type by shaving the feet. *See also* ARMENIAN BOLE.

BOLOGNESE LETTERS.   Manuscript lettering which originated at the legal school of the University of Bologna and was used as the basis for the Gothic types known as 'Rotunda.' It was introduced into Germany from Venice and was consequently often called 'Litterae Venetae' by the early German printers.

BOLT.   The folded or doubled edge of paper at the head, tail or fore-edge of a sheet in an uncut or unopened book. These are known as head bolts, tail bolts or fore-edge bolts. The folded edge at the back of a sheet is referred to, not as a 'bolt,' but as the 'last fold' or 'back fold.' *See also* FOLD TO PAPER, FOLD TO PRINT, OPEN EDGE.

BOM PROOF.   A proof which is specially printed and bound for submission to a book club.

BOMBAY LIBRARY ASSOCIATION.   Founded on 9th December 1944 with the object of promoting the library service and librarianship mainly within the municipal limits of the city of Bombay and Greater Bombay. Any person or institution interested in library work may become a member.

BONE FOLDER.   A flat piece of bone 6 to 9 inches long, about 1 inch wide and ⅛ inch thick with rounded corners and edges which is used for rubbing along the fold of a sheet of paper to bend the fibres of the paper firmly into position, and in book repairing. *See also* FOLDING STICK.

BONNANGE CARD CATALOGUE TRAY.   An obsolete form of tray invented by M. F. Bonnange. The cards are hinged near the bottom, the lower piece (which is thicker than the upper) having shoulders which fit into grooves in the sides of the tray.

BOOK. 1. A set of blank sheets of paper bound along one edge and enclosed within protective covers to form a volume, especially a written or printed literary composition presented in this way. 2. A division of a literary work, which is separately published and has an independent physical existence, although its pagination may be continuous with other volumes. 3. At a UNESCO conference in 1964 a book was defined as 'a non-periodical printed publication of at least forty-nine pages, exclusive of cover pages.' *See also* PAMPHLET. 4. A collection (*Fr.* assemblage) of manuscript or printed leaves fastened together to form a volume or volumes, forming a BIBLIOGRAPHICAL UNIT (*q.v.*). (It is distinct from periodicals, and from other forms of material, such as films, prints, maps, etc.) (*IFLA*). *See also* ADAPTATION, DOCUMENT, FASCICLE, PART, PRINTED BOOK, PUBLICATION, VERSION, VOLUME, WORK.

BOOK AUCTION SALE. A method of selling second-hand books; it dates from the early seventeenth century, and is the usual method of selling large libraries or individual copies of rare or valuable books. The prices realized are recorded in *Book auction records* or the American *Book prices current*.

BOOK BAND. A narrow strip, or band, of printed paper placed round a jacketed book to advertise it by drawing attention to it, e.g. its cheap price, an award which had been made in respect of it, the 'book of the film,' etc.

BOOK BARROW. A barrow from which books are sold, usually in a street market. The wheels of the barrow are intended to enable the display fitting and the books to be moved conveniently from the storage place to the sales position rather than from one sales position to another, although this is done in some cases.

BOOK BIN. An unenclosed receptacle in which books are placed, especially in a staff enclosure while awaiting attention such as discharging or shelving.

BOOK BOAT. A common means of providing a library service to residents on islands and land masses accessible only by boat. They are provided in Norway, Sweden and Denmark.

BOOK BOXES. Boxes in which books are transported.

BOOK CAPACITY. *Synonymous with* SHELF CAPACITY (*q.v.*).

BOOK CARD. A piece of card or plastic material on which are written the means of identifying a particular book (usually some or all of the following: charging symbol, accession number, class number, author, title) and which is used in charging (i.e. recording) the loan of the book. Book cards are usually made of manilla, of different colours for different departments or classes of books, but plastic is often used because of its better handling properties and greater durability. Also called 'Charging card,' and in America 'Book slip,' 'Charge slip' and 'Charging slip.'

BOOK CARRIER. *See* BOOK CONVEYOR.

BOOK CATALOGUE. A catalogue produced in book form. Also used as a synonym for PRINTED CATALOGUE (*q.v.*). Sometimes used synonymously for PAGE CATALOGUE (*q.v.*).

BOOK CLASSIFICATION. A general term covering bibliographical and bibliothecal classifications.

BOOK CLOTH. Cotton or linen cloth (usually coloured) used for book covers.

BOOK CLUB. A publishing activity issuing to subscribing members, specially, and cheaply, printed books of merit. The subjects of the books published may be restricted to one subject; the books have usually been published before, although in some cases very recently, and are limited in number in any one year.

BOOK CLUB EDITION. A book sold by a Book Club to its members. Such books may not be the same edition, reprint, issue or impression as are normally available through trade channels to the public; they are usually specially printed and bound, and except in the cases of clubs or societies whose purpose is to supply books of exceptional quality, of inferior materials.

BOOK COLLECTING. The assembling of books which because of their bibliographic interest, their contents (historic or factual), the history of the individual copies, or their rarity, have some permanent interest to the collector.

BOOK COLLECTION. *Synonymous with* BOOK STOCK (*q.v.*).

BOOK COLLECTOR. One who purchases books systematically often in a given field of knowledge or within the limits of some branch of historical bibliography.

BOOK CONVEYOR. A system of metal or other containers joined to an endless chain, or other device, which is capable of conveying books, correspondence, papers, etc., either horizontally or perpendicularly between the various parts of a large library on different floors. They are usually operated by electricity, and push button control ensures the automatic discharge of the containers' contents at specified service points. Also called 'Book carrier,' 'Book distributor.'

BOOK COUPON. *See* UNESCO COUPONS.

BOOK COVER. *See* COVER.

BOOK CRAFTS. The operations which are carried out in producing books and which require varying degrees of skill in their performance; these include paper-making, printing, design of books, design and production of illustrations, and binding.

BOOK DECORATION. The impressing of a design on the cover of a book, often by gold (but sometimes blind) tooling. The design so impressed.

BOOK DEVELOPMENT COUNCIL. An independent non-profit-making body, formed in April 1965, registered as a company and sponsored by the Publishers Association. Described as 'a British enterprise for international co-operation' it seeks to make available the skills of British publishing wherever they can be used, particularly in developing countries.

BOOK DISPLAY. A small exhibition of books usually on one or several related subjects, in (and sometimes outside) a library.

BOOK DISTRIBUTOR. *See* BOOK CONVEYOR.

BOOK DRIVE. A campaign to secure gifts of books or of money for buying books. (American.)

BOOK DROP. A box or chute provided so that readers can return books when a library is closed or where drive-in facilities are available.

BOOK END. *See* BOOK SUPPORT.

BOOK FAIR. 1. An exhibition of books and of book-making, sometimes including talks by authors, illustrators, booksellers and publishers. 2. Trade exhibitions of books with the object of selling and exchanging books. Some, particularly those held at Frankfurt and Leipzig before the Second World War, became world famous. The Frankfurt Book Fair has in recent years developed into an important international means of selling books and encouraging translation of books into other languages.

BOOK FORM. Said of a work published as a book but which has been issued previously in serial form, usually in a periodical.

BOOK FUND. The fund, or amount of money, which is available for the purchase of books, and possibly of non-book materials.

BOOK HAND. A style of artificial, calligraphic handwriting used for books (as distinct from the cursive styles used by individuals for records, memoranda, correspondence, etc.), before the introduction of printing. Uncial, Caroline minuscule, Gothic, and Humanistic are book hands. Bastard, and Chancery are not.

BOOK HOIST. *See* BOOK LIFT.

BOOK HOLDER. (*Reprography*) A device for holding open a bound volume in a level or near-level plane so that all parts of the image are in focus during reproduction.

BOOK HUNTER. One whose occupation is the tracing of specific titles in the second-hand market, sometimes at the request of a would-be purchaser.

BOOK ILLUSTRATION. The making of drawings or paintings to illustrate the text of a book. The resulting illustration.

BOOK JACKET. The paper wrapping covering a book as issued by the publisher. It serves the purposes of protecting the book, and if illustrated (as it usually is), of attracting attention. It bears the name of the author, the title, and usually has a BLURB (*q.v.*) on the first flap, and elsewhere, particulars of other books by the same author or issued by the same publisher. Also called 'Dust cover,' 'Dust jacket,' 'Dust wrapper,' 'Jacket,' 'Wrapper.'

BOOK LABEL. *See* BOARD LABEL, BOOK PLATE.

BOOK LIFT. A small device for carrying not more than 1 cwt. of books perpendicularly from one floor to another. Usually operated by electricity, it may be hand-operated by hauling on a rope if the distance is not more than about 25 feet; this is a slow and tedious method. A hand-operated lift is sometimes called a book hoist.

BOOK LIST. A list of books, usually on some specific subject and arranged in classified or author order.

BOOK NUMBER. 1. The number, letter, or other symbol or combination of symbols used to distinguish an individual book from every other book in the same class, and at the same time to arrange books bearing the same class number in the desired order on the shelves, by author, title, edition, date of publication, etc. It usually consists of the (a) AUTHOR MARK, (b) WORK MARK, (c) VOLUME NUMBER. Also called 'Book mark.' *See also* CALL NUMBER. 2. In the Colon Classification it follows the class number and precedes the COLLECTION NUMBER (*q.v.*) to form the CALL NUMBER (*q.v.*); it is the symbol used to fix the position of a book in relation to other books having the same ULTIMATE CLASS (*q.v.*). The Book Number individualizes the document among the documents having the same class number, and is used to mechanize the position of a document among those having the same ultimate class. *See also* ASSOCIATED BOOK.

BOOK OF ARMAGH. Written by Ferdomnach, a scribe, who died in 844, this MS contains portions of the New Testament. It is the first example of the Irish pointed hand to which a definite date can be given, and resembles the English pointed hand of the period.

BOOK OF HOURS. The name given to books of private devotions

designed for the laity; they were very popular and in general use throughout the Catholic Church from the fourteenth to the sixteenth centuries. Both before and after the discovery of printing they were often beautifully illuminated, and fine examples of them are today much coveted by collectors. Great personages were fond of having these books made specially for themselves, with decorations and illustrations of an individual appeal.

BOOK OF KELLS. *See* KELLS, BOOK OF.

'BOOK OF THE YEAR FOR CHILDREN' MEDAL. A bronze medal awarded by the Canadian Association of Children's Librarians for outstanding children's books, one in English and one in French, published in Canada during a calendar year and written by a Canadian or resident of Canada. The award is made only when an entry is worthy in quality; the first book in English to receive the award was Roderick Haig-Brown's *Starbrick Valley winter* (1947) and the first book in French was Emile S. J. Gervais' *Mgr. de Laval* (1954). The Medal was designed after the bas relief of Alfred Laliberté from the Hébert Memorial in Quebec City and shows the European mother, Marie Rollet Hébert, reading to her children.

BOOK PAPER. A name given to paper manufactured for books to distinguish it from newsprint, cover paper and writing paper.

BOOK PLATE. A label pasted in a book to mark its ownership and sometimes to indicate its location in a library. Private book plates are often ornate or artistic: simpler and smaller ones bearing merely the owner's name are called 'book labels.'

BOOK POCKET. The strong paper receptacle like the corner of an envelope pasted on the inside of the board of a book to take the book card. The BOARD LABEL (*q.v.*) frequently serves this purpose.

BOOK POST. A postal rate applying to the carrying of books: it is usually cheaper than the ordinary parcel rate providing the packages are made up in such a way that the postal authorities may examine them at will without breaking any seals and without inconvenience.

BOOK PREPARATION. *See* PROCESSING.

BOOK PRESS. A press, usually of wood or steel, into which books are placed during binding or repairing processes. *See also* BOOK STACK, BOOKCASE, DOUBLE-FACED SHELF, DOUBLE SIDED STACK, PRESS, TIER.

BOOK PROCESSING. *See* PROCESSING.

BOOK PROCESSING CENTER. A co-operative organization operated for a group of libraries where the ordering and processing of books (cataloguing, preparation, catalogues for use of public) is undertaken for all the participants, whether as a separate service or as one of other services. (American.)

BOOK PRODUCTION. The art and craft of making books including designing, choice and use of materials, illustration, printing and binding.

BOOK RACK. A shelf or small group of shelves used for displaying books.

BOOK RAILBUS. A means of taking books to isolated residents in northern Sweden. The railbus stops at every house alongside the railway.

BOOK RARITIES. Books of which few copies are known to exist; scarce books.

BOOK REST. A portable fitting similar to the music rest of a piano which is placed at a convenient angle for reading on a table or desk to hold a book when notes are being made from it.

BOOK REVIEW. An evaluation of a book published in a periodical or newspaper.

BOOK SATCHEL. A bag used in mediaeval times for carrying books. It frequently hung from a cleric's habit cord or on a warrior's belt.

BOOK SELECTION. The process of choosing books for inclusion in a library.

BOOK SHRINE. A box or chest, usually ornamented, in which valuable books were placed in mediaeval times. *See also* CUMDACH.

BOOK SIZES.

	Octavos:	Quartos:
Pott	$6\frac{1}{4} \times 4$	$8 \times 6\frac{1}{4}$
Foolscap	$6\frac{3}{4} \times 4\frac{1}{4}$	$8\frac{1}{2} \times 6\frac{3}{4}$
Crown	$7\frac{1}{2} \times 5$	$10 \times 7\frac{1}{2}$
Large Crown	$8 \times 5\frac{1}{4}$	$10\frac{1}{2} \times 8$
Large Post	$8\frac{1}{4} \times 5\frac{1}{4}$	$10\frac{1}{2} \times 8\frac{1}{4}$
Demy	$8\frac{3}{4} \times 5\frac{5}{8}$	$11\frac{1}{4} \times 8\frac{3}{4}$
Post	8×5	10×8
Small Demy	$8\frac{1}{2} \times 5\frac{5}{8}$	$11\frac{1}{4} \times 8\frac{1}{2}$
Medium	$9 \times 5\frac{3}{4}$	$11\frac{1}{2} \times 9$
Small Royal	$9\frac{1}{4} \times 6\frac{1}{8}$	$12\frac{1}{4} \times 9\frac{1}{4}$
Royal	$10 \times 6\frac{1}{4}$	$12\frac{1}{2} \times 10$
Super Royal	$10\frac{1}{2} \times 6\frac{3}{4}$	$13\frac{1}{2} \times 10\frac{1}{4}$
Imperial	$11 \times 7\frac{1}{2}$	15×11

See also OCTAVO, PAPER SIZES, SIZE. American book sizes are given below: in several instances there are minor differences between these and the British sizes with a common name. The sizes are not absolute.

Name	inches
Thirty-sixmo	$4 \times 3\frac{1}{3}$
Medium Thirty-twomo	$4\frac{3}{4} \times 3$
Medium Twenty-fourmo	$5\frac{1}{2} \times 3\frac{5}{8}$
Medium Eighteenmo	$6\frac{2}{3} \times 4$
Medium Sixteenmo	$6\frac{3}{4} \times 4\frac{1}{2}$
Cap Octavo	$7 \times 7\frac{1}{4}$
Duodecimo	$7\frac{1}{2} \times 4\frac{1}{2}$
Crown Octavo	$7\frac{1}{2} \times 5$
Post Octavo	$7\frac{1}{2} \times 5\frac{1}{2}$
Medium Duodecimo	$7\frac{2}{3} \times 5\frac{1}{8}$
Demy Octavo	$8 \times 5\frac{1}{2}$
Small Quarto (usually less)	$8\frac{1}{2} \times 7$
Broad Quarto (varies up to 13×10)	$8\frac{1}{2} \times 7$
Medium Octavo	$9\frac{1}{2} \times 6$
Royal Octavo	$10 \times 6\frac{1}{2}$
Super Royal Octavo	$10\frac{1}{2} \times 7$
Imperial Quarto	11×15
Imperial Octavo	$11\frac{1}{2} \times 8\frac{1}{4}$

(*The first column gives the vertical height.*)
For metric book sizes, *see* METRIC BOOK SIZES.

BOOK SLIDE.   A coverglass used as a lantern slide and bearing in ink particulars of a book or books available for borrowing at the close of a library talk.

BOOK SLIP.   *See* BOOK CARD.

BOOK STACK.   A room closed to the public, which is equipped to shelve large numbers of little-used books in as small a space as possible. Stack rooms are usually built adjacent to the points of service, have narrow gangways and steel shelving, and do not require natural lighting. *See also* BOOK PRESS, BOOKCASE, DOUBLE-FACED SHELF, DOUBLE-SIDED STACK, PRESS, TIER.

BOOK STAMP.   An ownership mark made by means of an ink impression from a metal or rubber stamp, embossed, on the title-page, cover or end-paper of a book.

BOOK STAND.   A small portable stand for carrying or displaying a few books.

BOOK STOCK.   The whole of the books comprising a library.

BOOK STORE.   1. A room or stack in which books are kept. 2. A book shop.

BOOK SUPPORT. An L or T shaped piece of iron or wood placed at the end of a row of books to keep them upright. Also called 'Book end.'

BOOK TALK. A talk about books, often given in a library by a librarian.

BOOK TRADE. The organized business of selling books. The term usually relates to the whole national organization involving book-sellers and their organizations together with the publishers and their organizations.

BOOK TRAY. A tray for carrying books. It has three sides no more than about 4 inches high provided with slots or handles to facilitate carrying.

BOOK TROLLEY. Synonymous with BOOK TRUCK (q.v.).

BOOK TROUGH. A short V-shaped shelf for displaying books on a counter or desk.

BOOK TRUCK. A wheeled trolley about 3 feet long, with two or three shelves accessible from each side which is used for conveying books to different parts of a building. Special adaptations are made for taking books to patients in hospital wards.

BOOK VAN (WAGON). A large motor van fitted up with shelves so that readers in outlying areas where there is no library may choose their books. A vehicle used for delivering books to county branches. Also called a TRAVELLING LIBRARY (q.v.) or (in America) a 'Bookmobile.'

BOOK WEEK. A local or national event in which librarians, often with the co-operation of booksellers and publishers, arrange book displays and lectures, with the object of stimulating interest in books, particu-larly amongst children. These are arranged on a national scale less often in England than in America, where in addition to the general book week in November, others dealing with a particular type of book are arranged, as Religious Book Week, Catholic Book Week. The idea of a children's book week originated with Franklin K. Mathiews, who was Chief Librarian of the Boy Scouts of America. He enlisted the support of Frederick G. Melcher, President of the R. R. Bowker Co.; together they secured the help of booksellers and librarians with the result that the first Children's Book Week was held in 1919.

BOOKAMATIC. The trade name for a method of TRANSACTION CARD CHARGING (q.v.). An Addressograph-Multigraph recorder, which is much cheaper than any of the machines used in other such systems, records the details of loan on a pre-numbered TRANSACTION CARD. Embossed plastic book cards and readers' cards are used in the machine to print the name and address of the reader and the author and title of the book on a transaction card which is kept in the library.

A transaction card bearing the same number and the date due for return is placed in the book. The book-card is kept always in the book and is only taken out to place it in the recorder so as to print the details of loan on the transaction card. *See also* CHARGING METHODS.

BOOKBINDER. A person whose occupation is the binding of books.

BOOKBINDING. 1. The act or process of binding a book, whereby the sheets are sewn or otherwise fastened into a permanent cover of book-binder's board, the sides and back of which are covered with leather or cloth, or other suitable material. 2. The strong covering of the book.

BOOKBINDING BOARD. A 'board' used as a component in making covers of hardback books.

BOOKBINDING STAMP. A tool with an embossed design which is used to impress a design on the cover of a book.

BOOKCASE. A case with shelves for books: it may or may not have doors. *See also* BOOK PRESS, BOOK STACK, DOUBLE-FACED SHELF, DOUBLE-SIDED STACK, PRESS, TIER.

BOOKETERIA. A self-service library, mainly of novels, placed in a modern store in parts of American towns which are not served by branch libraries. Borrowers issue books to themselves, place returned books in special parts of book shelves for assistants who attend each morning to discharge them, and leave any fines due. As far as is known, this idea was pioneered by Stewart W. Smith in Lincoln, Nebraska, in about 1947.

BOOKLET. A small book in a paper cover or in very light binding.

BOOKMARK. A piece of paper or other material placed between the leaves of a book to mark a place. Bookmarks are frequently used as a means of advertising. It may take the form of a piece of ribbon fastened in the 'hollow' back of a book, i.e. between the back folds of the sections and the spine. Also called 'Book marker.'

BOOKMARK LIST. A list of books printed in the form of a bookmark.

BOOKMOBILE. A large motor vehicle, equipped with shelves and a book-issuing desk, which the public may enter to select books for home reading. Also called a 'Mobile branch library' or TRAVELLING LIBRARY (*q.v.*). *See also* BOOK VAN.

BOOKS, USA, INC. A private, non-profit, educational organization formed late in 1963 to provide a means for American citizens and organizations to buy and have sent abroad collections of 'meaningful paperback books.' USIS officers and Peace Corps Volunteers distribute the ten-book packets to overseas libraries, reading rooms, schools and individuals. Thirteen different packets of books enable foreigners to learn more about the U.S. through reading substantial works about its political and economic systems, its culture, people and aspirations. A similar organization, Law Books, U.S.A., is confined to books dealing with the philosophy and spirit of the American legal system.

BOOKSELLER.   A dealer having a varied selection of books covering a wide range of subjects and of all types. Sometimes second-hand books are also stocked.

BOOKSELLERS' ASSOCIATION OF GREAT BRITAIN AND IRELAND.   Founded in 1895, membership of this Association is open to all booksellers who are approved by the PUBLISHERS' ASSOCIATION (q.v.). It exists to increase the sale of books, to protect the interests of booksellers, to provide classes and correspondence courses for the training of members and their assistants, to uphold the status of the trade, and to ensure adherence to the Net Book Agreement.

BOOKSHOP.   See BOOKSTALL.

BOOKSTALL.   A 'stand,' of temporary or permanent design, at which books are sold, the vendor usually being on the inside and the purchaser on the outside of the stand.   A bookshop is a larger place which the purchaser enters.

BOOKWORK.   The branch of the printing industry, particularly typesetting, which is concerned with book production.

BOOKWORM.   1. The larva of a moth or beetle which burrows into the covers and pages of books. 2. A person who reads voraciously.

BORDER.   1. (Bibliography) An ornamental enclosure of a title-page or a substantial part of it, or of a page of type, illuminated manuscript or body of printed matter; or merely an ornamental design placed on one or more sides of the above. See also BLOCK 4, COMPARTMENT, FRAME, RULE BORDER. 2. (Binding) Ornamentation placed close to the edges of the sides of a book-cover or the spine of a volume. To be distinguished from FRAME (q.v.). 3. (Printing) A continuous decorative design arranged around matter. It can consist of continuous cast strips of plain or patterned rule, or be made up of repeated units or FLOWERS (q.v.).

BOROUGH AUDITORS.   In a few boroughs, accounts are audited by three persons none of whom need have professional qualifications or experience. Two of these, known as elective auditors, are elected by local government electors, the third, known as the mayor's auditor, is appointed from among the members of the council. Collectively they are known as 'Borough auditors.' The term of office for all borough auditors is three years. None of these has the power of disallowance or surcharge as does a district auditor. A borough council whose accounts are subject to borough audit may pass a resolution to adopt either district or professional audit. *See also* DISTRICT AUDIT, MUNICIPAL AUDIT, PROFESSIONAL AUDITOR.

BOROUGH COUNCIL. A statutory local authority which provides local government services within its geographical area. It was entitled to provide public library services under the Public Libraries Act, 1892. Councils which had not adopted this Act by the time the 1919 Act became operative lost their power to become library authorities. For the conditions under which borough councils may become library authorities and so provide public library services, see Appendix 3. Abbreviated BC. *See also* NON-COUNTY BOROUGH.

BORROWER. *See* READER.

BORROWERS' INDEX. *See* BORROWERS' REGISTER I.

BORROWER'S NUMBER. The registration number assigned to a member of a library.

BORROWERS' REGISTER. 1. A list of members of a library entered in the order of joining and giving particulars as to name and address and the number (if any) of the tickets. This requires an index. 2. Borrowers' application forms filed in alphabetical order. This is the modern and more satisfactory method.

BORROWER'S TICKET (CARD). The membership card entitling the holder to borrow books from a library.

BOSS. A metal knob, often ornamented, fixed upon the covers of books, usually at the corners and centre, for protection and embellishment.

BOTTOM EDGE. The TAIL (*q.v.*) of a book. Also called 'Lower edge,' 'Tail edge.'

BOTTOM MARGIN. *Synonymous with* TAIL MARGIN (*q.v.*).

BOTTOM NOTE. *Synonymous with* FOOTNOTE (*q.v.*).

BOUND. 1. A book which is sewn or otherwise fastened into stiff boards. 2. (*Adj.*) In CO-ORDINATE INDEXING (*q.v.*) joined in modification of the meaning of a commonly used term; e.g. 'Free Energy' is a *bound* term (unit concept) while 'Free' and 'Energy' may be *free* terms in the same co-ordinate indexing system (*IBM*).

BOUND VOLUME. Any book that is bound; usually a number of issues of a periodical comprising a volume and bound.

BOUND WITH. A term used by cataloguers when referring to books published separately but subsequently bound together. When such a volume has been supplied with a collective title-page the main catalogue entry may be made from this, the individual publications being entered in a contents note and given analytical entries. Otherwise each item would be given its own entry 'Bound with . . .' and the first item in the collection quoted. In each case there would be only one CALL NUMBER (*q.v.*).

BOUNDARY STRAPS. *Synonymous with* DECKLE STRAPS (*q.v.*).

BOURDILLON REPORT. The Report of the Working Party appointed by the Minister of Education in March 1961, *Standards of Public Library Service in England and Wales*, 1962. Mr. H. T. Bourdillon was Chairman of the Working Party. This, together with the BAKER REPORT (*q.v.*) formed the basis of parliamentary discussions and the framing of the Public Libraries and Museums Bill of 1964.

BOURGEOIS. An obsolete name for a size of type equal to 9 pt.

BOUSTROPHEDON WRITING. Derived from *boustrophedon*, Greek for 'as the ox ploughs'; refers to ancient Greek writing in which alternate lines run from left to right and then from right to left – the pattern that would be made by an ox ploughing a field. The letters in the lines commencing at the right are reversed as if mirrored.

BOW BRACKET. *Synonymous with* BRACE (*q.v.*).

BOWDLERIZED. A text which is altered by changing or omitting words or passages considered offensive or indelicate: after Thomas Bowdler who in 1818 published an expurgated edition of Shakespeare.

BOWL. The full rounded and entirely enclosed portion of a type letter as in O, B, D, b, a; the part enclosing a closed COUNTER (*q.v.*).

BOX. (*Printing*) 1. An area within a larger type area, or within or between type columns, formed by rules or white spaces with the object of emphasizing what is printed within. 2. A rectangular or square border of one or more lines placed around type matter, and made up of rules which may be mitred or butted.

BOX FILE. A container made to stand on a shelf, and intended primarily to contain flimsy material such as correspondence or newspaper cuttings. The most durable kinds are those with wooden sides, board base and hinged lid, the whole being covered with cloth and/or paper and lined with paper. A spring clip is usually provided to keep the contents in position. Unless the lid fits tightly, overlaps the box, and does not warp, they are not dust-proof. *See also* PAMPHLET BOX.

BOX-IN. To place rules around type matter so that the characters when printed appear in a frame or box.

BOX LIBRARY. Boxes containing standard sets of books catering for different tastes and supplied in developing countries by community development organizations to community centres in rural areas for circulation from village to village.

BOXED. A work in two or three volumes inserted into a container to display them, keep them together, or protect them.

BOXHEAD. 1. A series of printed or ruled lines for headings in a ruled table. 2. A cut-in head with a frame around it. Also called 'Box heading.'

BOXHEAD RULING. The space at the top of a ruled column for the insertion of hand-written headings for each column.

BOYET STYLE. A style of book decoration practised by Luc Antoine Boyet, who worked in France in the eighteenth century for Count Hoym. It is characterized by a plain border, ornamental corners and edges, and a central monogram or device. Boyet is sometimes credited with introducing DOUBLURES (*q.v.*).

BOYS AND GIRLS HOUSE, TORONTO. Established in 1922 by the Toronto Public Library as a library for children, it is now an international centre for those concerned with library work for children.

BRACE. (*Printing*) A bracket ⁀ cast on its own body, usually to a definite number of ems. Formerly called 'Vinculum.' A *sectional brace* is made of several parts which can be assembled to the length required; the middle position is called a COCK (*q.v.*).

BRACKET SHELF. A shelf secured temporarily or permanently for display purposes at the end of a bookcase.

BRACKET SHELVING. Adjustable shelving where the shelves rest, or are fixed, on brackets, which are secured to the rear upright stanchions of steel shelving fixtures, and which also serve as book supports. Also called 'Suspension shelving.' Sometimes the brackets simply support the shelves from underneath; this type is also called 'Cantilever shelving.'

BRACKETS. Rectangular enclosing marks [ ]. Used in cataloguing to indicate something which does not appear in the original but is added by the cataloguer. To be distinguished from CURVES ( ), (*q.v.*). Angle brackets ⟨ ⟩ are used to enclose matter which itself appears in [ ] on the title-page. Also called 'Angular marks,' 'Square brackets.' *See also* CIRCULAR BRACKETS, CURVES.

BRADEL BINDING. A type of temporary binding said to have originated in Germany, and first adopted in France by a binder named Bradel.

BRADFORD SCIENTIFIC, TECHNICAL AND COMMERCIAL SERVICES. *See* BRASTACS.

BRADFORD'S LAW OF SCATTERING. *See* LAW OF SCATTERING.

BRAILLE. A system of reading and writing for the blind in which the letters are formed by raised dots embossed into the paper in groups of six, three high and two wide. Named after the inventor Louis Braille (1809–52), a blind Frenchman.

4*

BRANCH. A section of the Library Association's membership admission to which is dependent on the place in which a librarian is employed or works. There are at present twelve branches. Membership of only one branch is permitted. Aslib also has geographical branches. *See also* DIVISION, GROUP, LIBRARY ASSOCIATION, SECTION. In a college or university, a collection of books and other materials on one subject, housed in a separate area and serviced by its own staff. It is centrally administered and is usually on the same campus as the main library.

BRANCH AND MOBILE LIBRARIES GROUP. A Group of the Library Association; it was formed in January 1966 and is concerned with the particular outlook and needs of such kinds of service point.

BRANCH LIBRARIAN. The librarian in charge of a branch library. *See also* DEPARTMENTAL LIBRARY. (*County Libraries*). The librarian in charge of a branch library not covered by the definitions of AREA LIBRARIAN, DISTRICT LIBRARIAN, REGIONAL LIBRARIAN, REGIONAL OFFICER (*qq.v.*).

BRANCH LIBRARY. A library other than the main one (called the 'Central') in a system. It usually comprises adult lending and children's departments, a quick-reference collection and possibly a news-room, and is intended to meet the library needs of the surrounding population, particularly in the matter of books for home-reading. It is housed in premises set aside for the purpose, is specially equipped and furnished, and staffed by trained assistants. The book stock is a permanent one. Sometimes called a 'District Library.' In English county libraries, a *full-time branch* is open not less than thirty hours a week: a *part-time branch*, less than thirty but more than ten hours per week in premises specially equipped and furnished. A *sub-branch* is one staffed, stocked and administered from a larger branch in the vicinity. 'Branch' is a general or collective term which includes more than one of the types of service points known as Full-time Branch Library, Library Centre or Part-time Branch Library (e.g. 'branch library policy', 'staffing of branches') but excludes those which are not administered by paid staff.

BRANCHING CLASSIFICATION. A classification with two or more sub-classes, or main branches, each subdivided again, and perhaps again and again. It may be converted into a TABULAR CLASSIFICATION (*q.v.*). Also called a 'Ramifying classification.'

BRASS RULE. *See* RULE.

BRASTACS. (BRADFORD SCIENTIFIC, TECHNICAL AND COMMERCIAL SERVICE.) A scheme of library co-operation inaugurated in 1961 and centred on the Bradford Public Library, Darley

St., Bradford, 1, with the co-operation of the Library of the Institute of Technology. It operates similarly to the Sheffield Interchange Organization (*see* SINTO) and aims to make industry more information-conscious and help to bring about the establishment of more libraries. Books and periodicals are lent, and there is an information service. Member organizations should have a minimum of twenty-five books and take current periodicals.

BRAYER. Formerly a wooden pestle, round in shape and flat at one end with a handle on the other, used to spread ink on the block to an even depth and consistency before being taken up by the ink balls. Later, a hand-roller for distributing the ink before it is taken up by forme rollers. Also used when making a galley proof.

BREAK (BREAK UP). (*Printing*) To dispose of a forme of printing matter by separating material to be re-melted from furniture, blocks, rules, foundry type, etc. *See also* DISTRIBUTING.

BREAK-LINE. The last line of a paragraph where quads are needed to fill out the last space. In good type-setting it does not begin a new page. *See also* END A BREAK, END EVEN, RUN ON.

BREAKER. A part of the machinery used to make paper; it is a tub-like vessel into which the raw material is placed after boiling in the 'boiler' or 'kier' in order that it may be washed and further broken to reduce and separate the fibres. Also called 'Beater' or 'Hollander.'

BREECHES BIBLE. *See* GENEVA BIBLE.

BREVIARY. The book of daily Divine Office used in the Roman Catholic Church. It contains: 1. Calendar; 2. Psalter; 3. Proprium de Tempore (collects and lessons); 4. Proprium Sanctorum (collects, etc., for Saints' Days); 5. Commune Sanctorum (collects, etc., for Saints without special services); 6. Hours of the Virgin, burial services, etc., i.e. Small Offices. It contains neither the Communion Service nor the Mass.

BREVIER. An obsolete name for a size of type equal to about 8 pt.

BRIEF. 1. A letter of authority. 2. A letter of the pope to a religious community, or an individual upon matters of discipline, and differing from a BULL (*q.v.*) by being less solemn and ample, and in the form in which it is written. 3. A letter patent which used to be issued by the sovereign as head of the church, licensing a collection to be made in churches for a specified object or charity. 4. A written description of the requirements for a building to be designed, and supplied to an architect so that he may prepare plans. It sets out the purpose of the building and its various rooms or departments, indicating their size, shape and juxtaposition, and any special features to be provided.

BRIEF CATALOGUING.   Simplified cataloguing, especially in respect of details after the imprint and including the tracing, for books that are likely to go into a storage library, for pamphlets, and for other special categories. *See also* LIMITED CATALOGUING, SIMPLIFIED CATALOGUING.

BRILLIANT.   An obsolete name for a size of type about 4 pt.

BRING-UP.   To bring a block up to the correct printing height by using underlay or interlay.

BRIQUET.   A conventional representation on a bookbinding of a steel used with tinder for striking a light.

BRISCH-VISTEM SYSTEM.   A system of recording information on punched cards (called 'characteristics cards'), each of which has a thousand numbered squares and is reserved for a particular subject in accordance with a coded scheme of classification appropriate to the general subject area. Holes are punched to record information, each numbered square being allocated to a particular document or item of information; these are indexed alphabetically. Information is obtained by super-imposing cards allocated to the appropriate subjects, the co-incident holes indicating the items possessing the characteristics required. This system is now sold in Great Britain under the trade name VISIscan. *See also* PEEK-A-BOO.

BRISTOL BOARD.   A fine quality board made from rags and used for drawings or paintings. It is made by pasting two or more sheets of paper together, the substance being determined by the number of sheets.

BRITISH CATALOGUE OF MUSIC.   A catalogue of music and books about music published in Great Britain and consisting of entries made from material deposited under the Copyright Acts at the Copyright Receipt Office at the British Museum. Publication, quarterly, began in 1957 under the auspices of the Council of the British National Bibliography. A faceted scheme of classification, drawn up by Mr. E. J. Coates, formerly Editor of the *Catalogue*, is used for arranging entries. This was published in 1960 by the Council of the British National Bibliography.

BRITISH CATALOGUE OF MUSIC CLASSIFICATION.   The scheme, drawn up by Mr. E. J. Coates, which is used to classify the entries in the BRITISH CATALOGUE OF MUSIC (*q.v.*).

BRITISH COPYRIGHT COUNCIL.   Founded in 1954 as the British Joint Copyright Council. The name was altered and the scope and membership greatly increased in 1965. The aims of the Council are briefly (a) to defend and foster the true principles of copyright; (b) to

cherish as an ultimate aim the acceptance of those principles throughout the world; (c) to bring together the bodies who speak for authors,
artists, composers, actors, musicians and all others who are partners
in or justly interested in the protection of copyright; (d) to keep a
vigilant watch on any changes in law, administration, social practice,
or mechanical contrivance which may require an amendment to the
law; (e) to give attention to any matter relating to copyright brought to
notice by a member; (f) to increase public knowledge of the principles,
problems and importance of copyright law and practice. The membership of the Council is composed of British societies of authors,
artists, actors, musicians and others who are concerned with creative
activity.

BRITISH EDUCATION INDEX. Compiled by the Institutes of
Education in England; indexes articles on education in some fifty
British periodicals. It is published three times a year by the Library
Association and is cumulated into two-year volumes; it is intended to
complement the American *Education Index*.

BRITISH HUMANITIES INDEX. A quarterly index, with annual
cumulations, of articles appearing in over 330 British, and a few
Dominion, periodicals; it is published by the Library Association.
Prior to January 1962 it was known as the *Subject Index to Periodicals*,
and first appeared in 1915; no volumes were issued in the years 1923
to 1925 inclusive. Abbreviated BHI.

BRITISH INSTITUTE OF RECORDED SOUND LTD. A non-
profit-making company, registered as a charity, which exists to
promote the study and use of recorded sound in all its aspects. A collection of records, international in scope, has been built up since June
1955; this includes music of all countries and periods, literature and
drama, speeches and historical events, music hall and popular entertainment, language and dialect, bird song, and everyday sounds
doomed to disappear with changing times. Donations of records are
desired, private recordings are copied for preservation, and the
Institute itself copies B.B.C. transmissions in order to prevent them
from being lost to posterity. In addition to the record archive the
Institute has a reference library of books, periodicals and record
catalogues. Abbreviated BIRS. Publishes *Recorded Sound* (*q.*).

BRITISH MUSEUM LIBRARY. The chief British national library,
consisting of four departments: Printed Books; Manuscripts; Oriental
Printed Books and Manuscripts; Prints and Drawings. As the national
deposit library, it receives and preserves for public record a copy of
every piece of printed matter published in the United Kingdom, and

has benefited under the Copyrights Acts in this way ever since the Royal Library (which had enjoyed the right since 1662) was transferred to the British Museum in 1757 although these rights were not enforced until the middle of the nineteenth century. The Library contains over 6,000,000 printed books, about 60,000 Western and 30,000 Oriental MSS., 100,000 charters and rolls, etc. There is an associated British Museum (Natural History) Library at the Natural History Museum; this does not benefit from the Copyright Act. These are both reference libraries. Abbreviated BML.

BRITISH NATIONAL BIBLIOGRAPHY.   An organization which has issued since 4th January 1950 a weekly printed list of books published in Great Britain. Full catalogue entries are made from books received at the Copyright Office of the British Museum, classified by Dewey's *Decimal Classification* and published each week in classified order, but with appropriate subject headings. The last issue each month contains a monthly author index. Quarterly, half-annual, and annual and five-year cumulations are made. The publications are known as '*BNB*' or *British National Bibliography*. Entries are also available on international standard size cards (12.5 × 7.5 cms. or 5 × 3 inches).

BRITISH NATIONAL BOOK CENTRE.   A service of the NATIONAL CENTRAL LIBRARY (*q.v.*) for the interchange among British libraries, and between British and overseas libraries, of surplus library materials. British, Commonwealth and other overseas libraries have all benefited considerably from this service, which is operated through the distribution by BNBC of lists of books available (notified by libraries on cards to BNBC) first to British libraries and then to foreign libraries. The BNBC decides on allocation and then notifies the owning library where to send the books. Benefiting libraries are expected to offer in return either surplus material or, in the case of overseas libraries, new publications if available.

BRITISH NATIONAL COMMITTEE ON PALAEOGRAPHY.   A sub-committee on manuscripts of the Standing Conference of National and University Libraries (SCONUL). *See also* SCONUL.

BRITISH PAPER AND BOARD INDUSTRY RESEARCH ASSOCIATION.   This Association is concerned with research on pulping, and paper-making processes, the assessment of raw materials, performance of paper-making machinery, performance testing of paper and effluent treatment. It is grant-aided through the Ministry of Technology. Abbreviated BPBIRA. The Association publishes technical reports covering its research work, or setting out recommended test procedures; these are sent to members free of charge.

Unclassified reports are available to members. It also publishes *Library Notes* (to membs.), *Abstract Bulletin of the Institute of Paper Chemistry* (m. to mebs.), *What We Are Doing* (q. to membs.). *See also* PRINTING, PACKAGING AND ALLIED TRADES RESEARCH ASSOCIATION.

BRITISH RECORD SOCIETY. Formed in 1889 with the object of preserving records and making them accessible to scholars by the publication of indexes in a series known as the *Index Library*. Over 80 volumes have been published relating to various categories of record, and in the last few decades they have been concerned almost exclusively with indexing testamentary records.

BRITISH RECORDS ASSOCIATION. Inaugurated November 1932 to co-ordinate the work of the many individuals, authorities, institutions and societies interested in the conservation and use of archives in the United Kingdom. Its aims are (a) to serve as a link between all authorities, institutions or individuals concerned in the preservation, custody, study and publication of records; (b) to develop informed opinion on the necessity for preserving records of historical importance; (c) to provide a centre for the accumulation and dissemination of all kinds of technical information useful to individuals or institutions engaged in archive work, or in the publication of record sources; (d) to encourage the use of records as historical material, particularly as regards their publication. Abbreviated BRA. Publishes *Archives* (two p.a.).

BRITISH SOCIETY FOR INTERNATIONAL BIBLIOGRAPHY, THE. Founded in 1927 as the British section of the Institut de Bibliographie, known as BSIB, and amalgamated in 1948 with the Association of Special Libraries and Information Bureaux (ASLIB).

BRITISH STANDARDS INSTITUTION. The approved British body for the preparation and promulgation of national standards covering, inter alia, methods of test; terms, definitions and symbols; standards of quality of performance or of dimensions; preferred ranges; codes of practice. Abbreviated BSI. *See also* STANDARDS.

BRITISH TALKING BOOK SERVICE FOR THE BLIND. *See* NTBL.

BRITISH TECHNOLOGY INDEX. A current subject guide to the major articles published in 400 British technical journals; published monthly since January 1962, each twelfth issue being an annual cumulation. Published by the Library Association. Abbreviated *BTI*.

BRITISH UNION CATALOGUE OF PERIODICALS. A list of over 140,000 titles of periodicals of the world, from the seventeenth century to the present day, together with particulars of the holdings of over

440 British libraries. Compiled with funds made available by the Rockefeller Foundation, it was published in four volumes between 1955 and 1958. A *Supplement* to 1960 was published in 1962. It is being kept up-to-date by the National Central Library, additions and amendments being recorded in the quarterly *BUCOP: new periodical titles*. Familiarly called *BUCOP*.

BROAD. Applies to a sheet of paper which is divided by halving the long side (i.e. across the narrow way). This is the regular or common way of dividing a sheet. Hence a *broad folio*, quarto, or octavo. The opposite of OBLONG (*q.v.*). A *broad fold* is a sheet folded so that the longest dimension is horizontal; the grain then runs with the shorter dimension of the paper.

BROAD CLASSIFICATION. An arrangement of books in main classes with little or no sub-division, instead of in their more minute sub-divisions. *See also* CLOSE CLASSIFICATION.

BROAD FOLIO. *See* FOLIO.

BROADSHEET. A long, narrow advertising leaflet; usually the long quarto of the sheet of paper from which it is cut. It may be printed on both sides. Sometimes used synonymously with BROADSIDE (*q.v.*).

BROADSIDE. A large sheet of paper printed on one side right across the sheet, for sheet distribution, and usually intended to be posted up, e.g. proclamations, ballad sheets, news-sheets, sheet calendars, etc. *See also* BROADSHEET. Also used of a poster of which the width is greater than the depth.

BROCHURE. Literally 'a stitched work' (from the French 'brocher,' to stitch). A short printed work of a few leaves, merely stitched together, and not otherwise bound; a pamphlet.

BROKEN BACK. A book whose back has broken open from head to tail. Also called 'Broken binding.'

BROKEN LETTER. One, the face of which is damaged and cannot give a complete impression. Indicated in a proof by placing a small x in the margin. Also called 'Bad letter,' 'Battered letter,' 'Damaged letter,' 'Spoiled letter.'

BROKEN ORDER. The removal of a section, or sections, of the book stock from its proper sequence in the classification in order to facilitate use.

BROKEN-OVER. A PLATE (*q.v.*) or other separate sheet which is to be inserted in a book, and is given a narrow fold near the back, or binding, edge before sewing, etc., to ensure that it will lie flat and turn easily when the book is bound.

BROKERS' CIRCULAR. A circular published by a firm of stockbrokers, sometimes at regular intervals, containing particulars of securities.

BRONZING. Dusting with a fine metallic powder over a sheet freshly printed with ink, varnish or size to give a brilliant, lustrous effect.

BRONZING SIZE. A printing ink made specially for bronzing. The term is sometimes used for printing ink for subsequent printing with metallic ink.

BROTHERS OF THE COMMON LIFE. Monks who maintained monasteries in various parts of Germany and the Low Countries in the last quarter of the fifteenth century and set up printing presses in about sixty of them between 1475 and 1490. Their first dated book was issued in 1476 from the 'Nazareth' Monastery at Brussels.

BROWN CLASSIFICATION. The familiar name for James Duff Brown's *Subject Classification* (*q.v.*). *See also* ADJUSTABLE CLASSIFICATION.

BROWN LIBRARY, JOHN CARTER. A collection of 30,000 books dealing with the discovery and settlement of America to 1800; assembled by John Carter Brown (1797–1874) who was one of America's best-known book collectors. The library was passed on to Brown University, Providence, Rhode Island, U.S.A., in 1900, since when it has grown considerably and is one of the finest collections of Americana in existence.

BROWN MECHANICAL WOODPULP. A woodpulp for paper-making obtained by grinding steamed or boiled logs.

BROWNE BOOK CHARGING SYSTEM. A system of book charging which is attributed to Nina E. Browne, an American Librarian, who described it in 1895. It is, however, very little different from the method adopted about 1873 by Mr. L. G. Virgo, Librarian of Bradford Public Library. The reader has a limited number of tickets, each of which is available for one book only at a time, and which he gives up when books are borrowed and which are handed back when the books are returned. This simple, reliable and speedy method was replaced in America by the Newark and Detroit methods and others based on them, but, until photo-charging was introduced, was the most universally used method in Great Britain. 'Reverse Brown' uses a pocket book-card and a card ticket: this was described by Jacob Schwartz in 1897 and had been in use for a number of years. Since World War Two other methods have taken the place of Browne, but two modifications of this system have enabled it to meet the demands of busier public libraries; these are CHEQUE BOOK CHARGING METHOD and the ISLINGTON CHARGING SYSTEM (*qq.v.*). An adaptation with the object of reducing queues at the return counter was introduced at Gravesend in 1964 by the Librarian, Mr. E. N. Moore. All books issued within seven days are stamped with the same date for return, which is a Tuesday in order to spread the load from Saturday. The date stamp used also stamps a running number; the charges are not sorted but kept in the order of issue; guide cards bearing two figures are used between each ten charges and one bearing three figures is inserted for each hundredth book issued. In this way it is possible to find required charges without numbering them. A new sequence of numbers is begun each week. *See also* CHARGING METHODS, TOKEN CHARGING.

BROWSABILITY. The ability of an indexing system to lend itself to unsystematic or random searches. This ability is of interest or use to the searcher even though it may not produce a logical answer to the search question (*IBM*).

BROWSE. To investigate, without design, the contents of a collection of books or documents (*IBM*).

BROWSING ROOM. A room provided in an American college, university, or public library which contains novels and non-fiction books on all subjects, but no text books. It is intended for recreational reading and not for study, in order to help achieve which, furnishings are bright and informal. Books may or may not be borrowed for home reading. A development of the POPULAR LIBRARY (*q.v.*).

BRUSH COATED. (*Paper*). Paper given a smooth printing surface by applying the clay, or other, coating substance as a separate and later operation to the actual paper making, in order to make it perfectly smooth so as to take a high degree of finish. *See also* ART, COATED PAPER, MACHINE COATED.

BRUSH-PEN. A pen, with a fibrous point, made of reed, used for writing on papyrus.

BRUSSELS CONVENTION. Popular name for the revision (signed on 26th June 1948) of the BERNE COPYRIGHT UNION (*q.v.*). *See also* COPYRIGHT, INTERNATIONAL.

BRUSSELS EXPANSION. A familiar name for the UNIVERSAL DECIMAL CLASSIFICATION (*q.v.*).

BRYANT MEMORANDUM. The *Memorandum on the present program of the Library of Congress and related agencies*. It comments on the Federal and research library situation and the role of the Library of Congress. It was written in 1962, by Douglas Bryant, Associate Director of the Harvard Library, at the request of Senator Claiborne Pell of Rhode Island who introduced it into the *Congressional Record* for 24th May 1962. The reply by the Librarian of Congress, Mr. L. Quincy Mumford, appeared in the *Congressional Record* for 2nd October 1962.

BUCKET. A section in the memory of a computer. (*IBM*).

BUCKLE-FOLDER. A machine which folds printed sheets by passing them between two continuously revolving rollers placed one above the other until the leading edge touches a stop bar. The rollers continue to impel the rear half of the sheet until it is folded and so carried down between the lower revolving roller and a third one which is parallel to it. *See also* KNIFE-FOLDER.

BUCKLES. (*Binding*) Severe wrinkles near the head and back of the folded sections. *See also* SECTION.

BUCKRAM. A strong textile, either of linen or cotton, used for covering books. *See also* ART CANVAS.

BUCOP. Abbreviation for *British Union Catalogue of Periodicals* (*q.v.*).

BUDGET. The total amount of money which is available for library purposes after the estimate of anticipated needs has been approved by the appropriate authority.

BUDS. In bookbinding, an ornament filling a small panel on some rolls: it is a conventionalized form of a spray bearing buds.

BUILDING-IN MACHINE. A machine which, in book production, dries cased books in a matter of seconds by means of several applications of heat and pressure. This is an alternative to the slower method of the STANDING PRESS (*q.v.*).

BULK. 1. The thickness of a book exclusive of its covers; this will be less after, than before, binding. Book papers are measured by the thickness of a number of pages. The extremes between which papers of the same weight, but of a different class, vary in bulk may be seen from the following figures, based on 320 pp. of quad crown 100 lb.

Featherweight	53/32 in.	Pure Super – calendered	22/32 in.
Esparto M.F.	29/32 in.	Coated Art	21/32 in.
Pure M.F.	24/32 in.	Imitation Art	20/32 in.

2. The thickness of a sheet of paper related to its weight and measured in thousandths of an inch. 3. To 'bulk' a book is to make it appear bigger than it need be by using a thick but light-weight paper.

BULL. A formal papal letter under the leaden seal (Bulla).

BULLETIN. 1. A publication, generally a pamphlet, issued by a government, society or other organization at regular intervals and in serial form. 2. A periodical or occasional publication containing lists of books added to a library, and other library information.

BULLETIN BOARD. A notice board in a library on which are exhibited lists of books, announcements of forthcoming events, jackets of new books added to the library, and miscellaneous library information.

BUMPED OUT. (*Printing*) 1. Matter which is widely leaded. 2. A line of characters in which extra spacing has been inserted to square it up with the measure of a longer line.

BUMPER. A machine used to compact the sections of a book after they have been sewn together. Also called a 'Nipper' or 'Smasher'.

BURIN. An engraver's tool.

BURN-IN. (*Reprography*) The act of exposing sensitized material, or of increasing the exposure of a specific area of sensitized material.

BURN-OUT. (*Reprography*). The complete destruction of the diazo component through exposure to actinic lights.

BURNESS AWARD, JACK K. An award of $500, offered by the Newspaper Division of the Special Library Association and given by the Jack K. Burness Memorial Fund for distinguished newspaper librarianship.

BURNISHED EDGES. Coloured or gilt edges which have been made smooth and bright by a polishing tool.

BURSTING STRAIN. The measurement, expressed in pounds per square inch, of pressure required to rupture paper when being tested on a Mullen or Ashcroft machine.

BUSINESS ARCHIVES COUNCIL. A non-profit-making body supported by voluntary contributions from business firms, universities libraries and record offices, and managed by a committee representing all of these interests. Its objects are to preserve business records and encourage interest in business history. Publishes *Business Archives* (2 a year).

BUTT SPLICE. *See* SPLICE.

BUTTED. (*Printing*). Lines of type, or rules, placed end to end to make larger lines. Also called 'Butted slugs'.

BUTTED SLUGS. *See* BUTTED.

BUTTERFLY PLAN. An arrangement of bookstacks in a butterfly or fan shape. *See also* RADIATING STACKS.

BUTTING. 1. To produce a line of type in the form of a slug (using a Linotype, or similar machine,) which is longer than the machine normally makes (30 picas); the line is set on two slugs which are butted together – placed end to end. 2. To place two pieces of paper, cloth or leather with edges touching.

BYE-LAWS. Bye-laws may be made under the provisions of the Public Libraries and Museums Act 1964, s. 19, regulating the use of facilities provided by the authority under this Act and the conduct of persons in premises where those facilities are provided. Bye-laws may include provisions enabling officers of a local authority to exclude or remove from premises maintained by the authority any person who contravenes the bye-laws. A set of model bye-laws has been prepared at the Department of Education and Science. Before bye-laws can be effective they must be submitted by local authorities in England and Wales to the Secretary of State for confirmation. Bye-laws must be displayed in any premises maintained under the Act to which the public have access. The provisions in Northern Ireland and in Scotland are slightly different.

BYNAME. *See* NICKNAME.

BYTE. (*Information retrieval*) 1. A generic term to indicate a measurable portion of consecutive binary digits, e.g. an eight-bit or six-bit byte. 2. A group of binary digits usually operated as a unit. 3. An element of data which consists of eight data bits plus a parity bit, and represents either one alphabetic, or special, character, two decimal digits, or eight binary bits; a sequence of binary digits which is handled as a unit.

BYZANTINE BINDINGS. Book covers, rather than true bindings, finely wrought in gold and silver, and often inlaid with precious stones. They date from the foundation of Byzantium by Constantine the Great in the fourth century.

c. Abbreviation for CHAPTER (*q.v.*), caput or *circa* (*q.v.*), although in the last instance 'ca' is preferable. Also for the word 'copyright' when used in descriptive notes, though not legally valid in a copyright notice when © should be used.

© The symbol claiming copyright under Article III (1) of the Universal Copyright Convention (*see* COPYRIGHT, INTERNATIONAL); it is required by law to be placed before the name of the copyright proprietor and the year of first publication. The Inter-governmental Copyright Committee, meeting in Washington in October 1957, recommended positions in various kinds of publication where the symbol might be placed: amongst these was the title-page or the page immediately following, or at the end of a book or pamphlet; under the main title or the MASTHEAD (*q.v.*) of a newspaper, magazine or other periodical; on the face side of a map, print or photograph, either on the actual map or picture (but near the title or the margin) or on the margin.

C.D. SYSTEM. Abbreviation for the CLASSIFICATION DECIMALE UNIVERSELLE now known as UNIVERSAL DECIMAL CLASSIFICATION (*q.v.*).

C-LIBRARY. A 'circulating library' as distinct from a D-LIBRARY (*q.v.*).

CFSTI. Abbreviation for Clearinghouse for Federal Scientific and Technical Information. A section of the U.S. Department of Commerce; its function is to make available particulars of unclassified (i.e. non-secret) reports in the U.S.A., which it does by publishing a list *United States Government research and development reports* (USGRDR).

CNRS. Acronym for Centre Nationnel de la Recherche Scientifique et Technique. The most important centre in France for scientific documentation; it was set up in 1939 under the aegis of the Ministry of Education, and maintains a library of periodicals only. It collaborates with a number of documentation centres in compiling a location index of translations and the *Bulletin Signalétique* (formerly *Bulletin Analytique*) which contains brief abstracts of articles on a wide range of scientific subjects. Abbreviated CNRS.

CTFE. Acronym for Colleges of Technology and Further Education, a Group of the Library Association.

ca. Abbreviation for *circa* (*q.v.*).

CABINET. 1. An enclosed rack or frame for holding type cases, galleys, etc.; made formerly of wood but now also of pressed sheet steel. 2. A standard size of card, $4\frac{1}{4} \times 6\frac{1}{2}$ inches.

CABINET EDITION. *See* LIBRARY EDITION.

CABINET SIZE. *See* OBLONG.

CADASTRAL MAP. One drawn on a large scale to show ownership, extent and value of land for purposes of taxation.

CADENZA. An ornamental solo passage towards the end of a piece of music or the end of a section; in a concerto, the cadenza is usually towards the end of the first, or the last, movement. Cadenzas were originally improvised by the soloist who was thus given an opportunity to demonstrate his brilliance as an executant, but are sometimes written by the original or a later, composer. Sometimes they are provided with an accompaniment.

CADIG. Abbreviation for Coventry and District Information Group which was commenced on an informal basis in 1953, with a membership of fifteen, a formal constitution being adopted in 1962 when the membership had reached thirty. The Group aims to promote the rapid and relatively informal exchange of both written and verbal information. It is organized from the Reference and Technical Library of the Central Public Library, Derby Lane, Coventry, Warwickshire, where a union list of periodical holdings of the member libraries, totalling 2,500 items, is maintained. All local educational institutions for further education, the larger local firms, and the public libraries within twelve miles of Coventry are members. A small annual sub-scription is payable by member libraries to cover the costs of organi-zation and of arranging meetings held in member libraries, which include the public libraries of Leamington Spa, Rugby and Nuneaton, and the library of the University of Warwick.

CALCOGRAPHY. *See* CHALK DRAWING.

CALDECOTT MEDAL. An award made annually in America for the most distinguished American picture book for children. Named after Randolph Caldecott, the nineteenth-century English artist and book illustrator. The Medal was donated by Frederic G. Melcher and the award is administered by the Children's Services Division of the ALA. The Newbery-Caldecott Awards Committee of the CSD, which numbers 22 plus the chairman, makes the selection. The Medal was designed by Rene Paul Chambellan and is named after the nineteenth-century English artist and book illustrator Randolph Caldecott (1846–1886). It was first awarded (in 1938) to Dorothy P. Lathrop for *Animals of the Bible.*

CALENDAR. 1. A chronological list of documents in a given collection, e.g. charters, state papers, rolls, etc., giving the date and with annota-tions indicating or summarizing the contents of each. 2. An almanack giving lists of days, months, saints' days, etc., for a given year, or a special list of important days for certain purposes throughout the year e.g. a university or gardening calendar.

CALENDER. A machine consisting mainly of metal rollers between which paper is passed to give it a smooth surface. The degree of smoothness depends on the pressure of the rollers and the extent to which they close the pores.

CALENDERED PAPER. Paper that is given a smooth surface by roll-ing, when newly-made, between smooth cylinders under pressure. Paper which receives a minimum of calendering emerges as an antique. With more calendering it acquires a machine finish, then an English finish, and it finally becomes a super-calendered, glossy sheet. *See also* SUPER-CALENDERED PAPER.

CALF. A bookbinding leather made from calfskin and so used since at least 1450. It may have a rough or a smooth (the more usual) finish. Books which are full-bound can be further described as being diced, grained, marbled, mottled, scored, sprinkled, stained, or tree, accord-ing to the form of decoration used. Special styles are known as antique, divinity, law, reversed or roughened.

CALL CARD. *Synonymous with* CALL SLIP (*q.v.*).

CALL NUMBER. As the term implies, the number by which a reader requisitions a book. Usually the classification number (or in fixed location, shelf number) followed by the BOOK NUMBER (*q.v.*) or simply the AUTHOR MARK (*q.v.*). It is used to identify a particular book, and to indicate both its position on the shelves and its position relative to other books; it is marked on the lower part of the spine of a book as well as on catalogue cards and other records. In the Colon Classification, the call number consists of the class number, book number and COLLECTION NUMBER (*q.v.*). The class number fixes the position of a book's specific subject relative to other subjects.

CALL SLIP. A printed blank on which are entered the author, title and call number for books required in a reference or university library. Also called 'Call card', 'Requisition form'.

CALLIGRAPHIC INITIAL. An initial in a mediaeval illuminated manuscript made by a scribe rather than an artist. Such initials are in ink, and rarely brushed with colour or touched with gold.

CALLIGRAPHY. The art of fine handwriting: penmanship. A calligrapher is a trained penman. Calligraphic types are those designed in close sympathy with the spirit of good handwriting.

CALOTYPE. An early photographic process invented (c. 1839) by W. H. F. Talbot. Paper sensitized with silver iodide was brushed over with a solution of silver nitrate, acetic acid or gallic acid and exposed while wet. Translucent paper permitted a positive to be printed and led to the use of the glass plate. Also called 'Talbotype'.

CAMBRIDGE INDIA PAPER. Trade name for a grade of paper used for Bibles; made by James R. Compton & Bros. Ltd., Bury, Lancashire. So named to distinguish it from OXFORD INDIA PAPER (*q.v.*). *See also* INDIA PAPER.

CAMBRIDGE STYLE. The English style of book decoration characterized by double panels with a flower tool at each of the outer four corners.

CAMEO. A die-stamping process which results in the design being in plain relief on a coloured background.

CAMEO BINDING. A binding having the centre of the boards stamped in relief, in imitation of antique gems or medals. Also called 'Plaquette binding'.

CAMEO-COATED PAPER. An American dull-finished coated paper suitable for printing half-tones with a non-lustrous surface: it is particularly suitable for artistic engravings. The English equivalent is matt-finished art paper. *See also* ART.

CAMEO STAMP. The earliest form of tool for blind tooling used between the eleventh and early sixteenth centuries. It was oval in shape and engraved with a pictorial design; when impressed on the side of a book it resembled a cameo.

CAMERA CARD. An electric accounting machine-size card containing unexposed and unprocessed microfilm in an aperture of the card, and which is to be exposed and processed while in the aperture of the card in order to create an image of a document on the microfilm. A 'copy card' is a similarly-made card used to make a microfilm copy from a camera card which has been exposed and processed (the exposure of the copy card and its processing being carried out with the microfilm in the aperture). *See also* IMAGE CARD.

CAMERA MICROFILM. The developed microfilm used in a camera to photograph a document; so used to distinguish the film from a microfilm copy made therefrom. Also called 'First generation microfilm'. *See also* FIRST REPRODUCTION MICROFILM.

CAMERAGRAPH. A similar machine to the photostat, but reproducing work on both sides of the sheet.

CAMPBELL CITATION, FRANCIS JOSEPH. A citation and medal awarded by the ALA for outstanding contributions to library services for the blind.

CANADIAN ASSOCIATION OF LAW LIBRARIES. Founded in July 1962 as a Chapter of the American Association of Law Libraries with the objects of fostering a spirit of co-operation among Canadian law libraries and increasing their usefulness and efficiency. Any person engaged or interested in law library work may become a member; there are five classes of member: (a) Individual – any person officially connected with a law library or law book collection; (b) Institutional – any law library; (c) Associate – any person interested in a law library or law collection but not directly connected with it; (d) Honorary; (e) Life – persons retired from active work who were formerly individual members. Membership of classes (d) and (e) is by election; of the remainder by payment of appropriate fees. Abbreviated CALL. Publishes *CALL newsletter*, *Index to Canadian legal periodical literature*.

CANADIAN LIBRARY ASSOCIATION. Formed in 1946, this Association exists (a) to promote education, science and culture within the nation through library service; (b) to promote high standards of librarianship and the welfare of librarians; (c) to co-operate with library associations both within and outside Canada and with other organizations interested in the promotion of education, science and culture. Specialist activities of the Association are carried out by ten sections. Abbreviated CLA. Publishes *Canadian index to periodicals and documentary films* (m., 11 p.a.; annual cumulation); *Canadian library* (bi-m); *Feliciter* (membs.).

CANCEL. This term is loosely given to a part of a book (leaf, part of a leaf or leaves) on which there is a major error which cannot be allowed to remain, and to the leaf which is printed to take the place of the original. The original leaf, which would be more accurately described as the 'Cancelled leaf' (Cancellandum), is cut out by the binder and the corrected one (cancel, cancelling leaf, cancellans) pasted to its stub. Occasionally both leaves are found in a book, the binder having omitted to remove the cancelled leaf.

CANCEL A LOAN. To record the return of a borrowed book; to cancel the record of its loan.

CANCEL TITLE. A reprinted title-page to replace one cut out.

CANCELLAND. *Synonymous with* CANCELLANDUM (*q.v.*).

CANCELLANDUM. *See* CANCEL.

CANCELLANS. *See* CANCEL.

CANCELLATION. The removal of a leaf of a section of a book because of textual error, or for some other reason, leaving a portion of the leaf in the form of a stub. The portion left is known as a disjunct leaf. The portion of the leaf removed is known as the cancellandum and a leaf inserted to take its place is known as the cancellans. *See also* CANCEL.

CANCELLATION MARK. *Synonymous with* DELETION MARK (*q.v.*).

CANCELLED LEAF. *See* CANCEL.

CANCELLING LEAF. *See* CANCEL.

CANEVARI BINDING. A style of binding named after Demetrio Canevari (1539–1625), physician to Pope Urban VII, and usually consisting of a blind-tooled centre panel enclosing a sunken portion bearing a large cameo either glued to the leather or impressed on it.

CANON. An obsolete name for a size of type equal to about 48 pt. The name is probably derived from the use by early printers of this size of type for printing the Canon of the Mass.

CANTILEVER SHELVING. Shelving in which the shelves rest on cantilever brackets having lugs at the back which engage in slots in the upright. No uprights support the shelves at the front, all the weight being carried on the brackets. This provides a long line of shelving without the obstructions caused by the supporting brackets of the bracket type shelving. Deep shelving of this kind is excellent for bound volumes of newspapers or other large publications it is desired to shelve flat, but firmly secured book supports are essential for books which are to be stood up in the normal way. *See also* BRACKET SHELVING, SHELVING.

CAP. 1. Abbreviation for capital. 2. (*Binding*). Protection given to the leaves of a book while being tooled by hand, by wrapping and pasting brown paper around all the book except the boards. When so protected, the book is said to be capped.

CAP LINE. (*Printing*) 1. A line of type which is set in capital letters. 2. An imaginary line which runs along the top of capital letters. *See also* ASCENDER LINE, BASE LINE, MEAN LINE.

CAPITALES QUADRATA. *Synonymous with* SQUARE CAPITALS (*q.v.*).

CAPITALIZATION. The use of capital letters.

CAPITALS. The largest letters of any size of type: those kept in the upper of the two cases of printer's type. Sometimes called 'full capitals' to distinguish them from SMALL CAPITALS (*q.v.*). The headings used in this glossary are in capitals. The use of capitals is indicated in a MS. or proof by a treble underlining. Abbreviated caps. *See also* LOWER CASE LETTERS, SMALL CAPITALS, UPPER CASE LETTERS.

CAPPED. *See* CAP.

CAPSA. A cylindrical box used in Roman libraries to hold one or more rolls standing upright.

CAPSTAN. (*Binding*) An ornament, roughly resembling a capstan, which was common on English and French heads-in-medallions rolls.

CAPTION. 1. The heading at the beginning of the text or of a chapter, section, etc. 2. The wording which appears immediately underneath, or adjacent and relating to, an illustration. This is sometimes called 'Cut line', 'Legend', or 'Underline'.

CAPTION TITLE. The title printed at the beginning of a chapter or section, or at the top of a page. Where the title-page of a book is missing, this may be used to provide a title for the entry in a catalogue or bibliography; in such a case a note 'caption title' is normally used. Also called 'Head title', 'Drop-down title', 'Text title'.

CARAVAN LIBRARIES. Mobile libraries drawn by mechanical horses Landrovers or other vehicles which may perform other duties after taking the library to its site. They may be caravans or other trailers adapted for use as mobile libraries. Sometimes these libraries provide static library services in urban areas in emergency or until a permanent branch can be opened or erected. *See also* MOBILE LIBRARY.

CARBONIZED FORMS. Paper so coated with a pressure-transferable pigmented layer so that copies of all or part of original typescript or manuscript can be obtained without inserting separate sheets of carbon paper, and made up into unit books or used in sets or continuous forms. *See also* NCR.

CARBRO. A photographic colour print process (*Verry*).

CARD. A rectangular piece of card (*see* BOARDS 3) of international standard size, usually 5 × 3 inches, 12·5 cm × 7·5 cm (7·5 cm × 12·5 cm in continental countries), having a surface suitable for writing or typing on, and used for entries in catalogues and similar records. *See also* A7 LIBRARY CARD.

CARD CABINET. The case of drawers for accommodating a CARD CATALOGUE (*q.v.*). Also called a 'Card Catalogue Cabinet'.

CARD CATALOGUE. A catalogue, the entries of which are made on cards of uniform size and quality, and stored in any desired order on their edges in drawers, each card being restricted to a single entry and with details of class number or call number to enable the item to be found. *See also* A7 LIBRARY CARD, MAIN ENTRY, STANDARD SIZE CARD.

CARD CHARGING. The recording of issues of books by means of book-cards associated with readers' tickets or identification cards.

CARD DRAWER. A drawer for holding cards in a CARD CABINET (*q.v.*). Also called 'Card tray'.

CARD FOUNT. The smallest complete fount of type stocked and sold by a typefounder.

CARD INDEX. An index made on cards usually of standard size (5 × 3 inches) and kept on their edges in a drawer. *See also* CARD, STANDARD SIZE CARD.

CARD NUMBER. A symbol consisting of numbers, or a combination of letters and numbers, and possibly the date, used to identify particular entries on centrally produced printed catalogue cards such as those of the British National Bibliography or the Library of Congress, mainly to facilitate ordering.

CARD-OPERATED TYPEWRITER. A typewriter into which is fed punched cards and which, when the electric current is switched on, automatically types on paper in the ordinary way. Some machines similarly type from punched paper tape.

CARD RANDOM ACTION MACHINE. *See* CRAM.

CARD STOCK. A 'board', or heavy weight paper, usually over ·006 inch in thickness made to withstand heavy wear in tabulating or punched card machines, or in catalogues.

CARD TO CARD PRINTER. A machine which produces, by contact printing, duplicate card mounted microfilm.

CARD TRAY. *Synonymous with* CARD DRAWER (*q.v.*).

CARDATYPE. Trade name for a card-operated typewriter which reads punched cards and causes a typewriter to transcribe the punching on to some form of record.

CARDING. A North American term for making out cards for books and other library materials, either from the materials themselves or from lists, to be used when checking records for ownership or for bibliographic accuracy, and possibly later as part of the acquisition record.

CARDMASTER. 1. Trade name for a simple duplicating device specially designed for producing catalogue cards. Stencils are cut from mimeograph machine stencils, inserted in a holder and inked on a card-size pad. Also called a 'Chiang Small Duplicator'. 2. Trade name for a make of rotary card filing cabinet. *See also* ROTARY CARD FILE.

CARET (*Lat.*: 'it needs'). The mark (ᴧ) used in a MS. or proof to signify that something is omitted and indicate where an addition or insertion is to be made. Also called 'Insertion mark'.

CARNEGIE LIBRARY. A library built with the financial assistance of funds given by Andrew Carnegie.

CARNEGIE MEDAL. An award made by the Library Association to the writer of an outstanding book for children. The book must be written in English and have been published in the United Kingdom during the year preceding the presentation of the award. Named after Andrew Carnegie (1835–1918) the iron-master and philanthropist, it was first awarded in 1936 to Arthur Ransome for *Pigeon Post*. A list of the books awarded the Medal is published in the Library Association *Year book*.

CAROLINGIAN. A minuscule book hand developed in France in the eighth century from the Roman cursive, much influenced by the English half uncial. The Carolingian minuscule is the prototype of the modern styles of penmanship, and of lower case roman type. It belongs to the second dynasty of French Kings founded by Carl the Great (Charlemagne) and much of its success was due to Alcuin of York, a distinguished English scholar, churchman and poet, who took charge of the Abbey of St. Martin at Tours at the invitation of Charlemagne. It was the dominant book hand for nearly three centuries.

CARREL. A small room connected with a reference library, which is set aside for continuous research work by one reader and in which books, note-books, etc. may be securely locked during the temporary absence of the reader. This word is now used in America to indicate any table or other space reserved for one reader which provides by means of front and side screening a more or less secluded study and writing area, whether or not facilities are provided for locking up books. Such facilities for up to four readers are also called carrels. *Closed carrels* are cubicles which give complete seclusion. *Open carrels* give partial seclusion. *Suspended carrels* are those which are provided by fitting (suspending) writing areas similar to table tops into the uprights of steel shelving to give writing space in stack rooms. *See also* OASIS.

CARRIAGE. A flat frame bearing the guide rails on which the plank (supporting the stone on which rests the forme) of a hand printing machine moves to its printing position.

CART. A small book box, not on wheels, but divided into sections to display children's books face up. (American.) Called in Europe a KINDERBOX (*q.v.*).

CARTOBIBLIOGRAPHY. A bibliography of maps.

CARTOGRAM. A highly abstracted, simplified map the purpose of which is to demonstrate a single idea in a diagrammatic way. In order to do this outlines of land or the exact locations of other features are often altered.

CARTOGRAPHER. A maker of maps.

CARTOGRAPHER ENTRY. An entry under the name of the maker of a map.

CARTOGRAPHY. The science and art of making maps.

CARTOUCHE. 1. A frame, either simple or decorative, or a scroll, in which the title, name of the cartographer, and other particulars relating to a map are placed. The cartouche usually appears in a corner of the map, and in old maps was frequently adorned with country scenes, animals, human figures, armorial or architectural designs, etc. 2. A drawn framing of an engraving, etc. 3. (*Binding*) A small rectangular ornament formed on blind rolls by one or more lines, generally with a plain centre.

CARTOUCHE TITLE. The title which appears within the cartouche or scroll-like design on a map or engraving.

CARTRIDGE PAPER. A hard, tough paper made with a rough surface and in a number of grades.

CARTULARY. *Synonymous with* CHARTULARY (*q.v.*).

CASE. (*Binding*) The cover for a book which is made completely before being attached to a book by means of the endpapers and sometimes tapes in addition. (*Printing*) In hand composition, a tray divided by 'bars' into compartments in which printer's individual letters, numerals and spaces are kept and which is placed on the FRAME (*q.v.*) when in use, and in a cabinet when idle. The arrangement of the compartments is the same for all types and sizes. Cases may be in pairs, an upper and a lower containing respectively the capitals and small letters (hence *upper* case (u.c.) and *lower* case (l.c.)) or the whole fount may be in a double unit. *See also* CASING.

CASE BINDING. *See* CASE.

CASE BOOK. A book bearing a cloth cover, as originally issued by the publisher. Thus 'cased'.

CASED. *See* CASE BOOK.

CASING. The operation of inserting a sewn book into its case, or cover, which is made separately from the book, and pasted to the book by means of endpapers.

CASLON. A type face designed and cut in 1722 by William Caslon (1692–1766), England's first and greatest type-founder. It is an OLD FACE (*q.v.*) type and is one of the most widely used of all type faces in American and British printing. For a specimen alphabet, *see* TYPE FACE.

CASSIE. An old term, derived from the Fr. *cassé* (broken), for the outside and frequently damaged sheets of a ream of good paper. 'Cassie quires' are the two outside quires of a ream, also called 'Coding quires'.

CAST COATED PAPER. A very expensive American art paper with an exceptionally soft, absorbent and uniformly flat surface. It was developed about 1950.

CAST-UP. To calculate the cost of composing type.

CASTING BOX. (*Printing*) A machine, or device, for casting stereos.

CASTING OFF. The process of estimating the amount of space COPY (*q.v.*) will occupy when set up in a given size of type.

CASUAL MNEMONICS. Characters used mnemonically in a scheme of classification where letters in the notation are used to indicate subjects, the notation letter being the same as the first letter of the name of the subject. They are used in particular circumstances and not as part of the normal method of notation. *See also* MNEMONICS.

CATALOGUE. (*Noun*) A list of books, maps, or other items, arranged in some definite order. It records, describes and indexes (usually completely) the resources of a collection, a library or a group of libraries. To be distinguished from (1) a list, which may or may not be in any particular order and may be incomplete, and (2) a bibliography, which may not be confined to any one collection of books or to a particular group of libraries. Each entry bears details of class number or call number to enable the item to be found, as well as sufficient details (such as author, title, date of publication, editorship, illustrations, pagination and edition) to identify and describe the book. (*Verb*) To compile a list of documents according to a set of rules so as to enable the consulter to know what items are available, and from the class number, call number, or other means of identification, where they may be found. In a special library, in addition to entries under authors, subjects, and possibly titles, it may include (a) analytical entries; (b) abstracts – especially in scientific and technical libraries; (c) annotations indicating the treatment or coverage of the subject; (d) entries under subjects for work in progress and for individuals who are authoritative sources of information on specific subjects; (e) entries for pertinent information material in other parts of the organization or in other libraries.

CATALOGUE CARD. 1. A plain or ruled card on which catalogue entries may be made. 2. A card containing such an entry. *See also* STANDARD SIZE CARD.

CATALOGUE CODE. A set of rules for guidance of cataloguers in preparing entries for catalogues so as to ensure uniformity in treatment. Such codes may include rules for subject cataloguing, and for filing and arranging entries. Examples are: the *Anglo-American cataloguing rules*, *A.L.A. rules for filing catalog cards*, *Rules for a dictionary catalogue* by A. C. Cutter, and the Library of Congress *Rules for descriptive cataloging in the Library of Congress*. Examples of rules for cataloguing special materials are Music Library Association/American Library Association *Code for cataloguing music and phonorecords*, Guppy, H., *Rules for the cataloguing of incunabula*, Unesco, *International rules for the cataloguing of educational, scientific and cultural films and filmstrips*.

CATALOGUE DRAWER, CATALOGUE TRAY. One of the drawers of a card catalogue, in which catalogue cards are kept.

CATALOGUE RAISONNÉ. A catalogue of an author's work, especially of an artist's pictures, engravings, etc., usually arranged by subjects, with comments, elucidations, appraisals, and bibliographical details. Also called '*Classed catalogue*' and '*Classified catalogue*' (*qq.v.*).

CATALOGUER. A librarian who prepares an entry for a catalogue.

CATALOGUING. Strictly, the process of making entries for a catalogue; additionally it may cover all the processes involved in preparing books for the shelves, or simply the preparation of entries for the catalogue.

CATALOGUING, PRINCIPLES OF. There may be said to be seven basic principles of cataloguing, five (multiple approach, unique entry, inevitable association, probable association, specific entry) common to all types of entry, and two (adequate description, concise description) relating to book description. See under the names of the various principles.

CATALOGUING AND INDEXING GROUP. A Group of the

Library Association. It was formed in 1964 and came into official existence on 1st January 1965.

CATALOGUING DEPARTMENT. The department of a library which deals with the ordering, cataloguing and classification of books, together with their processing, i.e. preparation for issue to the library users. Where there is no ORDER DEPARTMENT (*q.v.*), the work of ordering and processing books is also done here. In some American libraries, the work of preparing the books for the shelves, other than cataloguing and classification, is carried out in a separate department.

CATALOGUING IN SOURCE. Cataloguing books before they are published, the entries being compiled from proof copies made available by the publishers, and the work being carried out by a centralized agency so that full cataloguing information is printed in the books concerned, and also so that catalogue cards are available for purchase on the day of a book's publication. A grant was made by the Council on Library Resources, Inc. to the Library of Congress in 1958 to test the financial and technical feasibility and the utility of such cataloguing. The Library of Congress reported in 1960 that the experiment which had been carried out in conjunction with other bodies indicated that such cataloguing was not practicable because of the very high cost of the programme to both publishers and the Library of Congress, disruptions of publishing schedules, the high degree of unreliability of catalogue entries based on texts not in their final form, and the low degree of utility which would result from the copying of these entries.

CATCH. A metal plate secured to a book cover and having a bar, over which the clasp fits. Sometimes a pin is used instead of there being a bar.

CATCH LETTERS. Groups of letters (usually three in a group) appearing in dictionaries, gazetteers, etc., at the tops of pages to indicate the first or last words of a page or column. Those on *verso* pages represent the first three letters of the first word on that page, those on the *recto* represent the first three of the last word on that page. Sometimes two groups of letters joined by a hyphen indicate the first and last words on a page.

CATCH STITCH. *Synonymous with* KETTLE STITCH (*q.v.*). Also a stitch made when sewing on tapes by passing the needle (after it comes out of the right side of the tape and before it goes across the tape) eye-end down under three or four threads below it and then into the loop so formed. The thread is then pulled up tight to form a knot in the centre of the tape before being drawn back into the middle of the section. This is done to avoid too great looseness.

CATCH TITLE. *Synonymous with* CATCHWORD TITLE (*q.v.*).

5

CATCHLINE. A line of type inserted temporarily at the top of matter by the compositor in order to identify it, and so printed on proofs. Also the name given to a short line of type in between two large displayed lines.

CATCHMENT AREA. (*County Libraries*). In library planning denotes the area from which readers may be expected to be drawn to a given library service point.

CATCHWORD. 1. The word occurring at the bottom of a page after the last line, such word being the first on the following page. Catchwords originally appeared at the last page of a quire of a MS. and served as a guide to the binder. Later, they appeared at the foot of every verso, sometimes every page, but in conjunction with the signature served no useful purpose and were discontinued in the nineteenth century. Also called 'Direction word'. 2. A word at the top of a page or column in encyclopaedias and works of a similar nature, denoting the first or last heading dealt with on the page. 3. In indexing, the word or words which govern the position of an entry in the index.

CATCHWORD ENTRY. An entry in a catalogue under some striking word in a book's title, other than the first, which is likely to be remembered.

CATCHWORD INDEX. One which uses a significant word from a title or text to index an item (*IBM*).

CATCHWORD TITLE. A PARTIAL TITLE (*q.v.*) consisting of some striking or easily remembered word or phrase. It may be the same as a sub-title or the ALTERNATIVE TITLE (*q.v.*). Also called 'Catch title'.

CATEGORICAL TABLES. In J. D. Brown's *Subject classification*, tables representing forms, standpoints, qualifications and other modes of dividing subjects. Each term in the tables is given a number (0 to 975). These are added (after a point which is used as a separating device) to subject numbers in any part of the classification:

> e.g. .1 Bibliography.
> .2 Dictionaries.
> .10 History.
> .33 Travel.
> .57 Museums.

Examples of the application of numbers from the Categorical Tables:

> Russia S 000.
> – Bibliography of S 000.1
> – History of S 000.10
> – Travel in S 000.33
> – Museums in S 000.57

London   U 900.
- Bibliography of   U 900.1
- Dictionary of   U 900.2
- History of   U 900.10
- Travel in   U 900.33
- Museums in   U 900.57

CATEGORY. (*Classification*) A term with varying meanings. 1. A 'point of view' according to which a subject can be divided. (*Wildhack*). Considered by some to be synonymous with FACET (*q.v.*). 2. 'A concept of high generality and wide application which can be used to group other concepts' (*Glossary and subject index*). *See also* FUNDAMENTAL CATEGORIES. 3. A comprehensive class or description of things (*IBM*). 4. A logical grouping of associated documents (*IBM*). 5. A class or division formed for purposes of a given classification. In faceted classification, special distinctions are made between categories, classes, facets and phases (*IBM*). *See also* FUNDAMENTAL CATEGORIES.

CATENA.   A series of extracts from the writings of the fathers, arranged with independent additions to eludicate scripture and provide a commentary thereon.

CATENATI.   Chained books.

CATER-CORNERED.   Paper which is cut diagonally, not square.

CATHEDRAL BINDING.   One decorated with Gothic architectural motifs, often including a rose window, done between 1815 and 1840 in England and France. In England the decoration was sometimes built up of large single tools: in France it was normally stamped on the covers. This was a revival by the nineteenth century binder Thouvenin of the ARCHITECTURAL BINDING (*q.v.*) style.

CATHOLIC LIBRARY ASSOCIATION.   Founded 1921 in the U.S.A. to initiate, foster, and encourage any movement toward the development of Catholic literature and Catholic library work. Abbreviated CLA. Publishes *The best in Catholic reading* (a) and many non-serial publications; *Catholic booklist* (a); *Catholic library world* (9 p.a.); *Catholic periodical index* (q.); *Handbook and membership directory* (a.) .

CAT'S PAW CALF.   (*Binding*). An acid strain pattern on a calf binding which resembles the paw marks of a cat.

CAWTHORNE PRIZE.   An award instituted in memory of the late Mr. Albert Cawthorne, formerly Chief Librarian of Stepney as a result of a gift of £300 worth of shares by his son, Mr. B. A. Cawthorne. The interest on these shares is awarded each year to the candidate obtaining the highest marks in Part I of the Library Association's professional examinations, and was first awarded to Mr. G. K. Barnett in 1965.

CEASED PUBLICATION. A work in several volumes, the publication of which was not completed, or a periodical, the publication of which has been discontinued.

CEDILLA. The mark under the letter ç to indicate that it has a sound other than that of *k*; in French it has the sound of *s* and in Spanish of *th*.

CELL. An area in a library formed by placing two free-standing book-cases against wall shelving. This arrangement was used by Sir Christopher Wren at Trinity College, Cambridge, in 1676. Usually called 'Alcove'.

CELLO-CLIPS. Clips, two of which can be affixed to the top edges of maps, large or heavy drawings, or plastic relief models, for suspension from horizontal rods.

CELLULOSE. The common term for chemical wood pulp, the basic substance of paper manufacture. It is the predominating constituent of plant tissues from which it must be separated before it can be used.

CELLULOSE ACETATE. *See* FILM BASE.

CELLULOSE TRIACETATE. *See* FILM BASE.

CEN *See* EUROPEAN COMMITTEE FOR CO-ORDINATION OF STANDARDS.

CENEL *See* EUROPEAN COMMITTEE FOR CO-ORDINATION OF STANDARDS.

CENSORSHIP. Prohibition of the production, distribution, circulation or sale of material considered to be objectionable for reasons of politics, religion, obscenity or blasphemy. This action is usually taken by persons empowered to act by federal, national, state or local laws, and takes the forms of preventing publications passing through the Customs or through the post, or of action in a law court to prevent their sale. *See also* INDEX LIBRORUM PROHIBITORUM.

CENTER FOR DOCUMENTATION AND COMMUNICATION RESEARCH. This organization is based on the School of Library Science at Western Reserve University, Cleveland, Ohio, U.S.A., and is concerned with machine literature searching. Abbreviated CDCR.

CENTER FOR RESEARCH LIBRARIES. An American co-operative scheme to house little-used materials integrated into a collection in which duplicates are eliminated in order to sponsor broader co-operation including co-operative acquisition. Proposed in 1941, it started in 1951. Members (now over twenty) share operating costs. It is situated in Chicago, and was known as the Midwest Inter-Library Center, abbreviated MILC until the Spring of 1965 when, because it served institutions in eleven States and the University of Toronto in Canada, it was decided to change its name. Its scope now extends to all research libraries in the U.S.A. and Canada, and potentially, Mexico. Abbreviated CRL. *See also* LIBRARY RESEARCH CENTER.

CENTESIMAL DEVICE. A method used in the Universal Decimal Classification to lengthen arrays where nine divisions are inadequate; the digits 11–99 are used to represent co-ordinate subjects instead of 1–9.

CENTRAL ADVISORY COUNCIL FOR EDUCATION (ENGLAND). This organization developed from a Consultative Committee which existed prior to the Second World War and was responsible for enquiries which resulted in such reports as the Hadow Report; it ceased to function during the war but was known as the Central Advisory Council for Education from 1946 until it was reconstituted in August 1963. Enquiries which have been undertaken in recent years have been published as *Early leaving, 15 to 18* (the Crowther Report), *Half our future* (the Newsom Report) and *Children and their primary schools* (the Plowden Report). There is a separate Council for Wales.

CENTRAL CATALOGUE. 1. A catalogue placed in the central library of a library system but containing entries for books in all the libraries. 2. A catalogue of the central library of a library system.

CENTRAL LIBRARY. 1. The chief library in a system, containing the office of the chief librarian, the administrative department, and the largest collections of books. Sometimes called the 'Main Library'; if a public library it is usually situated in the centre or busiest part of a town, if a non-public library it would be at the most important or effective place in the organization, possibly at the headquarters. 2. The library which is provided in a primary school for all the children to use as distinct from the class library which is placed in each class room. Also called a 'General library.'

CENTRAL MUSIC LIBRARY. A limited company which is housed at the Buckingham Palace Road Branch of the Westminster City Public Libraries and administered by the Westminster City Council. Founded on 21 October 1948 by an original donation of £10,000 from Winifred Christie Moór, it includes the former collections of Gerald Cooper, Edwin Evans and his father, Charles Woodhouse and Eric Blom. The large collection of sheet and bound music, as well as the books, are available for loan through public libraries. Thematic indexes are published with the financial support of the Arts Council and the British Council. Abbreviated CML.

CENTRAL SHELF LIST. 1. A shelf list recording all the books in the central library of a system of libraries. 2. A combined shelf list, housed in the central library, but recording all books in all the libraries of a library system.

CENTRALIZED CATALOGUING. 1. The cataloguing of books by some central bureau, and the distribution therefrom, of printed entries on catalogue cards, or otherwise. Notably the Library of Congress scheme and the British National Bibliography. 2. The cataloguing at one library of all the books of a library system comprising more than one library, thus achieving uniformity throughout the system.

CENTRALIZED PROCESSING. In the U.S.A., the Library Services Act has stimulated the setting up of processing centres for the purchase, cataloguing, classifying and processing of books, audio-visual and other material for a number of libraries. This has resulted in considerable economies and the freeing of professional staff for other duties.

CENTRALIZED REGISTRATION. The registering of readers at one library in a system, comprising several libraries, rather than at those at which the application forms are handed in.

CENTRE. In an English county library, a small static library service point, provided in premises which may at times be used for other purposes, open less than ten hours a week, having a stock which is changed from time to time, and staffed by voluntary or paid librarians.

CENTRE NATIONAL DE LA RECHERCHE SCIENTIFIQUE ET TECHNIQUE. *See* CNRS.

CENTRE NOTE. (*Printing*) A note, or reference, placed between columns of text as in a Bible. *See also* INCUT NOTE.

CENTRED DOT. (*Printing*) A period placed higher than the base line of a piece of type, as, c·e·n·t·r·e·d, to show multiplication ($1·2 = 2$), or to separate roman capitals in the classic form of inscriptions (M·A·R·C·V·S). Also called 'Space dot.'

CENTREING ARROWS. Markings on a document to aid positioning of the document when filming, and of the microfilm when mounting.

CENTREPIECE. (*Binding*) An ornament, usually ARABESQUE (*q.v.*), placed in the centre of the cover of a bound book and often used with cornerpieces, or cornerstamps. It was a favourite style of binding in the late sixteenth and early seventeenth centuries. Also used of a piece of metal usually embossed and engraved, and fastened on to the cover. Also called 'Centrestamp.'

CENTRESTAMP. *Synonymous with* CENTREPIECE (*q.v.*).

CENTRO DE DOCUMENTAÇAO CIENTIFICA. The Portuguese Scientific Documentation Centre was formed to survey the country's library resources and to rationalize holdings.

CENTRO DE DOCUMENTACIÓN CIENTIFICA Y TÉCHNICA. The Mexican Centre of Scientific and Technical Documentation.

CERNE, BOOK OF. An illuminated MS. of the Passion and Resurrection portions of the Gospels, written at Lichfield in the early 9th century, so named as it was formerly kept at Cerne Abbey, Dorset; it is now in the Library of Cambridge University. The style of decoration is severely calligraphic and the colours, used are light shades with only occasional gold; some pages are enlivened with beasts.

CEROGRAPH. A wax engraving process usually used for making maps. A drawing is made direct on wax spread over a copper plate which is then used as a mould from which an electrotype is made. Also called 'Cerotype.'

CEROGRAPHY. The process used for making cerographic prints. *See also* CEROGRAPH.

CEROTYPE. A print made by the cerographic process. *See also* CEROGRAPH.

CERTIFICATE OF ISSUE. The statement, printed in a LIMITED EDITION (*q.v.*), certifying the number of copies printed and sometimes bearing the autograph of the author and/or illustrator.

CETIS. Acronym for Centre Européen pour le Traitement de l'Information Scientifique; it was set up by EURATOM (Organisation Atomique Européene) to standardize documentary method and establish a European network of information in the field of nuclear energy.

cf. Abbreviation for *confer* (*q.v.*) (*Lat.*, meaning 'compare').

ch. Abbreviation for CHAPTER (*q.v.*).

CHAIN. (*Classification*) The succession of divisions subordinate one to another expressing the relation 'A includes B, which in turn includes C' (or, conversely, 'C is part of B, which is part of A'), e.g. Literature, English Literature, English Poetry, Shakespeare's Poetry, *Adonis*, constitute a chain of divisions in the class Literature. A hierarchy of terms, each containing or including all which follow it in the same series: a hierarchy of sub-classes of decreasing extension and increasing intension, devised by successive division. The chain of progression in a scheme of classification from general to specific may be:

    780 Music
       782 Dramatic music
         782·1 Opera
           782·154 Wagner *Die Meistersinger*

The indexer, using the principle of chain indexing, works his way back from the most specific step to more general terms, and in this case would provide these entries:

Operas by individual composers 782·154
Opera   782·1
Music: Dramatic   782
Music   780

CHAIN INDEX.   An alphabetic index wherein a heading is provided for each term, or link for all the terms used in a subject heading or classification (*IBM*). Each term represented by a given part of the classification symbol, followed by the term for each other part, appears as a heading in the reverse order of the symbol, so that the last term in the symbol becomes the first. If the symbol is comprised of four parts, there will be four entries: the first consisting of four terms; the second, of three after the first term of the previous entry has been omitted; the third, of two, and so on. The final one is the heading for the symbol with the widest connotation, and the most extension, relating to the subject in question. *See also* CORRELATIVE INDEX, RELATIVE INDEX.

CHAIN INDEXING.   *See* CHAIN.

CHAIN LINE.   *See* LAID PAPER.

CHAIN MARK.   *See* LAID PAPER.

CHAIN PROCEDURE.   (*Cataloguing*) A method of constructing subject index entries, without permutation of components, by citing terms contained in particular chains. *See also* CHAIN.

CHAIN STITCH.   *See* KETTLE STITCH.

CHAINED BOOKS.   Books chained to shelves or reading desks in libraries of the fifteenth to early eighteenth centuries to prevent theft. The practice began to die out by the middle of the seventeenth century when it became customary to shelve books upright.

CHAINED LIBRARY.   One in which the books were chained to shelves or reading desks.

CHALCOGRAPHY.   Engraving on copper or brass.

CHALK DRAWING.   One executed in crayon or pastel. The art of drawing with chalks or pastels is called chalcography.

CHALK ENGRAVING.   *Synonymous with* CRAYON ENGRAVING (*q.v.*).

CHALK OVERLAY.   A method of overlaying whereby an impression is taken on paper having a thin coating of chalk. This coating is then washed off the non-inked parts with diluted acid, thus leaving the inked design in relief. The resulting outline is then fitted as an overlay to the cylinder or platen so as to decrease or increase pressure. Also called 'Mechanical overlay.'

CHAMBER MUSIC. Seriously intended instrumental music for two or more instruments, played by one instrument to each 'part.' It excludes music for orchestra, chorus and other large combinations, vocal music and all instrumental music for one instrument. *See also* ORCHESTRAL MUSIC.

CHAMPLEVÉ. Enamelled bindings made by craftsmen between the eleventh and thirteenth centuries. Designs were cut into a thin sheet of gold or copper which formed the cover, the cavities being filled with enamel. On other bindings the enamel was limited to the decoration of borders and corners. This kind of binding was mainly carried out at Limoges. *See also* CLOISONNÉ.

CHANCERY. The department of the Lord Chancellor, from which issue documents under the Great Seal, such as Charters, Letters Patent, writs and the like, also the place where Charters, Letters Patent and documents of a like nature are enrolled.

CHANCERY LIBERATE. *See* LIBERATE ROLL.

CHANGED NAME. Used of a person who has written under a different name.

CHANGED TITLE. Used to describe a book that has been published under a different title to the one originally used.

Chap. Abbreviation for CHAPTER (*q.v.*).

CHAP-BOOK. A small, cheap book, in a paper binding, and of a popular, sensational, juvenile, moral or educational character. These were popular in the seventeenth and eighteenth centuries, and contained tales, ballads, historical incidents, biographies, tracts, interpretations of dreams, palmistry, astrology, etc. They were sold by chapmen, i.e., pedlars, hawkers. The word comes from the Anglo-Saxon root *ceap* (trade).

CHAPEL. An association of journeymen in the printing and binding trades. Chapels usually exist in printing works of medium and larger size. The secretary, or leader, called the Father of the Chapel, is appointed by the members and one of his duties is to collect and forward trade union dues. To 'call a chapel' is to hold a chapel meeting of the journeymen.

CHAPTER. A division of a book, usually being complete in itself in subject matter but related to the preceding and following ones.

CHAPTER HEADING (HEAD, HEADLINE). The heading placed at the text beginning a chapter. It is usually set below the normal top of the type area of the other pages; the type used is normally larger than that used for running titles, and is of a uniform size and position for each chapter.

5*

CHARACTER. 1. A letter of the alphabet, numeral, punctuation mark, or any other symbol cast as a type. Also called 'Sort.' 2. A personage, real or fictitious, figuring in an opera or work of imaginative literature, especially a novel or play. 3. A style of handwriting.

CHARACTER COUNT. A count of every letter, number, punctuation mark, word or sentence space, etc., in a piece of prose copy.

CHARACTERISTIC OF A CLASSIFICATION. A distinctive property, element, or feature, inherent in a character by which a class is defined. A *typical characteristic* is one by which an individual of a class is representative of that class. A *type* is a typical individual, one that has most distinctly the typical characteristic, or characteristics, distinctive of the class. A class may be a type, or *typical class*, if it is representative of a *class of classes* (*Bliss*). The attribute which forms the basis of division. Language, form, and historical period are common characteristics in the classification of literature. A term used to express the principles by which a group is divided (as, genus into species) e.g. the characteristic that divides the animal kingdom into two parts is the absence or presence of a backbone. The characteristic is said to be 'natural' when it exhibits the inherent properties of the things classified. When it does not affect the structure, purpose, or intrinsic character of the things to be divided, but separates according to an accidental quality it is said to be 'artificial.' Thus, in zoology, the presence of a backbone is a natural characteristic, while the habitat (land, sea, or air) is an artificial characteristic. The characteristics chosen as the basis of arrangement must be essential (i.e., the most useful) for the purpose of the classification. They must be used consistently, i.e. it is impossible to classify a subject by two characteristics at once. *See* CROSS CLASSIFICATION. Ranganathan's characteristics are: differentiation, concomitance, relevance, ascertainability, permanence, relevant sequence, consistency. Also called a 'Principle of division.'

CHARACTERS IN PICA. *See* ALPHABET LENGTH.

CHARCOAL DRAWING. One made with a charcoal crayon on paper with a rough surface. Such drawings are easily smudged, and to prevent this they are sprayed with a fixative.

CHARCOAL PAPER. A soft, rough-surfaced paper used for making charcoal drawings.

CHARGE. 1. The record of a loan, giving particulars of the book lent and the reader's name and address. 2. To 'issue' a book; to record the loan of a book; to make a 'charge.' 3. An amount of money which is authorised by s.8 of the Public Libraries and Museums Act 1964 for a service provided by a public library. Charges, not exceeding such amount as may be specified by the Secretary of State, may be made (a) for notifying a person that a book or other article reserved by him has become available for borrowing, (b) in respect of failure to return a book or other article before the end of the period for which it was lent. The latter has always been known as a 'fine.' A library authority may make a charge for the borrowing of any article, except that where the authority is under a duty to make facilities for borrowing available to residents, non-resident students and non-resident employees, such a person shall not be charged for borrowing (a) a book, journal, pamphlet or similar article, or (b) a reproduction made by photographic or other means of the whole or a part of any such article s.8 (3). A charge may be made for supplying book catalogues or indexes, or any similar articles, where they become the property of the persons to whom they are supplied s.8 (4), and also for facilities which go beyond those ordinarily provided as part of the library service s.8 (5). Where premises are provided under the Public Libraries and Museums Act 1964, charges may be made for admission to any event of a cultural or educational nature (s.20).

CHARGE A BOOK. The action of recording the loan of a book, or making a 'charge.'

CHARGE SLIP. *See* BOOK CARD.

CHARGING CARD. *See* BOOK CARD.

CHARGING DESK. *Synonymous with* STAFF ENCLOSURE (*q.v.*).

CHARGING MACHINE. A machine used for recording the loan of books to readers.

CHARGING METHODS. The methods by which loans of books are recorded. *See* BOOKAMATIC, BROWNE BOOK CHARGING SYSTEM, CHEQUE BOOK CHARGING METHOD, DETROIT SELF-CHARGING SYSTEM, DICKMAN CHARGING SYSTEM, ISLINGTON CHARGING SYSTEM, NEWARK CHARGING SYSTEM, PHOTOCHARGER, PUNCHED CARD CHARGING, TOKEN CHARGING, TRANSACTION CARD CHARGING.

CHARGING SLIP. *See* BOOK CARD.

CHARGING SYSTEM. The method used in keeping records of the loan of books. *See* CHARGING METHODS.

CHARGING TRAY. The steel or wooden tray which is used to hold the 'charges.'

CHART. 1. A map for the use of marine navigators showing the coastline, the position of rocks, sandbanks, channels, anchorages, and the depths of water in different parts of the sea expressed in feet or fathoms. 2. A graphical representation by means of curves, or the like, of the fluctuation of statistical records of such items as population, prices, production, barometric pressure, temperature, etc. 3. Information of any kind arranged in tabular form, or graphically by means of curves.

CHART PAPER.   A hard, tub-sized paper which must be strong, tough, pliable and subject to folding without cracking. It should be liable to stretch as little as possible during printing in view of register, smooth without gloss, suitable for pen and ink charting and therefore able to withstand erasure. *See also* PLAN PAPER.

CHARTER.   An instrument whereby a sovereign or legislature grants rights to a person or corporation.

CHARTER BOOKSELLER.   A retail bookseller who satisfies certain conditions laid down by the Booksellers Association with regard to service to the public.

CHARTER ROLL.   A parchment roll upon which charters were enrolled at the Chancery.

CHARTULARY.   1. A keeper of archives. 2. A place in which records or charters relating to a religious, civil or private state are kept. 3. The book in which they are listed or copied. Also called 'Cartulary.'

CHASE.   (*Printing*) A rectangular iron frame in which, by means of wedges, composed matter is secured and rendered portable. The wedges are called side- and foot-sticks and quoins. When they are adjusted, between the type matter and the chase, the whole becomes a forme, and is said to be 'locked up.' In SHEET WORK (*q.v.*) the forme which contains the text which will be on the inside pages of a printed sheet when folded, is called the 'inner forme' and that which contains those on the outside, the 'outer forme.'

CHASED EDGES.   *Synonymous with* GAUFFERED EDGES (*q.v.*).

CHAUCER TYPE.   A re-cutting, in 12-point, of the TROY TYPE (*q.v.*) designed by William Morris. It was first used in 1892. *See also* GOLDEN TYPE.

CHEAP EDITION.   An edition of a book issued at a cheaper price. Usually it is a reprint of an earlier edition, printed on poorer paper and bound in a cheaper cover.

CHECK-LIST.   1. A record on which is noted each number, or part, of a work 'in progress' as it is received. 2. A list of items giving brief information sufficient only for identification. 3. An enumeration of documentary holdings with a minimum of organization and bibliographic information (*IBM*).

CHECK MARKS.   Indications made by cataloguers on title-pages of books, as a guide to assistant cataloguers or typists, of items to b omitted in the entries, e.g. ( ) may mean, 'omit from all cards,' [ ] may mean 'omit from title card but include on subject cards.' They are pencilled on by the cataloguer as a guide to his assistants.

CHECKOUT ROUTINE. 1. A procedure used in machine documentation systems to determine the correctness of answers, involving the use of sample inquiries, the answers to which are known (*IBM*). 2. The necessary procedures demanded before removing a document from a collection (*IBM*).

CHELTENHAM. An unattractive type face designed by Bertram G. Goodhue (1869–1924) in 1896 and widely used by jobbing printers as it is a FOUNDERS' TYPE (*q.v.*).

CHELTENHAM CLASSIFICATION. A system devised for the library of the Ladies' College, Cheltenham, and used in a number of schools. The tables were published under the editorship of Miss E. S. Fegan and Miss M. Cant who were successive librarians of the College. Being aligned closely with the school curriculum, the contents of the main classes correspond with the traditional coverage of subjects as taught.

CHEMICAL WOOD. Wood reduced to pulp by a chemical process, cooking in acid (sulphite process), or an alkaline liquor (soda process), for use in the manufacture of paper. This produces a purer pulp than that obtained by the MECHANICAL WOOD (*q.v.*) process. A combined chemical and mechanical wood process results in a paper which is intermediate in quality between the two.

CHEMISE. A loose cover for a book with pockets for boards. These were sometimes used in the Middle Ages instead of binding.

CHEQUE BOOK CHARGING METHOD. An adaptation of the BROWNE BOOK CHARGING SYSTEM (*q.v.*) to enable it to deal more rapidly with great pressure at the entrance side of staff enclosures, which it does most satisfactorily. This was the problem facing librarians when they were seeking methods of avoiding queues in the middle 1950's and which resulted in the introduction of TOKEN CHARGING (*q.v.*) and of transaction charging systems. With this system a reader is issued with a small book of fifty perforated slips of paper, similar to a small cheque book, and each bearing the same number. When a book is borrowed, a slip torn from the cheque book by an assistant is placed with the book card to form a CHARGE (*q.v.*). On discharging a book, the numbered cheque book slip is destroyed. When writing overdue notices, the name and address of the borrower is obtained by referring to the list of cheque book numbers against which names and addresses have been entered. Delayed discharging (i.e. cancelling the loan record at a less busy time) is possible with this method. *See also* CHARGING METHODS.

CHEQUERING. (*Binding*) To divide a surface into squares of alternately different ornament or colours, by equidistant vertical and horizontal lines like a chess-board.

chi. (*Bibliography*) The Greek letter χ used to denote an unsigned gathering or leaf in respect of which no signature can be inferred and which is not the first gathering. *See also* pi.

CHIANG SMALL DUPLICATOR. *See* CARDMASTER.

CHIAROSCURO. 1. A black and white sketch. 2. A method of printing engravings, usually wood-engravings, from blocks representing lighter and darker shades, used especially in the fifteenth and sixteenth centuries. 3. A print produced by this means. 4. The earliest form of colour printing. It was a woodcut method, the colours being successively printed in register from separate blocks after an impression from the master block had been made.

CHIEF ASSISTANT. The senior assistant librarian next to the deputy librarian.

CHIFFON SILK. A thin, strong and durable silk material which can be used for mending and strengthening paper, especially of valuable books.

CHILDREN'S BOOK CIRCLE. An informal group of children's book editors and those who work in publishers' children's book departments. It was started in 1962 to provide an opportunity for such persons to exchange ideas on the publication of, and publicity for, children's books. The Eleanor Farjeon Award 'for distinguished services to children's books in the past year' was first made in 1966 (to Mrs. Margery Fisher for her reviews of children's books in *Growing Point*) in memory of Eleanor Farjeon, one of the greatest children's writers, who died in 1965. Anyone doing outstanding work for children's books, whether librarian, teacher, author, artist, publisher, reviewer, television producer – in fact, anyone – is eligible for the award which is a monetary prize of at least fifty guineas. Nominations for the award may be made by members of the Circle only.

CHILDREN'S BOOK TRUST. A non-profit-making Indian publishing venture inspired by Shankar Pillai, the Indian cartoonist. Situated in Delhi, it publishes books in English and Hindu which are sold at subsidised prices.

CHILDREN'S BOOK WEEK. *See* BOOK WEEK.

CHILDREN'S LIBRARY. The department reserved for the exclusive use of children. It usually contains lending and reference sections and periodicals.

CHILDREN'S SERVICES DIVISION. Became a Division of the American Library Association on 1 January 1957. It is concerned with the extension of library services to children in all types of library, and is responsible for evaluating and selecting book and non-book materials for, and improving the techniques of, library services to children from pre-school age through the eighth grade or junior high school age, when such materials or techniques are intended for use in more than one type of library. Abbreviated CSD. Publishes *Top of the News* (4 p.a. free to membs.) jointly with the Young Adult Services Division.

CHINA CLAY. A substance (Si O_2) found in large quantities in Cornwall and used in paper making to obtain finish, consistency and opacity, it is also used for coating papers.

CHINA PAPER. Very thin, silky and costly, waterleaf paper used for proofs for woodcuts and for woodcuts to be mounted on stronger paper. Also called 'Chinese paper' and 'Indian proof paper.'

CHINESE STYLE. A book printed on double leaves, i.e. with unopened folds at the fore-edges and the interior pages blank. In a catalogue entry double leaves would be indicated by, e.g. 18 *double* 1, or 36 pp. (*on double leaves*); if unnumbered, each double leaf is counted as two pages, e.g. [36] *pp.* (*on double leaves*). 'Japanese style' refers to a Japanese book printed in the same manner.

CHIP. A unit of microfilm containing a micro-image, or images, and coded identification. Chips are used in automatic retrieval systems.

CHIP BOARD. (*Binding*) A less expensive material than MILLBOARD or STRAWBOARD (*q.v.*) used for covering books.

CHI-RHO. Sacred monogram formed by the first two letters of the Greek word for Christ ☧.

CHIROGRAPH. A formal handwritten document.

CHIROXYLOGRAPHIC. A mediaeval block book in which the illustrations are printed from blocks and the text added by hand.

CHISWICK PRESS. The printing press founded by Charles Whittingham the Elder (1767–1840) in 1811, and continued even more successfully by his nephew of the same name (1795–1876) who controlled the Press from 1840. The elder Whittingham was famous for his attractive, popularly priced classics and for his handling of woodcuts; the nephew was well known for his association with the publisher William Pickering, whose printing he did after 1830. The name of the Press was first used in an imprint in 1811 and persisted for 150 years.

CHLORIDE PAPER. Sensitized photographic paper with an emulsion of gelatin-silver chloride of medium sensitivity. Mainly used for contact printing.

CHOROCHROMATIC MAP. One in which areal distribution is shown by distinctive colours or tints. This method is used for most geological, soil or political maps.

CHOROGRAPHIC MAP. One representing a large region, country, or continent, on a small scale.

CHOROPLETH MAP. One showing 'quantity in area' calculated on a basis of average numbers per unit of area, such as population in a country, by tinting civil divisions by graduated lines or colours, the degree of darkness of which is proportionate to the value represented.

CHOROSCHEMATIC MAP. One in which small semi-pictorial symbols such as dots or lines of various shapes, sizes and density are used over the area of the map to represent distribution without indication of quantity, of land utilization or vegetation.

CHRESTOMATHY. A collection of excerpts and choice selections, especially from a foreign language, with notes of explanation and instruction.

CHROMO. Pertaining to colours. 1. In colour printing there are many terms prefixed by this word, the combining word often giving the particular definition, such as chromo-collotype, chromo-lithography, chromo-xylography. 2. (Paper) A heavily coated paper used for chromo-lithography; it is more heavily coated than art paper.

CHROMOGRAPHY. A reproduction of a coloured illustration by lithography, or one of the many photo-mechanical processes.

CHROMO-LITHOGRAPHY. See COLOUR LITHOGRAPHY.

CHROMO-XYLOGRAPHY. Coloured woodcuts. See also CHIAROSCURO.

CHRONICLES. These differ from annals in being more connected and full, though like annals, the events are treated in the order of time.

CHRONOGRAM. A phrase, sentence or inscription, in which certain letters (usually distinguished by size or otherwise from the rest) express by their numerical values a date or epoch, e.g. stVLtVM est DIffICILes habere nVgas, which is:

V L V M D I I C I L V
5 50 5 1000 500 1 1 100 1 50 5 = 1718.

See also ROMAN NUMERALS.

CHRONOLOGICAL DEVICE. One of the distinctive principles for determining the sequence of subjects in the Colon Classification. It is a notational device which ensures chronological order by using a symbol to represent a date or origin.

CHRONOLOGICAL ORDER. Arrangement in order of date. Applies to order of entries in a catalogue (date of publication – imprint or copyright) or of the material itself (books, pamphlets or cuttings).

CHRYSOGRAPHY. The art of writing in gold letters, as practised by mediaeval writers of manuscripts.

CHURCH AND SYNAGOGUE LIBRARY ASSOCIATION. Formed on 11th July 1967 in Philadelphia to enable librarians of U.S.A. church and synagogue libraries (which total more than all the public, college and special libraries combined) to encourage and aid the development of improved church library service. Membership is open to voluntary and professional librarians, to library committee members, ministers, priests, rabbis, directors of Christian education, principals of synagogue schools, Sunday school superintendents, churches, publishers, booksellers and others interested in church and synagogue libraries. Although an ecumenical association, there are sections for different denominations; there are also Chapters based on geographic areas. Abbreviated CSLA. Publishes *CSLA Newsletter* (q., to membs.).

CICERO. A continental unit for measuring the width of a line of type. One Cicero equals 4·511 mm, or 12 Didot points. The name is said to be derived from the size of type used in Schoffer's edition of Cicero's *De Oratore* in the late fifteenth century. *See also* DIDOT SYSTEM, MEASURE, POINT.

CICRIS. Abbreviation for Co-operative Industrial and Commercial Reference and Information Service; a scheme started in 1951 at the instigation of Mr. R. D. Rates when Borough Librarian of Acton. The organization is now known as the West London Commercial and Technical Library Service. It was set up to assist commerce and industry in West London by librarians co-ordinating their selection and purchase of books, periodicals and other printed material in agreed fields, and making it available to one another. The public libraries of eight London Boroughs, nine technical colleges and over eighty firms and organizations co-operate, holding between them $1\frac{1}{2}$ million books and over 3,000 technical periodicals. Members should have a library and be willing to lend; there is a nominal annual subscription.

CIDESA. The International Centre for African Social and Economic Documentation. Set up in January 1961 at the instigation of CEDESA (the Centre de Documentation Économique et Sociale Africaine). Aims to collect and co-ordinate documentation on economic and social subjects concerning Africa with a view to furthering the progress of the continent in these fields. Membership is open to scientific and philanthropic institutions. Financed by members' dues. Publishes an annual bibliographic index.

CIPHER. 1. The initials of a name, or the arrangement of its letters in an ornamental manner, but disposed in such a way that it becomes a kind of private mark. 2. In machine searching as part of information retrieval, the codes whose notations, whether alphabetic or other symbols, are intentionally scrambled so as to keep the system of rules, and thus the common or source language, a secret.

circa. (*Lat.* 'about') Used to indicate uncertainty in a date, as *c.* 1934, about 1934.

CIRCLE OF STATE LIBRARIANS. The organization to which those employed in British government libraries and information bureaux may belong. It had its beginnings in 1914 when the PANIZZI CLUB (*q.v.*), named after Sir Anthony (Antonio) Panizzi who was Director of the British Museum, was formed. In those early days government librarians were only a minority of the membership of the Club, the objects of which were 'to provide opportunities for social intercourse between the Senior Officers of Reference and Research Libraries and to promote all measures tending to their higher efficiency.' After the First World War, the then Treasurer of the Panizzi Club (*q.v.*), Mr. A. E. Twentyman, Librarian of the Board of Education, took the initiative of reviving the Club and associating State Librarians as such with it. The name 'Circle of State Librarians' was used; it was an informal organization limited to officers-in-charge of Government libraries; it had only two officers (Chairman and Secretary), there was no committee, and no subscription was collected. In general, its objects were to encourage and maintain personal acquaintance and contact between its members and so facilitate co-operation in the ordinary day-to-day business of their libraries. Three meetings a year were held but these and other activities of the Circle were brought to a stop by the Second World War. The circle was revived in 1946 and membership was widened to admit 'those employed in a State Library or Information Service, who possess such professional qualifications or experience as will satisfy the Committee,' and who were engaged in the storing and dissemination of knowledge, such as archivists, intelligence officers of research departments and others whose interests and problems were similar to those of librarians. In 1953 the function of the Circle was again widened 'to cultivate a common interest in bibliographical problems arising in Government service' and the membership opened 'to all members of the Government service who are interested in the activities of the Circle.' Abbreviated CSL. Publishes a bulletin (2 a year, membs. only).

CIRCUIT EDGES. The edges of a book-cover which overlap the edges of the book. Used mostly for Bibles. Also called 'Divinity circuit,' 'Divinity edges,' 'Yapp edges.'

CIRCULAR BRACKETS. CURVES (*q.v.*), or Round Brackets, used in the Colon Classification to enclose the SUBJECT DEVICE NUMBER (*q.v.*) which forms part of the CLASS NUMBER (*q.v.*). The first '(' is called 'Starter' and the second ')' 'Arrester.' *See also* BRACKETS.

CIRCULAR ROUTING. *See* ROUTING.

CIRCULATING LIBRARY. A library which lends books for use outside the building. In England, the term usually indicates a commercial library where payment has to be made for the use of the books. *See also* SUBSCRIPTION LIBRARY.

CIRCULATION. The total number of books issued from a library in a given period.

CIRCULATION DEPARTMENT. The American term for the department of a public library which lends books for home-reading. Called a 'Lending department' in England.

CIRCULATION DESK. The American equivalent of the English STAFF ENCLOSURE (*q.v.*). Also called 'Charging desk,' 'Delivery desk,' 'Discharging desk,' 'Issue desk,' 'Lending desk,' 'Loan desk,' 'Receiving desk,' 'Return desk,' 'Slipping desk.'

CIRCULATION RECORD. A record of the books issued for home-reading.

CIRCULATION STATISTICS. A record of the number of books circulated (issued) for home-reading.

CIRCULATION WORK. The American term indicating the work of a department issuing books for home-reading.

CISE. Colleges, Institutes and Schools of Education – a Group of the Library Association.

CITATION INDEX. A list of articles that, subsequent to the appearance of the original article, refer to, or cite, that article. This method has been used extensively in the legal profession and is particularly applicable to scientific literature.

CITATION ORDER. The order of application of principles of division in determining an appropriate class number for a document. Also called 'Facet formula.'

CLAIM. Any communication sent to a bookseller or other supplier to hasten the delivery of overdue material.

CLANDESTINE LITERATURE. Publications which are printed,

published, and circulated secretly. They are usually of a political nature and seek to overthrow the government, or in time of war, act against the power in authority. Also called 'Secret literature,' 'Underground literature.'

CLANDESTINE PRESS. A printing press which operates secretly.

CLAPP-JORDAN FORMULAE. Formulae devised by Verner Clapp and Robert T. Jordan, and stated in 'Quantitative criteria for adequacy of academic library collections' (*College and Research Libraries* **26** (5) September 1965). They attempt to identify the principal factors affecting the academic needs for books and to ascribe suitable weights to each.

CLARENDON. The name of a particular type face, and also of a group of faces characterized by little difference between thick and thin strokes, narrowness, and angular semi-Egyptian serifs. 'Consort' and 'Fortune' are of this kind. They were originally designed to give bold emphasis, particularly for dictionaries so that the word defined stood out clearly, and although still used for this purpose are now being used in their own right. For a specimen alphabet, *see* TYPE FACE.

CLARENDON PRESS. Edward Hyde, first Earl of Clarendon (1609–74), gave the profits of the copyright of his *History of the Rebellion* to the University of Oxford to erect the first building in which the University's business of printing was wholly carried on – hence the name Clarendon Press. The business was transferred from the Sheldonian Theatre to this new building in 1713.

CLASP. A metal fastening hinged to one board and made to clip or lock into a loop or bar on the other board of a bound book or album. *See also* CATCH.

CLASS. (*Classification*) (*Noun*) 1. A group of concepts, or of things, assembled by some likeness which unifies them. This likeness is called the 'characteristic of a classification.' A class consists of all the things that are alike in essentials, characters, properties and relations, by which it is defined. 2. A group having the same or similar characteristics (*IBM*). 3. A major division of a CATEGORY (*q.v.*). *See also* FORM CLASSES, MAIN CLASS, SUMMUM GENUS. (*Verb*) To classify books according to a scheme of classification.

CLASS CATALOGUE. *Synonymous with* CLASSIFIED CATALOGUE (*q.v.*).

CLASS ENTRY. An entry in a catalogue under the name of a class, as distinct from one under a specific subject.

CLASS GUIDE. A guide to the shelves which gives the main class symbol and subject, and perhaps the same information for the main divisions of the class. It is usually placed at the end of a press or over the central tier.

CLASS LETTER. The first letter of a main class or division of a classification scheme the notation of which begins with a letter of the alphabet, it is used to designate a particular main class of the classification.

CLASS LIBRARY. The class room library in a primary school, so called to distinguish it from the 'general' or 'central' library provided in the same school for all to use.

CLASS LIST. A list of the books in a particular class, usually arranged in classified order.

CLASS MARK. The classification symbol placed on the spine of the book, on the title-page and added to a catalogue entry to indicate the book's place in the classification and on the shelves.

CLASS NOTATION. *Synonymous with* CLASS MARK (*q.v.*).

CLASS NUMBER. One or more characters showing the class to which a book belongs in the scheme of classification in use. In a RELATIVE LOCATION (*q.v.*), this number also shows the place of the book on the shelves and in relation to other subjects. It translates the name of its specific subject into the artificial language of the notation of the scheme of classification. The class number may be compounded of a variety of symbols used in a specified sequence, and followed by certain signs or symbols the purpose of which is to separate the constituent parts of the Class Number and/or to indicate the characteristic of the following symbol. 'Relation marks' are used for this purpose in the UDC – *see* UNIVERSAL DECIMAL CLASSIFICATION. In the Colon Classification the Class Number consists of the ten Arabic numerals; the twenty-six capital letters of the Roman alphabet; twenty-three small letters of the Roman alphabet (*i*, *l*, and *o* being omitted); some Greek letters; the punctuation marks; circular, or round, brackets (the first '(' being called Starter and the second ')' Arrester) and horizontal arrows. The digit 'O', the punctuation marks and the arrows are called 'Connecting symbols' and occur only as connectives or conjunctions in the Colon language.

CLASS SYMBOL. *Synonymous with* CLASS MARK (*q.v.*).

CLASSED CATALOGUE. *Synonymous with* CLASSIFIED CATALOGUE (*q.v.*). Also called 'Class catalogue.'

CLASSED LIBRARY. *Synonymous with* CLASSIFIED LIBRARY (*q.v.*).

CLASSER. As used by Bliss and Savage, one who allocates class numbers to books according to an existing scheme of classification. *See also* CLASSING, CLASSIFIER.

CLASSIC. An outstanding work, usually appearing in several versions and in translation, and sometimes adapted, being the subject of commentaries and other writings, and continuing in print even long after first publication. In classification it is often treated as if it were a class or a subject.

CLASSIC DEVICE. (*Classification*) In the Colon Classification, the digit x which is put after the class number to which a CLASSIC (*q.v.*) should be assigned and which precedes a Work Facet or Author Facet. This is done to bring together the different editions of a classic in a class, also the different editions of each of its commentaries, and to keep a classic and the commentaries thereon in juxtaposition. Also to keep each classic and its associated commentaries in juxtaposition to other classics in the same class.

CLASSICAL AUTHOR. For the purposes of the Colon Classification, an author, one at least of whose works is a classic. The Classic Device, consisting of the digit x placed after the number representing the ultimate class to which the classic should be otherwise assigned and adding after it an Author Facet, is employed to bring together the different editions of a classic in a class and also the different editions of commentaries on the classic.

CLASSIFICATION. 1. The arrangement of things in logical order according to their degrees of likeness, especially the assignment of books to their proper places in a scheme of book classification. 2. A scheme for the arrangement of books and other material in a logical sequence according to subject or form. 3. A 'coding' system within which the series of symbols indicating a concept, or semantemes, are subject to certain order relationships. *See also* BROAD CLASSIFICATION, CLOSE CLASSIFICATION, SUMMUM GENUS.

CLASSIFICATION CODE. A set of rules to help classifiers to class books.

CLASSIFICATION DECIMALE UNIVERSELLE. *See* UNIVERSAL DECIMAL CLASSIFICATION.

CLASSIFICATION FOR SOCIAL SCIENCES. Compiled by Barbara Kyle for the Unesco Social Science bibliographies at the request of the INTERNATIONAL COMMITTEE FOR SOCIAL SCIENCES DOCUMENTATION (*q.v.*). Referred to as the KC.

CLASSIFICATION MARK. *See* CLASS MARK.

CLASSIFICATION OF LIBRARY SCIENCE. A faceted scheme which was prepared by the CLASSIFICATION RESEARCH GROUP (*q.v.*) and published by Aslib in 1965. The Scheme is in two sections; the first (sections A/Z) contains the 'core' subjects of library science, while the second (classes 1/8) contains 'fringe' subjects which are disciplines in their own right but are of concern to librarians and information scientists. This scheme is used for arranging entries in *Library and Information Science Abstracts*.

CLASSIFICATION RESEARCH GROUP. An unofficial group of British librarians who have been meeting since February 1952 to discuss the theory and practice of classification. Its bulletins are published in the *Journal of Documentation*. Abbreviated CRG.

CLASSIFICATION RESEARCH STUDY GROUP. Founded in the U.S.A. in 1959 to promote basic and applied research in classification without allegiance to any particular system; to afford members an opportunity to exchange information on classification; to encourage publication of papers of interest in classification. Abbreviated CRSG. Publishes *CRSG News Notes* (2 p.a. to membs.).

CLASSIFICATION SCHEDULE. The printed scheme of a system of classification.

CLASSIFICATION SCHEME. A scheme by which books are classified or arranged in systematic order. The following are some of the better known schemes, the author's names being given in brackets: Bibliographic Classification (Bliss); Colon Classification (Ranganathan); Decimal Classification (Dewey); Expansive Classification (Cutter); Library of Congress Classification; Subject Classification (Brown); Universal Decimal Classification. The above are all general schemes. Some schemes for narrower fields of literature are: Barnard, C. C., *A classification for medical and veterinary libraries;* Stewart, J. D., *A tabulation of librarianship;* Foskett, D. J., *The London education classification;* Glidden, S. H., and Marchus, D., *A library classification for public administration materials;* Coates, E. J., *British catalogue of music classification;* Vickery, B. C., and Farradane, J. E. L., *Cranfield classification for aeronautics and allied subjects; Faceted classification for engineering*.

CLASSIFICATION SYSTEM. A particular scheme of classification. *See also* CLASSIFICATION SCHEME.

CLASSIFICATIONIST. 1. One who makes a scheme of classification. Called by Bliss and Savage a 'classifier.' 2. A theorist who organizes and divides documents according to a specific criterion. *See also* CLASSIFIER.

CLASSIFIED ARRANGEMENT. The arrangement of books in a library according to some scheme of classification.

CLASSIFIED CATALOGUE. A catalogue in which the entries are arranged in classified order of subjects, whether logically, in systematic order, exhibiting hierarchical relationship between subjects as in the SYSTEMATIC CATALOGUE (*q.v.*) – the more usual, or alphabetically, as in the ALPHABETICO-CLASSED CATALOGUE (*q.v.*). It is usually in two parts: the classified file of entries in systematic order, and the alphabetical subject index to the classified file. Also called 'Classed catalogue,' 'Classified subject catalogue.'

CLASSIFIED FILE.   The entries, in systematic order, of the CLASSIFIED CATALOGUE (*q.v.*). This is one (the main) part of this kind of catalogue, the other part being the alphabetical subject index. Also called 'Systematic file'. *See also* FEATURE HEADING.

CLASSIFIED INDEX.   1. One in which entries are not arranged in one strict alphabetical sequence, but under general headings, e.g. the names of binders would be arranged alphabetically, under the heading 'binders' and not in their correct places in the alphabetical sequence. 2. An index characterized by sub-divisions of hierarchic structure. An index using or displaying genus-species (class-subclass) relationships (*IBM*). *See also* CLASSIFIED CATALOGUE.

CLASSIFIED LIBRARY.   A library in which the books are arranged according to a recognized scheme of classification. Also called a 'Classed library.'

CLASSIFIED MATERIAL.   Memoranda, reports and other documents emanating from government departments, industrial and other corporations, research associations, etc., which are of a secret and confidential nature. They are classified as 'top secret,' 'secret,' 'confidential' and 'restricted' in a descending order of secrecy and are treated variously in libraries.

CLASSIFIED ORDER.   The arrangement of books and other materials, or of entries in a catalogue, in order according to a scheme of classification.

CLASSIFIED SUBJECT CATALOGUE.   *See* CLASSIFIED CATALOGUE.

CLASSIFIER.   As used by Bliss and Savage, one who names and defines classes and co-ordinates them into tables to form a scheme of book classification. The process of compiling the tables is called 'classifying.' These terms have generally related to the allocation of classification numbers to books, and are so used by Palmer and Wells. *See also* CLASSIFICATIONIST.

CLASSIFY.   To classify is to bring individuals with the same or similar characteristics together actually, or mentally, that is, conceptually. Also, in a secondary sense, to arrange classes in a classification, and to allocate the appropriate CLASS NUMBER (*q.v.*) to a book or other document according to a scheme of classification. *See also* CLASS.

CLASSIFYING. The act of fitting books or other material into an existing scheme of classification. Called by Bliss, Savage and Sayers 'classing.' *See also* CLASSER, CLASSING, CLASSIFICATIONIST, CLASSIFIER, FACET, FOCUS, PHASE.

CLASSING. As used by Bliss, Savage and Sayers, allocating class numbers to books according to a scheme of classification. *See also* CLASSER, CLASSIFYING.

CLASSROOM COLLECTION. 1. A temporary, or semi-permanent, collection of books deposited in a schoolroom by a public, or a school, library. 2. A number of books sent by a college library to a classroom for use by students and teachers. (American).

CLAY TABLETS. Cuneiform clay tablets were the earliest form of books, and were protected by an outer shell of clay which was inscribed with a copy, abstract, or title, of the contents.

CLEAN PROOF. One having very few, or no, printer's errors.

CLEAR BASE. *See* FILM BASE.

CLEARING HOUSE OF INFORMATION. Applied to an organization or special library which possesses only a small amount of published material but obtains information for users by means of the telephone and correspondence.

CLEARINGHOUSE FOR FEDERAL SCIENTIFIC AND TECHNICAL INFORMATION. *See* CFSTI.

CLEMENTS LIBRARY, WILLIAM L. In 1923 William L. Clements deposited the library of Americana which he had been collecting for over twenty years with the University of Michigan, Ann Arbor. It is primarily a 'collection of the sources of American history', and has been extended over the years by the addition of books and documents which promote that study. The stock totals 37,000 volumes, 25,000 maps and 200,000 MSS.

CLERICAL ASSISTANT. In America, a person who performs work requiring ability of a high order, but not knowledge of the theoretical or scientific aspects of library work.

CLICHÉ. 1. A common and stereotyped journalistic or literary phrase. 2. An electrotype or stereotype plate.

CLICHOGRAPH. *Synonymous with* KLISCHOGRAPH (*q.v.*).

CLINICAL LIBRARIAN. A person who, by aptitude, training and experience, is qualified to participate in the remedial, therapeutic and rehabilitative care of individuals in hospitals and institutions.

CLIP. The metal eye, of whatever form, fixed to one of the covers of a book in a medieval chained library, and to which the book's chain was fastened.

CLIPPING. A piece clipped, or cut from a newspaper or periodical. (American.) Called in England a 'Cutting,' 'Press cutting.'

CLIPPING BUREAU. A commercial organization which clips, or cuts, items from newspapers and periodicals on specific subjects and sends them to subscribers (American). Called in England a 'Cuttings bureau.'

CLIPPING SERVICE. The cutting of news items, etc. daily from newspapers and periodicals in an industrial, commercial or other organization, and sending them to officials who will find them useful. This is often undertaken in the library or information department.

CLIPPINGS FILE. A collection of cuttings from newspapers and periodicals, used to supplement the information to be found in books, and usually kept in classified or subject order in folders in a vertical file. Also called 'Cuttings file.'

CLOGGED. A half-tone, or line block, the impression from which has become smudged by the spaces between the dots or lines of the block becoming filled with ink. It may be due to dirty ink, dust, over-inking or the incorrect damping of a lithographic plate. Also known as 'filling in.'

CLOISONNÉ. Enamelled bindings made during the eleventh century, mainly by Greek and Italian craftsmen. The design was first outlined by soldering thin strips of metal on to a metal plate and then filling the compartments so formed with coloured enamels. *See also* CHAMPLEVÉ.

CLOSE. The second of a pair of punctuation marks, e.g. ')]. *See also* CIRCULAR BRACKETS, SQUARE BRACKETS.

CLOSE CLASSIFICATION. The arrangement of books in a classification system in as minute sub-divisions as possible; i.e. the full application of a scheme. Also called 'Exact classification.' *See also* BROAD CLASSIFICATION, MINUTE CLASSIFICATION.

CLOSE MATTER. Lines of type set without leads, or thinly spaced.

CLOSE ROLL. A parchment roll upon which letters close were enrolled at the Chancery.

CLOSE SCORE. A musical score in which the music of more than one part or instrument is written on one stave. Also called 'Short score,' 'Compressed score,' 'Condensed score.'

CLOSE UP. (*Printing*) To place lines or characters together by removing spacing-out leads or intervening letters.

CLOSED ACCESS. The now obsolete method of keeping readers from the book shelves; this necessitated the provision in lending libraries of printed catalogues and indicators to inform readers which books were 'in' or 'out.' Also called 'Closed shelves,' and 'Closed library.'

CLOSED BIBLIOGRAPHY. One which has been completed. The

opposite of PERIODICAL BIBLIOGRAPHY (*q.v.*). *Synonymous with* RETROSPECTIVE BIBLIOGRAPHY. SEE ALSO BIBLIOGRAPHY, CURRENT BIBLIOGRAPHY.

CLOSED ENTRY. 1. The catalogue entry for all the parts or volumes of a serial publication or work in several volumes, containing complete bibliographical information. Until the library has acquired a complete set, the bibliographical details are recorded in an OPEN ENTRY (*q.v.*). 2. A catalogue entry in which blank spaces are not left in the body of the entry or in the collation so that additional particulars of holdings may be entered subsequently. This is the normal form of catalogue entry.

CLOSED JOINT. (*Bookbinding*) The type of joint which is obtained when cover boards are laced on. Also called 'Tight joint.' *See also* FRENCH JOINT.

CLOSED LIBRARY. *See* CLOSED ACCESS.

CLOSED SHELVES. *See* CLOSED ACCESS.

CLOSED UP. When typesetting is divided between several compositors and each has completed his allocation, the matter is closed up.

CLOTH. A generic term applied to material which is not leather or obviously paper used for covering books. It was originally a material made of natural fibres of some kind. It was first used for this purpose in about 1820. *See also* CLOTH BINDING.

CLOTH BINDING. Used to describe a book which is bound entirely in cloth. A book so bound is called 'Cloth bound.'

CLOTH BOARDS. *See* BOARDS.

CLOTH-CENTRED. A duplex board or paper having a core, or centre, of muslin, linen or canvas (i.e. a cloth with paper on both sides), and used for maps, tables, membership tickets, envelopes, etc. Cloth-faced, -lined, or -mounted paper or card indicates that the cloth is not a core but is pasted on one side only, and is termed linen- or canvas-lined (-backed) according to the kind of cloth used.

CLOTH JOINT. Piece of cloth used to cover the joints on the inside of very heavy or large books.

CLOTH-LINED PAPER (BOARD). Paper or board which is reinforced with muslin or cloth affixed to one side. *Cloth centred paper, or board, is* made up of two sheets or furnish layers with muslin or cloth between them.

CLOTH PRINT. (*Reprography*) A print made on sensitized cloth. Prints are usually made on paper or film.

CLOTH SIDES. A book which has cloth sides but leather at the spine and possibly at the corners as well.

CLUMP. A thick piece of type metal, ranging in width from 5 pt. upwards, but usually 6 pt. or 12 pt., and of the height of leads. Clumps are used in whiting out, and as footlines at the bottoms of columns and pages.

COARSE SCREEN. *See* SCREEN.

COATED PAPER. 1. A general term for papers such as chromo, art, enamel, which have been prepared for different printing processes by applying a mineral such as china clay after the body paper has been made. Also called 'Surface paper.' 2. Any paper whose surface is coated with a mixture of clay and glue made of casein to give it a smooth surface. The term is used to distinguish it from loaded papers in which the clay is mixed with the pulp during manufacture. *See also* ART.

COATING. A thin layer of light-sensitive chemical applied to a base material such as cloth, paper, or transparent plastic, or a mineral such as china clay to a printing paper. *See also* COATED PAPER.

COBOOK GROUP OF LIBRARIES. *See* YORKSHIRE COBOOK GROUP OF LIBRARIES.

COBOOK SCHEME. *See* YORKSHIRE COBOOK GROUP OF LIBRARIES.

COCK. The middle portion of a Brace (*q.v.*). when cast in three pieces as ⌒ ⌄ ⌐.

COCK-UP INITIAL. An initial letter that extends above the first line of text but aligns with the foot of it.

COCKLE. (*Paper*) A puckered effect on paper, produced either naturally or artificially during the drying process. Paper and board will cockle and get out of shape with excessive heat or moisture; to prevent this these materials must be kept under temperature- and humidity-controlled conditions.

cod. Abbreviation for CODEX (*q.v.*).

codd. Abbreviation for codices.

CODE. 1. A system of conventional signs which are used as abbreviations to represent information. Rules for their use may be incorporated. Such symbols may represent specific subjects and may be presented in the form of holes punched into cards for the retrieval of information. 2. Any system of symbols by which messages in the normal, common, or source language are transferred into a target, or code, language in order to achieve some desirable advantage over the normal language or numerical expression. 3. In information retrieval, (*noun*) information presented in the 'language' that a computer can understand and handle; (*verb*) to put into machine language. 4. A system of symbols used in transmitting or storing information (*IBM*). 5. A system of arbitrary signs and symbols used to represent words or concepts, as distinguished from a cipher wherein arbitrary signs and symbols are used to represent single letters or syllables (*IBM*). 6. A systematic body of laws, regulations or rules (*IBM*). 7. A communication system for information (*IBM*). 8. In connexion with information retrieval systems, 'a set of discriminable physical marks or signals such as holes, notches, magnetic dots, pulses, etc.' (*Taube*). 9. 'A set of unambiguous rules, whereby messages are converted from one representation to another' (*Verry*). 10. A code, or notation, consisting of configurations of 'marks' (or code elements), each distinctively recognizable configuration of which is called a 'sort.' Also called 'Code character.' 11. 'A determinant for the location of holes on a punched card' (*Scheele*). 12. 'The translation of names of specific subjects into written symbols suitable for presentation in the form of a series of perforations . . . etc., permitting mechanical retrieval' (*Ranganathan*). 13. A set of rules for carrying out some such function as cataloguing. *See also* ALGORITHMIC CODE, CODE LANGUAGE, DESCRIPTOR, DIRECT CODING, INDIRECT CODING, NON-SEMANTIC CODE, SEMANTIC CODE, TABULATED CODE.

CODE ELEMENTS. *See* CODE.

CODE CHARACTER. *See* CODE 10.

CODE LANGUAGE. The symbols used to represent words or numerals in a natural, or source, language.

CODE MARK. An indication of purchase made in code on the back of a title-page.

CODED TAPE. A strip of paper, film, or other material containing an electronic or punched code for the activation of typewriter, typesetter or other machinery.

CODELESS SCANNING. A system of retrieval which has been developed from the L'UNITÉ (*q.v.*) system.

CODEN. 1. A code classification assigned to a document or other library item consisting of four capital letters followed by two hyphenated groups of arabic numerals, or of two arabic numerals followed by two capital letters, or of some similar combination. 2. The combination of letters, numbers and symbols assigned as a result of applying coding rules in order to produce a bibliographical citation. *See also* BISHOP'S RULES. The *ASTM coden for periodical titles* uses five-letter codes for the titles of periodicals and serials; the first four letters of each coden have some mnemonic relation to the title, and the fifth letter is arbitrary and will assist in maintaining as many mnemonic relationships as possible for similar periodical titles.

CODEX (*Pl.* Codices). An ancient book composed of pieces of writing material fastened so as to open like a modern book as distinct from the SCROLL or VOLUMEN (*qq.v.*) which it superseded. The name was originally given to two or more tablets of metal, wood or ivory, hinged together with rings; the inner sides were covered with wax and these were written on with a stylus. Later 'Codex' was given to books of this type made of papyrus, vellum or parchment, and later still to volumes consisting of many leaves of parchment or vellum, e.g. *Codex Alexandrinus*. Codices became general for law-books in classical Rome, and were used largely for MS. copies of the scriptures and classics. Codex means a block of wood, probably from the wooden covers. When a codex of the original form consisted of two leaves, it was called a Diptych, of three, a Triptych, and of more, a Polytych. Abbreviated cod. (*Pl.* codd.). There are a number of codices of the Bible, and these are often named after the place of discovery. The four most important of these are *Codex Sinaiticus* (4th or beginning of the 5th century – in the British Museum), *Codex Vaticanus* (4th century – in the Vatican), *Codex Alexandrinus* (5th century – in the British Museum) and the palimpsest *Codex Ephraemi* (5th century Greek text overwritten in a 12th-century hand – in the Bibliothèque Nationale, Paris). These originally contained the whole Greek text of the Old and New Testaments, but are now incomplete. The *Codex Bezae* (5th or 6th century – at Cambridge) containing only the *Gospels* and *Acts* is another important early copy of the *Bible*. All were written in uncials (i.e. capitals) and without breaks between words. The term 'codex' was also used for a collection of Roman laws; these included *Codex Theodosianus* and *Codex Justinianeus*.

CODEX ALEXANDRINUS.   This codex was given to Charles I in 1627 by the Patriarch of Constantinople, and formerly Patriarch of Alexandria. It has been in the British Museum since 1757. *See also* CODEX.

CODEX AMIATINUS.   One of three codices written by order of Ceolfrid, who became Abbot of Jarrow in 690, and taken by him on a journey for presentation to Pope Gregory II in 716. It is written in Latin uncials, and is one of the Vulgate. At one time it was preserved at Monte Amianta in the Abruzzi Mountains and is now in the Laurentian Library, Florence. *See also* CODEX.

CODEX ARGENTEUS.   The remains of the fifth- and sixth-century MSS. of the translation of the Bible into the Gothic tongue by Wulfilas (or Ulfila), Bishop of the Visigoths. It is written mainly in Greek, but with some roman and runic characters, in gold and silver on purple-stained parchment. On 187 leaves, it contains most of the

New Testament, and has been in the library of Uppsala University, Sweden, since 1669. Other fragments are in Milan and Wolfenbüttel.

CODEX BEZAE. On vellum, this codex was presented to Cambridge University Library by Theodorus Beza who acquired it from the Monastery of St. Iremaeus at Lyons. *See also* CODEX.

CODEX LAUDIANUS. This codex contains the Book of the Acts of the Apostles in Greek and Latin, and was brought from Italy to England in the seventh century, probably by Benedict Biscop. It is now in the Bodleian Library at Oxford. *See also* CODEX.

CODEX RESCRIPTUS APHRAËMI. A fifth century palimpsest MS. of the Bible with some works of Ephrem Syrus overwritten in the twelfth century. Fragments are in the Bibliothèque Nationale, Paris. Also known as *Codex Ephraemi*. *See also* CODEX.

CODEX SINAITICUS. The oldest extant Greek vellum codex, the text being written on 48-line columns. It was discovered in 1844, and the portion of 347 leaves (of an estimated total of 730) containing part of the Old Testament and all the New Testament was acquired by the British Museum in 1933. A further 43 leaves is in the Leipzig Library and is known as the *Codex Frederico-Augustaneus. See also* CODEX.

CODING. (*Information retrieval*) 1. The translation of the names of specific subjects or of recorded information into written symbols according to a pre-arranged system or code, which may if necessary be presented in the form of perforations; it must be legible to the eye or by machine and must have three characteristics: it must (1) suit the retrieving device used, (2) be capable of representing all likely subject descriptions, (3) be as compact as possible. 2. A list of successive computer operations in code for solving a given problem. Also, the act of writing a prepared list in code. *See also* CODE, MARGINAL HOLE-PUNCHED CARDS, NOTATION, SOUNDEX.

CODING QUIRES. *See* CASSIE.

CO-EXTENSIVENESS. Intensive classification to coincide with the specific nature of the subject of a book.

COFFIN. A square frame in a hand printing press in which is bedded a stone on which the FORME (*q.v.*) is placed.

COIL BINDING. *Synonymous with* SPIRAL BINDING (*q.v.*).

COILED BINDING. *Synonymous with* SPIRAL BINDING (*q.v.*).

COLD COMPOSITION. (*Printing*) Any method of composition which does not involve the casting of metal type. Typewriter and photographic methods are included. 'Cold type' is sometimes used to distinguish this method from 'hot metal' typesetting.

COLD TYPE. Composition by a composing machine which does not require hot metal, such as photographically or on a typewriter, JUSTOWRITER or VARITYPER (*qq.v.*).

COLE SIZE CARD. A graduated card for determining the sizes of books (not by measurement but by bibliographical description) when writing catalogue and bibliography entries. This size card, which was first issued in 1889 by the Library Bureau, was based on the size rules of the American Library Association, the more uniform and accurate use of which the size card was intended to achieve. The card was named after its designer, Dr. George Watson Cole (1850–1939), who was Librarian of the Henry E. Huntington Library from 1915 to 1924. *See also* HUNTINGTON LIBRARY. A description of the card may be read in *The Library Journal* **14**, 1889, pp. 485–6.

COLLABORATOR. One who is associated with another, or others, especially in the writing of books, being responsible for some aspect of, or contribution to, a work, but not responsible for the content as a whole.

COLLAGE. A picture or visual arrangement made partly or entirely of pieces of paper, wallpaper, illustrations, photographs or any other textured or figured material.

COLLATE. 1. To examine a book, whether bound or in the process of being bound, to see if the sections are complete and in the right sequence and to make sure that no maps, illustrations, etc., are missing. 2. To collect, compare and examine minutely and critically books and manuscripts to determine whether or not two copies are identical or variants. 3. Used in connection with tabulation machines to indicate the combining or merging of record cards into a desired sequence.

COLLATERAL REFERENCE. One which in an alphabetico-specific subject catalogue links two headings belonging to the same hierarchical level under a common generic term, and which would stand side by side if arranged in a classification scheme.

COLLATING MARK. A quad mark having a printing surface about 12-point deep by 5-point wide, which is printed so that after folding and gathering, the marks appear in descending order on the back of each section in such a way that the omission or duplication of a section becomes immediately apparent. Also called BACK MARK, BLACK STEP (*qq.v.*), 'Quad mark'.

COLLATION. 1. That part of a description of a book, apart from the contents, which describes the book as a physical object by specifying the number of volumes, pages, columns, leaves, illustrations, photographs, maps, format, size, etc. In a bibliographical description of an old book the number, which is expressed by the signature letters (*see* SIGNATURE 2), and composition of the sections is important. A *collation by gatherings* records the make-up of a book by stating the signature letters, e.g. A⁴, *², B–2A⁴, etc.; a *collation by pagination* records the make-up by the page numbers, e.g. [1]–[12], 1–374, etc. 2. The process of examining a new book to check its completeness, presence of all the illustrations, etc. 3. To check that a book is complete before binding or re-binding. 4. To compare two or more texts, either (a) to ascertain which is the first edition of a printed work, or (b) to establish a definitive or standard text. 5. To merge and combine two or more similarly ordered sets of items to produce an ordered set (*IBM*).

COLLATOR. 1. A fitting consisting of trays or divisions into each of which is put a number of small printed or duplicated sheets of paper in a required order so that one of each may be arranged in sequence quickly when required. This saves the labour and table space involved in laying the sheets out in piles in order to take one from each. 2. In electric accounting machines, one which combines or emerges files of cards into any desired sequence.

COLLECTANEA. Passages selected from one or more authors, generally for instruction. A collection or miscellany.

COLLECTED EDITION. An edition of an author's works published in one volume or in a number of volumes in a uniform style of binding.

COLLECTED WORKS. All the writings of an author, including those which have not been printed previously, published in one volume or a number of volumes in a uniform style of binding, usually with an inclusive title.

COLLECTING DRUM. A revolving drum which is fitted to a high-speed printing press or paper-making machine to catch the sheets of paper coming out of the machine and collect them in groups of from five to ten so that final delivery can be at a slower speed. They are then delivered together as a group which can be passed on at only a fifth of the speed otherwise required.

COLLECTION. 1. A number of books or other items on one subject, or of one kind, or collected by one person or organization. 2. (*Bibliography*) A number of works, or parts of them, not forming a treatise or monograph on a single subject, and regarded as constituting a single whole, as a collection of plays, essays, etc. 3. (*Cataloguing*) If written by one author, three or more independent works, or parts of works, published together; if written by more than one author, two or more

6

independent works, or parts of works, published together but not written for the same occasion or for the same publication.

COLLECTION NUMBER. In the Colon Classification, a suitable symbol to be determined by each individual library, and added to the CLASS NUMBER (*q.v.*) and BOOK NUMBER (*q.v.*) to indicate the collection to which the book belongs.

COLLECTIVE BIOGRAPHY. A volume, or volumes, consisting of separate accounts of the lives of people.

COLLECTIVE ENTRIES. In selective cataloguing, several entries on one card for pamphlets on the same or related subjects. They may be either author or subject entries.

COLLECTIVE TITLE. 1. A title under which articles written separately by several authors are published together. If there is no recognized author, compiler, or editing body, the main catalogue entry appears under the title of the work. 2. The title given to a work as a whole when that work consists of several works, each with its own title (*IFLA*).

COLLECTOR. One who puts together several works or parts of works. Usually called an editor.

COLLEGE LIBRARY. A library established, maintained, and administered by a college to meet the needs of its students and faculty.

COLLEGES, INSTITUTES AND SCHOOLS OF EDUCATION. Formerly a sub-section of the UNIVERSITY, COLLEGE AND RESEARCH SECTION (*q.v.*) of the LIBRARY ASSOCIATION (*q.v.*). Now an independent Group. Abbreviated CISE.

COLLEGES OF TECHNOLOGY AND FURTHER EDUCATION. Formerly a sub-section of the UNIVERSITY, COLLEGE AND RESEARCH SECTION (*q.v*) of the LIBRARY ASSOCIATION (*q.v.*). Since January 1970 it has been an independent Group. Abbreviated CTFE.

COLLOCATION. The arrangement of sub-classes of a classification by degrees of likeness.

COLLOGRAPHY. A similar production process to collotype except that a film base wrapped around a cylinder is used instead of a flat glass plate.

COLLOPLAS. Trade name for a process for making non-etched gravure cylinders in which a rubber surface on which the printing image is impressed hydraulically is substituted for the copper-coated etched cylinders used in photogravure. The method was announced in 1954 by Koch Processes Ltd., a member of the Photogravure and Allied Holdings Ltd. Group.

COLLOTYPE. A variety of photogravure. A print which gives accurate gradation of tone; it is made by a photo-mechanical process directly from a hardened emulsion of bichromated gelatine on glass. Phototype, Albertype, Artotype, Heliotype and Lichtdruck are forms of collotype. William Henry Fox Talbot, an English pioneer of photography, discovered in 1852 that a chromate gelatine layer was case-hardened by exposure to light, and the first person to employ this process for the production of printing plates was Alphonse Louis Poitevin in 1855. By coating a plate with chromated gelatine and printing and developing a photographic image on it, a surface could be obtained which, when damped, responds to ink in the same way as a lithographic stone. Also called a 'Gelatine print'.

COLOMBIER. Drawing and plate paper size 24 × 34½ inches. Also spelled 'Columbier'.

COLON. 1. A device used in the Universal Decimal Classification to link related class terms (*IBM*). 2. A device used in the Colon Classification to separate successive foci. Later, in the Colon Classification, a device to introduce the energy facet (*IBM*).

COLON ABBREVIATIONS. A scheme devised by C. A. Cutter to save the writing out in full of authors' forenames. It consists of the initial letters of the most used Christian names in each letter of the alphabet followed by a colon (vertically for men, horizontally for women), e.g.

         H: (Henry)
         J: (John)
         M.. (Mary).

COLON CLASSIFICATION. An elaborate, scholarly scheme designed by S. R. Ranganathan especially for Indian libraries. It is based on the classification of any subject by its uses and relations, which are indicated by numbers divided by the colon ':'. In this classification, ready-made class numbers are not provided for most topics, but are constructed by combining in assigned permutations and combinations the classes of the various unit schedules of which the scheme consists, colons separating the different units. Special schedules are provided for Geographical Divisions (a Local List), Language Divisions, and Chronological Divisions (Space Isolate, Language Isolate, and Time Isolate respectively). A schedule of common sub-divisions (Common Isolate), using the lower-case letters of the alphabet as its primary symbol is also provided. It was the first example of an analytico-synthetic classification, in which the subject field is first analysed into facets, and class numbers are then constructed by synthesis.

COLONIAL EDITION. An edition of a work, usually of fiction, often printed and bound at the same time as the ordinary edition, but usually on poorer paper, and bound in a poorer style. Issued for export to the Colonies.

COLOPHON (Gr. 'finishing, end'). 1. Particulars of printer, place and date of printing, title, name of author, and publisher's or printer's device, found at the end of manuscripts and or early printed books. It was first used in printed books by Fust and Schoeffer in the 'Mainz Psalter' of 1457, and gradually became common, but was superseded towards 1600 by the Publisher's Imprint. Its use in MSS. was occasional; it then gave the scribe's name and the date. *See also* IMPRINT. 2. The current meaning is the publisher's device, e.g. Hutchinson's bull, Heinemann's windmill or Thames and Hudson's dolphins.

COLOPHON DATE. The date give in the COLOPHON (*q.v.*), and so described when used in a catalogue or bibliography.

COLOUR FILTER. Coloured gelatine, glass or plastic, used in front of a camera lens to absorb certain colours.

COLOUR GRAVURE. The process of producing coloured illustrations in colour by PHOTOGRAVURE (*q.v.*). This method is used principally for mass circulation colour magazines and packaging materials. The colour picture is usually of almost continuous tone, the dark and light shades being obtained by varying depths of the etched cells.

COLOUR LITHOGRAPHY. A method of printing in colour by lithography using separate stones or plates for each colour.

COLOUR PRINTING. The art of producing pictures, designs, etc., in a variety of colours, shades and tones by means of printing from plates, or by lithography; chromatic printing.

COLOUR PROCESS. A set of two or more half-tones made by colour separation. Half-tone colour printing is commonly called process colour work.

COLOUR SEPARATION. 1. The process by which colours of an original work of art or colour print are analysed into the basic colours in such a way that printing plates may be prepared in order to print in succession and finally yield a print of correct colouring. This is done by placing filters in front of the camera lens when making negatives.

COLOUR SEPARATION NEGATIVE. A negative for use in colour printing which, by the use of a colour filter, has recorded a primary colour.

COLOUR TRANSPARENCY. A positive colour photograph on a transparent support, usually film.

COLOUR UNDER GILT. The edges of a book coloured (usually red) before gilding. Usually found in Bible binding. *See also* EDGES, RED UNDER GOLD EDGES.

COLOUR WORK. Printing processes used to print in two or more colours, such as two-, or four-colour half-tone; planographic and intaglio work in colour. Often called according to the number of plates used, 'Three-colour Process', 'Four-colour Process'.

COLOURED EDGES. *Synonymous with* SPRINKLED EDGES (*q.v.*).

COLOURED PLATE. A whole-page coloured illustration produced by any process.

COLOURED PRINTINGS. A cheap quality paper, having a high content of mechanical wood pulp; it is used, among other purposes, for the covers of pamphlets.

COLPORTEUR. A travelling bookseller or agent, usually of a religious group or society, who sells tracts and copies of the scriptures at low prices.

COLUMBIAN. An out-of-date name for a size of type equal to about 16 point.

COLUMBIAN PRESS. A printing press designed by George Clymer of Philadelphia and brought to England in 1817 where it became more successful than in the United States. The press derived its power from a system of levers which converted the lateral movement of the bar to the vertical movement of the iron beam from which the platen was suspended. The most conspicuous feature of the press was a cast-iron eagle which acted as an adjustable counter weight.

COLUMBIER. *See* COLOMBIER.

COLUMN. 1. A narrow division of a page of a book formed by vertical lines or spaces. 2. A narrow block of letterpress arranged in the form of a column. 3. (*Printing*) A vertical line or square bracket.

COLUMN INCH. (*Printing*) *See* AGATE LINE.

COLUMN PICTURE. Picture in a mediaeval illuminated manuscript the width of a column of text, whether at the head of a page, or interrupting the text at intervals.

COLUMNAR. A series or classification in which the terms, or classes, are arranged in a column. The classes may be co-ordinate, or they may be regarded as subordinate, each to that above it. (*Bliss*). *See* HORIZONTAL, TABULAR CLASSIFICATION.

COLUMNS. Some kinds of books such as encyclopaedias have the text printed in two or more parallel columns of type to the page. Where these, instead of the pages, are numbered, the collation in a cataloguing or bibliographical entry should make this clear, as: XI pp., 1480 columns.

COMAC.   Continuous Multiple Access Collator.   A punched card collating system for the storage and retrieval of information prepared for
the Air Force Office of Scientific Research, Directorate of Advanced
Studies, Washington, D.C. It is a mechanized Uniterm index, codes
punched on one card being matched against codes punched on another
card, the codes for the logical product or sum being punched on a
third card.

COMB PATTERN.   A pattern produced on marbled papers or other
surfaces from a vat in which colours have been combed to form a
pattern. *See also* MARBLED PAPER.

COMBINATION CODING.   *Synonymous with* INDIRECT CODING (*q.v.*).
See also MARGINAL-HOLE PUNCHED CARDS.

COMBINATION PLATE.   One in which both half-tone and line
methods have been used.

COMMAND PAPERS.   *See* PARLIAMENTARY PAPERS.

COMMAND RETRIEVAL INFORMATION SYSTEM.   A system
of images on scrolls of 16 mm or 35 mm microfilm, with 500,000
images on a scroll. Scrolls are placed in a special retrieving device
having a keyboard selector and a screen where an enlargement can be
viewed or copied as a micro image. Abbreviated CRIS.

COMMENTARY.   Explanatory or critical notes on an Act of Parliament,
a literary text or some other work. It may accompany the text or be
issued separately.

COMMERCIAL LIBRARY.   Similar to a commercial section but on a
much larger scale and housed in a separate room from the reference
library, and sometimes in a separate building.

COMMERCIAL SECTION.   The section of a reference library devoted
to providing material and information of a commercial nature.

COMMITTEE ON MANPOWER RESOURCES FOR SCIENCE
AND TECHNOLOGY.   Set up in February 1965, this Committee
replaced the Scientific Manpower Committee, and has as its terms of
reference 'to examine and report from time to time on manpower
resources for science and technology'. It reports jointly to the Secretary of State for Education and Science and the Minister of Technology. Abbreviated CMR.

COMMON AUXILIARIES.   *See* UNIVERSAL DECIMAL CLASSIFICATION.

COMMON FOLIO.   *See* FOLIO.

COMMON ISOLATES.   Symbols attached to many classes in the Colon
Classification and indicating literary form, e.g. *a* bibliography; *c* concordance; *v* history; *y*2 syllabus; P*v* history of linguistics; Plll*v* history
of English linguistics. When attached to a host class number without

a connecting symbol, as in the examples given, they are called *Anteriorising Common Isolates*, but when needing a connecting symbol *Posteriorising Common Isolates*.

COMMON RULING. Term used to denote the vertical lines (rules) printed on account-book paper. *See also* FEINT RULING.

COMMON SUBDIVISIONS. Form divisions which are used throughout a classification to sub-divide any subject. These have distinctive names in different classifications, e.g. AUXILIARY TABLES (*q.v.*) in Dewey and the Universal Decimal Classification; CATEGORICAL TABLES (*q.v.*) in Brown's *Subject classification*, and SYSTEMATIC SCHEDULES (*q.v.*) in Bliss's *Bibliographic classification*.

COMMONWEALTH AGRICULTURAL BUREAUX. This organization was set up to act as a clearing-house for information for scientists and research workers in agriculture throughout the world. The organization covers all the agricultural sciences, including forestry and animal health, and operates three Institutes and ten Bureaux. Abbreviation CAB.

COMMONWEALTH SCIENTIFIC AND RESEARCH ORGANIZA-TION. Established in Australia by the Science and Industry Act of 1949; it replaced the Council for Scientific and Industrial Research established in 1926 which itself replaced the Institute of Science and Industry which was formed in 1919. It is concerned with all fields of pure and applied science, excluding medicine, and operates through nearly forty subject divisions and sections. The functions are: carrying out scientific research for the promotion of primary and secondary industries in the Commonwealth and its Territories; training scientific research workers and awarding studentships; making grants in aid of scientific work; the recognition and support of research associations; maintaining Commonwealth standards of measurement; disseminating scientific and technical information, publishing scientific and technical reports. Compiles and publishes *Australian Science Index* (m.) and *CSIRO Abstracts* (m.). Most of the divisions and sections issue publications. Abbreviated CSIRO.

COMMUNITY LIBRARY. A major library unit containing an adequate, well-organized collection of books, serving a population of 55,000, open 48 to 66 hours a week, and having a professional and clerical staff. (American.)

COMPACT STORAGE. The storing of books on rolling or swinging stacks which have to be moved into another position to permit consulation, or of books or other material placed in drawers built into shelving and opening into a stack aisle. Such shelving is used normally in stack rooms, and increases capacity up to 114%. *See also* COM-PACTUS, DRAW-OUT SHELVES, ROLLING BOOKCASE, ROLLING PRESS, STOR-MOR, SWINGING BOOKCASE.

COMPACTUS. Trade name for a particular design of shelving invented by Ingold, a Swiss engineer. Steel bookcases are placed against one another and are moved sideways for consultation of the books by operating a lever which activates a clutch which grips a revolving cable set in the floor, or by pressing a switch which operates the same mechanism by electricity. The books on one side of each of two cases are exposed to view by this means. Also called 'Ingold-Compactus'.

COMPANY FILE. A file, kept especially in commercial, industrial, research and learned or professional association libraries, containing information relating to individual firms. The type of information kept depends on the type of library and the needs of its users but may include reports, company reports, house journals, catalogues, book-lets, cuttings, advertisements, stock exchange listings, etc. Also called 'Corporation file'.

COMPARTMENT. 1. In a book stack, sets of shelves arranged verti-cally between two uprights and placed back to back. (American.) 2. (*Bibliography*) A group of decorative borders comprising (a) a single carved or engraved piece with the centre portion cut out so as to resemble a picture frame into which the letterpress of a title or other matter is set; (b) a piece originally carved or engraved as (a) but later cut into four or more pieces; (c) four or more pieces cut or engraved separately but intended to form a single design when assembled; (d) such borders made from four pieces of cast type-ornaments but with ends cut obliquely to help form a border. *See also* FRAME.

COMPARTMENT PICTURE. An illumination, in a mediaeval illumi-nated manuscript, divided into sections each of which contains a picture.

COMPASS MAP. *See* PORTOLAN CHART.

COMPEND. A subject treated briefly, or in outline only.

COMPENDIUM. A work containing in a small compass the substance or general principles of a larger work; a brief, comprehensive sum-mary.

COMPENSATION GUARDS. Short stubs bound into a volume to balance the space taken up by folded maps or other bulky material so that this can be incorporated without distorting the shape of the book. Also called 'Filling-in guards'. *See also* GUARD, STUB.

COMPETITOR FILE. A record on cards, or a file of cuttings, publi-cations, reports about, or published by, competitor companies.

COMPILATION. A work compiled by assembling material from other books.

COMPILER. 1. A collector or editor of written or printed material gleaned from various sources or from one or more authors; and who arranges it for publication. 2. One who produces a musical work by collecting and putting together written or printed matter from the work of several composers. Also, one who chooses and combines into one work selections and excerpts from one or more composers (*MLA/ALA Code*).

COMPILER ENTRY. A catalogue entry for the compiler of a work.

COMPLETE BIBLIOGRAPHY. *See* BIBLIOGRAPHY 1.

COMPLETION. *See* CONTINUATION.

COMPLEX SUBJECT. In classification, one which reflects more than one distinct conventional class.

COMPLUTENSIAN POLYGLOT. The polyglot *Bible* in six volumes printed between 1514 and 1517 at Alcalá de Henares, a small town near Madrid, by Arnald Guillen de Brocar. It was the first of the great multi-lingual Bibles, and is by far the most important landmark in Spanish printing. The text is in Hebrew, Aramaic, Greek and Latin. Called Complutensian Bible because Complutum is the Roman name for Alcalá de Henares. *See also* POLYGLOT.

COMPONENT. An individual constituent word in a compound subject heading.

COMPOSE. To set type-matter ready for printing.

COMPOSER. One who composes, especially music.

COMPOSER ENTRY. 1. An entry in a catalogue for a musical composition under the name of the composer as the heading. Normally this is the main entry but it may be an added entry. 2. Sometimes used for the composer heading chosen for the entry, and not the entry itself.

COMPOSING RULE. A flat strip of steel or brass placed by the compositor between each line of type in his composing stick when setting type. Rules provide a flat surface for each line of type and facilitate the handling of the composed type. Also called 'Setting rule'.

COMPOSING STICK. *Also called* STICK (*q.v.*).

COMPOSITE AUTHORS. Name given to the several authors contributing to one work. Not to be confused with JOINT AUTHOR (*q.v.*).

COMPOSITE BOOK. 1. A book of a composite nature, where an editor has brought together several works by different authors into one volume. 2. A book on more than one subject. 3. A COMPOSITE WORK (*q.v.*).

6*

COMPOSITE SUBJECT. (*Classification*). One which consists of more than one element, e.g. the design of furniture for children's libraries.

COMPOSITE WORK. 1. A literary production on a single subject written by two or more authors in collaboration, the contribution by each forming a distinct section or part of the complete work. 2. A musical composition in which two or more composers collaborate similarly, each contribution forming a distinct section or part of the complete work.

COMPOSITION. Type setting: hence Compositor.

COMPOSITION FOUNT. Loosely used to indicate any type-face of a size of 14-point or less, used for book printing and 'tapped' on a type-composing machine.

COMPOSITOR. One who sets printer's type.

COMPOUND CATCHWORD. In indexing, a hyphenated word which must be treated as if the hyphen did not exist.

COMPOUND CLASS. In the Colon Classification, a class made of a Basic Class (i.e. Main, or Canonical, Class) and one or more Isolates.

COMPOUND HEADING. *See* MAIN HEADING.

COMPOUND SUBJECT. (*Cataloguing*) One which requires more than one word in the subject heading to express its meaning. A compound subject may consist of a phrase or a combination, the separate words of which are divided by punctuation. (*Classification*) One which reflects more than one facet within a conventional class, for example, within the class Building, Wooden Floor is a compound, reflecting both a material and a part.

COMPOUND SUBJECT HEADING. A heading which consists of (a) two words joined by a conjunction, as 'Punch and Judy'; (b) a phrase, as 'Council of Trent'; (c) words which are always associated together; e.g. 'Capital Punishment'; 'Political Economy'.

COMPOUND SURNAME. A name made of two or more proper names, generally connected by a hyphen, conjunction or preposition.

COMPREHENSIVE BIBLIOGRAPHY. One which lists, as far as possible, everything published on the subject. *See also* CURRENT COMPREHENSIVE BIBLIOGRAPHY.

COMPRESENCE. A linked set of FEATURES (*q.v.*) describing a given ITEM (*q.v.*), or of items defining a given feature.

COMPRESSED SCORE. *Synonymous with* CLOSE SCORE (*q.v.*). *See also* SCORE.

COMPUTERIZED REARRANGEMENT OF SPECIAL SUBJECTS. *See* CROSS.

CONCEPT CO-ORDINATION. 1. A system of multi-dimensional

indexing with single concepts to define a document uniquely (*IBM*). 2. A system of co-ordinate indexing for information retrieval. *See also* CO-ORDINATE INDEXING, UNITERM CONCEPT CO-ORDINATE INDEXING, ZATOCODING.

CONCEPT INDEXING. The process of deciding which are the concepts in a particular document that are of sufficient importance to be included in the SUBJECT INDEX (*q.v.*).

CONCERTINA FOLD. A method of folding paper, first to the right and then to the left, so that it opens and closes in the manner of a concertina. Also called 'Zig-zag fold'.

CONCILIUM BIBLIOGRAPHICUM. A bibliographical work begun by Herbert Haviland Field at Zurich in 1895. Cards were printed and distributed as soon as published for all publications (primarily periodical articles, with some books and pamphlets) on zoology, palæontology, general biology, microscopy, anatomy, physiology and kindred subjects, from all countries. It thus formed a complete bibliography. After the death of the founder in 1921, the Rockefeller Foundation made a grant for five years, hoping that the organization would receive finance internationally. The enterprise continued on subscriptions alone until 1940 when it ceased to function. It is often referred to as the ZURICH INDEX.

CONCISE DESCRIPTION, PRINCIPLE OF. The avoidance of duplication or unessential information in a catalogue entry. *See also* CATALOGUING, PRINCIPLES OF.

CONCORDANCE. 1. A book arranged so as to form an alphabetical index of all passages, or of all the more important words, in any work, with indications of the context of such passages and phrases in the text. 2. In machine indexing, an alphabetical index of words in a document, each word present in the text being an index entry. As no discrimination is exercised in preparing this type of index, the decisions that must be made can be performed well by machines.

CONCRETENESS, PRINCIPLE OF DECREASING. *See* DECREASING CONCRETENESS, PRINCIPLE OF.

CONCRETES AND PROCESSES. A method of indexing devised by K. Kaiser in which the main (first, or leading) word of the subject-entry is the main, 'concrete', subject, and the later one/s the secondary (or aspect) 'processes' sub-dividing it.

CONDENSED SCORE. *Synonymous with* CLOSE SCORE (*q.v.*). *See also* SCORE.

CONDENSED TYPE. Type which is narrow in proportion to its height. **This is an example.**

CONDITIONING. The maturing of paper, carried out in the paper mill by drying out or adding moisture to it so as to bring it 'into balance' with what is accepted as normal printing-room atmosphere and to enable it to be used on fast-running machines without danger of cockling. The process is carried out in a temperature of 60°–65° F. and a relative humidity of 65%; the paper will then contain about 7% moisture evenly distributed over the sheet, and the fibres will remain stable during printing.

CONDUCTOR'S PART. The printed music for an instrumentalist who also simultaneously conducts a concerted work. Also called 'Conductor's score'. *See also* SCORE.

CONDUCTOR'S SCORE. *Synonymous with* CONDUCTOR'S PART (*q.v.*). *See also* SCORE.

confer. (*Lat.* 'compare'.) To compare or refer to. Usually used in the abbreviated form (cf.).

CONFIDENTIAL FILE. Material in a special library which is kept securely, and apart from other material, and is only used under certain conditions. *See also* CLASSIFIED MATERIAL.

CONGER. A group of from ten to twenty wholesale booksellers who combined to share the publishing and selling of books, and to protect the sale of their books from undercutting and piracy. Congers were a feature of the London book trade in the late seventeenth and early eighteenth centuries.

CONGRESS, LIBRARY OF, CLASSIFICATION. *See* LIBRARY OF CONGRESS CLASSIFICATION.

CONJOINT AUTHORSHIP. *See* JOINT AUTHOR.

CONJUGATE. (*Bibliography*) This term is applied to two leaves which can be traced into and out of the back of a book and found to be one piece of paper.

CONJUNCTIVE. Pertaining to the joining or coupling of two documents, words, phrases, or elements of information in order to express a unity. Being neither disjunctive nor collateral (*IBM*).

CONNECTING SYMBOLS. *See* CLASS NUMBER and FUNDAMENTAL CATEGORIES.

CONNECTIVE CATALOGUE. *Synonymous with* SYNDETIC CATALOGUE (*q.v.*).

CONNOTATION. A term in classification indicative of all the qualities conveyed by, or comprised in, a class name; e.g. 'man' in connotation means the qualities (mammalian structure, upright gait, reason, etc.) that go to make up man, as opposed to *detonation*, where the term merely marks down or indicates. The phrase: 'That man is really a man' shows the denotative followed by the connotative use of the word. Connotation and denotation may be considered synonymous with intension and EXTENSION (*q.v.*).

CONNOTATIVE. *See* CONNOTATION.

CONSERVATIVE LIBRARY ASSOCIATION. Founded in the U.S.A. in 1964. Is devoted to collections that emphasise educational books, and to a conception of the freedom to read that includes books of the right as well as the left.

CONSIDERATION FILE. The accumulation of current selections for purchase. (American.)

CONSISTENT CHARACTERISTICS. *See* CHARACTERISTIC OF A CLASSIFICATION.

CONSOLIDATED INDEX. An index, in one sequence, to several volumes, a long run of a periodical or other serial publication, or to several independent works or serial publications.

CONSOLIDATED SYSTEM. A system of libraries established by the decision of several municipal governing bodies, or by the action of voters, and governed by the Board of Trustees of the system. The individual library units operate as branches of the system. (American.)

CONSTANT MNEMONICS. *See* MNEMONICS.

CONTACT. A copy of a photograph or document made in direct contact with the original.

CONTACT COPY. *See* CONTACT PRINTING.

CONTACT COPYING. A non-optical copying process whereby the original and the material of reproduction are brought into close contact during exposure. The resulting copy can be described as a 'contact print'. *See also* CONTACT PRINTING, LENSLESS COPYING. REFLEX COPYING, TRANSMISSION COPYING.

CONTACT PHOTOGRAPHY. A method of making a photographic copy of a document on only one side of which the record appears, whereby the light shines through the document being copied on to the sensitized paper. The resulting black-on-white negative is then placed together with a sheet of sensitized paper and the process repeated to make a positive. *See also* REFLEX COPYING.

CONTACT PRINT. *See* CONTACT COPYING.

CONTACT PRINTER. A machine for making contact copies (i.e. transmission prints or reflex copies) which are the same size as the original. *See also* REFLEX COPYING, TRANSMISSION COPYING.

CONTACT PRINTING. Any form of photographic or other copying method in which a sheet of sensitized material is held in firm and even contact with the original photographic negative or original document. The copying may be done by the direct or transmission method, or by the reflex method; the resulting print may be termed a 'contact copy'. *See also* REFLEX COPYING, TRANSMISSION COPYING.

CONTEMPORARY BINDING.   One that is contemporary with the printing of the book.

CONTENTS.   Strictly, a 'table of contents' but seldom used in this form. 1. A list of the 'preliminaries' and chapter headings of a book in their correct order, or of articles in a periodical, with the numbers of the pages on which they begin. 2. A list of the musical works contained in a printed collection of music or in an album of gramophone records, or of those recorded on a single record.

CONTENTS-BOOK.   A loose-leaf book in which a list of the contents of a volume or of a continuation is kept if too lengthy for a catalogue card.

CONTENTS LIST.   *Synonymous with* CONTENTS (*q.v.*).

CONTENTS NOTE.   A note appearing after the catalogue entry giving the headings of the chapters, parts, or volumes. In a descriptive bibliography it will indicate what is printed on each page included in the collation by gatherings.

CONTINUATION.   1. A book only partly written by the original author and continued by someone else. 2. A work issued as a supplement to one already published. 3. A part issued in continuance of a serial, series or book. An order to supply subsequent parts as issued is called a 'Continuation Order'.

CONTINUATION CARD.   1. A card used for ordering a CONTINUATION (*q.v.*). 2. A CONTINUATION LIST (*q.v.*). 3. An EXTENSION CARD (*q.v.*).

CONTINUATION LIST, CONTINUATION RECORD.   A list of all books such as annuals, series, and works issued in parts for which there are standing orders.

CONTINUATION ORDER.   An order to supply each succeeding issue of an annual or serial publication – a 'continuation' of an item already in stock. *See also* CONTINUATION.

CONTINUATION REGISTER.   *Synonymous with* CONTINUATION LIST (*q.v.*).

CONTINUOUS FEED.   The action of an automatic sheet feeder attached to a printing press, folding, or other machine, so that the supply of sheets can be replenished without interrupting the operation of the machine.

CONTINUOUS FLOW CAMERA.   Apparatus for taking photographs,

which automatically moves the originals and the film to be exposed after each exposure. Also called 'Flow camera', 'Rotary camera'.

CONTINUOUS-FORM LOAN RECORDS. Continuous stationery used in specially made writing cabinets called 'registers' where up to five copies of the records of loans are required in non-public libraries. A carbon, or self-carbon paper is used, and the sets of paper are supplied printed and perforated. After each loan is recorded the set of papers is torn off and the separate pieces of paper are filed in different sequences under author, borrower's name, accession number, date, etc. as desired. Each piece is usually of a distinct colour to enable insertion in the correct file to be done easily and without inserting in wrong files. Borrowers are permitted in some libraries to make out their own loan records.

CONTINUOUS PAGINATION. The use of one sequence of page numbering throughout a book or several parts or volumes.

CONTINUOUS PRINTER. A photographic printing apparatus for the reproduction of an original, from either a negative or positive on to sensitized film or paper, by a continuous movement of the material through the exposing and processing stages. During the exposing process, the film being copied and a roll of paper or film, are synchronized to move at the same speed past the printing aperture. *See also* OPTICAL PRINTER.

CONTINUOUS PROCESSING. Processing photographs or films in machines which automatically transport the photographic material through the required solutions, finally drying the product.

CONTINUOUS REVISION. An encyclopaedia, such as the *Encyclopaedia Britannica* which is not completely revised and published as a new edition. Minor alterations or extensive additions or revisions are carried out, additional or supplementary pages being inserted within the existing pagination by the addition of 'A.B.C.' etc. to the page numbers.

CONTOUR LINE. One drawn on a map to connect points having the same elevation.

CONTOURS. Lines drawn on a map to join all places at the same height above sea level. The intervals between contours may represent height differences from 50′ to several thousand feet dependent on the scale of the map. On physical maps the areas between contours are often shown in different colours progressing from various shades of green for lowlands through browns to red and finally white. Depths of the sea bed are indicated by Isobaths (*q.v.*).

CONTRACT SERVICES. Items appearing in a library's statement of income and expenditure to record funds (a) received from a governmental, library, or other, agency for specific services rendered, or (b) for services rendered to the library by individuals or agencies on the basis of a specific contract. (American.)

CONTRARIES. Any impurities in the waste paper, rags or other materials such as silk, feathers, wool, string, bones, pins, rubber, etc., to be used for paper- or board-making, and which are likely to be injurious.

CONTRAST. The difference between the high and low densities in a print or negative. (*Concepts* . . .)

CONTROLLED CIRCULATION. *See* ROUTING.

CONTROLLED CIRCULATION SERIAL. A serial publication which is usually issued without charge and is only available to those whom the author or those responsible for its publication specify.

CONTROLLED INDEXING. Implies a careful selection of terminology so as to avoid, as far as possible, the scattering of related subjects under different headings. *See also* WORD INDEXING.

CONVENIENCE COPY. (*Reprography*) A copy of a document made quickly and economically, but not necessarily of the highest standard of quality or permanence.

CONVENTION CONCERNING THE EXCHANGE OF OFFICIAL PUBLICATIONS AND GOVERNMENT DOCUMENTS BETWEEN STATES. A multilateral convention which was adopted by the General Conference of Unesco in December 1958, and came into force on 30th May 1961. It had been ratified or accepted by eighteen States by September 1963.

CONVENTIONAL FOLIAGE. A bookbinding ornament which is often quite unrealistic but obviously suggested by foliage.

CONVENTIONAL NAME. A name, other than the real or official name, by which a person, corporate body, thing or place has come to be familiarly known.

CONVENTIONAL TITLE. A UNIFORM TITLE (*q.v.*) which is constructed from terms describing the form or subject of a work, and arranged in a generally accepted sequence. It is used mostly in cataloguing music, where, e.g. terms are arranged in the order given to describe the musical form of the composition, its instrumentation (sonata, concerto, trio, piano quartet, etc.), its position in a sequence of the composer's works, its key, its opus (or equivalent) number, and descriptive title or soubriquet.

CONVERSION. The process of changing the representation of information to a form which is usable by a computer, e.g. converting it to machine 'language' on paper tape.

CONVEYOR BELT. A moving continuous belt of rubber, webbing or similar material, used to carry goods from one place to another. Used in libraries to convey books when handed in by readers from the place of receipt to the 'transaction' or 'discharging' room where they are examined and checked with lists of 'reserves' before being returned to the shelves.

CO-OPERATION, LOCAL. Amongst the numerous schemes providing various forms of co-operation among libraries in small geographical areas are the following, under which entries will be found:

BRASTACS	LADSIRLAC	SAALIC
CADIG	LINOSCO	SINTO
CICRIS	LIST	TALIC
HADIS	MANTIS	WALIC
HALDIS	MISLIC	WANDPETELS
HATRICS	NANTIS	YEWTIC
HERTIS	NELL	
HULTIS	NELTAS	

CO-OPERATIVE, INDUSTRIAL AND COMMERCIAL REFERENCE AND INFORMATION SERVICE. *See* CICRIS

CO-OPERATIVE CATALOGUING. The sharing by a number of libraries of the cost and/or labour of cataloguing to avoid the duplication of effort common to each. Not to be confused with CENTRALIZED CATALOGUING (*q.v.*).

CO-OPERATIVE PUBLISHERS. *See* VANITY PUBLISHERS.

CO-OPERATIVE PURCHASING. An arrangement between several libraries whereby one of them, or a separate organization, purchases books for all of them in order to obtain books at a cheaper rate than is possible for individual libraries, because of the smaller number of copies, and therefore the less-advantageous terms, which the small libraries obtain.

CO-OPERATIVE SYSTEM. A group of independent and autonomous libraries co-operating by informal or formal agreements or contracts which stipulate the common services to be undertaken. (American.)

CO-OPTED MEMBER. A member of a (libraries) committee who is not a member of the local council, but has special knowledge, or interest in social, educational, political, or public activities.

CO-ORDINATE. (*Classification*) Specific terms subordinated to the same genus. *See also* CO-ORDINATE CLASSES.

CO-ORDINATE CLASSES. (*Classification*) 1. Classes which are correlated so that classes leading up to a subject come before it and those which develop from it, or are next in likeness or character, come after it. 2. Classes which are of the same order of SPECIFICATION (*q.v.*) and grade of division in a classification. (*Bliss*).

CO-ORDINATE INDEXING. 1. An indexing scheme whereby the inter-relations of terms are shown by coupling individual words (*IBM*). 2. A system of information retrieval in which the indexing or recording of information in, or characteristics of, a document are accomplished by entering a reference number (page number, report number, etc.) on a card (or a column of a card) which is reserved for, and bears the heading of, an individual term to which it is devoted. KWIC Index, Scan-Column Index and Tabledex are all forms of compact book-form co-ordinate indexes. Also called 'Concept Co-ordination', 'Correlative indexing', 'Enriched co-ordinate indexing', 'Multiple aspect indexing', 'Synthetic indexing'. *See also* FREE INDEXING, MANIPULATIVE INDEX, UNITERM CONCEPT CO-ORDINATE INDEXING.

CO-ORDINATED DECENTRALIZATION. The management of a number of libraries as separate units, although they together form a library system (as faculty or departmental libraries within a university system), their varying activities being co-ordinated to provide a cohesive, efficient service to meet all the needs which may be made upon the library as a whole.

CO-ORDINATION OF TERMS. The modulation from one term to another by gradual steps in order that the process of evolving a classification may exhibit its hierarchy or schedule.

COPAL. A resinous substance obtained from various tropical trees, and used in the manufacture of varnish and printing inks.

COPIER-DUPLICATOR. A machine for making automatically one or several copies of an original document by a photocopying method without the use of a special master.

COPPER ENGRAVING. *See* ENGRAVING.

COPPER PLATE. A plate used for ENGRAVING (*q.v.*) in which the drawing is incised with a burin.

COPPERPLATE. A carefully written cursive script often used when inscribing the captions under engravings and used until recent times by writing masters as models for their pupils to copy.

COPY. 1. Matter for the printer to set up in type. 2. A single specimen of a printed book. 3. The material to be reproduced by photographic or other means; also the result of a reproduction process.

COPY-BOARD. The board on which the copy is secured whilst being photographed.

COPY CARD.   *See* CAMERA CARD.

COPY EDIT.   The checking of a MS. by a publisher or printer before marking it up for the typesetter, for accuracy of facts, grammatical construction, possible libel, HOUSE-STYLE (*q.v.*), etc.

COPY FITTING.   (*Printing*) Adjusting 'copy' to the space available by changing the space allotment, the length of copy, or the size of type. *See also* COPY 1.

COPY NUMBER (or COPY LETTER).   A figure or letter added to the call number of a book to distinguish different copies of the same book, e.g. 821C46, 821C46s, 821C46 (cop. 2). *See also* BOOK NUMBER, VOLUME NUMBER, WORK MARK.

COPY PREPARATION.   (*Printing*) The act of preparing for the compositor a MS. which has been 'copy edited', by making the MS. legible and accurate, indicating printing style, type to be used, etc.

COPY READER.   An employee at a printing works whose task is to prepare the copy for composition by marking the measure, sizes of type to be used for text, quotations, footnotes, etc. and check the author's consistency in the use of capitals, citation, spelling, punctuation and sentence structure.

COPY SLIP.   *See* PROCESS SLIP.

COPY-TAX.   *See also* LEGAL DEPOSIT.

COPYCAT.   A trade name of a particular machine for reproducing photographically sheets of printed, written or drawn matter the same size as the original.

COPYFLO.   Trade name for a xerographic continuous printer which will make fully automatic reproductions from roll or card-mounted microfilm. It is made by the Haloid Company, and a service unit has been installed in London by Rank Xerox Ltd. The machine prints on one side of the paper only and the paper is delivered flat up to 24 inches wide, or, in the case of a book, folded in such a way that the folds form the edges of each pair of printed pages as in Chinese books.

COPYHOLDER.   1. A device attached to composing machines or used in conjunction with a typewriter to hold a MS. or 'copy'. 2. An assistant who reads the 'copy' to a proof reader. 3. A device which may be a simple board or an elaborate vacuum frame designed to hold the copy before the camera (*Verry*).

COPYING PROCESS.   A process for making copies of documents on sensitized material. *See also* CONTACT COPYING, DIAZOTYPE PROCESS, ELECTROPHOTOGRAPHIC PROCESSES, NEGATIVE 3, OPTICAL COPYING, PHOTOGRAPHIC PHOTOCOPYING, POSITIVE PROCESS, RAPID COPYING, REFLEX COPYING, THERMAL PROCESS, TRANSMISSION PRINTING.

COPYIST.   A person who transcribed MSS. prior to the introduction of printing.

COPYRIGHT.   The exclusive right of an author or his heirs to produce and reproduce (e.g. to publish and receive royalties) in respect of a literary, musical or artistic work. It is valid for a limited number of years and the work must not be reproduced in whole or in part, without the copyright owner's permission. The Copyright Act, 1956, is the only source of copyright law in the United Kingdom and Northern Ireland. It repealed the Copyright Act, 1911, except sections 15, 34 and 37. Copyright differs in its meaning according to its usage in relation to the various works in which it can subsist, i.e. literary works, dramatic works, musical works, artistic works, sound recordings, cinematograph films, television broadcasts, sound broadcasts and published editions of works. The Act establishes separate codes of copyright in respect of these different types of work. In relation to literary, dramatic or musical works, copyright is the exclusive right to do certain 'acts restricted by the copyright'. These are set out in Section 2(5): (a) reproducing the work in any material form; (b) publishing it; (c) performing it in public; (d) broadcasting it; (e) causing it to be transmitted to subscribers to a diffusion service; (f) making any adaptation of it; (g) doing, in any adaptation of it, any of the acts specified in relation to it in paragraphs (a) to (e) above. Copyright subsists (1) in every unpublished work of which the author was a qualified person (defined in Section 1(5) as a British subject, a British protected person, a citizen of the Republic of Ireland, persons domiciled or resident in the United Kingdom, persons domiciled or resident in another country to which the provisions of the Act extend, or a body corporate); (2) in publication of the work. Copyright continues to subsist until fifty years from the end of the year in which the author died or in which a work was first posthumously published, performed, offered for sale to the public in record form, or broadcast. Section 15 makes new provision whereby copyright subsists in a 'published edition'; this protects the material form in which a work – even if it is not itself a copyright work – is presented to the public, and entitles the publisher to a copyright in a particular typographical arrangement. Copyright in this case subsists for twenty-five years from the end of the year in which the work was first published. If British publishers adopt the device of marking publications with the symbol © – which is usually done on the back of the title-page – and fulfilling the other requirements of the Universal Copyright Convention (i.e. the name of the copyright proprietor and the year of first publication), copyright in such publications is automatically secured in all countries which have ratified this Convention. *See also* BERNE COPYRIGHT UNION, COPYRIGHT, INTERNATIONAL.

COPYRIGHT DATE. The date copyright was granted for an individual work. This is usually printed on the verso of the title page of books. If several dates are given, they signify changes in the text, or renewals of copyright. The first copyright date indicates the date of the first edition of a book and corresponds to the imprint date of the original edition. *See also* BERNE CONVENTION, COPYRIGHT, COPYRIGHT, INTERNATIONAL.

COPYRIGHT DEPOSIT. The deposition of free copies of a book or musical composition in a COPYRIGHT LIBRARY (*q.v.*) according to law. *See also* LEGAL DEPOSIT.

COPYRIGHT FEE. Fee paid to the holder of a copyright for the right to use his material for a particular purpose, e.g. to include a poem in an anthology or to read it in public, or to play a piece of music, or a record of the same, in public.

COPYRIGHT, INTERNATIONAL. International copyright exists in most countries through their membership of the Berne Convention; first publication in any country of the Union (see BERNE COPYRIGHT UNION), ensures copyright throughout the other countries which are signatories. Any work published in a non-Union country has the same standing as a work published in a Union country if it is simultaneously published in a Union country. There are seven inter-American conventions in the U.S. International copyright exists only through reciprocal arrangements with members of the Union and is dependent upon compliance with the legal provisions of the respective countries. A Universal Copyright Convention came into operation in 1955. This was designed to secure support from the adherents of the Berne Convention and the various inter-American Conventions, as well as countries which subscribe to none of them. Whereas earlier conventions aimed to establish an international copyright code, the Universal Copyright Convention is designed to provide a basis and method of conciliation. It was prepared under the auspices of Unesco and signed at Geneva on 6th September 1952 by some thirty-nine States including the United Kingdom and the U.S.A. Ratifying states agree to extend the same protection to foreign authors, composers and artists as to their own nationals. It provides protection to literary, scientific, and artistic works for a minimum of twenty-five years. *See also* BERNE COPYRIGHT UNION.

COPYRIGHT LIBRARY. A library which is entitled under copyright laws to receive a free copy of any or every book published in the country. Section 15 of the Copyright Act, 1911 – which was not repealed by the Act of 1956 – provides that the publisher of every book (including 'sheet of letterpress, sheet of music, map . . .'), is, within one month after publication, to deliver, at his own expense, a copy of the book to the British Museum, and also if written demand is made before the expiration of twelve months after publication, to send a copy to the Bodleian Library, Oxford; the University Library, Cambridge; the National Library of Scotland, Edinburgh – except that law books are to be transmitted to the Faculty of Advocates to be vested in their Law Library (National Library of Scotland Act, 1925); Trinity College, Dublin, and with certain exceptions specified by the Board of Trade, the National Library of Wales, Aberystwyth. These exceptions are designed to exclude books published in small editions unless they are written in Welsh or relate wholly or mainly to the Welsh or other Celtic peoples or to the natural history of Wales.

COPYRIGHT LIST. A list of the books deposited in a library under the copyright laws.

COPYTRON. Trade name for an electrostatic reproduction machine made by the Charles Bruning Company, Inc.

COPYWRITER. A writer of advertisements.

CORANTO. 1. The earliest form of newspaper, consisting of one leaf in small folio, the text being in two columns on each side of the leaf. Published first in Holland and Germany, and in England in 1620 and 1621, such publications were known by the name coranto, whether published in England or on the continent. They were issued at least once a week as a half-sheet in folio, and only foreign news was printed. 2. Sometimes the word Coranto is used to include Newsbooks which were published until 1642. *See also* NEWSBOOK, RELATION. Nathaniel Butter began a *Newes* on 2nd August 1622, and in October 1622 commenced publishing with Nicholas Bourne and William Sheffard *A Coranto;* these were numbered serially.

CORDING QUIRES. *See* CASSIE.

CORDONNIER CARDS. *See* PEEK-A-BOO.

CORDOVAN LEATHER. Goatskin, originally tanned and dressed at Cordova, Spain. Used for MUDÉJAR BINDINGS (*q.v.*), and often dyed red. The English name is 'Cordwain.'

CORDS. Heavy strings to which the sections of large and heavy books are bound. Sometimes called BANDS (*q.v.*). *See also* TAPES.

CORDWAIN. *Synonymous with* CORDOVAN LEATHER (*q.v.*).

CORNER-MARKED CARD. A catalogue card bearing in the top right-hand corner information such as language, date of publication, editor, or translator, or a combination of these where there are many entries under the same heading. The purpose is to facilitate rapid perusal of a number of cards at one reading. Sometimes the original title of a translated work is written in the upper right-hand corner so that original and translations may be filed together.

CORNER MARKING. The original title of a translated work placed in the upper right-hand corner of a catalogue card so that the original and the translation will be filed together. A reference is required from the translation title to the original. Alternatively, translations may be entered on the same card as the original title, or in other words the original title may appear above the translation, a reference under the translation title being optional but desirable. In libraries, such as those of universities, where many books in translation are in stock, the supplying of original titles is a very expensive procedure.

CORNERPIECE. 1. (*Binding*) An ornament, usually arabesque, designed to be used at the corners of a bound book, usually to match a centre-piece or other decoration. Also used of metal corners attached to the binding. Also called 'Cornerstamp.' 2. (*Bibliography*) Interlacing bars, 'cusping,' or other separate ornament at the corner of a border around type, or lettering of an illuminated manuscript.

CORNERS. 1. The leather over the corners of a book in 'half' binding. *See also* LIBRARY CORNER, MITRED CORNER, SQUARE CORNER. 2. In printing, ornamental type metal connecting borders. 3. Pieces of metal or pasteboard to slip over the corners of a book to protect them in the post. Also called 'Cornerpieces.'

CORNERSTAMP. *Synonymous with* CORNERPIECE (*q.v.*).

CORPORATE AUTHOR. A corporate body such as a government or government department, a society (learned, social, etc.), or an institution which authorizes the publication of documents, and under the name of which, as the author, the documents will be entered in a catalogue. In certain kinds of corporate authorship, entries are made under the *place* followed by the *name* of the body.

CORPORATE BODY. An institution, organized body, or assembly of persons known by a corporate or collective name (*IFLA*).

CORPORATE ENTRY. A catalogue entry made under a government, government department, society or institution or other body, of a work issued by that body, or under its authority. It may be a main or an added entry.

CORPORATE NAME. The name by which a corporate body is known.

CORPORATION FILE. *See* COMPANY FILE.

CORRECTED EDITION.   A new edition of a book in which errors, etc., have been corrected.

CORRECTED PROOF.   A printer's proof on which errors in type-setting have been marked, using the generally accepted code of correction-marks. *See also* PROOF, PROOF CORRECTIONS.

CORRECTION MARKS.   The signs used on a printer's proof to mark errors in typesetting. These are set out in British Standard 1219: 1958 *Printers' and authors' proof corrections. See also* PROOF CORRECTIONS.

CORRELATION.   A systematic or reciprocal connexion – sometimes, the establishment of a mutual or reciprocal relation of or between (*IBM*).

CORRELATION OF PROPERTIES.   In classification the likeness between the various qualities which are common to all the things comprised by a genus.

CORRELATIVE INDEX.   An index enabling selection of documents or of references to them by correlation of words, numbers, or other symbols which are usually unrelated by hierarchic organization (*IBM*). *See also* CO-ORDINATE INDEXING.

CORRIGENDA. (*Sing.* CORRIGENDUM).   A printed list of corrections of errors which were noticed after matter was printed. It is usually printed on a slip and inserted among the PRELIMINARIES (*q.v.*) but sometimes a blank page is used. Also called 'Errata.' *See also* PASTE-IN.

CORRUPT A TEXT.   To tamper with a text by omission, addition, or alteration in order to convey a meaning which was not intended by the original author. This is sometimes done to standard or modern works for political propaganda.

CORYMBE.   A French system of information retrieval using continuous strips of 3 mm. film on which items of information are stored in the form of black on white images. There are identical images but white on black, and exact coincidence will cause a black-out and operate the selector.

COSTERIANA.   Fragments of books, having the appearance of early printing and asserted to have been printed before 1473, and consisting mostly of editions of the *Donatus*, or the *Doctrinale*. These were sup-posed to have been printed by Laurens Janszoon Coster of Haarlem (1405–84) who was thought at one time to have invented printing with movable types in or about 1440.

COTTAGE BINDING.   *Synonymous with* COTTAGE STYLE (*q.v.*).

COTTAGE STYLE.   A decorative binding in which the centre panel was often given a gable at head and foot, and the spaces filled with a variety of interlacings, sprays, and small 'tools.' Although this style may have originated in France, it is most characteristic of English bindings of the late seventeenth century to 1710. Also called 'Cottage binding.' *See also* MEARNE STYLE.

COTTON LINTERS. The short fibres adhering to the cotton seed after ginning (separating the seeds from the fibre), and also obtained as 'recovered' fibres from the cotton seed oil and cake factories. When purified it is used for paper-making. It can be used to replace 5-35 per cent of the rag content of fine papers without lessening the strength of the paper; it improves uniformity and the colour properties of the paper, and provides a cleaner, bulkier sheet. It is also used in the cheaper kinds of blotting paper used for interleaving diaries and account books.

COUCH ROLL. That part of a Fourdrinier paper making machine which removes some of the moisture from the sheet of paper during manufacture.

COUNCIL FOR MICROPHOTOGRAPHY AND DOCUMENT REPRODUCTION. *See* MICROFILM ASSOCIATION OF GREAT BRITAIN.

COUNCIL FOR SCIENTIFIC POLICY. Established in January 1965 'to advise the Secretary of State for Education and Science in the exercise of his responsibilities for the formulation and execution of government scientific policy.' It replaced the Advisory Council on Scientific Policy. Abbreviated CSP.

COUNCIL OF NATIONAL LIBRARY ASSOCIATIONS. Founded in 1942 'to promote a closer relationship among the national library associations of the United States and Canada by providing a central agency to foster co-operation in matters of mutual interest, by gathering and exchanging information among its member associations, and by co-operating with learned, professional and scientific societies in forwarding matters of common interest.' Abbreviated CNLA. *See also* Z-39.

COUNCIL OF PLANNING LIBRARIANS. Founded in the U.S.A. in 1960 by a group of planning librarians associated with schools of planning and planning agencies during the annual convention of the American Institute of Planners, to exchange information about professional practices in libraries with particular concern for those which are peculiar to planning libraries; to formulate and to administer projects which the Council decides are of service to the planning profession and librarianship; to advise on library organization for new planning programmes in institutions and agencies. Abbreviated CPL. Publishes *CPL Bibliographies* (irreg.), *CPL Newsletter*.

COUNCIL ON LIBRARY RESOURCES, INC. An independent,

non-profit making corporation which was established in September 1956 with the aid of a five million dollar grant from the Ford Foundation which also made a second grant of eight million dollars in January 1961. Its function is 'to assist in solving the problems of libraries generally and of research libraries in particular, conducting research in, developing and demonstrating new techniques and methods, and disseminating through any means the results thereof, and for making grants to other institutions and persons for such purposes; and for providing leadership in and wherever appropriate, co-ordination of efforts (1) to develop the resources and services of libraries and (2) to improve relations between American and foreign libraries and archives.' It assists through research, development and demonstration, in solving problems that are common to libraries generally rather than to provide assistance toward library activities which normally constitute local responsibilities. The council works principally through grants or contracts to qualified individuals or institutions. Abbreviated CLR.

COUNTER. 1. *Synonymous with* STAFF ENCLOSURE (*q.v.*). 2. (*Printing*) The interior 'white' of a letter; it may be entirely enclosed by a bowl as in 'O' or it may be the sunken part of the face as 'M' 'E' 'n'. The angular corner is known as the 'crotch'. The distance from the face to the bottom of the counter is known as the 'depth of counter'.

COUNTER DUTY. Duties performed in the counter or staff enclosure in a public department of a library.

COUNTERMARK. A smaller and subsidiary WATERMARK (*q.v.*) found in antique papers, usually in the centre, or lower centre of the second half of a sheet and opposite the watermark. Border or corner positions are not uncommon. It usually comprises the name or initials of the maker (in the U.K., and in later times, the mill number) and the date (first in 1545) and place of making, although small devices such as a small post-horn or cabalistic signs have been found.

COUNTERSUNK. A binding having a panel sunk or depressed below the normal level of the binding to take a label, inlay or decoration.

COUNTY BIBLIOGRAPHY. A bibliography of books and other forms of written record relating to a county.

COUNTY BOROUGH COUNCIL. The council of a local authority known as a 'county borough'. A county borough, like a county council, can provide all the services which are permitted to be provided by a local authority. *See also* BOROUGH COUNCIL, COUNTY COUNCIL, NON-COUNTY BOROUGH, Appendix 3.

COUNTY COUNCIL. A statutory LOCAL AUTHORITY (*q.v.*) with more powers than any other kind of authority except a County Borough: these are exercised within a county's geographical area. Public Libraries were provided in county areas by the County Education Authority under the Public Libraries Act, 1919, but under the Public Libraries and Museums Act, 1964, county councils are enabled to set up library committees directly responsible to the county council if they wish. Abbreviated CC. There were fifty-two administrative counties in England and Wales but Middlesex County Council and the London County Council disappeared with the formation of the Greater London Council on 1st April 1965. The London County Council has never been a library authority, as all the metropolitan borough councils in the area of the L.C.C. had provided public libraries by adopting the Public Library Acts prior to the Public Library Act, 1919, which first authorized county councils to provide public libraries.

COUNTY DISTRICT. A generic term, first used in the Local Government Act, 1933, to indicate an urban district, rural district, or non-county borough forming part of a geographical and administrative county, but having its own form of local government for certain purposes. A distinct local government area within the area of a county council.

COUNTY HEADQUARTERS. The administrative centre for a county library system. It usually has the main book reserve, operates a postal service direct to readers, provides offices for the senior administrative librarians, and may house a lending library. It is usually situated in the county town or the one where the administrative headquarters of the county council is.

COUNTY LIBRARIES GROUP. A Group of the Library Association; it exists to unite the interests of those working in county libraries of the UK, to provide for the expression of opinion and for liaison with the parent body. It was formed in 1927 as the County Libraries Section, the name being changed when the present constitution of the Library Association came into operation in 1963. Publishes *Readers' Guides* (a series of selective bibliographies) and *County Newsletter* (occasional, free to memb.).

COUNTY LIBRARY. A library provided (in England, Wales and Northern Ireland by resolution of the county council; in Scotland by the county education authority, in America according to state legislation), to supply the reading needs of people dwelling in rural areas who have no access to municipal collections. *See also* COUNTY COUNCIL. In America, a free public library service provided for county residents and financed from county tax funds; it may be administered as an independent agency or in co-operation with another library agency.

COUNTY RECORD OFFICE. A RECORD OFFICE (*q.v.*) which is required by law to be set up in England by every county council.

COUNTY REGIONAL BRANCH. A REGIONAL BRANCH (*q.v.*) in a county library system.

COUNTY SCHOOLS LIBRARY. An instructional materials library maintained in America by a county superintendent of schools who provides materials and services to contracting schools.

COURANTS. Dutch news publications, related but not numbered, known to have existed since the year 1607. *See also* CORANTO, NEWSBOOK.

COURT. A standard size for cards, $3\frac{1}{2} \times 4\frac{1}{2}$ inches; envelopes are $3\frac{3}{4} \times 4\frac{3}{4}$ inches.

COURT BARON. Court held by the Lord of a Manor in virtue of his right as a land holder, in which offences against the customs of the manor could be published but no punishments involving the life or limbs of the subject could be inflicted.

COURT HAND. 1. Style of writing used in legal and other public documents. Generally used of 'hands' from about 1100 to the end of the sixteenth century. 2. Sometimes used to mean legal hands of the same period only.

COURT LEET. Court of Record to punish all offences under High Treason, not incidental to a manor, but frequently held by a Lord of a Manor by virtue of a special grant.

COURT ROLL. A roll on which records of cases in private courts such as a Court Baron or Court Leet were kept.

COVENTRY AND DISTRICT INFORMATION GROUP. *See* CADIG.

COVER. 1. That which is placed securely on a sewn or stapled publication to protect it in use; it may be of paper or cloth, or board covered with paper, cloth or leather. The cover of a 'hard cover' book (as distinct from a 'paperback') is known as a 'case' or 'publisher's case'. 2. The outside sheet of a pamphlet, or the case of a book, used to protect the body of the work. 'Front cover,' and 'back cover' relate to the side pieces or outsides of the boards of the cover.

COVER DATE. The date which appears on the cover of a publication, usually a pamphlet. Should this be different to another inside the book, it may appear in the imprint part of a catalogue or bibliography entry as [*cover* 1965]. Where all the cataloguing data is on the cover, this procedure is unnecessary.

COVER INCLUDED IN PAGING. Where the cover is included in the pagination of a pamphlet the collation portion of the catalogue or bibliography entry may be in the form '28 pp (incl. cover)'.

COVER PAPER. A generic term usually indicative of a strong, coloured paper with good folding qualities suitable for brochure, booklet, pamphlet and price-list covers. Cover papers are available in a variety of embossings as well as plain. Sizes:

	inches
Cover Double Crown	$20\frac{1}{2} \times 30\frac{1}{2}$
Cover Medium	$18\frac{1}{2} \times 23\frac{1}{2}$
Cover Royal	$20\frac{1}{2} \times 25\frac{1}{2}$
Double Crown	20×30
Double Medium	23×36
Double Royal	25×40
Imperial	22×30
Quad Crown	30×40

COVER POCKET. *Synonymous with* POCKET (*q.v.*).

COVER TITLE. The title of a book placed on a publisher's case, or as distinguished from that printed on the title-page. Not to be confused with the BINDER'S TITLE (*q.v.*). *See also* BACK TITLE.

COVER TO COVER TRANSLATION. A serial publication which contains in each issue a translation of the whole, or a major part, of an issue of a serial publication in another language.

COVERS BOUND IN. The original covers of a publication bound in, or to be bound in, when a book is re-bound.

CRABS. Books returned to a publisher by a bookseller because he had been unable to sell them. Also called 'Returns'.

CRACKLE. *See* RATTLE.

CRADLE BOOKS. *See* INCUNABULA.

CRAM. Abbreviation for Card Random Access Mechanism, a unitized magnetic card system developed by the National Cash Register Company for recording and retrieving data. Data are recorded on cards 14 inches long by $3\frac{1}{4}$ inches wide, there being fifty-six parallel channels divided into seven sets of eight channels. The total capacity of each card is 160,000 bits (at 250 to the inch).

CRANFIELD CLASSIFICATION FOR AERONAUTICS AND ALLIED SUBJECTS. A scheme devised by B. C. Vickery and J. E. L. Farradane to provide a faceted classification for the materials in the library of the College of Aeronautics at Cranfield.

CRANFIELD PROJECT.   *See* Aslib Cranfield Research Project.

CRASH.   *Synonymous with* MULL (*q.v.*).

CRASH FINISH.   A cover paper which is similar to LINEN FINISH (*q.v.*) but has a coarser texture.

CRAYON DRAWING.   A drawing made with a soft, black crayon, usually for strong or impressionistic effects. It is suitable for illustrations, portraits, etc., and may be reproduced by half-tone.

CRAYON ENGRAVING.   A similar process to STIPPLE (*q.v.*) but aiming to produce the effect of a chalk drawing. Various specially grained roulettes, etching needles, and a *mattoir* (a form of miniature cudgel) are used through the etching ground to prepare the printing plate for biting with acid. The graver and roulette may be used afterwards directly on the surface of the plate. Stipple and crayon processes are sometimes used together in portrait work, stipple being used for the face and crayon for the body and clothing. Also called 'Chalk engraving'.

CREASING.   1. A linear indentation made by machine in a card or thick paper. By compressing the fibres it provides a hinge and increases the number of times the paper can be flexed at the crease before breaking. *See also* SCORING. 2. A printing fault, seen as deep creases; it may result from storing the paper at an incorrect humidity, or from other causes.

CREDIT LINE.   A statement giving the name of an artist, photographer, author, agency, or owner of an original or of copyright, and printed under a photograph, drawing, article or quotation which is reproduced or published.

CRESTING ROLL.   A ROLL (*q.v.*) which has, on one side of the design, a series of crests or tufts, the other side being approximately straight. *See also* HERALDIC CRESTING.

CRIBLÉ INITIAL.   A decorated initial used at the beginning of a chapter, specially by the sixteenth-century French printer Geoffrey Tory, in which the capital appears on an all-over ground of small dots, or sieve-like pattern.

CRIBLÉ METAL CUT.   A soft metal used late in the fifteenth century for block printing instead of wood, the metal being punched with holes (criblé) to relieve the black mass. *See also* MANIÈRE CRIBLÉE.

CRIS.   Abbreviation for Command Retrieval Information System. Trade name of the Information Retrieval Corporation for their mechanized storage and retrieval device which uses a scroll of microfilm as the information storage medium.

CRITICAL ANNOTATION.   *Synonymous with* EVALUATION (*q.v.*).

CRITICAL APPARATUS. *Synonymous with* APPARATUS CRITICUS (*q.v.*).

CRITICAL BIBLIOGRAPHY. 1. The comparative and historical study of the make-up of books (*Besterman*). 2. The science of the material transmission of literary texts (*Greg.*). Also called 'Analytical' or 'Historical' bibliography. *See also* BIBLIOGRAPHY.

CRITICAL CLASSIFICATION. The exercise of the classifier's personal opinion when classifying a book; if care is not taken to avoid bias or prejudice, this may result in wrong placing.

CRITICAL EDITION. A scholarly text of a work, established by an editor after original research, and the comparison of manuscripts, documents, letters and earlier texts. This editorial work is considerable, especially in textual criticism. The edition is characterized by the APPARATUS CRITICUS (*q.v.*) included. *See also* STANDARD EDITION, VARIORUM EDITION, DEFINITIVE EDITION.

CRITICISM NUMBER. *See* ASSOCIATED BOOK.

CROCKETED CRESTING. (*Binding*) A frame formed by roughly rectangular stamps ornamented with crockets (small curved designs) or with roughly triangular stamps, which, placed together and pointing outwards, give a cresting effect.

CROPPED. 1. In bookbinding, a term applied to a book when too much of its margin, especially the head-margin, has been trimmed off. *See also* BLED, CUT, SHAVED, TRIMMED, UNCUT. 2. A photograph of which a part of the top, bottom or sides is omitted from its reproduction, in order to bring it into proper proportions for the space it is to occupy.

CROPPER. A small printing machine working on the platen principle; so named after the English manufacturer H. S. Cropper & Co. who produced the 'Minerva' machine in 1867; this was similar to the 'Franklin Press' manufactured by George Phineas Gordon, a small master printer of New York.

CROSS. Abbreviation for Computerized Rearrangements Of Special Subjects; one of four computer-composed indexes included in each fortnightly issue of *Biological Abstracts* (*See* BIOSIS). It co-ordinates all abstracts pertinent to each of 503 major and subordinate subject headings used in arranging abstracts included in each issue of *BA*, the numbers of relevant abstracts being placed under each in ten columns as determined by the last figure of the abstract number.

CROSS-BARS. Metal bars used to divide a CHASE (*q.v.*) into sections of equal size, each of which contains the same number of pages. They enable the pages to be locked up more securely, and also make corrections in one section easier while not disturbing the others.

CROSS CLASSIFICATION.   1. The action of dividing when forming a scheme of classification by more than one characteristic in a single process of division, leading to confusion of ideas and terms and resulting in the parts having no real relationship to one another, and in placing related subjects in different divisions. 2. A TABULAR CLASSIFICATION (*q.v.*), or one that is reducible to tabular form, in which the classes or sub-classes of each series are crossed by the terms of a secondary series of specifications, so that the resulting sub-classes have the specifications of both series and are therefore common to both (*Bliss*).

CROSS DIRECTION.   Said of paper which is cut across, that is, cut at right angles to the direction in which the web of a paper machine moves. The cross direction of the paper is much weaker, and expands more, than in the direction parallel to the flow of the pulp on the machine. *See also* AGAINST THE GRAIN, GRAIN DIRECTION, WITH THE GRAIN.

CROSS DIVISION.   *Synonymous with* CROSS CLASSIFICATION (*q.v.*).

CROSS HATCHING.   (*Binding*) Two sets of parallel lines executed in opposite directions so that the lines cross.

CROSS-HEAD.   A short descriptive heading placed in the centre of a type line to divide the sections of a work, or the chapters of a book. Cross-heads are separated from the text by one or more lines of space, and normally indicate primary sub-divisions of a chapter. Subsequent sub-divisions are: shoulder-heads and side-heads. *See also* HEADING 4, SHOULDER-HEAD, SIDE-HEAD.

CROSS-INDEX.   To make an index entry under several headings, where appropriate, for the same item.

CROSS REFERENCE CARD.   The catalogue card on which a cross reference is entered.

CROSS REFERENCE, GENERAL.   *See* GENERAL REFERENCE.

CROSS REFERENCE SHEET.   A record on a pro forma sheet recording the filing of related material in other files. It may refer to (a) a specific publication, (b) part of a publication, (c) specific facts in a given publication.

CROSS REFERENCES.   In indexing and cataloguing, references or directions from one heading to another. 1. *Single* (*see* ——). An instruction to look elsewhere for *all* items relating to the subject matter which is sought. 2. *Reciprocal* (*see also* ——). An instruction to look elsewhere for *other* items relating to the subject matter sought. 3. *Multiple* (*see also* ——). An instruction to refer to several other places, usually to more specific entries. *See also* GENERAL REFERENCE.

CROTCH. (*Printing*) The angular corner of the COUNTER (*q.v.*) of a type letter.

CROWN. A sheet of printing paper measuring 15 × 20 inches.

CROWN OCTAVO. A book size, 7½ × 5 inches. *See also* BOOK SIZES.

CROWN QUARTO. A book size, 10 × 7½ inches. *See also* BOOK SIZES.

CROWTHER REPORT. 15 *to* 18: *a Report of the Central Advisory Council for Education* (*England*), 1959. Known as the Crowther Report after the Chairman Sir Geoffrey Crowther. The report deals with the educational needs of young people between the ages of 15 and 18 and was the result of a comprehensive study of those needs since March 1956.

CRUSHED LEVANT. A large-grained LEVANT (*q.v.*) leather binding with a smooth, polished surface, caused by crushing down the natural grain.

CRUSHED MOROCCO. Morocco, the grain of which has been smoothed by hand. *See also* GLAZED MOROCCO.

CRYPTOGRAPHY. Writing in cipher.

CRYPTONYM. A secret name.

CRYPTONYMOUS BOOK. One in which the name of the author is concealed under an anagram or similar device, e.g. Mesrat Merligogels (Master George Mills).

CUBE UNIT BUILDING. *See* MODULAR CONSTRUCTION.

CUBOOK. The volume of space required to shelve books of average size and allowing for vacant space 10 per cent of each shelf. A tier 3 feet wide by 7 feet 6 inches high (seven shelves) contains 100 cubooks. For a full treatment, see the *Library Journal* 59: 865–8, Nov. 15, 1934; 61: 52–4, Jan. 15, 1936.

CUE SYSTEM. A system, proposed to be used in bibliography and indexing, consisting of alphabetical codes placed above an entry to indicate the chronological, topical, and geographic aspects of the article referred to.

CUIR BOUILLI. Book decoration in which the leather cover is soaked in hot water, modelled and hammered to raise the design in relief; it sets very hard, and in the ninth century it was found to be so hard that boards were unnecessary.

CUIR-CISELÉ BINDING. A binding with a design cut into dampened leather instead of being stamped or tooled on it. A relief effect was then obtained by punching the leather around the design. Hammering from the back gave an embossed effect. A widely-practised method in fifteenth-century Germany.

CUL DE LAMPE. A form of decorative printing practised in the sixteenth century which used arabesque title-borders and tail-pieces

7

strongly suggestive of metal lantern-supports. A tail-piece. J. B. M. Papillon (1698–1776), the most distinguished member of a family of French wood-engravers, was renowend for the delicacy in his minute floral head- and tail-pieces (culs-de-lampe), which decorate many mid-eighteenth-century French books.

CUM LICENTIA.   *Synonymous with* CUM PRIVILEGIO (*q.v.*).

CUM PRIVILEGIO.   (*Lat.* 'with permission'). Printed by authority, either secular or ecclesiastical. Sole authority for printing.

CUMDACH.   A rectangular box (usually of bronze, brass or wood, and plated with ornamented silver or gold), which was made for the preservation of precious books. Also called 'Book shrine'.

CUMULATED BOOK CATALOGUE.   A compromise between the card and the book (printed) catalogue. Linotype slugs are preserved by the printer after a printing and subsequent entries are interpolated as necessary.

CUMULATED VOLUME.   A publication consisting of entries for a bibliography, catalogue, index, etc., which have previously appeared in periodically published parts, and re-assembled into one sequence.

CUMULATION.   The progressive inter-filing of items arranged in a predetermined order and usually published in periodical form, the same order of arrangement being maintained.

CUMULATIVE INDEX.   One which is built up from time to time by combining separately published indexes into one sequence.

CUMULATIVE LIST.   A list of books published separately and afterwards incorporated in other similar lists which in their turn may have been compiled in the same way.

CUNEIFORM WRITING.   Wedge-shaped letters in which Old Persian and Babylonian inscriptions were written, so termed from their wedge-like appearance and made by pressing the end of a stick or reed into the soft clay of the tablet at an angle and continuing the stroke in a straight line with constantly diminishing pressure.

CURATOR.   The superintendent of a museum, art gallery, etc.

CURATORS.   Name given to boards of people responsible for managing the various institutions of Oxford University. The Curators of the Bodleian Library, for example, number eighteen, namely, the Vice-Chancellor, the Proctors or their deputies, seven members of Congregation elected by that House, six professors elected by the professors of the various faculties, and two members of Congregation elected by Council, one of whom must be a Curator of the Chest; these are elected to serve for ten years, and are entrusted with the general control of the affairs of the library, including the appointment of a librarian, and of other officers, subject to the approval of Convocation, and are responsible for the expenditure of all sums accruing to them through the University Chest or otherwise.

CURIA REGIS. Under feudal organization a court of justice, or administration was called a 'curia'; Curia Regis was the Court of the Norman Kings of England.

CURIOSA. Term used in describing books of curious and unusual subject matter. Sometimes used euphemistically as a classification for *erotica*.

CURL. A deformation of a sheet of paper or board over its whole surface so that it tends to roll up into the form of a cylinder.

CURRENT AWARENESS JOURNAL. A periodical consisting of reproductions in facsimile of contents tables of many individual journals.

CURRENT BIBLIOGRAPHY. A list of books which is compiled at the same time as the books are published. It is usually published as a periodical. Sometimes called 'Open bibliography'.

CURRENT COMPLETE NATIONAL BIBLIOGRAPHY. A complete list of published or issued records of a nation; such a list can be complete only to a specified date. A current national bibliography is a listing of publications compiled at the time of publication and falling within the definition of a NATIONAL BIBLIOGRAPHY (*q.v.*).

CURRENT COMPREHENSIVE BIBLIOGRAPHY. The technique of making available, through current bibliographical services, informative lists of the totality of publications in particular catagories defined solely by (a) recency of publication; (b) type of issuing agency; (c) the geographical area or political jurisdiction within which they were produced; but not by their contents (e.g. literary form or subject-content) or distribution (e.g. location of copies). *See also* CURRENT SELECTIVE BIBLIOGRAPHY.

CURRENT NUMBER. The last-issued number of a newspaper or serial publication and bearing the most recent issue number and/or date. Also called 'Current issue'.

CURRENT PUBLICATION SURVEY. *See* LITERATURE SURVEY 2.

CURRENT SELECTIVE BIBLIOGRAPHY. The technique of making available, through current bibliographical services, informative lists of publications in particular catagories defined by (a) recency of publication, (b) some one or more characteristics of the publications. The usual characteristics are content (e.g. literary form, subject), distribution (e.g. location of copies), and value. *See also* CURRENT COMPREHENSIVE BIBLIOGRAPHY, SELECT BIBLIOGRAPHY.

CURRENTLY RECEIVED. Periodicals which are received on publication.

CURRICULUM MATERIALS CENTER. A centre, usually located in an American school central administration building, in which are kept professional books, current and back numbers of teaching professional periodicals, microfilms, recordings, supplementary textbooks, art prints mounted on cardboard, pamphlets, fabrics, filmstrips, models, and possibly high school and elementary school books (which may be borrowed for the children). The materials are issued to teachers only. The ALA *Standards* recommends that any district having over 10,000 students should have such a centre. Also called a 'District Materials Center'. *See also* INSTRUCTIONAL MATERIALS CENTER.

CURSIVE. 1. Running writing, letters within words being joined. 2. Sometimes used to differentiate smaller 'hands' from uncial. 3. A class of type face which is based on handwriting. It may be ITALIC (*q.v.*) in which there is a version of almost every named type face or script which is drawn to look as though handwritten. Kaufman Script, Trafton Script and Typo Script are names of script type faces. *See also* TYPE FACE.

CURVES. ( ) Signs used to denote inserted explanatory or qualifying words, phrases, clauses or remarks. To be distinguished from BRACKETS (*q.v.*). Also called 'Round brackets' and PARENTHESES (*q.v.*). *See also* BRACKETS, CIRCULAR BRACKETS.

CUSTODIAN. A person in charge of a special collection or of a building in which exhibits are displayed.

CUSTOM-BOUND. (*Binding*) A book which is bound to specific instructions, not in accordance with general instructions.

CUT. (*Noun*) 1. A design cut or engraved on wood, copper, or steel from which a print is made. 2. The impression from such a printing block. 3. An engraving, or plate, printed on the text page. 4. (*Verb*) To trim the edges of a book. 5. (*Adjective*) Of a book having cut edges. *See also* CUT EDGES, OPENED, PLATE.

CUT CORNER PAMPHLET FILE. A free-standing box file which has the upper back corners of the sides cut away to half the height of the box; the upper half of the back as well as the top are unenclosed. Such boxes are used for containing pamphlets on the shelves. *See also* PRINCETON FILE.

CUT DUMMY. Complete proofs of the illustrations of a book, arranged in proper sequence and containing the figure and galley numbers.

CUT EDGES. (*Binding*) The top, fore, and tail edges of a book cut solid by a guillotine. When gilt they are known as 'gilt edges'. *See also* EDGES.

CUT FLUSH.   A book having its cover and edges quite even, the cutting operation having been done after the cover (usually paperboards or limp cloth) had been attached to the book. Also called 'Stiffened and cut flush.' A book so made is described as with 'flush boards.'

CUT IN-BOARDS.   A book which has had the head, tail and fore-edge trimmed after the boards have been secured. *See also* CUT OUT-OF-BOARDS.

CUT-IN HEADING.   A paragraph or section heading set in a bold or otherwise distinguishing type in a space made available against the outer margin but within the normal type area. Also called 'Incut heading'. *See also* INCUT NOTE.

CUT-IN INDEX.   *Synonymous with* THUMB INDEX (*q.v.*).

CUT-IN LETTER.   One of a large size, and occupying the depth of two or more lines of type as at the beginning of a chapter or paragraph. *See also* COCK-UP INITIAL, DROP LETTER.

CUT-IN NOTE.   *Synonymous with* INCUT NOTE (*q.v.*).

CUT-IN SIDE NOTE.   *Synonymous with* INCUT NOTE (*q.v.*).

CUT LINE.   Matter appearing below an illustration. More often called a 'Caption'.

CUT-OUT HALF-TONE.   *See* HALF-TONE.

CUT OUT-OF-BOARDS.   A book which has had its edges cut or trimmed before the boards are affixed. This method is used for books with a hollow back, the boards of which are not laced on but fit closely in the grooves. *See also* CUT IN-BOARDS, LACING-IN.

CUT TO REGISTER.   Watermarked paper which has been so cut that the watermark appears in the same position in each sheet.

CUTTER AUTHOR MARKS.   A system of author marks devised by Mr. C. A. Cutter, and consisting of from one to three letters at the beginning of an author's name, followed by numbers which increase as the names proceed along the alphabet. Author's names beginning with a consonant other than S have one letter, with S or a vowel have two letters, and Sc have three letters, followed in each case by a number, e.g.:

Ab2	Abbot	G42	Gilman	Sal	Saint
A12	Aldridge	Sch51	Schneider	Swl	Swain
G16	Gardiner	Sch86	Schwarts		

Their purpose is to enable books to be arranged alphabetically by using a relatively brief symbol. *See also* BOOK NUMBER, CUTTER-SANBORN THREE-FIGURE TABLE.

CUTTER CLASSIFICATION. *See* EXPANSIVE CLASSIFICATION.

CUTTER NUMBERS. *See* CUTTER AUTHOR MARKS.

CUTTER-SANBORN THREE-FIGURE TABLE. An extension of the Cutter Author Marks for individualizing authors by using a combination of letters and three numbers (two for J, K, Y, Z, E, I, U, O; one for Q and X) in numerical order.
For example:

Rol 744	Roli 748	Roman 758
Role 745	Roll 749	Romani 759
Rolf 746	Rolle 751	
Rolfe 747	Rollo 755	

CUTTING. A piece cut from a newspaper or periodical. Also called 'Clipping' (American), 'Press cutting'.

CUTTINGS BUREAU. *See* CLIPPING BUREAU.

CUTTINGS FILE. *Synonymous with* CLIPPINGS FILE (*q.v.*).

CYANOGRAPHY. A blue-printing method of copying on only one side of the paper drawings and documents which do not include half-tone prints; the process is based on iron compounds and produces copies with white lines on a blue ground.

CYBERNETICS. The science of control and communication processes in animals and machines.

CYCLIC CLASSIFIED CATALOGUE. *See* ROTATED CATALOGUE.

CYCLIC INDEX. *Synonymous with* ROTATED INDEX (*q.v.*).

CYCLOPAEDIA. *Synonymous with* ENCYCLOPAEDIA (*q.v.*).

CYLINDER DRIED. Paper which has been dried on the paper-making machine by being passed over steam-heated cylinders, as distinct from other methods of drying. Also called 'Machine-dried'.

CYLINDER PRESS. A printing press which makes the impression by a cylinder as opposed to a platen. It has a revolving impression cylinder under which is a flat bed containing the type or plates which moves backwards and forwards. These presses can be of two types; the Wharfedale or stop-cylinder press in which for every sheet printed, the cylinder makes almost one complete revolution and stops while the bed returns, an opening in the cylinder allowing the bed to return freely, and the Miehle or two-revolution press in which a smaller and continuously revolving cylinder revolves once to print one sheet then rises and revolves once more while the type bed slides back into position. This type of machine is the best letterpress machine for colour-printing and book-work. *See also* FLAT-BED PRESS, PLATEN PRESS, ROTARY PRESS.

d.c.   Abbreviation for a page of printed matter set in Double Column; Double Crown (paper 20 × 30 inches); Double Cap (i.e. double foolscap) printing paper, 17 × 27 inches.

D-LIBRARY.   A 'duplicating library', which processes and stores photo-reduced copies of books and other documents which are not lent for use outside the library. The objects are to save space in storing multiple copies, avoid loss through wear, mutilation, and theft, and avoid costs of, and wasted effort recording and discharging loans and binding books. *See also* C-LIBRARY.

D.M.C.   District Materials Center. *See* CURRICULUM MATERIALS CENTER.

D.S. (document signed).   A document of which only the signature is autographic.

d.w.   Abbreviation for dust wrapper. *See* BOOK JACKET.

DAGGER (†).   The second reference mark in footnotes, coming after the asterisk. When placed before an English, or after a German, person's name, it signifies 'dead' or 'died'. *See also* REFERENCE MARKS.

DAGUERREOTYPE.   A means of making a photographic image on a copper plate coated with a light-sensitive layer of silver. The process was invented by Louis Jacques Mandé Daguerre (1789–1851) in 1833 following the death of J. N. Niepce, with whom he had been in partnership, but not made public until 1839. The earliest daguerreotypes are unique in that they cannot be copied, but the process was superseded in the 1850s by a negative positive process by which an unlimited number of copies may be made. The process is considered to be the first really practicable photographic method. Daguerre was a French scene-painter who became well known as a result of the diarama he built in Paris in 1822; after 1826 he devoted himself to developing photographic processes.

DAILY.   A serial publication issued every day, except perhaps on Sunday.

DAMAGED LETTER.   A piece of type, the printing surface of which has been damaged. When appearing in a printer's proof it is marked by a X in the margin. Also called 'Bad letter', 'Battered letter', 'Broken letter', 'Spoiled letter'.

DAMPERS.   The damping rollers which are an important part of lithographic printing presses; they damp the printing plate after each impression with a fluid, known as a damping mixture, the composition of which varies according to the material used for the forme (stone, zinc, steel, aluminium, etc.), in order to prevent the ink adhering to the plate, which it would do if the plate became too dry. In a hand-press damping is done with a sponge.

DANDY ROLL. A cylinder of wire gauze which presses upon the drained but still moist pulp just before it leaves the wire cloth of the paper-making machine for the rollers. The weaving of the wire of the dandy roll leaves its impression on the paper and determines whether it is to be wove paper (with the impression of fine, even gauze) or laid paper (with the impression of parallel lines). When devices or monograms are worked into the fine wire of the roll, 'watermarks' are produced.

DANIEL PRESS. A private printing press established by the Rev. C. H. O. Daniel at Frome in 1846, revived at Worcester College, Oxford, in 1874 and used until he died in 1919 for the private publication of family verses as well as small pamphlets and books. In 1877 he discovered the punches, matrices and types which had been used by Dr. Fell at the University Press between 1667–74 and used them at his press. *See also* FELL TYPES.

DANSK CENTRAL FÖR DOKUMENTATION. (Danish Centre for Documentation.) Exists to give advice on the use of the Universal Decimal Classification and on the organization of special libraries.

DASH. A short strip of rule cast in the following lengths, and used for punctuation: the two-em dash——; the one-em dash—; the en rule –; and the hyphen - . These may be used for decoration or for the clearer laying out of printed matter, but usually longer rules or ornamental rules are more often used for these purposes. *See also* BORDER, FRENCH RULE, RULE, SWELLED RULE, SWUNG DASH.

DASH ENTRY. Said of an entry for a book – following one or two long dashes (one for the author, the second for the title) – which continues, indexes, or supplements a monograph. Such an entry follows the entry for the main work.

DATA. (*Information retrieval*) A general term for information. It is used to distinguish input and output information from instructions, and also to indicate the absence, or presence, of a certain condition, such as a magnetic field.

DATA COMPILATION. The regular and systematic recording on standard-size cards or record sheets, of facts as they are discovered in a variety of miscellaneous publications.

DATA PROCESSING. Recording information by some means whereby it (or only some of that stored on the same record) may be obtained immediately by some mechanical or semi-mechanical process. There are two basic modes of data processing: conventional and inverted. In the conventional mode, an 'item record' (which may be a punched card, section of a magnetic tape or magnetic disc) bears a number of codes representing characteristics describing the 'item of information' which may be a document, test, sale or employee. In the inverted data processing mode the process is reversed, 'items of information' being stored on records reserved for recognized characteristics.

DATA STORAGE AND RETRIEVAL SYSTEM. One which stores items for later re-use rather than modification, and which usually maintains the file items unaltered.

DATE. The statement in a book, either at the foot of the title-page, or on the reverse thereof, of the year in which the book was published. *See also* COLOPHON, COPYRIGHT DATE, DEDICATION DATE, FALSE DATE, IMPRINT DATE, MAINZ PSALTER.

DATE CARD. *See* DATE LABEL.

DATE DUE. The date on which a book is due for return to a library.

DATE GUIDE. A guide bearing numerals representing the dates on which books are due for return and placed in front of the appropriate charges in the issue trays.

DATE LABEL. The label placed in a lending library book and dated to indicate when it is due for return. In a few libraries dates of issue are used instead. Also called in America a 'Date slip' or 'Dating slip'. Sometimes a loose card, called a 'Date card' is used. *See also* TRANS-ACTION CARD.

DATE LINE. The line in any paper or magazine on which the date of issue appears.

DATE OF ISSUE. The date on which a book was issued.

DATE OF PUBLICATION. 1. The year in which a book was published. It is usually printed at the foot of, or on the back of, the title-page. In old books a date often formed part of the colophon. 2. The day and/or month and year of publication in the case of a newspaper or other periodical.

DATE SLIP (DATING SLIP). The American name for a DATE LABEL (*q.v.*).

DATE STAMP. 1. The date a library book is due for return (or of issue) which is stamped on a transaction card or date label. 2. The machine or dater used to make the impression.

DAY OF PUBLICATION. *See* PUBLICATION DAY.

DE LUXE BINDING. A fine leather binding, lettered and tooled by hand. So-called de luxe bindings are often machine products.

DE LUXE EDITION. An edition of a book in which especially good materials and fine workmanship have been used.

DE VINNE. A type face cut for Theodore Low De Vinne, 1828–1914, a distinguished American printer. He was a co-founder with

7*

Robert Hoe in 1884 of the Grolier Club and printed its first publication, a reprint of the *Star Chamber Decree*, 1637. He encouraged New York printing house owners to form a union which, when combined with similar groups from other cities, became known in 1887 as the United Typothetae.

DEAD FILE. In acquisition work, a file containing (1) cards for books received and catalogued, (2) cards for books not available as gifts or by purchase despite considerable correspondence, (3) completed or filled cards for serial publications.

DEAD MATTER. Type which has been set up and is waiting to be distributed. *See also* GOOD, KILLING, LIVE MATTER, MATTER.

DECALCOMANIA. 1. A transfer or design printed on special paper for transfer to pottery or some other permanent base. 2. The paper for printing such transfers on. 3. The process of printing illustrations on glass, wood, pottery, etc. Abbreviated DECAL.

DECET. 1. A combination of ten singers or musicians. 2. The music for same.

DECIMAL CLASSIFICATION. There have been several schemes which have employed decimals in some way but the one usually referred to by this name is that compiled by Melvil Dewey and published in 1876, in which it is the notation that is used decimally. In this scheme it is possible to extend the printed scheme at any point to any desired extent. It divides knowledge into ten main classes and is the most used classification for general libraries. Abbreviated DC. Since 1951 the revision of the schedules has been undertaken within the Library of Congress Library. Some major changes were made in the sevententh edition. There were some relocations and re-casting of schedules; form divisions were retitled 'standard sub-divisions' in recognition of the fact that many are modes of treatment rather than forms. The index is new in concept and execution. The scheme is kept up to date between editions by means of the bulletin issued by the revisers under the title *Decimal classification: additions, notes and decisions* (free to users from LC). The Dewey numbers have been printed on LC catalogue cards since April 1930; they also appear on the cards supplied by the H. W. Wilson Company. *See also* ABRIDGED DECIMAL CLASSIFICATION, DEWEY DECIMAL CLASSIFICATION, UNIVERSAL DECIMAL CLASSIFICATION.

DECIMAL DIVISION. The expansion of a portion of a classification schedule and giving the resulting terms a numerical notation on the decimal principle.

DECIMAL NOTATION. A notation used to identify subjects in a

scheme of classification; it consists of numerals used decimally so as to permit the logical subdivision of subjects, or a chain of classes, indefinitely. The notation of the Dewey Classification is of this kind. *See also* NOTATION.

DECIMAL NUMBER. The number of a book, or of a term, in a classification schedule, which is determined by the decimal principle. This method is used in both the Dewey Classification and the Universal Decimal Classification.

DECIMO-OCTAVO. *Synonymous with* Octodecimo, EIGHTEENMO (*q.v.*)

DECIMO-SEXTO. *Synonymous with* SEXTO-DECIMO.

DECK. 1. One floor of a stack containing book shelves, lifts, and workrooms (American). 2. The American term for a collection of cards, commonly a complete set of cards, which have been punched for a definite service (*IBM*). Often called in Britain a 'Pack'.

DECKLE. 1. Abbreviation for DECKLE EDGE (*q.v.*), and for deckle strap. 2. The frame or border, usually of wood, which confines the paper pulp to the mould when making paper by hand. 3. In the papermaking machine, the distance between the two deckle straps.

DECKLE EDGE. The feathery edge at the borders of a sheet of handmade or mould-made paper; it is caused by the deckle or frame which confines the paper pulp to the mould. It is also found in machine-made papers, being caused in these by the rubber deckle straps at the sides of the paper machine, or by artificial means such as a jet of water. Also called 'Feather-edge'.

DECKLE STRAPS. Endless rubber bands which run on both sides of the wire cloth of a paper-making machine in order to keep the wet pulp within the desired limits of width. Also called 'Boundary straps'.

DECKLET. A set of cards forming a single record (*IBM*).

DECODER. In information retrieval, the locator which searches and extracts items from the DOCUMENT STORE (*q.v.*).

DECORATED COVER. The front cover of a book which bears distinctive lettering or an illustration or design.

DECORATIVE. A class of type faces which have exaggerated characteristics of the other three classes, ABSTRACT, CURSIVE and ROMAN (*qq.v.*), or distinctive features which preclude them from being included in those classes. They are usually fussily ornamental, but included in this group is OLD ENGLISH (*q.v.*).

DECREASING CONCRETENESS, PRINCIPLE OF. A general principle for choosing an order of application of the characteristics of a classification. Ranganathan has developed a general facet formula which reflects this principle and is popularly known by the abbreviation

PMEST standing for the five 'fundamental categories' Personality, Matter, Energy, Space and Time.

DEDICATION.   The author's inscription to a person or persons testifying respect, and often recommending the work to his (or their) special protection and favour, it usually appears on the recto of the leaf following the title-page. In sixteenth- and seventeenth-century books the dedication often took the form of a dedicatory letter written by the author to his patron.

DEDICATION COPY.   A copy of a book presented by the author, and so inscribed, to the person to whom the work is dedicated.

DEDICATION DATE.   The date given at the beginning or end of a dedication.

DEDICATORY LETTER.   *See* DEDICATION.

DEEP-ETCHED HALF-TONE.   *See* HALF-TONE.

DEEP ETCHING.   In photo-engraving, additional etching made necessary to secure proper printing depth where this cannot be accomplished by routing, as in places where dense black lines are used, or where line negatives and half-tone negatives are combined in the same place (*United Typothetae*). *See also* ETCHING.

DEFAULTER.   A reader who fails to return a book or pay a fine. Such people are usually black-listed.

DEFENSE DOCUMENTATION CENTER.   The U.S.A. centre which was commenced in 1960 as ASTIA, the name being changed in 1963. Abbreviated DDC.

DEFINITION.   (*Classification*) Concise description in distinct terms for essentials and characteristics (*Bliss*).

DEFINITIVE EDITION.   The final authoritative text of the complete works of an author – the nearest possible approach to what the author intended – edited usually after the author's death. It is characterized by its editorial introduction, notes and sometimes APPARATUS CRITICUS (*q.v.*). Not to be confused with a VARIORUM EDITION (*q.v.*). Applies also to the works of a composer of music.

DEGRESSIVE DESCRIPTION.   *Synonymous with* SELECTIVE CATALOGUING (*q.v.*).

del, delt.   Abbreviation for delineavit (*Lat.*). Used on engravings, maps, etc. to indicate the name of the artist or cartographer responsible for the original drawings.

DELAYED DISCHARGING.   Delaying the cancellation of a loan until after the reader returning a book has entered the library to choose another book. This is done as a normal part of the routine in some libraries, but in others discharging is only delayed during very busy periods, it being the usual practice to discharge books immediately they are returned. *See also* CHEQUE BOOK CHARGING METHOD, DISCHARGING BOOKS, ISLINGTON CHARGING SYSTEM, TRANSACTION CARD CHARGING.

dele. *See* DELETE.

deleatur (*Lat.* 'delete'). *See* DELETE.

DELEGATION OF POWERS. The handing over by a local authority, with or without restrictions, to the library committee, of all powers relating to the management of the library, except the power of levying, or issuing a precept for, a rate, or of borrowing money.

DELETE. To blot out, to erase, to omit. A mark, like the Greek letter δ, used in correcting proofs, is put in the margin to show that certain letters or words crossed through are to be deleted. Often abbreviated 'del', 'dele', or δ (representing the lower case initial letter of the Latin 'deleatur', delete).

DELETION MARK. The mark used in correcting a proof to indicate matter to be omitted. Also called 'Cancellation mark'. *See also* DELETE.

DELIQUESCENCE. Tendency to absorb atmospheric moisture (*Verry*).

DELIVERY DESK. *Synonymous with* CIRCULATION DESK (*q.v.*).

DELIVERY HALL. The centrally-placed focal point in a library where books may be issued and returned, and where the catalogue may be consulted.

DELIVERY ROOM. In American libraries, the room in which books are returned and issued.

DELIVERY STATION. A library service point at which no books are shelved but to which books requested by readers are sent to await collection.

DELIVERY VAN (*County Libraries*). A vehicle intended and adapted primarily for the transport of books in boxes or trays, and providing no facilities for the selection of books. Some delivery vans are designed to be used on occasion as DISPLAY VANS (*q.v.*), but this term is not now included in the County Libraries Section's list of definitions.

DEMCO SELF-CHARGING SYSTEM. A simplification of the NEWARK CHARGING SYSTEM (*q.v.*) in which reader's tickets are not used. The borrower enters his ticket number on the next vacant line of the book card; this is checked by the assistant who stamps the date label.

DEMONYM. A popular or ordinary qualification used as a pseudonym, as 'An Amateur', 'A Bibliophile'.

DEMOPLETH MAP. A type of CHOROPLETH MAP (*q.v.*) which shows distribution by civil divisions.

DEMY. A standard size of printing paper, $17\frac{1}{2} \times 22\frac{1}{2}$ inches, and of writing and drawing paper (also called 'small demy') $15\frac{1}{2} \times 20$ inches. *See also* OCTAVO, PAPER SIZES.

DEMY OCTAVO. A book size, $8\frac{3}{4} \times 5\frac{5}{8}$ inches. *See also* BOOK SIZES.

DENOTATION. *See* CONNOTATION.

DENOTATIVE. *See* CONNOTATION.

DENSITOMETER. A photoelectric instrument for measuring the density, or degree of blackness, of a photographic image. A reflection-densitometer is used to measure the density of an opaque surface (print) before setting the camera and screen for half-tone exposure. Measuring the optical density of ink films during printing is done with a similar instrument.

DENSITY. In documentary reproduction, the degree of photographic opacity. (*Concepts* . . .) The degree of opacity of films and blackness of prints (the light-absorbing quality of a photographic image); it is usually expressed as the logarithm of opacity.

DENTELLE. Lace-like tooling on the borders of a book cover, placed near the edges and pointing towards the centre. The most notable binders working in this style were the Derome family and Pierre-Paul Dubuisson who was appointed binder to Louis XV in 1758.

DENTELLE A L'OISEAU. Dentelle bindings in which birds are introduced into the design of the borders; chief executant was N. D. Derome. *See also* DEROME STYLE.

DENUDATION. (*Classification*) The formation of a chain of classes by the application of successive characteristics of division.

DEPARTMENT. 1. A section of a library devoted to one subject as in a DEPARTMENTALIZED LIBRARY (*q.v.*), or to one kind of service, as a 'Reference library'. 2. An administrative section of a library which has one function or series of functions, such as 'Cataloguing department'. In America sometimes called a 'Division'.

DEPARTMENT HEAD. A member of the professional staff of an American library who is directly responsible to the Chief Librarian, or Director, for a division of the library organization having its own staff. In a library organized under the divisional system, a head of one of the divisions of the central library.

DEPARTMENT OF SCIENTIFIC AND INDUSTRIAL RE-SEARCH. The British organization of this name, which was created in 1915, was responsible to a committee of the Privy Council concerned with Scientific and Industrial Research. In 1956 the Department was reconstituted by statute, and placed under an Executive Council appointed by the Lord President of the Council. It was governed by the Council for Scientific and Industrial Research known as the Research Council and was entrusted with developing and encouraging research and disseminating the results of such research. It ran fifteen research stations whose resources were concentrated on research that was clearly in the national interest and could not reasonably be done elsewhere. Regional Technical Information Centres were provided in nine cities; they were autonomous bodies set up and supported by local organizations and mostly assisted by grants from D.S.I.R. Financial aid was given to industrial research associations and similar research organizations which in the main operated a variety of services for the benefit of their members, although in some instances these services were extended to non-members. It also made grants available to universities and colleges for specific research. In October 1963 the Trend Committee recommended (*Report*. Command Paper 2171) the dissolution of DSIR and the creation of two bodies – one a Science Research Council, for the support of research projects at universities in pure and applied science; the other, an Industrial Research and Development Authority to take over most of the research stations managed by the Department and responsibility for the support of industrial research. Adoption by the Government of recommendations based on the Report was announced in February 1964. A Natural Environment Research Council was to work in the field of environmental sciences and natural resources, supporting research in geophysics, geology, oceanography, fisheries, hydrology, forestry, terrestrial ecology, and nature conservation.

As a result of an Order in Council, made under the Science and Technology Act, 1965, the DSIR was dissolved as from 1st April 1965, and its functions, and also those of the National Institute for Research in Nuclear Science, were taken over by other bodies and government departments. On the same date the Science Research Council came into being; this took over the functions of the former DSIR in respect of research grants to universities and post-graduate training awards not within the fields of the other councils. Those parts of the DSIR concerned with research and development in aid of industry, together with the staffs concerned, were transferred to the Ministry of Technology which took over ten of the fifteen DSIR research stations (Building Research Station, Fire Research Station, Forest Products Research Laboratory, Laboratory of the Government Chemist, Hydraulics Research Station, National Engineering Laboratory, National Physical Laboratory (including National Chemical Laboratory), Torry Research Station, Warren Spring Laboratory and Water Pollution

Laboratory) and responsibility for financial support to forty-eight industrial research associations.

The Ministry of Technology took over the DSIR information functions concerned with disseminating technical information in industry. The NATIONAL LENDING LIBRARY FOR SCIENCE AND TECHNOLOGY (*q.v.*), and the more general scientific information work as well as the overseas liaison responsibilities of DSIR were transferred to the Department of Education and Science. The Road Research Laboratory became a responsibility of the Minister of Transport, and the Tropical Products Institute of the Minister of Overseas Development. The Geological Survey and Museum was transferred later to the Natural Environment Research Council. The scope of the work of the research establishments remained substantially the same.

DEPARTMENT OF TECHNICAL PROCESSES. *See* PROCESSING DEPARTMENT.

DEPARTMENTAL CATALOGUE. A catalogue consisting of entries for books in one department only of a library.

DEPARTMENTAL LIBRARY. A library in a college or university which is apart from the main library and restricted to one subject or group of subjects. Also called 'Branch library', 'Faculty library', 'Laboratory collection', 'Office collection', 'Seminar collection'.

DEPARTMENTALIZED LIBRARY. A large library in which all the material on each broad subject, whether for reference or lending, is kept in separate rooms or clearly defined sections. Also called SUBJECT DEPARTMENT (*q.v.*).

DEPENDENT WORK. A term used by cataloguers to indicate a work which is related in some way to a work by another author already published. It may be a modification, adaptation or amplification of the earlier work; the term includes such writings as abridgements, commentaries, continuations, dramatizations, librettos, parodies, revisions, selections, sequels and supplements.

DEPOSIT COPY. A copy of a newly published book, pamphlet or periodical, etc., which is sent to one or more libraries, as required by law, and sometimes to complete copyright protection in the country. *See* DEPOSITORY LIBRARY.

DEPOSIT LIBRARY. A library service point stocked with a small collection of books which is changed periodically, and which is open for a few hours only daily, or on selected days of the week. These are usually established in new housing areas to provide a temporary book service until a permanent library can be provided, and in factories and institutions.

DEPOSIT STATION. *Synonymous with* DEPOSIT LIBRARY (*q.v.*).

DEPOSITORS. Readers who pay a deposit, in lieu of obtaining a guarantee, to enable them to borrow books from a library.

DEPOSITORY CATALOGUE. A copy of a national library catalogue, such as that of the Library of Congress, which is deposited in selected libraries.

DEPOSITORY LIBRARY. In England, a library which is entitled by law to receive a free copy of every book published. In America, a library which is entitled to receive all, or selected, United States government publications, or designated to receive free a full list of Library of Congress catalogue cards.

DEPTH CLASSIFICATION. 1. Classifying so minutely that the most specific subject in all its aspects is identified and dealt with fully and accurately. 2. Classification schedules that have been sufficiently worked out to meet the needs of MICRO-THOUGHT (*q.v.*), of libraries for specialist materials and users, and of documentation.

DEPTH OF FIELD. The distance between the nearest and farthest objects from a camera which are acceptably sharp, at a given lens aperture.

DEPTH OF STRIKE. *See* BEVEL.

DEPUTY LIBRARIAN. The chief assistant librarian. One who becomes acting chief librarian in all absences of the principal. Formerly called 'Sub-librarian'. Sometimes called 'Associate librarian' in America.

DEQUEKER SYSTEM. (*Information retrieval*) The first information searching system to be introduced. It consisted of cards with rows of holes punched in the body of the cards and filed on their edges in a cabinet. Rods were inserted through the holes corresponding to the codes for the subject of an enquiry, and a half-turn of a handle operated a mechanism to raise slightly above the level of the remainder of the cards those bearing the codes required. *See also* EDGE-NOTCHED CARDS, MARGINAL-HOLE PUNCHED CARDS, PUNCHED CARDS, SLOTTED CARDS.

DERIVATIVE BIBLIOGRAPHY. Used synonymously for selective or subject bibliographies of the secondary type, and sometimes for retrospective bibliographies. *See also* BIBLIOGRAPHY, PRIMARY BIBLIOGRAPHY, RETROSPECTIVE BIBLIOGRAPHY, SECONDARY BIBLIOGRAPHY.

DEROME STYLE. A style of book decoration practised by the Derome family in France in the eighteenth century. It is mainly confined to symmetrical corner tooling of a very richly engraved floreated scroll work, pertaining very closely to the roccoco style of the Louis period. Nicholas Denis Derome (1731–88) who worked for Count Hoym is famous for his Dentelle borders. *See also* DENTELLE.

DESCENDER. The vertical descending stem of lower-case letters such as j, p, q, etc.; that part which extends below the 'X'-HEIGHT (*q.v.*). *See also* ASCENDER.

DESCRIPTIVE BIBLIOGRAPHY. The kind of bibliography which makes known precisely the material condition of books, that is, the full name of the author, the exact title of the work, the date and place of publication, the publisher's and printer's names, the format, the pagination, typographical particulars, illustrations and the price, and for old books, other characteristics such as the kind of paper, binding, etc. Also called 'Analytical bibliography'. *See also* HISTORICAL BIBLIOGRAPHY.

DESCRIPTIVE CATALOGUING. That part of the cataloguing process which is concerned with the choice and form of main and added entries, transcription of title-page details, collation, etc. The term was coined by the survey committee at the Library of Congress in 1940. *See also* SUBJECT CATALOGUING.

DESCRIPTOR. (*Information retrieval*) 1. An elementary term. 2. A simple word or phrase used as a subject (*IBM*). 3. A word, translatable into a code, or symbol, which is given to a document to describe it and by means of which it can be discovered when required. Also called 'Code', 'Semantic factor'. It may be a subject heading or a class number. *See also* UNIT RECORD.

DESCRIPTOR FILE. A file, or sequence, of UNIT RECORDS (*q.v.*), i.e. DESCRIPTORS (*q.v.*) followed by their relevant supplementary information.

DESCRIPTOR LANGUAGE. A standardized indexing vocabulary comprising descriptors and used to describe documents, or their contents. A controlled descriptor language economizes on the number of symbols used in the descriptor file, standardizes subject description, maximizes the probability of retrieving all documents relative to an enquiry and none that are irrelevant, and provides for specific reference and generic survey to the extent needed by the users.

DESENSITIZATION. Applying a solution, called an 'etch', (of nitric acid and gum arabic for stone; gum arabic, chromic acid and phosphoric acid for zinc, gum arabic and phosphoric acid for aluminium) to a lithographic printing plate after an image has been transferred to it, to desensitize the non-image areas, remove stray traces of grease from them, and increase the moisture-retaining capacity.

DESIDERATA. 1. A list of subjects on which the author of a book requires information. If only one is required the singular form 'desideratum' is used. 2. A list of books required.

DESIGN. (*Verb*) To plan the entire format of a book. (*Noun*) The specification for the format of a book.

DESIGNATION MARK. Letters corresponding to the initial letters of the title of a book, and the volume number (if any), which are sometimes printed alongside the SIGNATURE MARK (*q.v.*) on each section to help the binder identify the sections belonging to a particular title. *See also* DIRECTION LINE.

DESK. *Synonymous with* STAFF ENCLOSURE (*q.v.*).

DESK SCHEDULE. A schedule arranged to show the assignments of staff to each desk or department in a library. (*American.*)

DESK-TOP LIBRARY. *See* PACKAGE LIBRARY.

DESTINATION SLIPS. Pieces of paper which project from books in the Order Department or Cataloguing Department to indicate by their colour or marking to which libraries they are allocated.

DETROIT SELF-CHARGING SYSTEM. A simplified form of the NEWARK CHARGING SYSTEM (*q.v.*), the borrowers themselves making some of the records.

DEVICE. An emblem or monogram used by a printer or publisher to identify his work. It is usually used as part of the printer's IMPRINT (*q.v.*) or publisher's name on the title-page or spine.

DEVIL. *See* WILLOW.

DEWEY DECIMAL CLASSIFICATION. The classification devised by Melvil Dewey (1851–1931) in 1873, and first published anonymously in 1876, since when it has been revised seventeen times. Knowledge is divided into the following main classes: O, General works; 1, Philosophy; 2, Religion, 3, Sociology; 4, Philology; 5, Natural Science; 6, Useful Arts; 7, Fine Arts; 8, Literature; 9, History. The notation is a pure one, being based on three figures and used decimally. Subdivision by form is facilitated by the use of a table of common subdivisions with a mnemonic notation; the linguistic numbers from 420–499 and the geographical numbers from 940–999 are used mnemonically to subdivide by language and place. The relative index is original, and shows the relation of each subject indexed to a larger subject (or class or division), or after the entry word the phase of the subject is indicated. This scheme is used in most public, school, and many non-public, libraries. The schedules were considerably extended in each successive edition until the fifteenth 'Standard' Edition (1951) which was published after Dewey's death and was a much attenuated edition, being designed for a small library. In this, the simplified spelling which Dewey had always used was discontinued. Since 1951 the revision of the schedules has been undertaken within the Library of Congress Library. Some major changes were made in the seventeenth edition. There were some re-locations and re-casting of schedules; form divisions were retitled 'standard sub-divisions' in recognition of the fact that many are modes of treatment rather than forms. The index is new in concept and execution. The scheme is kept up to date between editions by means of the bulletin issued by the revisers under the title *Decimal classification: additions, notes and decisions* (free to users from LC). The Dewey numbers have been printed on LC. catalogue cards since April 1930; they also appear on the cards suppled by the H. W. Wilson Company. *See also* UNIVERSAL DECIMAL CLASSIFICATION.

DEWEY MEDAL, MELVIL. Donated by Forest Press, Inc., this annual award, consisting of a medal and citation of achievement, is made to an individual or a group for recent creative professional achievement of a high order, particularly in those fields in which Melvil Dewey was so actively interested, notably library management, library training, cataloguing and classification, and the tools and techniques of librarianship. The award is administered by the ALA Awards Committee which appoints a jury of five to make the selection. The Medal was first awarded (in 1953) to Ralph R. Shaw.

DIACRITICAL MARK. A mark, such as an accent, placed over or under a letter to express some special phonetic value.

DIAERESIS. Two dots placed over the second of two consecutive vowels to show that they are to be pronounced separately, as Chlöe, coöperate. In English it is now an obsolescent symbol, having been replaced by the hyphen (co-operate); the Americans now use neither.

DIAGONAL FRACTION. The separation of the numerator from the denominator by an oblique stroke instead of a horizontal one, e.g. 1/2.

diagr. (*Pl.* diagrs.) Abbreviation for DIAGRAM (*q.v.*).

DIAGRAM. As distinct from an illustration proper, a diagram gives only the general outline or plan of the thing represented. Abbreviated diagr.

DIAMOND. An out-of-date name for a size of type equal to about 4½ point.

DIAPER. A binding pattern consisting of a simple figure constantly repeated in geometrical form: the pattern may consist of figures separated by the background only, or of compartments constantly succeeding one another, and filled with a design. The design is done with a 'diaper roll'.

DIAPHRAGM CONTROL. A device for indicating the correct aperture for any camera extension and screen ruling when using a PROCESS CAMERA (*q.v.*).

DIAPOSITIVE. A positive copy (of a document) made on transparent material. *See also* NEGATIVE, POSITIVE.

DIAZO. A contraction of diazonium, the chemical compound used in ammonia-developing reproduction papers, cloths and films which will reproduce anything printed, drawn, or written on a translucent or transparent material when exposed to ultra-violet light and developed in ammonia fumes. *See also* DIAZOTYPE PROCESS. Also used of a dye-coated paper which will produce a copy directly by exposure to a transparent or translucent original. The sensitive dye is bleached by exposure to light, the unbleached portions can be developed by a liquid developer or ammonia fumes, according to the type of paper used.

DIAZOTYPE PROCESS. A copying process whereby paper treated with a diazo compound is placed against the document to be copied and an exposure made by means of powerful arc lamps. The exposed paper is developed by passing it through a chamber containing ammonia fumes or over rollers damped with a specially prepared solution. It enables a positive black and white copy to be made in one operation but cannot reproduce facsimiles of double-sided documents. Blue, brown or red lines may be produced as well as black. A print made by this method may be called a 'Diazo print' or 'White print'. The base materials for diazo printing may be paper, film, or cloth. Before prints can be made by the diazo process, which can be done on the cheapest of sensitized papers, a translucent master must first be made. Non-reversible images are generally produced by this method, i.e. negative and positive images will produce the same kind of image. The process originated in 1923. Also called 'Dyeline'. *See also* AZOFLEX, OZALID.

DICED. Binding with tooling to resemble dice or small diamond squares.

DICHOTOMY, CLASSIFICATION BY. *See* BIFURCATE CLASSIFICATION.

DICKMAN CHARGING SYSTEM. A slightly simplified and mechanized development of the Newark system to obviate the necessity for making records in longhand, thus lessening the possibility of mistakes.

DICTIONARY. 1. A book explaining the words of a language, the words being arranged in alphabetical order; it usually gives the orthography, pronunciation and meaning of each word. A dictionary of the words in a restricted field of knowledge usually gives only the meaning. 2. In information retrieval, *synonymous with* THESAURUS (*q.v.*).

DICTIONARY CATALOGUE. A catalogue in which all the entries (author, title, subject, series, etc.) and references are arranged in a single alphabet – like a dictionary. As distinct from other alphabetical catalogues, subject entries are made under specific subjects. In some instances, the arrangement of sub-entries may depart from a strictly alphabetical order in order to provide a logical, or other convenient, arrangement, the main headings still retaining the alphabetical order.

DICTIONARY INDEX. A series of entries with verbal headings arranged in alphabetical order. Also called 'Alphabetico-specific subject catalogue'.

DIDONE. A category of type face having a sharp contrast between the thick and thin strokes. The axis of the curves is vertical, the serifs of the lower-case ascenders are horizontal and there are no brackets to the serifs. Of such are Bodoni, Corvinus, Extended and Modern. The term Didone has replaced MODERN FACE (*q.v.*).

DIDOT. A MODERN-FACE (*q.v.*) type cut in 1784 by Firmin Didot (1764–1836) the most famous of a French family which is important in the history of printing. Most eminent as a type-founder, he was mainly responsible for developing the type which is now familiar. He revived and developed the stereo-typing process, and produced singularly perfect editions of many classical English and French works. He and other members of his family fixed the standard for book types in France in the nineteenth century.

DIDOT NORMAL. The standard on the Continent of Europe for the height of type from the feet to the printing surface. It is 0·9278 inches. *See also* TYPE HEIGHT.

DIDOT POINT. *See* DIDOT SYSTEM.

DIDOT SYSTEM. A system of type measurement originated by François Ambroise Didot (1730–1804), the French typefounder, in 1775. One Didot point equals 0·0148 inches; one English point equals 0·013837 inches. The Didot System was generally adopted in France early in the nineteenth century and by German typefounders between 1840 and 1879. *See also* CICERO, POINT.

DIE. An engraved stamp used for stamping a design.

DIE SINKING. The process of making dies; die cutting.

DIE STAMPING. A printing process that gives a raised effect. Sometimes the die does not carry the ink, and the raised paper alone makes the letter discernible. *See also* EMBOSSING.

DIE SUNK. A depression produced by the application of a heated die or block.

DIFFERENCE. *See* PREDICABLES, FIVE.

DIFFERENTIAL RATING. A local rate levied (in addition to the county rate) to provide staff and maintain a library building in order to satisfy the reading requirements of the area covered by the local rate. *See* FLAT RATE.

DIFFUSION TRANSFER. A photocopying method which produces a positive by chemical diffusion from the negative, e.g. Agfa rapid, Gevacopy (*Verry*).

DIFFUSION TRANSFER PROCESS. *See* TRANSFER PROCESS.

DIGEST. A methodically arranged compendium or summary of literary, historical, legal, scientific, or other written matter.

DIGESTER. (*Paper*) The vessel in which rags, esparto or wood are boiled, with chemicals, often caustic soda, to break down the fibres. *See also* BOILER.

DIGIT. 1. Each of the symbols comprising a BOOK NUMBER (*q.v.*) in the Colon classification. 2. In classification, a distinctively recognizable configuration of marks (e.g. letters – both capital and lower case – numbers, punctuation marks and any other symbols), or code elements, included in a notation, therefore synonymous with 'sort'. 3. In computer codes, each item comprising a symbol; in the symbol ABA553 there are six digits but only four 'sorts' or 'characters' (A, B, 3, 5). Each conventional set of sorts is called a 'species' (the capitals, the numerals). *See also* CODE. 4. The printers' symbol ☞. Also known as 'Fist', 'Hand' or 'Index'.

DIGRAPH. *Synonymous with* DIPTHONG (*q.v.*).

DIME NOVEL. An American term for a type of paper-covered fiction which was popular during the second half of the nineteenth century. A cheap, sensational, novel.

DIN. The characters used before figures to identify standards issued by the Deutscher Normenausschuss (DNA), the German standards institution. The DIN standards for sizes of paper were later adopted by the International Standards Organization.

DIPLOMATIC. The science of the critical study of official as opposed to literary sources of history, i.e. of charters, acts, treaties, contracts, judicial records, rolls, chartularies, registers and kindred documents.

DIPHTHONG. Two letters joined together and representing one sound, as æ, Æ, œ, Œ. Also called 'Digraph'.

DIPTYCH. *See* CODEX.

DIRECT CODING. The assignation of a separate meaning to each individual part of a search medium, as e.g. each hole in an edge-punched card or each individual punching position in a machine-punched card. *See also* INDIRECT CODING, MARGINAL-HOLE PUNCHED CARDS.

DIRECT CONTACT COPYING.   A process for documentary copying which requires the action of light on a sensitized coating on paper. One method uses infra-red light waves acting on a heat sensitive coating which is placed in firm contact with the document to be copied. The infra-red rays are passed through the copy paper to the original and in so doing are absorbed by the text image, the resultant heat blackening the corresponding areas of the copy paper to produce a positive copy. This is called a THERMAL PROCESS (*q.v.*). The other method uses ultra-violet light waves and sensitive paper coated with diazo compounds. The original must have printing on one side only and must have opaque images on translucent paper capable of passing ultra-violet light. The original is placed, under pressure, on the paper with the image side up and ultra-violet light is played across the original with the result that the translucent portions of the original disintegrate the diazo compounds, making them incapable of acting as a colouring agent. The dry paper is then passed through gaseous ammonia, the dye remaining in the image area being brought out and resulting in a readable, dry positive. This is a DIAZOTYPE PROCESS (*q.v.*).

DIRECT COPYING.   *See* LENSLESS COPYING.

DIRECT HALF-TONE.   A half-tone for which the screen negative is made directly from the subject, not from a photograph or drawing.

DIRECT IMAGE FILM.   The type of film which produces a negative or positive copy from the same kind of original, in one step.

DIRECT POSITIVE.   1. A photographic paper which gives a positive copy by direct exposure to a positive original. 2. The positive print prepared without an intermediate negative. Also called 'Self positive'.

DIRECT POSITIVE PROCESS.   One where the exposed film is developed to a positive, instead of to a negative, by using a reversal developing process.

DIRECT PRINTING.   Printing in which the impression is made direct from forme to paper, as in letterpress, and is not offset on to the paper from another medium. *See also* LETTERPRESS, OFFSET.

DIRECT SUB-DIVISION.   When determining subject headings for a dictionary catalogue in respect of a book limited to one locality, the heading is sub-divided by the name of a county, province, city or other locality without the interposition of the name of the country; e.g. GEOLOGY – SURREY. Indirect sub-division interposes the name of the country; e.g. GEOLOGY – ENGLAND – SURREY.

DIRECTION DES BIBLIOTHÈQUES DE FRANCE. This organization, which is under the control of Le Ministère de l'Éducation Nationale was founded in 1945 when it took over from the Ministry the responsibilities for the employment and training of professional librarians. It is responsible for the administration and functioning of the big French national libraries and the municipal libraries as well as the libraries of the University of Paris and 15 other universities. The Direction provides instruction and issues certificates and diplomas to staff employed in libraries which come under its control.

DIRECTION LINE. Used to indicate the line of characters when the abbreviated title of a book called DESIGNATION MARK (*q.v.*) follows the signature mark, or letter, which is printed at the foot of the first page of each sheet, to guide the binder when gathering. Originally, the line on which a CATCHWORD (*q.v.*) was printed. Also called 'Signature line', 'Title signature'. *See also* DESIGNATION MARK, SIGNATURE AND CATCHWORD LINE.

DIRECTION NUMBER. The number which appears on the DIRECTION LINE (*q.v.*) at the bottom of a leaf of an old book, i.e. below the lowest line of type.

DIRECTION WORD. *See* CATCHWORD.

DIRECTORY. A book containing lists of names of residents, organizations or business houses in a town, a group of towns or a country, in alphabetical order, and/or in order of situation in roads, or of firms in trade classifications arranged in alphabetical order; or of professional people, manufacturers or business houses in a particular trade or profession.

DIRTY PROOF. A proof containing many errors or typographical imperfections; a proof that has been returned to the printer with many corrections.

DIS. *See* DISTRIBUTING.

DISC. Popular name for a gramophone (in America, a 'phonograph') record.

DISC INKING. The inking system which is found particularly in some platen printing machines. A round disc revolves on its own gearing at the head of the machine and the inking rollers pass over the disc before descending on the type-forme. *See also* PLATEN PRESS.

DISC NUMBER. A symbol, consisting of letters and numbers allocated to a DISC (*q.v.*) by the manufacturer for purposes of identification. It is printed on the label on the disc and is used in lists and catalogues as a means of identification.

DISCARD. A book that is withdrawn from circulation in a library because it is out-of-date or in too worn or dirty a condition.

DISCHARGE. (*Verb*) The act of cancelling the record of the loan of a book or other item on its return to the library. *See also* CHARGE.

DISCHARGING BOOKS. The act of cancelling the record of books on loan by re-inserting the book-cards in them on their return, or otherwise cancelling the loans to indicate that they have been returned. *See also* SLIP.

DISCHARGING COUNTER. The staff enclosure which is set aside for the work of discharging books, i.e., cancelling the record of a loan.

DISCHARGING DESK. *See* CIRCULATION DESK.

DISCOBUS. A vehicle which carries gramophone records for loan.

DISCOGRAPHY. A list of gramophone records (popularly called 'discs') giving details of composer, title, performer/s, maker, and maker's catalogue number.

DISCOUNT. The reduction from the list price of goods. With regard to English published books this is limited to 10% off the published price to those who sign the NET BOOK AGREEMENT (*q.v.*) although some booksellers who do not sign the agreement offer more. It is only available to libraries which provide a free service to the whole of a community. In the U.S.A. discounts are much greater; each publisher has his own discount schedule which is applicable to wholesalers, retailers, schools, libraries, etc. It is usually a sliding scale based on the quantity ordered.

DISCOURSE. *Synonymous with* RELATION (*q.v.*).

DISCRETE RECORD. A marginal-hole punched card, a machine sortable punched card, a piece of film, or a length of tape. If these records represent single documents and bear all the results of analysing a single document such records are said to result in a 'document system', whereas if they represent a single subject (or aspect) and contain information as to which documents in a file have this subject in common, the result is an 'aspect system'.

DISJOINED HAND. Handwriting in which the letters are not connected to one another. Also called 'Script writing'. The opposite of JOINED HAND (*q.v.*).

DISJUNCT LEAF. The stub which remains in a book after the removal of the remainder of the leaf because it contained matter which could not be allowed to remain. *See also* CANCELLATION.

DISPLAY STAND. A piece of furniture built to stand on the floor of a library on which to display books.

DISPLAY TYPE. Large or heavy-faced type used for headings, title-pages, posters or advertisements. They may include sizes between 18 and 24 point but usually comprise 30, 36, 42, 48, 60, 72 and more exceptionally 84 and 96 point.

DISPLAY VAN. A vehicle which may be used primarily or occasionally to display books either to persons within the van or to those passing along the outside of it. *See also* DELIVERY VAN.

DISPLAY WORK. The setting of short lines in varying faces and sizes of type, as distinct from a solid area of type. Advertisements, titles and headings are 'display' work.

DISSECTION. (*Classification*) The formation of an array of co-ordinate classes.

DISSEMINATION OF INFORMATION. The distribution, or sending, of information whether specifically requested or not, to members of an organization by a librarian or information officer. The means used normally include news bulletins, abstracts, individual memoranda or letters, and personal interviews or telephone calls, but may also include notes accompanying articles, memoranda, cuttings or reports and the underlining of sentences or marking of paragraphs in same.

DISSERTATION, ACADEMIC. A thesis or treatise prepared as a condition for the award of a degree or diploma.

DISTINCTIVE TITLE. One that is peculiar to a particular publication.

DISTRIBUTED RELATIVES. A secondary aspect of a subject which is used to show a relationship when classifying a document, and which will not be used as the main, but as a subordinate, subject when determining the class number. The same sub-heading may be used to subdivide many headings.

DISTRIBUTING. 1. Putting loose type back into their respective boxes and cases after use, or for melting, after use in the forme. This is done after machining and when type is not to be kept standing for reprints. Commonly called 'dissing'. Abbreviated 'dis'. *See also* BREAK. 2. In presswork, the uniform spreading of ink on the face of the printing forme.

DISTRIBUTION IMPRINT. The statement on the verso of the title-page of a book, which names the branches or representatives through which the publisher's books are distributed.

DISTRIBUTOR ROLLERS. The rollers on a printing press which

spread ink on the ink slab, roll it to the correct consistency and transfer it to the rollers which ink the type-forme. They are made wholly of metal, or of rubber or composition on a metal core. Also called 'Distributing rollers'.

DISTRICT. (*County Libraries*) A part of the County Library area other than a REGION or AREA (*qq.v.*) and usually comprising a town and its adjacent rural area organized as a library unit.

DISTRICT AUDIT. The accounts of all local authorities other than boroughs are subject to District Audit, and certain accounts of boroughs are also subject statutorily to district audit. These are such accounts as the rate accounts and education accounts. District auditors are appointed by the Minister of Housing and Local Government, and their powers and duties are prescribed in the Local Government Act, 1933. *See also* AUDIT, MUNICIPAL AUDIT.

DISTRICT CENTRAL LIBRARY. (*County Libraries*) The principal library in a DISTRICT (*q.v.*), usually situated in the main centre of communications. If it has no branches or centres, it is a DISTRICT LIBRARY.

DISTRICT LIBRARIAN. One in charge of a county branch library serving directly residents in an area larger than the town in which it is situated, but possibly excluding residents of that town.

DISTRICT LIBRARY. 1. *Synonymous with* BRANCH LIBRARY (*q.v.*) in an urban library system. 2. In a British county library system, a branch situated in a market town or other focal area, at which books are not distributed or services provided to the service points in surrounding areas, but is used by residents in those areas, although possibly excluding the residents in the town itself if this is not within the county library area. *See also* REGIONAL BRANCH, REGIONAL HEAD-QUARTERS.

DISTRICT MATERIALS CENTER. *Synonymous with* CURRICULUM MATERIALS CENTER (*q.v.*).

DITTOED. Something that is duplicated on a spirit duplicator, strictly one produced on the American machine of this kind, called a Ditto. A generic name (as 'Roneoed' for items produced on a wax stencil duplicating machine).

DITTOGRAM. A printed character, or group of printed characters, repeated in error.

DIURNAL. A periodical which is published or issued every day.

DIURNALL. *See* NEWSBOOK.

DIVIDE LIKE THE CLASSIFICATION. The mnemonic use after the point (.) of symbols from various parts of a classification schedule in order to sub-divide a subject, as e.g. in 016 of Dewey's *Decimal Classification*:

016	Bibliography	of special subjects
016·1	„	of philosophy
016·17	„	of ethics
016·22	„	of the Bible
016·54	„	of chemistry

DIVIDED CATALOGUE. A catalogue in which the entries are separated into two or more sequences in order to simplify filing and consultation, which may become complicated in a large dictionary catalogue. All subject and form entries and their necessary references may form an alphabetical subject catalogue and the remaining entries form an author-title catalogue.

DIVIDING STROKE. *Synonymous with* LINE DIVISION MARK (*q.v.*).

DIVINITY CALF. A plain dark brown calf binding often used in the mid-nineteenth century for theological or devotional books. The boards were sometimes bevelled and the edges red.

DIVINITY CIRCUIT. The American equivalent of Yapp, or CIRCUIT EDGES (*q.v.*).

DIVINITY EDGES. *See* CIRCUIT EDGES.

DIVISION. 1. In some libraries, a section of a Department. 2. In some libraries, a Department. 3. A unit in a library system which is concerned with a particular function, as a 'Catalogue division', or with a definite subject, as 'Science division'. 4. In the American Library Association and the Special Libraries Association, sections of the membership which exist to further the work of libraries and librarianship and the well being of librarians within the limitations of each division. These divisions may represent a type of organization or a subject field; each has its own officers and organizational machinery. *See also* BRANCH, GROUP, SECTION.

DIVISION. (*Classification*) 1. The process of dividing classes or groups of a classification scheme into their more minute parts. 2. The result so formed. 3. A subject or topic which is subordinate to a class. 4. Breaking down a FACET (*q.v.*) into its foci. *See* FOCUS. *See also* EXHAUSTIVE DIVISION, MAIN CLASS.

DIVISION HEAD. In American libraries a member of the professional staff directly responsible to a department head, and in charge of a subdivision of a department.

DIVISION LIBRARY. In an American university or college, a collection of books attached to, and administered by, a division or a group of related departments, usually with some form of co-operative arrangement with the general library, or as a part of the library system.

DIVISIONAL TITLE. A page preceding a section or division of a book, and bearing the name or number of the section or division. The reverse is usually blank.

DIVISIONAL TITLE-PAGES. *See* GENERAL TITLE.

do. Abbreviation for ditto, the same.

DOCUMENT. 1. A record – made on a more or less flat surface or on a surface admitting of being spread flat when required, made of paper or other material fit for easy handling, transport across space, and preservation through time – of thought created by mind and expressed in language or symbols or in any other mode, and/or a record of natural or social phenomena made directly by an instrument without being passed through the human mind and woven into thought created and expressed by it. (*S. R. Ranganathan.*) 2. Material of any kind, regardless of its physical form and characteristics, on which information has been recorded. 3. A record, usually inscribed or written, which conveys information, and which is relied on to establish facts. It is now taken to include any form of graphic, acoustic or haptic record (book, cutting, map, manuscript, drawing, periodical, etc.). 4. A work recorded in language or symbols, or by other means (*IFLA*). 5. Any form of recorded information, whether indited, alphanumeric, pictorial or auditory.

DOCUMENT ADDRESS. (*Information retrieval*) A class number or other symbol indicating the whereabouts of a document in a STORE. *See also* UNIT RECORD.

DOCUMENT CARD. A UNIT CARD (*q.v.*). A card carrying all the bibliographic and index information for an item. Used in ZATOCODING (*q.v.*) and other edge-notched card systems as well as in serially searched files (*IBM*). Cards used in machine-sorting systems are also called document cards. Frequently each card represents a document or part of a document.

DOCUMENT CATALOGUE. A catalogue of documents.

DOCUMENT COPYING. *See* DOCUMENTARY REPRODUCTION.

DOCUMENT RETRIEVAL. The process of providing relevant documents on a specified subject when required. This cannot be done until (a) the documents have been classified or indexed in some way, (b) the classification or index decisions stored by some means, (c) these decisions have been searched.

DOCUMENT RETRIEVAL SYSTEM. One which provides a complete copy of a required document instead of merely a citation or reference. An aspect of INFORMATION RETRIEVAL (*q.v.*).

DOCUMENT STORE. In information retrieval, a place where documents are kept.

DOCUMENT SYSTEM. A method of machine indexing that presumes a discrete record, e.g. a marginal-hole punched card, a machine-sortable punched card, a piece of film, or a length of tape which represents a single document and contains, in searchable form, all of the results of an analysis of a single document. *See also* DISCRETE RECORD, ITEM ENTRY.

DOCUMENTALIST. One who practises documentation. An information officer or intelligence officer who is concerned with the collection and dissemination of knowledge, rather than the librarian who is concerned with the techniques of handling records of knowledge, making them available and possibly exploiting them. He is concerned with assembling information contained within documents together with data from other sources to form a new compilation.

DOCUMENTARY INFORMATION. Information about documents, or information recorded in documents. Either kind of information may be 'retrieved' according as to whether the purpose of the retrieval is to indicate where the needed information can be found, or what it is.

DOCUMENTARY REPRODUCTION. The copying of documents or pages of books by photographic or non-photographic means so that the copy has the appearance of the original, and without first of all copying the text letter by letter on a typewriter or by typesetting. *See also* DIAZOTYPE PROCESS, ELECTROPHOTOGRAPHIC PROCESSES, LENSLESS COPYING, PHOTOCOPY, PSEUDO-PHOTOGRAPHIC PHOTOCOPYING, REFLEX COPYING, SILVER PROCESSES, THERMAL PROCESS, TRANSFER PROCESS.

DOCUMENTATION. 1. The act of collecting, classifying and making readily accessible the records of all kinds of intellectual activity. 2. The recording of knowledge and the sources of knowledge, organizing such records systematically so that they may be found quickly, and disseminating by various means both the knowledge and the sources of the knowledge. 3. The recording, organization and dissemination of specialized knowledge (*Aslib*). 4. The science of collecting, storing and organizing recorded informational materials or documents for optimum access. 5. Includes the activities which constitute special librarianship plus the prior activities of preparing and reproducing materials and the subsequent activity of distribution. 6. The selection, classification and dissemination of information. 7. The science of ordered presentation and preservation of the records of knowledge serving to render their contents available for rapid reference and correlation. 8. The procedure by which the accumulated store of learning is made available for the further advancement of knowledge. 9. The art of facilitating the use of recorded, specialized knowledge through its presentation, reproduction, publication, dissemination, collection, storage, subject analysis, organization, and retrieval. 10. Collection and conservation, classification and selection, dissemination and utilization of all information (*IBM*). 11. The designation of the total complex of activities involved in the communication of . . . specialized information . . . including the activities which constitute special librarianship plus the prior activities of preparing and reproducing materials and the subsequent activity of distribution. (*Mortimer Taube*) 12. The group of techniques necessary for the ordered presentation, organization and communication of recorded specialized knowledge, in order to give maximum accessibility and utility to the information contained. (*J. D. Mark and R. S. Taylor*) 13. The identification, the investigation, the assembling and the use of documents (*French Union of Documentation Services*).

DOCUMENTATION CENTRE. A place where publications are received, processed, preserved, summarized, abstracted and indexed; where bulletins relating to such material are prepared for distribution to those interested; where research is undertaken, bibliographies prepared, and copies or translations made.

DOCUMENTATION LIST. Bibliography with an emphasis on the inclusion of periodical articles and on the reader being served by a specialist engaged in research, business, deliberation or administration.

DOCUMENTATION WORK. The preparation of a DOCUMENTATION LIST (*q.v.*).

DOCUMENTOGRAPHY. Bibliography, but widened in scope in order to give details of materials included in mixed files containing printed matter, articles from reviews, manuscripts, typescripts, photographs, maps and plans such as are collected in documentation centres. A faster method of recording material, developed so that it may be more easily consulted as soon as the material is processed.

DOCUMENTS. Things admissible to archives (see ARCHIVES 2) being manuscripts made of any suitable materials, scripts produced by writing machines or by means of type, type-blocks, engraved plates or blocks, or film, together with all other material evidence whether they include alphabetical or numerical signs which form part of or are annexed to, or may reasonably be assumed to have formed part of, or been annexed to, a manuscript or script record, and which were drawn up or used in the course of an administrative or executive transaction (whether public or private) of which they formed part, and which were subsequently preserved in the custody of the person or persons responsible for that transaction and for their legitimate successors.

DOCUMENTS DEPOSITORY. In America, a library which is legally designated to receive without charge copies of all or selected U.S. government publications, or a library which is designated to receive without charge a full set of Library of Congress printed cards.

DOG-EARED. Said of a book, portfolio, or similar article having the corners of the leaves turned down and soiled by careless or long continued usage.

DONATION RECORD. A record of gifts; it may be kept in a book or on cards.

DONATUS DE OCTOBUS PARTIBUS ORATIONIS. See BLOCK BOOKS.

DONORS LIST. The record of donors arranged alphabetically and kept on cards, one card to each person. (American.)

DORKING CONFERENCE. See INTERNATIONAL CONFERENCE ON CLASSIFICATION FOR INFORMATION RETRIEVAL.

DORMITORY DISTRICT. The part of a town which is residential and in which no industry is carried on.

DORMITORY LIBRARY. A collection of books placed in a dormitory of an American college or university. The books are usually intended for recreational reading but may also be recommended texts.

DORSE. The reverse side of a MEMBRANE (*q.v.*).

DOS-A-DOS BINDING. Two or more books – usually small ones – bound back to back so that the back cover of one serves as the back cover of the other and the fore-edges of one are next to the fore-edges of the other.

DOT-ETCHING. *Synonymous with* RETOUCHING (*q.v.*).

DOT MAP. One which shows density of distribution by dots of uniform size, each dot representing a given quantity.

DOTTED RULE. A strip of metal of type height with a face showing a dotted line which may vary from fine dots close together to a sequence of short dashes. *See also* RULE.

DOTTING WHEELS. Small hand-tools of varying shapes used by artists when engraving metal plates.

DOUBLE. 1. In printing, a word, etc., erroneously repeated. 2. A sheet of paper twice the unit size, e.g. double crown (20 × 30 inches), ordinary crown being 15 × 20 inches. *See also* PAPER SIZES.

DOUBLE-BOOK. A book printed on half sheets.

DOUBLE COLUMNED. A page of printed matter set to half the width

8

of a normal page line, with an em or more space, or a RULE (*q.v.*), between the columns. Abbreviated d.c. Also said to be set in 'Half-measure'. Double columns are used in such works as dictionaries, encyclopaedias and Bibles.

DOUBLE CROWN. A sheet of paper measuring 20 × 30 inches.

DOUBLE DAGGER (‡). The third reference mark for footnotes, coming after the DAGGER (*q.v.*). Sometimes called a 'Double obelisk'. *See also* REFERENCE MARKS.

DOUBLE DOCUMENT. A defect in microfilming whereby a rotary camera photographs simultaneously two documents in such a way that one covers or overlaps the other. Adjustment of the document stop will usually prevent this.

DOUBLE ELEPHANT. *See* ELEPHANT.

DOUBLE ENTRY. Entry in a catalogue under more than one subject, or under subject and place, and under the names of subordinate contributors such as joint authors, editors, illustrators, translators, etc., using the same form of entry with suitable headings added. Also, entry for a pseudonymous work under the real name of the author as well as under the pseudonym.

DOUBLE-FACED CATALOGUE CABINET. A catalogue in which drawers are placed to face both sides, or which, although made as one unit, is in effect two catalogues placed back to back.

DOUBLE-FACED SHELF. A shelf which is accessible on both sides.

DOUBLE LEADED. *See* LEADED MATTER.

DOUBLE LEAVES. The leaves of CHINESE STYLE (*q.v.*) books. These are recorded in a catalogue entry in the form '18 double l' or '36 pp. (on double leaves)'. Should the leaves be unnumbered, each is counted as two pages, as: [36] pp. (on double leaves).

DOUBLE LETTER. *Synonymous with* LIGATURE (*q.v.*).

DOUBLE NUMERATION. A system of numbering whereby illustrations, charts, etc., are related to the chapter, the numbers of which are the key numbers, e.g. Fig. 7.5 indicates the fifth figure in the seventh chapter.

DOUBLE OBELISK. *Synonymous with* DOUBLE DAGGER (*q.v.*).

DOUBLE PICA. An out-of-date name for a size of type equal to about 22 points.

DOUBLE PLATE. An illustration which stretches across two pages of a book when open. *See also* FOLDING PLATE.

DOUBLE PRINTING. Two impressions on the same sheet.

DOUBLE QUOTES. Pairs of superior commas " . . . " used to indicate quoted matter. *See also* SINGLE QUOTES, TURNED COMMA.

DOUBLE REGISTER. Two ribbons fastened in a book to serve as book-markers.

DOUBLE RULE. A RULE (*q.v.*) having two lines of different thickness of face. *See also* PARALLEL RULE.

DOUBLE SETTING. A resetting of part of a book after some of the type had been distributed in order to print more copies than had at first been intended, the decision to print more having been made during machining.

DOUBLE-SIDED STACK. A book-case or stack with shelves on both sides.

DOUBLE-SPREAD. Two facing pages on which printed matter is spread across as if they were one page. When printing an illustration this way two blocks must be used unless the spread comes in the middle of a section. *See also* CONJUGATE, OPENING.

DOUBLE TITLE-PAGE. Used where a work has both a right-hand and a left-hand title-page. Usually one of these serves for the series or the complete volumes of a set, and the other is limited to the individual volume.

DOUBLE WEIGHT PAPER. Sensitized photographic paper between 0·0112 and 0·0190 inches inclusive. *See also* PHOTOGRAPHIC PAPERS.

DOUBLETTE. *See* REPLICA.

DOUBLURE. 1. An ornamental inside lining of a book cover of leather or silk, usually with a leather hinge, and often elaborately decorated. 2. Ornamental end-paper. Also called 'Ornamental inside lining'.

DOUBTFUL AUTHORSHIP. Authorship ascribed to one or more persons with no convincing proof. *See also* ATTRIBUTED AUTHOR.

DOVES PRESS. One of the most famous British private presses. It was directed by T. J. Cobden-Sanderson, who founded it with Sir Emery Walker, at Hammersmith, London, in 1900. Their partnership was dissolved in 1909 but Cobden-Sanderson continued to operate until 1916. The most important publication was the Doves Bible, published in five volumes between 1903–5. The name 'Doves' was taken from Doves Place, a passage off the Upper Mall, Hammersmith. The name was first used for the Doves Bindery which Cobden-Sanderson started in 1893 at 15 Upper Mall.

DOWNWARD REFERENCE. A direction from a more- to a less-comprehensive heading in an alphabetico-specific subject catalogue. The reverse of UPWARD REFERENCE (*q.v.*).

DRAGON'S BLOOD. Any of several resinous substances, mostly dark red in colour. It is used in powdered form in photo-engraving for etching line plates. Dragon's blood powder is brushed up against the slightly raised lines of the image or design on the metal plate from four sides, and 'burned in', thus protecting these lines against the action of the etching solution or acid (*United Typothetae*).

DRAW-OUT SHELVES. A form of compact storage consisting of shelves wide enough to take two rows of books, one facing each way, fixed across, or in place of, ordinary shelves. When it is desired to consult the books these shelves are drawn out, as if they were drawers, into the gangway. An example of this kind of shelf is 'Stor-mor', made by W. R. Ames of San Francisco, California.

DRAWER HANDLE. A tool of a Corinthian volute which was commonly used in English Restoration book decoration. So called from its similarity to the handle of a small drawer.

DRAWN-ON COVERS. The binding of square-backed magazines and paperbacks, the cover being attached by gluing to the spine of the book. When the end-papers are pasted down, it is said to be *drawn-on solid*.

DRESSED FORME. A forme of pages of type with furniture between and around them, the page-cord having been removed. *See also* FORME, NAKED FORME.

DRESSING. 1. Fitting the FURNITURE (*q.v.*) between and around the pages in a chase prior to locking up the FORME (*q.v.*). 2. Fitting an illustration block into type so that text and illustration can be printed together.

DRIVE OUT. (*Printing*) 1. Said of type-matter which is spaced widely between the words so as to occupy more lines. 2. An instruction to the compositor to insert wide spaces between words. *See also* KEEP IN.

DROP. (*Printing*) To unlock a forme and remove the furniture and chase after printing, the type then being either distributed or 'kept standing', i.e. tied up and stored.

DROP-DOWN TITLE. The short title on the first page of text. It should be the same as the RUNNING TITLE (*q.v.*). *See also* CAPTION TITLE.

DROP FOLIO. A folio number or page number at the bottom of a page.

DROP GUIDES. *See* FEED GUIDES.

DROP INITIALS. *See* DROP LETTER.

DROP LETTER. Large initial used at the beginning of a chapter or article, and running down two lines or more. *See also* COCK-UP INITIAL, CUT-IN LETTER.

DROP SLIP. Publications ordered from a JOBBER (*q.v.*) but sent direct, at the jobber's request, by the publisher to the library. (American.)

DROPPED HEAD. The first page of a chapter or book where the first line commences a third or more down the page.

DROPPED LETTER. A character which becomes removed during the course of printing and drops out of the forme causing an omission in the matter when printed.

DRY AMMONIA PROCESS. The AMMONIA PROCESS (*q.v.*) of reprography. Also called DRY PROCESS (*q.v.*).

DRY END. The drying end of a paper-making machine. The other end is known as the WET END (*q.v.*).

DRY FLONG. *See* FLONG.

DRY OFFSET. 1. Printing by letterpress onto a rubber cylinder from which the impression is offset on to paper. The resulting advantages are reduced make-ready, the possibility of using uncoated paper for fine half-tones, etc. The process is not lithographic and no water need be used. 2. A printing process by which photo-engraved plates are printed by the offset transfer principle, the inked impression from a relief-etched magnesium plate being made on a rubber blanket cylinder and offset from this on to the paper as this is carried round the impression cylinder.

DRY-POINT ETCHING. An etching made directly on copper by means of a sharp needle called a point. In dry-point work, the etching is all done by hand and not by a mordant applied to a wax-covered plate in which the design has been cut, as is the rule in ordinary etching. Etchings often have dry-point lines, which have been added after the acid etching has taken place. The beauty of this method is due to the burr caused by the point on each side of the channel being left and not removed as in an engraving. The effect of this in printing is to produce the velvety line which is characteristic of a dry-point.

DRY PROCESS. A method for producing copies of documents which does not employ wet chemicals. Some diazotype prints are made by a dry process. The usual developing process used in electrophotography is dry. *See also* DOCUMENTARY REPRODUCTION, DUST DEVELOPMENT.

DRY SILVER. A silver halide process in which the latent image is made visible by the application of heat rather than the use of chemicals. *See also* SILVER PROCESSES.

DRYING END. The end of a paper-making machine where there are the steam-heated drying cylinders over which the damp web of paper (containing about 70 per cent of water) is passed before it reaches the calender rolls.

DUAL-SPECTRUM. A two-stage copying process developed by the 3 M Company. The master is first made by the action of ultra-violet light, and the subsequent copy is produced from the master by infra-red light. Each stage may involve manual operations or the second may be done automatically.

DUCALI BINDINGS.   Venetian bindings of the decrees of the Doges which are decorated with a combination of Oriental and Western techniques. The method was to cover the board with a paper com-position, the centre and corners being recessed, then to paste on thinly pared leather and add a coating of coloured lacquer to complete the background. Gold-painted arabesques provided the final decoration.

DUCK-FOOT QUOTES.   The common name for Continental quotes or inverted commas. The form « » is used by French printers, but the Swiss and German printers use them in reverse, i.e. » «. They were first used in 1546 by Guillaume Le Bé of Paris, and are consequently also known as 'Guillemets'.

DULL-COATED.   Paper which is coated but not polished: it is suitable for fine half-tones, being smooth but having no gloss. The term 'dull finish' is sometimes applied to the low or natural finish of COATED PAPER ($q,v,$) or uncoated papers which have not been glazed; practic-ally identical with 'matt art' paper. *See also* ARTS.

DULL FINISH.   *See* DULL-COATED.

DUMMY.   1. A copy, generally made up of blank leaves, trimmed and sewn but not bound, to represent the actual bulk of a book about to be published. 2. A complete layout of a job showing the arrangement of matter to be printed on every page, and giving particulars of type, illustrations, etc. 3. A temporary catalogue card, usually handwritten and distinctively coloured, which serves as a substitute while a main or other entry, or a block of cards, are out of the catalogue for amend-ment. *See also* SHELF DUMMY.

DUMMY BANDS.   Imitation RAISED BANDS ($q.v.$) on the spine of a book. Also called 'False bands'.

DUO.   A method of making microcopies on film in which the film makes two passages through the film printer, printing on one half of the film first, and then on the other.

DUODECIMO (12 mo.).   1. A sheet of paper folded four times to form a section of twelve leaves (24 pp.). As a sheet cannot be folded for bind-ing without a portion being cut, the smaller cut-off portion has to be inserted after folding into the larger folded portion to provide the page sequence. Alternatively a sheet and a half sheet can be used. If the printer lays down two rows of six pages the result is known as 'Long twelves', but if three by four pages, 'short' or 'square' twelves. Where the width of the pages is greater than the height, the term 'broad twelves' is used. Also called 'Twelvemo'. 2. A book printed on paper folded to form sections of twelve leaves. *See also* OBLONG.

DUOSTAT. Trade name for the equipment made by Photostat Ltd., and the process for making copies of documents using direct positive paper.

DUOTONE. Two-colour half-tone printing.

DUOTYPE. Two half-tone plates of the same black and white original, both made from the same half-tone negative, but etched separately so as to give different colour values when superimposed during printing.

DUPLEX. 1. Photographic paper which has a coating of emulsion on both sides. 2. An image-positioning technique used in rotary camera microfilming, whereby the use of mirrors or prisms enables an image of the front side of a document to be photographed on one half of the film, while an image of the back side of the same document is photographed simultaneously on the other half of the film. 3. Any make of camera which will copy as described in 2.

DUPLEX HALF-TONE. A screen reproduction in two printings from half-tone blocks made from a monochrome original, one being used as a colour tone. The method is used in both letterpress and offset work to give the impression of a mellow monochrome picture, being richer and better toned than is possible from a single-colour half-tone block.

DUPLEX LEDGER. *See* LEDGER WEIGHT.

DUPLEX PAPER. 1. Paper having two different coloured surfaces. 2. Any paper composed of two sheets pasted together. Duplex papers are usually made by bringing the two layers, generally of different colours or quality, together in the wet state and pressing or rolling them together, thus forming a homogeneous mass. *See also* TWIN WIRE PAPER. If three papers are brought together in the way described the resulting paper is known as Triplex.

DUPLICATE. A second, or subsequent, copy of a book already in stock. Strictly it should be identical in edition, imprint, etc., but the kind of library and the intrinsic value placed on variations of bibliographical details or contents determines the exact meaning of 'duplicate' in specific libraries. (*Reprography*) In microcopying, a copy-film usually made from a master film negative or a printing master. Duplicators may be either negative or positive in character.

DUPLICATE ENTRY. Entry in an index or other form of record of the same subject matter under two or more distinct aspects of it or under two headings.

DUPLICATE PAGING. Description of a book which has paging in duplicate, as e.g. a book with the original text on the verso and the translation on the recto. This would be recorded in the collation part of a catalogue entry as: *148, 148 pp.*, possibly with the note: 'Opposite pages numbered in duplicate'.

DUPLICATE PAY COLLECTION.   A selection of duplicate copies of new novels which are available only on payment for each book borrowed. After a time these books become part of the ordinary stock which is lent without charge. Also called 'Rental collection'.

DUPLICATE TITLE.   Used of a reprint which has a reproduction of the original title-page in addition to its own.

DUPLICATED SIGNATURES.   Two sets of signatures which are identical.

DUST COVER.   *Synonymous with* BOOK JACKET (*q.v.*).

DUST DEVELOPMENT.   A development process used in document copying by which latent electrostatic images are made visible by treatment with a developing powder. *See also* XEROGRAPHY.

DUST JACKET.   *Synonymous with* BOOK JACKET (*q.v.*).

DUST WRAPPER.   *Synonymous with* BOOK JACKET (*q.v.*).

DUSTER.   *See* WILLOW.

DUTCH GOLD.   *Synonymous with* DUTCH LEAF (*q.v.*).

DUTCH LEAF.   A thin sheet obtained by beating an alloy of copper and zinc; it is sometimes used in tooling as a substitute for gold leaf. It quickly discolours. Also called 'Dutch gold'.

DUTCH PAPER.   *Synonymous with* VAN GELDER PAPER (*q.v.*).

E. P. DUTTON – JOHN MACRAE AWARD. $1,000 offered by the E. P. Dutton Co. for advanced study in serving the needs of culturally deprived children and youth.

DWARF BOOK.   *Synonymous with* BIBELOT (*q.v.*).

DYADIC ALPHABET.   A two-letter alphabet.

DYE-LINE FILM COPY.   A print made by the transmission process on diazo film. *See also* DIAZOTYPE PROCESS, TRANSMISSION PRINTING.

DYE-LINE PROCESS.   *Synonymous with* DIAZOTYPE PROCESS (*q.v.*).

DYFLEX.   Trade name for Remington Rand equipment for making diazo prints using a reversed copy on DIRECT POSITIVE PAPER (*q.v.*).

DYNAMIC MAP.   One which expresses movement such as transport, migration, or military manoeuvres. The symbols used are mainly flow lines and arrows but change is sometimes expressed by isopleths or choropleths.

E.A.M.   Abbreviation for electronic accounting machine.

E.A.M. CARD.   An electric accounting machine card, i.e. a tabulating card, into which coded holes are punched. Often called a 'punched card'. When holes have been punched it is called a 'Master data card'.

EDP. Abbreviation for ELECTRONIC DATA PROCESSING.

e.g. Abbreviation for *exempli gratia* (*Lat.* 'for example'). Also for edges gilt.

E.S. Abbreviation for engine-sized. *See* ENGINE-SIZING.

EAST AFRICAN LIBRARY ASSOCIATION. Founded in 1956 to encourage the promotion, establishment and improvement of libraries, library services, books and book production in East Africa; to improve the standard of librarianship and the status of the library profession; to bring together all who are interested in libraries and librarianship. Abbreviated EALA. Publishes *East African Library Association Bulletin* (2 p.a. membs. only).

EAST PAKISTAN LIBRARY ASSOCIATION. Founded in 1958 to: (a) promote library services in East Pakistan; (b) provide and promote library training facilities and research in library science; (c) improve the status and conditions of service of library personnel; (d) co-operate with library organizations and associations with similar aims in and outside the country with a view to advancing the cause of library service. Membership is open to those engaged in library work and others interested in libraries and librarianship. Abbreviated EPLA. Publishes *The Eastern Librarian* (q.).

EASY BOOK. A book for the youngest readers; usually more illustrative than textual.

ÉCRASÉ LEATHER. Leather which has been crushed mechanically to give it a grained appearance.

Ed. (edit.). Abbreviation for EDITED, EDITION, EDITOR (*qq.v.*).

EDGE DECORATION. The application of ink, colour (sprayed, sprinkled or marbled), or gold leaf to the edges of a book.

EDGE FOG. Light or dark areas along the edge of a developed film or print, caused either by the unintentional admission of light to the sensitive material, or to the effects of age or unsatisfactory storage conditions.

EDGE-NOTCHED CARDS. Punched cards which have up to four rows of holes drilled around the edges. These are punched out to record information; the cards fall off the needle when it is inserted in the hole reserved for the information required. One edge-notched card is allocated to each document and each punchable position is reserved for one feature. This limits the usefulness of the system. Also called 'Edge-punched cards'. *See also* FEATURE CARD-SYSTEM, MARGINAL-HOLE PUNCHED CARDS, SLOTTED CARDS.

8*

EDGE-PUNCHED CARDS. *Synonymous with* EDGE-NOTCHED CARDS (*q.v.*).

EDGE-ROLLED. Said of leather-bound books the broad edges of which have been tooled 'blind' or 'gold' with a FILLET (*q.v.*). *See also* TOOLING.

EDGES. (*Binding*) The three outer edges of the leaves of a book; they may be finished in a number of ways. *See also* CUT EDGES, EDGE-ROLLED, GAUFFERED EDGES, GILT EDGES, GILT TOP, MARBLED EDGES, RED EDGES, RED UNDER GOLD EDGES, SPRINKLED EDGES, TOOLED EDGES, TRIMMED 2, UNCUT, WHITE EDGES.

EDIAC. Acronym of Electronic Display of Indexing Association and Content. A device which displayed the logical sum of all other words used in indexing any document indexed by the first word entered in the device.

EDIT. To prepare or arrange the work of one or more authors for publication, whether in book form or as a periodical or newspaper.

EDITED. 1. A literary work by one author, or several authors, which has been prepared for publication by one or more persons other than the author of the whole work. 2. A work consisting of separate items, often written by different people, which has been assembled or prepared for publication by an EDITOR (*q.v.*).

EDITIO MINOR. A lesser, but important, edition of a book or work previously printed, but sometimes the first separate printing of a work previously included in a larger volume. *See also* EDITIO PRINCEPS.

EDITIO PRINCEPS. 1. The first edition of a book printed from the old manuscript, when printing first began. *See also* EDITIO MINOR. 2. The first edition of any new work, but for this the term 'first edition' is more commonly used.

EDITION. 1. The whole number of copies of a work printed from the same type or plates and issued at one time or at intervals. An edition may comprise a number of impressions. A statement of the edition of a book is often placed on the title-page or on the verso thereof, together with particulars of any previous editions on the verso. 2. A number of copies printed at any one time, when either the text has undergone some change, or the type has been partly or entirely reset, or the format has been altered. The term is applied also to the copies forming the original issue known as the 'first edition', as well as to subsequent editions. (B.S. 1413: 1947). 3. The embodiment of a work in a particular typographical form. Different editions may embody an identical text, or varying texts (*IFLA*). 4. One of the various editions of a newspaper printed at different times on the same day, or periodically summarizing the news of the period since the previous edition was issued, or to celebrate some particular event. 5. One of the successive forms in which a musical composition is issued and in which alterations have been incorporated either by the composer or by an editor. *See also* ABRIDGED EDITION, AUTOGRAPHED EDITION, DEFINITIVE EDITION, EXPURGATED EDITION, FINE PAPER COPY, FIRST EDITION, GRANGERIZING, IMPRESSION, ISSUE, LARGE PAPER EDITION, LIBRARY EDITION, LIMITED EDITION, NEW EDITION, NUMBERED AND SIGNED EDITION, PARALLEL EDITION, POLYGLOT, REPRINT, REVISED EDITION, SUBSCRIBERS' EDITION, UNEXPURGATED EDITION, VARIORUM EDITION.

EDITION BINDERY. A bindery in which books are bound for publishers; one in which EDITION BINDING (*q.v.*) is undertaken. *See also* CASE, PUBLISHER'S COVER.

EDITION BINDING. A binding, usually a casing, ordered and paid for by the publisher as a part of the normal publishing of trade editions, and used for all the copies of a title published by him, as distinct from individual binding carried out for the bookseller or purchaser. Also called 'Publisher's binding'.

EDITION DE LUXE. A special edition of a book containing extras not in ordinary editions, such as additional plates, or printed on large paper, etc.

EDITION STATEMENT. That part of a catalogue entry which relates to the edition of the book catalogued, as: 2nd rev. ed.

EDITIONS FILE. A list on cards of editions which a library wishes to purchase.

EDITOR. 1. A person who prepares someone else's work for publication. The editorial work may be limited to mere preparation of the matter for printing, or may involve considerable revisionary and elucidatory work, including an introduction, notes and other critical matter. 2. A person who is responsible for, and supervises, the publication of a newspaper, journal, periodical or book.

EDITOR REFERENCE. A reference in a catalogue from the name of an editor, or from an entry under an editor's name to another entry where more complete information is to be found.

EDITORIAL. An article expressing a paper's own policy and beliefs on current matters.

EDITORIAL COPIES. Copies of a new publication sent out by the publisher for review, notice, or record. *See also* ADVANCE COPY, REVIEW COPY.

EDUCATIONAL FILM LIBRARY ASSOCIATION. Founded in the U.S.A. in 1943 to promote the production, distribution and utilization of educational films and other audio-visual materials. Abbreviated EFLA. Publishes *EFLA Bulletin* (9 p.a. to membs.); *Service Supplements* (bi-m. to membs.).

EDUCATIONAL RESOURCES INFORMATION CENTER. *See* ERIC.

EDUCOM. Abbreviation for Interuniversity Communications Council. An American non-profit corporation started in mid-1965 with a five-year grant of $750,000 from the Kellogg Foundation to facilitate 'collaboration among institutions of higher learning in their efforts to utilize the emerging communications sciences'.

EDWARDS OF HALIFAX. *See* FORE-EDGE PAINTING.

EGGSHELL. A paper with a non-glossy, soft, smooth finish. Most antique papers have an eggshell finish.

EGMONT. A light-faced roman type-face designed by S. H. De Roos and available from Intertype since 1937. It has a very small x-height, with tall ascenders and short descenders; there is vertical stress, rather thin flat serifs extending both ways on the top of the ascenders. For a specimen alphabet, *see* TYPE FACE.

EGYPTIAN. A group of display faces having slab-serifs and little contrast in the thickness of the strokes. They developed from the Antique face cut by Vincent Figgins prior to 1815 and were extensively used by jobbing printers in the nineteenth century. Early san serif types were also known as Egyptians but the name gradually became limited to slab-serif types, 'grotesque' being given to san serifs. Modern Egyptian faces are Beton, Cairo, Karnak, Luxor, Playbill, Rockwell, etc. These are also called block-serif abstract faces. *See also* BOLD FACE, CLARENDON.

EICHNER DRY COPY. A method of producing facsimile copies of single-sheet documents by feeding them through an Eichner machine in contact with copying paper. It is an indirect thermographic process. *See also* THERMOGRAPHY.

EIGHTEEN-MO. 1. A book in which the sections are folded four times so that each leaf is an eighteenth of the sheet. Also called 'Octodecimo'. 2. A sheet of paper so folded.

EJECTOR. In the Linotype and Intertype casting machines, the mechanism for ejecting cast lines.

ELEANOR FARJEON AWARD. *See* CHILDREN'S BOOK CIRCLE.

ELECTIVE AUDITOR. *See* BOROUGH AUDITORS.

ELECTORS' ROLL. *Synonymous with* REGISTER OF ELECTORS (*q.v.*).

ELECTRIC STYLUS. An electrically heated stylus used over a strip of metallic foil to impress the CALL NUMBER (*q.v.*) on to the spine of a book.

ELECTRO. Abbreviation for ELECTROTYPE (*q.v.*).

ELECTROFAX. Trade name for an electrophotographic process which was developed by the Radio Corporation of America Laboratories in 1954. The chief difference between this method and xerography is that a sensitive zinc-oxide coating is applied to a paper base and forms the actual copy paper whereas xerography uses a sensitive plate as an intermediate from which the image is finally transferred. In the machines on the British market, development techniques are by liquid and brush development.

ELECTROGRAPHIC PROCESSES. *Synonymous with* ELECTRO-PHOTOGRAPHIC PROCESSES (*q.v.*).

ELECTRONIC PHOTO-ENGRAVING MACHINES. Machines which produce half-tone printing plates automatically. The engraving is done on metal or plastic by a cutting or burning stylus used in conjunction with a scanning device which traces the original by means of a photographic cell. They utilize the action of light to give instructions, through electronic apparatus, to a mechanical instrument which removes unwanted areas of the plate. Trade names of such machines are: Elgrama, Fairchild Scan-a-Graver, Luxographe, Klischograph, Photo-Lathe.

ELECTROPHOTOGRAPHIC PROCESSES. XEROX and ELECTROFAX (*qq.v.*) are electrophotographic processes used in documentary reproduction. Both produce dry permanent copies at high speeds and can also make masters for the diazo, hectographic and lithographic processes. Xerox uses selenium plates or drums, and the copy can be made on any kind of paper. Electrofax uses paper coated with zinc oxide in place of the drum and on this the print is made. Small table machines are made for using the Electrofax method, and this type of machine is being used to make printing masters for offset lithography from normal paper copies.

ELECTROPHOTOGRAPHY. A documentary copying process which uses layers of photosemiconductors on the base material. A print so made may be called an electrophotocopy. *See also* ELECTROPHOTO-GRAPHIC PROCESSES, PHOTOGRAPHY.

ELECTROSTATIC PROCESSES. *Synonymous with* ELECTROPHOTO-GRAPHIC PROCESSES (*q.v.*).

ELECTROTYPE. A facsimile plate of a type forme or another plate, produced by taking an impression in wax, lead or plastic, depositing in this mould a thin shell of copper or other metal by an electro-plating process, backing it with type metal, and mounting it type high on wood. Half-tones (except the very coarsest) demand electros, which may also be made from line blocks and composed type. Abbreviated 'Electro'.

ELEPHANT. A size of paper varying from 28 × 23 inches to 34 × 28 inches. 'Double elephant' printing and writing papers vary from 36 × 24 inches to 46 × 31 inches; drawing papers are 26¾ × 40 inches (not an exact multiple of 'Elephant'). 'Long elephant' is a term employed for wallpaper 12 yards long and usually 22, 22½ or 30 inches wide.

ELEPHANT FOLIO. A folio volume larger than an ordinary folio but not so large as ATLAS FOLIO (*q.v.*). About 14 × 23 inches and formerly used for service books, maps, etc.

ELIOT PRIZE ESSAY AWARD, IDA AND GEORGE. $100 offered by the (American) Medical Library Association for the essay published in any journal during the previous year which has done most to further medical librarianship.

ELISION MARKS. *Synonymous with* OMISSION MARKS (*q.v.*).

ELITE. The smaller of the two common sizes of typewriter type, having twelve characters to the inch as against ten for the larger 'pica' size.

ELROD. *See* LUDLOW.

ELZEVIER. Name of the house of Elzevier, Dutch booksellers and printers; founded by Lodewijck (Louis) Elzevier (1542–1617) at Leyden in 1583 it continued until 1791, being directed by members of the Elzevier family. Of the books emanating from this firm, the most famous are the 32 mo. pocket-sized editions of the Latin classics begun in 1629. Books of this size printed elsewhere were known as 'Elzevirs'. Also spelled Elsevier and Elzevir. The distinctive type-face they used had a great influence on book design.

EM. The square of the body of any size of type; the printer's unit of square measure. A standard unit of typographic measurement, for which a 12 point em is the basis. This equals 0·166 inch, and there are approximately six 12-point ems to one inch. Sometimes called 'Pica.' This unit is used for computing the area of a printed page no matter what size of type is to be used for setting the text; thus if the area is 20 ems wide and 30 ems deep, the width is 240-point and the depth 360-point. It is also used to indicate the amount of indenting required. So called because the space taken up by the letter m is usually square. *See also* EN, PICA.

EM DASH. The dash—as here—used in punctuation. *See also* DASH.

EM QUADRAT. A square of metal used to fill out short lines of type to the required length; its width is equal to the BODY (*q.v.*). It is a type body cast less than type height, and is always the square of the size of type it accompanies, e.g. an em quadrat of 12-point type is 12 × 12 points. Em quadrats are often made in multiple. Used normally before the first word of a new paragraph. Usually called 'Em quad' or 'Mutton' (slang). The second and subsequent lines of these definitions are indented two ems. *See also* EN QUADRAT.

EMAGE. The area of a block of text, or of a text page, measured in terms of ems of its type size.

EMBLEM BOOK. A type of book in which designs or pictures called emblems, expressing some thought or moral idea, were printed with accompanying proverbs, mottoes, or explanatory writing; or in which verses are arranged in symbolic shapes such as crosses.

EMBOSSED. (*Binding*) A design which is raised in relief. (*Printing*) Lettering, or a design, which is raised above the surface of the paper.

EMBOSSED BOOK. A book in which the text is printed in embossed characters, such as Braille, for the use of the blind.

EMBOSSING. Relief printing by the use of a sunken die and a raised counterpart, called female and male, the surface of the paper being raised in relief. It may also be done by the use of certain substances dusted on the printed surface and caused to be raised by heating. Also called 'Process embossing', 'Relief printing', 'Bas relief printing'. *See also* DIE STAMPING, THERMOGRAPHY.

EMBOSSING PLATE. A plate cut or etched below its surface and used for producing a design, usually lettering, in relief on a sheet of paper. *See also* EMBOSSING.

EMBOSSING PRESS. A machine used in binderies for impressing lettering and designs on book covers.

EMBROIDERED BINDING. Binding in which the covering material is embroidered cloth. Also called 'Needlework binding'.

EMULSION. The chemicals with which a photographic film or paper is coated. In documentary reproduction the emulsion used on papers is usually silver halide suspended in a medium such as gelatine.

EN. Half the width of an EM (*q.v.*) but the same height.

EN QUADRAT. A square of metal half the width of the body of a type, and half an EM QUADRAT (*q.v.*), usually inserted after a punctuation mark when not ending a sentence. Usually called 'En quad' or 'Nut' (slang).

EN RULE. A dash the width of an en space. *See also* DASH.

ENAMEL PAPER. A highly finished paper coated on one side.

ENAMELLED BINDINGS. *See* CHAMPLEVÉ, CLOISONNÉ.

ENCHIRIDION (*Pl.*, – ONS or – A.). A hand-book, specifically a manual of devotions.

ENCODE. 1. To put into symbolic form. 2. In information retrieval, to transform a document, message or abstract by means of a specific notation.

ENCODING. (*Informational Retrieval*) A process whereby a message is transformed into signals that can be carried by a communication channel.

ENCYCLOPAEDIA. A work containing information on all subjects, or limited to a special field or subject, arranged in systematic, (usually alphabetical), order. Encyclopaedias may be in one volume, in which case very brief information will be given, or they may be in forty or more volumes in which the various matters will be comprehensive, usually written by experts, and sometimes containing bibliographies and illustrations. The term was first used in a book title in Johann Heinrich Alsted's *Encyclopaedia cursus philosophici*, Herborn, 1608. It was one of the last encyclopaedias written in Latin and compiled on a systematic plan; in future they were to be in the vernacular languages with the entries in alphabetical order. The first of this kind to be published in English was John Harris's *Lexicon technicum, or, An universal English dictionary of the arts and sciences*, London, 1704. One of the earliest encyclopaedias was the Spanish Archbishop Isidore of Seville's *Etymologiarum sivi originium libri XX* which was completed in 623. More than a thousand manuscripts of this have survived, and in printed form it had an undiminished appeal as late as the seventeenth century.

END A BREAK. An instruction to the compositor that the last line of a TAKE (*q.v.*) or section of copy is to be filled out with quad spacing after setting the last word. *See also* BREAK LINE, END EVEN, RUN ON.

END EVEN. An instruction to the compositor that the last line of type in a TAKE (*q.v.*) or section of copy is to be spaced out so that the last word is at the end of a line. *See also* BREAK-LINE, END A BREAK, RUN ON.

END LEAF. The piece of paper covering the turned-in covering material and the joint, or hinge reinforcement, of a re-bound book. (American.)

END-MATTER. The items which follow the text of a printed book. These include appendices, bibliography, notes, supplements, indexes, glossary, imprint or collation, advertisements. *See also* BACK MATTER.

ENDNOTES. Notes printed at the end of a chapter or end of a book. In certain types of book such as those intended for the general reader, or printed lectures, endnotes are preferable to footnotes.

ENDPAPER. A sheet of paper at each end of a book which is inserted by the binder to help fasten the sewn sections to the cover. One half, the 'paste-down endpaper', is pasted on to a cover of the book (with the tapes between); the other, the 'free endpaper' or 'fly-leaf' is pasted with a narrow strip of paste at the fold to the end leaf of a section. Endpapers are best left plain but are frequently used for maps and tables. *See also* DOUBLURE, MAP ENDPAPER.

ENGINE-SIZING. Hardening paper by adding a moisture-resistant substance as casein, starch or resin to the pulp before the stuff flows on to the machine wire. This is the usual method of sizing the cheaper papers and produces a weaker paper than TUB-SIZING (*q.v.*). Engine-sized paper is abbreviated ES. *See also* SURFACE SIZING.

ENGLISH. An out-of-date name for a size of type equal to about 14 point.

ENGLISH FINISH PAPER. A calendered paper with a smooth but not highly glossy finish.

ENGLISH STOCK. A group of publications of which the STATIONERS COMPANY (*q.v.*) held the sole rights of printing and distributing. Perpetual rights were given in a patent granted in 1603 by James I to the Master, Wardens and Assistants of the Company. The publications included almanacs, ABC primers, prognostications, psalters, psalms in metre and catechisms and were sold in large numbers.

ENGRAVED TITLE-PAGE. A supplementary title-page usually wholly engraved on copper which faces the usual printed title-page. These were popular in the seventeenth century and were frequently elaborate allegorical pictures or symbolic designs.

ENGRAVER'S PROOFS. Proofs of engravings used for verifying the quality of the work and for dummying up in pages.

ENGRAVING. 1. The art or process of making letters or designs on wood, metal or other substances, by cutting or etching, for the purpose of printing or stamping by an intaglio or recess process on paper or other material. 2. An engraved plate, or an impression made from an engraved plate. 3. An engraved inscription. 4. The act of taking an impression from an engraved plate. *See also* AQUATINT, ETCHING, LINE ENGRAVING, MEZZOTINT, WOOD ENGRAVING.

ENLARGED EDITION. *Synonymous with* REVISED EDITION (*q.v.*).

ENLARGEMENT. A copy, usually of a photograph or microphoto-graph, having a larger scale than the original. Also called 'Blow-up', 'Projection print'.

ENLARGER-PRINTER. An optical machine for producing images larger than the one being copied; it incorporates processing facilities for the rapid reproduction of copies, and can be operated under conditions of normal room-lighting.

ENRICHED CO-ORDINATE INDEXING. *Synonymous with* CO-ORDINATE INDEXING (*q.v.*).

ENROLLED ACCOUNT. An account which has been entered on a roll, usually for audit.

ENROLMENT. Entry of a document upon a roll.

ENSLA. Eastern Nigeria Division School Libraries Association. *See* NIGERIA LIBRARY ASSOCIATION.

ENTITY. In co-ordinate indexing, a thing mentioned as subject-matter.

ENTRANCE COUNTER. The side of a staff enclosure at which readers enter a library and return any books they have borrowed.

ENTROPY. The unavailable information in a group of documents. The degree of disorganization in an informational assemblage (*IBM*).

ENTRY. 1. The record of a book publication, or other item in a catalogue or other library record. In a catalogue it may be the main entry or an entry under subject, or an ADDED ENTRY (*q.v.*) or an INDEX ENTRY (*q.v.*). It may give a description of the item and also the location. 2. Sometimes used to indicate the cataloguing process which is concerned with determining the headings to be used for the BODY OF THE ENTRY (*q.v.*) or that part of the description of an item which follows a heading. 3. (*a*) A unit of an index consisting of a heading (and qualifying expression, if any) with at least one reference to the location of the item in the text or with a 'See' cross-reference. (*b*) In a complex entry, when references are numerous enough for systematic grouping, sub-headings are used to introduce sub-entries, each with the relevant reference(s). 4. An item in an index to a literary composition (MS., book, periodical, etc.) which refers to a single specific place in the text, and possibly indicates the nature of the material to be found there. 5. The physical form which an entry may take; in information retrieval called a TALLY (*q.v.*). *See also* ADDED ENTRY, ANALYTICAL ENTRY, GENERAL SECONDARY, HEADING, MAIN ENTRY, REFERENCE, SERIES ENTRY, TITLE ENTRY.

ENTRY WORD. 1. The first word, other than an article, of a heading in a catalogue; the one by which the entry is arranged. *See also* HEADING. 2. The word determining the place of an entry or group of related entries in the catalogue (*IFLA*).

ENUMERATIVE BIBLIOGRAPHY. A list of recorded items compiled within limits set by the compiler; these may be geographical, chronological or topical.

ENUMERATIVE CLASSIFICATION. A classification which attempts to list specific subjects. Owing to the difficulty of enumerating all possible specific subjects, most of such classifications are necessarily selective. The Library of Congress Classification is of this kind.

EPHEMERA. 1. Pamphlets, cuttings and other material, of ephemeral interest and value. 2. Such material of earlier periods which has acquired literary or historical importance.

EPHEMERIDES. *See* EPHEMERIS.

EPHEMERIS (*Pl.* EPHEMERIDES). 1. An almanac or calendar. 2. An obsolete term for a diary having been so used since the fourth century B.C. 3. A title-word of many seventeenth and eighteenth century periodicals. 4. An astronomical almanac giving the daily positions of stars and other heavenly bodies.

EPIGRAPH. A sentence or quotation at the commencement of the chapter of a book to indicate the sentiment or idea.

EPISTEMOLOGY. The science of organized ideas in their exact correspondence with outward things, or knowledge.

EPISTOLARIA. A liturgical book containing the Epistles.

EPITHALAMIUM. A poem or song in honour of a wedding, or of a bride and bridegroom.

EPITHET. A descriptive, significant name; an additional name or title expressing an attribute of the person referred to, and used to distinguish him from others of the same name. In catalogue entries, the epithet follows the personal name under which the entry is made.

EPITOME. A work that has been abridged or summarized from some larger work for a particular purpose, the essential matter of the original being retained. To be distinguished from an ADAPTATION (*q.v.*).

EPONYM. 1. One who gives, or is supposed to give, his name to a people, place or institution; also the name of that personage. 2. A distinguishing title formed from the name of a person to designate a period, people or place, e.g. Victorian era.

EPOPEE. An epic poem. Epic poetry.

ERA. Acronym for Electronic Reading Automation. A machine which will identify the numerals 0–9 and some fractions, the plus sign, and twelve specified capital letters at a speed of 200–300 characters a second. It is made by Solartron.

ERIC. Acronym for Educational Resources (formerly Research) Information Center, a national organization, supported financially by the U.S. Office of Education, which acquires, abstracts, indexes, stores, retrieves, and disseminates the most significant educational research documents.

ERIC/CLIS. The Clearinghouse for Library and Information Sciences of the Educational Resources Information Center of the U.S. Department of Health, Education and Welfare. Established in March 1967 at the Library School of the University of Minnesota, Minneapolis, Minnesota, this organization has a field of responsibility defined as 'the operation of libraries and information centers, the technology used to improve their operations and the education and training of librarians and information specialists'.

EROTICA. Indecent or obscene books. *See also* CURIOSA, FACETIAE.

ERRATA (*Sing.* ERRATUM). *Synonymous with* CORRIGENDA (*q.v.*).

ESCAPIST LITERATURE. Light literature such as thrillers, adventure stories and romances which are read for entertainment, as a relief from more serious reading, and as a distraction.

ESPARTO. A coarse grass, also termed 'Alfa', growing in countries around the Mediterranean, particularly southern Spain and northern Africa, which is used for making the better (but not the best) grades of book paper, featherweight and coating papers. The best grade is known as 'Spanish', the cheaper grades as 'Tripoli'. Esparto papers are distinguished by their refined silky texture and bulk, and their close uniform surface or finish. Their finish is their chief characteristic; this together with their bulkiness makes them eminently suitable for fine printings and other papers required to take a good impression from plates.

ESSAY PERIODICAL. A periodical publication, prevalent in the fifteenth century, each issue of which usually consisted of a single essay. The *Spectator* and the *Rambler* are examples.

ESSENTIAL CHARACTERISTICS. *See* CHARACTERISTIC OF A CLASSIFICATION.

ESTABLISHED. Said of a catalogue heading when an authority card or catalogue entry of any kind is made for it.

ESTHER J. PIERCY AWARD. *See* PIERCY AWARD, ESTHER J.

ESTIENNE, ROBERT. Born 1503 and son of Henry Estienne who founded in 1501 the famous firm of Parisian scholar-printers. Founded his own business in 1524, and was appointed in 1539 and 1540 printer to the king in Latin, Greek and Hebrew. The fine press-work of his books matches the careful editing of the classical texts, dictionaries and translations. From 1550 until his death in 1559 he worked at Geneva, where he printed several of Calvin's works. The most important member of the greatest family of scholar-printers of all ages, his chief and most secure claim of many to immortality, is that based on his Thesaurus, *Dictionarius sivi Latinae thesaurus*, Paris, 1531. He established the principle, contrary to his mediaeval predecessors, that a Latin dictionary must be based on classical authorities. He undertook the compilation of a series of Latin-French and French-Latin dictionaries which helped to create the classical French language: these were translated into German, Dutch and English, and were the progenitors of all bilingual dictionaries.

ESTIMATES. Annual calculations of amounts of money needed to provide a service. In the case of local authorities the estimates in respect of each committee are submitted to the financial officer who presents them to the finance committee which forwards complete estimates for the whole of the authority's activities to the council for adoption. *Special estimates* are those for completely new items which could not be anticipated when the annual estimates were prepared. *Supplemental estimates* (sometimes called *supplementary estimates*) are those made during the course of the financial year for amounts in excess of the figure which was included in the annual estimates and are due to a variety of causes such as an increase in the cost of materials or labour, or unanticipated difficulties in the carrying out of work, or urgent and unanticipated developments in the service. Increased expenditure cannot be incurred until supplemental estimates have been approved.

et al. Abbreviation for *et alii* (*Lat.* 'and others'). Used in a second or subsequent reference to a work in footnotes. It follows the name of the first of three or more collaborators whose work has previously been cited. Also for *et alia* 'and other things', *et alibi* 'and elsewhere'.

et infra. (*Lat.* 'and below'.) Used to indicate that something which follows may be of smaller size, as '24 vols., 8vo. *et infra*', meaning that the largest is 8vo. *See also infra.*

et seq. Abbreviation for *et sequens* (*Lat.* 'and the following one'). *Pl. et seqq.* abbreviation for *et sequentes, et sequentia* 'and those that follow'. *See also seq.*

etc. Abbreviation for *et cetera* (*Lat.* 'and the other, the rest'). Also abbreviated '&c.'

ETCHING.   1. The process of producing a design upon a plate of steel, copper, glass or zinc by means of drawing lines with an etching needle through an acid-resisting wax coating upon the polished surface of the plate, and then covering this surface with an acid which corrodes the metal in the lines thus laid bare. 2. A plate with an etched design upon its surface. 3. The art of producing impressions on paper or other material from an etched plate. 4. The impression produced by 3. *See also* DEEP ETCHING, DRY-POINT ETCHING.

ETHNIC NUMBERS. Numbers added to a classification symbol so as to arrange books by language or race. They are usually applicable throughout a classification scheme. Also called 'Linguistic numbers'.

ETHNOMUSICOLOGY.   The study of the native music of a people or of a race.

ETRUSCAN ALPHABET.   The most significant offshoot from the Greek alphabet and adapted to the language of the Etruscans. It developed, probably in the eighth century B.C. and lasted until the first century A.D. The Latin alphabet was derived from it.

ETRUSCAN STYLE.   A calfskin binding style, so called because of the contrasting colours or shades of leather (light brown or terra-cotta) and decoration (dark brown or black tooling); the terra cotta shades and decoration combined represent Greek and Etruscan vases. Such bindings usually have a rectangular central panel on each cover, or occasionally a plain oval with a classical urn in the middle and are tooled in black, surrounded by a border of Greek palmated leaves in black, with outer borders of classical design (Grecian key or Doric entablature) tooled in gold. The spines also are decorated with classical ornaments. This style was used by and probably originated by William Edwards of Halifax towards the end of the eighteenth century, and was practised until about 1820.

EUNICE ROCKWELL OBERLY MEMORIAL AWARD. *See* OBERLY MEMORIAL AWARD, EUNICE ROCKWELL.

EUROPEAN COMMITTEE FOR COORDINATION OF STAN-DARDS.   Founded in March 1961 in Paris in succession to a Common Market committee which had been set up in October 1957, also in Paris. Its aims are to establish standardization documents common to the countries of the European Economic Community and those of the European Free Trade Association for the purpose of harmonizing the standards of these countries so as to promote the development of trade and the exchange of services between them. National standardization organizations are members. Abbreviated CEN. Electrotechnical matters are dealt with by the parallel organization CENEL.

EUROPEAN DOCUMENTATION AND INFORMATION CEN-TRE.   Founded in 1952; registered under German law in 1957. Aims to group the active forces in all the European countries which are ready to defend in public the fundamental principles of European Christian culture, and to assist in the permanent co-operation of the personalities of the cultural, political and economic life of the European countries. Individuals and national centres may become members. Abbreviated CEDI (Centre Européen de Documentation et d'Information).

EUROPEAN ORGANIZATION FOR NUCLEAR RESEARCH. Established on 29th September 1954 'to provide for collaboration among European states in nuclear research of a pure scientific and fundamental character, and in research essentially related thereto'. Governments may become members. Abbreviated CERN. Publishes *CERN Courier* (m.).

EUROPEAN TRANSLATIONS CENTRE. Conceived in 1960, this information centre concentrates on East European scientific and technical literature with the following objectives: (a) to create a permanent link between national centres dealing with translations and to undertake studies connected with them, (b) to keep a title index of available translations and to issue a regular Translation List, (c) to collect non-commercial translations from countries that are willing to contribute such translations. It is based on the Technological University of Delft, Holland, and comprises sixteen national translations centres as well as the main centre. Publishes a quarterly comprehensive index of all existing translations (into chiefly English, French and German) which are processed at the Centre, the fourth issue being a yearly cumulation entitled *World index of scientific translations*, and *List of translations notified to ETC* (fortnightly). Abbreviated ETC.

EVALUATION. An estimate of the value of a work as a contribution to the literature of a subject.

EVALUATIVE ABSTRACT. *See* ABSTRACT.

EVE STYLE. *See* FANFARE (FLOURISH) STYLE.

EVEN PAGE. A page of a book bearing an even number; usually the VERSO (*q.v.*).

EVEN RIGHT-HAND MARGIN. Said of type-written matter where the lines have been justified and all have the same length, thus giving an even right-hand margin as well as the usual even left-hand margin.

EVEN SMALL CAPS. An instruction to the compositor that all the copy so marked is to be set in small capitals without any large capitals as would be done in 'caps and smalls'. Abbreviated even s. caps, or even s.c. Also called 'Level small caps'.

EVEN WORKING. The setting of 'copy' so that it will occupy a full sheet of, say, 32 pages. If an additional portion of a sheet is required for completion, say eight pages, this is called 'uneven working'. *See also* ODDMENTS.

EVOLUTIONARY ORDER. (*Classification*) The method by which subjects are shown in the order of their history or development, 'in natural history putting the parts of each subject in the order which that theory assigns to their appearance in creation. As science proceeds from the molecular to the molar, from number and space through matter and force to matter and life, etc., etc.' (*Cutter*) Cutter's Expansive Classification follows this order, as also in a rough way does Brown's Subject Classification. No scheme is, or can be, evolutionary throughout.

ex libris. 1. Latin phrase, meaning *from the books of* (i.e. from the library of); frequently used on book plates, the owners' name being written or printed after 'ex libris'. 2. Surplus books from a subscription or other library.

EXACT CLASSIFICATION. *Synonymous with* CLOSE CLASSIFICATION (*q.v.*).

EXACT SIZE. The measured size of a book expressed by centimetres or inches rather than by a signature symbol. Also called 'Absolute size'.

EXCERPT. A verbatim extract from a book, or piece of music, whether printed or manuscript. An extract or selection.

EXCHANGE. 1. The exchange by barter or trade of duplicate material with other libraries. 2. The exchange of publications with other institutions.

EXCHANGE CENTRE. An administrative office which negotiates the exchange of books between libraries, arranging for books to be sent from libraries where they are surplus to libraries where they are needed. *See also* BRITISH NATIONAL BOOK CENTRE.

EXCHEQUER SERIES. *See* LIBERATE ROLL.

EXHAUSTED EDITION. An edition which has become out-of-print.

EXHAUSTIVE DIVISION. Dividing as exhaustively and minutely as possible in order to give specific places in a scheme of classification.

EXHIBITION CASE. A glass-fronted case built against a wall, possibly amongst wall shelving; or a glass-topped showcase on legs, in which selected books, documents, illustrations or other items are exhibited.

EXHIBITION VAN. (*County Libraries*) A vehicle fitted with shelving or other method of displaying books from which local librarians, teachers, etc., select the stocks for their centres, but which does not serve the public direct.

EXHIBITS ROUND TABLE AWARD. $500 offered by the Exhibits Round Table of the American Library Association to an individual or group for aiding or improving some aspect of librarianship or library service on the basis of need in the profession or in the operation of professional library associations.

EXIT COUNTER. The side of a staff enclosure at which readers leave a library and have books issued or 'charged' to them.

EX-LIBRARY COPY. A catalogue description of a book originally in a public or circulating library.

EXOTICS. A general name used in the printing industry for Cyrillic, Arabic and other non-latin letter-forms.

EXPANSIVE CLASSIFICATION. The scheme of classification devised by C. A. Cutter, which began to appear in 1891, it is one of the most minute and scholarly of schemes for a general library, but it is now out-of-date. It consists of seven expansions (the seventh, uncompleted, being very detailed and suitable for a very large library) each of which covers the whole field of knowledge but in varying detail, and can be used according to the size of the library. Later expansions cannot be used in the same library, however, without re-classifying a number of the books, as the fundamental symbols had to be altered as the expansions progressed. The order of the schedules is evolutionary, the main classes being:

A	General Works.	R	Useful Arts, Technology.
B	Philosophy.	V	Athletic and Recreative Arts.
Br	Religion	Vv	Fine Arts. Music.
D	Historical Sciences.	X	Arts of Communication by
H	Social Sciences.		Language.
L	Sciences and Arts.		

The intervening letters in the above schedule are given to the more important divisions. The notation is a pure alphabetical one, permitting sub-division at any point in the scheme by the use of the alphabet, but form divisions and the Local List for sub-dividing geographically have numerical notations which can be used mnemonically.

EXPLANATORY GUIDE CARDS. Guide cards giving an explanation of the arrangement of the catalogue cards and placed at the beginning of groups of cards for voluminous authors, anonymous classics, sacred books, etc.

EXPLICIT. The closing phrase of a manuscript or early printed book indicating its completion and sometimes giving the author's name and the title of the work. It is the author's or scribe's colophon taken over from the manuscript, and may appear instead of, or in conjunction with, the printer's colophon. It is a contraction for *explicitus est* 'it is unfolded'.

EXPRESSIVE NOTATION. One of Ranganathan's canons of notation – that the notation should be designed to show that two terms are in the same array, or the same chain.

EXPURGATED EDITION. An edition with those parts left out that might be objected to on moral or other grounds. *See also* ABRIDGED EDITION, BOWDLERIZED.

EXTENDED SCORE. *Synonymous with* OPEN SCORE (*q.v.*). *See also* SCORE.

EXTENDER. That part of a type letter which projects above or below the main body of the letter. Also called 'Extruder'. *See also* ASCENDER, DESCENDER.

EXTENSION. (*Classification*) The extension of a term or class indicates all the different items included in the term; in other words, the compass of the term. The intension indicates their *qualities*. Extension and intension vary conversely; when one is great the other is small.

EXTENSION AGENCIES. Activities of the library services which are undertaken outside the main library buildings. These include REGIONAL BRANCHES, COMMUNITY LIBRARIES, SUB-BRANCHES, DEPOSIT STATIONS AND BOOKMOBILES. (*qq.v.*). (American.)

EXTENSION CARD. Second and subsequent catalogue cards used when the entry is too long to go on one card. It contains the classification number and the entry word from the first card, and is numbered 2, 3, etc. Also called a 'Continuation card', 'Run-on card'.

EXTENSION CENTRE LIBRARY. A branch library which is placed in an American University of college extension centre where college-level classes or other educational services are provided, usually through a specific division of an educational institution.

EXTENSION WORK. Activities which are undertaken with the object of reaching groups of people who might otherwise be unaware of the library, such as lecture societies, reading circles, discussion groups; and the provision of books for prisons, clubs, hospitals, literary societies, etc.

EXTERNAL BIBLIOGRAPHY. *See* HISTORICAL BIBLIOGRAPHY.

EXTERNAL READER. A person who is permitted to use a library provided primarily for the use of privileged persons, such as the members of a professional body or association.

EXTRA BINDER. A craftsman who uses the best materials and employs the soundest methods of construction; he usually decorates each binding with a design specially made for it.

EXTRA BINDING. In binding, a trade term for the best work. Applicable to any book well 'forwarded', lined with marbled or other special paper, silk head-bands, and gilt with a narrow roll round the sides and inside the 'squares'.

EXTRA-ILLUSTRATED. A book which has had additional illustrations and printed matter inserted since publication. *See also* GRANGER-IZING.

EXTRA LIGHTWEIGHT PAPER. Sensitized photographic paper between 0·0023 and 0·0031 inches inclusive. Also called 'Ultra thin paper'.

EXTRA THIN PAPER. Sensitized photographic paper between 0·0032 and 0·0037 inches inclusive. *See also* PHOTOGRAPHIC PAPERS.

EXTRA TICKET. *Synonymous with* SUPPLEMENTARY TICKET (*q.v.*).

EXTRACT. *See* ABSTRACT 5.

EXTRACT TYPE. Type which is different from that used for the text, normally being smaller, and used to enable quoted (or extracted) material such as poems, bibliographies, extracts, etc., to be easily distinguished from the text itself.

EXTRACTED ARTICLE. *Synonymous with* SEPARATE (*q.v.*).

EXTRAPOLATION. (*Classification*) The addition of new subjects to the end of an ARRAY (*q.v.*). This flexible aspect of notation is facilitated by the OCTAVE DEVICE (*q.c.*). *See also* INTERPOLATION.

EXTRUDER. *Synonymous with* EXTENDER (*q.v.*).

EXTRUDERS. The collective term for the ASCENDERS and DESCENDERS (*qq.v.*).

f. Abbreviation for 'following'. *Pl.* ff.

FABRIANO PAPER. An Italian paper used for special and fine editions.

FABRIC BINDING. One in which a fabric has been used instead of leather and vellum. Velvet, silk, satin, and canvas have been the most popular materials, and have been used more frequently in England than elsewhere. Velvet, a most extensively used fabric, was plain, embroidered, or even gilt-tooled. Embroidered bindings, in a form of split-stitch work known as *opus anglicanum* on satin, were popular in the fifteenth century.

FABRIKOID. The trade name for the pyroxylin-coated book cloth made by du Pont.

FABROLEEN. Trade name for a cheaper variety of LINSON (*q.v.*), made of specially prepared paper and used for case-making. *See also* CASE.

fac. Abbreviation for FACSIMILE and FACTOTUM (*qq.v.*).

FACE. 1. The entire unbroken front of shelving on one side of a double case or on one side of a room or gallery. 2. (*Printing*) The printing surface of type. It comprises STEM, BOWL, SERIF, COUNTER, CROTCH and KERN (*qq.v.*). Measured set-wise, i.e. left to right, a face may be condensed (compressed) or extended (expanded); measured body-wise, it may be small, ordinary, medium or large, according to the actual size of the short and long letters. 3. (*Printing*) A particular design or style of a fount of type. *See also* TYPE FACE.

FACE UP. (*Printing*) Said of full-page illustrations which are printed on the right-hand side of an opening, i.e. on the recto of a leaf.

FACET. In classification, the whole group of divisions (*see* DIVISION 4), or foci (*see* FOCUS *noun*), produced when a subject is divided according to a single characteristic. Five kinds of facet are discernable in any class: these relate to personality, matter, energy, space and time. Facets may be divided into *subfacets* (called by Ranganathan 'arrays'). *Dependent facets* do not appear in the classification except as a further division of a more fundamental facet. Modifications of basic facets are called *differential facets*. Each division of a facet is said to be an Isolate Focus, or simply an Isolate. Sometimes used to denote any single ISOLATE (*q.v.*) or any basic class. Also called 'Category'. *See also* AUTO-BIAS DEVICE, CHARACTERISTIC OF A CLASSIFICATION. 2. An aspect, or orientation, of a topic (*IBM*).

FACET ANALYSIS. (*Classification*) The analysis of any subject to determine what characteristics should be used to divide it, relating them to the five fundamentals. *See also* FACET.

FACET FORMULA. (*Classification*) A formula for the application of division; used so that the order of applying characteristics may be consistently maintained. *See also* CITATION ORDER.

FACET INDICATOR. A symbol which separates parts of a notation of a scheme of classification and indicates exactly what facet is to follow. Facet indicators were made possible in the Colon Classification by adopting the five FUNDAMENTAL CATEGORIES (*q.v.*), each of which is introduced by its own symbol. It may be a different kind of character in a mixed notation, e.g. a letter whereas other characters in the notation are figures, in which case every letter would indicate a facet. *See also* NOTATION.

FACETED CLASSIFICATION. 1. A scheme of classification which reflects in its structure the analysis of subjects according to a number of fundamental concepts, particularly those denominated: personality, matter, energy, space, time. It lists constituent parts of specific subjects, which parts must be assembled in a predetermined order to express the specific subjects. All modern schemes of classification are faceted to a certain degree: e.g. they provide tables of constant numbers for divisions relating to time and to space. A classification scheme which allows the classifier to build up the notation for a particular book from various unit schedules is called a 'faceted', 'synthetic' or 'analytico-synthetic' classification. 2. Classification schemes whose terms are grouped by conceptual categories and ordered so as to display their generic relations. These categories or 'facets' are standard unit-schedules and the terms, or rather the notation for the terms from these various unit-schedules, are combined at will in accordance with a prescribed order of permutation or combination (*IBM*).

FACETED INITIAL. In a mediaeval illuminated manuscript, an initial letter given the appearance of being faceted.

FACETED NOTATION. (*Classification*) A NOTATION (*q.v.*) representing the classification of a book in which a distinctive symbol is used to separate the facets which comprise it.

FACETED SUBJECT CLASSIFICATION FOR ENGINEERING. A scheme constructed by Mrs. Jean Aitchison in 1957 at the Whetstone Library of the English Electric Group for use in the Central Reports Files of internally published reports and in the abstract bulletins published by the Library.

FACETIAE. Coarsely witty books; objectionable or indecent works collectively. *See also* CURIOSA, EROTICA.

FACING PAGES. The two pages which are visible when a book is open. An OPENING (*q.v.*).

facsim. Abbreviation for FACSIMILE (*q.v.*). Also abbreviated 'fs.', 'fac.'.

FACSIMILE. 1. A copy of an original, reproduced in its exact form and style. 2. Used in cataloguing to indicate that the book catalogued contains a facsimile. Abbreviated 'fs', 'fac.', 'facsim.', 'facsims.' (pl.). 3. An electronic system for transmitting pictures and graphic materials over very high frequency air waves.

FACSIMILE BINDING. A binding which closely resembles an older binding.

FACSIMILE CATALOGUE. One which incorporates facsimiles of maps, pictures, designs, etc., as part of each catalogue entry which is made on larger cards than the normal size, or in loose leaf binders.

FACSIMILE EDITION. An exact copy of a book made photographically, by xerography, or by an offset process. Used to avoid the cost of setting up type in order to produce a new edition of an out-of-print book. Previously, a copy, as near the original as possible typographically, published to make widely available a book which existed only as an incunabulum or as a manuscript.

FACSIMILE REPRINT. A reproduction of a work, however printed, and reproducing exactly the appearance of the original.

FACSIMILE TRANSMISSION. The rapid transmission of printed pages from one point to another, using electronic devices. The process involves converting the original picture into an electrical impulse which is then transmitted over telephone lines, private lines, microwave, or a combination of these communication media. The receiving unit reconverts the electrical impulse into an exact duplicate of the original document on a screen or in the form of a hard copy.

FACT RETRIEVAL SYSTEM.   One which yields specific information in response to a search request. An aspect of INFORMATION RETRIEVAL (*q.v.*).

FACTOTUM.   An ornament of wood or metal having a space in the centre for the insertion of a capital letter of an ordinary fount of type; used to print ornamental initial letters at the commencement of a chapter. It is sometimes called a 'Factotum initial'. Abbreviated: fac.

FACTUM.   1. A statement of facts, or of the points in a case of controversy; a memorial (OED). 2. A statement of fact. A memorandum summarizing the chief facts of a case.

FACULTY LIBRARY.   *Synonymous with* DEPARTMENTAL LIBRARY (*q.v.*).

FACULTY OF ADVOCATES, EDINBURGH.   *See* NATIONAL LIBRARY OF SCOTLAND.

FAIR CALF.   *Synonymous with* LAW CALF (*q.v.*).

FAIR COPY.   A carefully made typescript or manuscript without mistakes or corrections, made after examining a draft.

FAIR COPYING DECLARATION.   An agreement by over 140 publishing organizations, including scientific societies under which the reproduction of articles for use by individual research workers is permitted. It developed from The Royal Society's Scientific Information Conference, held in 1948. The signatories regard it as fair dealing for a non-profit making organization, such as a library, archives office, museum or information service, to make a *single* reproduction of a part of an issue of a periodical on behalf of a person who represents in writing that he desires it solely for the purpose of private study, research, criticism or review, and providing he undertakes not to sell or reproduce for publication the copy supplied. The declaration does not apply to books and other non-periodic or non-serial publications.

'FAIR DEALING'.   A circumstance under which the copying of copyright material may be undertaken. This permits the making of a single copy for the purposes of research or private study.

FALSE BANDS.   *Synonymous with* DUMMY BANDS (*q.v.*).

FALSE DATE.   A date given wrongly, either intentionally or in error. In a catalogue entry the correct date is given in brackets following 'i.e.'.

FALSE DROP.   (*Information retrieval*) 1. Citation that does not pertain to the subject sought. An alien, usually in a manipulative or co-ordinate index (*IBM*). 2. An irrelevant reference made in indexing documents for concept co-ordinate indexing. *See also* UNITERM CONCEPT CO-ORDINATION INDEXING.

'FALSE FIRST' EDITION. An edition of a book said to be the first when in fact there had been an edition published previously by another publisher.

FALSE HYPHEN. One placed by the printer between two parts of a word which is broken at the line end.

FALSE IMPRINT. *Synonymous with* FICTITIOUS IMPRINT (*q.v.*).

FALSE LINK. (*Classification*). In chain indexing, a step in the notational hierarchy where the notational chain is lengthened by a symbol without an appropriate term being supplied. In the Dewey Decimal Classification, for example, where a zero is needed to introduce a standard sub-division or geographical table number, the zero having no verbal equivalent, but being merely an indicator that a form or geographical division is about to be employed. *See also* CHAIN INDEX SUBORDINATION, UNSOUGHT LINK.

FALSE SORT. The recalling, or retrieving, of information, especially with co-ordinate indexing, which is not required; this can be reduced by the careful choice of indexing terms when recording (indexing) documents. Also called in America 'False drops' and 'False reports'.

FALSTAFF. A fat face type. *See* FAT FACES.

FAMILY. The complete group or collection of all the sizes and styles of type of the same design: they have common characteristics and differ only in size, set or thickness of lines, e.g. the Gill Sans family, comprising: Gill Sans, **Gill Sans Bold,** Gill Sans Light, **Gill Sans Bold Condensed, Gill Sans Extra Bold.**

FAMILY NAME. A surname.

FAN. A book decoration style characteristic of Italian bindings in the seventeenth century, and of Scottish bindings, in which a design like a fan is tooled on the sides making a full circle in the centre, and often quarter circles in the corners. It is a development of the centre and cornerpiece bindings.

FANCY TYPE. Printing type of various sizes, ornamental in design; usually used for display purposes.

FANFARE STYLE. The later Eve style of decorating bookcovers, being a complication of geometrical interlacings and a multitude of scrolls, wreaths, sprays and flowers, filling all available space on back and sides of the book. It was practised in the late sixteenth century. Also called 'Flourish style'.

FARJEON AWARD, ELEANOR. *See* CHILDREN'S BOOK CIRCLE.

FARMINGTON PLAN. A scheme whereby over sixty American research libraries have agreed co-operatively to purchase books published in foreign countries in order to ensure that at least one copy of new books and pamphlets likely to interest research workers is acquired by an American library. Such books are promptly listed in the Union Catalogue at the Library of Congress and made available by inter-library loan or photographic reproduction. The plan was drawn up at Farmington, Connecticut, by K. D. Metcalf, J. P. Boyd and Archibald Macleish, and began to operate in January 1948. It is now supervised by the ASSOCIATION OF RESEARCH LIBRARIES (*q.v.*).

FASCICLE. Parts of a work which for convenience of publishing or printing, is issued in small instalments. They are usually incomplete in themselves and do not necessarily coincide with the formal division of the work into parts. They usually consist of sections, or groups of plates, protected by temporary wrappers, and may or may not be numbered or designated as a 'part', 'fascicule', 'lieferung', etc. Also called 'Fascicule', 'Fasciculus'.

FASCICULE. *Synonymous with* FASCICLE (*q.v.*).

FASCICULUS. *Synonymous with* FASCICLE (*q.v.*).

FAST BACK. *Synonymous with* TIGHT BACK (*q.v.*).

FAT FACES. Type faces which have extra thick perpendicular strokes whether straight or curved, such as Elephant, Ultra Bodoni, and Falstaff.

FAT MATTER. 'Copy' which can be set up in type easily since many lines of type will not be full. Novels which are largely dialogue are 'fat'. This is the opposite to difficult copy which is known as 'lean matter'. *See also* MATTER.

FAULTY MARGIN. An unequal margin due to imperfect registering.

FAVOURED FOCUS. Any simple or compound FOCUS (*q.v.*) which represents the subject of specialization of a library or the isolate in which its collection is more numerous than in other co-ordinate sub-classes.

FAVOURED LANGUAGE. The language in which most of the books in a library are written.

FEATHER-EDGE. *Synonymous with* DECKLE EDGE.

FEATHER ORNAMENT. (*Binding*) Engraved ornament which resembles feathers, on clasps or catches.

FEATHERING. 1. A fault in printing which results in a feathering effect visible when ink spreads beyond the printed impression via the fibres of the paper. It is caused by an excess of solvent in the ink, or an unsuitable paper. 2. Thinning down the overlapping edges of two pieces of paper which are to be joined when repairing a book.

FEATHERWEIGHT PAPER. Light, bulky, printing paper with 75% air space; it is made largely from esparto and has little or no calendering. It is slightly porous and not easy to handle. *See also* ANTIQUE.

FEATHERWORK. A type of book decoration which originated in Irish eighteenth century bindings, in which curved lines formed freehand with a gouge radiate from one point to produce a delicate and very rich pattern resembling feathers.

FEATURE. A characteristic of a thing indexed. *See also* CHARACTERISTIC OF A CLASSIFICATION, COMPRESENCE, ITEM, TERM.

FEATURE CARD. A plain or punched card allocated to a 'feature' in CO-ORDINATE INDEXING (*q.v.*) – a characteristic of the document indexed – on which are recorded the different items in a SET OF DOCUMENTS (*q.v.*) which have this same characteristic. Also called 'Term card' because a feature referring to subject matter is known as a 'term'.

FEATURE CARD SYSTEM. A method of information retrieval in which a card is reserved for a feature (variously called 'aspect', 'dimension', 'facet'), characteristic, or piece of information. Each card is printed with the same grid of punchable positions, which are numbered, and each of these corresponds to a particular document. The document number is punched in each appropriate feature card. When it is required to know which document, or documents, possess certain features, or combination of features, the feature cards are withdrawn from the file and placed one on the other. Light shining through the holes will reveal the documents possessing the features required. The number of features can be increased indefinitely simply by adding an additional card but when the number of documents exceeds the number of punchable positions (numbering 10,000 on cards of manageable size) a new set of feature cards must be commenced. *See also* EDGE-NOTCHED CARDS, MARGINAL-HOLE PUNCHED CARDS, SLOTTED CARDS.

FEATURE HEADING. The verbal part of a subject heading used in the systematic file of a CLASSIFIED CATALOGUE (*q.v.*), i.e. that part which is a translation into words of the last element of a classification symbol. The verbal part usually follows the symbol, and may be utilized to specify subjects for which no exact notation is provided in the scheme of classification.

FEATURING. The provision in a classified catalogue of the hierarchic 'chain', setting out the classificatory steps (class, number and heading) leading to the individual entries at any particular number. This practice has been adopted in both the *British National Bibliography* and the *British Catalogue of Music*, and should help in understanding and utilizing fully the construction of the class number and the arrangement of the catalogue.

fecit. (*Lat.* 'he or she made (did) this.'). Frequently added after the artist's name on a drawing, engraving or sculpture. *See also* sculpt.

FEDERAL LIBRARY COMMITTEE. Set up in March 1964 with the object of improving co-ordination and planning among the Government's research libraries. The decision was made after consideration of a report of the survey of Federal libraries conducted for the Brookings Institution by Dr. Luther H. Evans.

FEDERATION INTERNATIONALE DE DOCUMENTATION. The organization (formerly the Institut International de Documentation and the Institut International de Bibliographie) which publishes the UNIVERSAL DECIMAL CLASSIFICATION (*q.v.*) and many other publications in the field of information and documentation in which it is the major international non-governmental scientific organization. Abbreviated FID. *See also* INTERNATIONAL FEDERATION FOR DOCUMENTATION.

FEDERATION OF ASIAN LIBRARY ASSOCIATIONS. Founded 9th November 1957 to promote the library movement and library co-operation in Asia. Its activities now appear to be in suspense. Abbreviated FALA. Published *FALA News Letter*.

FEED BOARD. The platform on a printing machine on to which single sheets of paper are passed from the pile on the stock table and from which they are passed to the impression cylinder.

FEED GUIDES. One, or more, of several kinds of device for holding a sheet of paper in a uniformly straight position before it is taken, possibly by the grippers, to the place at which it will come into contact with the printing surface. On a cylinder press these are called 'Drop guides'.

FEEDBACK. (*Information retrieval*) Partial reversion of the effects of a given process to its source. Control of a system by the output of the system – that is, a self-correcting or self-compensating control (*IBM*).

FEEDER. The various pieces of automatic apparatus by means of which sheets of paper are fed to, and positioned on, printing presses and paper processing machines of various kinds.

FEET. The base of a piece of movable type formed by the 'groove' or 'heel-nick' which runs set-wise across the bottom surface of the body. Type not standing squarely is said to be 'off its feet'.

FEET OF FINE. In law, the foot of a fine was that one of the parts of a tripartite indenture recording the particulars of a fine, which remained with the court, the other two being retained by the parties. When the undivided sheet was placed so that this counterfoil could be read, it was actually at the foot of the parchment.

FEINT RULING. Term used to indicate the horizontal lines (rules), or cross-rules, printed on account-book paper or exercise books. *See also* COMMON RULING.

FELL TYPES. Types cut by the Dutch typefounder Walpergen between 1667 and 1672 and introduced by Dr. John Fell to Oxford University Press during and after 1671 when this press was revived. Dr. Fell was Dean of Christ Church and later Bishop of Oxford. The beautiful Fell types which are used by the OUP for books requiring an OLD STYLE (*q.v.*) type are still cast from the collection of type-punches and matrices made by Dr. Fell, having been re-discovered by the Rev. C. H. O. Daniel in 1877, and used by him on his private press at Worcester College. Dr. Fell was the second of the Press's great patrons, the first being Archbishop Laud. He took charge of printing and publishing on behalf of the University from 1672 until his death in 1686.

FELT MARK. An imprint left on paper by the felt of the papermaking machine due to the pressure of the felt on it.

FELT SIDE. The side of a sheet or roll of paper which has not come in contact with the wire during manufacture; therefore the smooth side of a sheet instead of the WIRE SIDE (*q.v.*). Also known as the 'Top side'.

FELTBOARD. A piece of cardboard or thin wood covered with felt or similar cloth and used for displays. Letters or pictured symbols to be displayed are covered with similar materials and adhere to the board when pressed against it. When flannel is used instead of felt it is called a 'Flannelboard' or 'Flannelgraph'.

FENCE. (*Classification*) Part of the NOTATION (*q.v.*) which merely separates facets without indicating the type of facet which is to follow. These were replaced in the fourth edition of the Colon Classification with FACET INDICATORS (*q.v.*).

FERE-HUMANISTICA. *See* GOTHIC or BLACK LETTER, TYPE.

FERROPRUSSIATE PROCESS. *See* BLUE PRINT PROCESS.

FERROTYPE PROCESS. A method for making direct positive prints in the camera on black or chocolate-coloured enamelled iron plates, called ferrotype plates. This method was popular for while-you-wait photography but the image is in reverse, there being no intermediate negative. *See also* GLOSSY PRINT.

FESTOON DRYING. A method of drying paper in a drying chamber in which warm air is circulated. The paper is hung in loops over rods which travel slowly through the chamber.

FESTSCHRIFT. A memorial or complimentary volume usually consisting of a number of contributions by distinguished persons, often students and colleagues of a person and issued in his honour. The subject matter of the various contributions is usually concerned with the subject in which the individual distinguished himself. It may also honour an institution or society especially on the occasion of an anniversary. LC cards give the contents of Festschriften when there are fewer than twenty-six contributions. Also called 'Memorial volume'.

ff. Abbreviation for *folgende Seiten* (*Ger.* 'following pages'); for a proper name (e.g. ffolkes); for *fecerunt* (*Lat.* 'they made it'); for folios (e.g. 200ff., i.e. 200 leaves, not pages) and foliation.

FIBRES. The plant cells, largely composed of cellulose, which are contained in the rag, grass, wood or other vegetable matter from which paper is made. The length and strength of these fibres, and the way in which they are interwoven, determine the quality and strength of the paper.

FICHE. A card. *See also* MICROFICHE.

FICTION RESERVE. *See* JOINT FICTION RESERVE.

FICTITIOUS IMPRINT. An imprint that is misleading with the object of evading legal or other restrictions, concealing the anonymity of the author, or concealing a piracy publication, etc. Also called 'False imprint'. Fictitious and imaginary imprints may be given in catalogue entries (1) as given, or (2) in the conventional form. When the real imprint is known, it is given in [] after the fictitious imprint.

FIELD. A fixed column or group of columns in a punched card allocated for punching specific information. The total area of a punched card available for information storage (*IBM*).

FIELD VISIT. A direct, personal, contact by a librarian or library consultant with a library agency, individual, group, organization, institution or governmental body, with the object of securing a better library service. (American.)

FIELD WORK. In county library work, the visiting of local branches in order to maintain official contact between these and headquarters.

FIGURE. 1. An illustration, map, chart, graph, etc., forming part of a page of text with which it is printed from a block imposed with the type, as distinct from a PLATE (*q.v.*). 2. A graphic symbol or character to represent a number. *See also* MARGINAL FIGURE.

FIGURE INITIAL. In a mediaeval illuminated manuscript, an initial letter which is made by representations of the bodies of human beings or animals.

FIGURED BASS. On a music score, a line of bass notes with figures under or over them from which indications the player of a harpsichord or organ could tell what chords the composer intended to be used, and could construct his own accompaniment. Also called 'Basso continuo', 'Thorough bass'.

FIGURES, OLD STYLE. *See* HANGING FIGURES, OLD STYLE, RANGING FIGURES.

FILE. (*Noun*) 1. A collection of written, typed or printed material or information arranged in some systematic order. 2. A holder or cabinet designed to hold such material. 3. A homogeneous collection of a single type of file items. *See also* ADVERTISEMENT FILE, BIOGRAPHY FILE, COMPANY FILE, COMPETITOR FILE, CONFIDENTIAL FILE, GEOGRAPHIC FILING METHOD, JOB FILE, LATERAL FILING, LEGAL FILE, MAP FILE, MEDIA FILE, OPEN BACK FILE, ORGANIZATION FILE, PATENT FILE, SUSPENSION FILE, TICKLER SYSTEM, TRANSFER FILE, VERTICAL FILE. 4. In information retrieval, a collection of entries on a TALLY (*q.v.*). (*Verb*) To arrange written, typed or printed material in order.

FILE ITEM. The smallest module or piece of information to be handled as a unit in a file.

FILESEARCH. A commercial system of information retrieval using 1,000-foot rolls of 35 mm film each containing approximately 32,000 pages with coded indexing beside each page. Coding of the film and retrieval of the documents utilize an intermediate FLEXOWRITER (*q.v.*). It is made by FMA Inc.

FILIGREE. Initials and borders decorated with fine lines around the edges.

FILIGREE LETTER. An initial letter with a decorated or filigree outline or background.

FILING. The action of arranging papers, non-book materials and other documents, and records of such, or other, items, into pre-determined sequences; also the subsequent insertion of additional items in their correct places.

FILING CARS. Desks on casters with a small table and a chair on a swivel, used when filing cards in catalogues. (*American*.)

FILING CHAIR. A chair used to reduce fatigue for a filing assistant working at a very large card catalogue. It, often together with a small table, is mounted on a light platform on wheels. The filing assistant while seated moves the chair along by pushing against the catalogue case. Also called 'Filing car'.

FILING CODE.   A code of rules for arranging the entries in a catalogue, or other material in a file. *A.L.A. Rules for filing catalog cards* (Chicago: ALA, 1968) and *Filing rules for the dictionary catalogs of the Library of Congress* (Washington: U.S. *Government Printing Office*, 1956) are such codes.

FILING MEDIUM.   That part of the entry or an added heading-word, phrase or symbol under which a card is filed. Also called ENTRY WORD, FILING TERM, FILING WORD (*qq.v.*).

FILING TERM.   *Synonymous with* FILING MEDIUM (*q.v.*).

FILING TITLE.   1. The title under which are filed catalogue, or bibliography, entries for work known by a number of different titles. 2. The portion of a title which is longer than an essential part by which the book is well known, and under which the catalogue entry is filed, e.g. *David Copperfield*, the full title of which is *The personal history of David Copperfield*. The filing title is indicated by putting a small stroke under the filing letter – in this case the 'D'. Augmented headings, conventional titles in the entries for music scores, and corner markings, are all forms of filing title. *See also* UNIFORM TITLE.

FILING WORD.   *Synonymous with* ENTRY WORD (*q.v.*).

FILLET.   1. A plain line or lines impressed upon the back or side of a book-cover. A 'French fillet' is three gilt lines unevenly spaced. 2. The wheel-shaped tool, with which these lines are impressed. Also called 'Roulette' or 'ROLL' (*q.v.*). *See also* TOOLING.

FILLING IN.   A printing fault in which the spaces in type characters, or the spaces between the dots of a half-tone block, fill with ink. This may be caused by using too much, or an unsuitable, ink, the forme being too high or the rollers incorrectly set, or by using an unsuitable paper, especially one which gives off fluff. *See also* CLOGGED.

FILLING-IN GUARDS.   *Synonymous with* COMPENSATION GUARDS (*q.v.*).

FILM BASE.   The plastic material which is coated with chemicals to make it sensitive to light. Cellulose acetate and cellulose triacetate are widely used for this purpose because of their dimensional stability, transparency, and relative non-inflammability. These materials may be edge-printed 'safety'. Cellulose nitrate was once used almost universally as a film base, but because of its inflammability is seldom used nowadays. Called 'Clear base' before being coated with photographic emulsion. *See also* BASE STOCK.

FILM JACKET.   A transparent holder into which individual frames, or strips, of 16 or 32 mm. microfilm may be inserted for storage.

FILM LIBRARY.   A collection of films. A few public libraries lend films to local societies and many preserve films of local interest as part of their local collection.

FILM LIBRARY INFORMATION COUNCIL. A national, professional organization of film librarians in public libraries in the U.S.A. and Canada. It was formed on 12th May 1967 during the American Film Festival in New York with the aim of promoting wider and better use of audio-visual materials in the communities served by public libraries. Abbreviated FLIC. Publishes *Film Library Quarterly*.

FILM LIBRARY INSTANTANEOUS PRESENTATION. *See* FLIP.

FILM PRODUCTION LIBRARIANS GROUP. A sub-committee of ASLIB (*q.v.*).

FILM SCRIPT. The story, dialogue and acting instructions for a film.

FILMAC. Trade name for microfilm reader-printers made by the Minnesota Mining and Manufacturing Co.

FILMOREX. 1. A system for the electronic selection of microfilm cards. Each card has a micro-reproduction of the document or abstract and a field of twenty 5-digit code numbers giving the bibliographic reference and the subjects treated (*IBM*). 2. A system devised in 1950 by Dr. Jacques Samain, Chef de Service of the Centre National de la Recherche Scientifique, Paris, for the storage and retrieval of microprint with the relative coding on the same piece of microfiche size 72 × 45 mm. The Filmorex Selector sorts through the microfiches at the speed of 600 per minute; those selected can be read with a microfilm reader and enlarged prints can be made from them.

FILMSET. Matter which has been composed by using photographic film and a PHOTO-COMPOSING MACHINE (*q.v.*).

FILMSETTING. The setting of type by photographic means using film as a medium. Each key on a filmsetting machine operates the placing of a negative of a letter of the alphabet (or other character) in position to be printed photographically in its correct order on a sheet of film. This sheet of film represents whole pages which can then be imposed in the proper position and printed down on to the lithographic printing plate. *See also* FOTOSETTER, LINOFILM, MONOPHOTO, PHOTON.

FILMSORT. Trade name for: 1. A microfilm system of information retrieval including the punched cards used therewith and allied products; it consists of aperture punched cards to which a microfilm frame is glued. Filmsort is produced by the Microfilm Products Division of Minnesota Mining and Manufacturing Company. The system has been applied primarily to the storage and retrieval of engineering drawings. 2. Jacket cards for filing and storing microfilm cut into strips.

FILMSTRIP. A strip of 16 mm or 35 mm film varying in length up to about fifty frames and bearing pictures, text or captions, and used as a visual aid to teaching. The positive images, in black and white or in colour, and usually on 35 mm film, are projected one at a time by means of a film strip projector. Some film strips are equipped with a tape or a recording that contains not only the narration but also a subsonic signal that activates a solenoid to advance the filmstrip to the next frame on being given a cue.

FILMSTRIP PROJECTOR. An electrically operated machine designed to accept filmstrips, usually 35 mm. Some also have slide holders to take 35 mm and larger mounted single transparencies. They are available with manual and/or remote control.

FILTER. Coloured transparent material used to absorb certain colours when taking black-and-white or colour photographs and in making separation negatives for colour printing.

FINAL PROOF. Also called 'Page proof'. *See* PROOF.

FINAL TITLE STRIP. The wording at the end of a film which indicates its contents.

FINDEX. Trade name for a system of punched cards used to record information, and kept in a framework. Holes in the cards are joined together by a punch to form slots of varying length and so record information. To ascertain any information recorded, rods are inserted into selected holes in the frame (corresponding to those in the cards) which is then inverted by hand. This causes punched cards to fall out of alignment. The framework is then turned to its original position after inserting a rod to prevent cards from dropping back into alignment; this permits the projecting cards to be examined.

FINDING AIDS. Classification schemes, catalogues, indexes of various kinds and of different varieties of library materials, etc., which have been devised to enable stored material, or information, to be obtained (retrieved) when required.

FINDING LIST. A very brief list of books, usually limited to author, title and class mark.

FINDING UNIT. The catalogues, bibliographies and circulation and information desks, which are usually grouped together in a university library. *See also* LIBRARY KEYS.

FINE. A charge made for retaining a book longer than the time allowed. This is referred to as a 'charge' in s.8 of the Public Libraries and Museums Act, 1964. *See also* CHARGE.

FINE CALCULATOR. *Synonymous with* FINE COMPUTOR (*q.v.*).

FINE COMPUTOR. A simple device for calculating the amount of fine due on a book which has been retained longer than the period allowed.

FINE COPY. Used to describe a second-hand book the condition of which is better than 'good' but poorer than MINT (*q.v.*).

FINE EDITION. *Synonymous with* DE LUXE EDITION (*q.v.*).

FINE-FACE RULE. A printer's brass RULE (*q.v.*) of hair-line thickness.

FINE PAPER COPY. Name applied to a book printed on better and larger paper than the ordinary edition.

FINE SCREEN. A screen with ruling above 120 lines per inch. *See also* SCREEN.

FINIS. (*Lat.*). The end, conclusion. Frequently printed at the end of a book.

FINISH. (*Paper*) The degree of smoothness of the surface of paper; printing papers may be described as, e.g. antique or super-calendered, writing and drawing papers as vellum or rough. 'Hot pressed' (H.P.) means plate glazed finish. *See also* NOT, PAPER FINISHES. (*Block-making*) The treatment of the outer edges of blocks as e.g. squared up, vignetted. (*Binding*) Ornamenting and lettering a bound book.

FINISHER. 1. A bookbinding craftsman who performs the processes (polishing the leather, lettering, embellishing) which are carried out on a hand-bound book after the sections have been secured within the case. 2. A machine which applies varnish, lacquer, liquid plastic or other fluid to cover materials by spraying, by roller, or by a printing plate.

FINISHING. That branch of binding concerned with the book after it has been put into its cover. Includes tooling, lettering, polishing. The workman who does this is called a 'finisher'. *See also* FORWARDING.

FINISHING HOUSE. *Synonymous with* SALLE (*q.v.*).

FINISHING ROOM. *Synonymous with* SALLE (*q.v.*).

FIRM ORDER. In acquisition work, an order placed with a dealer specializing in material which is difficult to obtain, authorizing him to search for and supply certain items within fixed price limits, or to supply items at a cost not to exceed a stated amount. Generally an order which will not be withdrawn.

FIRST ASSISTANT. In American libraries, a member of the professional staff of a department, division or branch having a minimum staff of three professional persons.

FIRST EDITION. The whole number of copies first printed from the same type and issued at the same time. Later printings from the same type are known as Reprints. Sometimes small typographical errors in a first edition are corrected during the printing, qualifying the later

9*

printings for the classification 'Corrected Edition', 'New Edition' or 'Revised Edition', but described as 'First issue of the first edition'. *See also* EDITION, IMPRESSION, ISSUE, NEW EDITION, REPRINT, REVISED EDITION.

FIRST ENGLISH EDITION. The first edition published in England of a book written in English and which had already been published abroad.

FIRST GENERATION MICROFILM. *Synonymous with* CAMERA MICROFILM (*q.v.*).

FIRST IMPRESSION. All the copies of a book printed at the first printing and before any alterations or additions have been made to the text. Subsequent printings made soon after the first, and before a reprint is made after a lapse of time, are called 'Second impression', 'Third impression', etc.

FIRST INDENTION. The eighth typewriter space from the left edge of a catalogue card, or the first, or outer, vertical line on a catalogue card ruled for handwriting. It is at this position that the author heading begins; should it run over the line, it continues at the 'Third indention'. Also called 'Author indention' and 'Outer indention'. *See also* SECOND INDENTION, THIRD INDENTION.

FIRST-LINE INDEX. An index in which the first lines of poems, hymns, songs are arranged in alphabetical order.

FIRST LINING. The piece of mull which is glued with a flexible glue to a book after it is sewn and nipped; it extends to within $\frac{1}{4}$ in. from the head and tail of the book and projects $1\frac{1}{4}$ in. on either side for affixing to the end-papers to give strength and firmness to the book. A strip of brown paper, the full size of the spine, is then stuck over it; this is known as the 'second lining'. The purpose of this lining is to give strength and firmness to the back of the book.

FIRST NAME. The first of the forenames or Christian names; a personal name as distinct from family or clan name.

FIRST PRINTING. The first quantity of a book to be printed; equivalent to FIRST IMPRESSION (*q.v.*).

FIRST PROOF. Also called 'Galley proof'. *See* PROOF.

FIRST PUBLISHED EDITION. The first edition published for sale to the public, and implying that it was preceded by an edition printed for private, official or otherwise restricted, circulation.

FIRST REPRODUCTION MICROFILM. A microfilm copy made from the CAMERA MICROFILM (*q.v.*). Also called 'Second generation microfilm'. *See also* GENERATION.

FIRST SEPARATE EDITION. The first edition to be printed within its own covers, of a publication which had previously been published with other matter.

FIRST VERTICAL. The left of the two vertical lines printed on a catalogue card intended for hand writing and serving as a guide to where the author heading and the second and subsequent lines of the entry should begin. *See also* FIRST INDENTION, SECOND VERTICAL.

FIRST WORD ENTRY. Entry under the first word of a book's title other than an article.

FIRSTS. First editions.

FIST. *Synonymous with* HAND (*q.v.*).

FIVE LAWS OF LIBRARY SCIENCE. 1. Books are for use. 2. Every reader his book. 3. Every book its reader. 4. Save the time of the reader. 5. A library is a growing organism. (*S. R. Ranganathan.*)

FIVE PREDICABLES. *See* PREDICABLES, FIVE.

FIXED FIELDS. In information retrieval, locations on a search medium, such as a punched card, that are reserved for information of a particular type, form or length. *See also* FREE FIELDS.

FIXED LOCATION. An antiquated method of arrangement by marking a book with shelf and other marks so that its position on a particular shelf should always be the same. The bookcases, tiers and shelves are each marked distinctly to make finding easy and these markings are often incorporated in the book number. Also called 'Absolute location'. The opposite of RELATIVE LOCATION (*q.v.*).

FIXED SHELF. One which cannot be adjusted.

FIXED-FUNCTION PLANNING. Planning a building in such a way that each room or department is designed and constructed for its specific purpose, thus giving the architect opportunities for displaying his architectural abilities. Walls dividing the rooms are permanent, and normally an essential part of the structure. The opposite of modular planning. *See also* MODULAR CONSTRUCTION.

FIXING. In photography and some documentary reproduction processes, the immersion of a film or paper after exposure to light, in a solution so as to remove any light-sensitive chemicals which have not been acted upon by exposure to light and 'fix' the film or paper to prevent further development.

fl. Abbreviation for *flores* (flowers), *floruit* (*q.v.*).

FLAG. *Synonymous with* MASTHEAD (*q.v.*).

FLANGE. The margin round a half-tone plate or line block to provide for fixing to the block.

FLANNELBOARD. *See* FELTBOARD.

FLANNELGRAPH. *See* FELTBOARD.

FLAT. (*Printing*) The sheet containing offset negatives or positives in the proper arrangement, from which the printing plate is made. Also, a flat printing plate.

FLAT BACK. A book which has not been rounded before being placed inside its CASE (*q.v.*), its back being at right angles to the sides. Also called 'Square back'. *See also* BACKING, ROUND BACK, ROUNDING.

FLAT-BED CAMERA. *Synonymous with* PLANETARY CAMERA (*q.v.*).

FLAT-BED CYLINDER PRESS. A printing machine with a flat bed on which the forme is placed under a rotating cylinder.

FLAT-BED PRESS. A printing machine having the printing forme on a bed with a flat surface, as distinct from a press with a curved surface.

FLAT-BED WEB PRESS. A machine for printing from a flat forme on to an endless roll of paper.

FLAT COPY. A photograph having no contrast and therefore normally unsuitable for process work. *See also* PROCESS ENGRAVING.

FLAT DISPLAY. A book display which features the front covers rather than the spines of the books.

FLAT PROOF. A print made from each plate in a colour series, using the colour in which that plate is to be printed in the series. *See also* PROOF, PROGRESSIVE PROOF.

FLAT PULL (ROUGH PULL). The proof taken on the machine without UNDERLAY or OVERLAY (*qq.v.*).

FLAT RATE. A rate levied over the whole of a county area to provide an adequate library service in all parts without the levying of additional local rates. *See also* DIFFERENTIAL RATING.

FLAT STITCHED. A publication which is sewn by the FLAT STITCHING (*q.v.*) method.

FLAT STITCHING. Sewing a pamphlet or book, which must have a flat back, in such a way that the wire or linen thread used passes through the inner margins as close to the folds of the sections as possible from the front right through to the back. *See also* SADDLE STITCHING, SIDE-STITCH.

FLATNESS. A condition of paper or board when it has no COCKLE, CURL (*qq.v.*) or wave.

FLEUR-DE-LIS LOZENGE. A lozenge stamp consisting of a flower with fleur-de-lis, or a variation of this design, filling the corners.

FLEURON. A conventional flower or an anomalous type of ornament of floral or foliage character, generally of roughly lozenge shape, used in decorating book-bindings. *See also* FLOWERS.

FLEXIBLE BINDING. A binding that allows the book to lie flat when open. This is largely achieved by using a FLEXIBLE SEWING (*q.v.*) and flexible glue.

FLEXIBLE CLASSIFICATION. A classification which permits the insertion of new subjects without destroying the sequence or logic of the arrangement. Flexibility is mainly a function of the notation.

FLEXIBLE NOTATION. A NOTATION (*q.v.*) which has the quality of allowing, by the addition of one or more symbols, the insertion of any new subject into any place in the classification without dislocating the sequence of either the notation or the classification schedule. *See also* NOTATION.

FLEXIBLE SEWING. Sewing a book on raised bands or cords, and passing the thread entirely round each band. It is the strongest form of sewing. A style of binding which allows the book to lie perfectly flat when open.

FLEXOWRITER. Trade name for a machine, similar to a typewriter, which will punch holes in a roll of paper tape to represent type characters as well as provide a typed page. The rolls of tape can be stored, and if later fed into the machine will cause it to operate electrically and type characters on paper in the traditional way.

FLIP. Abbreviation for Film Library Instantaneous Presentation. Trade name for a mechanized storage and retrieval device which uses a reel of coded microfilm, made by the Benson-Lehner Corporation, and storing 72,000 pages on 1,200-foot rolls of film.

FLOATING LIBRARY. A mobile library accommodated on a boat which takes books to isolated residents or hamlets on islands and places which are inaccessible except by river or sea. Books are left in boxes and placed in the care of a responsible person, or readers are allowed to choose from those displayed on shelves in the boat.

FLONG. A pulp-like board used for making the moulds for casting stereotypes. *Wet flong* is made (usually in the foundry of a printing establishment) from layers of tissue paper and blotting paper pasted together with a special paste and beaten onto the type or blocks in the forme and then dried. *Dry flong* is a similar material which, either in a completely dry state, or damp, is placed together with the forme in a hydraulic press. The use of paper in place of plaster of paris for moulding was introduced by Genoux of Lyons in 1829; a British patent, based on this method, was taken out by Moses Poole in 1839.

FLOOR CASE. *Synonymous with* ISLAND STACK (*q.v.*).

FLOOR DUTY. Being available to readers in a library in order to assist them with their choice of books; this is made possible for senior librarians by freedom from routine duties at the staff enclosure, departmental librarian's desk, or readers' adviser's desk.

FLORENTINE WOODCUTS.   These are often characterized by the combination of black-line and white-line methods in the same block; e.g. black is used as the colour of the ground, any stones, plants or other objects being represented by white lines on a black ground, while the upper part of the illustration follows the Venetian style of black lines on a white ground.

FLORET.   1. A binder's finishing tool with a flower or leaf design. 2. A flower or leaf-shape type used to separate sentences or paragraphs.

floruit.   (*Lat.* 'He flourished'). The period during which a person, whose birth and death dates were not exactly known, was believed to have been alive or flourished. Indicated by 'fl' before the dates or period.

FLOURISH.   1. A mark or flourish after a signature, often made as a protection against forgery. Also called a 'Paraph'. 2. A curved line or ornament, made of brass or cast metal, and used with lines of type.

FLOURISH STYLE.   *Synonymous with* FANFARE STYLE (*q.v.*).

FLOW CAMERA.   *Synonymous with* CONTINUOUS FLOW CAMERA (*q.v.*).

FLOW-LINE MAP.   One which shows movement, the direction or route followed being indicated by a line representing the railway or waterway concerned, while the width of the line represents the quantity of material conveyed.

FLOWER-HEADED RIVET.   (*Binding*) A rivet with an ornamental head with a design resembling a daisy.

FLOWERS.   Printer's ornaments which can be made up into decorative borders, strips, head and tail pieces. They may be floral, arabesque, geometric or pictorial in design. The best of them derive from book-binders' arabesque stamps. *See also* FLEURON, TYPE FLOWERS, TYPE ORNAMENTS.

FLUSH.   (*Printing*) Denotes the absence of INDENTION (*q.v.*). The instruction 'set flush on left' means that the matter is to be set evenly at the left margin, 'flush right' that all lines align at the right margin.

FLUSH BINDING.   A binding in which the covers do not project beyond the leaves, the whole having been placed in a guillotine and trimmed after the covers were secured.

FLUSH BOARDS.   A style of binding in which boards are glued to the paste-downs and a paper cover glued to the boards. The whole is then put into a guillotine and CUT FLUSH (*q.v.*). *See also* FLUSH TRIM.

FLUSH PARAGRAPH.   A paragraph having no indention, spacing being used to separate paragraphs.

FLUSH TRIM.   A style of binding in which the top, fore and bottom edges are cut after the paper, board or lining cloth covers have been put on. The covers are thus flush with the edges and do not overlap. Such books are said to be 'cut flush'. Also called 'Flush work'. *See also* FLUSH BOARDS.

FLUSH WORK.   *Synonymous with* FLUSH TRIM (*q.v.*).

FLY-LEAF.   A blank leaf at the beginning or end of a book, being the half of an ENDPAPER (*q.v.*), which is not stuck down to the board, or cover, of a book. Also called 'Free endpaper'. The half which is stuck down to the board, is called a PASTE-DOWN (*q.v.*). If there are other blank leaves, these are also known as fly-leaves.

FLY-SHEET.   1. A two- or four-page tract. 2. An endpaper.

FLY-TITLE.   *Synonymous with* HALF TITLE (*q.v.*).

fo.   Abbreviation for FOLIO (*q.v.*).

FOCUS.   (*Classification*) (*Noun*) 1. A generic term used to denote an ISOLATE (*q.v.*) or a class or any of its equivalents in the other PLANES (*q.v.*). 2. Any specific division (*see* DIVISION 4) of the subject according to one characteristic, i.e. any single division of a FACET (*q.v.*). (*Verb*) To decrease the EXTENSION (*q.v.*) and increase the intension within any facet, and so to arrive at a specific division of a facet. *See also* CLASSIFYING, FACET, PHASE.

FOIL.   1. Metal or pigment forming a very thin film on a thin backing material which is used with a stylus or a block when lettering or BLOCKING (*q.v.*) a book. 2. (*Reprography*) Diazo-sensitized plastic film.

FOIL BLOCKING.   *See* BLOCKING FOIL.

fol.   Abbreviation for FOLIO (*q.v.*). Less usual than 'fo', or 'Fo'.

FOLD.   *Synonymous with* BOLT (*q.v.*).

FOLD SYMBOLS.   The symbols used to indicate the way the paper of which a book is made is folded, and consequently the number of leaves in the section. These are F., Fo (Folio); 4to (Quarto); 6to (Sexto); 8vo (Octavo); 12mo (Duodecimo, Twelvemo); 16mo (Sextodecimo, Sixteenmo); 18mo (Octodecimo, Eighteenmo); 24mo (Vicesimo-quarto, Twenty-fourmo); 32mo (Trigesimo-secundo, Thirty-twomo); 64mo (Sixty-fourmo). They are often used to indicate the size of modern books.

FOLD TO PAPER.   An instruction that a sheet of printed paper is to be folded so that the edges of the leaves and the bolts are all level. *See also* BOLT, FOLD TO PRINT

FOLD TO PRINT.   An instruction that a printed sheet is to be folded in register, i.e. the edges of the printed areas are to be placed over one another exactly before the sheet is folded. *See also* FOLD TO PAPER.

FOLDED BOOK. One consisting of a long strip of paper folded like a sheet map, concertina fashion, the ends being attached to stiff covers. Used commonly in the Orient, but in the rest of the world mainly for books of a pictorial character giving views of places or panoramas. Also called 'Folding book'.

FOLDED LEAF. A leaf of a bound book which is so large that it has to be folded one or more times to keep it within the area of the page size. The abbreviation *fold.* is added to the appropriate term in the collation to indicate that illustrative matter is folded, as: 80 *l.* (3 *fold.*)*; fold. frontis; 2 fold. family trees; 60 maps (2 fold. in pocket). See also* FOLDING PLATE, GATEFOLD, THROW OUT.

FOLDER. 1. A publication consisting of one sheet of paper folded to make two or more leaves but neither stitched nor cut. 2. A large sheet of stout paper, usually manilla, folded once, and having a projection or tag for a heading at the top of the back portion, into which papers are placed for storage in a filing box or cabinet.

FOLDING. The folding of flat printed sheets into sections. The number of pages in a folded sheet is always a multiple of four (i.e. two leaves). After the last folding all the sections are secured by SEWING (*q.v.*) or stapling.

FOLDING BOOK. *Synonymous with* FOLDED BOOK (*q.v.*).

FOLDING GUIDES. Short lines printed on imposed sheets to indicate where they are to be folded.

FOLDING MACHINE. A machine for folding printed sheets to make sections for bookbinding. *See also* BUCKLE-FOLDER, KNIFE-FOLDER.

FOLDING PLATE. An illustration bound into a book but folded so as not to project beyond the pages of the book. Called a 'folded plate' by cataloguers. *See also* DOUBLE PLATE.

FOLDING STICK. A strip of white bone used when folding paper by hand to crease the paper without damaging it. *See also* BONE FOLDER.

FOLDINGS. A general term referring to printed sheets which have been folded to form sections. The following table gives the usual foldings.

Folio	(Fo)	folded once		giving	2 leaves		4 pages	
Quarto	(4to)	„	twice	„	4	„	8	„
Sexto	(6to)	„	three times	„	6	„	12	„
Octavo	(8vo)	„	three	„	„	8	„	16	„
Duodecimo (twelvemo)	(12mo)	„	four	„	„	12	„	24	„
Sectodecimo (sixteenmo)	(16mo)	„	four	„	„	16	„	32	„
Octodecimo (eighteenmo)	(18mo)	„	five	„	„	18	„	36	„

Vicesimo-quarto							
(twenty-fourmo)	(24mo) folded five times giving 24 leaves 48 pages						
Trigesimo-secundo							
(thiry-twomo)	(32mo)	„	five	„	„	32 „	64 „
Trigesimo-sexto							
(thirty-sixmo)	(36mo)	„	six	„	„	36 „	72 „
Quadrigesimo-octavo							
(forty-eightmo)	(48mo)	„	six	„	„	48 „	96 „
Sexagesimo-quarto							
(sixty-fourmo)	(64mo)	„	six	„	„	64 „	128 „

FOLGER SHAKESPEARE LIBRARY. This research centre for advanced scholars was opened in Washington, D.C., in 1932. It contains the world's largest collection of research materials on William Shakespeare and one of the Western Hemisphere's finest collections of materials on the British civilization of the sixteenth and seventeenth centuries. The stock numbers 250,000 volumes. Henry Clay Folger, an American industrialist and his wife Emily Jordan Folger selected the material forming the original collection. The collection was bequeathed to the American people, together with an endowment which was sufficient to maintain and expand it. The trust is administered by the Trustees of Amherst College, Folger's alma mater. The library is a modern building on Capitol Hill although the interior preserves the architectural conventions of the Tudor period.

FOLIAGED STAFF. A bookbinding ornament consisting of a staff or branch entwined with foliage.

FOLIATE. To number the leaves of a book.

FOLIATE INITIAL. In a mediaeval illuminated manuscript, an initial letter decorated with, or composed of, foliage.

FOLIATED. Used to describe the marking of every leaf – not page – of a manuscript or printed book with a consecutive number, or foliation.

FOLIATION. (*Verb*) Allotting folio or section numbers or other markings to pages. (*Noun*) The numbering of leaves of a MS. or book. Foliation was comparatively rare until the last quarter of the fifteenth century: it consisted originally of the word 'Folio', or an abbreviation thereof, followed by a roman numeral. Arabic figures were used in Italy between 1475 and 1500, and outside Italy after 1500. Eventually the Arabic figures stood alone. Sometimes columns of print were numbered instead of leaves. The numbering of pages (pagination) began to replace foliation towards the end of the sixteenth century but was not finally established until the eighteenth century. Abbreviated ff.

FOLIO.   1. Relates to the format of a book; a book printed on sheets of paper folded once, each sheet making two leaves or four pages. For an accurate indication, the paper size should also be stated, e.g. *crown folio*. In practice, a double-size sheet could be used and folded twice, or a quad-size sheet folded three times to give the same size page. *See* FOLDINGS. 2. The individual leaf of a book. A sheet is usually folded into two parallel with the narrow way (i.e. halving the long side) and when so folded is called 'regular', 'common', or 'broad' folio. 3. An indication of the size of a book, usually 30 cm. The actual size depends on the size of the sheet of paper and on the way it is folded. Abbreviated *Fo.*, *fo.*, *fol.*, or 2°. *See also* BOOK SIZES, ELEPHANT FOLIO. 4. A sheet of paper in its full size, i.e. flat unfolded, hence a folio ream is a ream of paper supplied flat. 5. The number of a leaf written or printed at the top or more usually, the bottom.

FOLIO EDITION.   One issued in FOLIO (*q.v.*) form.

FOLLOW COPY.   When written on a MS. this is a direction to the compositor to follow precisely the spelling and punctuation, however incorrect it may appear. When written on printed matter it indicates that the style and setting of the original are to be followed as closely as possible.

FOLLOW THROUGH.   *Synonymous with* the 'letter-by-letter' system of ALPHABETIZATION (*q.v.*).

FOLLOW-UP FILE.   An American term for a chronological file of cards, correspondence or copies of orders sent, to facilitate checking overdue orders or letters.

FOLLOW-UP NOTICES.   The American term for second and subsequent overdue notices.

FONDS.   The chief archive unit in the continental system and the basis of all rules as to arrangement of the contents of archives. An archive group consisting of archives resulting from the work on administration which was an organic whole, complete in itself, capable of dealing independently, without any added or external authority, with every side of any business which could normally be presented to it.

FONT.   *See* FOUNT.

FOOLSCAP.   A sheet of printing paper measuring $13\frac{1}{2} \times 17$ inches, usually folded to give a size of $13\frac{1}{2} \times 8\frac{1}{2}$ inches. Formerly known as 'large foolscap.'

FOOLSCAP FOLIO.   A book size $13\frac{1}{2} \times 8\frac{1}{2}$ inches. *See also* BOOK SIZES.

FOOLSCAP OCTAVO.   A book size $6\frac{3}{4} \times 4\frac{1}{2}$ inches. *See also* BOOK SIZES.

FOOLSCAP QUARTO. A book size $8\frac{1}{2} \times 6\frac{3}{4}$ inches. *See also* BOOK SIZES.

FOOT. 1. The bottom edge of a book. *See also* HEAD. 2. The margin at the bottom of a page of type. 3. The under-surface of type. The plane, parallel to the face on which the BODY (*q.v.*) rests. *See also* FEET.

FOOTLINE. 1. The line at the bottom of a page, especially the blank line or DIRECTION LINE (*q.v.*) i.e. the line containing the folio, signature, or page number just below the lowest line of type. 2. The horizontal ruled line near the bottom of a ruled page or sheet. 3. Supplementary material at the bottom of a page to be used in connection with matter appearing above it.

FOOTNOTE. A note at the foot of a page, usually in smaller type than the text, giving a reference, an authority, or an elucidation of matter in the text above. *See also* REFERENCE MARKS. Also called 'Bottom note'.

FOOTSTICK. *See* CHASE.

FORE-EDGE. The front edge of a sheet of paper or of the sections of a book opposite the folded edge through which the sewing passes. Also called 'Front edge'.

FORE-EDGE FOLD. *See* BOLT.

FORE-EDGE MARGIN. The space between the type matter and the fore-edge of a book or periodical. Also called 'Outside margin'. *See also* MARGIN.

FORE-EDGE PAINTING. A picture painted on the fore-edges of a book which is seen to the best advantage when the pages are splayed out. A 'double fore-edge' has two paintings which can be seen singly by fanning the leaves first one way, and then the other. Gold is usually applied after the paintings have been done. A 'triple fore-edge' has a visible painting in addition. This form of decoration is particularly associated with William Edwards of Halifax, a binder who opened a bookshop in London for his sons James and John in 1785, although the earliest known *dated* disappearing fore-edge painting is on a Bible dated 1651, where the painting of the Leigh arms is signed 'Lewis fecit, Anno Dom. 1653'. Edwards pioneered the idea of painting landscapes on fore-edges, first of all in brown or grey monochrome, and later in a full range of colours.

FORE-EDGE TITLE. A title hand-written on the fore-edge of a book so that it could be identified when standing on a shelf with its fore-edge outwards, the normal position in the sixteenth century.

FOREL. 1. Heavy, rough parchment used for covering old books. Also called 'Forrel', 'Forril'. 2. A case or cover in which a book or MS. is kept for protection, or into which it is sewn.

FOREL BINDING.   English book-bindings in which oak boards were covered with roughly dressed deerskins. They were made by monks in the eighth and ninth centuries.

FORENAME.   A name that precedes the family name, clan name, or surname. A Christian, or personal, name. It is a name or part of a name which designates a person as an individual and distinguishes him from others bearing the same family name, surname or clan name. Also called GIVEN NAME (*q.v.*), 'Personal name'.

FORENAME ENTRY.   The entry in a catalogue for a book under the author's forename or personal name instead of the surname or family name as is usual. Books by the following are so entered: saints, popes, persons known by the first name only, sovereigns, ruling princes and members of the immediate families of sovereigns.

FOREWORD.   *Synonymous with* PREFACE (*q.v.*).

FORM.   1. A classification term applied to the manner in which the text of a book is arranged, as a dictionary, or the literary form in which it is written, as drama, poetry, etc. *See also* FORM CLASSES, FORM DIVISIONS. 2. *Form in music* indicates the structure of a musical composition which may be indicated by 'sonata', 'symphony', etc. 3. American spelling for FORME (*q.v.*).

FORM CLASSES.   Those parts of a classification in which the books are arranged according to the form in which they are written, e.g. poetry, drama, fiction, essays, etc., the subjects of the books being ignored.

FORM DIVISIONS.   Adjuncts to a classification which enable books to be arranged (within their subject) according to the form in which they are written. They usually have a mnemonic notation which can be applied to any part of a scheme. There are two kinds of form division: OUTER FORM indicates books of which the contents is arranged in a particular way, such as in classified or alphabetical order as in dictionaries, or according to the form of writing or presentation, as essay, bibliography, periodical. Subjective, or INNER FORM, indicates modes of approach such as the theory, history, or philosophy of a subject.

FORM ENTRY.   An entry in a catalogue under (1) the name of the form in which a book is written, e.g. Poetry, Drama, Fiction, or (2) the form in which the subject material is presented, e.g. Periodicals.

FORM HEADING.   1. A heading used in a catalogue for a FORM ENTRY (*q.v.*), e.g. 'Encyclopaedias'. Also called 'Form subject heading'. 2. A heading derived from and describing the category of document (*See* DOCUMENT 2) entered under it rather than its author, title or subject, e.g. Encyclopaedias (*IFLA*).

FORM NUMBER.   (*Classification*) A symbol used to indicate the literary form in which a work is written. It is obtained in connexion with the Colon Classification by translating the name of the form of exposition into appropriate symbols in accordance with the Scheme's Form Schedule, and may be used as part of the BOOK NUMBER (*q.v.*).

FORM SUB-HEADING. 1. A sub-heading used for sub-arranging in a catalogue entries for books on the same subject by their literary or practical form, e.g. Electronics – Bibliography. 2. A sub-heading, not consisting of an author's name or of a title, designed to delimit a group of entries according to some common characteristic of form, e.g. Laws, Treaties, under the name of a country (*IFLA*).

FORM SUBJECT HEADING. *Synonymous with* FORM HEADING (*q.v.*).

FORMAL ANONYMA. Works, like periodicals, which do not involve the idea of concealed authorship. These are catalogued by Library of Congress and many other libraries in the style known as HANGING INDENTION (*q.v.*). *See also* TRUE ANONYMA.

FORMAT. 1. A term used to describe the appearance and make-up of a book; its size, shape, paper, type, binding, illustrations, etc. 2. Strictly, the number of times a sheet of paper has been folded to form a section of a book, e.g. quarto (folded twice giving four leaves). *See also* FOLDINGS, FOLIO.

FORME. The combination of chase, furniture and type when 'locked up' ready for machining; i.e. the pages imposed in a chase. The forme containing the text, which will be on the inside pages of a printed sheet when folded, is called the 'inner forme' and that which contains those on the outside, the 'outer forme'. Spelt in America without the 'e'. *See also* DRESSED FORME, NAKED FORME.

FORME GAUGE. *See* GAUGE.

FORREL. *Synonymous with* FOREL (*q.v.*).

FORRIL. *Synonymous with* FOREL (*q.v.*).

FORTNIGHTLY. A serial publication issued every second week. Also called 'Bi-weekly', 'Semi-monthly'.

FORTY-EIGHTMO (48mo). A sheet of paper folded six times to form a section of forty-eight leaves (96 pp.). Also called 'Quadrigesimo-octavo'.

FORWARDING. The processes of binding a book after it is sewn until it is about to be placed in its cover ready for FINISHING (*q.v.*). The workman doing this is called a 'Forwarder'.

FOSDIC. Acronym for Optical Scanning Device for Input to Computers, a storage and retrieval system using 16 mm. microfilm. It was developed by the (American) National Bureau of Standards for the National Weather Record Center.

FOTOSETTER. A machine for typesetting by photography, constructed by the Intertype company and used since 1947. It works mainly on the same principle of circulating matrices as the Intertype slug-casting machine. A keyboard releases matrices from the magazines in which they are stored. A matrix, known as a *Fotomat*, has a photographic negative character embedded in its side; otherwise it is similar to an ordinary toothed Intertype matrix. The type lines are made up separately photographed characters, justification being pre-arranged and automatic, and interlinear spacing obtained by adjusting the micrometer film feed dial as necessary. Four magazines, each with 114 characters, can be mounted on the machine at the same time; eight lenses enable the camera to set eight different sizes of type from each of these four magazines – 3,648 characters in all.

FOUL CASE. A case of type in which some of the separate pieces of type have been put into wrong compartments.

FOUL PROOF. One with many corrections marked on it. In America a proof pulled after corrections have been made.

FOUNDERS' TYPE. Type cast by a type-founder as distinct from type cast by the printer on such machines as the Monotype, Linotype, Ludlow or Intertype.

FOUNDRY. The department of a printing works where matrices are made from the type-formes and blocks, and where stereo plates are cast. Other operations concerned with the casting or fabricating of type and other printing surfaces are also carried out here; the casting and routing machines, type-metal, stereo-metal and similar materials and the necessary tools are to be found here.

FOUNDRY PROOF. A proof pulled before the forme is sent to the foundry to be stereotyped.

FOUNDRY TYPE. *Synonymous with* FOUNDERS' TYPE (*q.v.*).

FOUNT. 1. A full set of type of one style and size containing the correct number of the various characters, i.e. upper and lower case, numerals, punctuation marks, accents, ligatures, etc. A type family includes founts of roman, italic, semi-bold, semi-bold condensed, and sanserif. *See also* SORT, TYPE FACE 2. 2. The whole collection of tools used by a binder's finisher.

FOUNT SCHEME. *See* BILL OF TYPE.

FOUR-COLOUR PROCESS. An extension of the THREE-COLOUR PROCESS (*q.v.*), by adding black or grey to give greater depth or solidarity. Also called 'Full colour'.

FOURDRINIER MACHINE. The first machine for making a continuous roll of printing paper. It was invented by Nicolas Louis Robert in 1797, developed in England by Bryan Donkin on behalf of Henry and Sealy Fourdrinier but not perfected until 1804. The principle of this machine is the basis for contemporary machines. The fluid pulp flows from a tank to a moving wire mesh belt during which it is strained and the fibres shaken into a web by agitation. This web of pulp then passes between couch rolls which give it enough strength to be transferred from the wire-cloth to an endless felt on which it passes through successive pairs of press rolls and so to drying cylinders. Thus all the separate processes carried out in the vat, mould, couch and press are combined in one machine. Originally the paper was then cut into sheets and loft-dried in the traditional way, but later additions to the Fourdrinier machine enabled the web of paper to be passed round a series of heated drums and so dried before being drawn through the rolls of a calender to impart the desired finish.

FOURNIER. A type face cut about 1730 by the French engraver and type-founder Pierre Simon Fournier *the younger* (1712–68). A MODERN FACE (*q.v.*) type which is characterized by its very fine hair-line serifs. For a specimen alphabet, *see* TYPE FACE.

FOURNIER POINT. A unit of type measurement, one point being 0·0137 inch, established by P. S. Fournier in 1737. It was superseded by the Didot Point. *See also* DIDOT SYSTEM.

FOXED. Prints and pages of old books with yellowish-brown spots caused by dampness.

FOXING. *See* FOXED.

FRAKTUR. (*Printing*) The group name for German blackface type or bold face type. *See also* BOLD FACE.

FRAME. 1. A wooden stand with a sloped top on which cases of type are placed for the compositor's use. 2. (*Binding*) Ornamentation consisting of a simple hollow rectangle placed some distance from the edges of the cover of a book. To be distinguished from BORDER (*q.v.*). 3. (*Bibliography*) The complete borders which are not COMPARTMENTS (*q.v.*). They comprise (a) enclosures made up of separate cuts or ornaments which show no evidence of having been carved or engraved for use together as a border; (b) those made up of separate cast type-ornaments, commonly used for book decoration. 4. (*Reprography*) An area containing an image in a film or microprint. 5. A geometric subdivision of the microfiche grid. A micro-image and its margins are contained within a frame. The standard size of a microfiche frame is 11·25 mm × 16 mm (single) or 23 mm × 16 mm (double).

FRAME MARGIN. (*Reprography*) The non-image area between the micro-image and the frame. *See also* FRAME 4.

FRAME SIZE. The size of the frame, or exposable area, of film.

FRAMED-CUT. A completely carved decorative full-page cut except for a small panel into which is set a letterpress title. Also called 'compartment', 'title-cut' or 'woodcut title-page with panel'.

FRANCIS JOSEPH CAMPBELL CITATION. *See* CAMPBELL CITATION, FRANCIS JOSEPH.

FRANKPLEDGE. In Old English, 1. The system by which every member of a 'tithing' – a company of ten householders – was answerable for the good conduct of, or damage done by, any one of the other members. 2. One of the mutually responsible members of a tithing. Occasionally, the tithing itself.

FRATERNITY LIBRARY. A library in a fraternity on an American college or university campus. It may be one of a circulating collection from the main library, or it may be owned by the fraternity.

FRED. Acronym for Figure Reading Electronic Device. A machine made by E.M.I. which can read a specially designed type-face consisting of the numerals and six letters, at the rate of 10,000 characters a second.

FREDERIKSBERG TYPE. The name given to a type of public library building, the main lending library of which consists of a large ground floor room with a gallery all round, and with reference and reading rooms and children's library on one side or the other of the lending library. The charging desk is placed in the entrance hall. So named after the Frederiksbergs kommunebiblioteker, Denmark, designed by the municipal architect, H. C. Andersen.

FREE. 1. In CO-ORDINATE INDEXING (*q.v.*), alone, not bound or joined to a separate modifier. *See also* BOUND 2. 2. (*Binding*) Said of a stamp, of whatever form, which has no boundary line, or frame, round it; such stamps may be in intaglio or relief.

FREE ENDPAPER. That portion of an endpaper which is not pasted down to the cover but adhered to the end section of a book. Also called 'Fly-leaf'. *See also* ENDPAPER.

FREE HAND. Writing of any period not conforming to definite rules, such as the regular use of set abbreviations.

FREE FIELDS. In information retrieval, location on a search medium, such as a punched card, which is not reserved for information of a particular type, form or length. *See also* FIXED FIELDS.

FREE INDEXING. In CO-ORDINATE INDEXING (*q.v.*), the assignment as index terms for a given document, of words or phrases chosen from a set of words or phrases considered by the indexer to be appropriate indexing terms even though they may not appear in the document.

FREE LANCE. A journalist or photographer not holding a salaried position on the staff of any one particular paper but who contributes to several papers at will.

FREEDLEY MEMORIAL AWARD, GEORGE. Established in 1968 by the THEATRE LIBRARY ASSOCIATION (*q.v.*) to honour the late founder of the Association, theatre historian and first curator of the Theatre Collection of the New York Public Library. The award, in the form of a plaque, is made on the basis of scholarship, readability, and general contribution to knowledge. It was first awarded (in 1969) to Louis Sheaffer for his *O'Neill, son and playwright*.

FRENCH FILLET. *See* Fillet.

FRENCH FOLD. A sheet printed on one side only and then folded into a section, the bolts being left uncut. *See also* ORIHON.

FRENCH JAPON. *See* JAPANESE PAPER.

FRENCH JOINT. A joint formed by keeping boards a short distance from the back, splitting the boards and placing tapes between, thus allowing greater play at the hinge and permitting the use of a much thicker leather or cloth than otherwise. *See also* CLOSED JOINT.

FRENCH RULE. (*Printing*) A rule made of brass or type metal and widening to a diamond shape in the middle.

FRENCH SEWING. (*Binding*) Sewing without TAPES (*q.v.*).

FRET. A continuous border pattern made up of interlaced bands or fillets. Such patterns may be used for the decoration of pages or tooled on book covers.

FRIAR. A light patch left on a forme or printed sheet due to imperfect inking. *See also* MONK.

FRINGED FOLIAGE ORNAMENT. (*Binding*) A finisher's ornament of roughly lozenge shape, with a design of conventional foliage, the characteristic feature of which is a shallow fringe round its edge.

FRISKET. A light rectangular iron frame about the size of a TYMPAN (*q.v.*) which is covered with brown paper and attached to the upper part of the tympan. The frisket sheet is folded over the tympan, the centre part of the brown paper which would otherwise cover the printing surface being cut out, before the tympan is turned over the forme. Its purpose is to prevent the sheet of paper being dirtied or blackened by the CHASE (*q.v.*), and FURNITURE (*q.v.*), to hold the sheet to the tympan and to lift the sheet from the FORME (*q.v.*) after printing.

front. (frontis.). Abbreviation for FRONTISPIECE (*q.v.*).

FRONT BOARD. The piece of millboard or strawboard which is used for the front cover of a book.

FRONT COVER. *Synonymous with* OBVERSE COVER (*q.v.*).

FRONT EDGE. *Synonymous with* FORE-EDGE (*q.v.*).

FRONT MATTER. *Synonymous with* PRELIMINARIES (*q.v.*).

FRONT-PROJECTION READER. A reader in which an enlargement of a microform is projected onto the front of an opaque screen and read by reflected light. *See also* BACK-PROJECTION READER.

FRONTISPIECE. Any pictorial representation at the front of a book, usually facing the title-page, and as a rule unnumbered and unpaged. In cataloguing, the abbreviation *front.* or *frontis.* is given in the collation only when there is no other illustrative material and the frontispiece cannot be better described as *port, map,* etc.

fs. Abbreviation for FACSIMILE (*q.v.*).

FUGITIVE COLOURS. Coloured printing inks which change or fade when exposed to normal light. Reds, greens and blues are particularly susceptible to fading.

FUGITIVE FACTS FILE. A file of facts which it has been difficult to obtain in answer to readers' inquiries, and which are likely to be asked for again. (American.)

FUGITIVE MATERIAL. Such publications as pamphlets, programmes and duplicated material produced in small quantities and of immediate, transitory or local interest.

FULDA MS. A MS. of the Gospels and other books of the New Testament written in Latin uncials and dating from *c.* 546.

FULL BINDING. A binding in which the covering material covers back and sides. Usually applied to a leather bound book. A book so bound is described as 'full bound' or 'whole bound'. *See also* HALF LEATHER, QUARTER LEATHER, THREE-QUARTER LEATHER.

FULL BOUND. A book wholly covered with leather.

FULL CATALOGUING. The style of cataloguing in which the entries give all the information provided for by the rules of the code adopted. In 1951 the Library of Congress decided to catalogue fully only certain categories of books in order to speed up the cataloguing processes. The following illustrate the kinds of categories included although individual items within the groups are assigned to full, or limited, cataloguing on the basis of their individual value: (1) basic reference and research tools in all subjects, e.g. encyclopaedias, dictionaries, bibliographies, etc.; (2) scholarly works in all fields of knowledge, including records of research, scholarly editions and translations of classical writings, publications of learned societies, institutes, governments, etc., which embody the results of research; (3) incunabula, rare books, and other works valuable for their bibliographical interest; outstanding examples of the art of book-making; art books containing exceptionally valuable reproductions. Other categories of books are dealt with by a method of LIMITED CATALOGUING (*q.v.*). *See also* SHORT CATALOGUING.

FULL COLOUR. When an ample amount of ink has been used in printing; in distinction from grey colour, when only a small quantity of ink is used (*United Typothetae*).

FULL FACE. Sometimes used *synonymously with* BOLD FACE (*q.v.*). Also used to denote FULL ON THE BODY (*q.v.*).

FULL-GILT. A book with all edges gilded.

FULL LEATHER. *See* FULL BINDING.

FULL MEASURE. Type set throughout the whole length of a line, whether of type column or page. *See also* MEASURE.

FULL NAME. A name in which all the names of an individual are given in full.

FULL-NAME NOTE. The full name of an author which is given in the bottom right-hand corner of Library of Congress catalogue cards when a short form of the name (e.g. omitting an indication of a Christian name or giving only the initials) is used for the heading. Similar notes are given in the same position for the name in religion, the original name, a pseudonym which covers joint authors, the real name, secular name, or stage name.

FULL ON THE BODY. A fount of capitals designed to occupy the complete body area, AS THIS. Also called 'Full face'.

FULL OUT. (*Printing*) To commence printed matter flush without indention.

FULL POINT. The punctuation mark used at the end of a sentence, between figures to mark decimals, and elsewhere in typography. Also called a 'Full stop'.

FULL SCORE. *See* SCORE.

FULL STOP. *Synonymous with* FULL POINT (*q.v.*).

FULL-TIME BRANCH LIBRARY. (*County Libraries*) One housed in premises set aside for the purpose, and specially equipped and furnished, open not less than thirty hours a week. *See also* BRANCH LIBRARY.

FULL TITLE. *Synonymous with* MAIN TITLE (*q.v.*).

FUNDAMENTAL CATEGORIES. (*Classification*) Personality, Matter, Energy, Space, and Time (PMEST) are the five fundamental categories of facets which Ranganathan has developed into a general facet formula which represents the PRINCIPLE OF DECREASING CONCRETENESS (*q.v.*), Personality being regarded as the most concrete category and Time as the most abstract. *See also* CATEGORY. 'Each facet of any subject, as well as each division of a facet, is considered as a manifestation of one of the five fundamental categories' (*Ranganathan*).

Placed in reverse order to that given above they would be in the order of increasing sequence of concreteness. The Connecting Symbols and Symbols of the Facet are given below.

Fundamental category (F.C.)	Connecting symbol (C.S.)	Symbol for the Facet
Personality	, (comma)	[P]
Matter	; (semicolon)	[M]
Energy	: (colon)	[E]
Space	. (dot)	[S]
Time	. (dot)	[T]

See also DECREASING CONCRETENESS, PRINCIPLE OF.

FURNISH.   The materials from which a paper is made, e.g. the furnish of a litho paper might be: esparto, 60 per cent; chemical wood, 30 per cent; loading, 10 per cent.

FURNISH LAYER.   Paper or board made up of one or more plies of the same furnish, combined while still moist, without the use of adhesive. Two, three, or more, furnish layers similarly combined are known as 'Two-layer, Three-layer, or Multi-layer paper or board' (in some countries as 'Biplex' or 'Duplex', 'Triplex', or 'Multiplex' respectively) according to the number of layers. The external furnish layers of the three-layer papers may be of the same composition, while the multi-layer papers may have two or more furnish layers of the same composition.

FURNITURE.   The wood or metal material used by the printer to form margins and to fill in large gaps between the type matter especially where there is a small amount of type to a page as on a dedication or title-page, and to help secure the printing material in the CHASE (*q.v.*).

FUTHARK.   *See* RUNES.

g.e.   Abbreviation for GILT EDGES (*q.v.*).

GKD NOTATION.   An abbreviation for the Gordon-Kendall-Davison notation which is used simply to describe structural formulae in chemistry. Also called the 'Birmingham notation'.

G.S.G.S. SERIES OF MAPS.   A series of maps published by the Directorate of Military Survey of the British War Office (formerly known as the General Staff, Geographical Section) covering Europe, Africa and Asia, and the East Indies.

g.t. (or g.t.e.).   Abbreviation for GILT TOP (*q.v.*).

GALLEY.   A long narrow and shallow steel tray about 22 inches long and open at one end, into which type is transferred from the compositor's stick or from the type-setting machine to await making up into pages. It is from the type in this galley that the galley proof (also called a 'galley') is taken. *See also* PROOF.

GALLEY PRESS. A printing press made for the pulling of galley proofs. *See also* PROOF.

GALLEY PROOF. *See* PROOF.

GAP. (*Information retrieval*) A hiatus in a collection, commonly of serials or regularly issued proceedings (*IBM*).

GARALDE. A category of type face in which the axis of the curves is inclined towards the left. There is generally more contrast between the relative thickness of the strokes than in the Humanist designs (*See* HUMANIST I), the serifs are bracketed, the bar of the lower-case 'e' is horizontal, and the serifs of the lower-case ascenders are oblique. These designs are based on those of Aldus and Garamond, and were formerly called OLD FACE or OLD STYLE (*qq.v.*). Bembo, Caslon and Vendôme are garalde faces.

GARAMOND. An elegant OLD FACE (*q.v.*) type – and one of the most venerable – named after Claude Garamond (d. *circa* 1561), a pupil of Geoffroy Tory, and the first, and perhaps the finest, of the French letter-cutters and type-founders. His roman fonts were very beautiful; these and his italic, which he admits was based on the Aldine italic, have a delightfully unconventional design. They were cut about 1540. Garamond types are very legible and unusually pleasing; the face is of light and clean design, showing a very slight difference between the thick and thin strokes. For a specimen alphabet, *see* TYPE FACE.

GASCON. *See* LE GASCON STYLE.

GATEFOLD. An illustration, map, or other insert which is larger than the page of the publication into which it is bound, so that it must be unfolded for viewing. (American.) *See also* FOLDED LEAF, FOLDING PLATE, THROW OUT.

GATHERING. (*Verb*) The process of assembling and arranging in correct order the various sections which go to make up a book, preparatory to SEWING (*q.v.*). (*Noun*) A SECTION (*q.v.*).

GAUFFERED EDGES. The gilt edges of the leaves of a book which have been decorated by impressing heated engraved tools to indent a small repeating pattern. This style was popular in the sixteenth and seventeenth centuries. Also called 'Chased', 'Gauffred', 'Goffered'.

GAUFFERING. The decoration of the gilded edges of a bound book with heated finishing tools which indent a small repeating pattern. Also called 'Chased edges', 'Goffered edges'.

GAUGE.   (*Printing*) A strip of metal or wood with a notch which is used by the make-up man to denote the exact lengths of pages or widths of margins. Also called 'Forme gauge'.

GAZETTE.   A record of public events which is published periodically. A journal or newsheet. A publication issued by a government or university to convey official information, decisions or statements.

GAZETTEER.   A geographical dictionary with a varying amount of descriptive, geographical, historical or statistical information.

GELATIN-DYE-TRANSFER.   A range of processes in which dye images produced photographically are transferred from a light sensitive matrix to a receiving sheet. *See also* TRANSFER PROCESS, VERIFAX.

GELATINE PRINT.   Another name for COLLOTYPE (*q.v.*).

GENEALOGICAL TABLE.   A representation of the lineage of a person or persons in tabular or diagrammatical form.

GENERAL ABSTRACT.   *See* ABSTRACT.

GENERAL BIBLIOGRAPHY.   *See* BIBLIOGRAPHY 1.

GENERAL CLASSIFICATION.   A classification which arranges the whole field of knowledge – the visible and invisible universe – in logical order.

GENERAL CROSS REFERENCE.   *Synonymous with* GENERAL REFERENCE (*q.v.*).

GENERAL INFORMATION REFERENCE.   A general reference in a catalogue from a specific subject on which there are no individual books to a more general subject which includes the specific subject.

GENERAL LIBRARY.   1. A library which is not limited to a particular field or subject. 2. The main library in a primary school. Also called CENTRAL LIBRARY (*q.v.*). 3. The main library of a university library system. (American.) 4. An agency, undertaking library functions at a state level, which administers a state library's general collections. (American.)

GENERAL REFERENCE.   A *See also* reference in an index or catalogue which directs the user to a number of headings under which entries on specific subjects may be found. These are often used to avoid bulking out the catalogue with a number of specific references. Also called 'General cross reference', 'Information entry', 'Multiple reference'. *See also* CROSS REFERENCES, SPECIFIC REFERENCE.

GENERAL SEARCH.   *Synonymous with* HIERARCHICAL SEARCH (*q.v.*).

GENERAL SECONDARY.   An entry for a person or a corporate body whose connexion with the publication catalogued cannot be indicated in the heading by the use of some specific designation as arranger, editor, etc.

GENERAL TITLE. One which is provided for a book consisting of several works which have previously been published separately and whose title-pages are called 'Divisional title-pages'.

GENERAL WORKS. A group name, sometimes used as a heading in a scheme of classification, for books of a general nature, i.e. dealing with many different subjects. Sometimes called a GENERALIA CLASS (q.v.).

GENERALIA CLASS. The main class of a classification which is reserved for books on many subjects such as encyclopaedias.

GENERATION. (*Reprography*). An indication of the remoteness of a copy from the original document. The original picture of the document is called a 'first generation' copy (or microfilm); copies made from this are called 'second generation', and copies made from this, 'third generation', etc.

GENERIC. Pertaining to a genus or class of related things (*IBM*).

GENERIC DESCRIPTOR. A DESCRIPTOR (q.v.) related to a genus or class of related things.

GENERIC SEARCHING. (*Information retrieval*) In machine searching for indexed material, where the machine has a 'memory unit' which will hold references to allied ideas, then searching under broader headings than the more specific ones under which a document is indexed.

GENEVA BIBLE. A version of the English Bible, translated by William Whittingham, Anthony Gilby, Thomas Sampson and possibly others, and printed by Rouland Hall, Geneva, 1560. It was produced by Marian exiles and was never sanctioned by the Archbishop of Canterbury; after the death of Archbishop Matthew Parker in 1575, it was openly printed in London (first English edition, 1576) and was the Englishman's private Bible until Cromwellian times. The General Assembly of the Scots Kirk adopted the Geneva Bible (1579) as its official version. Being the first English Bible printed in roman type it did much to help the English reading public to become familiar with the roman face. It was the first Bible in English to be divided into verses. Because of the rendering of Genesis iii. 7, it is sometimes referred to as the 'Breeches Bible'.

GENEVA CONVENTION. Popular name for the Universal Copyright convention. *See* COPYRIGHT, INTERNATIONAL.

GENUS. *See* PREDICABLES, FIVE.

GEOGRAPHIC DIVISION. Sub-division in classification or in subject headings by country, region or locality.

GEOGRAPHIC FILING METHOD.   Arranging material, or entries in a catalogue, list or bibliography, according to place, either by place-names or by a geographic classification scheme. Also sub-arrangement by place (either alphabetically by place-name or by classification) in any method of filing. Alphabetical filing may be by specific place.

GEOGRAPHICAL ENTRY.   The name given to catalogue entries for topographical books and geographical guides, which go under the name of the district to which they refer.

GEOGRAPHICAL NUMBERS.   Numbers added to a classification symbol to arrange the books geographically. They are usually applicable throughout a classification scheme.

GEOLOGICAL SURVEY.   An organization which publishes geological maps of Britain through the ORDNANCE SURVEY (*q.v.*).

GEOMETRIC.   A group of LINEALE (*q.v.*) type faces which are based-on a circle, a triangle or on geometric shapes. They are usually MONO LINE (*q.v.*), and the 'a' is often single-storey.

GEORGE FREEDLEY MEMORIAL AWARD.   *See* FREEDLEY MEMORIAL AWARD, GEORGE.

GERMANIC HANDWRITING.   A pre-Carolingian, or pre-Caroline handwriting, which was greatly limited in time and space (eighth to ninth centuries A.D.). A 'national' style of handwriting which developed after the dissolution of the Roman Empire, and was a development of the Latin cursive. *See also* CURSIVE, HANDWRITING.

GET EN MOL.   *See* JETÉ EN MOULE.

GET IN.   1. To set 'copy' in less space than estimated. 2. To set type very close, or to set it so that it will fit within a required area by using thin spacing.

GHOST WRITER.   One who writes or prepares a book such as an autobiography, or articles for, and in the name of, another (usually well-known) person.

GIANT BOOK.   A three-dimensional cardboard blow-up of the outside of a book for purposes of display. *See also* BLOW-UP.

GIFT BINDING.   Any book bound in leather for presentation such as a school prize, or part of an edition bound in leather at the publisher's order for the gift market.

GIFT BOOK.   *See* KEEPSAKES.

GIFT CARD.   A record made for each gift; it corresponds to an order card made for a purchased book.

GIGGERING.   Polishing a blind impression on a leather binding by rubbing a small hot tool on it.

GILL.   A type-face named after Eric Gill (1882–1940) the English sculptor, artist and type designer: it is characterized by the absence of serifs and is therefore known as 'Gill Sans'. Although excellent for display captions it is not wholly suitable for book work as it becomes tiring to read after a time. Gill designed two type faces which are excellent for this purpose: 'Joanna' (1930) and 'Perpetua' (1929–30), the last being his most widely-used type. This most pleasing type is used for display as well as for text. In 1934 he designed a special type for Sterne's *Sentimental Journey* published by the Limited Editions Club of New York. This was the basis for Linotype's 'Pilgrim' which appeared in 1953. For alphabet specimens, *see* TYPE FACE.

GILT EDGES. (*Binding*) The edges of a book which have been trimmed by a guillotine, covered with gold leaf and burnished. 'Antique gold edges' are those which have an unburnished gilt finish. Edges are sometimes tooled with a diapered pattern after binding. *See also* EDGES.

GILT EXTRA. (*Binding*) A binding with more than the normal amount of gilt ornamentation.

GILT IN THE ROUND. A book, the fore-edges of which have been gilded after rounding, the fore-edge appearing as a solid gilt surface.

GILT IN THE SQUARE. A book, the fore-edges of which have been gilded before rounding with the result that there is a tendency for the sections at the beginning and the end of the book to show a white edge.

GILT ON THE ROUGH. Gilding on the uncut edge of a book, or on one that has not been cut solid. It provides the elegance of gold without any sacrifice of margin but does not, like smooth gilt edges, keep the dust out. This was a popular style in France in the nineteenth century and continues popular there. *See also* MARBLING UNDER GILT, ROUGH GILT, SOLID GILT.

GILT TOP. The top edge of a book trimmed smooth and gilded, the remaining edges being trimmed only. Also called 'Top edges gilt'. Abbreviated g.t., g.t.e., or t.e.g. (top edges gilt). *See also* EDGES, GAUFFERED EDGES, SOLID GILT.

GIRDLE BOOK. A book used in the middle ages and early Renaissance which had secured to it an extra protective cover of soft leather made in such a way that the book could be hung from the girdle or habit cord of a cleric.

GIVEN NAME. The personal name (in Western races the 'Christian' name) given to an individual to distinguish him from other members of his family or clan. This name is given at baptism and/or inserted on a birth certificate.

GLAIR. An adhesive substance (made by heating up the white of eggs and vinegar or water) used as a size to retain gold in 'finishing' and edge-gilding books.

GLASSINE. A transparent glossy-surfaced paper obtained by excessive beating of the stock, or by acid treatment. It is made in white and a variety of colours, and is used for panels for window-envelopes, as jackets to protect new books, and for general wrapping purposes.

GLAZED MOROCCO. Morocco, the grain of which has been smoothed by calendering to impart a polished appearance. *See also* CRUSHED MOROCCO.

GLOSS. In ancient MSS. an explanation or interpretation of a word or expression, placed in the margin or above the line, and often in a more familiar language. Also used for an explanation inserted in the margin or text of a book to clarify a foreign or difficult passage. *See also* SIDE NOTE.

GLOSS INK. A printing ink consisting of a synthetic resin base and drying oils; this composition ensures that penetration and absorption into the paper is retarded and that it dries with a brilliant, glossy surface. Specially suitable for use with coated papers and for printing by letterpress or lithographic methods.

GLOSSARIAL INDEX. An index to a book which gives a description or definition of the word indexed as well as its page number.

GLOSSARIST. *Synonymous with* GLOSSOGRAPHER (*q.v.*).

GLOSSARY. 1. An alphabetical list of abstruse, obsolete, unusual, technical, dialectical or other, terms concerned with a subject field, together with definitions. 2. A collection of equivalent synonyms in more than one language.

GLOSSATOR. A writer of glosses to texts; a commentator; especially a mediaeval commentator on the texts of civil and canon law. *See also* GLOSSOGRAPHER.

GLOSSIST. *Synonymous with* GLOSSOGRAPHER (*q.v.*).

GLOSSOGRAPHER. A writer of glosses to a text, or of commentaries on a text; an annotator. Also called a 'Glossarist', 'Glossist', 'Glottographer'. *See also* GLOSSATOR.

GLOSSOGRAPHY. The writing of glosses or commentaries; the compiling of glossaries (*OED*).

GLOSSY PRINT. A photographic print with a shiny surface. These are necessary for the making of satisfactory half-tone blocks. They are usually made on smooth bromide and contact paper that is glazed on a heated metal or ferrotype plate, highly polished chromium-plated steel, stainless steel or plastic which is now often in the form of an electrically heated drum that is kept constantly revolving during operation. Also called 'Ferrotype'.

GLOTTOGRAPHER. *Synonymous with* GLOSSOGRAPHER (*q.v.*).

GLUEING OFF. The process of applying glue to the spine of a book, either after sewing, or instead of sewing, and just prior to placing it within its case.

GLYPHIC. Styles of type face which are chiselled, rather than calligraphic, in form. Of such are Albertus, Augustea and Latin.

GLYPHOGRAPHY. A process of making printing plates by engraving on a copper plate covered with a wax film, then dusting with powdered graphite, producing a surface that is used to make an electrotype (*United Typothetae*).

GOATSKIN. Leather manufactured from the skins of goats; the best skins come from the River Niger, the Levant or Morocco, and are named after the places from which they come.

GOFFERED EDGES. *Synonymous with* GAUFFERED EDGES (*q.v.*).

GOLD. Used in the form of thin leaves or foil for lettering or tooling books.

GOLD CUSHION. A pad, used by binders' finishers, to which a sheet of gold leaf adheres and from which the finisher takes the small pieces required for each book. The pad is usually filled with blotting paper, felt, or similar material, and covered with leather.

GOLD KNIFE. A knife used by binders' finishers to cut gold leaf while on the gold cushion. It has a long, flat blade, and is sharpened on both sides.

GOLD STAMPED. A book with a design stamped in gold on the binding by means of a stamp. *See also* BLOCK 3, PANEL STAMP, TOOLING.

GOLD TOOLING. *See* TOOLING.

GOLDEN COCKEREL PRESS. An English private press, founded in December 1920 by Harold Midgely Taylor at Waltham Saint Lawrence, Berkshire, to print and publish (in a co-operative manner, and under the conditions of a 'village industry') new works of literary significance by young authors; and to print and publish fine editions of books of established worth. When Mr. Taylor retired in January 1924 owing to illness, the Press was purchased by Robert Gibbings, illustrator and woodcutter who operated it until 1933. The press is still active. Most of the printing is done in Caslon Old Face.

GOLDEN TYPE. The first of three types cut by William Morris for his Kelmscott Press. It was a 14-point roman based on an early fount used by Nicholas Jenson and was first used in 1891. In 1891 he designed the TROY and, in 1892 the CHAUCER, types (*qq.v.*). *See also* KELMSCOTT PRESS.

GONE TO BED. *See* GONE TO PRESS.

GONE TO PRESS. A term used to indicate that formes or plates have been sent for machining and that it is too late to make any but vital corrections or alterations. Any which occur at this stage are often included in corrigenda. In a newspaper office the term 'Gone to bed' is generally used.

GOOD. Said of composed type which has been printed off and which, because it may be used at a later date, is not distributed but kept standing.

GOTHIC MINUSCULE. The style of handwriting which, by the end of the twelfth century, had degenerated from the Carolingian Minuscule into a hand consisting of long, angular, pointed letters. It was on this that most of the early European printers based their first types.

GOTHIC TYPE. Type resembling the Gothic script used as a book hand in the later middle ages. Gothic types are usually divided into four groups: (1) *Text, Lettre de forme* (Ger. *textura*), or (pointed) church type; (2) *Gothico-antiqua, lettre de somme* (Ger. *fere-human-istica*), the simple round gothic; (3) *Rotunda*, the ordinary round text-type; (4) *Bastard, lettre de batarde* (Ger. *bastarda*), or cursive type. It is now loosely used to include all bold sans serif and grotesque type faces. Also called 'Black letter type'.

GOTHICO-ANTIQUA. *See* GOTHIC TYPE.

GOTTLIEB PRIZE, MURRAY. $50 and publication offered by the (American) Medical Library Association for the best essay submitted on some phase of medical history.

GOUDY. A type face named after the American type-designer, Frederic W. Goudy who flourished in the early years of the present century. Probably his most famous type is Kennerley.

GOUFFERED. *See* GAUFFERED EDGES.

GOUGE. A bookbinder's finishing tool used for producing a curved line on a book cover at a single application. It has a set of arcs of concentric circles.

GOVERNMENT DOCUMENT. A publication issued at government expense or published by authority of a governmental body. As used in America, any publication in book, serial or non-book form bearing an imprint of a government, whether federal, state, local, or foreign, and of inter-governmental organizations, such as Unesco, etc. *See also* OFFICIAL PUBLICATION.

GOVERNMENT LIBRARY. A library maintained out of central

government funds. Government libraries normally fall into three broad groups: National libraries, departmental libraries and the libraries of research stations.

GOVERNMENT PUBLICATIONS. Publications of an official character, or of an instructional, descriptive, or historical nature, which are published by the government publishing department for parliament or one of the government departments. *See also* PARLIAMENTARY PUBLICATIONS.

GRABHORN PRESS. Founded by the Grabhorn brothers, Edwin and Robert, of San Francisco, this press has established a leading reputation for gifted and original work since their first commission from the Book Club of California in 1921. The Grabhorns' work is lively and virile and they are particularly skilful in colour-printing, especially from wood-blocks.

GRACE. Abbreviation for the Graphic Arts Composing Equipment – a photocomposition machine that converts information from magnetic tape into latent typographical images on photosensitive film or paper. *See also* MEDLARS.

GRADATION IN SPECIALITY. Bliss's 'principle by which the several sciences and studies distinguished by their conceptional scope and their relations to the real order of nature, are arranged in serial order from the most general to the most special.' The modulation of more fundamental classes into their derivatives in the same way that special sciences depend on, and to some extent are derived from, the general sciences.

GRAIN. The direction in which the fibres lie in a sheet of paper. *See also* AGAINST THE GRAIN, WITH THE GRAIN.

GRAIN DIRECTION. The direction in which the majority of the fibres in a sheet of paper lie. The moving web of a paper-making machine causes the fibres in the pulp to lie parallel with one another in the direction of the web movement. Also called 'Machine direction'. It is important to determine the 'direction' of paper used for lithography, postage stamps, account books or close register work, to avoid differences in expansion. Hand-made papers expand or shrink equally in all directions due to the shaking which occurs during manufacture and which felts the fibres in all directions. *See also* AGAINST THE GRAIN, WITH THE GRAIN.

GRAINED LEATHER. A tanned skin on which the natural grain (visible on the side on which the hair grew) has been worked up to raise and accentuate it. Graining is also artificially produced by stamping a skin with engraved metal plates.

GRAINING.   1. The process of producing the natural grain markings of leather by boarding, i.e. the pushing or pulling of a fold in the skin with the aid of a board covered with cork, which grips that portion of the skin with which it is in contact. 2. The art of producing an artificial grain on leather by stamping it with metal plates or passing it through rollers on which the desired grain markings are engraved.

GRAMOPHONE LIBRARY.   A collection of gramophone records. Such collections are maintained by public libraries, the records being lent to local gramophone or musical societies, clubs, schools, or private individuals.

GRAMOPHONE RECORD.   A recording of a musical composition, or vocal statement, or reading, made on a thin, flat, circular plastic material which is placed on a machine to reproduce the sounds recorded. Called popularly, a 'disc', and also in America, a 'Phonograph record'.

GRAMOPHONE RECORD NUMBER.   A symbol, usually consisting of one or more letters and numbers, and allocated by the manufacturer to an individual recording for purposes of identification. It is printed on the label on the record.

GRANGERIZING.   The practice of inserting in a bound volume illustrations, letters, documents, etc., not issued as part of the volume but referred to in the text. Such additional matter is mounted or inlaid on sheets of good quality paper and inserted in the appropriate parts of the book which is usually re-bound. The practice dates from 1769, when James Granger published a 'Bibliographical History of England' with blank leaves for the reception of illustrations. Such a volume is said to to be 'Extra-illustrated' or 'Grangerized'.

GRAPHIC.   Styles of type faces which suggest that the characters have not been written but drawn. Of such are Cartoon, Libra and Old English (Monotype).

GRAPHIC LENGTH.   A characteristic of the length of notation symbols used in a scheme of classification, whereby there is ability to remember easily a sequence because of their visual appearance. A pure notation (one consisting of the same kind of characters, as all figures or all letters) is easier to remember than a mixed notation comprising figures, letters or symbols. *See also* PHONIC LENGTH.

GRAVER.   A BURIN (*q.v.*).

GRAVURE.   A French word, meaning cutting or engraving; used as a continuing word, like photogravure, rotogravure, etc. (*United Typothetae*). An abbreviation for PHOTOGRAVURE (*q.v.*).

GREAT PRIMER.   An out-of-date name for a size of type equal to about 18 point.

GREATER LONDON COUNCIL.   The new administrative area comprising thirty-two London boroughs each with a population range of 169,000 to 340,000 and replacing as from 1st April 1965 the London County Council, the Middlesex County Council and eighty-five other local authorities. The status of the City of London remains but with the powers of a London Borough Council. The Middlesex County Libraries were transferred to the new boroughs in the former area of the Middlesex County Council.

GREEK FASHION.   Book bindings with raised HEADBANDS (q.v.), i.e. those which project beyond the boards at the head and tail of the spine. The Greek technique of forwarding was used in the West only for Greek books.

GREEK LIBRARY ASSOCIATION OF CYPRUS.   Founded in April 1962 for the purposes of uniting librarians and improving libraries and librarianship in Cyprus. Membership is open to all persons working in libraries in Cyprus.

GREEN BOOK.   An official report published by the Italian government; so called because published in a green paper cover. See also BLUE BOOK.

GREEN PAPER.   A document issued by any Department or Ministry of the British Government. It sets out government propositions so that full consultation and public discussion may take place while policy is still in a formative stage. Green Papers are intended to meet the need for better communication between Government and public rather than to present proposals as in a White Paper. See also BLUE BOOK, PARLIAMENTARY PAPERS, WHITE PAPER.

GRID.   (Binding) An ornament which is frequently used on heads-in-medallions rolls, and consists of two horizontal lines with a few short vertical bars between them, the sides having a foliage character.

GRIGG COMMITTEE.   Popular name of the Committee on Departmental Records of which Sir James Grigg was Chairman. It was set up in 1952 by the Master of the Rolls and the Chancellor of the Exchequer to review the arrangements for the preservation of Government Department's records and to make recommendations. The Committee's report was presented in 1954; and the recommendations it contained were accepted by Government in principle; the Public Records Act 1958 which came into force on 1 January 1959 repealed the former acts of 1838, 1877 and 1898. This Act transferred the direction of the Public Record Office from the Master of the Rolls to a Minister of the

Crown, the Lord Chancellor, who was given a general responsibility for public records.

GRIPPER EDGE. *See* LAY EDGES.

GRISA. Groupe de Recherche sur l'Information Scientifique (Scientific Information Processing Research Team). A working party of CETIS (*q.v.*).

GROLIER-AMERICANA SCHOLARSHIPS. Donated by the Grolier Foundation, and made to two library schools, one of which is a graduate library school and the other with a programme of library education at undergraduate level, for scholarships for a student in each institution who is in training for school librarianship. It is awarded annually in the form of $1,000 cash for each school, and administered by the American Association of School Librarians whose Grolier-Americana Scholarships Awards Committee considers applications received previously from directors of library schools. The schools selected choose the student to whom the scholarship is to be given. The Scholarship was first awarded in 1957 to the Department of Librarianship, Western Michigan University and to the School of Library Service, Columbia University.

GROLIER AWARD. Donated by Grolier Inc., and consisting of $1,000 cash and a citation of achievement, this award is made annually to a librarian in a community or in a school who has made an unusual contribution to the stimulation and guidance of reading by children and young people. It 'is usually given for outstanding work with children and young people through high school age, for continued service, or in recognition of one particular contribution of lasting value'. Selection of the recipient is made by a jury of five appointed by the ALA Awards Committee (which administers the Award), and representing the following ALA divisions: AASL, CSD, YASD and one member representing the ALA Awards Committee who serves as chairman. The Award was first made in 1954 to Siddie Joe Johnson.

GROLIER NATIONAL LIBRARY WEEK AWARD. $1,000 donated by Grolier Inc., and offered by the ALA Committee on National Library Week to the state library association sponsoring the most effective statewide Library Week programme.

GROLIERESQUE. The style of binding which is associated with Jean Grolier (1479–1565). It depends for its effect on light and graceful geometrical 'strapword' (interlaced double fillets), and influenced ornate binding for two centuries. *See also* MAIOLI STYLE.

GROOVE.   The cut-out portion of the base of a piece of movable type. Also called 'Heel-nick'. It has no particular purpose in printing. *See also* FEET.

GROOVES.   (*Binding*) 1. The shoulders formed on the sides of books in backing, to allow the boards to lie even with the back when secured. 2. Incisions in the back edge of a board to take the cords on which the sections are sewn.

GROSS SQUARE FOOTAGE.   The sum of the areas of a library at each floor level included within the principal outside faces at exterior walls, but not including architectural setbacks, or projections. (American.)

GROTESQUE.   Sans serif display types of unconventional design which are not usually pleasing to behold. A name given at the beginning of the nineteenth century to the earliest SANS SERIF (*q.v.*) types, which have been revived and come into favour for display work. During the 1920's and 1930's the following sans serif faces became popular: Futura, Gill, Granby, Vogue. These are a group of LINEALE (*q.v.*) type faces with nineteenth-century origins. Some contrast in the thickness of the strokes exists, and there is a squareness in the curves. The ends of the curved strokes are usually horizontal. The G is spurred and the R usually has a curled leg. *See also* NEO-GROTESQUE.

GROUND.   An acid-resisting compound used on etching plates to protect the non-image-bearing portions from the action of the acid. It is composed of beeswax, asphaltum, gum mastic and pitch.

GROUNDWOOD PULP.   *Synonymous with* MECHANICAL WOOD (*q.v.*).

GROUP.   A section of the membership of the Library Association, and formally constituted in accordance with the bye-laws of the Association. Each group is concerned with a particular subject interest in librarianship. Members are entitled to join two groups: more on payment of small additional subscriptions. *See also* BRANCH, DIVISION, LIBRARY ASSOCIATION, SECTION. Aslib also has subject Groups.

GROUP NOTATION DEVICE.   The device of using ordinal decimal fraction numbers of two or more digits (but the same number of significant digits) to represent a number of co-ordinate isolates or array-isolates, when they are too many to be represented economically by SECTOR DEVICE (*q.v.*) alone.

GROWING FLOWER.   A common ornament on bookbinders' finishers' rolls, consisting usually of a flattened elliptical base from which springs a stem bearing leaves and at the top two flowers, the tops of which curl outwards.

GRUB STREET.   According to Dr. Johnson, 'originally the name of a street near Moorfields, much inhabited by writers of small histories, dictionaries, and occasional poems. . . .'

GUARANTEE.   The undertaking signed by a guarantor when undertaking to be responsible for any losses incurred as a result of the guaranteed person using the library.

GUARANTOR.   A person who signs a voucher for a reader who is not a ratepayer, guaranteeing to make good any financial losses caused by the person guaranteed by reason of his using the library.

GUARD.   1. A strip of linen or paper pasted by a binder (1) on to or into the sections of a book to prevent the sewing tearing through the paper, (2) on the inner edge of an illustration, the guard being sewn through. 2. One or more pieces of paper or linen placed together to equalize the space taken by a folded map or other insert or by material pasted to the pages of a cuttings book. Also to enable additional illustrations, maps or leaves to be added after binding. Also called 'Stub'.

GUARD BOOK CATALOGUE.   See PAGE CATALOGUE.

GUARD SHEET.   A sheet of paper, usually thinner (and often transparent) than that on which the book is printed, bearing a letterpress description or an outline drawing to protect and/or elucidate the illustration which it accompanies. The guard sheet is not normally included in the pagination.

GUARDING.   Fixing a guard to a section, map or illustration, etc. Strengthening the fold between two conjugate leaves with an adhesive, pasted, or glued-on strip of paper.

GUIDE BOOK.   A handbook for travellers and visitors which gives information about a country, region, or building.

GUIDE CARD.   A card with a projecting tab used in a card catalogue or file to indicate the arrangement and to facilitate reference.

GUIDE-LETTER.   A letter printed in the space to be filled by the rubrisher or illuminator of an early printed book as a guide to prevent him inserting a wrong letter.

GUIDE SLIP.   See PROCESS SLIP.

GUILLEMETS.   See DUCK-FOOT QUOTES.

GUILLOTINE.   A machine for cutting paper, with a knife having a perpendicular action.

GUM ARABIC.   A solution used to preserve offset plates, and in lithographic printing. See also DESENSITIZATION.

GUMMING UP.   Applying a solution of gum arabic to an offset plate to protect it from grease and oxidation.

GUTENBERG BIBLE.   See MAZARIN BIBLE.

GUTTER.   The adjoining inner margins of two facing pages of type; the margins at the sewn fold of a section. 2. The combined marginal space formed by the two inner margins of confronting pages of a book (B.S. 4187: 1967). 3. (*Binding*) The trough between the edge of the board and the backed spine of a bound book. *See also* BACKING, GROOVE, JOINT 3, SPINE.

GUTTER MARGIN. *Synonymous with* BACK MARGIN (*q.v.*).

GUTTERING. The ridges that sometimes occur (as a result of use) along the spine of a binding which has a tight or a flexible back.

GYPSOGRAPHIC PRINT. *Synonymous with* SEAL PRINT (*q.v.*).

h.t. Abbreviation for HALF-TITLE (*q.v.*).

HABILITATIONSSCHRIFTEN. A 'probationary treatise embodying the results of original research that is submitted to the faculty in order that its author be recognized as a Privatdozent at the university'. (*Cassell's New German and English Dictionary*.)

HACHURES. Vertical and horizontal lines used on a map to indicate by their length and closeness the direction and steepness of variations in height of the earth's surface, the lines being crowded together to represent the steepest slopes. *See also* HATCHING.

HADIS. A co-operative grouping of organizations, based on the Huddersfield Public Libraries, and functioning since 1959 within a radius of ten miles from Huddersfield, each of which possesses at least fifty books and takes three current periodicals. There is no headquarters; members requiring books or information contact member organizations directly. The focal point is an executive committee, and particularly its officers. Publishes *Query* (q.) and occasional publications.

HAGAR PRESS. The German counterpart of the ALBION PRESS (*q.v.*).

HAGIONYM. The name of a saint taken as a proper name.

HAGUE SCHEME. A scheme of book classification compiled by Dr. Greve. *See also* SISO.

HAIR LINE. A thin stroke of a letter or type character.

HAIR SPACE. (*Printing*) The thinnest spacing material. It is cast less than type height and is used between letters or words. Hair spaces vary in thickness from eight to twelve to an em, according to body size, thus in 6 pt. the hair space is $\frac{1}{2}$ pt.; in 12 pt. it is $1\frac{1}{2}$ pts.; in 18 pt. it is 2 pts.; and in 24 pt. it is 3 pts. Thissentenceishairspaced.

HALDIS. The Halifax and District Information Service; formed in 1966 at the College Library, Percival Whitley College of Further Education, Francis Street, Halifax, Yorkshire, whereby organizations which have literature, and are willing to inter-lend and pay a nominal annual subscription, may co-operate with one another.

HALE AWARD, SARAH JOSEPHA. A medal awarded to a distinguished author whose work and life reflect the literary tradition of New England. Donated by the friends of the Richards Free Library.

HALF BANDS. Ridges on the spine of a bound book, at the top and bottom, smaller than bands. They usually mark the position of the KETTLE STITCH (*q.v.*).

HALF BINDING. *See* QUARTER BINDING.

HALF BOUND. *Synonymous with* HALF LEATHER (*q.v.*).

HALF CLOTH. A book with a cloth spine, usually with the title printed on a paper label, and having paper covered 'board' (i.e. strawboard) sides. May also be called 'Half linen'.

HALF-DARK TYPE. *Synonymous with* MEDIUM FACE TYPE (*q.v.*).

HALF FRAME. The use of a mask in the gate of a camera to reduce the image to half size, e.g. to 24 × 18 mm. from 24 × 36 mm.

HALF LEATHER. A term used to describe a book with a leather spine and corners, but with the rest of the sides covered in cloth. *See also* LEATHER BOUND, QUARTER LEATHER.

HALF-LINE BLOCK. A printing block made by interposing a half-line screen (i.e. parallel lines without cross-lines) between the original line drawing and the negative. The result is lighter in tone than the original.

HALF LINEN. *See* HALF CLOTH.

HALF-MEASURE. *See* DOUBLE COLUMNED.

HALF MONTHLY. A periodical issued twice a month, or fortnightly.

HALF SEE SAFE. An expression used by a bookseller when ordering copies of a book from a publisher to indicate that, while all copies will be paid for, he may ask the publisher to take back half of them in exchange for copies of another title. *See also* SEE SAFE.

HALF-SHEET IMPOSITION. *Synonymous with* HALF-SHEET WORK (*q.v.*).

HALF-SHEET WORK. Printing (with two machinings) a sheet of paper on both sides with the same forme. The paper is then cut in half to give two copies. *See also* SHEET WORK. Also called 'Half-sheet imposition'.

HALF-STAMP. (*Binding*) A finisher's stamp the design of which is the same as, or similar to, one half of a fleuron, pineapple, etc. It is generally used for the compartments at the edges of the frame in lozenge compartment bindings. Sometimes used back to back to form the lozenges in the centre.

HALF-STUFF. (*Paper*) Partially broken and washed STOCK (*q.v.*) which has been reduced to a fibrous pulp, usually before it is bleached. The finished pulp, ready for the vat or paper machine is termed 'whole-stuff'. *See also* PULP, STOCK, STUFF, WHOLE-STUFF.

HALF-TITLE. The brief title of a book appearing on the recto of the leaf preceding the title-page. It serves to protect the title-page and help the printer to identify the book to which the first sheet belongs. The wording of long titles is often abbreviated. The use of such a page dates from the latter half of the seventeenth century although a blank sheet had been used to protect title-pages for a very long time. It is often abbreviated h.t. Also called 'Bastard title', 'Fly-title'. *See also* SECOND HALF-TITLE.

HALF-TONE. The name given to the process by means of which photographs, drawings, designs, etc., are reproduced in tone as opposed to solid black and white: also to the actual prints made by it. The printing plate is of copper or zinc and the image is reduced to a series of dots varying in intensity with the tone values of the original. This is done photographically in conjunction with a mechanically ruled screen which is coarse with few dots to the square inch for printing on coarse papers, and many to the square inch for fine, smooth papers. Etching removes the background, leaving the dots representing the image to be printed by relief process. A *Squared-up half-tone* is one finished with straight sides at right angles. Half-tones are also finished as Circles or Ovals. A *Vignetted half-tone* is one which has no sharp edge to the design, and 'fades' out. A *Cut-out half-tone* is one from which the background is entirely removed. A *Deep-etched half-tone* is one from the highlights of which the dots characteristic of a half-tone are entirely removed, leaving the paper virgin white in the reproduction.

HALF-TONE PAPER. An ART (*q.v.*), imitation art, or other super-calendered or coated paper suitable for the printing of half-tones.

HALF-TONE SCREENS. Transparent plates of glass used for making half-tone blocks. They are ruled diagonally with opaque lines usually, but not necessarily, at right angles to each other, the thickness of the lines and of the intervening spaces being approximately equal. The number of lines to the inch varies, 'fine' screens having more than 'coarse' ones. The smoother the paper used, the finer must be the half-tone block. *See also* SCREEN.

HALF UNCIAL. The last stage in the development of the Roman period of Latin manuscript handwriting, being a somewhat informal kind of letter based on minuscule forms and used from the fifth to the ninth centuries. It is specially associated with the calligraphic revival by Alcuin in the ninth century. Most of the letters were minuscules, only a few of the capitals, such as N and F, remaining.

HALF YEARLY. A periodical which is issued at six-monthly intervals. Also called 'Semi-annual'. *See also* BI-ANNUAL.

HALIFAX AND DISTRICT INFORMATION SERVICE. *See* HALDIS.

HALSEY W. WILSON LIBRARY RECRUITMENT AWARD. *See* WILSON LIBRARY RECRUITMENT AWARD, HALSEY W.

HAMMOND INCORPORATED LIBRARY AWARD. An annual Award of $500 cash and a citation, donated by the C. S. Hammond Company, and made to a librarian who has effectively encouraged the use of maps and atlases or promoted an interest in cartography. The Award is administered by the ALA Awards Committee, the selection being made by a jury of five representing various divisions of the ALA. The first recipient was Mrs. Clara E. Le Gear in 1963.

HAMPSHIRE INTER-LIBRARY CENTER. *See* HILC.

HAND. The printers' symbol ☞. Used to attract attention. Also called 'Digit', 'Fist', 'Index'.

HAND COMPOSITION. The setting up of printer's type by hand as distinct from machine setting.

HAND GRAVURE. A method of copperplate printing. After inking and before each impression is taken, the surface is wiped by hand (*United Typothetae*).

HAND-MADE PAPER. Paper made by dipping a mould into the pulp vat and taking up sufficient 'stuff' to form a sheet of paper of the required substance. A shaking movement causes the fibres to mix together. The pulp is composed of rag fibres; when the best linen rags are used the resulting paper is the most durable obtainable. Also called 'Vat paper'.

HAND PRESS. A press in which the forme is inked, the paper fed and removed, and the pressure applied, by hand; used to distinguish it from one worked by power; often used in printing offices to pull proofs by hand and for short runs on small sheets of paper. It is the direct descendant of the earliest type of printing press.

HAND ROLLER. *See* BRAYER.

HAND SET. Type which has been set by hand, as opposed to type set by machine.

HAND SEWING. The sewing by hand through the folds of sections of a book, using a sewing frame. *See also* SEWN.

HAND STAMP. A brass letter, or motif, set in a wooden handle, and used by a binder's finisher in lettering the cover of a hand-bound book.

HANDBILL. A poster, or placard, printed by hand.

HANDBOOK. A treatise on a special subject; often nowadays a simple but all-embracing treatment, containing concise information, and being small enough to be held in the hand; but strictly, a book of science or technology written primarily for practitioners and serving as a book for constant revision or reference. Also called a 'Manual'.

HANDWRITING. Books were produced by writing by hand before the use of wood blocks early in the fifteenth century (see BLOCK BOOK). After European countries had shaken off the political authority of the Roman empire, and the educated communities had been scattered and dissolved, the Latin 'cursive' or 'running' script changed and several 'national' hands, or styles of the Latin cursive minuscule developed. The five principal national hands are South Italian or Beneventan, Merovingian (in France), Visigothic (in Spain), Germanic pre-Carolingian, and Insular (in Ireland and England). The earliest of the five periods into which Latin manuscript handwriting can be divided is the Roman period (second to eighth centuries) and this can be divided into five groups: *Quadrata*, or *Square capital*, hand; *Rustic capital* hand; *Uncial* hand; *Later cursive* hand; and *Half uncial* hand (*qq.v.*).

HANGING FIGURES. The numerals of certain type-designs which range within the limits of the EXTRUDERS (*q.v.*), e.g. the Caslon figures 3456789 as distinct from the 12 and 0 of the same face. Old-face types usually have hanging figures, although in some, e.g. Plantin, RANGING FIGURES (*q.v.*) are available as an alternative.

HANGING INDENTION. 1. A paragraph of which the first line is set to the full width of the measure, the second and all subsequent lines of the paragraph being indented one or more ems from the left-hand margin as for this definition. *See also* PARAGRAPH INDENTION. Also called 'Hanging paragraph'. 2. In cataloguing, the form of indention in which the first line begins at the 'author indention' ('first indention') and succeeding lines at the 'title indention' ('second indention'). This method is used by the Library of Congress and many other libraries for 'formal anonyma', i.e. works like periodicals which do not involve the idea of concealed authorship. It is a method which tends to emphasize the first word of the title.

HANGING PARAGRAPH. *Synonymous with* HANGING INDENTION (*q.v.*).

HANS CHRISTIAN ANDERSEN AWARD. *See* ANDERSEN AWARD, HANS CHRISTIAN.

'HANSARD'. *See* PARLIAMENTARY PAPERS.

HARD BOUND. Bound in cloth- or paper-covered boards. Also called 'Hard cover'.

HARD COPY. 1. A human-readable copy produced from information that has been transcribed to a form not easily readable by human beings (*IBM*). 2. A record on card or paper, to distinguish it from a record on microfilm or magnetic tape. It may be a contact copy or an enlargement. 3. A printed copy of machine output in readable form for human beings; e.g. reports, listings, catalogues, documents, summaries.

HARD COVER. *See* HARD BOUND.

HARD PACKING. Thin card, or hard or stiff paper, used to cover the cylinder of a printing press in order to obtain a sharp impression, with little indentation of the paper, when printing on smooth hard paper.

HARDBACK. A book published in stiff covers. The opposite of PAPERBACK (*q.v.*).

HARLEIAN STYLE. An English style of book decoration with a centre motif composed of small tools usually arranged in a lozenge-shaped design, and having an elaborate if sometimes rather narrow border decorated by means of one or more rolls. These 'Harleian' bindings were made by Thomas Elliott for Robert and Edward Harley, the First and Second Earls of Oxford.

HARRIS AWARD, JOHN. Offered by the New Zealand Library Association 'for the written record of notable library work, whether in the bibliographical, critical, historical or administrative fields, which will be a contribution to New Zealand librarianship'. The work should be the result of original research. The Award consists of an 'appropriate diploma, plus the sum of £25'. It was first made to Mr. W. J. McEldowney, a former Honorary Secretary of the NZLA, in 1963.

HARVARD SYSTEM. A method of citing papers from scientific books and periodicals. The items making up a reference are as follows: (i) author's name and initials; (ii) year of publication, in parentheses, with *a*, *b*, etc. if more than one paper in the year is cited; (iii) full title of paper (roman type); (iv) name of periodical, contracted as in the *World List of Scientific Periodicals* (italic type); (v) volume number (in bold arabic figures); (vi) number of first page of paper; e.g.

> Gregory, P. H. (1940). The control of narcissus leaf disease. *Ann. appl. Biol.* **27**, 338.
>
> Jensen, H. L. & Betty, R. C. (1943). Nitrogen fixation in leguminous plants. *Proc. Linn. Soc.* N.S.W. **68**. I.

One of the chief advantages of this system is that footnotes can be dispensed with, a list of references being printed at the end of the article in alphabetical order of authors' names. In the text, references are given by printing the author's name and the date of publication in parentheses as (Gregory, 1940), (Jensen and Betty, 1943) but if the author's name is part of the text the date only is given in (). When three or more authors have collaborated in a paper, all the names are given in the first citation, but subsequently only the first name followed by '*et al.*' need be used.

HATCHING. A row of parallel, diagonal lines. Often found on the half bands or on the heads and tails of the spines of bindings from the sixteenth century onwards. Also used for the 'azured' shading on the centres of finishers' tools. *See also* CROSS HATCHING, HACHURES.

HATRICS. Abbreviation for Hampshire Technical Research Industrial and Commercial Service which was set up in 1964 and has its headquarters at the Commercial Library of the Central Library, Civic Centre, Southampton. It is the intention of the various institutions concerned with the acquisition and distribution of technical, scientific and commercial information in Hampshire to communicate directly with one another through the medium of a directory of resources. There are no membership limitations. An annual subscription of three guineas is payable.

HAWNT REPORT. The Report on *The Public library service in Northern Ireland*, 1966, (Belfast, H.M.S.O., Cmd. 494), so named after Dr. J. S. Hawnt, the Chairman of the Advisory Committee appointed in September 1964 by the Minister of Education, Government of Northern Ireland, 'to consider the public library service . . . and make recommendations for its development, having regard to the relationship of public libraries to other libraries'.

In many respects the Committee's recommendations follow closely those of the ROBERTS REPORT (*q.v.*), but there was the important difference that the Hawnt Committee considered that financial arrangements were altogether unable to meet the demands of a modern library service; proposals were therefore made for government grants. The powers and duties of local library authorities were enumerated. It was considered that a Provincial Library should be created and that the Belfast Central Library should become this Provincial Library and function under a Provincial Joint Committee, leaving the branch libraries under the control of the Belfast Corporation. A minority report, however, could not accept this dismembering of the Belfast Public Libraries as the price of establishing the Provincial Library.

HAYSTAQ. Name of an information searching procedure with electronic computers used by the U.S. Patent Office (*IBM*).

HEAD. 1. The margin at the top of a page. 2. The top of a book or of a page. 3. The top of the spine of a book where the headband is placed. 4. The top edge of a book. *See also* FOOT.

HEAD AND TAIL. The top and bottom edges of a book.

HEAD MARGIN. The blank space above the top line of printed matter. 'Heads' relates to the top margins.

HEAD ORNAMENT. An ornament specially designed for the top of a page: it may incorporate the lettering of the chapter heading, or provide an *island space* in which to print it. It is sometimes called a 'Headband' or 'Head piece'. *See also* TAIL ORNAMENT.

HEAD PIECE. *Synonymous with* HEAD ORNAMENT (*q.v.*).

HEAD TITLE. The title, even in abbreviated form, given as a heading above a page of type. *See also* HEADLINE.

HEADBAND. (*Binding*) The band, usually of coloured silk threads, at the head of a book, placed between the sections and the cover, and projecting slightly beyond the head. Originally it was a cord or leather thong similar to the ordinary bands, around which the ends of the threads were twisted, and laced-in to the boards. Nowadays headbands are usually made of coloured silks and are sewn on after the book has been forwarded thus having no purpose other than decoration. The two were formerly distinguished as 'headband' and 'tailband' but both are now called 'headbands' or 'heads'. 2. (*Printing*) A printed or engraved decorative band at the head of a page or chapter. Also called 'Head piece', 'Head ornament'.

HEADCAP. The thickened end of the spine at head and tail of the leather spine of a book; this is caused by placing a piece of sized Italian hemp inside the turn-in at the head and tail of the spine after the leather has been fitted to the book. If headbands are used, they are left visible. *See also* HEADBAND, TAILCAP.

HEADING. 1. (*Cataloguing*) The commencement of a catalogue entry – usually written or printed on a separate line and sometimes in larger type than the remainder of the entry – the first sequence of characters (forming a name, word or phrase) which determine (a) the exact position of an entry in a catalogue, (b) group-related entries together in a catalogue. It is generally the author, subject, or first word not an article, of the title, but may be the class number. *See also* ENTRY WORD, FORM HEADING, FORM SUB-HEADING, SUB-HEADING, UNIFORM HEADING. 2. (*Indexing*) The word(s) or symbol(s) selected from, or based on, an item in the text – specifically the initial word or keyword – arranged in alphabetical or other chosen order. (B.S. 3700:1964). Such words or symbols express the subject or idea to which reference is given and appear at the beginning of the entry. 3. The entry word followed by any other (or others) necessary for its meaning. 4. The word or words at the top of a page, chapter or section. 5. (*Book production, Printing*) Sub-headings which divide chapters and comprise CROSS-HEADS, INCUT NOTE, MARGINAL NOTES, SHOULDER-HEADS, SIDE-HEADS (*qq.v.*). 6. (*Information retrieval*) The word, name or phase at the beginning of an entry to indicate some special aspect of the document (authorship, subject content, series, title, etc.) (*IBM*).

HEADLINE. The heading at the top of the page giving the title of the book (usually on the verso) or the subject of the chapter or of the page (usually on the recto). Also called 'Page head'. *See also* CAPTION TITLE, HALF TITLE, PAGE HEADLINE, RUNNING TITLE, SECTION HEADLINE. When giving the title of the book, even in abbreviated or different form, it may be called 'Head title'.

HEADQUARTERS. *See* COUNTY HEADQUARTERS.

HEADS. *See* HEAD MARGIN.

HEAT COPYING. Making copies of documents by a heat process. *See also* THERMAL PROCESS, THERMOGRAPHY.

HEAT DEVELOPMENT PROCESS. A term sometimes applied to the THERMAL DIAZO PROCESS (*q.v.*) and to processes using VESICULAR FILM (*q.v.*).

HECTOGRAPH PROCESS. A duplicating process in which the impression is transferred from a gelatine bed on to paper (gelatine hectograph), or from a master sheet on which the matter to be reproduced has been imprinted through a hectograph carbon and which is transferred to paper by means of a solvent such as industrial methylated spirit. This modern development is known as spirit duplicating.

HECTOGRAPHY. Reproducing an image by the hectograph process.

HEEL-NICK. *See* GROOVE.

HEIDELBERG. The name of a fully automatic printing press made by the Schnellpressenfabrik A.G., Heidelberg. The first press was a platen press made in 1914, in which the paper was fed by revolving wings. The Cylinder Heidelberg, first marketed in 1936, is a single-revolution machine in which the cylinder, moving at a constant speed, makes one revolution for each impression.

HEIGHT TO PAPER. The exact height of type from the bottom (or feet) of the type to the printing surface. Types of the exact height will print evenly; those which are too high receive too much pressure while those too low receive little or no pressure. Also called TYPE HEIGHT (*q.v.*).

HEILIGENBILDER. *See* HELGEN.

HELGEN. Woodcuts printed on paper at the end of the fourteenth century and beginning of the fifteenth. They were usually very simple black-line pictures, often hand-coloured, with little or no shading, and consisted of pictures of the saints or other religious subjects. They were intended to illustrate the teachings of the wandering monks who distributed them to the illiterate peasantry. Also called 'Heiligen-bilder'.

HELIOGRAPH. A print made by Albrecht Breyer of Berlin who used the REFLEX COPYING (*q.v.*) process in 1839. He placed silver chloride papers in contact with the printed pages to be copied.

HELIOGRAPHIC MATERIALS. Those used to make a HELIOGRAPH (*q.v.*) print.

HELIOGRAPHY. 1. An obsolete name for photography. 2. In photo-engraving, the art of fixing the images produced by the *camera obscura*.

HELIOGRAVURE. Any photo-engraving process by which intaglio engravings are made.

HELLBOX. (*Printing*) The box into which damaged or broken type made on a casting machine is thrown for melting down and recasting.

HELPFUL ORDER. The order of items in a classification schedule which displays the subjects in such a way that the order itself leads the user to the specific subject needed.

HEMI-CELLULOSES. (*Paper*) Impure forms of cellulose consisting of organic substances, comprising, in the main, sugars, starches and carbohydrates. These are associated with cellulose (which is formed from the elements carbon, hydrogen and oxygen, and obtained from the atmosphere by the process known as photosynthesis) in plant fibres. A high hemi-cellulose content in pulp is desirable as this provides a paper with good bonding and folding qualities.

HEMP. A fibre derived from the tissue of an annual plant which is grown extensively in America, Asia and many parts of Europe. Hemp, hemp refuse, twines and old ropes are used to make brown wrapping paper and cable insulating paper.

HER MAJESTY'S STATIONERY OFFICE. The government publisher in Britain, variously named 'Her Majesty's' or 'His Majesty's' according to whether the ruling monarch is a queen or king. The HMSO prints all parliamentary publications and many others but arranges with commercial printers to print much that is published. The printing of stationery and the purchase of books is undertaken for government departments and libraries as well as the publishing for all government departments. HMSO publishes more titles than any other British publisher. It is also the agency in the United Kingdom for publications of Unesco, the United Nations and the U.S. Government Printer. *See also* NON-PARLIAMENTARY PUBLICATIONS, PARLIAMENTARY PAPERS, PARLIAMENTARY PUBLICATIONS.

HERALDIC CRESTING. Cresting on bindings, the projections of which terminate in heraldic (usually Tudor) emblems. *See also* CRESTING ROLL.

HERTFORDSHIRE COUNTY COUNCIL TECHNICAL INFORMATION SERVICE. *See* HERTIS.

HERTIS. Abbreviation for Hertfordshire County Council Technical Information Service. A scheme, conceived in 1956, and based on the College of Technology, Hatfield, whereby library facilities in the colleges of further education, integrated with those of the separately administered County Library, are made available to industry. These college libraries are provided, not under the public library acts but the Education Act, 1944. Industrial members subscribe from three to twenty guineas to the scheme and receive weekly particulars of books added to the libraries and of articles in current periodicals appropriate to their fields of interest. Books, periodicals and other material may be borrowed, and information obtained, by the members.

HEURES. *See* BOOK OF HOURS.

HEURISTIC TECHNIQUES. In machine indexing, simulations of human methods of learning and problem solving. Functionally heuristic programmes are designed to discover solutions to problems which they do by setting up goals and sub-goals, which are then put in order and tested to determine whether in fact any of the solution sequences fully satisfy the requirements of the problem.

HIERARCHIC. 1. Arranged in serial rank rather than ordinal position. 2. Pertaining to a generic classification or organization of materials (*IBM*).

HIERARCHICAL NOTATION. (*Classification*) A NOTATION (*q.v.*) which is designed to show that two terms are in the same array, chain, hierarchy or facet. The chains and arrays of symbols reflect the hierarchy of terms. All main classes are represented by symbols of equal length, and new main classes are inserted by the introduction of new digits. Also called 'Expressive notation', 'Structural notation'.

HIERARCHICAL SEARCH. An examination of entries in a subject catalogue under heads which constitute a CHAIN (*q.v.*): it is conducted in an upward direction from the most, to the least, specific heading. Also called 'General search'. *See also* ALPHABETICAL COLLATERAI SEARCH, SUBSTITUTION GENERIC, SYSTEMATIC COLLATERAL SEARCH.

HIERARCHY. The order of precedence in which subjects are set out in the schedule of a scheme of classification. Where each element in a sequence of terms has a unique predecessor as in the traditional classificatory tree (*see* PORPHYRY, TREE OF), this is known as *strong hierarchy*; each given class is immediately subordinate only to a single genus. *Weak hierarchy* is where an element may have more than one predecessor; a given descriptor (e.g. plastic transparency tray) may be immediately subordinate to more than one generic descriptor (plastic tray, transparency tray).

HIEROGLYPH. A character, originally in the form of picture-writing engraved in stone by the ancient Egyptians, to convey thoughts or information. Any symbol or character used in any form of picture-writing. The meaning of the ancient Egyptian symbols was discovered in 1799 by Champollion when he deciphered the Rosetta Stone, now in the British Museum, on which was a parallel text in hieroglyphics, demotic script and Greek.

HIEROGLYPHICS. 1. Ancient Egyptian picture-writing; hence symbols or characters used in any picture-writing. 2. The form of communicating information or ideas by hieroglyphs.

HIEROGRAM. A sacred character or written symbol.

HIEROGRAPHIC. Pertaining to sacred writing.

HIERONYM. A sacred name used as a surname.

HIGHLIGHT. The white, or light, parts of a photograph, drawing or half-tone block.

HILC. Abbreviation for Hampshire Inter-Library Center which originated at the end of 1951 as a joint enterprise between the three colleges of Amherst, Mt. Holyoke and Smith in western Massachusetts. It is devoted mainly to the storage of little-used serials which are completely integrated. Members contribute funds which, with money obtained from the sale of duplicates, provide for limited acquisition of rarely consulted serials and expensive sets. The Center also subscribes to 300 journals not in member libraries which are circulated to each college library for three months and then retained at the Center and are available on request. It is based on the University of Massachusetts Library.

HINGE. (*Binding*) A strip of paper or fabric, placed between the two halves of an endpaper, where the body of the book is fixed to the covers, to give strength. In America this term is used to indicate the part of the book identified by the groove along the front and back covers when they join the back strip or spine, allowing the book to be opened easily. *See also* JOINT.

HINGED. Plates, maps or other separate sheets to be inserted in a book, which have been given a narrow fold on the inner edges so that there is little chance of the sheets tearing away from those to which they are attached; also so that they will lie flat, and turn easily in use, when bound.

HINGED AND JOINTED PLATES. Two adjoining plates from which a strip has been cut away at the binding edge and then joined together by means of a common strip of linen or paper to form a hinge and joints.

HISTORIATED INITIAL. An initial, capital or border of a mediaeval MS. or early book decorated with figures of men and/or animals, rather than illuminated with flowers or conventional designs; a representation of a person or scene, illustrating the text it introduces. *See also* INHABITED INITIAL.

HISTORICAL BIBLIOGRAPHY. Dealing with the history and methods of book production – printing, binding, paper making, illustrating and publishing. Also called 'analytical', 'applied', 'critical', 'descriptive', 'external', or 'material' bibliography.

HISTORICAL MANUSCRIPTS COMMISSION. Founded 1869 to discover and publish papers of historical importance. Until recently its principal activity was the publication of printed Reports and Calendars. Since 1945, and especially since the new warrant of 1959, its activities have proliferated: it maintains the NATIONAL REGISTER OF ARCHIVES (*q.v.*), new series of publications are appearing or planned, including a list of *Record repositories in Great Britain,* joint publications in conjunction with record societies, publication of papers of nineteenth-century prime ministers, a guide to scientists' papers under a joint Royal Society/HMC committee, and a summary guide, list by list, to the contents of the National Register of Archives. *Reports to the Crown* now appear every five years and an Annual Report is published. *Sectional List 17* (*gratis* from HMSO) gives the Warrant and details of publications.

HISTORY CARD. A card inserted in a catalogue and giving particulars, under the name of a corporate body, of dates of foundation, incorporation, changes of name, affiliation with other bodies, etc. Also called 'Information card'.

HISTORY ENTRY. An entry in a catalogue which gives changes of name, affiliations, etc., concerning a person or corporate body, or in the wording of a title, together with significant dates. Such entries precede specific entries under the appropriate headings.

HISTORY FILE. *Synonymous with* ORGANIZATION FILE.

HIT. Term used in mechanized retrieval systems to represent an apparent answer found by the machine (*IBM*).

HOLDINGS. 1. The stock (books, pamphlets, periodicals, micro-records, and other material) possessed by a library. 2. Specifically, the volumes, or parts of serial publications, possessed by a library.

HOLDINGS CARD. A catalogue card which shows the volumes or parts of a work which the library has. It is usually the main entry card.

HOLIDAY GUIDE. A publication giving particulars of a town which caters for holiday makers.

HOLIDAY ISSUE. Books issued in excess of the usual number and for a longer period than usual to persons going on holiday.

HOLING. The drilling, or punching, of holes in the boards of a book to take the slips or cords ready for lacing. Also called 'Holing out.'

HOLING OUT. *Synonymous with* HOLING (*q.v.*).

HOLLANDER. (*Paper*) A beater or beating engine of the type made in Holland towards the end of the seventeenth century.

HOLLOW. The space between the back of a book itself (i.e. the folded and sewn sheets) and the spine of a HOLLOW BACK (*q.v.*) book.

HOLLOW BACK. A binding in which there is a space between the back of the book itself and the cover, caused by the leather, cloth or other material being attached at the joints, and not glued to the back of the book itself. Also called 'Loose back', 'Open back'. Sometimes a tube of thin card or paper is flattened and pasted between section folds and cover spine. When the cover is glued to the back it is known as a TIGHT BACK (*q.v.*).

HOLLOW QUADS. Large quads which are cast with hollow parts to make them lighter and save metal. Also used of type which is occasionally cast similarly for the same reason.

HOLKHAM BIBLE PICTURE BOOK. A MS. probably made in London for a Dominican patron between 1326 and 1331 and now in the British Museum. It has no contemporary title and consists of forty-two leaves all but two of which are illustrated with 231 pictures.

HOLOGRAPH. 1. A document or manuscript wholly in the hand-writing of its author. Hence, holograph reprint, a reproduction of a MS. by mechanical means. 2. A recording on photo-sensitive film, made without the use of lenses, by combining two or more laser beams of different colour to form a single beam. When the holograph is viewed in white light a three-dimensional, multi-colour picture is revealed.

HOLOGRAPHY. The process of making holographs. *See* HOLOGRAPH 2.

HOLOTHEME. All the notions (things or characteristics mentioned as subject matter) considered as subject-matter.

HOME BINDERY. 1. A binding department maintained by a library committee and under the control of the librarian. 2. A method of developing the book-buying habit in Asia. It is run by a single publisher who has a strong and varied list of publications, or by a wholesale bookseller, and incorporates features of book clubs in the West. New subscribers who undertake to purchase at a specially low price a specified number of books in a year from a large selection offered, are entitled to buy the season's best sellers at extremely low prices.

HOME READING DEPARTMENT. *Synonymous with* LENDING DEPARTMENT (*q.v.*).

HOMO. *See* MARLIS.

HOMOGRAPH. One of several words having the same spelling but a different meaning, e.g. Birmingham (Alabama), Birmingham (England); skate (fish), skate (sport); game (sport), game (fowl). These should be avoided in subject headings and indexes where possible, but when unavoidable, a qualifying, or defining word or phrase should be added to each in order to clarify the meanings and to separate entries on different subjects. Sometimes these are called homonyms. *See also* HOMONYM.

HOMOLOGY. The principle used in forming schedules in a classification which uses the similarity of essential characteristics as a basis of division.

HOMONYM. 1. An identical name (surname and forenames) for two or more people. A namesake. Also an identical corporate, or other, name. 2. One of several words which may have a different origin and meaning but the same sound and a different spelling, e.g. pail (bucket), pale (stake), pale (wan).

HOMONYMIC, HOMONYMOUS. Having the same name.

HOMOTOPIC ABSTRACT. An abstract of an article published in the same issue of a journal as the article abstracted.

HONORIFIC TITLE. A title conferred on a person to indicate royalty, nobility, rank, or an honour. The whole name is sometimes incorporated with that of an organization or activity with which the person was associated. Examples: John XIV, *Pope*; Mountbatten, *Earl*, *Field-Marshal*; Princess Mary Home; Bishop Creighton House; Sir Halley Stewart Trust; Lord Roberts Workshops. A 'title of honour'.

HOOKED ON OWN GUARD. The method of securing a single-leaf illustration by folding its binding edge, so as to form a guard, around the fold of the section before sewing. *See also* GUARD 1 (2), PLATE GUARDED AND HOOKED.

HORAE. *See* BOOK OF HOURS.

HORIZONTAL. A series or classification in which the terms, or classes, are arranged in a horizontal line. The several classes are then usually regarded as co-ordinate; but a series of successively subordinate classes and sub-classes might also be so arranged, instead of in a column (*Bliss*). *See also* COLUMNAR, TABULAR CLASSIFICATION.

HORN BOOK. A children's primer which appeared towards the end of the sixteenth century. It consisted of a thin sheet of vellum or paper mounted on an oblong piece of wood and covered with transparent horn. The wooden frame had a handle by which it was hung from the child's girdle. The sheet bore the alphabet, the vowels in a line followed by the vowels combined with consonants in tabular form, the Roman numerals, the Lord's Prayer, and the exorcism 'in the name of the Father and of the Sonne and of the Holy Ghost, Amen!' A simpler and later form of Horn book, consisting of the tablet without the horn covering, or a piece of varnished cardboard, and resembling a horn book without the handle, was called a battledore.

Hors texte. Illustrations to a book which are without text matter. A plate. They are usually numbered with roman numerals to avoid confusion with numbered illustrations in the text (which are usually in line) and with the pagination of a book.

HOSPITAL LIBRARIES AND HANDICAPPED READERS GROUP. A Group of the Library Association which was formed in 1962 following the activities of the Guild of Hospital Librarians between 1934 and 1953 and sporadic meetings of hospital librarians subsequently. It seeks to provide facilities for librarians concerned with meeting the reading needs of those who are physically or mentally handicapped (whether in hospital or not), to meet and exchange views and impart information, and to arrange for reports and books of particular interest to members to be written and published. Publishes *Book Trolley* (q.).

HOSPITAL LIBRARY. A library provided for the use of hospital patients and sometimes the staff, either by the hospital authority, a voluntary organization, or a public library. In England the Ministry of Health contributes a fixed sum per occupied bed towards the cost of the service.

HOSPITALITY. (*Classification*) The quality of a notation which enables new subjects to be inserted in their appropriate place. A feature of the notation of the Colon Classification in which it is virtually infinite, and is achieved by combining the decimal fraction principle with the faceted principle. *Hospitality in array*, i.e. the ability to accommodate co-ordinate topics, is achieved by (1) the octave device, (2) group notation, (3) the chronological device, (4) the subject device, and (5) the alphabetical device. *Hospitality in chain,* i.e. the simultaneous specification of all the facets of a subject, if necessary, and the ability to specify new facets in their correct sequence, is secured by (1) decimal fractions, (2) faceted notation, (3) the apportionment of 'sectors', or zones, of notation to different array within the same facet, (4) auto-bias, (5) intra-facet relation and (6) phase relations.

HOST BOOK. As used in connexion with the Colon Classification, a book about which another is written, as e.g. a criticism or a reply; the latter is called an ASSOCIATED BOOK (*q.v.*).

HOST DOCUMENT. A MACRO-DOCUMENT (*q.v.*) when considered from the point of view of a document forming part of it; e.g., a periodical would be considered a macro-document, and each article in it a micro-document; the periodical would then be the host document for each of the articles in it.

HOT MELT. In bookbinding, a glue which is applied hot and sets immediately when used on a cool surface.

HOT-PRESSED. Good quality rag paper which is given a glazed, smooth finish by being pressed with hot metal plates. Abbreviated H.P. *See also* FINISH, NOT, ROUGH.

HOUSE CORRECTIONS. Corrections, or alterations, made to a script or proof by the publisher or printer's proof reader, as distinct from those made by the author.

HOUSE JOURNAL. A periodical produced by a commercial or industrial organization, either for internal distribution amongst the staff and employees or externally to customers. Its purpose is to interest readers in the technical side of the organization's activities, rather than the social or personal side, which is more the concern of the 'House magazine'. Also called 'House organ'.

HOUSE MAGAZINE. *See* HOUSE JOURNAL.

HOUSE OF COMMONS BILLS. Public Bills, printed by HMSO on pale green paper for consideration in the House of Commons. *See also* PRIVATE BILLS.

HOUSE OF COMMONS PAPERS. Reports and returns which have to be presented to the House under the provisions of various Acts of Parliament, reports from government departments compiled by direct order of the House, and reports of the Standing Committees and Select Committees of the House.

HOUSE OF LORDS PAPERS AND BILLS. A series of publications consisting almost entirely of Public Bills but also a few Papers. Public Bills are printed by H.M.S.O. on pale green paper.

HOUSE OF LORDS RECORDS OFFICE. Contains over 1,500,000

records of Parliament as a whole dating back to 1497. They are in the custody of the Clerk of the Parliaments. The Search Room is open to the public who may also be granted access to the Journals of the House of Commons (from 1547), and to the other surviving records of the Commons (from 1572). Records of Parliament prior to 1497 are preserved in the PUBLIC RECORD OFFICE (*q.v.*).

HOUSE ORGAN.   *See* HOUSE JOURNAL.

'HOUSE' PAPERS.   *See* PARLIAMENTARY PAPERS.

HOUSE STYLE.   The typesetting style normally used in a printing establishment. *See also* STYLE MANUAL, STYLE OF THE HOUSE, STYLE SHEET.

HUDDERSFIELD AND DISTRICT INFORMATION SERVICE. *See* HADIS.

HULL SCHEME.   *See* HULTIS.

HULL TECHNICAL INTERLOAN SCHEME.   *See* HULTIS.

HULTIS.   The Hull Technical Interloan Scheme (known between 1953 and 1961 as the Hull Scheme for the Interloan of Technical Publications) by means of which libraries of all kinds in Hull pool their resources for mutual benefit. It is centred on the Commercial and Technical Library at the Central Library of the City of Kingston upon Hull and its activities are sponsored and controlled by the Public Libraries Committee through the Chief Librarian. Any organization with twenty-five books and three current periodicals is entitled to membership for which no charge is made.

HUMANIST.   1. A group of type faces, formerly known as 'Venetian' and derived from the fifteenth-century style of minuscule handwriting characterized by a varying stroke thickness achieved by means of an obliquely-held broad pen. In faces in this group the cross stroke of the lower case 'e' is oblique, the axis of the curves is inclined to the left, there is little contrast between thin and thick strokes, the serifs are bracketed, and the serifs of the ascenders of the lower case letters are oblique. Examples of this category of type faces are Verona, Centaur and Kennerley. *See also* TYPE FACE. 2. Also a group of LINEALE (*q.v.*) type faces based on the proportions of roman capitals and Humanist or GARALDE (*q.v.*) lower-case letters, rather than on the early grotesques which are another group of Lineales. They have some contrast between the thick and thin strokes, and the 'a' and 'g' are two-storey.

HUMANISTIC HAND.   A mediaeval hand-writing less angular than Gothic, based on Old Roman capitals and the Carolingian minuscule. It was a result of the Renaissance in the fifteenth century which brought a general awakening of interest in classic, and pre-Christian literature. Also called 'Neo-Caroline'.

HUNDRED ROLLS, of A.D. 1274. Public records of great importance for local history, containing an inquisition into the state of every hundred (a division of a county) and answers, on oath, to questions relating to the public exchequer.

HUNTINGTON LIBRARY. One of the most famous of scholars' libraries of Americana and English literature. It is situated in San Marino, California, U.S.A., and is surpassed only by the British Museum and the Bodleian libraries, in the quality and importance of its British books. The library is in a building which was opened in 1920 and was especially designed to protect and preserve the valuable collection of books in the grounds of Huntington House (formerly the home of Henry Edwards Huntington, 1850–1927) which houses the Art Gallery containing some of the world's famous pictures. The stock totals 390,000 volumes and 3,000,000 MSS.

HYDROGRAPHIC CHART. A chart of coasts and harbours.

HYPHEN. The shortest rule used for punctuation. It is used to join compound words, or as the link at the end of a line to join the parts of a word which cannot be set in one line. *See also* DASH.

HYPO. Abbreviation for hyposulphite of soda (formerly known as sodium thiosulphate) which is used in photography for fixing prints.

HYPOSOMETRIC MAP. One on which the successive altitudes are indicated by the system of colour tints.

i.e. Abbreviation for *id est* (*Lat.* 'that is').

i.q. Abbreviation for *idem quod* (*Lat.* 'the same as').

ISBN. Acronym for INTERNATIONAL STANDARD BOOK NUMBER. *See* STANDARD BOOK NUMBER.

IASLIC. Acronym for Indian Association of Special Libraries and Information Centres. Founded in September 1955 with the following aims: to encourage and promote the systematic acquisition, organization and dissemination of knowledge; to improve the quality of library and information services and documentation work; to co-ordinate the activities of, and to foster mutual co-operation and assistance among, special libraries, scientific, technological and research institutions, learned societies, commercial organizations, industrial research establishments, as well as other information and documentation centres to the fullest extent; to provide contact for libraries, information bureaux, documentation centres, scientists, research workers, specialists and others having a common interest;

to improve the technical efficiency of the workers in special libraries and information and documentation centres, and to look after their professional welfare; to act as a centre of research in special librarianship and documentation techniques; to act as a centre of information in scientific, technical and other fields. Various categories of membership exist. Publishes working papers irregularly, technical pamphlets and monographs; also *IASLIC Bulletin* (q.).

ib., ibid. Abbreviation for *ibidem* (*Lat.* 'in the same place', 'the same reference'). Used in a footnote reference to avoid repeating the title of a work referred to immediately above. It can be used in successive references to the same work.

ICONOGRAPHY. 1. The study of the portraits, statues, coins, and other illustrative material relating to a person, place or thing. 2. The detailed listing of such material. 3. The art of illustrating, or representing, by figures, images, diagrams, etc.

id. Abbreviation for *idem* (*Lat.* 'the same [author or publication]'). Used in footnotes to avoid repeating an author's name, or other identity of a book or periodical when being referred to successively.

id est. (*Lat.* 'that is to say'). Abbreviated i.e.

IDA AND GEORGE ELIOT PRIZE ESSAY. *See* ELIOT PRIZE ESSAY, IDA AND GEORGE.

IDEAL ARRANGEMENT. (*Classification*) The mental operation resulting in placing things in order corresponding to an idea, or series of ideas, in the mind and in accordance with the mental picture of the things to be arranged. *Actual arrangement* is the physical placing in order, of specimens which can be seen or touched, such as botanical specimens, postage stamps or books.

IDENTIFICATION CAPTION. (*Reprography*) The identification symbol or phrase, both on the document and on the frame of microfilm, which is visible to the unaided eye.

IDENTIFICATION CARD. Used in place of a borrower's ticket in the NEWARK CHARGING SYSTEM (*q.v.*) and TRANSACTION CARD (*q.v.*) systems generally.

IDEOGRAM. *Synonymous with* IDEOGRAPH 2 (*q.v.*).

IDEOGRAPH. 1. An individual signature or trade mark. 2. A symbol or picture used in writing, e.g. in Chinese, to represent an object or an idea, and not, as in the phonetic system, the sounds which make up the name of these.

IDEOGRAPHY. The representation of ideas by graphic symbols ('ideograms'). A highly developed form of picture-writing in which ideas are conveyed by pictorial representation.

IFLA. Acronym for INTERNATIONAL FEDERATION OF LIBRARY ASSOCIATIONS (*q.v.*).

ILL. Abbreviation for INTER-LIBRARY LOAN (*q.v.*).

ill. (illus.). Abbreviation for illustrated, ILLUSTRATION/S (*q.v.*).

ILLATIVE ABSTRACT. *See* ABSTRACT.

ILLUMINATED BINDING. A term used for all bindings which included extra colours, but particularly to those where a design was blocked in blind and the outline afterwards filled in with colour. Originally a French innovation, this style was practised in Britain from about 1830 to 1860.

ILLUMINATED BOOK. A book or manuscript, usually on vellum, decorated by hand, with designs and pictures in gold, silver and bright colours, not primarily to illustrate the text, but to make with it a unified whole.

ILLUMINATED INITIAL. A first letter of a word or paragraph decorated with colours, especially gold.

ILLUMINATION. The painting of initial letters at the commencement of a chapter of a MS. in gold, silver, or colour.

illus. Abbreviation for illustrated, illustration, illustrator.

ILLUSTRATIONS. Photographs, drawings, portraits, maps, plans, plates, tables, facsimiles, diagrams, etc., placed in a book to elucidate the text. Abbreviated illus.

ILLUSTRATIONS COLLECTION. A collection of photographs, prints, drawings or reproductions of pictures assembled either for general use in public libraries or in institutions as an aid to their work or an essential part of the organization's activities. Called 'picture collections' in America; in Britain this term usually relates to a collection of original pictures or to a collection of reproductions of same. *See also* PICTURE FILE, PICTURE COLLECTION.

ILLUSTRATOR. A person who makes drawings and designs to illustrate a book or periodical.

ILLUSTRATOR ENTRY. A catalogue entry for an illustrator whose work is of sufficient importance to be catalogued.

IMAGE. 1. A design or picture to be reproduced by a printing process as an illustration. 2. (*Reprography*). That area within the frame (*see also* FRAME 4) which, after exposure and processing, contains the whole of the representation of the original.

IMAGE CARD. An APERTURE CARD (*q.v.*) which contains an image on exposed and processed microfilm in an aperture of the card. *See also* APERTURE CARD, CAMERA CARD.

IMAGIC. A thermal document-copying process which is not yet a commercial process. Designed by Mr. A. Games, the process is operated through distillation.

IMBRICATION.   A style of book decoration in which the pattern consists of overlapping leaves or scales.

IMITATION ART.   *See* ART.

IMITATION BINDING.   A modern binding made to represent an old style.

IMITATION EMBOSSING.   *Synonymous with* THERMOGRAPHY (*q.v.*).

IMITATION LEATHER.   Paper or cloth embossed or finished to represent leather.

IMITATION PARCHMENT.   A variety of tough paper first made by W. E. Gaine in 1857. It may be (a) rendered transparent, strong, grease-proof, and sometimes water-proof, by prolonged beating of the pulp, or (b) passed through a bath of sulphuric acid which 'toughens' the fibres.

impensis (*Lat.* 'at the expense of').   Used in an IMPRINT (*q.v.*) or COLOPHON (*q.v.*) of an early printed book to indicate the publisher, or bookseller or patron who was financially responsible for its publication.

IMPERFECT.   A book which is found to have pages or sections omitted, duplicated, misplaced or inserted upside down, damaged or missing.

IMPERFECTIONS.   Printed sheets rejected by the binder on account of being in some respect imperfect, and for which others are required to make the work complete.

IMPERIAL.   A sheet of printing and drawing paper measuring 22 × 30 inches.

IMPERIAL WAR MUSEUM LIBRARY.   One of the national libraries maintained by the British government. It is concerned only with collecting material relating to the Great War and later military operations involving Great Britain and the Commonwealth. There are three separate collections – Reference, Film, Photographic.

IMPORT.   A book published in one country and imported into another. The importer may act as one of several importers or may have sole distribution rights over a given area. He may or may not arrange to have his own name placed on the title page as distributor or publisher either in addition to or in place of the original publisher's name, and he may do this by means of a small label.

IMPOSING STONE.   *See* STONE.

IMPOSITION.   The arrangement of the pages of type in the chase so that they will read consecutively when the printed sheet is folded. On correct imposition depends not only the right order of the pages but also REGISTER 3 (*q.v.*).

IMPRESSED WATERMARK. A watermark produced, not by the usual method, but by placing a stereo, in bronze, rubber, or other substance, on the press roll of the paper-making machine, and so leaving a design in the paper where it was more compressed. *See also* WATERMARK.

IMPRESSION. 1. (*Printing*) The copies of a book printed at the same time from the same type or plates. A *new impression* is one taken from the same standing type, or stereotype, as the original. An edition may consist of several impressions providing no alterations are made. Also called a 'Printing'. 2. A number of copies printed at any one time. B.S. 1413:1947 recommends that when a book is reprinted or reproduced from the same setting of type, the word 'impression' should be used and not the word 'edition'. *See also* EDITION, FIRST EDITION, ISSUE, REPRINT, REVISED EDITION. 3. The pressure applied to a forme of type by the cylinder or platen. 4. (*Binding*) The effect of impressing a block or type into the cover of a book. 5. A single copy of a print or map. 6. (*Illustration*) A print taken, by means of the special engraving press, from an engraved plate. *See also* STATE.

IMPRESSION CYLINDER. The roller of an offset printing press which presses the paper into contact with the blanket cylinder; or any cylinder around which the paper is carried during its contact with type or plates.

imprimatur (*Lat.* 'let it be printed'). The licence for publication, granted by a secular or ecclesiastical authority, carrying the name of the licenser, and the date (which may differ from that of the imprint). Usually printed at the beginning of a book: when on a separate leaf this is called a 'licence leaf'. Now rarely found except in the form of the words 'permissu superiorum' on works by Roman Catholic priests. This is distinct from copyright. Where state or church censorship exists, the imprimatur becomes an approval of what has been published.

IMPRINT. 1. The statement in a book concerning the publication or printing of a book. Also called 'Biblio'. The PUBLISHER'S IMPRINT is the name of the publisher and the date and place of publication, it usually appears at the foot of the title-page, and sometimes more completely on the back. The PRINTER'S IMPRINT gives the printer's name and the place of printing, it usually appears on the back of the title-page, on the last page of text, or on the page following. It is compulsory in all books printed in the United Kingdom (2 & 3 Vict. c. 12 S2). *See also* COLOPHON, DISTRIBUTION IMPRINT. 2. (*Cataloguing and bibliography*) That part of an entry which gives the above particulars, though it is customary to omit the *place* of publication if it is the capital city of the country. When the imprint is covered by a label (usually giving the name of a publisher or agent in a country other than that of origin) the data for the catalogue entry is taken from the label. 3. (*Binding*) The name of (a) the owner; (b) the publisher appearing at the bottom of the spine; (c) the binder stamped on the cover of a book, usually at the bottom of the inside of the back board. 4. (*Printing*) The name of an OLD FACE type which is much used for book work. For a specimen alphabet see TYPE FACE.

IMPRINT DATE.　The year of publication as specified on the title-page.

IN BOARDS.　1. When a book is cut after the mill-boards are attached, it is said to be cut in boards. *See also* BOARDS. 2. A cheap style of binding common in the eighteenth and early nineteenth centuries, consisting of pasteboards covered with paper (usually blue sides and white spine). It was superseded by cloth. Occasionally used in the early twentieth century.

IN PENDENTIVE.　(*Printing*) Typesetting in which successive lines are set in decreasing width, the first (and possibly second) line being set to the full measure, the subsequent ones being indented left and right of a central axis so that the last line of a page or paragraph is only a single word. It has the effect of a triangle resting on its apex.

IN PRINT.　Said of a book which is available from the publisher.

IN PROGRESS.　A term used in catalogues and elsewhere to indicate that a work in several volumes is not complete but still in course of publication. *See also* CHECK-LIST.

IN QUIRES.　A book in unbound sheets. *See also* IN SHEETS.

IN SHEETS.　Printed sheets of a book, either flat or folded, but unbound. This term is gradually replacing 'in quires' with which it is synonymous. *See also* SHEETS.

IN SLIP.　Matter set up and proof-pulled on galleys before being made up into pages.

IN STOCK.　Said of a book, copies of which are held by a book-seller for sale.

IN THE PRESS.　A book which is in the actual process of being printed.

IN THE TRADE.　Books published by, and obtainable from, commercial publishing firms rather than from government or private presses. (*American*).

INCIDENTAL MUSIC.　Music written for performance during the presentation of a theatrical play or film whether it has an essential connexion with the plot, or story, or not.

incipit (*Lat.* '(Here) begins'). The commencement of a mediaeval MS. or early printed book. The identity of the work and of the author may be found here if it is not given on the title-page or in the colophon.

INCOMPLETE. Said of a book from which a part has been omitted during manufacture.

INCUNABULA (*Sing.*, INCUNABULUM; Anglicized, INCUNABLE). Books printed before 1500, this date limitation probably deriving from the earliest known catalogue of incunabula: an appendix to Johann Saubert's *Historia bibliothecae Noribergensis . . . catalogus librorum proximis ab inventione annis usque ad a. Chr.* 1500 *editorum,* 1643. 'Incunabula' derives from the Latin 'cunae' (cradle) and indicates books produced in the infancy of printing; more specifically those which were printed before the use of loose type was common. It is said that Philippe Labbé (1607–67), a Parisian bibliographer, was the first to use the term 'incunabula' for the act of printing, not for the books themselves. The word was not used with this latter meaning until the late eighteenth century. Before the use of movable type, books were handwritten, and later printed from engraved wooden blocks (xylographic books).

INCUNABULIST. One who is well versed in a knowledge of incunabula.

INCUT HEADING. *See* CUT-IN HEADING.

INCUT NOTE. A side note which is let into the outer edge of a paragraph of text instead of appearing in the margin. Usually set in smaller and heavier type than the text. Also called 'Cut-in note', 'Cut-in side note', 'Let-in note'. *See also* CENTRE NOTE.

INDENT. To begin a line of type a little way in, as at the beginning of a fresh paragraph.

INDENTION. 1. (*Printing*) The leaving of a blank space at the beginning of a line or a new paragraph. *See also* HANGING INDENTION. 2. (*Cataloguing*) The distances from the left edge of a catalogue card at which the various parts of the entry begin. The purpose is to ensure uniformity in setting out the various parts of an entry. The 'first indention', at which the author's surname begins, is normally the first vertical line, or eighth typewriter space from the left-hand edge of the card; the 'second indention', at which the title begins, is then the second vertical line, or the tenth typewriter space, and the 'third indention' – for the second (indented) line of a two-line analytic author and title heading on a UNIT CARD (*q.v.*), or for any other indented entry beyond the second indention – the twelfth typewriter space. Akers' *Simple Library Cataloging* recommends 12 and 14 as the spacing for the second and third indentions; this is satisfactory for simple entries, but 10 and 12 are better for catalogues in larger libraries. *See also* FIRST INDENTION, SECOND INDENTION, THIRD INDENTION.

INDENTURE. A document drawn up in duplicate and divided so as to leave a tooth-like edge on each part.

INDEPENDENTS. Books or pamphlets published separately and afterwards bound together.

INDEX. 1. A systematically arranged list giving enough information for each item to be traced by means of a page number or other symbol indicating its position in a sequence. 2. A detailed alphabetical list or table of topics, names of persons, places, etc., treated or mentioned in a book or series of books, pointing out their exact positions in the volume, usually by page number (sometimes with an additional symbol indicating a portion of a page) but often by section, or entry, number. 3. In 1964 The British Standards Institution issued *Recommendations for the Preparation of Indexes for Books, Periodicals, and Other Publications* (BS. 3700: 1964), and defined an index as, 'A systematic guide to the text of any reading matter or to the contents of other collected, documentary material, comprising a series of entries, with headings arranged in alphabetical or other chosen order and with references to show where each item indexed is located.' 4. 'Within the fields of library practice and documentation, an index is a guide to the contents of any reading matter or other documentary materials which provides a systematic, sustained subject analysis of the contents of such materials arranged according to alphabetical, chronological, numerical, or other chosen order. Each entry is followed by page number, paragraph number, or other indicator showing the exact location of the reference.' (ASA Z39.4–1959). 5. A much broader connotation is now given to this term due to contemporary practices of compiling finding-guides to the contents of, and shelved position of, material in a library collection, sometimes using mechanical methods (even computers) for this purpose. From many points of view an index is synonymous with a catalogue, the principles of analysis used being identical, but whereas an index entry merely locates a subject, a catalogue entry includes descriptive specification of a document concerned with the subject. 6. (*Information retrieval*) That which specifies, indicates or designates the information, contents or topics of a document or a group of documents. Also a list of the names or subjects referring to a document or group of documents (*IBM*). 7. (*Verb*) To prepare an organized or systematic list which specifies, indicates or designates the information, contents or topics in a document or group of documents (*IBM*). *See also* Auto-Abstract, Controlled Indexing, Index Librorum Prohibitorum, Kwic Index, Permutation Indexing, Uniterm Concept Co-ordination Indexing, Word Indexing. 8. The printers' symbol ☞. Also called 'Digit', 'Fist', 'Hand'.

INDEX BOARD. A quality of single- or twin-wire pulp board, white or coloured, used for cutting into standard sizes for index cards and record work generally. They may be described as pulp board with a good, even and well-finished surface suitable for writing. They are smooth, hard-sized and of even Look Through (*q.v.*). Sizes: Index Royal $20\frac{1}{2} \times 25\frac{1}{2}$ inches. Index Royal and a half $25\frac{1}{2} \times 30\frac{1}{2}$ inches.

INDEX ENTRY. The entry which is included in an index.

INDEX EXPURGATORIUS. An index to passages to be expunged or altered in works which are otherwise permitted. This term is loosely used for the list of books that the Roman Catholic Church forbade its members to read, or permitted them to read only in expurgated form; this is the Index Librorum Prohibitorum (*q.v.*).

INDEX LANGUAGE. The language that is used in the subject index which is part of an information retrieval system. It may be an alphabetical or classified arrangement of terms, or a variation of these. Each term or heading actually used in the index language, of whatever kind, is called an 'index term'. Also called 'Descriptor language'. Its 'vocabulary' is the complete collection of sought terms in the natural language.

INDEX LIBRORUM PROHIBITORUM. A list of books which Roman Catholics were prohibited by ecclesiastical authority from reading or keeping without permission. Such books could not be imported into countries where Roman Catholic control was considerable. The list was commonly called the 'Index' or 'Roman Index', and was also known as 'Index Expurgatorius'. The *Index* was printed first by Antonio Blado in Rome in 1559 and is the classic example of censorship. From late Roman times there had been censorship of books considered to be dangerous to religion and morals, and although bishops, universities and inquisitions had circulated lists of prohibited books this was the first really effective means of censorship. The 'Congregation' which was first set up in 1558 to prepare the *Index* continued to be responsible for its publication. The Index was last brought up to date in 1947; Cardinal Ottaviani, pro-prefect of the Doctrinal Congregation declared in April 1965 that no more books would be put on the Index. On 14 June 1966 the Vatican announced that it had been abolished; although it ceased to be legally binding, Roman Catholics were reminded of their duty to avoid reading books dangerous to faith and morals.

INDEX MAP. A small-scale key map to an atlas or series of maps, which shows how the total area has been divided up by the individual maps.

INDEX TAB. A small piece of paper, card or fabric attached to, and projecting from, the fore-edge of a leaf and bearing in progressive order from top to bottom letters or words. Its purpose is to assist the speedy finding of the information required. *See also* THUMB INDEX.

INDEX TERM. *See* INDEX LANGUAGE.

INDEX TRANSLATIONUM. A Unesco publication which lists translations of literary, scientific, educational and cultural works published in pamphlet or book form. Resumed as an annual in 1949, it continues a similar publication issued regularly from July 1932 to October 1940, as a quarterly publication (thirty-one issues being published) by the former International Institute of Intellectual Co-operation. The present ('New' Unesco) series began with a volume number No. 1, 1948, dated 1949 © 1950.

INDEXING. The art of compiling an INDEX (*q.v.*). *See also* SOCIETY OF INDEXERS.

INDIA PAPER. Originally a soft absorbent paper, cream or buff in colour, imported from China for proofs of engravings. In 1875 the name was used for a thin opaque paper made from hemp or rag. *See also* BIBLE PAPER, CAMBRIDGE INDIA PAPER, OXFORD INDIA PAPER.

INDIA PROOF. A proof of an engraving taken on India or other fine paper. Sometimes wrongly applied to the whole first edition.

INDIA PROOF PAPER. *See also* CHINA PAPER.

INDIAN ASSOCIATION FOR SPECIAL LIBRARIES AND INFORMATION CENTRES. *See* IASLIC.

INDIAN BIBLE. The first Bible printed in the American Colonies was a translation by John Eliot into the Indian language.

INDIAN INK. A very black waterproof writing and drawing fluid having great density, used for drawings designed for reproduction and for records where permanence is desired.

INDIAN LIBRARY ASSOCIATION. Founded in 1933, with the following objects: the furtherance of the library movement in India, the promotion of the training of librarians, and the improvement of the status of librarians. Published *Abgila* (=annals, bulletin and granthalaya of the Indian Library Association) (q.).

INDICATIVE ABSTRACT. *See* ABSTRACT.

INDICATOR. A frame, glazed on the public side, which indicated the numbers of the books 'in' and 'out' in a closed access library.

INDICATOR DIGIT. A symbol used in the notation of a scheme of classification to announce a change of method of division. *See also* DIVISION 4.

INDIRECT CODING. The use of combinations of holes or of punching positions in edge-punched or machine-punched cards because of the need to provide rotations for more subjects, or meanings, than there are individual positions available. Also called 'Combination coding'. *See also* DIRECT CODING.

INDIRECT SUBDIVISION. *See* DIRECT SUBDIVISION.

INDIVIDUAL ENTRY. Entry in a catalogue under a person or place as subject.

INDUSTRIAL LIBRARIES. Libraries provided by, and in, industrial firms.

INEDITA. Unpublished works.

INEDITED. A work published without editorial changes; it may contain indelicate passages which might have been altered or omitted in editing.

INEVITABLE ASSOCIATION, PRINCIPLE OF. In descriptive cataloguing, the principle that applies to any name, whether it be of person, book (title), corporate body, periodical, etc., that contains a word that will inevitably be remembered by anyone who asks for that person, book, subject, corporate body or periodical. The principle dictates that the entry chosen for that name will be the word inevitably remembered. *See also* CATALOGUING, PRINCIPLES OF.

INFECTIOUS DISEASES. Certain infectious diseases are 'notifiable diseases'; these have been re-defined in Section 47 of the Health Services and Public Health Act 1968 and comprise cholera, plague, relapsing fever, smallpox and typhus. The Secretary of State for Social Services is empowered to make other diseases notifiable by regulation and the Public Health (Infectious Diseases) Regulations 1968, which consolidated into one instrument, with amendments, all previous regulations relating to the notification and prevention of infectious diseases, provide for the notification of acute encephalitis, acute meningitis, acute poliomyelitis, amoebic dysentery, anthrax, bacillary dysentery, diphtheria, infective jaundice, leprosy, leptospirosis, malaria, measles, ophthalmia neonatorum, paratyphoid fever, scarlet fever, tetanus, tuberculosis, typhoid fever, whooping cough and yellow fever. A local authority may, with the approval of the Secretary of State, and after advertisement, extend the category of notifiable diseases in its area. Chickenpox and glandular fever have been made notifiable in this way from time to time. Notice of the occurrence of all these diseases must be sent by the medical practitioner to the medical officer of the local authority. A local authority may provide a disinfecting station and may, in certain circumstances, disinfect premises and articles likely to retain infection. Persons who have books known to have been exposed to infection from a notifiable disease must not return the books to the Library but must notify the appropriate local authority so that they may be disinfected. A person who knows he is suffering from a notifiable disease shall not take any book, or cause any book to be taken, from a public library. A person shall not permit any book which has been taken from a public library, and is under his control, to be used by any person whom he knows to be suffering from a notifiable disease.

INFERIOR CHARACTERS. Small figures and letters cast below the level of the base line, as in chemical formulae, thus: H_2SO_4. *See* SUPERIOR FIGURES (LETTERS).

INFIMA SPECIES. The class with which the division of a classification ends. *See also* SUBALTERN GENERA AND SUMMUM GENUS.

INFLUENCE PHASE. One of Ranganathan's three main 'phase relations'; it is the relationship of one subject influencing another. The other two are BIAS PHASE and TOOL PHASE (*qq.v.*). The process of determining the appropriate class for a document; where one thing influences another, the document is classified under the thing influenced. *See also* PHASE.

INFORMATION. The essential ingredient of any control system (*Edwards*).

INFORMATION AREA. (*Reprography*) The printed, or written, area of a document or micro-print which contains the information; it usually excludes the margins.

INFORMATION CARD. *Synonymous with* HISTORY CARD (*q.v.*).

INFORMATION CENTRE. Usually an office, or a section of a bibliographical centre, research bureau or documentation centre, which gives information about books or on a subject with which the organization providing the facilities of the centre is concerned. Staffing varies, but may include any or all of the following: research officers, librarians, bibliographers or trained information officers. It may include the functions of a special library and extend its activities to include collateral functions such as: technical writing, functions performed by machine methods, and library research for clients.

INFORMATION CLEARING HOUSE. A name sometimes given to a special library possessing a limited amount of published material, but which collects and gives information by telephone, correspondence and the use of other libraries. (American.)

INFORMATION DEPARTMENT. The department of an organization, the primary function of which is to give information when requested.

INFORMATION DESK. A desk in a library or other building staffed by one or more persons whose function is to give information. This may vary from little more than directions to various parts of the building to a full information service (even if only of a quick-reference nature) based on an appropriate collection of reference books and other appropriate material.

INFORMATION ENTRY. *Synonymous with* GENERAL REFERENCE (*q.v.*).

INFORMATION FILE. 1. A list of sources of information which is not readily found and which may in the first instance have been difficult to obtain. 2. Extracts, illustrations, pamphlets, and articles torn from periodicals and other fugitive material filed, usually in a vertical file, in some systematic order for ready reference.

INFORMATION ITEM. *Synonymous with* TOPIC (*q.v.*).

INFORMATION LIBRARIAN. The librarian in charge of an INFORMATION LIBRARY (*q.v.*).

INFORMATION LIBRARY. A library which serves as the basis of an INFORMATION SERVICE (*q.v.*).

INFORMATION OFFICER. One whose function is to give information; he often works in close co-operation with a librarian, giving information from his own knowledge (often being a specialist in the field of knowledge concerned) and from published materials which are collected, administered and made available by a librarian.

INFORMATION PROCESSING. *See* PROCESSING 1.

INFORMATION RESOURCE. As defined for the purposes of the NATIONAL REFERRAL CENTER (*q.v.*): any organization, facility, or individual willing and able to give authoritative responses to scientific or technical inquiries out of an existing store of knowledge or expertise.

INFORMATION RETRIEVAL. Finding documents, or the information contained in documents, in a library or other collection, selectively recalling recorded information. Methods of retrieval vary from a simple index or catalogue to the documents, to some kind of punched card or microfilm record which requires large or expensive equipment for mechanically selecting the material required. Classification, indexing and machine searching are all systems of information retrieval. *See also* DATA PROCESSING, RETRIEVAL, TERMATREX SYSTEM. Abbreviated IR.

INFORMATION SCIENCE AND AUTOMATION DIVISION. A

11*

Division of the American Library Association since 28 January 1966. Is concerned with the application of electronic data processing techniques and the use of automated systems in all areas of library work; within this field it fosters research, promotes the development of appropriate standards, disseminates information, and provides a forum for the discussion of common problems. Abbreviated ISAD. Publishes *Journal of information science and library automation* (q.).

INFORMATION SCIENTIST. An INFORMATION OFFICER (*q.v.*) who has a science degree and may be qualified in the administration of a library of scientific literature. He should be capable of evaluating information gathered and of exercising an advisory function. *See also*, INSTITUTE OF INFORMATION SCIENTISTS.

INFORMATION SERVICE. A service provided by, or for, a special library which draws attention to information possessed in the library or information department in anticipation of demand; this is done by preparing and circulating news sheets, literature surveys, reading lists, abstracts, particulars of articles in current periodicals, etc. which it is anticipated will be of interest to potential users of the service.

INFORMATION TRANSFER EXCHANGE. *See* PROJECT INTREX.

INFORMATION WORK. The collection, evaluation and organized dissemination of scientific and technical information. It includes (a) abstracting technical writings; (b) translating same; (c) editing the products of (a) and (b); (d) indexing, subject classification and retrieval of information; (e) searching literature, preparing bibliographies, reports, etc.; (f) obtaining, providing, and advising on scientific and technical information; (g) disseminating information; (h) research on problems in information work.

INFORMATIVE ABSTRACT. *See* ABSTRACT.

infra. (*Lat.* 'below'). Used in footnotes and sometimes in the text to refer to an item mentioned subsequently.

INGO-PACT. Ingold's world patent for compact shelving. *See* COMPACTUS.

INGOLD-COMPACTUS. *See* COMPACTUS.

INGRAIN. A rough and shaggy quality of tinted paper used for pamphlet covers and wall hangings.

INHABITED INITIAL. In a mediaeval illuminated manuscript, an initial letter containing figures of human beings, beasts, or both. *See also* HISTORIATED INITIAL.

INITIAL LETTER. A capital letter, being the first letter of a word, sentence or paragraph, larger than the subsequent letters, and so set to give emphasis or for decoration. In typography, its size is indicated by the number of lines of body type it occupies, as '3-line initial'. Sometimes called 'Ornamental initial'. *See also* FACTOTUM.

INK BALL. A large, round sheepskin or buckskin pad stuffed with wool, or horsehair and cotton, and fastened to a wooden handle. It was used from the fifteenth century until about 1820 (when superseded by rollers) for inking set-up type in the forme. The pressman used them in pairs holding one in each hand.

INK BLOCK. A piece of beech wood fastened to the hind-rail of a printing press and used for spreading the ink. *See also* INK SLAB.

INK SLAB. The part of some printing machines, consisting of a large, flat, steel bed, on to which the ink is placed and from which the distributing rollers take, mix and spread it, before transferring it to the forme. *See also* INK BLOCK.

INLAID. 1. A piece of printing, a MS., or an illustration, which is inset in a frame or border of paper, the overlapping edges having first been shaved thin in order to prevent bulkiness at the joins. 2. A leather binding in which the cover has had leather of another colour or kind set in.

INLAY. 1. The paper used to stiffen the spine of a book when being re-bound. 2. A picture or decoration inlaid in the cover of a book. *See also* ONLAY. 3. A MS., letter, leaf, plate or document mounted in a cut-out frame to protect it and permit both sides to be read.

INLAYING. In bookbinding, pasting down a differently coloured leather to that of the cover as part of the decoration; usually within an outlined tool form, border or panel. *See also* ONLAYING.

IN-LINE PROCESSING. (*Information retrieval*) A technique by which an item may be fully processed, with random access to all of the entries which that item may affect. The processing of data without sorting or any prior treatment other than storage (*IBM*).

INLINE LETTERS. Jobbing and display work letters in which hand-tooling of the main strokes results in a white line forming their central part when printed. This gives the effect of blackness relieved by white. *See also* OPEN LETTERS.

INNER FORM. *See* FORM DIVISIONS.

INNER FORME. A forme containing the pages of type which will, when printed, become the inside of a printed sheet in SHEET WORK (*q.v.*). The reverse of 'outer forme'.

INNER INDENTION. *Synonymous with* SECOND INDENTION (*q.v.*).

INNER LONDON LIBRARY COMMITTEE. The organization on which the Inner London Boroughs (formerly the Metropolitan Boroughs but reconstituted on 1 April 1965) are represented. It maintains from levies paid by these boroughs the catalogue previously known as the LONDON UNION CATALOGUE (*q.v.*).

INNER MARGIN. *Synonymous with* BACK MARGIN (*q.v.*).

INPUT. (*Information retrieval*) That which is put in – that is, the information transferred from external storage to the internal storage of the machines (*IBM*).

INSCRIBED COPY. *See* PRESENTATION COPY.

INSDOC. The Indian National Science Documentation Centre was founded by the Indian Government in 1952 with the following objects: (1) to receive and retain all scientific periodicals; (2) to inform scientists and engineers of articles of interest by means of a monthly bulletin of abstracts; (3) to answer specific enquiries; (4) to supply photocopies or translations to individual workers; (5) to be a national depository for published and unpublished Indian scientific reports; (6) to be a channel through which Indian scientific work is made known and available to the rest of the world. The Centre comes under the Council for Scientific and Industrial Research and has been placed under the administrative control of the Director, National Physical Laboratory. Publishes *Insdoc list of current scientific literature* (*f.*), which serves to give information concerning articles published outside India before the publications are received by surface mail in India, and is compiled from microfilm copies of the tables of contents of scientific periodicals which are received by airmail.

INSERT. An additional sentence or a paragraph added to a proof to be inserted in a revise or final proof.

INSERTION MARK. *Synonymous with* CARET (*q.v.*).

INSERTION MOTIF. An ornament such as a pillar or a bar, etc., dividing two columns of text, or one scene from another, in a mediaeval illuminated manuscript.

IN-SERVICE TRAINING. A scheme consisting of practical work and a course of lectures given on one or more occasions every week or so, whereby trainees or the more junior members of a staff are given instruction in the routines carried out in the library and on wider and more general aspects of librarianship.

INSET. 1. An illustration, map or other item, not part of the printed sheets, included when binding a pamphlet or book. They may or may not be sewn in. 2. A folded sheet laid inside another. It may be part of a printed sheet cut off before folding and inserted in the middle of the folded sheet to complete the succession of the pages. If so, it is also called 'offcut'. 3. An advertisement or separate leaf, not an integral part of the publication inserted in a magazine or booklet. 4. An extra page or set of pages inserted in a proof, or a book. 5. A small map, illustration, etc., set within the border of a larger one.

INSET MAP. A small map printed within the border of a larger one.

INSIDE LINING, ORNAMENTAL. *Synonymous with* DOUBLURE 1 (*q.v.*).

INSIDE MARGIN. *Synonymous with* BACK MARGIN (*q.v.*).

inst. Abbreviation for instant, and meaning 'of the current month' when following a date. *See also* ult.

INSTALMENT. A part of a literary work, published serially in a periodical; sometimes a portion of a work which is published in 'parts' or 'numbers'. This term is falling into disuse, largely because the publication of a work 'in parts' is becoming less common.

INSTITUT INTERNATIONAL DE DOCUMENTATION. Formerly the Institut International de Bibliographie. Now the Fédération Internationale de Documentation. *See* UNIVERSAL DECIMAL CLASSIFICATION.

INSTITUTE OF ARAB MANUSCRIPTS. Founded in April 1946 by the Arab League to make more widely known the Arab contribution to universal culture which is to be found in more than three million volumes scattered in public and private libraries throughout the world. By the middle of 1958 microfilms and over 80,000 enlargements had been made of over 15,000 rare and valuable manuscripts. These are available for consultation at the Institute in Cairo, through inter-library loans or by providing enlargements.

INSTITUTE OF INFORMATION SCIENTISTS. A professional organization formed in 1958 to promote and maintain high standards in scientific and technical information work and to establish a professional qualification for graduates engaged therein. The Institute claims that there is a clear distinction between the work of a librarian and of an information officer, and arising from the latter's use of specialized scientific knowledge in evaluating, interpreting and collating information, a course of full-time instruction was started at the (London) Northampton College of Advanced Technology which is now the City University. The course now leads to the degree of M.Sc. Previously part-time classes had been held there under the aegis of the Institute, and students who had successfully completed the Institute's examination were awarded a Certificate. Part-time classes continue and the Certificate continues to be awarded by an external examination to such students. Outline membership conditions: a *Student Member* must have obtained a General Certificate of Education at two 'A' levels including an approved scientific subject and be employed in information work. An *Associate* must have a science or engineering degree, obtained the Certificate of the Institute and have one year's approved experience in information work, or five years' experience in scientific or technical work other than in information work after 'A' levels. *Members* must have a degree and have had two years' experience in information work and achieved distinction in this. *Fellows* are elected at the discretion of the Council.

INSTITUTE OF LIBRARY RESEARCH. Established in 1966 by the University of California to conduct research into library problems and develop methods for improving library work (using the numerous libraries of the University and campuses of the University as a laboratory) and advance education for librarianship.

INSTITUTE OF REPROGRAPHIC TECHNOLOGY. A professional association, inaugurated in England on 23 November 1961 to promote scientific knowledge and research in reprographic work. Abbreviated IRT. Publishes *Repro* (q.).

INSTITUTION. An organization or society established for some scientific or social purpose and supplying some public or educational need. For purposes of cataloguing it is distinguished from a society or an association by requiring for its efficient functioning a building with plant and equipment whereas a society may function without these, and as efficiently in one place as another.

INSTITUTO BRASILEÑO DE BIBLIOGRAFÍA E DOCUMENT-AÇAO. Founded in 1954 in Rio de Janeiro with the assistance of Unesco. It is a unit of the Conselho Nacional de Pesquisas, and provides a science reference library and documentation training courses. Abbreviated IBBD.

INSTITUTO DE DOCUMENTACIÓN E INFORMACION CIEN-TIFICA Y TECNICA. A national documentation centre established in 1963, with the technical assistance of Unesco, at Havana, Cuba, being attached to the Comisión Nacional de la Academia de Ciencias de la República de Cuba. Publishes a *Boletín*.

INSTRUCTION. (*Information retrieval*) A machine word consisting of characters which are recognized by the computer and therefore capable of causing machine action. A set of characters which specifies an operation and usually indicates the location of the data to be processed.

INSTRUCTIONAL MATERIALS CENTER. A room, in an American elementary or high school, in which all learning materials (books, periodicals, vertical file materials, slides, films, filmstrips, transparencies, gramophone records, tapes, models, art reproductions,

8 mm. loops, and any necessary machinery to operate them) are kept and from which they may be borrowed, or used, by teachers or pupils. Also called 'Learning Resources Center'. *See also* CURRICULUM MATERIALS CENTER.

INSTRUMENTAL CUES. Abbreviations and/or thematic indications in a music score or PART (*q.v.*), and serving as a guide to the instrumentation, or as an entry signal, for the performer. These are common in 'parts' of concerted music and essential in the scores for piano-conductor. *See also* SCORE.

INSULAR HANDWRITING. The most beautiful of all national styles of handwriting which developed from the semi-uncial book hand of the early Christian missionaries to the British Isles and, unlike the Continental styles, from the cursive minuscule. The two principal varieties of this script are (a) the Irish hand which was used from the sixth century to the Middle Ages and developed into the modern Irish script, and (b) the Anglo-Saxon semi-uncial style which developed from (a) in the seventh and eighth centuries. *See also* CURSIVE, HANDWRITING.

INTAGLIO. (*Printing*) A design engraved or incised in the surface of a hard plate. An intaglio plate for printing is usually of copper and has the design engraved with a graver or etched by acid. (*Binding*) The impression of a ROLL (*q.v.*) in which the sunk part of the leather forms the design.

INTAGLIO PRINTING. Printing done from an intaglio (incised) plate, into which the design or image is countersunk or depressed; after being inked and wiped, leaving ink only in the engraved parts, it is placed with a damp sheet of printing paper on the press, layers of felt are added, and pressure applied. The thickness of the ink transferred to the paper varies with the depth of the incisions on the plate; this ink being layered on the plate can be felt on the resulting print (as distinct from the planographic and letterpress methods) and is a means of identifying the method of printing. Copperplate printing, steel die embossing and impressions taken from dry-point plates are forms of intaglio printing, as are etchings, line engravings, mezzotints, aquatints, photogravures and dry-point etchings. The opposite of LETTERPRESS (*q.v.*) and RELIEF PRINTING (*q.v.*).

INTAMEL. The International Association of Metropolitan City Libraries, a section of IFLA (*q.v.*) which was formed in 1968 with the object of encouraging members (libraries in metropolitan areas serving not less than 400,000 population) (a) to participate in international co-operation; (b) to exchange books, staff, and information particularly in connection with deposits and collections of international and foreign literature; (c) to participate in IFLA and its Public Libraries Section.

INTEGER NOTATION.   One in which the notation of a scheme of classification consists of whole numbers as opposed to decimal *fraction notation*. There is no method of allowing for interpolation of new subjects in an integer notation except by leaving gaps where it is estimated that future expansion might take place.

INTEGRAL.   A leaf which is part of a section, as distinct from one which is printed independently from a section but inserted in it.

INTEGRAL NOTATION.   The NOTATION (*q.v.*) of a scheme of classification which uses numbers arithmetically (as does the Library of Congress scheme) and not decimally. Also called an 'arithmetical' notation.

INTEGRATION.   The bringing together in a conventional manner of the various details which comprise a catalogue entry.

INTEGRATIVE LEVELS.   A theory propounded by the biologist Joseph Needham who considers 'the existence of levels of organization in the universe, successive forms of order in a scale of complexity' and suggests that 'a sharp change in the organizational level often means that what were wholes on the lower level become parts on the new, e.g. protein crystals in cells, cells in metazoan organisms, and metazoan organisms in social units'.

INTEGRITY OF NUMBERS.   The view that the numbers or other symbols used to denote items in a scheme of classification should not be drastically altered in later revisions of the scheme.

INTELLOFAX SYSTEM.   An aperture card combined with a punched card system of recording information enabling a portion of the card to be used for index and selection purposes by EAM (*q.v.*) equipment. The installation of this system at the Central Intelligence Agency in America is possibly the largest single installation of such EAM aperture punched cards. The system was instituted in 1954. Each card contains a set of subject and area codes in punched form identifying the coverage of a document together with a pre-printed abstract to be copied for presentation to the requester.

INTENSION.   *See* EXTENSION.

INTER-AMERICAN BIBLIOGRAPHICAL AND LIBRARY ASSOCIATION.   Founded on 3 October 1930 in Washington as the Inter-American Bibliographical Association. The present title and revised statutes were adopted on 21 December 1934. Its aims are to furnish information on bibliographical sources to investigators, research workers, students and writers; act as a clearing house for requests about organizations, libraries, or individuals known to have access to, possess, or know of, particular bibliographical resources; undertake bibliographical, library, archival work in co-operation with related agencies in all American countries and publish bibliographical and library aids. Abbreviated IABLA. Publishes conference proceedings, books, *Doors to Latin America* (q. to membs.) which is a guide to books published in the U.S.A.

INTER-AVAILABILITY OF TICKETS. Arrangements whereby the membership tickets of one library may be used to borrow books from another library.

INTERCALATION. The act of inserting a heading for a new subject between two existing headings of a classification.

INTERCALATION DEVICE. (*Classification*) The part of a NOTATION (*q.v.*) which indicates the incorporation of part of a notation from an entirely different scheme of classification, e.g. ( ) could be used in this way to embrace the figures 33 which in the U.D.C. scheme indicate economics.

INTEREST-PROFILE. A list of terms selected from a thesaurus indicating the area of interest of the user of an information service; it is used in the selection of documents in a Selective Dissemination of Information System. Also called USER-PROFILE. *See also* SDI.

INTERESTS RECORD. A record of the interests of individuals habitually using a library. It is compiled from statements made on their membership application forms, from requests for books or information, deliberate interviews, or contacts, and in an organization of fixed and limited numbers such as a firm or research laboratory, by reading correspondence. It is maintained, usually in subject order, to determine what current matter shall be routed or abstracted and to whom lists of additions and other information shall be disseminated.

INTERFIX. (*Information retrieval*) 1. A device to signal relationships between concepts. Thus for a series of compounds, A, B, C, ... insertion of the interfixes 1 and 2 (for example A_1, B_1, B_2, C_2 ...) signals that the compounds with the same numerical interfix are in one mixture and those with a different one are in a different mixture (*IBM*). *See also* LINKS, MODULANT, ROLES. 2. A neutral symbol attached to a DESCRIPTOR (*q.v.*) to indicate other descriptions with which it is interlocked.

INTERLACING. Ornament composed of bands, etc., woven together.

INTERLAY. An UNDERLAY (*q.v.*) consisting of a sheet of paper or other material placed between a printing plate and its mount in order to raise the plate to its proper height for good printing.

INTERLEAF. An extra leaf, usually blank, inserted between the regular leaves of a book. The blank leaves may be provided for the writing of notes, or if they are thin tissues, to prevent the text and illustrations from rubbing. The latter may be pasted to the inner margins, or they may be loose. The plates so protected are known as tissued plates. Such a book is said to be interleaved.

INTERLEAVING. Tissue or blank paper used for interleaving illustrations and letterpress. Also thin blotting paper used for interleaving diaries.

INTERLENDING. The lending of books between libraries.

INTER-LIBRARY LOAN. A book lent between libraries of the same or different systems for a particular reader. *See also* REGIONAL BUREAUX.

INTERLIBRARY REFERENCE SERVICE. A form of co-operation whereby reference work is done by one library for patrons of another which is not an integral part of the same system. (American.)

INTERLINEAR BLANK. *Synonymous with* INTERLINEAR MATTER (*q.v.*).

INTERLINEAR MATTER. Characters providing explanations, translations or subsidiary matter, written or printed in smaller characters between the ordinary lines of text to which they relate.

INTERLINEAR SPACE. Space between lines of type. Also called 'Interlinear blank'.

INTERLINEAR TRANSLATION. A translation printed between the lines of the original text to which it relates.

INTERMEDIATE COPY. (*Reprography*) A copy of a document which serves as an intermediate stage in producing the final copy, as e.g. a readable negative (white on black) from which a black on white copy is made.

INTERMEDIATE FILE. *See* MARLIS.

INTERMEDIATE LIBRARY. A department containing specially selected books and duplicates of some of those in the adult and junior departments for the use of adolescents.

INTERN. In America, a graduate who works in a library full-time while attending part-time at a school of librarianship. *See also* INTERNE.

INTERNATIONAL ADVISORY COMMITTEE ON BIBLIOGRAPHY, DOCUMENTATION AND TERMINOLOGY. A Unesco Committee which as from 1 January 1961 succeeded the two Unesco international advisory committees on Bibliography and for

Documentation and Terminology in Pure and Applied Science. Publishes *Bibliography, Documentation and Terminology*.

INTERNATIONAL AND COMPARATIVE LIBRARIANSHIP GROUP. A Group of the Library Association which was formed in October 1967 to further the study of library services in countries overseas. Publishes *Focus on international and comparative librarianship* (*q.*).

INTERNATIONAL ASSOCIATION FOR MASS COMMUNICATION RESEARCH. Established in Paris in 1957 to promote throughout the world the development of research on problems relating to the press, radio, television and films. It has amongst its objects the establishment of a list of research institutes, and the collection of data on current research projects and current bibliographical material. Abbreviated IAMCR.

INTERNATIONAL ASSOCIATION FOR THE DEVELOPMENT OF LIBRARIES IN AFRICA. Developed in 1960 from the Association pour le Développement des Bibliothèques Publiques en Afrique with the intention of working in every African State for the development of (a) national libraries responsible for acquiring and preserving all printed matter produced in the country so that it shall be available for perusal; (b) public and school libraries to propagate culture at all levels of society and work actively for the education of their communities; (c) reference libraries for universities, institutes, research centres, etc. Abbreviated AIDBA. *See also* ASSOCIATION FOR THE DEVELOPMENT OF PUBLIC LIBRARIES IN AFRICA.

INTERNATIONAL ASSOCIATION OF AGRICULTURAL LIBRARIANS AND DOCUMENTALISTS. Founded 1955 to promote internationally, and nationally, 'agricultural library science and documentation as well as the professional interest of agricultural librarians and documentalists'. It succeeded the International Committee of Agricultural Librarians (founded 1935). Abbreviated IAALD. Publishes *Quarterly Bulletin of the IAALD*.

INTERNATIONAL ASSOCIATION OF DOCUMENTALISTS AND INFORMATION OFFICERS. Founded 1962 in Paris to promote contacts between people of all nationalities whose work concerns the problems of documentation, and to defend their professional interests. Individuals may become members. Abbreviated AID (Association Internationale des Documentalistes et Techniciens de l'Information). Publishes *AID News* (m.), *AID Bulletin* (q.).

INTERNATIONAL ASSOCIATION OF LAW LIBRARIES. Founded in New York in 1959 'to promote on a co-operative, non-profit and fraternal basis the work of individuals, libraries, and other institutions and agencies concerned with the acquisition and bibliographic processing of legal materials collected on a multi-national basis, and to facilitate the research and other uses of such materials on a world-wide basis.' Abbreviated IALL.

INTERNATIONAL ASSOCIATION OF METROPOLITAN CITY LIBRARIES. *See* INTAMEL.

INTERNATIONAL ASSOCIATION OF MUSIC LIBRARIES. Founded in Paris in 1951, the object of this Association is 'to constitute a representative international organization charged with stimulating and co-ordinating all the activities, national and international, of music libraries, and to study and facilitate the realization of all projects dealing with music bibliography and music library science.' It aims to arrange for co-operation in the compilation of music bibliographies, exchange material, and train music librarians. Abbreviated IAML. Publishes *Fontes artis musicae* (3 a year). It has a British branch which was founded in 1953 and was primarily responsible for the inauguration of the *British catalogue of music* in 1957; publishes *Brio* (q.).

INTERNATIONAL ASSOCIATION OF TECHNOLOGICAL UNIVERSITY LIBRARIES. Founded in Brussels in May 1955 to act as an organ for international co-operation between member libraries and to stimulate and develop library projects of international and regional importance. It is a section of IFLA (*q.v.*). Abbreviated IATUL. Publishes *Reprints* (irr.) and *Newsletter* (6 p.a.).

INTERNATIONAL ASSOCIATION OF THEOLOGICAL LIBRARIES. Formed at a conference of the International Federation of Library Associations (IFLA) in Brussels in 1955 of which it was a subsidiary. Abbreviated IATL. It ceased to function in 1960.

INTERNATIONAL BUREAU OF FISCAL DOCUMENTATION. Created as a foundation of the International Fiscal Association (IFA) this Bureau aims at complete co-operation with the Association. The Bureau's objects include the foundation and maintenance of an international documentation bureau for the supply of information on fiscal legislation and the application of fiscal law, and particularly the study of fiscal science. It seeks to realize this by establishing a library on fiscal legislation, supplying both general and detailed information, providing research facilities, issuing a journal, and continuing co-operation with the publications of other interested bodies. Abbreviated IBFD. Publishes *Documentation service* (f.) a literary survey covering books and periodical articles, and other publications.

INTERNATIONAL CATALOGUE CARD. The size of card which has been adopted internationally for use in card catalogues: it is 5 × 3 inches (7·5 × 12·5 centimetres).

INTERNATIONAL CENTRE FOR AFRICAN ECONOMIC AND SOCIAL DOCUMENTATION. Founded January 1961 to gather together and co-ordinate documentation on economic and social material concerning Africa with a view to facilitating and promoting the progress of the Continent in these fields. Publishes *Bibliographical index* (a.).

INTERNATIONAL CHILDREN'S CENTRE. Founded in Paris in 1950 by the United Nations Children's Fund (UNICEF) and the French Government to study childhood problems in the various countries. A Centre of International Documentation on Pediatrics and Child Welfare was set up at the Chateau de Longchamp. The library has 5,000 books, 1,000 files of periodicals and about 10,000 files of reprints in addition to government and international organization documents. Catalogue cards, indexing not only books but periodical articles, etc., are supplied to other libraries and individual research workers on a subscription basis. Abbreviated ICC. Publishes *Le Courrier* (6 p.a.), *Biologia Neonatorum* (q.), *L'Enfant au Milieu Tropical* (m.).

INTERNATIONAL CLASSIFICATION. The brief name for Fremont Rider's scheme of classification for a general library, *International classification for the arrangement of books on the shelves of general libraries*, first published in 1961. Its main outline is similar to the Library of Congress classification; form and geographical subdivisions are enumerated in each main class; the notation consists of three letters and can be extended by 'book numbers' which are a combination of letters from the BISCOE DATE TABLE (*q.v.*) plus the initial letter of the author's name; no auxiliary tables are provided, neither are alternative locations. The schedules have 14,000 places.

INTERNATIONAL COMMITTEE FOR AFRICAN SOCIAL AND ECONOMIC DOCUMENTATION. *See* CIDESA.

INTERNATIONAL COMMITTEE FOR SOCIAL SCIENCES DOCUMENTATION. Founded in November 1950 in Paris at a meeting called by Unesco following recommendations of two committees of experts in 1948 and 1949. Registered in accordance with French law. Collects, keeps up-to-date and disseminates information on the different documentation services in the social sciences, and helps establish bibliographies and documentary tools which its surveys show to be necessary. The Committee sponsors or undertakes the following categories of bibliography: those on inter-disciplinary problems within the social sciences; guides to bibliographical sources of use to social scientists, but not restricted to them; retrospective regional bibliographies in the social sciences. It also sponsors the regular publication by Unesco in English and French of separate bibliographies of sociology, of political science, of economics, of social and cultural anthropology. It initiated, with the help of the Nuffield Foundation, investigation into the need for, and production of, a scheme of classification for the four Unesco bibliographies dealing with sociology, political science, economics, and social anthropology. The Kyle Classification for Social Sciences is the result. The membership consists mainly of representatives of international associations specializing either in the social sciences or in documentation and bibliography. It is financed by a grant from Unesco, and its activities include the compilation of current bibliographies and directories. Abbreviated ICSSD. Publishes *International Political Science Abstracts* (q.), *Confluence* (2 p.a.), *International Bibliography of the Social Sciences* . . . (annually).

INTERNATIONAL CONFERENCE ON CATALOGUING PRINCIPLES.   An outstanding conference of cataloguers, bibliographers and library officers with cataloguing expertise was held in Paris, 9–18 October 1961, consequent upon a proposal made by the council of IFLA in 1957 to seek agreement on certain basic cataloguing principles. It was sponsored by IFLA with the object of reaching 'agreement on basic principles governing the choice and form of entry in the alphabetical catalogue of authors and titles'. A *Preliminary Official Report* was issued by the Executive Secretary, A. H. Chaplin, and published in *Libri*, Vol. 12, No. 1, 1962. The full report was published separately in 1963 by IFLA. Abbreviated ICCP.

INTERNATIONAL CONFERENCE ON CLASSIFICATION FOR INFORMATION RETRIEVAL.   Held at Dorking, England, 13–17 May, 1957. The *Proceedings* of the Conference were published by Aslib who organized it as the British member of FID in co-operation with the Classification Research Group and the University of London School of Librarianship and Archives.

INTERNATIONAL CONFERENCE ON INFORMATION PROCESSING.   Held 15–20 June 1959 in Paris; organized by Unesco with the help of experts from various countries, with the object of bringing experts together to share their knowledge and experience. The conference was mainly concerned with the workings and uses of computers. The International Federation of Information Processing Societies was set up and was later known as the INTERNATIONAL FEDERATION FOR INFORMATION PROCESSING (*q.v.*).

INTERNATIONAL CONFERENCE ON SCIENTIFIC INFORMATION. Held 16–21 November 1958 in Washington, under the general sponsorship of the American Documentation Institute, the U.S. National Science Foundation and the National Academy of Sciences in collaboration with Unesco and the International Federation for Documentation. It was designed to summarize the state of scientific information. Abbreviated ICSI.

INTERNATIONAL CONGRESS ON REPROGRAPHY. The first congress was held in Cologne 14–18 October 1963. It was organized by the German Society for Photography with the object of bringing together research workers and specialists who are engaged in the development of facsimile reproduction processes in order to discuss their experience and plans.

INTERNATIONAL COPYRIGHT. *See* COPYRIGHT, INTERNATIONAL.

INTERNATIONAL COPYRIGHT ACT, 1886. This was passed to enable the original Berne Convention to be carried out in the Dominions. *See* COPYRIGHT, INTERNATIONAL.

INTERNATIONAL COUNCIL FOR BUILDING DOCUMENTATION. Abbreviated CIDB. *See* INTERNATIONAL COUNCIL FOR BUILDING RESEARCH STUDIES AND DOCUMENTATION.

INTERNATIONAL COUNCIL FOR BUILDING RESEARCH, STUDIES AND DOCUMENTATION. Founded in 1953. Superseded the International Council for Building Documentation (CIDB) which had been established in 1950. Aims to encourage, facilitate and develop international co-operation in building research, studies and documentation, covering technical, economic and social aspects of building. Abbreviated CIB. Has published *ABC: abridged building classification for architects, builders and civil engineers: a selection from the Universal Decimal Classification system by the International Building Classification Committee* in single language editions in English, Dutch, French, German, Hungarian, Italian, Norwegian, Serbo-Croatian, Swedish and Danish. Publishes also the 'CIB Directory' – in full: *Directory of building research and development organisations; Organisations in Europe; CIB member organisations outside Europe; International organisations*, Rev. ed. 1963, in English, and *CIB bulletin* (q.) in English with a Spanish version published by a CIB member Institute in Spain.

INTERNATIONAL COUNCIL FOR RESEARCH IN THE SOCIOLOGY OF CO-OPERATION. Established in 1953. Its aims embrace the development, encouragement and exchange of information concerning the work and research done in its field. Each of the national research centres affiliated to the Council pursues a triple policy of research, documentation and integrated consultation in the social and economic context of its country. Thus the second point comprises the setting up of co-operative libraries and documentation centres to aid research workers, the establishment of an International Library of the Sociology of Co-operation comprising works published in English, French, German and Italian, and giving aid in the publication of research work arising from these activities. Publishes amongst many works *International archives of sociology of co-operation*. Abbreviated ICRSC.

INTERNATIONAL COUNCIL OF MUSEUMS. Founded in Paris in 1946 on Unesco's initiative. The Council's aims include the establishment of an international organization representing museums and the museum profession, and the development of international co-operation between them. Maintains a Museum Documentation Centre which also acts in that capacity for the Museums Division of Unesco. Abbreviated ICOM. Publishes *ICOM News*.

INTERNATIONAL COUNCIL OF SCIENTIFIC UNIONS. Founded in 1919 in Brussels as the 'International Research Council'; re-named in 1931. Its aims are to co-ordinate and facilitate activities of international scientific unions in the field of natural sciences, encourage international scientific activity in subjects which do not fall within the purview of any existing organizations, maintain relations with the UN and its specialized agencies, and make contacts and mutual arrangements with other international councils or unions, where common interests exist. In 1952 the Council set up the ICSU Abstracting Board which, with a Unesco subvention, aims to assist scientific abstracting reviews to co-operate with one another. Additionally, Unesco makes a financial contribution to bibliographical publications issued by the Council and its members. Abbreviated ICSU.

INTERNATIONAL COUNCIL ON ARCHIVES. Founded in June 1948 by professional archivists meeting in Paris under the auspices of Unesco. Aims to hold periodical international congresses, establish and maintain relations among archivists of all nations, and among all professional agencies and institutions whose activities relate to the conservation, organization or administration of archives; to further technical and administrative aspects of public and private archives wherever located and to facilitate access to archives, their objective study and the knowledge of their contents. International associations, institutions, and individuals may become members. Financed by members' dues and by Unesco subvention. Abbreviated ICA. Publishes *Archivum, Répertoire Sélectif des guides d'archives, Guide international des archives, Guide to sources for the history of Latin America.*

INTERNATIONAL DOCUMENTATION CENTRE. Situated at Hogelby Hus, Tumba, Sweden, the function of this information centre is to microfilm books and periodicals both in-print and out-of-print in anticipation of demand and to order. Copies are made on 3×5 inches microfiche and on filmstrip. Abbreviated IDC.

INTERNATIONAL FEDERATION FOR DOCUMENTATION. The English name of the Fédération Internationale de Documentation (FID) by which the International Institute of Bibliography became known in 1938. This organization developed from the UDC (*q.v.*) and exists (a) to group on an international basis, organizations and individuals interested in the problems of DOCUMENTATION (*q.v.*) and to co-ordinate their efforts; (b) to promote the study and practice of documentation in all its branches and forms, and to create an international network of documentation; (c) to establish guiding principles for the member organizations in their work; (d) to organize the exchange of information relevant to the work of member organizations; (e) to convene conferences dealing with the problems of documentation; (f) to publish, sell and distribute periodical and non-periodical publications dealing with documentation; (g) to co-operate with other international organizations concerned with related subjects; (h) to take such other legal and appropriate measures as may be conducive to the attainment of the above objects. The development of the UNIVERSAL DECIMAL CLASSIFICATION (*q.v.*) is its major activity but it is concerned with other aspects of documentation especially since the Warsaw Conference in 1959. Publishes *Revue de la Documentation* (q.), *FID News Bulletin* (m.).

INTERNATIONAL FEDERATION FOR INFORMATION PROCESSING. Formerly the International Federation of Information Processing Societies which was set up as a result of an international congress on information processing organized by Unesco and held in Paris in 1959. The members of the Federation are national societies, the adhering society in the United Kingdom being the British Computer Society. The Federation organized its first congress in Munich 1962, and a full report was published in 1963 by the North Holland Publishing Company under the title *Information processing,* 1962. Aims: to sponsor international conferences and symposia on information processing; to establish international committees to undertake special tasks falling within the scope of member societies; to advance the interests of member societies in international co-operation. Registered in accordance with Belgian law. Abbreviated IFIP. Publishes *IFIP Newsletter* as part of *ICC Newsletter* (International Computation Centre, Rome).

INTERNATIONAL FEDERATION OF INFORMATION PRO-CESSING SOCIETIES. Became known in 1962 as the INTERNATIONAL FEDERATION FOR INFORMATION PROCESSING (*q.v.*).

INTERNATIONAL FEDERATION OF LIBRARY ASSOCIA-TIONS. Abbreviated IFLA. Founded June 1929 in Rome to promote and facilitate international co-operation in librarianship and bibliography. Also known by the French name Fédération Internationale des Associations de Bibliothécaires (FIAB). The work of IFLA is done through annual Council meetings and seventeen sections and committees studying practical questions of international librarianship such as union catalogues, international loans, exchange of publications, national and university libraries, public libraries, work with children, library buildings, library education, reprography, bibliographical work, etc. Its membership comprises five international associations (AIL, ALJH, IAALD, IALL and IATUL (*qq.v.*)) and the Ibero-American Commission of Librarians' Associations, and national Associations in seventy-six countries. Following the appointment of a full-time secretary in 1963 it now has its headquarters in England. During the twenty-ninth session of the Council, held in Sofia (Bulgaria) in September 1963, an Association of the Libraries of International Organizations was formed within the framework of IFLA. Publishes *Libri* (q.), *Actes du Conseil de la FIAB* (a.), *IFLA News* (q.). *Inspel* (2 or 3 times p.m. by the Section of Special Libraries). IFLA developed from the International Library and Bibliographical Committee.

INTERNATIONAL FEDERATION OF NATIONAL STANDARDI-ZATION ASSOCIATIONS (ISA). A body which was liquidated during the Second World War and superseded by the INTERNATIONAL ORGANIZATION FOR STANDARDIZATION (*q.v.*).

INTERNATIONAL FEDERATION OF RECORD LIBRARIES. Founded in Milan on 27th May 1963 and registered in accordance with French Law. It aims (a) to facilitate co-operation between gramophone record libraries and contribute to the development of their activities; (b) to contribute to the organization of the profession of record librarian. Membership is open to international associations and to national committees comprising institutions and individuals. It is financed by members' dues. Abbreviated FIP (Fédération Internationale des Phonothéques).

INTERNATIONAL FEDERATION OF SOUND ARCHIVES. Founded in 1963 'to encourage co-operation between sound archives. To aid in the development of the activities of sound archives. To aid in establishing professional standards for librarians of recorded sound. To engage in any or all activities related to the field of recorded sound'.

INTERNATIONAL FEDERATION OF TRANSLATORS. Founded in Paris with Unesco support in December 1953 to bring together representative groups of translators in order to defend their material and moral interests, encourage the establishment of such groups in countries where they do not exist, represent translators at the international level, follow the development of theoretical and practical questions relating to translation, and contribute to the spread of culture. Organizes congresses and pursues various projects through committees relating to terminology, registers of specialist translators, copyright, training, etc. Registered in accordance with French law. Abbreviated FIT. Publishes *Babel* (q.).

INTERNATIONAL INSTITUTE OF ARTS AND LETTERS. Founded on 20th December 1931 in Paris to achieve worldwide co-operation in the cultivation and promotion of arts, letters and sciences, with the object of increasing knowledge and of contributing in other ways to human progress. Members (Fellows, Corresponding and Associate) are selected from those qualified by outstanding achievements in the field of culture in forty countries.

INTERNATIONAL MICROGRAPHIC CONGRESS. Originally, the National Microfilm Association (U.S.A.) considered setting up foreign chapters but later decided to sponsor an international microfilm organization. Finance was provided and formal incorporation papers issued in the state of Michigan in September 1962. Officially, therefore, IMC dates from then. The first international meeting, however, was held during the NMA Convention in April 1964. Membership (full) is open to national microfilm associations but there is also individual membership provided that the individuals are also members of their national organization, if there is one. Broadly, the aims are international co-operation in all matters concerning microfilm – standardization, publications, meetings, exchange of information, etc. Abbreviated IMC. Publishes *IMC Journal* (q., distributed through national associations), and *The International Directory of Micrographic Equipment* (1967).

INTERNATIONAL MILLIONTH MAP. A 'map' of the world on a 1:1,000,000 scale; so far, about 300 of the projected 1,500 sheets have been completed.

INTERNATIONAL MUSICOLOGICAL SOCIETY. Founded in Basle, 1927, by amalgamating the *Internationale Musikgesellschaft* and the *Union Musicologique*. Reconstituted in 1949, the Society aims to establish relations between musicologists in different countries; serve as a central information and bibliographical office. Abbreviated IMS. Publishes *Acta musicologica* (q.). and congress reports.

INTERNATIONAL ORGANIZATION FOR STANDARDIZATION. Constituted in London under its present statutes in October 1946 to replace the pre-war International Federation of National Standardizing Associations (ISA) and the United Nations Standards Co-ordinating Committee. Aims to promote development of standards in the world with a view to facilitating international exchange of goods and services, and to developing mutual co-operation in the sphere of intellectual, scientific, technological and economic activity. Over 100 technical committees of experts appointed by national standard bodies who are members formulate recommendations to national member associations. Abbreviated ISO. Publishes *ISO journal* (m.), *ISO memento* (a.), both for member bodies only.

INTERNATIONAL PAPER SIZES. The international 'A' series of paper sizes are now widely used throughout the world. In Britain many organizations have adopted them and there is both a British Standard (B.S. 3176) and an international recommendation (ISO/R 216) covering them.

'A' SERIES OF TRIMMED PAPER SIZES

Desig-nation	SIZE		Desig-nation	SIZE	
	mm	inches		mm	inches
4 A	1682 × 2378	66.22 × 93.62	A 5	148 × 210	5.83 × 8.27
2 A	1189 × 1682	46.81 × 66.22	A 6	105 × 148	4.13 × 5.83
A 0	841 × 1189	33.11 × 46.81	A 7	74 × 105	2.91 × 4.13
A 1	594 × 841	23.39 × 33.11	A 8	52 × 74	2.05 × 2.91
A 2	420 × 594	16.54 × 23.39	A 9	37 × 52	1.46 × 2.05
A 3	297 × 420	11.69 × 16.54	A 10	26 × 37	1.02 × 1.46
A 4	210 × 297	8.27 × 11.69			

INTERNATIONAL PUBLISHERS ASSOCIATION. Founded in Paris in 1896 as International Publishers Congress to consider problems common to the publishing and bookselling trades, and to uphold and defend the complete freedom of publishers to publish and distribute literary works, and secure international co-operation between them. Congresses are held periodically in different countries. A permanent office is maintained at Geneva. Membership is open to professional book and music publishers associations. Activities include help to secure signatories to the BERNE CONVENTION and UNIVERSAL COPYRIGHT CONVENTION (*qq.v.*) and to keep the flow of books between countries free of tariffs and other obstacles, provision of aid to emerging countries, and consideration of international copyright and translation rights. Publishes reports and congress proceedings. Abbreviated IPA.

INTERNATIONAL READING ASSOCIATION. Founded in the U.S.A. on 1st January 1956 to encourage the study of reading problems at all levels, and also to stimulate and promote research in developmental, corrective and remedial reading. Abbreviated IRA. Publishes *The Research Teacher, Journal of Reading* (both 8 p.a.), *Reading Research Quarterly*.

INTERNATIONAL SECTION FOR PERFORMING ARTS LIBRARIES AND MUSEUMS. Founded in September 1954 at Zagreb with the object of developing co-operation among libraries, as well as museums, public, private and specialized collections concerned with the theatre, dance, cinema, marionettes, mime, festivals, son et lumière, radio and television. Membership is open to individuals and organizations. It is financed by grants from the International Federation of Library Associations. Seven congresses have been held in different capital cities since 1960. Publishes *Spectacles-Documents* (bulletin) in *Recherche Théâtrale* (3 a year). Congress proceedings.

INTERNATIONAL STANDARD BOOK NUMBER. *See* STANDARD BOOK NUMBER.

INTERNATIONAL STANDARDS. There are a number of international standards organizations which have the task of seeking to unify the various national standards. The two most important are International Organization for Standardization (ISO) and International Electrotechnical Commission (IEC). Some ISO recommendations of interest to librarians include:

ISO/R 4 International code for abbreviation of titles of periodicals

ISO/8 Layout of periodicals

ISO/R 18   Short contents list (of periodicals or other documents)

ISO/R 77   Bibliographical references (Essential elements)

ISO/R 169   Sizes of photocopies (on paper) readable without optical devices

ISO/R 193   Microcopies on transparent bases. Recommended bases, dimensions

ISO/R 214   Abstracts and synopses

ISO/R 215   Presentation of contributions to periodicals

ISO/R 216   Trimmed sizes of writing paper and certain classes of printed matter

ISO/R 218   Microcopies – scale of 35 mm microfilm for international exchange

See also AMERICAN NATIONAL STANDARDS INSTITUTE, INC., BRITISH STANDARDS INSTITUTION, DIN, INTERNATIONAL ORGANIZATION FOR STANDARDIZATION, PAN AMERICAN STANDARDS COMMISSION, STANDARDS.

INTERNATIONAL UNION FOR THE PROTECTION OF LITERARY AND ARTISTIC WORKS. Founded 9th September 1886 to ensure effective protection to authors of literary and artistic works, and to ensure and develop the international protection of literary and artistic works. Membership is open to governments. Organizes diplomatic conferences. Has a specialized library of 12,000 vols. Publishes *Le droit d'auteur* (m.), *Copyright* (m.).

INTERNATIONAL YOUTH LIBRARY. An Associated Project of Unesco, founded in 1949 in Munich. It developed out of the first post war exhibition of international children's books organized in Munich by Mrs. Lepman in 1946. The stock totals over 100,000 books from more than fifty countries, about 80 per cent of the books being donated by the publishers. Abbreviated IYL.

INTERNE. An assistant librarian who, for a period of about a year, exchanges positions with someone holding a similar position in another country. Also spelt 'intern'.

INTERPOLATED NOTE. An explanation or description added to an entry by the compiler of a catalogue or bibliography to clarify the original material. Such information is inserted within SQUARE BRACKETS (*q.v.*).

INTERPOLATION. (*Classification*) The insertion of a new topic at any point in a scheme of classification. A non-structural type of notation renders this readily possible. *See also* EXTRAPOLATION.

INTERPRETER. An electric accounting machine which prints information recorded by holes punched on cards. The printing of such information is called 'interpreting'.

INTER-REGIONAL SUBJECT COVERAGE SCHEME. Under this scheme each of the Regional Bureaux became responsible on 1st January 1959 for seeing that one library in its area purchases every new book and pamphlet published in the United Kingdom, which is included in the *British National Bibliography*; the allocation of sections of the Dewey Classification is as follows:

000–099	Northern	400–499	East Midlands
100–199	Wales	800–899	„ „
200–299	South-Western	500–599	West Midlands
300–349	Yorkshire	600–699	North-Western
350–399	Scotland	700–799	London
		900–999	South-Eastern

These books are not recorded in the National Union Catalogue at the National Central Library as it is known that they are available in a particular region; requests for books are sent to the appropriate regional bureau. The books purchased under this scheme are intended to be provided primarily for preservation.

INTER-RELATED LOGIC-ACCUMULATING SCANNER. An atypical punching pattern used on punched cards, developed at the U.S. Patent Office. Abbreviated ILAS.

INTERROGATION MARK. A punctuation sign (?) placed at the end of a direct question. Also used between parentheses to indicate an author's questioning of the accuracy of a statement. Also called 'Interrogation point', 'Mark of interrogation', 'Question mark'.

INTERSECTING FRAME. (*Binding*) One or more decorative frames, the sides of which (or some of them) are extended, where they meet each other, to the edges of the cover.

INTERSPACING. *Synonymous with* LETTER SPACING (*q.v.*).

INTERTYPE. A typesetting machine casting type in a slug, similar to, but differing in detail from, the LINOTYPE (*q.v.*).

INTERUNIVERSITY COMMUNICATION COUNCIL. *See* EDU-COM.

INTRA-FACET RELATION. *See* PHASE.

INTREX. *See* PROJECT INTREX.

INTRODUCTION. 1. A short essay or statement, usually being a general survey of the subject preparing the reader for the treatment to follow, of a commendatory nature, and written by an authority in the field with which the book deals. Its order in the PRELIMINARIES (*q.v.*), is after the Preface and immediately before the first page of text.

Sometimes it is the first chapter. 2. Included in the title of a book, it indicates that it is an introductory book on the subject, intended for students, and possibly a popular treatment, but not as elementary as a PRIMER (*q.v.*). If dealing with a learned or highly scientific subject, it may be comprehensible only by specialists.

INTRODUCTION DATE.   The date given at the beginning or end of an INTRODUCTION (*q.v.*).

INVERPOS PAPER.   Trade name for a type of SILVER HALIDE PAPER (*q.v.*) which gives a positive image without the necessity for first making a negative when making copies by LENSLESS COPYING (*q.v.*).

INVERSION, PRINCIPLE OF.   In classification, placing the facets in schedule order in such a way that the most concrete, intensive or significant is last.

INVERSION OF TITLE.   The turning about of a title to bring a particular word to the front. This practice is frequently adopted in dictionary catalogues.

INVERTED BACONIAN SCHEME.   A scheme of classification in which the order of the main classes in Francis Bacon's philosophical system outlined in his *The advancement of learning* (1605) – history poesy, philosophy – are inverted, as in the schemes of Dr. W. T. Harris and Melvil Dewey.

INVERTED COMMAS.   Pairs of superior commas, or sometimes single commas, placed at the beginning and end of quotations. *See also* QUOTES.

INVERTED ENTRY.   An index entry which has been re-arranged to bring the most important word or words to the front. For example, 'CO-EFFICIENT OF EXPANSION, APPARENT'.

INVERTED HEADING.   A catalogue heading which has had the order of the words inverted to bring the most important word to the front, as CHEMISTRY, ORGANIC.

INVERTED TITLE.   *See* INVERSION OF TITLE.

INVOICE.   A list of items supplied, together with the prices charged for each. An itemized bill.

IONAMETER.   *See* pH Value.

IRA.   Acronym for INTERNATIONAL READING ASSOCIATION (*q.v.*).

IRISH ASSOCIATION FOR DOCUMENTATION.   Founded 1947 with the aim of co-ordinating documentation services in Ireland. Most special and large public libraries have contributed to the *Union list of current periodicals and serials in Dublin libraries*, 1960 (Supplement 1962), which records more than 6,000 titles and gives locations.

IRISH CENTRAL LIBRARY FOR STUDENTS.   Founded by the

Carnegie United Kingdom Trust in 1923; control was transferred to An Chomhairle Leabharlanna (The Library Council) in 1948. Supplements the regular library services of local authorities, educational institutions and learned societies, and the services of public and special libraries generally, by providing books for study and research both from its own stock and by means of inter-library loans. Abbreviated ICLS.

IRISH STYLE.   An eighteenth-century style of book decoration distinguished by a large centre lozenge of inlaid fawn leather.

ISAD.   Acronym for INFORMATION SCIENCE AND AUTOMATION DIVISION (*q.v.*).

ISADORE GILBERT MUDGE CITATION.   *See* MUDGE CITATION, ISADORE GILBERT.

ISARITHMS.   *Synonymous with* ISOPLETHS (*q.v.*).

ISEPHODIC MAP.   One which shows the equal cost of travel, places of equal freight rates being connected by isephodes similar to isochrones.

ISLAND BOOKCASE.   *See* ISLAND STACK.

ISLAND CASE.   A bookcase (usually double-sided) which is so placed that readers can walk all around it.

ISLAND STACK.   A book STACK (*q.v.*) which is placed away from the wall so that readers can walk all round it. Also called 'Island bookcase'.

ISLIC.   *See* ISRAEL SOCIETY OF SPECIAL LIBRARIES AND INFORMATION CENTRES.

ISLINGTON CHARGING SYSTEM.   A method of recording the loan of books introduced at the Islington Public Libraries in 1963. Readers are provided with plastic identity cards bearing their name and address in raised characters: these they insert in a machine called a Recorder to print their name and address on a small slip of paper. This is used together with a book-card to record a loan. Otherwise the system is exactly the same as the BROWNE BOOK CHARGING SYSTEM (*q.v.*). It has the advantage of permitting delayed discharging. *See also* CHARGING METHODS.

ISOBARS.   Lines on a map which connect places with the same barometric pressure.

ISOBATHS.   Lines on a map joining points on the sea bed which have an equal depth. Such lines show the relief of the sea bed, just as CONTOURS (*q.v.*) show the relief of the land by joining places of equal altitude. Areas between isobaths are coloured in varying shades of blue.

ISOCHRONIC MAP.   One which shows possible progress of travel in all directions from a given centre in certain specified time intervals.

ISOCRYMES. Lines on a map which connect places with the same degree of frost.

ISOGONES. Lines on a map which connect places with equal angles of magnetic variation. Also called 'Isogonic lines'.

ISOGONIC CHART. One which shows lines connecting places of equal magnetic declination or variation.

ISOGRAMS. *Synonymous with* ISOPLETHS.

ISOHALINES. Lines on a map joining points in the oceans which have equal salinity.

ISOHELS. Lines on a map which connect places with the same amount of sunshine over a certain period.

ISOHYETS. Lines on a map which connect places with the same amount of rainfall over a certain period.

ISOHYPSES. Lines on a map which connect places with the same elevation.

ISOLATE. (*Classification*) 1. A generic term applicable to all the three planes – Idea, Notation, Words – in the Colon Classification, and indicating a division of a FACET (*q.v.*). Also called 'Isolate focus'. In addition to COMMON ISOLATES (*q.v.*), there are Time, Space and Language isolates used to indicate periods of time, geographical division, and languages respectively. 2. The name of anything that can exist and behave as a unit or a word expressing its behaviour. Isolates are taken from the literature of a subject. 3. A single component ('ingredient') of a compound subject.

ISONEPHS. Lines on a map which connect places with the same amount of cloud over a certain period.

ISOPLETH MAP. A quantitative aerial map on which the geographical distribution of the elements is shown by lines of equal value, such as contours, isobars, isohyets and isotherms. *See also* ISOPLETHS.

ISOPLETHS. Lines on a map which connect places of equal density or value of distribution of any specific element. Also called 'Isorithms' and 'Isograms'. If they connect places of equal temperature they are called 'isotherms'; of equal rainfall, 'isohyets'; of barometric pressure, 'isobars'; of magnetic variation, 'isogones'; of sunshine, 'isohels'; of frost, 'isocrymes'; of clouds, 'isonephs'; of equal elevation, 'isohypses'. They connect an average number of individual units. Lines which connect a continuous value, such as temperature, are called 'isarithms'.

ISOSEISMAL LINES. Lines on a map joining places which have suffered an equal intensity of shock from an earthquake. Such lines usually form closed curves round their seismic focus.

ISOTHERMS. Lines on a map which connect places with the same temperature at a particular instant or having the same average temperature over a certain period.

ISRAEL LIBRARY ASSOCIATION. Founded in 1952 to raise professional standards of all types of libraries and improve the working conditions of librarians. Membership is open to anyone who has held a permanent position in a library for one year or who has graduated from the Graduate Library School of the Hebrew University in Jerusalem. Abbreviated ILA. Publishes *Yad-la-kore* (*The Reader's Aid*) – contains abstracts in English of the main articles.

ISRAEL SOCIETY OF SPECIAL LIBRARIES AND INFORMATION CENTRES. Registered in August 1966 to encourage and promote efficient utilization of knowledge through special libraries and information centres, to facilitate written and oral communication among its members, and to co-operate with other bodies with similar or allied interests in Israel and abroad. Abbreviated ISLIC. Publishes *Bulletin, Contributions to information science* (3 p.a.).

ISSUE. 1. All the charges or other records representing books on loan. 2. The number of books so issued. 3. The copies of a book in which the original sheets are used but which differ in some respects from copies previously issued (e.g. a new title-page or other difference in the preliminaries, an additional appendix, the inclusion of a list of publisher's announcements). 4. The number of impressions (copies) of an old map or print made at a given time without any change being made in the plate. 5. A particular publication, complete in itself, of a serial or periodical which is issued at intervals or in parts. *See also* EDITION, FIRST EDITION, IMPRESSION, NEW EDITION, REPRINT, REVISED EDITION.

ISSUE DESK. *See* CIRCULATION DESK.

ISSUE GUIDES. Pieces of card, plastic or metal which project above the issue (the projection being numbered or lettered according to the method of arrangement) to facilitate the finding of records of books on loan. *See also* CHARGE.

ISSUE NUMBER. The number given to a separately issued part of a serial to distinguish it from other issues. Numbers may run consecutively from the first issue onwards, but if the issues are divided into volumes, a new sequence of issue numbers commences with each volume; in this case they are printed on the cover, and also in each issue immediately after the volume number.

ISSUE TRAY. A tray containing the ISSUE (*q.v.*).

ital. Abbreviation for italic.

ITALIAN STYLE.   *See* ALDINE (ITALIAN) STYLE.

ITALIC.   Sloping type, as distinguished from the normal, upright, Roman type, used to emphasize any special point, or for the names of publications, ships, etc. It was first used by Aldus Pius Manutius in 1501, and was originally called Aldine or Chancery, and was based on a humanistic Italian handwriting of a somewhat earlier period. *This is italic* and is indicated in a MS. prepared for the printer by a single underlining. Abbreviated ital.

ITALTYPE.   A slug-composing machine which was made in Italy in the early 1950s. INTERTYPE (*q.v.*) and LINOTYPE (*q.v.*) matrices can be used as well as the maker's Italtype matrices.

ITEM.   (*Information retrieval*) In an index, the reference to the document. Also the document itself, whether a book, serial, abstract, article, photograph or microform, etc. *See also* COMPRESENCE, FEATURE, TERM.

ITEM CARDS.   Cards used to record information by means of coloured tabs, holes or notches in connexion with some form of CO-ORDINATE INDEXING (*q.v.*). *See also* FEATURE CARD.

ITEM ENTRY.   In information retrieval, the entry of particulars of a document under a heading or symbol identifying the document. This is the traditional method used in library catalogues. It is also the method used on edge-slotted cards. Also called 'Document system'. *See also* TERM ENTRY.

IVORY BOARD.   A good quality card, made from wood, and used for printing.

JACKET.   *Synonymous with* BOOK JACKET (*q.v.*).

JACKET BAND.   A strip of paper wrapped round a book-jacket to emphasize some sales aspect.

JACKETED FILM.   Microfilm which has been inserted in a FILM JACKET (*q.v.*).

JACONET.   Cotton material, glazed on one side, and used to line and strengthen the spines of books.

JANE ADDAMS AWARD.   *See* ADDAMS AWARD, JANE.

JANNON, JEAN.   A master printer in Paris in 1610, who, due to his Protestant leanings, went to Sedan where he printed for the Calvinist Academy and issued one of the finest and earliest of French specimen books in 1621. His types were used solely for the Academy and the Prince of Sedan during the next twenty years at the end of which period he returned to Paris to set up a business, but went again to Sedan to print for the Academy because of oppression and the confiscation of some of his punches and some matrices; these were sent to the Imprimerie Royale which had recently been set up by Cardinal Richelieu. They remained there until 1898 when they were revived and used for various de luxe editions published by the Imprimerie Nationale, as the Imprimerie Royale became known after the Revolution, and which attributed their design to Claude Garamond whose style he undoubtedly used for his work. His types had a considerable influence because of their use at Sedan over many years, and much later, because of their revival at the end of the nineteenth century.

JANSENIST STYLE. A very simple binding named after Cornelius Jansen, the seventeenth century Bishop of Ypres, decorated only by a centre-piece (often armorial) and corner fleurons, or devoid of ornamentation on the outside of the covers, but with elaborate DOUBLURES (*q.v.*) tooled with DENTELLE (*q.v.*) borders.

JAPANESE PAPER. A paper, or tissue, in varying substances, having a silky texture; it is handbeaten from the bark fibres of the mulberry tree, or in imitation thereof. Used for printing, etchings, photogravures, books; also used for binding. 'French Japon' is a good imitation, it is less expensive but not so strong.

JAPANESE STYLE. *See* CHINESE STYLE.

JAPANESE VELLUM. An extremely costly, strong hand-made Japanese paper with a firm glossy surface, and a creamy tint. It is much used for engravings, and diplomas, or where a very durable paper is required. It will not withstand india-rubber, and must be handled very carefully. An imitation is made by treating thick ordinary paper with sulphuric acid.

JENSON. A type face named after Nicolas Jenson (1420–80), a French printer who went to Venice in 1468 and had his own printing works there. 'The world's first great type designer, perhaps the greatest in all typographical history' – *McMurtrie*. He used his 'perfect roman letter' in *De praeparatione evangelica* by Eusebius, 1470; this served as the model for Morris's Golden type and for Benton's Cloister. Jenson was working in Venice, and his type became a pattern for all future type designs. The Monotype Centaur, designed by Bruce Rogers, is based on Jenson. The letters are open, dignified, clear and legible, of even colour and perfect harmony. The contrast between thick and thin strokes is slight; the serifs are blunt with very small brackets.

JETÉ EN MOULE. ('Cast in a mould'). Mould metal type for use in printing. Also called 'Get en mol'.

JEWISH LIBRARIANS ASSOCIATION. FOUNDED in 1946 in the U.S.A. to advance the interests of Jewish libraries and the professional status of Jewish librarians; to promote publications of Jewish biblio-graphical interest. Abbreviated JLA. It was merged in June 1966 with the Jewish Library Association to form the ASSOCIATION OF JEWISH LIBRARIES (*q.v.*) of which it is an autonomous Division.

JEWISH LIBRARY ASSOCIATION. Founded in 1962 in the U.S.A. 'to promote and improve library service and standards in Jewish communities; to serve as a centre for the dissemination of Judaica, library information and guidance; to encourage the establishment of new Judaica libraries'. Published *Newsletter* (3 a year). It was merged in June 1966 with the Jewish Librarians Association to form the ASSOCIATION OF JEWISH LIBRARIES (*q.v.*) of which it is an autonomous Division.

JOANNA. A light roman type designed by Eric Gill in 1930. It is remark-able for its small capitals which do not reach the height of the ascen-ders, themselves not tall. It is eminently suited for book work.

JOB FILE. A collection of SEARCH RECORDS (*q.v.*). The record of the results of the enquiries may be kept separately from the search records. In either case they serve as a record of information and may save searching on a subsequent occasion when the enquiry is repeated.

JOB PRESS. A small platen printing press which is used for producing small items such as handbills.

JOB PRINTER. One who prints small items such as labels, leaflets, forms, stationery, handbills, etc., in small quantities.

JOBBER. In America, a wholesale bookseller who stocks many copies of various kinds of books issued by different publishers and supplies them to retailers and libraries. There are two types of jobber (1) those who stock mainly current text-books, trade, and technical books, and (2) those who stock only remainders.

JOHN CARTER BROWN LIBRARY. *See* BROWN LIBRARY, JOHN CARTER.

JOHN HARRIS AWARD. *See* HARRIS AWARD, JOHN.

JOHN NEWBERY MEDAL. *See* NEWBERY MEDAL, JOHN.

JOINED HAND. Handwriting in which the letters are all joined to one another. The opposite of DISJOINED HAND (*q.v.*).

JOINER'S PRESS. The name given to the earliest hand printing presses which were introduced about 1440. Made of wood, they were similar to wine presses, the pressure needed to press the paper on to type being applied by means of a screw turning on to a flat platen.

JOINT. 1. One of the two parts of the covering material that bend when the covers of a book are opened. 2. The strips of cloth, leather or other material that are used to reinforce the end-papers. 3. The grooves, formed by the backing process, which are made to receive the boards when binding a book. *See also* HINGE.

JOINT AUTHOR. One who writes in collaboration with another, or several other writers. The parts written by each are not always indicated; in fact, the contribution of each is usually not distinguishable.

JOINT AUTHORSHIP. (*Cataloguing*) Describes the authorship of books in which two or more persons collaborate, the parts written by each not being specified.

JOINT BOARD. Two or more library authorities which are authorized by an order of the Secretary of State made after consultation, and with the agreement of the authorities concerned, to be a library authority and provide a library service covering the areas of the separate library authorities before the formation of the joint board. Provision for their formation is made in Section 5 of the Public Libraries and Museums Act, 1964. *See also* LIBRARY AREA, LIBRARY AUTHORITY, Appendix 3.

JOINT CATALOGUE. One containing entries for the books in two or more libraries.

JOINT COMMITTEE. A committee composed of representatives of two authorities and possibly co-opted members, which administers one or more libraries serving both areas. The committee has such of the powers of a library authority, except that of borrowing money, as the two authorities agree to confer upon it.

JOINT CODE. The popular name for the code of cataloguing rules prepared by a joint committee of the British and American library associations. *See also* ANGLO-AMERICAN CODE.

JOINT FICTION RESERVE. A scheme whereby a number of libraries agree to hold novels permanently. The authors are allocated according to alphabetical sequence amongst the co-operating libraries by agreement. The first scheme of this kind was started in Metropolitan London and included the keeping of all copies which were redundant in Metropolitan libraries as well as buying all new titles by the allocated authors. A similar scheme was adopted in the Northern Regional Bureau and on 1st January 1962 a National Joint Fiction Reserve scheme (abbreviated NJFR) which is a co-operative effort of all regional bureaux outside London and the South-Eastern began to operate. Each region is responsible for a certain section of the alphabet. This scheme provides only for the purchase and retention of new publications and is not retrospective. Allocation by author amongst the regions is as follows:

A–C	North-Western	K–M	West Midlands
D–F	Northern	N–S	Yorkshire
G–J	East Midlands	T–Z	South-Western

See also ASSOCIATION OF METROPOLITAN CHIEF LIBRARIANS.

JOINT REPORT.   Familiar name for *School libraries in post-war reconstruction: a joint report* published in 1945.   It was the result of co-operation between the School Library Association and the School Libraries Section of the Library Association. This section ceased to exist in 1945 in order to make possible a single association for school librarians.

JOINT WORK.   A work by two or more authors in which the individual contributions are not distinguishable (*IFLA*).

JOSEPH W. LIPPINCOTT AWARD.   *See* LIPPINCOTT AWARD, JOSEPH W.

JOURNAL.   1. A newspaper or periodical. Particularly a periodical issued by a society or institution and containing news, proceedings, transactions and reports of work carried out in a particular field. 2. A record of a person's activities day by day.

JOURNALESE.   Words and phrases commonly used by journalists. Hackneyed phrases.

JOURNALISM.   The profession of compiling, writing for and editing newspapers, periodicals, etc.

JOURNALIST.   One who edits or contributes to a newspaper or periodical.

JOURNALS OF THE HOUSE OF COMMONS and of the HOUSE OF LORDS.   *See* PARLIAMENTARY PAPERS.

JUDICIAL WRIT.   One issuing from a Court of Law.

JUMBLED TYPE.   *Synonymous with* PIE (*q.v.*).

JUNIOR ASSISTANT.   A young assistant librarian who does not supervise the work of other assistants.

JUNIOR BOOK.   A book for children.

JUNIOR DEPARTMENT.   *Synonymous with* JUNIOR LIBRARY and CHILDREN'S LIBRARY (*q.v.*).

JUNIOR LIBRARIAN.   One who works with children, or in a children's library.

JUNIOR LIBRARY.   *Synonymous with* CHILDREN'S LIBRARY (*q.v.*).

JUSTIFICATION.   (*Cataloguing*) The provision of data, especially in the form of a note, introduced into an added entry, cross-reference, or subject heading for the sole purpose of making clear why the particular entry was provided. An entry treated in this way is said to be justified.

JUSTIFYING. (*Printing*) In typesetting, equally spacing out words to a given measure, so that each line will be of the same length.

JUSTOWRITER.   The trade name for an American machine for composing typewriter characters. Two electrically-driven machines are used, each having a typewriter keyboard. As words are typed on paper on the first machine, a moving tape is punched with a code for each character and the spacing needed to justify each line. When this tape is run through the second machine, interpretation of the punched code produces automatically typed and justified lines. The finished and corrected page is suitable for reproduction by photo offset or photogravure.

JUTE.   A plant which contains weaker and less durable fibres than flax or hemp. and which are somewhat easily rotted by water. Jute paper was originally made from old rope, burlap, jute or manilla clippings, but is now usually made from sulphite stock (woodpulp used for making kraft paper) and is the material from which heavy wrapping paper and large bags for such materials as cement, coal and potatoes are made. 'Jute tissue' is made from old sacks and similar material and is used for tailors' patterns.

JUTE BOARD.   A strong, light-weight board, made from jute fibres, and used for binding books.

JUVENILE BOOK.   Trade name, now rarely used, for a book for children.

JUVENILE DEPARTMENT.   *Synonymous with* CHILDREN'S LIBRARY (*q.v.*).

JUVENILE LIBRARY.   *Synonymous with* CHILDREN'S LIBRARY (*q.v*).

K.C.   Stands for the Kyle Classification, the familar name of the CLASSIFICATION FOR SOCIAL SCIENCES (*q.v.*) compiled by Barbara Kyle.

KAISER INDEX.   *See* KAISER'S SYSTEM.

KAISER'S SYSTEM.   A method of subject indexing propounded by J. Kaiser in his *Systematic indexing*, 1911. He emphasized that subject indexing policy must be entirely guided by the purpose for which the collection of documents had been formed. In determining subject headings, classificatory order has been introduced into the dictionary arrangement.

KALVAR.   A dry copying process in which Kalvar materials are used in paper and film. It is used for the duplication of microfilm; being speedy in exposure and development it is the most conveniently processed commercially available film, and has great possibilities of further development and application. It uses a non-silver emulsion, has some characteristics similar to diazo, and does not require the wet processing or washing stages.

KARD-A-FILM. Trade name for a Remington Rand system for filing strips of roll film. Slotted cards in three sizes have translucent protectors into which two or three strips of 16 mm or 35 mm film may be placed.

KATE GREENAWAY MEDAL. An award, made by the Library Association annually with the intention of recognizing the importance of illustrations in children's books, to the artist who in the opinion of the Library Association has produced the most distinguished work in the illustration of children's books during the year preceding the award. The work must have been originally published in the United Kingdom. It was first awarded in 1956 to Edward Ardizonne for *Tim all alone*. A list of books awarded the medal is published in the Library Association *Year book*.

KEEP DOWN. (*Printing*) To use capitals sparingly.

KEEP IN. (*Printing*) 1. To set matter closely so that it does not take up more space than necessary. 2. Type matter with narrow openings between the words. *See also* DRIVE OUT.

KEEP OUT. (*Printing*) To set matter widely spaced so that it takes up as many lines as possible.

KEEP STANDING. An order not to distribute the type after running off, pending possible reprinting.

KEEP UP. (*Printing*) To use capitals freely, even promiscuously.

KEEPSAKE. 1. A lavishly printed and ornately bound gift book, often consisting of poetry; many such books were issued annually in the first half of the nineteenth century. 2. Printed commemorative publications issued by clubs or other organizations for special occasions. 3. Before the end of the seventeenth century it was the custom in some English printing establishments to honour visitors by printing their names and the date in an ornamental style – usually in a framework of flowers and rules – and present it to them as a memento. The guest witnessed the setting of the type and pulled the press. The practice became more general during the eighteenth century but declined in the last quarter; it was reserved for distinguished persons in the nineteenth century, for the most exalted of whom the printing was done on silk or satin.

KELLS, BOOK OF. An illuminated MS. of the Latin Gospels, found in the ruins of the Abbey of Kells, Ireland, and thought to date from the eighth or early ninth century. It has been in the Library of Trinity College, Dublin, since 1661. It is an important example of Hiberno-Saxon art.

KELMSCOTT PRESS. A private press founded and directed by William Morris between 1891 and his death in 1896, although the Press continued until 1898. The three founts of type used (Golden, 1890; Troy, 1891; Chaucer, 1892) were designed by Morris and cut by E. P. Prince in the years stated but not used until 1892. The books issued were excellent examples of book production. The Golden Type face was named after Caxton's *Golden Legend* in which it was to have been used first. It was, however, first used in 1891, and for six books, before the *Golden Legend* was printed in 1892. *See also* JENSON.

KEPT BOOK. *Synonymous with* RESERVED BOOK (*q.v.*).

KERFS. Shallow saw-cuts, about $\frac{1}{32}$ inch deep, made between $\frac{1}{4}$ and $\frac{1}{2}$ inch from the ends of the gathered sections of a book. The loops of the kettle stitches formed by the sewing of the sections, or the cords, fit snugly into the kerfs and leave the back of the sewn sections smooth.

KERN. (*Printing*) Any part of the face of a type letter which extends over the edge of the body and rests on the shoulder of the type adjacent to it, as fi, fl.

KERNED. Said of a type letter which has part of the face projecting beyond the metal body on which it is cast.

KETTLE STITCH. The stitch made at the head and tail of a book in hand sewing, by which the thread of one section is fastened to the thread of the one on each side. The term is frequently regarded as being a corruption of 'catch up stitch', but it may be derived from the German *Ketten-stich* (chain stitch) or *Kettel stich*, (the stitch that forms a little chain). Also called 'Catch stitch'.

KEY. 1. The block or forme in letterpress printing, and the plate or stone in lithography, which acts as a guide for position and registration of the other colours. Also called KEY PLATE (*q.v.*). 2. A binder's tool for securing the bands when sewing.

KEY PLATE. 1. The plate of maximum detail in a set of colour plates to which other plates in the same set are registered during the printing process. 2. Any printing plate that is used to get others into register. Also called KEY (*q.v.*)

KEY TERM. *Synonymous with* KEYWORD (*q.v.*).

KEYBOARDING. Producing type, proofs, tape or film by manual operation of a keyboard machine.

KEYPUNCH. A manually operated mechanical device which punches holes in pre-determined positions to record information on punched cards used with an electric accounting machine system. The punching of such holes is called 'keypunching'. The checking of the correctness of such punching is performed on a machine known as a Keyverifier.

KEYS, LIBRARY. *See* LIBRARY KEYS.

KEYSORT. Trade name for a manual system of recording information in connexion with information retrieval; it consists of EDGE-NOTCHED CARDS (*q.v.*).

KEYVERIFIER. *See* KEYPUNCH.

KEYWORD. (*Information retrieval*) Grammatical element which conveys the significant meaning in a document. Word indicating a subject discussed in a document (*IBM*). *See also* CATCHWORD.

KEY-WORD-IN-CONTEXT. *See* KWIC.

KEY-WORD-OUT-OF-CONTEXT. *See* KWOC.

KIER. The part of paper-making machinery used to boil the raw material (rags, esparto, etc.) especially under steam pressure. Also called 'Boiler'.

KILL. (*Printing*) Direction to the printer to melt down, or distribute, composed type matter which is no longer wanted. *See also* DEAD MATTER, LIVE MATTER.

KILLING. (*Printing*) Distributing set-up type after use so that it may be used again.

KINDERBOX. A box about 2 feet square and 8 inches deep, divided into four compartments and standing on short legs. It holds large-page books for young children and is placed in an adult lending library or a children's lending library. Called in the U.S.A. a 'Cart'. Some models accommodate larger books upright in narrow divisions below the floor of the box proper, i.e. at floor level.

KING REPORT. The report of a committee of which Dr. Gilbert W. King was chairman, set up in 1961 to survey the application of automatic devices to the work of the Library of Congress and other general research libraries. It specifically contemplates (a) that L. of C. catalogues may be so mechanized that they can be consulted electronically on viewing screens subject to the viewers' complete manipulation; (b) that the collections to which the catalogues refer will be so mechanized through photographic or electronic micro-reproduction as to place them within the individual user's electronic control. The Report *Automation and the Library of Congress: a survey sponsored by the Council on Library Resources, Inc.* was published in January 1964.

KIRKUS SERVICE, THE. A periodical, started in January 1933 as *The New York Office* and known by several titles until the present one was adopted in 1967, containing book reviews which often appear before the books are published. It was originally designed to furnish advice to booksellers but is now aimed primarily at librarians.

KLISCHOGRAPH. A German electronic photoengraving machine for producing plastic, zinc, copper or magnesium half-tone plates. The original to be reproduced is placed face down on a glass plate on a table and a blank plate, face up, placed above it and clamped into position. A scanner under the table picks up reflected light by means of two electric cells and transmits impulses through amplifiers to the engraving head above the plate and thence to the V-shaped engraving needle which digs dots of a size and depth varying in relation to the brightness of the original. The engraving head is stationary, the plate and original being reciprocated under it, the scanner returning to its position as each line is completed ready for the next line. Blocks can be engraved for monochrome and for three- and four-colour printing. The machine was invented by Dr. Rudolph Hell of Kiel and is also known in Great Britain as the 'Clichograph'.

KNAPP FOUNDATION. The Knapp Foundation of North Carolina, Inc. and the Knapp Foundation of New York were established in 1929 by the late Joseph Palmer Knapp, prominent business leader, publisher, and for 50 years a director of the Metropolitan Life Insurance Company. These foundations have contributed substantial sums for many studies and projects for the advancement of health, welfare and education in America.

KNAPP SCHOOL LIBRARIES PROJECT. A demonstration project which was funded with a grant of $1,130,000 from the Knapp Foundation, Inc. It was in operation from 1st March 1963 until 29th February 1968 and had as its objects: (1) to demonstrate the educational value of school library programmes, services, and resources which fully meet the national standards for school libraries; (2) to promote improved understanding and use of library resources on the part of teachers and administrators, by relating the demonstration situations to teacher education programmes in nearby colleges; (3) to guide and encourage citizens, from as many communities as possible, in the development of their own library programmes through planned activities enabling them to study demonstration situations; (4) to increase interest and support for school library development among educators and citizens generally, by disseminating information about the demonstration programmes and evaluating their effectiveness in reaching the stated goals. The Project was organized and directed by the American Association of School Librarians, a Division of the American Library Association. In November 1967 the Foundation made the sum of $1,163,718 available for a second five-year project called the School Library Manpower Project; this 'is designed to attack three aspects of the problem of developing fully and using properly school library manpower – task and job analysis, education for school librarianship and recruitment from specific manpower pools'.

KNIFE-FOLDER. A folding machine which has a blunt-edged knife parallel with and above the slot formed by two parallel and constantly revolving rollers. When a sheet of paper is placed above these with an edge against a stop the knife descends and presses the sheet between the rollers which carry it away, the fold being made where the knife made contact. *See also* BUCKLE-FOLDER.

KNOWLEDGE CLASSIFICATION. A classification used for any branch of knowledge, but which cannot be adapted for classifying books until a generalia class, form classes and divisions, a notation, and an index have been added.

KODAGRAPH. Trade name for an Eastman Kodax reader designed to take micro-opaques up to $14 \times 8\frac{1}{2}$ inches. It has a green filter on the surface of the reading screen to prevent reflections.

KOREAN LIBRARY ASSOCIATION. Founded on 16th April 1955 to contribute to cultural advancement and social improvement in Korea by accelerating the spread of libraries and the betterment of the library service. Its objects are: to study the principles of library organization and administration; to publish books and other materials about library services; to train library personnel and improve their working conditions; to provide guidance to any individual or organization in planning a library; to prepare selected lists of Korean books; to activate the national reading movement; to devise specifications for standard library furniture and equipment; to organize and operate a professional reference library; to co-operate with international organizations concerned with library services. Membership is open to libraries and also to individuals who have acquired more than eighteen academic credits in library science. Abbreviated KLA. Publishes *KLA Bulletin* (m.).

KRAFT PAPER. A strong calendered brown paper of medium colour and with prominent chain-lines (*see* LAID PAPER) used specially for wrapping purposes. It is sometimes strengthened with hessian or tar to make waterproof wrapping paper of great strength. *See also* BLEACHED KRAFT.

KRAFT ROTACOL. *See* ROTARY CARD FILE.

KURSIV. *See* CURSIVE.

KWIC. Abbreviation for Key-Word-in-Context. 1. A method of PERMUTATION INDEXING (*q.v.*) which relies on mechanical means for selecting the terms. It was developed by Mr. H. P. Luhn of International Business Machines, and uses a computer to permute automatically words in periodical article titles, and to group titles in which the same words occur. An example of this kind of index is *Chemical Titles* published by the American Chemical Society since 5th January 1961. The system consists of a thesaurus of key words and associated words, coded and put on punched cards that operate a computer searching a magnetic tape. When search keywords and coded tape match, the computer prints out the keyword and the words following it, and the number of the document. When the index is printed, the keywords in each index line are printed at the middle of the type measure and thus, with a double space preceding each, appear under one another in alphabetical order in a column. The full measure of the line is filled by printing as much of the title immediately before and after the keyword as can be accommodated. 2. A listing, usually of titles, or significant sentences from an abstract, with the keywords put in a fixed position within the title or sentence and arranged in alphabetic order in a column (*IBM*). 3. An index based on the cyclic permutation of words; each 'substantive' term being brought to a predetermined position and alphabetized. *See also* CO-ORDINATE INDEXING, KWOC, WADEX.

KWOC. Abbreviation for Key-Word-Out-of-Context, a refinement of KWIC (*q.v.*). Titles are printed in full under as many Key-Words as the indexer considers useful; these may be chosen from a thesaurus or list of standard headings as well as from the title, and there is no limit to the source of Key-Words. The Key-Words are separated from the title on a line of their own and act as subject headings. If the title is itself amended to give a concise but clear indication of the item's subject content it becomes a NOC (Notation of Content). *See also* WADEX.

KYLE CLASSIFICATION. *See* CLASSIFICATION FOR SOCIAL SCIENCES.

l.c. Abbreviation for lower case. *See* LOWER CASE LETTERS.

l.p. Abbreviation for LARGE PAPER COPY or EDITION (*q.v.*).

L.S. Abbreviation for LIBRARY SCHOOL (*q.v.*).

L.S. *See* LOCUS SIGILLI *and* A.L.S.

LABEL. A small strip of leather, usually of a different colour to that used for the binding of a book, placed on the spine and displaying one or more of the following: title, author's name, volume number, date. Also called 'Lettering pieces'. When two labels are used they are described as 'double lettering pieces'. Labels of paper were used on books bound in boards covered with paper.

LABEL TITLE-PAGE. The title and author's name printed near the top of an otherwise blank page, or protecting leaf, at the beginning of a book. Often called 'label title', the name is given to the first form of title-page in early printed books (1470–1550). The earliest extant example is a Papal Bull of Pius II, printed in 1463 at Mainz, probably by Fust and Schöffer.

LABORATORY COLLECTION. *Synonymous with* DEPARTMENTAL LIBRARY (*q.v.*).

LACAP. Acronym for Latin America Co-operative Acquisitions Program. Organized in 1960 as a result of the extension of the FARMINGTON PLAN (*q.v.*) to Latin America and the organization of the SALALM (*q.v.*) which recommended its formation; it is a co-operative enterprise that provides its participants with a steady flow of the printed materials currently published in all the countries of Latin America. The University of Texas, the New York Public Library and Stechert-Hafner Inc. were the initiators of the scheme which was first called a 'Project'.

LACE BORDER. *See* LACEWORK 2.

LACED ON. *See* LACING-IN.

LACEWORK. 1. A border decoration on bindings, done by tooling, to represent lace. *See also* DENTELLE. 2. Borders framing whole-page illustrations in nineteenth-century French books, the border-decoration consisting of punching the pattern out of the paper as in paper doyleys.

LACING-IN. (*Binding*) Attaching the boards by the operation of passing the slips or cords on which the book is sewn, and after they have been splayed out and moistened with paste, through holes pierced in the boards.

LACUNA (*Pl.* LACUNAE). Gaps in the stock of a library, which await filling.

LADSIRLAC. Abbreviation for Liverpool and District Scientific, Industrial and Research Library Advisory Council which was sponsored by the Liverpool City Council in 1955 in order to give extra-mural services to industry over and above the normal services offered through public, technical and special libraries. Membership is by payment of an annual subscription. In 1962 LADSIRLAC, in association with the Department of Scientific and Industrial Research and the Liverpool City Council, inaugurated a Technical Information Centre, the cost of which was met by DSIR and local industry: this deals with production enquiries and provides (a) liaison between local industry and research associations, and (b) technical information. LADSIRLAC also provides Industrial Library Services which are separately financed jointly by the Liverpool City Council and local industry: these comprise postal borrowing services, literature searches, a technical information bulletin and a translations advisory service.

LAID IN. Used in a note to a catalogue entry to indicate the inclusion in a gramophone record album or musical publication, of a leaflet or pamphlet relating to the music and its performance. *See also* ANALYTICAL BOOKLET.

LAID PAPER. Paper which, when held up to the light, shows thick and thin lines at right angles. They are caused by the weave of the dandy roll, or in hand-made paper by the mould having long thin wires placed very close together and fastened to thicker ones at intervals of about one inch. The horizontal thin ones are called 'wire-lines' or 'wire-marks' and the vertical thick ones 'chain-lines', 'chain-marks' or 'wide-lines'. To obtain the best impression when printing, the wire-lines should run across the page and the chain-lines down it.

LAMBSKIN. A bookbinding leather with a smooth finish; it is similar in appearance to calf but less durable.

LAMINATED. A sheet of paper to which a sheet of clear plastic has been permanently adhered on one or both sides. Book jackets, leaves of books, or paper covers are treated in this way to give them increased durability.

LAMINATION. A method of preserving frail papers or the thin or perishing leaves of books by placing them between two sheets of thin transparent thermo-plastic material which when subjected to heat under pressure protects the paper by making it impervious to atmospheric conditions. *See also* SILKING.

LAMPBLACK. Pure carbon deposit; formerly the most important black pigment used in manufacturing printing inks. It was produced by burning pitch resin in a vessel in a tent made of paper or sheepskins. The smoke was deposited on the inside of the tent which was then beaten to cause the black to fall on to the floor. Impurities were removed by heating it several times until red-hot in an iron box with a small aperture at the top.

LAMPOON. A satirical attack generally of a scurrilous but humorous character, upon a person, and written in prose or verse.

LAND UTILIZATION SURVEY OF BRITAIN. Maps, the publication of which began in 1933, based on, and showing everything which appears on, the fourth edition of the 'Popular' series of Ordnance Survey maps, but showing in addition in contrasting colours the use to which land is put.

LANDSCAPE. *Synonymous with* OBLONG (*q.v.*).

LANDSCAPE BINDING.   A type of binding which has landscape views on its covers, the landscape views being drawn freehand with Indian ink or acid and later coloured, or printed by some means. They date between 1777 and 1821.

LANGUAGE NUMBER.   A facet which may form part of a BOOK NUMBER (*q.v.*) in the Colon Classification. It is obtained by translating the name of the language in which the book is written into appropriate symbols in accordance with the language schedule given in Chapter 5 of the Schedules. *See also* ETHNIC NUMBERS.

LANGUAGE OF THE TEXT.   The language in which the text of a book is printed and which is not determinable from the title, e.g. *Faust*. In such a case the cataloguer may (1) add a note, e.g. 'Text in German and English'; (2) integrate a translator statement, e.g. 'Tr. into English by . . .'; (3) augment the heading, e.g. 'Goethe, Johann Wolfgang von. Faust. English.'

LANGUAGE SUB-DIVISION.   (*Classification*) Sub-division of a subject according to the language in which it is written, or sub-division of a language division in the philological class of a scheme of classification.

LANSTON.   *See* MONOTYPE.

LAP SPLICE.   *See* SPLICE.

LAPIDARY TYPE.   A fount of capital letters similar to those on Roman monumental inscriptions. Examples were cut by Erhard Ratdolt at Augsburg in 1505. *See also* SQUARE CAPITALS.

LARC ASSOCIATION.   A non-profit-making association formed in the U.S.A. early in 1969 to advance library automation.

LARGE FOLIO.   A general term to indicate a large-sized folio book. *See also* FOLIO 3.

LARGE PAPER COPY, or EDITION.   An impression of a book printed on larger and better quality paper than the usual trade edition, thus having wider margins. *See also* FINE PAPER COPY, LIMITED EDITION, SMALL PAPER COPY.

LARGE POST.   A sheet of printing paper measuring $16\frac{1}{2} \times 21$ inches.

LARGE ROYAL.   A sheet of printing paper measuring 20×27 inches.

LAST FOLD.   *See* BOLT.

LATER CURSIVE.   A Latin manuscript handwriting which came in sequence between UNCIAL and HALF UNCIAL (*qq.v.*). Its main characteristics are ligatures (joined letters) and the uneven height of the letters, some of which ascended or descended beyond the normal letter limits – which had not previously occurred. This distinction between tall and small letters marked the first stage in the development of minuscules (lower-case letters).

LATERAL FILING. Equipment which consists of pockets of tough paper, or linen, which are suspended (and usually move laterally within limits) from two rails placed one behind the other and running from left to right. They are made into fittings which will rest on shelves or as a complete filing cabinet the size of a book TIER (*q.v.*). The pockets usually have caption or heading holders on them, and there being no fronts or covers, the contents are immediately accessible. Filing capacity is much greater per cubic foot than in any other form of filing, whether vertical or in boxes on shelves. The specially-made cabinets have cupboard doors, roller, or spring blind fronts to keep out dust and provide security.

LATERALLY REVERSED. In documentary copying, reflecting the original as in a mirror. Also called 'Left-to-right-reversed'.

LATTICE. (*Information retrieval*) The network of inter-relationships between specific subjects (*IBM*). A partially ordered system in which any two elements have a greatest lower bound and a least upper bound. *See also* BOUND.

LATTICE STAMP. (*Binding*) A decorative ornament, the distinguishing feature of which is a central diamond formed of lattice or crisscross work.

LAURA INGALLS WILDER MEDAL. *See* WILDER MEDAL, LAURA INGALLS.

LAW BINDING. *See* LAW CALF.

LAW BOOKS, U.S.A. *See* BOOKS, U.S.A., INC.

LAW CALF. A leather binding using plain uncoloured calf or sheepskin. Mainly used for law books but now largely superseded by buckram cloth. Also called 'Fair calf', 'Law sheep'.

LAW OF SCATTERING. A 'law' deduced by Dr. S. C. Bradford (and later corrected by B. C. Vickery) who found that about a third of the articles on a subject are printed in the journals devoted to that subject, a further third appear in a larger number of journals devoted to related subjects, and the remaining third in an even larger number of journals in which such articles would not normally be expected to be published. According to the law of scattering, if Tx represents the number of journals having x references, T_{2x} the total number of journals having $2x$ references, and T_{3x} the total number of journals having $3x$ references, etc., then: $Tx : T_{2x} : T_{3x} = 1 : n : n^2$ where n may be any number depending on the value chosen for x.

LAW SHEEP. *Synonymous with* LAW CALF (*q.v.*).

LAY EDGES. The edges of a sheet of paper which are laid against the front and side lay gauges of a printing or folding machine. The front edge is known as the 'gripper edge'.

LAYOUT. 1. A plan, prepared for or by a printer, to show the arrangement of the matter, type faces, sizes of type, position of illustrations and captions, for a piece of printing. 2. The plan of an entire book.

LAYSTOOL. A stool on which white paper and printed sheets were laid close to the printing pressman's hand. By the nineteenth century a 'horse' with a sloping top had been evolved to take the paper and make it easier to pick sheets off the heap.

LE GASCON STYLE. Modified FANFARE bindings of the early seventeenth century, in which the strapwork is retained, the enclosed spaces differentiated by inlaid leather of different colours, and the sprays lighter. Fine dotted scrolls are frequently enclosed in the geometrical compartments and often extended into lines and curves of remarkable lustre and elegance. These scrolls and other ornaments are given dotted lines known as pointillé, instead of unbroken lines. Not practised after about 1660.

LEAD, TO. To insert leads between type or re-set on a larger body. A page of printed matter where the lines are well spaced out is said to be 'well leaded'.

LEAD MOULDING. A process for making electros or half-tone plates in which the base is lead instead of wax. Soft lead is forced into the forme under great (hydraulic) pressure and a mould of fine quality obtained. A copper shell is then deposited on the mould in the same manner as in wax moulding.

LEADED MATTER. (*Printing*) Having the lines of type separated by 'leads', or cast on a larger body, as 8 pt. type on 9 pt. body, to achieve the same effect. In the latter case, the type is called 'Long-bodied'. Type without 'leads' is said to be 'set solid'. 'Double-leaded' means a double space (usually 4 points) between lines of type. *See also* EM, PICA.

LEADER. 1. A short newspaper article expressing views or comments rather than (but often based on) news, and usually indicating the policy or editorial views of the proprietors of the paper. Fully, a leading article. 2. A portion of film at the beginning of a roll of film, and which is used for the threading of the film in a camera, processing machine, or projector.

LEADER WRITER. The writer of newspaper editorials, or leaders.

LEADERETTE. A short editorial article in a newspaper or periodical.

LEADERS. A sequence of dots or hyphens to lead the eye from one word to another as in tabular work, or across a page as in a table of contents.

LEADING LINE.   The top horizontal line on a standard ruled catalogue card; the one on which the author heading is entered.

LEADS.   Thin strips of lead which are less than type high, used to separate lines of type or to space them further apart. Type set on a larger body, such as 8 point on a 9 point body to give the same effect without the use of separate leads between each line, is called *long-bodied type*. Leads are usually made 1, 1$\frac{1}{2}$ (thin), 2 (middle), 3 (thick), and 4 points thick; when 6 and 12 point or more they are called 'clumps' and may be made of wood or metal. When clumps are made of wood they are called 'reglets'. Spacing material of greater dimensions than 18 point is known as 'furniture'.

LEAF.   A sheet of paper, printed, and folded once forms a section of two leaves or four pages, and is called folio; folded twice, it forms a section of four leaves or eight pages and is called quarto. A leaf consists of two pages, one on each side, either of which may or may not be printed on. Usually the recto has an odd number, and the verso the subsequent number, but in reprints this may not be the case. Books with un-numbered leaves or pages may be described in a catalogue or biblio-graphical entry as containing a specific number (ascertained by count-ing) of pages or leaves – preferably the latter if the book was published before pagination was general – in the form '320 l'. *See also* FOLDINGS, FOLIATION, SECTION.

LEAFLET.   A small sheet of paper folded once and printed on to make two to four pages following in the same sequence as in a book, but not stitched or bound. Often used to indicate a small, thin PAMPHLET (*q.v.*).

LEAN-FACE TYPE.   Type, the stems and other strokes of which have not their full width.

LEAN MATTER.   *See* MATTER.

LEARNING RESOURCES CENTER.   Sometimes used in America in the late 1960s for a school library. Also called 'Instructional Materials Center'.

LEATHER.   The cured and dyed hide of goat, pig or sheep. Used exten-sively for binding books.

LEATHER BOUND.   A book bound in leather, either FULL, HALF, QUARTER, or THREE-QUARTER (*qq.v.*).

LEATHER JOINTS.   Leather inner joints affixed (usually stuck in but sometimes sewn) to the endpapers of large hand-bound books to give greater strength. They were occasionally used in the seventeenth century in Europe; between 1750 and 1800 they were a fairly common feature of the best English morocco and russia bindings, and were usually heavily decorated with fillets, rolls and small tools.

LEATHERCLOTH. A fabric or plastic material which has been finished to simulate leather.

LEATHERETTE.   Paper or cloth having a surface in imitation of leather.

LECTERN.   A sloped woodern ledge on which books were laid flat and chained, and at which they were consulted, in mediaeval libraries.

LECTURE SCRIPT.   The text of a lecture.

LECTURE SERIES.   The name given to a series of lectures delivered in connexion with lecture trusts such as the Bampton, Gifford, or Hibbert, and afterwards published.

LEDGER CATALOGUE.   *Synonymous with* PAGE CATALOGUE (*q.v.*).

LEDGER CHARGING.   An antiquated method of recording books on loan by entering book-numbers against names or ticket numbers in adjacent vertical columns on loose sheets or in a bound ledger.

LEDGER WEIGHT.   (*Reprography*) Photographic paper of moderately heavy weight; used when greater body and mechanical durability are required. 'Duplex ledger' is coated on both sides for reproducing books; the paper used may have a wood, fibre or rag (linen ledger) base.

LEFT-TO-RIGHT REVERSED.   *Synonymous with* LATERALLY REVERSED (*q.v.*).

LEGAL DEPOSIT.   A method whereby certain libraries are entitled by law to receive one or more copies of every book or other publication which is printed or published in the country. Under English law the publisher must deliver to the British Museum within one month of publication, a copy of every book published, and the expression 'book' includes every part or division of a book, pamphlet, sheet of letterpress, sheet of music, map, plan, chart or table separately published, but not second and subsequent editions unless these contain additions or alterations in the letterpress or in the maps, prints or engravings. A copy must also be sent if requested in writing to the libraries of the universities of Oxford and Cambridge, to Trinity College, Dublin, to the National Library of Scotland (but law books to the Faculty of Advocates Library) and to the National Library of Wales (with certain classes of books excepted). Also called 'Copyright deposit', 'Copytax'. *See also* COPYRIGHT LIBRARY.

LEGAL FILE.   A collection of material relating to law cases; it may include briefs, decisions, or histories of cases.

LEGEND.   1. The title or short description printed under an illustration or engraving, or on a coin or medal. Also called 'Caption' and 'Cut-line'. 2. An explanation of symbols on a map. 3. A story based on tradition.

LEGISLATION. *See* PUBLIC LIBRARIES ACTS.

LEGISLATIVE HISTORY. A chronological account of the stages through which a particular bill has passed before enactment as a law. This would include all 'readings', committee debates and decisions, and 'floor' debates in both houses. The events leading to the bill, the efforts of organizations concerned in furthering it, any evidence given, and any history subsequent to enactment are also sometimes included.

LEMMA. The argument or subject written at the head of a literary composition.

LEMONNIER STYLE. A style of book decoration practised by Jean Christophe Henri Lemonnier, who worked for Count Hoym in France in the eighteenth century. It is characterized by pictorial mosaics of landscapes, bouquets, etc.

LENDING DEPARTMENT. The department of a library containing books for home-reading. Called a 'Circulation department' in America.

LENDING DESK. *See* CIRCULATION DESK.

LENDING LIBRARY. *Synonymous with* LENDING DEPARTMENT (*q.v.*).

LENSLESS COPYING. A general term for copying methods which do not use a camera. The apparatus used consists of a light-box with a ground-glass screen and pressure pad on top of it. Sensitized paper is placed in the closest possible contact with the original and exposed to light. If the original is translucent and has text on one side only it is placed next the light source with the sensitized surface of the copying paper against the back of the original: the light shines through the white paper of the original but does not pass through the text because the black print absorbs it. After development (which in many makes of copier is done in the copying machine) the result is a readable negative (i.e. white on black) which can be used as if it were a positive. This method is known as *direct copying* and sometimes, inadvisably because all non-camera methods rely on the closest contact between the original and the sensitized paper, as *contact copying*. When the original is opaque with text on both sides the REFLEX COPYING (*q.v.*) method is used, a normal white on black negative with the image in reverse being made. A black on white positive is made from this.

LET-IN NOTE. *Synonymous with* INCUT NOTE (*q.v.*).

LETTER BOOK. A book in which correspondence was copied by some means resulting in a facsimile copy. This was often done by writing the original letter with copying ink, placing it against a dampened sheet of thin paper (leaves of which comprised the book) and applying pressure.

LETTER BY LETTER. *See* ALPHABETIZATION.

LETTER SPACING. The insertion of spaces between the letters of a word or words to lengthen the MEASURE (*q.v.*), improve the appearance of the setting, or in special instances emphasize a word or sentence. This is letterspaced.

LETTER WRITER. 1. One who writes letters for illiterates. 2. A writer who has become famous for the letters he has written and possibly published.

LETTERA FONDA. *See* ANTIQUA.

LETTERED PROOF. The proof of an engraving in which the title and the names of the artist, engraver, printer, etc. are printed under the illustration.

LETTERING. The emplacement of the library CALL NUMBER (*q.v.*) on the spine of a book.

LETTERING ON THE SPINE. When the lettering on the spine of a book or bookjacket does not go across it, the direction may be up or down according to the choice of the publisher with consequent inconvenience to library users. In 1926 the Publishers Association and the Associated Booksellers of Great Britain and Ireland recommended that 'when a volume stands on the shelf the lettering reads from bottom to top', but in 1948 reversed their decision, recommending that the lettering should be downward so that the title can be easily read when the book lies flat, face upward. Librarians tend to prefer the earlier recommendation. *Periodicals of reference value* . . . (B.S. 2509:1959) recommends that the lettering of periodicals should be 'across the spine if the title is short enough; otherwise along the spine in such a way as to be readable when the publication is lying flat with the *front* cover uppermost.'

LETTERING PIECE. A piece of leather secured to the spine of a book to receive its title. *See also* LABEL.

LETTERPRESS. 1. The text of a book as distinguished from its illustrations. 2. Matter printed from type as distinct from plates. 3. A method of relief printing as opposed to intaglio or planographic.

LETTERS CLOSE. Letter addressed usually by the sovereign to some individual or group of individuals and closed with a seal.

LETTERS PATENT. An open letter issued generally under the great seal of the sovereign or some other magnate as a guarantee to the person or corporation named therein.

LETTRE DE BATARDE. *See* GOTHIC TYPE.

LETTRE DE FORME. *See* GOTHIC TYPE.

LETTRE DE SOMME. *See* GOTHIC TYPE.

LETTRE RONDE. *See* ANTIQUA.

LEVANT. A high-grade Morocco leather used for binding books, and made from the skin of the Angora goat.

LEVEL SMALL CAPS. *Synonymous with* EVEN SMALL CAPS (*q.v.*).

LEVER PRESS. Any printing press on which the impression is made by moving a lever, but the term is usually applied to the type of press used for proofing, etc., in which the lever is pulled down.

LEVIGATION. The action of using the LEVIGATOR (*q.v.*).

LEVIGATOR. A heavy steel disc which is rotated by hand over a lithographic stone when preparing its surface, sand and water being used as the abrasive.

LEXICOGRAPHER. The compiler of a dictionary.

LEXICOGRAPHIST. A LEXICOGRAPHER (*q.v.*).

LEXICOGRAPHY. The act, or process, of compiling a dictionary.

LEXICOLOGY. The branch of knowledge which is concerned with words, their history, form and meaning.

LEXICON. A dictionary of the words of a language, the words being arranged in alphabetical order; especially one giving the meaning in another language. It is chiefly applied to a dictionary of Greek, Syriac, Arabic or Hebrew but is also used for encyclopaedias and subject dictionaries.

LIABILITY SLIP. A slip recording the loan of a book for use on the the library premises. It is cancelled, or returned to the reader, when the book is returned.

LIAISON OFFICER. A librarian who carries out duties calling for a personal link between a county librarian and local persons or bodies. The duties may include visiting branches and centres, advising local librarians, training branch staffs, attending local committee meetings, taking charge of branches in emergency, and other tasks calling for the attendance in person of a senior member of the headquarters staff.

LIBERATE ROLL. A record of the writs authorizing delivery of money of out the Treasury. Chancery Liberate are rolls of letters issued, and the Exchequer series rolls of letters received; both are copied from the same originals.

LIBRARIAN. One who has charge of the contents of a library, making the stock and library services available to those who need them or are entitled to them.

LIBRARIAN-IN-CHARGE.　The librarian placed in charge of a particular department.

LIBRARIANSHIP.　The profession of librarian.

LIBRARIES OF NORTH STAFFORDSHIRE IN CO-OPERATION. *See* LINOSCO.

LIBRARII.　Used in mediaeval times to signify scribes.

LIBRARY.　1. A collection of books and other literary material kept for reading, study and consultation. 2. A place, building, room or rooms set apart for the keeping and use of a collection of books, etc. 3. A number of books issued by one publisher under a comprehensive title as the 'Loeb Classical Library', and usually having some general characteristic such as subject, binding, or typography. *See also* BRANCH LIBRARY, CENTRAL LIBRARY, CHILDREN'S LIBRARY, CIRCULATING LIBRARY, COLLEGE LIBRARY, DELIVERY STATION, DEPOSIT LIBRARY, DEPOSITORY LIBRARY, LENDING DEPARTMENT, REFERENCE DEPARTMENT, SCHOOL LIBRARY, SPECIAL LIBRARY, SUBSCRIPTION LIBRARY, UNIVERSITY LIBRARY.

LIBRARY & INFORMATION SCIENCE ABSTRACTS. An extended and enlarged form of LIBRARY SCIENCE ABSTRACTS (*q.v.*), which commenced publication in January 1969 by the Library Association jointly with Aslib. Abbreviated *LISA*. Published bi-monthly.

LIBRARY ACTS.　*See* PUBLIC LIBRARIES ACTS.

LIBRARY ADMINISTRATION.　The administration of a library is the force behind the machinery of its working routine. To oversee the work of a library in all its relations, and to plan for and promote its usefulness, is the work of the library administrator, and it embraces the supervision and development of the work of all departments and the solution of their various problems; library administration must of necessity begin where library organization ends.

LIBRARY ADMINISTRATION DIVISION.　A Division of the American Library Association; it was established in 1957 'to guide and to conduct the activities of the ALA which pertain to library administration in general.' Has five sections. Abbreviated LAD.

LIBRARY ADVISORY COUNCILS.　The formation of national advisory councils, one for England (excluding Monmouthshire) and the other for Wales and Monmouthshire, was provided for by Section 2 of the Public Libraries and Museums Act 1964. It is their duty 'to advise the Secretary of State upon such matters connected with the provision or use of library facilities whether under this Act or otherwise as they think fit, and upon any questions referred to them by him.' The Secretary of State appoints the members of the councils, their chairmen, and an officer of the Department of Education and Science as Secretary. *See also* LIBRARY AUTHORITY, LIBRARY REGION, APPENDIX 3.

LIBRARY AGREEMENT. *See* NET BOOK AGREEMENT.

LIBRARY AREA. The administrative area of a local authority acting as a library authority under the Public Libraries and Museums Act 1964: the administrative area of the authority, or, in the case of (a) a county council, so much of its administrative area as excludes the library area of any other library authority, (b) a joint board established under s.5 of the Act, the areas which, if the authorities constituting the board were library authorities, would form their library areas (s.4). *See also* JOINT BOARD, LIBRARY AUTHORITY.

LIBRARY ASSISTANTS' ASSOCIATION. *See* ASSOCIATION OF ASSISTANT LIBRARIANS.

LIBRARY ASSOCIATION. The British professional association for the examination and certification of librarians, for the regulation of the profession of librarianship, for the promotion of the better administration of libraries and the encouragement of bibliographical study and research and for the accumulation and dissemination of information concerning libraries. It was founded as the Library Association of the United Kingdom on 5 October 1877 at the conclusion of the First International Conference of Librarians, which was held at Brussels from 2–5 October under the presidency of Mr. John Winter Jones, the joint secretaries being E. W. B. Nicholson and H. R. Tedder. The *American Library Journal* was adopted as the official journal, the word 'American' being dropped. Publication of the *Monthly Notes* was commenced on 15 January 1880 and *The Library* was adopted as the official journal on 10 December 1880. On 30 January 1896 the name of the Association was changed to The Library Association, and the Association was granted its Royal Charter on 17 February 1898. The *Library Association Record* commenced publication as the official journal of the Association in January 1899. It became a wholly professional association in 1962 when new bye-laws came into operation. Members are automatically allocated to membership of one of twelve Branches according to their place of residence, and may become members of two Groups (more by paying a small annual subscription for each); the latter exist to further particular aspects of librarianship. The Association is controlled by a Council elected by the members. The Association's motto is *Ingenia hominum res publica* (The thoughts of men are the common wealth). Abbreviated LA. Publishes *British Humanities Index* (q.), *British Technology Index* (m.), *Journal of*

Librarianship (q.), *Library Association Record* (m.), *Proceedings of the Annual Conference* (a.), books, pamphlets and booklists. Some of the groups and branches publish conference reports, a periodical and occasional reports and papers.

LIBRARY ASSOCIATION OF AUSTRALIA. Founded in 1949, being re-constituted from the Australian Institute of Librarians which had been founded in 1937. A Royal Charter of Incorporation was granted by Her Majesty the Queen on 29 January 1963; in this the objects of the Association are expressed as: '(a) to promote, establish and improve libraries and library services; (b) to improve the standard of librarianship and the status of the library profession; (c) to promote the association for the foregoing objects of persons engaged in or interested in libraries or library services'. The Association conducts examinations in librarianship and in archive administration, and confers on members proficient in librarianship the distinction of Fellow ('FLAA') or Associate ('ALAA') of the Library Association of Australia. The Association has Branches in the Australian States and Territories, and Sections devoted to special fields of library work. The Sections may have Divisions in each State and in the Australian Capital Territory. The following sections have been formed: Archives, Children's Libraries, Public Libraries, Special Libraries, University and College Libraries. Institutions engaged or interested in libraries or library services may become members; individuals may become 'private' or 'professional' members. Abbreviated LAA. Publishes *Australian Library Journal* (q.).

LIBRARY ASSOCIATION OF CHINA. Founded in 1953 with the following aims: to help the Chinese Education Ministry to administer and direct the Summer Library Workshop; to publish the *Bulletin;* to constitute a collection of works for the use of librarians; to encourage the organization of book exhibitions; to carry out research on the libraries of China. Publishes *Bulletin* and books on librarianship.

LIBRARY ASSOCIATION OF IRELAND. Founded 1928, incorporated 1952. This Association represents the profession of librarianship in Eire; it provides postal tuition for, and conducts examinations for, the professional qualification (FLAI). Membership is open to all engaged in, or interested in, the profession of librarianship in Ireland or elsewhere. Abbreviated LAI. Publishes *An Leabharlann* (q.).

LIBRARY ASSOCIATION OF MALAYSIA. Founded on 6th May 1960 to (a) unite all persons engaged in library work or interested in libraries in Malaysia; (b) promote the better administration of libraries; (c) encourage the establishment, development, and use of libraries in Malaysia; (d) encourage professional education and training for librarianship; (e) publish such information as will be of service to members; (f) undertake such activities, including the holding of meetings and conferences, as are appropriate to the attainments of the foregoing objects. Individual membership is open to all persons engaged in library work or interested in libraries in Malaysia; institutional membership is open to all libraries and other institutions which share the objects of the Association; honorary membership is conferred on persons who have distinguished themselves in library work. The Association was known as the Library Association of the Federation of Malaya from 6th May 1960 to 8th July 1964. Abbreviated PPM (Persatuan Perpustakaan Malaysia). Publishes *Perpustakaan* (semi-a.).

LIBRARY ASSOCIATION OF RHODESIA AND NYASALAND. Aims to unite all persons engaged in library work, improve standards in all aspects of librarianship, bibliography and documentation and act as an advisory body in these matters.

LIBRARY ASSOCIATION OF SINGAPORE. Founded in 1954 as the Malayan Library Group and successively known as: Library Association of Malaya & Singapore (from November 1958); Library Association of Singapore (1960); Library Association of Malaysia, Singapore Branch (from January 1965); Library Association of Singapore (since January 1966). The objects of the Association and membership conditions are similar to those of the LIBRARY ASSOCIATION OF MALAYSIA (*q.v.*). Abbreviated PPS (Persatuan Perpustakaan Singapura), LAS. Published *Majallah Perpustakaan Singapura* (three issues 1961–1964), *Perpustakaan Malaysia* 1965 (superseded *Malayan Library Journal* and *Majallah Perpustakaan Singapura*), *Perpustakaan* (1966).

LIBRARY AUTHORITY. In England, a library authority is any local council responsible for local government which has adopted the library acts, whether it be the council of an urban district, non-county borough, London borough, county borough, county or the Common Council of the City of London. Any other local authority which was a library authority immediately before 1 April 1965 when the Public Libraries and Museums Act 1964 came into operation, ceased to be a library authority. For a summary of this Act, see Appendix 3. Every library authority in England has the duty 'to provide a comprehensive and efficient library service' for all residents and non-resident employees and students, and for that purpose 'to provide and maintain such buildings and equipment, and such books and other materials, and to do such other things, as may be requisite.' In Ireland, the library authority in counties and rural districts is the county council; in incorporated boroughs, the council or the municipal commissioners; in towns, the town commissioners. In Scotland, the library authority in counties is the county education authority; and in burghs, the magistrates *and* the council. For a summary of the Public Libraries and Museums Act 1964, see Appendix 3. *See also* LIBRARY AREA, REVIEW DATE.

LIBRARY BINDING. A specially strong binding to enable library books to withstand considerable use. This is achieved by a number of means, but particularly by guarding sections, sewing the sections on tapes and using specially durable cloth.

LIBRARY BOARD. *Synonymous with* BOARD OF LIBRARY TRUSTEES (*q.v.*).

LIBRARY CENTRE. *See* BRANCH LIBRARY.

LIBRARY CLERK. One who performs duties involving simple tasks related to library functions but limited to strict adherence to specific routines and procedures. The work is carried out under close supervision of a librarian or LIBRARY TECHNICAL ASSISTANT (*q.v.*). (American.)

LIBRARY COLLECTION. The total accumulation of material of all kinds assembled by a library for its clientele. Also called 'Library holdings', 'Library resources'.

LIBRARY COMMISSION. 1. An American organization created by an act of legislature, operating in one state but independent of the state library. It exists to promote library services by establishing, organizing and supervising public, and sometimes school, libraries, and by lending books and other material to communities which do not possess libraries. 'State Library Agency' is replacing this term. 2. Occasionally, a Board of Library Trustees.

LIBRARY COMMITTEE. The committee responsible for the provision of a library service.

LIBRARY CONSULTANT. An adviser to a librarian, a lay group or a body responsible for providing a library service.

LIBRARY CORNER. (*Binding*) The turning in of cloth at the corners of books so as to take up the excess in two diagonal folds, one under each turn-in. In this way the cloth is not cut, and the corner given additional strength. *See also* MITRED CORNER, SQUARE CORNER.

LIBRARY COUNCIL. England and Wales are divided into library regions, and each region has a library council consisting of persons representing each of the authorities in the region and such other persons as may be provided for by a scheme which is drawn up in respect of each library region by the Secretary of State after consulting the library authorities within the region. The library councils have 'a duty to make and supervise the working of arrangements for facilitating the co-operation of those authorities with one another and with other bodies within or outside the region having functions in relation to libraries.' The scheme referred to, provides (a) for the constitution, incorporation and functioning of the library council, and (b) for the observance by each of the authorities of any requirements made by the library council, including requirements as to the payment by the authority of contributions towards the expenses of the council. The scheme may also contain provisions directed to the promotion of inter-library co-operation within and outside the region as may appear to the Secretary of State to be expedient. The scheme is the subject of Section 3 of the Public Libraries and Museums Act 1964. Sub-section (5) of this section authorises the Secretary of State to require any library council to enter into and carry into effect arrangements with another such council or with any other body having functions in relation to libraries, with a view to improving the efficiency of the public library service or promoting its development. *See also* LIBRARY ADVISORY COUNCILS, LIBRARY AUTHORITY, Appendix 3.

LIBRARY DISCOUNT.   Discount on the cost of books purchased for a library.

LIBRARY ECONOMY.   The practical application of library science to the founding, organizing and administering of libraries.

LIBRARY EDITION.   1. A vague term indicating the edition of a book, series or set of books, often all the works of an author, in a substantial and uniform format to distinguish it from another less substantial edition, possibly in paper covers. Sometimes called 'Cabinet edition'. 2. An edition printed on good paper and in a specially strong binding for library use.

LIBRARY EXTENSION.   The provision of lectures, film shows, etc. in the library, arranging talks, book-displays, etc. outside the library buildings in order to draw attention to the library services and book stocks. In America, the promotion of libraries and the development of library services by state, regional or local agencies.

LIBRARY EDUCATION, GRADUATE.   Library education for which post-baccalaureate library science credit is given by an institute of higher education. (American.)

LIBRARY EDUCATION, UNDERGRADUATE.   Library education

for which undergraduate credit is given by an institution of higher education. (American.)

LIBRARY EDUCATION DIVISION.   Established as a Division of the American Library Association on 21 June 1946. Has specific responsibility for continuous study and review of library education, conduct of activities and projects within its areas of responsibility. Abbreviated LED. Publishes *LED Newsletter* (q., free to membs.).

LIBRARY HAND.   A handwriting used by librarians with the object of achieving uniformity and legibility in manuscript catalogues and other records. The formation of letters and the slope were determined with clarity in mind, and many librarians used this handwriting before the use of typewriters became common.

'LIBRARY HAS'.   A note to a catalogue entry indicating a library's holdings of a serial publication.

'LIBRARY HAS' CARD.   The card bearing the statement of a library's holdings of a SERIAL (*q.v.*); it is made on a separate card which is attached to the main entry card when there is more than one break in the continuity of the library's holdings.

'LIBRARY HAS' STATEMENT.   A statement on a catalogue card, usually for a SERIAL (*q.v.*) which records the date of first publication, and to indicate what issues of the serial the library possesses in the form 'Library has . . .' These entries are made only when the library does not have a complete set, and appear only on the main entry card. *See also* 'LIBRARY HAS' CARD.

LIBRARY HISTORY GROUP.   A Group of the Library Association, formed in 1962 to unite members interested in the history of libraries in order to further the aims set forth in the Charter of the LA, to encourage the discussion of, and promote interest in, all matters relating to library history, and encourage original work in the history of librarianship in the British Isles. Publishes *Library History* (q.).

LIBRARY HOLDINGS.   *Synonymous with* LIBRARY COLLECTION (*q.v.*).

LIBRARY INFORMATION SERVICE FOR TEES-SIDE.   *See* LIST.

LIBRARY KEYS.   Said of the card catalogue, the circulation and information desks, the bibliographies and indexes to periodicals, etc., grouped together in what is called a 'Finding unit' in university libraries.

LIBRARY MATERIALS.   Books, periodicals, pamphlets, reports, micro-forms, maps, MSS., gramophone records, tapes and all other audio-visual records.

LIBRARY OF CONGRESS.   The national and parliamentary library of the United States of America. Established on 24th April 1800 in Washington, it has become a library for government officers and also for the public. The stock totals 67 million pieces. *See also* NATIONAL UNION CATALOG.

LIBRARY OF CONGRESS CARD. A printed catalogue card on which a full catalogue entry is given, also notes, tracings, and Dewey and L. of C. classification numbers. Such cards have been issued by the Library of Congress since 1901, and available for purchase. Each card bears a serial number which is used by libraries when ordering printed cards for their catalogues. These numbers are printed in the respective books if published in the U.S.A., usually on the back of the title-page.

LIBRARY OF CONGRESS CLASSIFICATION. The scheme of classification used in the national library of the U.S.A. It has been held to be the greatest and most modern of utilitarian schemes. The outline of the scheme was drawn up by Dr. Herbert Putnam, in 1897, and is based in some respects on the Dewey Decimal and Cutter's Expansive schemes, the schedules being worked out by specialists in the various subjects. The main tables have been published, each with its own relative index, as completed, and revised from time to time. The result is a series of special schedules of greater detail than any other scheme. The outline, which is purely arbitrary is as follows:

A	General Works. Polygraphy.
B	Philosophy. Religion.
C	Auxiliary Sciences of History.
D	Universal and Old World History [and Topography] (*except America*).
E–F	America.
G	Geography. Anthropology. Folk-lore. Manners and Customs. Sports and Games.
H	Social Sciences. Economics. Sociology.
J	Political Science.
L	Education.
M	Music.
N	Fine Arts.
P	Language and Literature.
PN–PZ	Literary History. Literature.
Q	Science.
R	Medicine.
S	Agriculture. Plant and Animal Industry. Fish Culture and Fisheries. Hunting. Sports.
T	Technology.
U	Military Science.

V   Naval Science.

Z   Bibliography and Library Science.

The scheme does not conform to the theoretical rules for classification, being compiled to meet the needs of the library's huge collection of books. It typifies the enumerative method of classification and retains all powers of growth in the hands of the compiler. It is too detailed and complex for use in any but the largest library but the subject schedules are most useful for special and university libraries. There are no tables for sub-division by form or place which can be used in any part of the scheme. The notation is mixed, consisting of two letters and four figures used arithmetically, blanks being left in the alphabet and in the numbers for future insertions.

LIBRARY OFFICER. As defined by the Public Libraries and Museums Act 1964, 'an officer of a local authority employed by the authority solely or mainly for the purposes of any functions exercisable by it in relation to the public library service'; 'officer' includes a servant (s.25).

LIBRARY ORGANIZATION. Library organization must obviously precede library administration. Decision upon the methods and lines along which the library is to be run, and getting these methods into working order is the basis of library organization. Plans for, and erection of, the library building, executive decisions with regard to selection, appointment and duties of the staff, the planning and putting into practice of a definite system upon which the work of the library is to be carried on – these are successive stages in library organization. Organization is the act or process of organizing; i.e. creating a systematic union of individuals in a body whose officials, agents and members work together for a common end. Administration is the act of administering such a union; i.e. directing an office, service, employment, etc. Organization creates the machine; administration runs it.

LIBRARY PRACTICE. A common method of carrying out a routine or providing a service in libraries.

LIBRARY PROCESSING. *See* PROCESSING.

LIBRARY PUBLIC RELATIONS COUNCIL. Founded in the U.S.A. in 1939 to investigate, discuss, and promote every phase of library public relations. Abbreviated LPRC.

LIBRARY RATE. The amount of money per pound sterling of rateable value of a local authority area which is required to provide a public library service. A separate rate is not levied, the portion required for library purposes being raised as part of the general rate by the council of a local authority, i.e. of a county, London borough, county borough, non-county borough, or urban district.

LIBRARY REGION. One of a number of areas into which England and Wales are divided to facilitate co-operation between library authorities. *See also* LIBRARY COUNCIL, Appendix 3.

LIBRARY RESEARCH CENTER. Established in 1961 at the University of Illinois to conduct applied research in the public library field. *See also* CENTER FOR RESEARCH LIBRARIES.

LIBRARY RESEARCH CIRCLE. A group meeting under the auspices of the Indian Library Association to consider such matters as the elements of classification and the rationalization of terminology.

LIBRARY SCHOOL. An organized course, or courses, in librarianship attended by full-time and/or part-time students. It may be a separately managed institution in its own building but is usually a department of an institution for further education, or a faculty within a university. Abbreviated LS.

LIBRARY SCIENCE. The knowledge and skill concerned with the administration of libraries and their contents; library economy and bibliography.

LIBRARY SCIENCE ABSTRACTS. A publication of the Library Association (quarterly since January 1950) giving abstracts of books and articles in periodicals on librarianship published throughout the world. Abbreviated *LSA*. *See also Library & Information Science Abstracts.*

LIBRARY SERVICE. The facilities provided by a library for the use of books and the dissemination of information.

LIBRARY SERVICES ACT. An act passed by the Congress of the U.S.A. in 1956 authorising federal grants during five years to help bring public library services to rural areas of less than 10,000 population. It was extended in 1960 for a further period of five years, i.e. until 30 June 1966. The act is administered under the aegis of the Library Services Branch of the U.S. Office of Education. Funds may be used for salaries, books and other library materials, library equipment, and general operating expenses but may not be used for erecting buildings or purchasing land. *See also* LIBRARY SERVICES AND CONSTRUCTION ACT.

LIBRARY SERVICES AND CONSTRUCTION ACT. Passed in the U.S.A. in 1964, this act broadens the coverage of the LIBRARY SERVICES ACT (*q.v.*) by (1) making federal grants available for any urban or rural area without library services 'or with inadequate services', (2) authorizing federal grants for constructing library buildings where facilities are lacking.

LIBRARY SHELVING. Shelving which is made to meet the special needs of libraries. This is usually made in standard shelf lengths of 3 feet (centre of upright to centre of upright) and the shelves should be easily adjustable.

LIBRARY SIGN. The sign consisting of a torch of learning with a red cartouche, bearing in white lettering the words 'Public Library', which is placed outside branches of English county, and many non-county, libraries, and on mobile library vehicles.

LIBRARY SOCIETY OF PUERTO RICO. Sociedad de Bibliotecarios de Puerto Rico. Founded to extol the position of the librarian and to promote a greater recognition of the profession in Puerto Rico; to obtain a better qualification from its associates, and to promote an interest in the profession with the object of drawing the best talent into it, and also to strive to get the authorities concerned to make available the means to offer courses in library science in the country; to work for a greater expansion of the library services in Puerto Rico, and to advocate for the establishment of public libraries in all the communities in the island; to stimulate a greater exchange among the librarians both local as well as from abroad. Publishes *Bulletin of the Library Society of Puerto Rico*.

LIBRARY STAMP. A rubber stamp bearing the name of the library; this is used to indicate the ownership of books, periodicals and other publications.

LIBRARY TECHNICAL ASSISTANT. One whose duties are based on skills required by a library clerk, but, in addition, possesses a proficiency developed in one or more functional areas or in certain limited phases of library services. Such an assistant works under the supervision of a librarian, and may supervise and direct library clerks or clerical staff. *See also* LIBRARY CLERK. (American.)

LIBRARY TECHNOLOGY PROGRAM. Established on 1st May 1959 by the American Library Association with a grant from the Council on Library Resources for a period of two years, and later extended for five years from 1st July 1961 and then annually. Until 1st July 1966 it was known as the Library Technology Project. Purpose: to explore ways and means by which modern technology and the principles of scientific management can be used to streamline library operations and improve services, and to disseminate the results of its studies and investigations in these areas to the library profession. In order to carry out these objects LTP (1) tests and evaluates library equipment, supplies, and systems, and conducts systems studies, (2) develops new or improved items of library equipment and promotes improvements in existing equipment by calling desirable modifications to the notice of manufacturers, (3) works to develop performance standards for library equipment and supplies, to improve the quality of library products, and to furnish purchasing guidelines to librarians, and (4) provides an individualized information service to the library profession so that the results of LTP research may be utilized as effectively and as widely as possible. Abbreviated LTP. Publishes *Library Technology Reports* (6 p.a.).

LIBRARY TICKET. One indicating membership of a library and serving as the authority for borrowing books.

'THE LIBRARY WORLD' PUBLICITY AWARDS. These annual Awards were first made in 1965. Publications submitted for adjudication must have been issued during the previous year. There are two groups: (1) libraries in Great Britain and Northern Ireland, and (2) libraries overseas. Each group is divided into three sections as follows: (a) annual reports; (b) booklists and other bibliographical publications; (c) library publicity generally or specially. The awards take the form of certificates which are awarded to the first three winners in each section and group.

LIBRARY TRUSTEES. *Synonymous with* BOARD OF LIBRARY TRUSTEES (*q.v.*).

LIBRETTIST. The author of the text of an opera or other extended choral composition.

LIBRETTO. The words to which an opera or other lengthy musical composition for voices is set.

LIBRI MANUSCRIPTI. Books written by hand, as were all books before the invention of printing.

LICENCE LEAF. *See* IMPRIMATUR.

LICHTDRUCK. A kind of COLLOTYPE (*q.v.*).

LIFTED MATTER. Type or blocks removed from the forme and put on one side for use in other pages or in another job.

LIGATURE. Two or more letters joined together, or differing in design from the separate letters, and cast on one type body, as st, ct, ffl, ff, fi, fl to save space, avoid the unsightly juxtaposition of st, ct, ffl, ff, fi, fl, and to reduce the risk of damage to kerned letters. The term also refers to the joining stroke which connects the characters. Also called 'Double letter', 'Tied letter'. *See also* LOGOTYPE.

LIGHT FACE. The weight of type-face which is lighter than medium – the ordinary book weight – having thinner strokes. The opposite of BOLD FACE (*q.v.*). Most type families are made in varying weights, usually called light, medium, bold, extra bold; but 'medium' is normally understood when referring to a type face and is therefore only expressed when it is essential to distinguish it from the other weights.

LIGHTWEIGHT PAPER. Sensitized photographic paper between 0·0044 and 0·0059 inches inclusive. *See also* PHOTOGRAPHIC PAPERS.

LIKENESS. The quality of similarity or alikeness which is used in classification in order to group together objects or ideas according to their likeness.

LILLIPUT EDITION. *See* MINIATURE BOOK.

LIMITATION NOTICE. The statement in a book published in a LIMITED EDITION (*q.v.*) indicating the number of copies printed which comprise the edition, or part of the edition. The statement would define the special character of the edition, such as printed on 'large paper' or hand-made paper, and provide for the number of the individual copy to be written in.

LIMITED CATALOGUING. A term used by the Library of Congress for the standard of descriptive cataloguing which began to be applied in 1951 by the Library of Congress to certain categories of books in order to speed up cataloguing processes. Limited cataloguing is practised in order to reduce the work and time involved in recording more details than are required to identify and locate works which are not of sufficient bibliographic and reference utility to compensate for the time expended. The following illustrate the kinds of categories which are subject to limited cataloguing: (1) trade publications in general: current fiction, biography, history, drama, poetry, religion, travel, juvenile books, etc.; (2) minor publications of governments, institutions and other corporate bodies, e.g. the miscellaneous pamphlets, leaflets, and informational literature issued by such organizations; (3) text books, technical manuals, handbooks, etc.; (4) translations from English into a foreign language. It will be noted that the scheme does not apply to music, maps and other non-textual materials. Details of the limitations are given on pages 74–5 of *Cataloguing Rules of the American Library Association and the Library of Congress. Additions and Changes, 1949–58.* Washington, Library of Congress, 1959. *See also* FULL CATALOGUING.

LIMITED EDITION. An edition, printed on special paper and often with a special binding, which is printed in limited numbers (seldom more than 1,500, usually about 200 to 500, but often as few as ten) and sold at a higher price. Each copy bears a printed certificate (usually facing the title-page) indicating the size of the edition on which is written the actual copy number. Sometimes copies are signed by the author. Library of Congress catalogue cards usually bear details in a note, usually in quoted form, for editions of 500 copies or less, and numbered – and especially numbered and signed copies – are usually especially noted. Works in editions of 100 copies or less usually go to rare book collections, and fine limited editions which are not wanted in such collections are shelved in special locked collections for protection. *See also* LIMITATION NOTICE.

LIMITED EDITIONS CLUB.   An American subscription book club, founded in 1929 by George Macy, which produces well-designed and well-printed books.

LIMP BINDING.   Said of a book which is not bound in boards but with flexible cloth or leather.

LIMP CLOTH.   A term used to describe a style of publisher's binding. *See also* LIMP COVERS.

LIMP COVERS.   Thin book covers made without boards and covered with cloth or leather. They are flexible and bend easily.

LIMP LEATHER.   A full leather binding made without using stiff boards and therefore flexible. Often used for Bibles.

LINDISFARNE GOSPELS.   Written in Latin, this is the earliest and most beautiful extant manuscript in English half-uncials; it is supposed to have been written by Eadfrith, Bishop of Lindisfarne, about 700. Also known as the 'Durham Book'.

LINE.   1. The imaginary base-line of a piece of movable type, running set-wise on or about which all the characters are positioned. *See also* SET 2. 2. A row of printed or written characters extending across a column or page. *See also* MEASURE. 3. A FILLET (*q.v.*) used in bookbinding. 4. Reproduction of a drawing which prints only solid areas and lines, there being no tones.

LINE BLOCK.   A metal printing block made photographically direct from a black and white drawing without any intermediate tones other than tints, and mounted type-high for letterpress printing. *See also* ZINCOGRAPHY.

LINE-CASTING MACHINE.   A type-casting machine which casts a line of type in one slug. Intertype and Linotype are machines of this kind.

LINE COPY.   A copy of a document which has no tone values. Also called 'Line reproduction'. *See also* LINE ORIGINAL.

LINE CUT.   *Synonymous with* LINE ENGRAVING (*q.v.*).

LINE DIVISION MARK.   A mark, usually a vertical or oblique line, used in bibliographical transcription to indicate the end of a line of type in the original.

LINE DRAWING.   A black ink drawing made in line or stipple with indian ink, pencil, crayon, or brush, from which a line block may be made.

LINE END STROKE. *Synonymous with* LINE DIVISION MARK (*q.v.*).

LINE-ENDING. 1. Term used to indicate the last letter of a line of type when giving an exact bibliographical description of a title-page, the ending of each line being indicated by a vertical or oblique stroke or two such strokes. 2. An ornament (of which there are a great variety) filling the space at the end of a line in a mediaeval illuminated manuscript. Also called 'Line-filling'.

LINE ENGRAVING. 1. Engraving in which the effects are produced by lines of different width and proximity, cut into copper, steel, zinc or other similar material. 2. A plate produced by the line engraving process. 3. A picture printed from a line engraving.

LINE ETCHING. *Synonymous with* ETCHING (*q.v.*).

LINE-FILLING. *Synonymous with* LINE-ENDING (*q.v.*).

LINE ORIGINAL. An original document for copying, and having no tone values. A copy of such an original may be called a 'Line copy' or 'Line reproduction'.

LINE REPRODUCTION. *Synonymous with* LINE COPY (*q.v.*). *See also* LINE ORIGINAL.

LINEALE. Styles of type face where the characters have no serifs. Such faces were formerly known as 'sans-serif'. They may be subdivided into GROTESQUE, NEO-GROTESQUE, GEOMETRIC AND HUMANIST (*qq.v.*).

LINED. Said of a book which has a piece of material (strips of parchment which overlapped the joints and were pasted down under the endpapers of seventeenth- and eighteenth-century bindings) lining the spine to give it strength.

LINEN. A cloth made from flax for covering books.

LINEN FACED. Paper with a linen finish on one or both sides.

LINEN FINISH. Paper, the surface of which is made to resemble linen by placing it between plates of zinc and sheets of linen under pressure. *See also* CRASH FINISH.

LINEN-GRAINED. A book-cloth which is patterned to resemble linen.

LINEN PAPER. 1. Paper made from rags; originally from linen rags. 2. LINEN FACED (*q.v.*).

LINGUISTIC NUMBERS. *Synonymous with* ETHNIC NUMBERS (*q.v.*).

LINING. A piece of material, usually mull, placed in the spine of a book when binding it to give it strength. Also called 'Back lining'. *See also* FIRST LINING, SECOND LINING, TRIPLE LINING.

LINING, ORNAMENTAL INSIDE. *Synonymous with* DOUBLURE 1 (*q.v.*).

LINING FIGURES. (*Printing*) Arabic numerals which do not have ascenders or descenders, but which are the same size as capital letters, stretching from base-line to cap line thus: 1234567890. Also called 'Ranging figures'. *See also* HANGING FIGURES.

LINING PAPER. 1. That portion of an endpaper which is pasted down on the inner cover of a book. The other portion of the endpaper is known as the 'free endpaper'. *See also* ENDPAPER. 2. Coloured or marbled paper used as an ENDPAPER (*q.v.*).

LINING-UP TABLE. *Synonymous with* REGISTER TABLE (*q.v.*).

LINK LETTERS. *See* LINKS.

LINKED BOOKS. Separately bound books where the relationship between each other is indicated in various ways, such as collective or series title-pages; continuous paging, series or signatures; mention in contents or other preliminary leaves.

LINKS. In co-ordinate indexing, grouping devices; generally but not necessarily, symbols appended to item numbers. They show that terms are related. Also called 'Interfixes', 'Link letters', 'Punctuation', 'Association'.

LINOCUT. 1. A piece of linoleum engraved by hand, mounted on a wooden block at type height and printed from as if from a woodcut. Linocut blocks are very durable and can be electrotyped. Illustrations comprising broad flat masses and bold lettering are suitable for this method. 2. The impression made from a linocut block.

LINOFILM. A photo-composing machine built by the Mergenthaler Linotype Co., of New York and demonstrated in 1954. The machine has two units, a keyboard unit and a photographic unit. The standard typewriter keyboard unit has additional keys for hair-spacing, line erasing, quadding and fount selection; this punches a code into a paper strip and so specifies roman, italic, or bold in upper or lower case or small capitals, spaces and lines. Justification is achieved by a mechanical computer automatically punching into the strip. This strip is fed into the photographic unit which interprets electrically the specification of the punched strip and produces a positive with black letters on a clear base.

LINOLEUM BLOCK. An engraved piece of linoleum from which a LINOCUT (*q.v.*) is made.

LINOLEUM DRY-POINT. An impression made from a linoleum block on which the design has been made with a dry-point tool.

LINOSCO. Abbreviation for Libraries of North Staffordshire in
13*

Co-operation. This scheme of local library co-operation was formed in 1959 following several years of informal co-operation in the North Staffordshire area. Four public libraries, twelve university and college libraries and seven special libraries are members, and the organization is based on the Horace Banks Reference Library, Pall Mall, Hanley, Stoke-on-Trent, Staffs., where a union list of 2,600 periodical titles is maintained. Although the lending of books and periodicals between member libraries is the main purpose of LINOSCO, the committee has been concerned with the training of library assistants and has initiated the holding of classes. Meetings of the librarians of the co-operating libraries are held twice yearly at member libraries in rotation: at these, matters of national and local professional interest, as well as co-operation are discussed. *See also* MISLIC.

LINOTYPE. A typesetting machine casting a line of type in a slug. It was invented by Ottmar Mergenthaler (1854–99). The machine carries a large number of single matrices in a magazine; these are released as the keyboard is operated and assembled in sequence with double-wedge spaces separating the words. The spaces are used to justify the completed line as it is brought to the orifice of a mould, and there cast in a type-high slug. Linotype machines have been in use since 1890, and are the kind most used for printing newspapers.

LINOTYPE CALEDONIA. *See* TYPE FACE.

LINSON. The trade name for a particularly tough variety of paper used extensively for publisher's casing. It can be embossed to represent linen and is available in a wide variety of colours and finishes. It is used increasingly as an alternative to cloth, being much cheaper. It is one of a number of binder coverings made by Grange Fibre of Leicester.

LINT. Dust, or loose fibres, which separate from the raw material during paper-making.

LIPPINCOTT AWARD, JOSEPH W. Donated by Joseph W. Lippincott in 1937, and suspended between 1940 and 1947, this annual Award of $1,000 cash ($500 through 1959), a medal and a citation of achievement, is made to a librarian for distinguished service in the profession of librarianship, such service to include outstanding participation in the activities of professional library associations, notable published professional writing, or other significant activity on behalf of the profession and its aims. The Award is administered by the ALA Awards Committee, the selection being made by a jury of five appointed by the ALA Awards Committee. The first recipient was Mary U. Rothrock in 1938.

LIST. Abbreviation for Library Information Service for Teesside. Formed in 1964 to inter-lend books and periodicals between members. Libraries with a minimum of five technical periodicals and five technical books are entitled to become members. The scheme is operated from the Central Library, Victoria Square, Middlesbrough.

LIST, PUBLISHER'S. A list of books published by one publisher and still in print.

LIST OF CONTENTS. A contents-list or list of 'preliminaries'. *See* CONTENTS, TABLE OF.

LIST OF ILLUSTRATIONS. This follows the 'Table of Contents' and indicates the position in the book of the illustrations, both full-page and 'in the text'. *See also* PRELIMINARIES.

LIST OF SIGNATURES. *See* REGISTER 2.

LIST PRICE. The price of a book as quoted by the publisher in his catalogue.

LITERAL. An error made in setting type, usually through confusion of similar letters or an unclear manuscript, and involving no more than a letter-for-letter correction, such as a full point for a comma, or a transposition.

LITERAL MNEMONICS. *See* MNEMONICS.

LITERARY AGENT. One who arranges the sale and publication of authors' work with publishers of books, newspapers and periodicals, and who negotiates subsidiary rights such as dramatic, broadcasting, and film rights. An agent also acts for publishers by arranging for the writing of scripts which they need. The author pays the agent on a commission basis for his services.

LITERARY GUILD. One of the original American book clubs; it manufactured its own editions.

LITERARY MANUSCRIPT. A record or document produced by hand and indicating literary rather than textual excellence. Also called 'Textual manuscript'. *See also* ARTISTIC MANUSCRIPT.

LITERARY PROPERTY. The product of an author's creative effort in the form of manuscripts or published work which have an existing or potential financial value.

LITERARY WARRANT. 1. The volume of books which have been written on any topic. 2. (*Classification*) The quantity of expressed and embodied knowledge in any given field, waiting to be organized. 3. (*Information retrieval*) A subject which has appeared in the literature, is represented by the descriptors used in the retrieval system if it is desired to retrieve documents specifically relevant to that subject, and with minimum 'dilution' by other documents.

LITERARY WORK. A work, other than a SACRED WORK (*q.v.*), written in a literary form, e.g. a poem, drama, novel, etc. and having outstanding qualities such as beauty of form, emotional or intuitive appeal.

LITERATURE REVIEW. A survey of progress in a particular aspect of science over a given period (e.g. one, five, or ten years); it may range from a bibliographical index or mere list of references, to a general critical review of original publications on the subjects covered.

LITERATURE SEARCH. A systematic and exhaustive search for published material on a specific subject, together with the preparation of annotated bibliographies or abstracts for the use of the researcher. This is an intermediate stage between reference work and research, and is differentiated from both. It is often the first step in a research project, patent search, or laboratory experiment and sometimes reveals that the proposed action is unnecessary, having been carried out previously by others; if this is not the case the search usually gives valuable information on similar or identical work previously undertaken. In some libraries a separate room called a 'search room' is set aside and equipped with appropriate bibliographical 'tools' such as volumes of abstracts, periodical indexes, etc. for the carrying out of searches.

LITERATURE SURVEY. 1. A bibliography relating to a specific subject and listing of material either in a given collection, or in more than one library, or of literature on the subject. 2. A listing, with full bibliographical references, of recently published books and articles on a given subject in current journals, prepared usually by librarians or information officers in industrial organizations or research associations for the information of members of, or users of, the organization. It serves to keep those to whom it is circulated up-to-date in the literature of the subjects with which they are concerned. Brief annotations are often provided. Also called 'Current publication survey'.

LITHO CRAYON. A special crayon for drawing on lithographic plates.

LITHO PAPERS. Papers made especially for lithographic printing. Made basically from esparto, they have dimensional stability to ensure correct register, and are usually placed the narrow way across the printing machines, for any stretch must be the narrow way of the sheet.

LITHOGRAPH. A print or illustration produced by LITHOGRAPHY (*q.v.*).

LITHOGRAPHIC PRESS. A press for printing from a lithographic stone or plate. It is similar in appearance to a stop-cylinder press used for bookwork, and operates in much the same way.

LITHOGRAPHIC PRINTING. A planographic printing process

whereby the areas of the printing surface (the non-image areas) are hydrophic (i.e. have an affinity for water) and the printing (image) areas are hydrophobic (i.e. repel water and attract grease). *See also* LITHOGRAPHY.

LITHOGRAPHIC RIBBON. A special ribbon used for typing direct on to lithographic plates.

LITHOGRAPHY. The process of drawing designs on stone with a special greasy crayon, chalk, paint or ink, and of producing printed impressions therefrom; also any process based on the same principle in which a thin flexible metal plate or plastic is used instead of stone. The stone is saturated with water, the printing ink is then applied and adheres only to those portions covered by the crayon or other drawing medium. A separate drawing is required for each colour in the resulting print. In direct lithography the drawing is in reverse; in offset lithography the drawing is first made the right way round on transfer paper, printed on to a rubber-covered cylinder and 'offset' on to the paper. Lithography was invented by Aloys Senefelder, a Bavarian, in 1798. From the Greek 'Lithos' = stone. *See also* AUTO-LITHOGRAPHY, OFFSET LITHOGRAPHY, OFFSET PRINTING, PHOTO-LITHOGRAPHY, PHOTO-OFFSET.

LITHOGRAVURE. A process of photo-engraving on stone.

LITHO-OFFSET. *See* LITHOGRAPHY, OFFSET PRINTING.

LITHOPHOTOGRAPHY. *Synonymous with* PHOTO-LITHOGRAPHY (*q.v.*).

LITHOPRINT. *Synonymous with* OFFSET PRINTING (*q.v.*).

LITHOTINT. An obsolete method of lithography by which the effect of a tinted drawing was produced. Also a picture so produced.

LITTERAE VENETIAE. *Synonymous with* BOLOGNESE LETTERS (*q.v.*).

LIVE MATTER. A forme of letterpress or illustrations, ready for printing, electrotyping or stereotyping. It may be held for future use. *See also* GOOD, MATTER, STANDING TYPE.

LIVERPOOL AND DISTRICT SCIENTIFIC, INDUSTRIAL AND RESEARCH LIBRARY ADVISORY COUNCIL. *See* LADSIRLAC.

LIVRES À VIGNETTES. Books printed in the eighteenth century which were illustrated by vignette copper-plate engravings. The kind of engraving used was a mixture of etching with some gravure work.

ll. Abbreviation for leaves of a book, lines of type, *leges* (laws).

LOADED PAPER. *See* COATED PAPER.

LOADING. The adding of clay, chalk, or similar materials to STUFF (*q.v.*) when in the beater of a paper making machine, or flowed into the stock as it goes through the sluice-gate of the Fourdrinier machine.

It fills the spaces between fibres and so imparts solidity to the paper and provides a better printing surface.

LOAN. 1. A large sum of money raised by the local authority and repayable within a specified time for local government developments such as the erection of libraries, purchase of furniture, etc. 2. A book, or a number of books, on loan to an individual, a group of persons, an institution or a library.

LOAN COLLECTION. A collection of books, prints or pictures which are available for use at home as distinct from a collection which may only be referred to on the premises.

LOAN DEPARTMENT. A department from which loans of books and other materials are made, or in which such materials are kept. *Synonymous with* LENDING DEPARTMENT (*q.v.*).

LOAN DESK. *See* CIRCULATION DESK.

LOAN FEE. A charge made for the use of library materials.

LOAN PERIOD. The period which is allowed for reading a book away from a library.

LOAN SANCTION. Authority given by the Minister of Housing and Local Government to local authorities permitting them to borrow money in order to discharge their statutory powers and duties.

loc cit. Abbreviation for *loco citato* (*Lat.* 'in the place already cited'). Used in a footnote reference to avoid using the title or short title of the periodical referred to. It should be used less sparingly than *op. cit.* (*q.v.*).

LOCAL AUTHORITY. The unit of administration in Britain which is responsible for providing, either on its own behalf and as it is entitled to do by law, or on behalf of the central government, certain services within the area of its geographical boundaries. Not all services may be provided by each kind of local authority (county, county borough, non-county borough, urban district and parish); those having the widest powers are counties and county boroughs. A local authority with power to provide public libraries is called a LIBRARY AUTHORITY (*q.v.*).

LOCAL BIBLIOGRAPHY. A bibliography of books and other forms of written record relating to a geographical area smaller than a county. It normally includes books by and about people born in, or who have resided in, the area, as well as books relating strictly to the geography, natural history, architecture and social history of the area.

LOCAL COLLECTION. A collection of books, maps, prints, illustrations and other material relating to a specific locality, usually that in which the library housing the collection is situated. *See also* LOCAL GOVERNMENT (RECORDS) ACT, 1962.

LOCAL DIRECTORY. A directory relating to a specified locality; it may be limited in scope in any way, e.g. to telephone addresses or businesses, but usually includes particulars of residents and businesses, the entries being arranged in street order with 'trade' entries in classified order in addition.

LOCAL GOVERNMENT (RECORDS) ACT, 1962. This Act amends the law relating to the functions of local authorities respecting records in written or other form. It (1) empowers local authorities to promote the adequate use of their records by allowing inspection, copying, indexing, publication, exhibition, etc.; (2) enables local authorities to acquire local records by gift or purchase – or accept on deposit – records which, or (in the case of a collection) the majority of which, appear to be of local interest, and may deposit them with itself or other authorities, (3) authorizes the appointment of sub-committees to deal with records, (4) provides funds for dealing with records of local interest whether under the authority's control or not. The clerk to the council is custodian 'subject to any direction which the council may give'.

LOCAL LIBRARIAN. A voluntary worker at a village or other centre of a county library.

LOCAL LIST. 1. A list prepared by W. P. Cutter and appended to his *Expansive classification*, giving geographical and political divisions, with numbers, for use in arranging material geographically or to indicate relationship. 2. A list of places which may be used to permit sub-division by place in a scheme or classification. 3. A list of books relating to a particular locality.

LOCAL UNIT CARD. The basic catalogue entry, or UNIT CARD (*q.v.*), which is made at a library normally purchasing printed catalogue cards, in respect of a book which is not catalogued by the British National Bibliography, the Library of Congress, the H.W. Wilson Company or some other printed card issuing agency, or for a book which is to be catalogued locally, either temporarily until printed cards are received, or permanently. *See also* WILSON CARDS.

LOCATION. The place on the shelves or elsewhere in which required material may be found. It is indicated on records, for example on catalogue entries, by the LOCATION MARK (*q.v.*).

LOCATION INDEX. A record used in county libraries for tracing the whereabouts of particular books. It consists of book cards bearing the names or numbers of the centres to which the books have been sent, and is arranged in alphabetical order.

LOCATION MARK. A letter, word, group of words or symbol used on a catalogue entry, book list or bibliography, sometimes in conjunction with the CALL NUMBER (*q.v.*), to indicate the collection, library or position at which the book or item in question is shelved. Also called 'Location symbol'.

LOCATION REGISTER. A collection, or list, of records of books, documents, or other items, which are arranged by the FIXED LOCATION (*q.v.*) method or in a CLOSED ACCESS (*q.v.*) library. The arrangement of the items on the register may be by author, title, or accession number.

LOCATION SYMBOL. *See* LOCATION MARK.

LOCATIVE ABSTRACT. *See* ABSTRACT.

LOCKING UP. (*Printing*) Tightening up a forme of type matter in the metal frame known as a chase, preparatory to putting it on the press.

locus sigilli. (*Lat.* 'the place of the seal'). Usually abbreviated L.S. and printed within a circle at the place for a signature on legal documents.

LOFT-DRIED. Hand- or mould-made papers which are dried by suspension in a dry, airy loft.

LOG. A registry of items, e.g. on an accession list (*IBM*).

LOGICAL NOTATION. One in which each symbol of a classification scheme may be divided without limit by a sequence of similar symbols, each having the same value but representing a further step in the subdivision of the subject as represented by the preceding symbol or group of symbols.

LOGO. *Synonymous with* MASTHEAD (*q.v.*).

LOGOGRAM. An initial letter or number used as an abbreviation.

LOGOGRAPHIC WRITING. The earliest form of picture writing in which a single symbol was used to represent an entire word.

LOGOGRAPHY. A method of casting logotypes. It was first patented by Henry Johnson in 1780 who had a fount of 3,500 words and syllables, but the idea never developed owing to opposition from compositors of the time.

LOGON. (*Information retrieval*) That which enables one new distinguished group or category to be added to a representation.

LOGOTYPE. Several letters, or a word, cast on one type, or as a single matrix. Used in the printing of directories or other works in which such combinations are frequently repeated. *See also* LIGATURE.

LOMBARDIC HANDWRITING. An offshoot of the Italian semicursive minuscule which was derived from the Roman cursive style used throughout Italy in the seventh to ninth centuries. *See also* CURSIVE, HANDWRITING.

LONDON AND HOME COUNTIES BRANCH. The largest and
oldest Branch of the Library Association, having been formed in
July 1923.

LONDON AND SOUTH EASTERN LIBRARY REGION. Formed
early in 1969 by the amalgamation of the LONDON UNION CATALOGUE
(*q.v.*) and the SOUTH EASTERN REGIONAL SERVICE (which were formed
forty years previously) consequent upon the reorganizing of the
London Borough boundaries in 1965. This Bureau operates in
respect of the 82 public library systems in Greater London and the
nine counties of the South-East; it caters for a population of over
15,000,000 and is believed to be the largest scheme for library co-
operation in the world. Abbreviated LASER.

LONDON BOROUGHS COMMITTEE. The committee on which are
represented all the thirty-two London Boroughs (which were formed
after the borough boundaries were revised, and the London County
Council and the Middlesex County Council ceased to exist, on 1st
April 1965) plus the Common Council of the City of London. It
performs similar functions to the Metropolitan Boroughs Standing
Joint Committee which it superseded, viz. the co-ordination of local
government services throughout Greater London.

LONDON UNION CATALOGUE. The union catalogue of the (London) Metropolitan Public Libraries. From 1st November 1934 until
the reorganization of the London boroughs on 1st April 1965 it was
controlled by the Metropolitan Boroughs Standing Joint Committee
which levied on all metropolitan libraries a like amount of money for
its upkeep, and administered by the Association of Metropolitan
Chief Librarians on behalf of the MBSJC. It is maintained on the
premises of the National Central Library, and although not strictly a
regional bureau, functions as one, arranging for the loan of books
between the London libraries and other libraries throughout the
country. *See also* LONDON AND SOUTH EASTERN LIBRARY REGION.

LONG. *See* BROAD, OBLONG.

LONG-BODIED TYPE. Type which is cast on bodies larger than usual,
e.g. 10-point on 12-point. This avoids the use of LEADS (*q.v.*).

LONG DESCENDER. Letters g, j, p, q and y with extra long descenders; these are available as alternatives in some faces as, for example,
Linotype Caledonia and Times Roman. *See also* ASCENDER, DESCENDER.

LONG ELEPHANT. *See* ELEPHANT.

LONG GRAIN. Paper in which the fibres lie in the longer direction of
the sheet. *See also* GRAIN DIRECTION, SHORT GRAIN.

LONG LETTER. A character, such as f, j or k, which has either

ASCENDER or DESCENDER (*qq.v.*) or both. *See also* SHORT LETTER, which has neither.

LONG PAGE. A page of a book with more lines of type than most of the others. *See also* SHORT PAGE.

LONG PRIMER. An old name for a type size, about 10 point.

LONG REAM. 500 or 516 sheets of paper. *See also* REAM, SHORT REAM.

LOOK-THROUGH. The examination of paper by holding it up against strong light. By this means, the dispersion of fibres can be seen, and consequently the strength of the paper judged; it is also a means of seeing whether the paper is laid or wove, and if its texture is marred by impurities. *See also* WILD LOOK-THROUGH.

LOOSE. A book, the sections of which are badly loosened from the case, the sewing having broken.

LOOSE BACK. *Synonymous with* HOLLOW BACK (*q.v.*).

LOOSE LEAF BINDING. A binding which permits the immediate withdrawal and insertion of pages at any desired position, as in a loose leaf binder.

LOOSE LEAF CATALOGUE. A SHEAF CATALOGUE (*q.v.*).

LOOSE-LEAF SERVICE. A serial publication which is revised, supplemented, cumulated, and indexed by means of new replacement pages inserted in a loose-leaf binder; such publications are used where the latest statements and revisions of information are important, as with legal, political, social and scientific material. *See also* SERIAL SERVICE.

LOWER CASE LETTERS. Minuscules or 'small' letters such as a.b.c.; those other than capitals. The name originated from the fact that printers kept their type in two large cases, one above the other, each divided into sections containing one SORT (*q.v.*). The upper case contained the capital letters, majuscules, and the lower one the others. Abbreviated l.c. *See also* CAPITALS, SMALL CAPITALS, UPPER CASE LETTERS.

LOWER COVER. *Synonymous with* REVERSE COVER (*q.v.*).

LOWER EDGE. The TAIL (*q.v.*) of a book. Also called 'Bottom edge', 'Tail edge'.

LOWER MARGIN. *Synonymous with* TAIL MARGIN (*q.v.*).

LOXODROME. *See* PORTOLAN CHART.

LOZENGE. (*Binding*) A diamond-shaped figure, or a square figure, placed on one of its corners; it is usually decorated.

LUBETZKY CODE. A draft, issued in 1960, under the title of *Code of cataloguing rules, author and title entry*. This was written on entirely fresh lines (but firmly grounded in the Panizzi and Cutter traditions) under the direction of the (American) Catalog Code Revision Committee. In 1953, his critique of the second (1949) American edition of a code incorporating the Library of Congress rules, and superseding the A.A. Code, had been published under the title *Cataloging rules and principles*. Samuel Lubetzky was at the time the specialist in bibliographic and cataloguing policy at the Library of Congress.

LUDLOW. A machine which casts slugs for display work. Composing is done by hand, a special composing stick being used; when the characters are all in position, the stick is placed into the machine which casts a line as a slug. It is frequently used in conjunction with the Elrod machine which casts rules, leads, borders and plain slugs.

LULOP. *London Union List of Periodicals*. First issued in 1951, this publication records the periodicals available in the municipal and county libraries in Greater London. It gives the extent of the permanent files of periodicals processed, and also a guide to places where files or current issues only are available.

LUMBECKING. The PERFECT (*q.v.*), or flexible, method of binding whereby the separate sheets are not kept together by sewing but by adhesive only.

LUMINOTYPE. The original name for the UHERTYPE (*q.v.*) photocomposing machine.

LUMITYPE. A method of FILMSETTING (*q.v.*).

LUNDIA SHELVING. A patented design of adjustable shelving of Swedish origin made under licence in a number of countries. Two designs of wooden shelving are made. One is of traditional appearance and the other is cantilever shelving which gives the impression of unbroken rows of books. In the former the shelves are grooved at the ends to slide over rods the bent ends of which have been inserted into holes bored into uprights near the front and back edges. There are therefore no shelf supports on the underside of shelves to impede the shelving of books, and the shelves are quite rigid. Interlocking fixing bars enable the whole shelving, including uprights, top shelf and plinth to be assembled securely without using tools. The cantilever shelving consists of brackets (which may be of different lengths) placed in slotted metal uprights which are fixed to the wall. Some brackets are made so as to allow shelves to be placed at different angles, instead of at an angle of 90° to the upright, so as to permit books to be displayed flat or shelved flat. This is most suitable for large volumes which need to be shelved flat and for book and periodical displays, but as with most shelving of this type, book supports are essential if books are stood up on their bottom edges.

LUTHERAN CHURCH LIBRARY ASSOCIATION. Founded in 1958 in the U.S.A. 'to promote the growth of church libraries in Lutheran congregations by publishing a quarterly journal, *Lutheran Libraries*, furnishing booklists, assisting member libraries with technical problems, providing meetings for mutual encouragement, assistance and exchange of ideas among members'. Abbreviated LCLA.

LUTTRELL PSALTER.   An English Psalter of the East Anglian School, illuminated (as was usual at the time) by mainly grotesque beasts and monkeys (babewyns) but also with agricultural scenes, games and sports, and also incidents from the lives of the saints. It was written about 1340 for Sir Geoffrey Louterell of Lincolnshire who is depicted on a charger, his wife and daughter being in the same group. It is in the British Museum.

LUX.   As from 1st January 1969, the metric measurement of light value, one lumen or foot-candle being equal to 10·76 lux.

LUXURY BINDING.   *Synonymous with* DE LUXE BINDING (*q.v.*).

LYONESE (LYONNAISE) STYLE.   A style of binding with broad interlaced geometrical strapwork usually painted, lacquered, or enamelled in different colours; so called because it appeared on books bound at Lyons in the latter part of the sixteenth century. Also a style in which the binding is decorated with large corner ornaments and with a prominent centre design, roughly lozenge shaped, the all-over background being filled in with dots.

M.   Roman figure for 1,000 used as an abbreviation by printers.

MAGB.   Acronym for MICROFILM ASSOCIATION OF GREAT BRITAIN (*q.v.*).

M.F.   (*Paper*) Abbreviation for MACHINE FINISH (*q.v.*).

M.G.   (*Paper*) Abbreviation for MACHINE GLAZED (*q.v.*). *See also* PAPER FINISHES.

MACHINE COATED.   (*Paper*) Paper which has been coated with clay or a similar substance during the actual making of the paper to give it a smooth printing surface. When the coating is applied as a separate and later operation, it is called 'brush coated'.

MACHINE COMPOSITION.   Type setting by machine as distinct from setting by hand.

MACHINE DIRECTION.   *Synonymous with* GRAIN DIRECTION (*q.v.*). *See* AGAINST THE GRAIN.

MACHINE-DRIED.   *Synonymous with* CYLINDER DRIED (*q.v.*).

MACHINE FINISH.   Paper which has been made smooth, but not glossy, by receiving the normal finish of a Fourdrinier paper-making machine: this passes the paper over heated drums and through steel calendering rollers. Abbreviated M.F. This is the normal paper for letterpress printing where half-tones are not to be used. *See also* PAPER FINISHES.

MACHINE GLAZED. Said of a paper in which the 'glaze' or polish is produced on the paper-making machine, and not by means of super-calenders or a glazing machine. The only paper-machine which glazes in the process of making is the single-cylinder machine or 'Yankee' in which the web of paper is dried on the one large steam-heated cylinder with a highly polished surface. Machine-glazed papers are identified by being glazed on only one side (the under), the other being in the rough condition in which it comes from the wet end of the machine. Papers made on such machines are very varied in character and uses, for example, manillas for envelopes; litho, poster, kraft and sulphite bag papers and cheap wrappings and tissues. Abbreviated M.G.

MACHINE INDEXING. A process which assigns terms to individual documents with machine assistance.

MACHINE LANGUAGE. Information in the physical form that a computer can handle, e.g. properly coded information punched on paper tape or cards, or in electrical or magnetic form on magnetic tape.

MACHINE-LANGUAGE CODING. 1. Linguistic or numerical patterns susceptible of being handled by data processing equipment. 2. A special type of notation used for a specific data processing machine. 3. Coding in the form in which instructions are executed by the computer. Contrasted to relative, symbolic and other non-machine-language coding (*IBM*).

MACHINE-MADE PAPER. The continuous web, or roll, of paper made on cylinder machines or on the Fourdrinier machine.

MACHINE PROOF. A proof taken when corrections which were marked on galley and page proofs have been made, and the forme is on the printing machine. This proof affords the last opportunity for correcting mistakes before machining takes place. Also called 'Press revise'.

MACHINE REVISE. A proof printed when the forme is on the printing machine, in order that a comprehensive revise may be made of the whole of the details of workmanship, including those which the reader has not had an opportunity of verifying. Also called 'Machine proof'.

MACHINE SORTING. Sorting punched cards into a pre-determined order by machine.

MACHINE SYSTEM. A machine using the kind of electrical and

electronic equipment that was designed initially for accounting and other data processing procedures; these are punched card or computer systems and capable of accepting a store of information appropriately coded, storing it until required, and then producing selected items in usable form. They can be used in information retrieval for recording full bibliographic information or for the indexing function only.

MACHINE WIRE. *Synonymous with* WIRE (*q.v.*).

MACHINING. (*Printing*) 1. That part of printing concerned with actually printing on the paper. The other major processes in producing a book are composition and binding. Called 'Press work' in America. 2. The actual process of printing by running the forme through the machine so that the paper receives an impression from the printing surface.

MACKLE. A printed sheet with a blurred impression, owing to some mechanical defect in the printing.

McMEEKING REPORT. *Report of the Advisory Committee on Further Education for Commerce, 1959.* Called McMeeking Report after the chairman, Mr. J. G. McMeeking.

MACRO-DOCUMENT. A book, treatise, or document embodying macro-thought. *See also* MACRO-THOUGHT, MICRO-DOCUMENT.

MACROFORM. A reproduction of a document which can be read with the unaided eye. *See also* MICROFORM.

MACROGRAPH. A photographic reproduction of an object that may be slightly reduced, or of natural size, or magnified up to about ten diameters.

MACRO-THOUGHT. (*Classification*) A subject of great extension, usually embodied in the form of a book. *See also* MACRO-DOCUMENT, MICRO-THOUGHT.

MADE-UP COPY. A book which has had imperfections made good by the insertion of portions from other copies of the same edition.

MADE-UP SET. A work in a number of volumes which is made up by assembling volumes of more than one edition. It is catalogued as a regular set except that the various editions are specified in a note unless they can be mentioned in the body of the entry.

MAGAZINE. 1. A periodical publication as distinct from a newspaper. 2. A receptacle above the keyboard of a Linotype, or similar typecasting machine, for containing the matrices ready for assembling into lines of type or slugs.

MAGAZINE CASE. A cover for periodicals, usually having some contrivance for holding the magazine – cord, rod, etc. Also called 'Periodical case' and 'Reading case'.

MAGAZINE RACK. A fitting for displaying magazines.

MAGAZINE ROOM. A room used exclusively for the reading of periodicals. Sometimes called 'Periodical room'. *See also* NEWSROOM.

MAGNACARD. Trade name for a retrieval system developed by Magnavox in the U.S.A.; it has a magnetic information carrier system comprising a special rectangular card 25·4 × 76·2 mm with a magnetic coating. The storage capacity of the card is in excess of 5,000 bits – about 1,000 decimal digits. Cards are sorted at the rate of 6,000 cards a minute.

MAGNAPRINT. Trade name for a microfilm reader-printer made by the Recordak Corporation.

MAGNAVUE. Trade name for a mechanized storage and retrieval system using coded film chip storage media; made by the Magnavox Corporation.

MAGNETIC TAPE. Tape coated with a magnetic material which can store information. *See also* CRAM, MAGNACARD.

MAIN CARD. The catalogue card bearing the MAIN ENTRY (*q.v.*).

MAIN CATALOGUE. A colloquialism for what may be considered the most important catalogue in a library; it is usually the one with the most entries or the 'main entries'; it may be the classified catalogue without the author and subject indexes.

MAIN CLASS. The principal division of a scheme of classification, e.g. in Brown's *Subject Classification*: Matter, Life, Mind, Record; or Dewey's General works, Philosophy, Religion, Social Sciences, Language, Pure science, Technology, The Arts, Literature, History. These are divided into 'Divisions' which are divided into 'Subdivisions' which are in turn divided into 'Sections', each division proceeding by gradual steps, and each new heading becoming more 'intense'.

MAIN ENTRY. 1. The basic catalogue entry; usually the entry under the author's name. The main entry has the fullest particulars for the complete identification of a work. In card catalogues – especially dictionary ones – the main entry bears the TRACING (*q.v.*). It may bear in addition the tracing of related references and a record of other pertinent official data concerning the work. For music, the entry under the composer's name. 2. The entry chosen for the basic entry, whether it be a personal or corporate name, or the title of an anonymous book, collection, composite work, periodical or serial, or a uniform title.

MAIN HEADING. (*Indexing*) A description sometimes used (for a heading) in contradistinction to a subheading. (a) *Simple heading*. A heading consisting of a single word or a word with a hyphened prefix (e.g. anti-, co-, ex- mid-, non-, pre-) which alone would either have no meaning or have a different meaning. (b) *Compound heading*. A heading comprising two or more elements (with or without connecting hyphen) of which at least the first element could stand alone with its own meaning, e.g.

air-sea rescue   John o'Groats
Henry VIII   Underwater-to-air missiles

(British Standard 3700:1964).

(*Cataloguing*) The first part of a composite heading whcih includes one or more subheadings. That part of a heading which precedes a subheading.

MAIN LIBRARY. *See* CENTRAL LIBRARY.

MAIN STROKE. The principal stroke, heavy line, or stem of a type letter.

MAIN SUBJECT. A book may treat of several subjects, or may be considered by classifier or cataloguer to need cross references from a subsidiary to the one most important subject. The subject which is given priority and to which references are made is the 'main subject'.

MAIN TITLE. That part of the title which precedes the SUB-TITLE (*q.v.*).

MAIN TITLE-PAGE. The title-page from which the details for a catalogue entry are taken. *See also* ADDED TITLE-PAGE, HALF TITLE-PAGE.

MAINZ PSALTER. In Latin, this famous masterpiece of printing was printed by Johann Fust and Peter Schoeffer in Mainz and is dated 14th August 1457. It is the first printed book to give the name of the printer and the date of printing. *See also* MAZARIN BIBLE.

MAIOLI STYLE. The style of book decoration executed for Thomasso Maioli or Mahieu, (actually Thomas Matthieu a Frenchman), a contemporary of Grolier, in the middle of the sixteenth century. A distinguishing characteristic is that the Arabic ornaments are frequently in outline, whereas those of Grolier are ajuré, and of Aldus, solid. The style is generally composed of a framework of shields or medallions, with a design of scrollwork flowing through it, portions of the design usually being studded with gold dots.

MAJUSCULE. Large letter whether capital (upper case) or UNCIAL (*q.v.*). *See also* MINUSCULE.

MAKE-READY (MAKING-READY). The process of preparing a forme ready for printing. Levelling up and lining up by patching with paper, or cutting away on the impression cyclinder or platen BED (*q.v.*) and by underlaying or interlaying the blocks so that the impression from type and blocks on paper will be clear, clean and of uniform colour. The amount and position of make-ready is determined by a trial pull. The time which this process takes is an important item in every printing bill. It is upon the care with which a job is made-ready that the quality of the printing depends. Make-ready is of paramount importance in colour and half-tone work. *See also* OVERLAY and UNDER-LAY.

MAKE-UP. (*Printing*) 1. A general term for taking the type from the galleys, putting it into page form, insetting illustrative cuts, dividing the matter into page lengths, and adding running heads, titles of sub-divisions, folios, footnotes, etc., and securing with page-cord. The pages of type are then ready for locking in the CHASE (*q.v.*). 2. Some-times used instead of 'layout' to indicate the dummy showing the desired arrangement of letterpress and illustrations. 3. A list of the contents of a book supplied by the publisher to the binder to serve as an instruction as to the positioning of plates, plans, folded leaves, map endpapers, etc. *See also* MAKE-UP COPY, PUBLISHER'S BINDING.

MAKE-UP COPY. A set of folded sheets, plates, plans, etc. in correct order and sent by the publisher as an instruction to the binder. *See also* MAKE-UP.

MANCHESTER TECHNICAL INFORMATION SERVICE. The information service provided by the Scientific and Technical Library and Information Service of the Manchester Public Libraries. The scheme began operation in 1948 and is not restricted either by geo-graphical location or membership. There is no formal organization. Information is available to any firm or institution in the United King-dom, and there is no membership subscription. Close co-operation exists between the Manchester College of Science and Technology and the Bureau of Industrial Liaison (formerly the Manchester Joint Research Council). No fees are charged for information, only the re-funding postages on loans and payment for photocopies and publi-cations. The service is often referred to as MANTIS but the scheme is usually referred to in full.

MANIÈRE CRIBLÉE. A fifteenth-century 'relief' method of producing illustrations by means of a plate of soft metal such as copper, pewter or zinc in which the drawing was made with a graver and which, being sunk below the level of the plate, would appear as white lines on a black ground when printed. Intermediate tones were pro-duced by punching dots in the surface of the plate at more or less regular intervals. Also called 'Schrothlatt'.

MANILLA PAPER. A superfine tough quality of wrapping and label paper made from manilla hemp; also applied to cheap imitations made from wood pulp.

MANIPULABLE TEXT.   The characters, markings, or other forms of record, which are used on punched cards, punched tape, magnetic tape or photographic film to record original text material in such a way that it can be identified and retrieved by machine.

MANIPULATIVE INDEX.   An index in which manipulations other than turning pages, reading entries, following cross references, and locating documents are necessary. Mechanized indexes using punched cards, and the various co-ordinate indexing systems are examples (*IBM*).

MANN CITATION, MARGARET.   Instituted in 1950, and administered by the Cataloging and Classification Section of the Resources and Technical Services Division of the American Library Association, this citation is made to a librarian in recognition of distinguished contributions to librarianship through publication of significant professional literature, participation in professional cataloguing associations, or valuable contributions to practice in individual libraries. The first recipient of the Citation was Miss Lucile M. Morsch in 1951.

MANORIAL COURTS.   Administrative and legal courts concerned with matters affecting a particular manor. The *Court Customary* was principally concerned with the agricultural organization of the township, while the *Court Leet* had a minor criminal jurisdiction.

MANORIAL DOCUMENTS.   Documents relating to manors and the management of estates. Manorial Documents Rules were made in 1926 (S.R. & O. 1926, No. 1310) to implement the provisions of the Law of Property Act, 1922, as amended, by which the Master of the Rolls has power to transfer manorial documents to the Public Record Office or a public library, museum, or historical or antiquarian society.

MANTIS.   Abbreviation for Manchester Technical and Commercial Information Services. *See* MANCHESTER TECHNICAL INFORMATION SERVICE.

MANUAL.   *Synonymous with* HANDBOOK (*q.v.*).

MANUALE.   A case to protect a VOLUMEN (*q.v.*).

MANUSCRIPT.   A document of any kind which is written by hand, or the text of a music or literary composition in hand-written or type-script form, and which, in that form, has not been reproduced in multiple copies. An *illuminated manuscript* is one which has been decorated as described under ILLUMINATED BOOK (*q.v.*). Abbreviated MS. (*Pl.* MSS.).

MANUSCRIPT CATALOGUE.   One written by hand, or typed.

MANUSCRIPT LIBRARIAN. A librarian who has charge of a collection of manuscripts of all kinds, i.e. unprinted materials (whether written by hand or typed) other than books written by hand before the invention of printing (*libri manuscripti*).

MANUSCRIPT MUSIC BOOK. A book of MUSIC PAPER (*q.v.*).

MANUSCRIPT NOTE. A hand-written note in a book.

MANUSCRIPT SOCIETY, THE. An international organization of autograph collectors; founded in 1947, it aims to foster the greater use of original manuscript source material in the study, teaching, and writing of history; to facilitate the exchange of information and knowledge among researchers, scholars and collectors; to encourage the meeting of autograph collectors and stimulate and aid them in their various collecting specialities. Assistance is given to individuals and organizations in the matter of preservation and conservation, and in various other pertinent matters. A three-day meeting is held annually in an American city which is of interest to members because of manuscript resources. Membership is open to individuals and organizations and includes private collectors, dealers, librarians, historical societies, archivists, colleges and universities. Publishes *Manuscripts* (*q.*).

MAP. A plane representation of the earth's surface, or a part of same, indicating physical features, political boundaries, etc. *See also* MAPS. Also a similar representation of the heavens, showing the position of the stars, planets, etc. Also called an 'Astronomical map'. The first book to contain a printed map or diagram of the whole world was Isidore of Seville's *Etymologiarum sive Originum libri XX*, Augsburg, 19th November 1472. The earliest and most important maps to be printed from engraved copper plates in England were those of Christopher Saxton, who issued county maps between 1574 and 1579.

MAP ENDPAPERS. Endpapers on which maps are printed. *See also* ENDPAPER.

MAP FILE. A sequence of sheet or folded maps arranged in classified order, or alphabetically by place name. Sheet maps are kept in shallow drawers, often with hinged fronts which fall down and so reduce wear when consulting the maps, or in specially made vertical cabinets. *See also* PLAN CABINET.

MAP PAPER. *See* PLAN PAPER.

MAP PROJECTION. The arrangement of parallels and meridians so as to enable part, or the whole, of the spheroidal surface of the earth to be represented on a plane-surface.

MAP ROOM. A room devoted to the storage and consultation of maps.

MAPS.   For different kinds of maps, *see* ARTISTIC MAP, AVERAGE SLOPE MAP, ASTRONOMICAL MAP, CADASTRAL MAP, CARTOGRAM, CHOROCHROMATIC MAP, CHOROGRAPHIC MAP, CHOROPLETH MAP, CHOROSCHEMATIC MAP, DEMOPLETH MAP, DOT MAP, DYNAMIC MAP, FLOWLINE MAP, HYPSOMETRIC MAP, INTERNATIONAL MILLIONTH MAP, ISEPHODIC MAP, ISOCHRONIC MAP, ISOGONIC MAP, ISOPLETH MAP, RELATIVE RELIEF MAP.

MARBLED EDGES.   The three edges of a book cut solid, and stained to resemble marble. *See also* EDGES, SPRINKLED EDGES, STAINED EDGES, STIPPLED EDGES.

MARBLED PAPER.   Surface-coloured paper used by bookbinders. Marbling is done by floating white paper, or dipping the edges of a sewn book before inserting into the cover, on a bath of gum tragacanth, the surface of which has been sprinkled with various colours, and combed out to a desired pattern.

MARBLING.   The process of colouring the endpapers and edges of a book in imitation of marble.

MARBLING UNDER GILT.   Marbled edges of a book overlaid with gold. Usually the marbling is not very noticeable until the edges are fanned out. The style was first used in France in the seventeenth century, its invention being accredited to Le Gascon. Sometimes it is found in English bindings of the middle of the eighteenth century and later. *See also* GILT ON THE ROUGH, ROUGH GILT, SOLID GILT.

MARCIA C. NOYES AWARD.   *See* NOYES AWARD, MARCIA C.

MARGARET MANN CITATION.   *See* MANN CITATION, MARGARET.

MARGARET SCOGGIN SCHOLARSHIP.   *See* SCOGGIN SCHOLARSHIP, MARGARET.

MARGIN.   1. The unprinted area between printed or written matter and the edges of a page. The proportional width of the margins is a very important element in a properly balanced book-page. A good ratio is: head (top) margin 2; fore-edge (outside) 3; tail, also called 'lower' or 'bottom' (bottom) 4; back (inside) $1\frac{1}{2}$. 2. The area of a map, drawing or print, between the line enclosing the information area and the edge of the paper. 3. On microfilm, the area of background between the line enclosing the information area and the edge of the film frame.

MARGINAL FIGURE.   A figure printed in the margin of a book to indicate the number of a line of type for purposes of easy reference. *See also* RUNNERS.

MARGINAL-HOLE PUNCHED CARDS.   Cards which have rows of holes punched round the margins or over a large part of the card's area. These holes are notched or slotted to record information which is obtained, when required, by inserting needles, like knitting needles, in the holes and allowing cards on which the required information is recorded to fall away. They are also known as hand-sorted punched cards, edge-punched cards, edge-notched punched cards, Keysort cards, etc. In *direct* coding each marginal position is reserved for a specific piece of information or subject. In some designs of card, *combination* coding (the joint notching of two or more card positions) is possible. When the combination is such that the number of selection operations needed to isolate a subject is minimized, the coding scheme is called a 'Selector code'. *See also* DEQUEKER SYSTEM, EDGE-NOTCHED CARDS, SLOTTED CARDS.

MARGINAL NOTE. A note or GLOSS (*q.v.*) written or printed on the margin of a page opposite the portion of text to which it refers. Notes are called *footnotes* when printed at the bottom of the page, and *Shoulder-notes* when printed at the top corner of the page. Also called 'Marginalia'. *Synonymous with* SIDE NOTE (*q.v.*).

MARGINALIA. *Synonymous with* MARGINAL NOTES (*q.v.*).

MARK OF INTERROGATION. *Synonymous with* INTERROGATION POINT (*q.v.*).

MARK-SENSE. (*Information retrieval*) (*Verb*) To indicate a punch position by means of an electrically conductive pencil mark in such a way that a suitably designed machine can make the punch automatically (*IBM*).

MARKED PROOF. *See* PROOF.

MARKERS. In American libraries, those who process books by writing call numbers on the spines, insert book pockets, labels, etc.

MARKET LETTER. A bulletin issued by a stockbroker or investment house at regular intervals.

MARKING. 1. The placing of call numbers on books and other library materials. 2. The placing of a mark of ownership, with a note about disposition, on each item of a serial publication, as each is checked.

MARKING-UP. In book-binding, dividing the spine into equal portions and marking the position of the cords.

MARKOV PROCESS. *See* STOCHASTIC PROCESS.

MARKS. *See* CODE.

MARKS OF OMISSION. *Synonymous with* OMISSION MARKS (*q.v.*).

MARKS OF REFERENCE. *See* REFERENCE MARKS.

MARLF. Acronym for Middle Atlantic Regional Library Federation which was formed in 1969 to encourage the development of co-operation between libraries in the states of Delaware, Maryland, New Jersey, New York, Pennsylvania and West Virginia.

MARLIS. Abbreviation for Multi-Aspect Relevance Linkage, an information system which consists basically of three units; (a) Intermediate File, (b) the Ultimate Store, and (c) the Homo. The Intermediate File is a store of records on each of which is inscribed (a) one or more addresses in the Ultimate Store, and (b) code symbols characterizing the items at these addresses. These code symbols relate to only a few characterizing features of the items in the Ultimate Store. Examples of features entered on the Intermediate File records are (1) words (descriptors) selected as descriptive of the subject content of the items characterized, (2) the authors of these items, (3) their titles, dates and physical size. The code symbols on the Intermediate File records permit linear arrangement according to usual sequences as alphabetical or numerical. The Ultimate Store may take various physical forms, but consists essentially of a collection of items which are called 'volumes' because of the large amount of information each contains. Each 'volume' (of whatever form) bears a symbol, which is its address, and by which it is identified in the Intermediate File. Homo is the almost human computing unit of the system.

MASS BOOK. *See* MISSAL.

MASTER. The plate, or stencil in duplicating processes, from which copies are made. In photocopying, the negative from which a positive print is made.

MASTER CATALOGUE. A catalogue in which every main entry is a master card forming the official complete and up-to-date record of catalogued stock, and providing essential information for the cataloguers who maintain it. Being the union catalogue of the whole system it is usually kept in the cataloguing department or in the central library.

MASTER DATA CARD. *See* EAM CARD.

MASTER FILM. Any film, but usually a negative, which is used for making further copies.

'MASTER' HOLE. An extra hole punched beside each group of holes representing a particular field in a punched card, the master hole being punched to the edge of the card only if any other hole in the field is so punched. This permits rapid selection or rejection of cards whether punched or not punched, in any field, without having to needle the field hole by hole.

MASTER MICROFILM CARD. An APERTURE CARD (*q.v.*) containing microfilm, usually a negative, which is used for making further copies.

MASTHEAD. The statement of the name, ownership, address and frequency of publication, printer's name and address, and sometimes postage and subscription rates of a periodical publication. It is usually on the last or the editorial page of a newspaper, and on the editorial or contents page of a magazine. Also called 'Flag' and 'Logo'.

MATCHING. In computer technology, the comparison of two sets of codes to ascertain their similarity or difference.

MATERIAL BIBLIOGRAPHY. *See* HISTORICAL BIBLIOGRAPHY.

MATRIX (*Pl.* MATRICES). (*Printing*) 1. The mould from which a stereotype (stereo) or electrotype (electro) is made. The mould is made by placing wet flong (a material, about $\frac{1}{16}$ inch thick, made of alternate layers of tissue paper and blotting paper) over the type of which an impression is needed and then beating it with a stiff brush. It is then subjected to pressure, removed and dried. 2. A mould from which type is cast in a typesetting machine. 3. A copper mould which has been struck with a punch and from which individual type letters are cast. Also called a 'strike'. *See also* ELECTROTYPE, STEREOTYPE. (*Information retrieval*) A rectangular array of elements ... used to facilitate the study of problems in which the relation between these elements is fundamental.

MATT ART. *See* ART.

MATTER. 1. Type, whether in the process of setting up, or standing. It may be *live* matter (not yet printed from) or *dead* matter (awaiting distribution), *open* matter (leaded) or *solid* matter (without leads). The ancient terms, *fat* and *lean* matter, are still used to indicate the proportion of open spaces or break lines. The *fat*, of course, gives the compositor far less work to do than the *lean*. 2. Manuscript of copy to be printed. *See also* GOOD.

MAUD REPORT. The report of the Committee on the Management of Local Government which was set up by Sir Keith Joseph, when Minister of Housing and Local Government, on 3rd March 1964; so named after Sir John Maud, the Chairman. The terms of reference of the Committee were 'to consider in the light of modern conditions how local government might best continue to attract and retain people (both elected representatives and principal officers) of the calibre necessary to ensure its maximum effectiveness'. The report itself occupies volume 1 of the 5 volumes the overall title of which is *Management of local government*; volumes 2–4 are enquiries carried out for the Committee and entitled *The local government councillor*, *The local government elector* and *Local government administration abroad*. Volumes 1–4 were published in May 1967; volume 5 *Local government administration in England and Wales*, comprising further research enquiries carried out for the Committee, was published in July 1967. After Sir John Maud was created a life peer in 1967, the report became known as the Redcliffe-Maud Report.

MAYOR'S AUDITOR. *See* BOROUGH AUDITORS.

MAZARIN BIBLE. The 42-line Bible printed in Latin by Johann Gutenberg, Johann Fust and Peter Schoeffer at Mainz between 1450–5 and one of the earliest books to be printed from movable type. So called because the copy which first attracted the attention of bibliographers was discovered by Debure the French bookseller, in 1760, among the books of Cardinal Mazarin (1602–61) who was a well-known bibliophile. Mazarin's library is now in the Collège Mazarin, Paris. Forty-eight copies of this Bible are known, of which thirty-six are printed on paper and twelve on vellum; twenty-one in all are perfect. The British Museum possesses one of each, both perfect. Also known as the 'Gutenberg', or '42-line Bible'. *See also* MAINZ PSALTER.

MEAN LINE. (*Printing*) An imaginary line running along the top of all x-height letters, i.e. those without ascenders, a, c, e, etc. *See also* ASCENDER LINE, BASE LINE, CAP LINE.

MEARNE STYLE. The style of book decoration used during the seventeenth and early eighteenth centuries in England. This style is named after Samuel Mearne, the stationer and binder to Charles II and is a development of the Fanfare and Le Gascon styles. Red and black inlay was used with great effect, and the centre panel was often in the COTTAGE STYLE (*q.v.*). The ALL-OVER (*q.v.*) style was also often used. Also called 'Restoration style'. *See also* RECTANGULAR STYLE.

MEASURE. The width to which printed matter is set, i.e. the length of line. It is usually counted in 12-point ems, e.g. the full measure of the lines of type in this entry is 25 ems, i.e. $4\frac{1}{6} \div \cdot 166$ (or $\frac{1}{6}$) inches. *See also* DIDOT SYSTEM, EM, POINT.

MECHANICAL BINDING. A binding which uses a mechanical device such as a spiral binding of metal or plastic to hold the pages together.

MECHANICAL OVERLAY. *See* CHALK OVERLAY.

MECHANICAL PREPARATION. The preparation of books and other library materials for use. It includes rubber stamping and other forms of ownership marks, pasting labels, book pockets, and, where preparation is carried out in a cataloguing department, includes lettering books with class numbers and making out book-cards. (American.) *See also* PROCESSING CENTRE.

MECHANICAL SELECTION. (*Information retrieval*) The retrieving, or finding, of required information which has been recorded or indexed by machine punching or coding in such a way that when required no visual searching has to be done, but the records are scanned and extracted by machine. Also called 'Automatic selection'.

MECHANICAL WOOD. The lowest grade of wood pulp used in the

manufacture of paper, and prepared by the purely mechanical process of grinding. This method produces a higher yield than the chemical process but the resulting pulp is less pure. It is suitable only for newsprint: it has good printing qualities and is opaque but impermanent. Also called 'Groundwood pulp'. *See also* CHEMICAL WOOD.

MECHANICAL WOOD PULP. *Synonymous with* SEMI-CHEMICAL PULP (*q.v.*).

MECHANIZATION. Adding a notation to a classification schedule in order to mechanize the arrangement and re-arrangement.

MECHANIZED INDEXING. The accomplishment of indexing operations by mechanical means. This includes the preparation and compilation of indexes, and the sorting, assembling, duplication and interfiling of catalogue cards carrying index entries. *See also* AUTOMATIC INDEXING.

MECHANIZED LIBRARY. *See* VERAC.

MEDIA. Abbreviation for Magnavox Electronic Data Image Apparatus, a unit system type of information retrieval. (*See* MICROFILM.) It is somewhat similar to, but less expensive than, the MINICARD (*q.v.*) system. Film chips are 16 × 32 mm and contain two pages of text as well as a number which is legible without magnification; this number can also be obtained in binary code form for machine retrieval of the chips. It is made by the Magnavox Corporation.

MEDIA. Printed and audio-visual forms of communication and any necessary equipment required to render them usable.

MEDIA AIDE. An individual engaged in clerical or secretarial duties in a MEDIA CENTRE (*q.v.*).

MEDIA CENTRE. Sometimes used in the late 1960s in America for a school library, or learning centre in a school, where a full range of print and audio-visual media, necessary equipment, and the services of a media specialist, are accessible to students and teachers.

MEDIA FILE. Information prepared for buyers of advertising space in newspapers and periodicals, and giving particulars of circulation, column and type sizes and rates.

MEDIA PROGRAMME. All the instructional and related services provided for students and teachers by a MEDIA CENTRE (*q.v.*) and its staff.

MEDIA SPECIALIST. An individual who has broad professional preparation in educational media.

MEDIA STAFF. The personnel who carry out the work of a MEDIA CENTRE (*q.v.*) and its programme.

MEDIA TECHNICIAN. An individual who has training in the

preparation of materials and the operation and maintenance of apparatus.

MEDIAAN SYSTEM. A Belgian system of line measurement used in conjunction with the Fournier system of measuring type bodies; 12-point equals 0·1649 inch or 4·18 mm.

MEDICAL LIBRARY ASSISTANCE ACT. A 1965 amendment to the American Public Health Service Act, which expands the duties of the Board of Regents of the National Library of Medicine and the Surgeon General, provides 'a program of grants to assist in meeting the need for adequate medical services and facilities'. The programme, as outlined in the bill, will (1) assist in the construction of new, and the renovation, expansion, or rehabilitation, of existing medical library facilities; (2) help train medical librarians and other information specialists in the health sciences; (3) award special fellowships to physicians and scientists for the compilation of existing, and the creation of additional publications to facilitate the distribution and utilization of knowledge and information in the health sciences; (4) aid in research and investigations in medical library science and in the development of new techniques, systems, and equipment for information storage and retrieval; (5) help improve and expand the basic resources of medical libraries and related facilities; (6) aid in the development of a national system of regional medical libraries each of which would supplement the services of other medical libraries within the region served by it; and (7) provide financial support to biomedical scientific publications.

MEDICAL LIBRARY ASSOCIATION. Founded in the U.S.A. in 1898 to foster medical and allied scientific libraries, and exchange medical literature among its institutional members; to improve the professional qualifications and status of medical librarians; to organize efforts and resources for the furtherance of the purposes and objects of the Association. There are several subject groups and regional groups. Abbreviated MLA. Publishes *Bulletin* (q.) and *Vital Notes on Medical Periodicals*, 1952– .

MEDICAL RESEARCH COUNCIL. Established under this title in 1920, this Council is responsible to the Secretary of State for Education and Science for the promotion of research in medicine and the allied sciences. The Council is advised by a Clinical Research Board, a Biological Research Board and a Tropical Medicine Research Board and by about sixty special committees. The Council's largest establishment is the National Institute for Medical Research but there are eighty-one research units in addition. Abbreviated MRC.

MEDICAL SECTION. Formed on 24th September 1948 as a Section of the Library Association.

MEDIUM. 1. The weight of type-face midway between light and bold. This is the kind normally used for periodicals and book work. 2. An alternative name for Ben Day tint. *See* BEN DAY PROCESS. 3. The liquid, usually linseed oil, in which the pigment of printing ink is dispersed and by means of which it leaves an impression on paper. 4. A standard size of printing paper, 18 × 23 inches. 5. A finish given to paper that is neither highly calendered nor antique, but intermediate between the two extremes. Also called 'Medium finish'. 6. In music, the means (instrument/s or voice/s) by which musical sounds are produced, as indicated in the score.

MEDIUM CATALOGUING. Entries which are more complete than in Short or Selective Cataloguing but not so complete as in Full Cataloguing.

MEDIUM FACE. The weight of type-face half-way between light and bold. It is the kind that is normally used for periodicals and book work. Also called 'Half-dark type'.

MEDIUM FINISH. *See* MEDIUM 5.

MEDIUM WEIGHT PAPER. Sensitized photographic paper between 0·0084 and 0·0111 inches inclusive. *See also* PHOTOGRAPHIC PAPERS.

MEDLARS. Acronym for Medical Literature Analysis and Retrieval System which is operated at the NATIONAL LIBRARY OF MEDICINE (*q.v.*). It was initially a 2½-year project which was inaugurated to initiate and develop an electronic data processing, information, storage, and retrieval system in the field of medicine. The operation of this mechanized bibliographical system used the specially-designed Graphic Arts Composing Equipment (GRACE). MEDLARS is producing *Index Medicus* monthly and *Index Rheumatology* semimonthly, recurring bibliographies and demand bibliographies.

MELVIL DEWEY MEDAL. *See* DEWEY MEDAL, MELVIL.

MEMBERSHIP VOUCHER. An application voucher for membership of a lending library.

MEMBRANE. Single skin or parchment either forming part of a roll, or complete in itself. Its reverse side is called the Dorse.

MEMOIR. 1. A biography of a person written by someone else. 2. A monograph, or dissertation, on some noteworthy subject.

MEMOIRS. 1. A narrative of events based on the observations, experiences and memories of the writer; an autobiographical record. 2. A collection of researches and accounts of experiments, or dissertations on a learned subject, published by a learned society, especially in the form of a record of proceedings or transactions.

MEMORIAL.   1. A written statement of views in the form of a petition for submission to an authoritative body. 2. Usually in pl., a chronicle or document containing a historical narrative.

MEMORIAL VOLUME.   A publication, often consisting of contributions by several writers, in memory of a person or event. Also called 'Festschrift'.

MEMORIALIST.   A person presenting, or signatory to, a memorial.

MENDING.   Minor repairs to the leaves of a book not involving the replacement of any material or separation of the book from the cover. Not to be confused with REPAIRING (q.v.).

MERCATOR'S PROJECTION.   A chart enabling a mariner to steer a course by compass in straight lines; invented by Gerardus Mercator, all the meridians are straight lines perpendicular to the equator and all the parallels are straight lines parallel to the equator. It was first used by Mercator in a world map in 1569, and made navigation by dead reckoning easier. Edward Wright made its use practicable by publishing a set of tables for constructing the network of charts, and this development has made it possible to use Mercator's projection for all nautical charts.

MERCURIUS INTELLIGENCE.   See NEWSBOOK.

MERGE.   (Information retrieval). (Verb) To combine two files, already in sequence, into a single file (IBM).

MEROVINGIAN HANDWRITING.   The style of handwriting used in France from the sixth to the eighth centuries; a national style of cursive minuscule script which developed from the Latin cursive after the dissolution of the Roman Empire. See also CURSIVE, HANDWRITING.

MERRILL ALPHABETING NUMBERS.   A scheme devised by Mr. W. S. Merrill for arranging books in rough alphabetical order. The table is reprinted in the Introduction to Brown's *Subject Classification* and consists of 100 numbers allocated as the following first sixteen from the table show:

01	A	09	Beno	
02	Agre	10	Bix	
03	Als	11	Bou	The numbers
04	Ap	12	Brim	are applied
05	Ash	13	Bum	fractionally.
06	B	14	C	
07	Ban	15	Carr	
08	Bax	16	Chan	

MERRYTHOUGHT. (*Binding*) A finisher's stamp in the form of a merrythought, or wishbone, usually decorated with cusps or foliage ornament.

MeSH. Acronym for Medical Subject Headings, the 'vocabulary' of the (American) National Library of Medicine; it is used in connection with MEDLARS (*q.v.*), the Library's catalogue and the *Index Medicus*.

METABOLIC MAP. A map which shows the interrelations and correlations of biochemical reactions in metabolic sequences.

METAL FURNITURE. *See* FURNITURE.

METALLOGRAPHY. A lithographic process in which metallic plates are used instead of stone.

METALWORK. (*Binding*) A decorative ornament which is obviously an imitation of wrought and curved ironwork.

METHODICAL CATALOGUE. *Synonymous with* SYSTEMATIC CATALOGUE (*q.v.*).

METONYMY. The use of an attribute of a thing instead of the thing, e.g. 'crown' for a king. Reversed metonymy, i.e. the use of a descriptor naming the thing to indicate the attributes of the thing, is common.

METRIC BOOK SIZES. The following are the metric book sizes recommended in *Page sizes for books* (BS 1413:1970).

	Trimmed sizes in mm	Untrimmed sizes in mm	'Quad' Paper sizes in mm
Metric Cr. 8vo.	186 × 123	192 × 126	768 × 1008
Metric Lge. Cr. 8vo.	198 × 129	204 × 132	816 × 1056
Metric Demy 8vo.	216 × 138	222 × 141	888 × 1128
Metric Royal 8vo.	234 × 156	240 × 159	960 × 1272
A5	210 × 148*	215 × 152.5	RA0860 × 1220*

The trimmed and untrimmed sizes of case-bound books are those of a folded sheet after and before trimming 3 mm from the edges of a page (head, tail and foredge). The measurements followed by a * are ISO sizes. The ISO sizes which are internationally recommended for general printing are not suitable for books and cannot, in practice, be used. The trimmed page size for a paperback should be 180 × 110 mm.

METRO. The New York Metropolitan Reference and Research Library Agency, Inc. is a part of the movement to develop research and reference in the State of New York. It was founded in 1964 as a result of the activities of a committee of librarians from public, academic and special libraries in Metropolitan New York City. METRO began to function in 1966. It was granted a charter by the New York State Board of Regents. Its principal purpose is 'to improve reference library services in the New York metropolitan area by promoting and facilitating the utilization of existing resources and by developing additional resources'. It sponsors studies of research library needs and encourages inter-library co-operation; over thirty libraries are involved.

METRON.   A unit of metrical information which supplies one element (i.e. of evidence) for a pattern.

METROPOLITAN BOROUGH.   The official term used to indicate a borough in the area of the former London County Council. These boroughs ceased to exist on 1 April 1965 when the Greater London Act came into operation. The thirty-two boroughs in Greater London are known as London Boroughs and are so referred to in the Public Libraries and Museums Act 1964. *See also* BOROUGH COUNCIL, GREATER LONDON COUNCIL.

METROPOLITAN BOROUGH COUNCIL.   A BOROUGH COUNCIL (*q.v.*) within the former Metropolitan area of London. These ceased to exist after 1 April 1965 owing to the re-organization of local government in London. *See also* ASSOCIATION OF METROPOLITAN CHIEF LIBRARIANS, LIBRARY AUTHORITY, METROPOLITAN BOROUGH, Appendix 3.

MEZZOTINT.   1. A process of engraving on copper or steel in which the entire surface of the plate is slightly roughened, after which the drawing is traced and the plate smoothed in places by scraping, burnishing, etc., to produce the desired light and shade effect. 2. An engraving produced by the mezzotint process.

MICHEL STYLE.   The style of book decoration practised during the nineteenth century by Marius Michel and his son in France. The designs are often based on natural forms and the ornament is generally expressed in colour, outlined in blind, and very often without the use of gold.

MICROBIBLIOGRAPHY.   The production of subject bibliographies or indexes provided with supplements containing the full text in microprint of the material they list.

MICROCARD.   1. A term, trade-mark of the Microcard Corporation and covered by an American patent, which refers exclusively to 5 × 3 inch cards with images arranged in a specific manner. 2. The term is more generally used to indicate an opaque card of varying size on which microcopies have been reproduced photographically. A micro-card resembles a MICROFICHE (*q.v.*) in that the microcopies are arranged in rows and catalogue details, readable with the naked eye, are at the top of the card. It differs from other microforms in that the prints are positive as well as being opaque, and cannot be directly reproduced. A microcard is not readable without optical aid in the form of a specially-made reader.

MICROCITE. Trade name for a retrieval system which provides micro images of documents to which separate indexes are keyed. It was developed by the (American) National Bureau of Standards.

MICROCOPY. A copy of a document, or image, the scale of which is greatly reduced (compared with the original) by means of an optical device, and which needs an enlarger to enable it to be legible. Also called 'Microrecord'.

MICRODESENSITOMETER. A densitometer designed to measure the density of very small areas of a photographic image.

MICRO-DOCUMENT. Communication on a specialized topic, and usually short, e.g. a periodical or newspaper article, news-cutting, separate, or pamphlet which embodies micro-thought. *See also* MACRO-DOCUMENT, MICRO-THOUGHT.

MICROFICHE. A flat sheet of photographic film standardized (B.S. 4187:1967 and ISO/R 193) at 105 × 148 mm (nominally 4 × 6 inches) and 75 × 125 mm (nominally 3 × 5 inches), displaying at the top a catalogue entry, or title, readable with the naked eye, and bearing in horizontal and vertical rows micro-images of the complete text of a publication. The standard size of a frame is 11·25 × 16 mm (single) and 23 × 16 mm (double). Where a document is too long to be recorded on one microfiche, each subsequent one is called a 'Trailer' microfiche. Microfiche can be (a) a positive copy printed from strips of microfilm, (b) an actual frame cut from microfilm (usually 77 mm film), or (c) made directly with a step-and-repeat camera. Such sheets may be stored vertically like catalogue cards but require envelopes to protect them from damage. Envelopes can be opaque, with details written on, or transparent in which case the transparencies do not have to be removed from the envelopes. They can be inserted in the reading machines which are needed to be able to make use of the sheets. *See also* ULTRA-MICROFILM.

MICROFILM. A microphotograph on cellulose film. It may be negative or positive and may be 16, 35 or even 70 mm wide and of any length, depending on the number of exposures thereon.

For information retrieval purposes the length of the film may vary from 100 to 2,000 feet long; in addition to the roll film form the material used may be a small chip of film, normally 16 or 35 mm wide and from one to three inches long and known as the *unit system*, or it may be the *matrix system* which is based on cut sheets of film bearing micro images in a two-dimensional array, the film sizes being in the general area of 6 × 6 to 8 × 8 inches. Within each of these categories the systems may be further sub-divided into the so-called '*address*' *systems*, in which each item of the collection bears a number or title, and retrieval of the document results from a request for that document by identification, and another type of system which provides documents on the basis of a general description of their contents. The *unit system*, which includes the Aperture or PEEPHOLE CARD (*q.v.*) lends itself to system designs which will retrieve material quicker than the roll film systems. The *matrix system* makes possible even quicker access to material providing it is used as an address system only.

For special purposes, e.g. copying newspapers, or engineering drawings, or the preparation of MICROFICHE (*q.v.*), film of 70 mm wide is used.

Microfilm should be stored in a relative humidity of below 60 per cent and violent heat variations should be avoided: air conditioning is therefore desirable. Cabinets can be obtained which incorporate chemical drying and humidifying agents, but with these there is a risk of damage to the film. Microfilm should be stored on its edge, in a small metal or cardboard canister if in spool form, and placed in cabinets consisting of shallow drawers, or if in strip form, in transparent sheaths. Machines are necessary for reading microfilm.

MICROFILM ASSOCIATION OF GREAT BRITAIN. Inaugurated as the Council for Microphotography and Document Reproduction in England in 1961, the name being changed in 1965. Aims: to (a) assist in the promotion of the effective use of microfilm and document reproduction in industry, business, local government, education and all spheres of private and public administration, (b) to raise the standard of microfilm and document reproduction techniques and applications, (c) encourage wider understanding of these subjects and contribute to the development of improved facilities, (d) maintain contact with other bodies, both national and international, with similar aims and objects, for the exchange of information, (e) represent and promote the interests of all those concerned with handling information in microfilm. Abbreviated MAGB. Publishes *Microdoc* (q.).

MICROFILM FLOW CAMERA. A flow camera for taking automatically microcopies of documents, usually on film. *See also* CONTINUOUS FLOW CAMERA, MICROCOPY.

MICROFILM PRINT. An enlarged print made, normally on paper, from microfilm.

MICROFILM READER. An apparatus for the reading of microrecords by means of their enlarged projection on an opaque or transparent ground-glass screen, or white paper, or on a wall. It may be a machine for reading a microcopy on opaque material (microcard) in which light falls on the microcopy and is projected on to the screen by an optical system, or a machine for reading a microcopy on film (microfilm or microfiche).

MICROFILM READING GLASS. A magnifier for reading microcopies with or without artificial lighting equipment.

MICROFILM ROLL. A roll of MICROFILM (*q.v.*).

MICROFILM STRIP. A short length of MICROFILM (*q.v.*). *See also* FILMSTRIP, MICROSTRIP.

MICROFORM. A generic term indicating any form of micro record, whether on film, paper or other material.

MICROGRAPH. 1. A graphic record of the image, formed by a microscope, of an object. 2. An instrument constructed for producing extremely small copies of writing, printing or engraving, or for executing minute writing or engraving.

MICRO-IMAGE. *Synonymous with* MICROCOPY (*q.v.*).

MICROLEX. The trade name for readers, and for $6\frac{1}{2} \times 8\frac{1}{2}$ inch opaque laminated microcards, which are produced photographically by the Microlex Corporation, New York. Sheet negatives are made by moving the sheet film automatically after each exposure to produce rows of micro-images. Positive prints are then produced and laminated back to back. Each side of the card contains 200 pages of text. The method is used for the publication of legal reports and journals.

MICRO-OPAQUE. A copy of the whole, or part, of a book or other document made by means of microphotography, the print being on opaque paper or card. May be made solely by photographic means or by a printing method. Also called 'Opaque microcopy'. *See also* MICROCARD, MICROFORM, MICROPRINT.

MICRO-OPAQUE READER. A device for reading a MICRO-OPAQUE (*q.v.*).

MICRO-OPAQUE TAPE. A form of microtext which can be stuck on index cards used as a filing medium.

MICROPHOTOGRAPHY. Photography on so reduced a scale that a

14*

visual aid is required to discern the features of the resulting micro-photograph; 16 mm or 35 mm cellulose film is used, and the final form of the microcopy may be FILM STRIP, MICROFICHE, MICROFILM (*qq.v.*). The opposite of PHOTOMICROGRAPHY (*q.v.*).

MICROPRINT. A positive microphotograph size 9 × 6 inches and bearing a representation of 100 pages of a book. Reproduction is by a lithographic method on opaque paper. Microprint was invented by Mr. Albert Boni. *See also* MICROCARD, MICROFICHE, MICROFILM, MICRO-FORM, MICRO-OPAQUE, MICRORECORDING, MICROSLIDE, MICROSTRIP.

MICRORECORD. A copy of a document, the scale of which is reduced compared with the original, and which needs an enlarger to enable it to be legible. Also called 'Microcopy'.

MICRORECORDING. A form of photocopying in which the copy, either on film or paper, is reduced in size so much that it must be read in a 'reader' or by projection. The resultant copy may be made on roll film, sheet film or opaque paper, and is sometimes called 'Microtext'. *See also* MICROCARD, MICROFICHE, MICROFORM, MICROSLIDE, MICROSTRIP.

MICROREPRODUCTION. 1. The process of making microcopies of documents, the images being too small to be read by the unaided eye, on either opaque or transparent materials. 2. The copies so produced.

MICROSCOPIC EDITION. *See* MINIATURE BOOK.

MICROSEAL. Trade name for the microfilm aperture cards made by Microseal Inc.

MICROSECOND. A millionth of a second; a unit of measurement used to determine the speed at which a computer operates. *See also* NANOSECOND.

MICRO-SKANER. Trade name for pocket-size reader for microcards. Batteries provide illumination and a 20x enlargement is given.

MICROSLIDE. A single frame of microfilm which has been mounted for use in a microfilm projector.

MICROSTRIP. 1. Micro-images made from 16 mm or 35 mm film on to a roll of gummed paper, cut into sections and stuck on to standard size cards. 2. A strip of microfilm about 8 inches long which has been cut from a roll of film. It usually contains ten pages of text together with a title sheet. (*Concepts . . .*) Also called 'Microfilm strip', 'Strip microfilm'. 3. Trade name for positive prints from microfilm on strips of printing paper specially made for the purpose, and having a backing paper that peels off to expose a sticky surface permitting it to adhere to a card. 'Microtape' is a trade name for similar material.

MICROTAPE. *See* MICROSTRIP.

MICROTEXT. *See* MICRORECORDING.

MICRO-THOUGHT. (*Classification*) A subject of small extension, and therefore of great intension, usually embodied in the form of an article in a periodical, or of a section or a paragraph in a book, or of a pamphlet. *See also* EXTENSION, MACRO-DOCUMENT, MACRO-THOUGHT.

MICROTRANSPARENCY. A microcopy, usually on a film base, which is read by light passing through the film on its way to the eye of the reader. It is usually in the form of MICROFICHE or MICROPRINT (*qq.v.*).

MICROXEROGRAPHY. The creation of micro-images by means of xerography. Negative as well as positive images are possible.

MIDDLE ATLANTIC REGIONAL LIBRARY FEDERATION. *See* MARLF.

MIDDLE SPACE. *See* QUAD.

MIDWEST INTER-LIBRARY CENTER. Founded on 4th March 1949 to (1) provide more adequate research materials for the needs of mid-western scholarship and research; (2) provide for economical and efficient utilization of resources to avoid needless duplication and expense. The Midwest Inter-Library Center which was formed to carry out these objectives operated over a central block of twelve mid-western states and had as its two initial activities: (1) the co-operative collecting and housing of little-used material for the use of the region as a whole; (2) the development of a programme for filling out and enriching the resources of the region. Over twenty libraries (mainly university) co-operated in this scheme. Abbreviated MILC. Its name was changed on 25th January 1965 to the CENTER FOR RESEARCH LIBRARIES (*q.v.*).

MIEHLE. (*Printing*) The commonest type of TWO-REVOLUTION MACHINE (*q.v.*). Robert Miehle, a young Chicago machine-minder (d. 1932), made an important contribution to printing machine design by controlling the momentum of the bed (with the forme on it) at the instant of reversal by means of an enlarged star wheel and rack.

MILDRED L. BATCHELDER AWARD. *See* BATCHELDER AWARD, MILDRED L.

MILLBOARD. A kind of strong PASTEBOARD (*q.v.*) but made from old rope, sacking, wood pulp, and paper. Used for the covers of books which are heavy or have to stand hard wear. Also called 'Binder's board'.

MIMEOGRAPH. A trade name for a duplicator using wax stencils, and made by the A. B. Dick Co. of America. The term 'mimeographed' is incorrectly used for any form of duplication by means of wax stencils.

MINAFILE. Trade name for a type of vertical storage in which each unit consists of eight vertical drawers or containers, similar to steel transfer cases open at the top. The units can be built on to each other to any desired height, and will hold prints or photographs smaller than 15 × 10 inches in size.

MINIATURE.   1. A coloured initial letter or picture in an illuminated manuscript. 2. A greatly reduced copy of a document, but not so much as a MICROCOPY (*q.v.*), which is usually read or reproduced by means of optical aids. 3. A small highly-detailed drawing, painting, or portrait, especially on ivory or vellum.

MINIATURE BOOK.   A very small book, generally 3 inches (10 cm) or less in height, conceived as a whole on a tiny scale, printed with small type on suitable paper, bound in a binding which is tooled delicately, and, if illustrated, having drawings or reproductions which are in keeping with the size of the book. Many distinguished printers and publishers have issued such books. They include Bibles, books of devotion, almanacs, the poets, the classics, books for children, etc. The height is recorded in a catalogue entry in millimetres, not centimetres. Also called 'Lilliput edition', 'Microscopic edition'.

MINIATURE-PAINTER.   A painter of miniatures. Also called a 'MINIATURIST'.

MINIATURE SCORE.   *See* SCORE.

MINIATURIST.   *Synonymous with* MINIATURE-PAINTER (*q.v.*).

MINICARD.   A microfilm system of information retrieval, worked out in 1954 by the Eastman Kodak Corporation, in which images and codes are recorded on microfilm. Each piece is 16 × 32 mm in size and can contain up to twelve images photographed up to a reduction of 1/60 as well as the coding. A machine sorter, working on the same principle as a punched card sorter directs the minicards in the appropriate storage magazine, and a machine selector scans the code field passing the required minicards into a special magazine. They can then be examined in a reader; enlarged prints can be made if required. A file of two million Minicards, equivalent to 1,000 normal filing cabinets full of documents, will occupy a cabinet about 15 × 30 × 50 inches in size. The large capital required to acquire the Minicard machinery suggests installation only for regional or national purposes.

MINIM.   1. Single downstroke of a pen. 2. A sign in a musical score to indicate a note equal to two crochets or half a semi-breve.

MINIMATRIX SYSTEM.   *See* TERMATREX SYSTEM.

MINION.   An out-of-date name for a size of type equal to about 7 point.

MINISTER'S ACCOUNTS.   Accounts rendered by stewards, bailiffs or other manorial officials to the lord of the Manor.

MINISTRY OF TECHNOLOGY. This Ministry is responsible for Government interest in applied science and technology and has general responsibility for guiding and stimulating a major national effort to bring advanced technical and new processes into British industry. It administers ten of the fifteen research stations of the former DEPARTMENT OF SCIENTIFIC AND INDUSTRIAL RESEARCH (*q.v.*), and took over that department's responsibilities towards government-aided research associations. It incorporates the Atomic Energy Authority and is responsible for the National Research Development Corporation. The Minister of Technology is advised by the Advisory Council on Technology.

MINITEXT EDITION. Microprint version of a document whose text layout has been arranged to fit a given size page (*IBM*).

MINT. A book which is in the same condition as when it came from the publisher.

MINUSCULE. 1. A small style of writing developed from cursive. 2. LOWER CASE LETTERS (*q.v.*).

MINUTE CLASSIFICATION. *Synonymous with* CLOSE CLASSIFICATION (*q.v.*).

MINUTE MARK. A printer's symbol ' to represent feet (measurement) and minutes; it is also placed after a syllable on which the stress falls.

MINUTES OF PROCEEDINGS OF THE HOUSE OF LORDS. *See* PARLIAMENTARY PAPERS.

MISBOUND. A LEAF (*q.v.*), leaves or a SECTION (*q.v.*) which has been folded wrongly or misplaced by the binder.

MISCELLANEA. *Synonymous with* MISCELLANY (*q.v.*).

MISCELLANY. A collection of writings by various authors or on a variety of subjects. Also called 'Miscellanea'.

MISLEADING TITLE. One which does not indicate the subject-matter, or the form, of the work. In cataloguing when such a title is not clarified by the TRACING (*q.v.*), it can be amplified in the catalogue entry as: (a) *Doctor Zhivago, a novel;* (b) *A life of one's own* [autobiography]; or an explanatory note may be added.

MISLIC. Mid-Staffordshire Libraries in Co-operation. Established in 1963 and operating in parts of Staffordshire south of the LINOSCO (*q.v.*) scheme down to the environs of Birmingham. As well as co-operating in the interlending of material, the co-operative purchase of books costing over £7 is arranged to avoid unnecessary duplication.

MISPRINT. A typographical error.

MISSAL. A book containing the service for the celebration of the mass throughout the year. Sometimes loosely used for any book of devotions.

Before the invention of printing, the writing of missals was a branch of art which reached a high state of excellence in the monasteries. The books were written upon vellum in the most beautiful style of penmanship, and were adorned with the utmost magnificence. Also called 'Mass book'. *See also* BOOK OF HOURS.

MISTLETOE TOOL. (*Binding*) A finisher's tool which appears to have been first used on Irish bindings in about 1766; it is particularly common on the panels of spines of Irish bindings about 1780. In some forms it is embossed, and seems to be a feather rather than a mistletoe leaf.

MITRED. (*Binding*) A junction of lines at an angle of 45 degrees such as is necessary at the turn-in of covering material on the inside of the covers. Lines, in finishing, which meet each other at right angles without over-running. The connexion at the angles of an outer FRAME 2 (*q.v.*) to an inner frame or PANEL 1 (*q.v.*) by the diagonal use of FILLETS 1 (*q.v.*) or a ROLL (*q.v.*).

MITRED CORNER. (*Binding*) Turning the covering material over the inside of the board in such a way, by cutting, that the turn-ins meet without overlapping. *See also* LIBRARY CORNER, SQUARE CORNER.

MIXED NOTATION. *See* NOTATION.

MNEMONIC CHARACTERISTIC. The use of symbols in such a manner that they have a more or less constant meaning when applied anywhere in a classification scheme.

MNEMONICS. Symbols of the notation of a classification. When they are drawn from lists of divisions, tables or parts of schedules they are called by Ranganathan 'scheduled mnemonics'. Related ideas or 'associations' as used by Ranganathan in classifying, are called 'unscheduled mnemonics' or 'seminal mnemonics' to distinguish them from 'scheduled mnemonics'. Mnemonics may be *constant*, i.e. always denoting the same aspects or form wherever used throughout a scheme of classification, or *variable*, i.e. occasionally alternated or altered to suit the special needs of a specific subject. Dewey's common form divisions now called 'Standard subdivisions' are variable whereas the form marks of the Universal Decimal Classification are constant. *Systematic* mnemonics are those which reflect a consistent order; they are mainly a result of synthesis. *Literal* mnemonics depend on the use of letters in notation in such a way that the symbol for a class is the initial letter of the same class.

MOBILE BRANCH LIBRARY. *See* TRAVELLING LIBRARY.

MOBILE LIBRARIAN. A librarian whose duties are mainly carried out in a travelling or mobile library.

MOBILE LIBRARY. (*County Libraries*) A vehicle devised, equipped and operated to provide, as far as reasonably practicable, a service comparable to a part-time branch library.

MOBILIBRARY. *Synonymous with* MOBILE LIBRARY (*q.v.*).

MODELLED INITIAL. In a mediaeval illuminated manuscript, an initial letter given a rounded or three-dimensional aspect.

MODERN FACE. Printers' types, French in origin dating from 1698; but not popular until after the Revolution when Didot (France), Bodoni (Italy), Figgins, Thorne and Fry (England) cut various versions. 'Moderns' were popular throughout the nineteenth century. They are characterized by vertical emphasis, there being a considerable difference between thick and thin strokes and curves thickened in the centre. The fine bracketed serifs are at right angles to the strokes. Examples are: Bodoni (most foundries); Walbaum (Monotype). The following is in 12 pt. Bodoni:

ABCGEFGHIJKLMNOPQRSTUVWXYZ
abcdefghijklmnopqrstuvwxyz   1234567890

For specimen alphabets of other faces, *see* TYPE FACE. The term 'Didone' has superseded 'Modern face' for this category of type faces. *See also* ARABIC FIGURES, OLD FACE, TRANSITIONAL.

MODIFICATION. (*Cataloguing*) Variation in the presentation of information in catalogue entries by, for example, inversion of the initials of a manufacturing firm to bring the last name to the front, the omission of the first part of a geographic name if it indicates a type of governmental administration, the use of a uniform title (perhaps a translation from an original 'foreign' form) to bring all entries for the same work together. (*Indexing*) A word or phrase(s) inserted after a heading to indicate an aspect or character of the information given in the text at the place referred to, to limit its meaning or subdivide the entries, e.g. Land, claims and cessions of, by the states, 319 *sq*.

MODIFIERS. *See* ROLES.

MODULANT. An INTERFIX (*q.v.*); a standardized suffix added to the root of a word (Ruby English) to bring out the different aspects of a word's basic meaning (U.S. Patent Office). *See also* ROLES, RUBY ENGLISH.

MODULAR CONSTRUCTION. A system of building construction introduced for libraries by A. S. Macdonald in 1945 whereby the cubage between the exterior walls, foundations and roof is divided into equal, rectangular prisms of space, bordered on bottom and top by floors and ceilings and on the vertical edges by structural columns. This enables the area of departments to be varied at will and makes it possible to provide stack rooms horizontally or vertically in close proximity to the departments, and to extend or contract them as desired. A modular library is one constructed on this principle.

MODULAR PLANNING. Planning a building so that it consists of a number of modules (units), having no permanent internal walls dividing the floor area into rooms. Each floor is supported by pillars at regular intervals and these pillars are often partly hollow to accommodate plumbing, electric wiring and air conditioning ducts. Except for core service areas (lifts, staircases, etc.) which are enclosed by permanent walls, the whole of the floor area can be sub-divided into rooms and departments by placing free-standing book cases, partitions and furniture where desired, and can be varied at will. Also called 'Unit construction'.

MODULATION OF TERMS. A phrase used to indicate the development of terms, or headings, of a classification. A term should modulate into the term following it.

MONK. An ink blot or splash on a printed sheet; the term originated in the days when formes were inked with ink balls. *See also* FRIAR.

MONOCHROME. Any illustration in one colour.

MONOGRAPH. A separate treatise on a single subject or class of subjects, or on one person, usually detailed in treatment but not extensive in scope and often containing extensive bibliographies. Frequently published in series.

MONOGRAPH SERIES. A series of monographs with a collective title, often issued by a university or society.

MONOLINE. A type face in which all the strokes of the characters appear to be of the same thickness. Most LINEALE and SLAB SERIF (*qq.v.*) types are of this kind. *See also* GEOMETRIC.

MONOPHOTO. Trade name for a photo-typesetting, or film-setting, machine manufactured by the Monotype Corporation which produces characters on film instead of metal. The machine is virtually a complex photographic enlarger; one image of a character can therefore be easily enlarged to a great number of sizes. These are related to the traditional typographic sizes which can be set from 6 point to 12 point in one point steps and from 12 point to 24 point in two points steps. The space between lines can be varied by as little as half a point, e.g. 10 point type can be set as if on a body of $10\frac{1}{2}$, 11, $11\frac{1}{2}$, 12, $12\frac{1}{2}$ points, and so on. *See also* FILMSETTING.

MONOTYPE. Separate paper-perforating and type-founding machines invented by Tolbert Lanston for composing and casting single types. Individual types are cast on the casting machine from paper rolls perforated on the perforating machine in which a keyboard is incorporated.

MONTAGE. The combination of several photographs, drawings, or parts of pictures, blended to form a single illustration for decorative, display or advertising purposes.

MONTHLY. A periodical which appears once a month, with the possible exception of certain months, usually one during the summer.

MOOERS' LAW. 'An information retrieval system will tend *not* to be used wherever it is more painful and troublesome for a customer to have the information than for him not to have it.'

MOON TYPE. A system of reading for the blind in which the letters are formed by raised lines based on a greatly modified form of Roman capital letters. It is more easily learned than Braille and is consequently used by adults who have become blind late in life and find it difficult to master Braille. It is named after Dr. William Moon, a blind clergyman who lived at Brighton.

MORDANT. Acid or other corrosive, used in etching plates.

MORGUE. A collection of obituary notices of famous living people kept up to date in newspaper offices.

MOROCCO. 1. Leather manufactured from the skins of goats and largely used in bookbinding. 'Niger' morocco is tanned with a vegetable tannin, and being durable, flexible and relatively thin, is suitable for bookbinding. 'Persian' morocco lacks strength and durability and is unsuitable for bookbinding. 2. Leather made from sheepskin and lambskin but finished to look like goatskin.

MORTICE (MORTISE). An open space cut out of a printing plate or block so that type may be inserted in it. A block so prepared is said to be 'pierced'.

MOSAIC. A book decoration formed by inlaying or onlaying small pieces of leather of various colours to form a pattern. The technique is particularly associated with the work of the eighteenth-century French binders Padeloup le Jeune and Le Monnier.

MOSAIC MAP. A photographic representation of the earth's surface and the buildings, etc. thereon, made from two or more aerial photographs placed side by side.

MOTHER'S ROOM. A room in a public library in which are kept books for mothers to take home to read to children who have not themselves learned to read, and also books on child psychology, child care and other subjects concerned with the upbringing of children.

MOTORISED SHELVES. A form of compact shelving in which the bookcases are moved by electrical, or mechanical, power.

MOTTLED CALF.   A calf binding which has been mottled with colour or acid dabbed on with sponges or wads of cotton.

MOTTLED FINISH.   A paper with a variegated colour surface produced by mixing two slightly differently dyed shades of fibres, or by a drip of colour on the wet pulp.

MOULD.   (*Paper*) A rectangular wooden frame over which brass wires or wire cloth is stretched to serve as a sieve in order to permit water to drain away from the pulp fibres to form a sheet of paper. A wooden frame called a DECKLE (*q.v.*) fits round the edges of the mould and forms a tray with raised edges; this keeps the required thickness of pulp fibre on the wires until the excess water has drained away. (*Printing*) A device in two parts used for casting movable type.

MOULD-MADE PAPER.   An imitation hand-made paper made from rag FURNISH (*q.v.*) on a machine.

MOUNT.   A card or paper on to which something is pasted to protect, preserve, or display it.

MOUNTED.   A cutting, print, photograph, page, or similar item which is pasted on a mount.

MOUNTED PLATE.   An illustration printed on a separate sheet of paper and pasted to a page of a book.

MOVABLE LOCATION.   *See* RELATIVE LOCATION.

MOVABLE TYPE.   (*Printing*) Type cast as single units as distinct from slugs or blocks on which are a number of characters. It was the use of movable type towards the end of the fifteenth century, instead of engraved blocks, which led to the rapid development of printing. *See also* INCUNABULA, SLUG, XYLOGRAPHY.

MS.   Abbreviation for MANUSCRIPT (*q.v.*).

MUDÉJAR BINDINGS.   Spanish bindings in Cordovan leather, done between the thirteenth and fifteenth centuries by Moorish inhabitants of Spain known as mudéjares who were allowed religious freedom and to practise their crafts, of which bookbinding was one. The main design was a blind-tooled pattern of double outline interlacings with stamped strips of dots, curves, rings, etc. to form a background.

MUDGE CITATION, ISADORE GILBERT.   Instituted in 1958, and administered by the Reference Services Division of the American Library Association, this Citation is given annually to a person who has made a distinguished contribution to reference librarianship. This contribution may take the form of an imaginative and constructive programme in a particular library, the writing of a significant book or articles in the reference field, creative and inspirational teaching or reference services, active participation in professional associations devoted to references services, or in other noteworthy activities which stimulate reference librarians to more distinguished performance. The first person to receive the Citation was Mary Neill Barton in 1959.

MULL. . A thin loosely woven cotton cloth glued on to the backs of books to help hold the sections together. Known as 'super' in America.

MULTI-ASPECT INDEXING. Recording the various subjects a document deals with under the various subject headings (to which a card has been assigned), or by some other means. Usually punched cards are used because of the greater speed possible when retrieving information. *See also* Co-ordinate Indexing.

MULTICOUNTY LIBRARY. A library established by the joint action of the governing bodies, or by vote of the residents, of the counties concerned, and governed by a single board of library directors. (American.)

MULTI-DIMENSIONAL CLASSIFICATION. The characterization of each document from more than one point of view. This can be accomplished for the physical placing of documents only when there are as many copies as there are classificatory points of view. When classification schemes also serve as guides to the physical collection of documents, as in a classified catalogue, copies of catalogue cards (each representing a document) are placed at the different numbers for each point of view. Although each catalogue card represents a single document, one such document may be represented by several cards. *See also* Rigid Classification.

MULTI-DIMENSIONAL RETRIEVAL. Bringing together references to any one concept or set of concepts on demand, on one card or other form of Tally (*q.v.*). Edge-punched cards and tallies used in a variety of mechanical methods are used for this purpose.

MULTI-LAYER PAPER. *See* Furnish Layer.

MULTIPLE APPROACH, PRINCIPLE OF. A fundamental fact that books may be approached from the points of view of author, title, subject, series, etc.; this always has to be borne in mind by cataloguers. *See also* Cataloguing, Principles Of.

MULTIPLE MEANING. *Synonymous with* Polysemia (*q.v.*).

MULTIPLE REFERENCE. *Synonymous with* General Reference (*q.v.*).

MULTI-TIER STACK. A self-supporting metal framework extending from basement to roof and designed to carry the weight of the deck floors and the book load. The columns are placed close together and permit the use of thin slab concrete or metal plate floors as well as shelf supports. Local bye-laws in many English towns do not permit this type of construction.

MULTI-VOLUME BOOK.   A work in more than one volume.

MUNICIPAL AUDIT.   Borough councils may adopt in its entirety the system of district audit, or may choose to have professional audit which means that the accounts are audited by practising auditors whose qualifications are prescribed in the Act.* In practice, district audit and professional audit are the only two effective systems which are operated, but boroughs have additionally, the right to appoint three 'Borough auditors', two of whom are elected by the local government electors for the borough, and one is appointed by the mayor. This system is very little used except as a tradition in a few boroughs.

MUNICIPAL LIBRARY.   A public library serving an urban area and financed, maintained, and administered by any local government authority other than a county or urban district council. The use of the word 'municipal' is becoming less common, and has no legal meaning or connexion. In America, one which may also be similarly provided by a village or school district. In Australia, a public library.

MUNIMENT ROOM.   A room in which archives are kept.

MURRAY GOTTLIEB PRIZE.   *See* GOTTLIEB PRIZE, MURRAY.

MUSIC LIBRARY.   One devoted to music.

MUSIC LIBRARY ASSOCIATION.   Founded in the U.S.A. in 1931 to promote the development of music libraries, to encourage studies in the organization and administration of music in libraries. Abbreviated M.L.A. Publishes *Notes* (q.), *Supplement for Members* (irreg. to membs.), *Cumulated Index of Record Reviews* (irreg.).

MUSIC PAPER.   Paper ruled with staves of five lines for the writing of music. When made up into a book it is called a manuscript music book.

MUSIC SCORE.   *See* SCORE.

MUSICAL DESCRIPTION.   A description of the separate parts for instruments or voices used *simultaneously* during a musical performance. To be distinguished from a BIBLIOGRAPHICAL DESCRIPTION (*q.v.*) which is only concerned with *successive* parts and/or volumes (i.e. the various editions) of a musical composition.

MUSICAL WORK.   A composition to be played by one or more musical instruments or to be sung by one or more human voices.

MUSICOLOGY.   The study of music as a branch of knowledge or field of research.

MUSIKRITER.   A machine that will type music scores. It was invented

* The Local Government Act, 1933.

by Miss Lily Pavey of Camberwell, London, and first manufactured by the Imperial Typewriter Co. in 1964.

MUTTON. *See* EM QUADRAT.

n.c. Abbreviation for 'not catalogued'; relates usually to a volume of miscellaneous pamphlets which are not individually catalogued.

NCR. Abbreviation for No Carbon Required and also for the National Cash Register Company who have developed the type of paper indicated. It is used as business stationery and avoids the necessity of using carbons to make copies; the paper appears normal but is back-coated with a chemical which by contact with another paper through pressure causes an outline of the pressure to be reproduced. It is clean to handle.

NCRLC. Abbreviation for National Committee on Regional Library Co-operation. Formed in 1931. Functions: (a) to act as an advisory body on all matters concerning existing or potential regional areas, (b) to provide liaison between the various regional bureaux and the National Central Library. The Committee consists of representatives of the regions, the National Central Library, the Library Association, and the Association of University Teachers. The Committee was responsible for instituting the INTER-REGIONAL SUBJECT COVERAGE SCHEME and the PROVINCIAL JOINT FICTION RESERVE (*qq.v.*). *See also* JOINT FICTION RESERVE.

n.d. *See* NO DATE.

NFSAIS. Acronym for NATIONAL FEDERATION OF SCIENCE ABSTRACTING AND INDEXING SERVICES (*q.v.*).

NLL. Acronym for National Lending Library for Science and Technology (*q.v.*).

NLL cards. An international card catalogue of published aero-dynamic measurements first proposed by the National Lucht-en-ruimtevaart Laboratorium at Amsterdam and now being issued regularly.

NLLST. Acronym for National Lending Library for Science and Technology (*q.v.*).

n.p. 1. Abbreviation for no place of publication, no printer's name, no publisher's name. *See also* NO DATE. 2. Abbreviation for 'new paragraph'; an instruction to the compositor that a new paragraph is to be begun. It is indicated in a manuscript or proof by the letters 'n.p.' in the margin and [or // in the text before the first word of the new paragraph.

NTBL. Abbreviation for Nuffield Talking Book Library for the Blind which was established in 1935 as the Talk Book Library for the Blind, the name being changed in 1954. In 1960 the Nuffield Foundation gave a grant to convert the information then on records on to tape. The Library is administered by the Royal National Institute for the Blind and St. Dunstan's through their joint Sound Recording Committee, and maintained by the funds of these two voluntary charities. Membership is free and open to blind persons over the age of 21 who are registered with their local Blind Welfare Authority. The 'books' are specially recorded in the Committee's own studio; they are mainly fiction but a number of recordings of biographies, travel books and other non-fiction subjects are also produced. The 'books' are lent free and played on special recording machines which are non-commercial and rented from the Library. Now known as the British Talking Book Service for the Blind.

n.y.p. Not yet published.

NACL. Acronym for NATIONAL ADVISORY COMMISSION ON LIBRARIES (*q.v.*).

NAKED FORME. Pages of type secured by page-cord. *See also* DRESSED FORME, FORME.

NAME AUTHORITY FILE. The list of name headings used in a given catalogue, and the references made to them from other forms. *See also* AUTHORITY LIST, SUBJECT AUTHORITY FILE.

NAME CATALOGUE. A catalogue arranged alphabetically by names of persons or places, or both, whether used as authors or subjects.

NAME ENTRY. In indexing, an entry under the name of a person, place, or institution.

NAME INDEX. An index of names of authors or other persons.

NAME PALLET. *See* BINDER'S TICKET.

NAME REFERENCE. Where alternative forms of names are available, a reference to the one adopted for the heading in a catalogue.

NANOSECOND. A billionth of a second, a unit of measurement used to determine the speed at which computers operate. *See also* MICROSECOND.

NANTIS. Abbreviation for Nottingham and Nottinghamshire Technical Information Service which was formed in 1962 to improve the existing co-operation between libraries and information services in the Nottinghamshire area, to speed the flow and interchange of books and information, and to strengthen the local resources of material available. Membership is open to any library, information service, research organization, trade organization, industrial or business firm in the City of Nottingham and County of Nottinghamshire. Associate membership is open to similar organizations in the industrial areas surrounding Nottinghamshire. The service is intended to be financially self-supporting, members paying an annual subscription of £3 and associate members £5. Research associations and industrial trade organizations are admitted to free membership by reason of their special position as the corporate representatives of industry. The headquarters of the organization is at the Commercial and Technical Department of the Nottingham City Library.

NARRATION. *Synonymous with* RELATION (*q.v.*).

NARROW. A book whose width is less than two thirds its height.

NATIONAL ACADEMY OF SCIENCES – NATIONAL RESEARCH COUNCIL. A private, non-profit organization of scientists, dedicated to the furtherance of science and to its use for the general welfare. The Academy was established in 1863 under a Congressional charter signed by President Lincoln, and is required to advise the Federal Government on scientific matters; it is not a governmental agency. The National Research Council was established by the Academy in 1916, at the request of President Wilson, to enable scientists generally to associate their efforts with those of the limited membership of the Academy in service to the nation, to society and to science in the U.S.A. and overseas. Income is received from both public and private sources, and by contributions, grant, or contract. Funds are used to stimulate research and its applications, to survey the broad possibilities of science, to promote effective utilization of the scientific and technical resources of the U.S.A., and to further the general interests of science. Abbreviated NAS–NRC. Publishes *Industrial Research Laboratories of the United States*, 11th ed., 1960. *Scientific and Technical Societies of the United States and Canada*, 7th ed., 1961.

NATIONAL ADVISORY COMMISSION ON LIBRARIES. Established in the U.S.A. by Executive Order of 2nd September 1966, and issued by President Johnson. The Commission was charged to make a comprehensive study and appraisal of the role of libraries as sources of scholarly pursuits or centres for the dissemination of knowledge, and make recommendations designed to ensure an effective and efficient library system for the nation. The report was submitted to President Johnson on 15th October 1968. It recommended that it be declared national policy, enunciated by the President and enacted into law by Congress, that the American people should be provided with library and informational services adequate to their needs, and that the Federal Government, in collaboration with State and local governments and private agencies, should exercise leadership assuring the provision of such services. Abbreviated NACL.

NATIONAL AGRICULTURAL LIBRARY. One of the three national libraries in the U.S.A., the others being the Library of Congress and the National Library of Medicine. It was formed as a result of the Organic Act of 1862 which placed upon the Department of Agriculture the duty of 'acquiring and preserving all information concerning agriculture', the nucleus of the library being the transfer of the book and journal collection amounting to 1,000 volumes from the Agricultural Division of the Patent Office. The library was designated the National Agricultural Library in 1962. Its services are provided to personnel of the Department of Agriculture in Washington, and the field, state agricultural agencies, agricultural colleges and universities, research institutions, industry, individual scientists, farmers and the general public in every part of the world. The stock numbers 1,300,000 volumes. In 1969 the library moved to a fifteen-storey building in Beltsville, Maryland. Abbreviated NAL.

NATIONAL ARCHIVES AND RECORDS SERVICE. A grouping of five co-ordinate offices: the Office of Federal Records Centers, the Office of the Federal Register, the Office of the National Archives, the Office of Presidential Libraries, and the Office of Records Management. It supersedes the National Archives Establishment and is responsible to the Administrator of General Services of the U.S. government for promoting improved current records management and disposal practices in federal agencies; for selecting, preserving and making available to the government and the public the permanently valuable non-recurrent records of the federal government; for the preservation, publication and administration of the historical materials in the Franklin D. Roosevelt Library at Hyde Park, N.Y.

NATIONAL ART LIBRARY. The library of the Victoria and Albert Museum in South Kensington, London. One of the national libraries maintained by the British government.

NATIONAL ASSOCIATION OF LOCAL AND GOVERNMENT OFFICERS. The trade union to which most librarians and other officers employed by local authorities and 'utility' services (e.g. gas and electricity undertakings) belong. It is the largest trade union for 'black-coated' workers. Abbreviated NALGO.

NATIONAL BIBLIOGRAPHY. A bibliography of books produced in the language of one country, irrespective of the country in which published, about the country by natives of the country irrespective of residence, and of books produced in that country, whatever their language.

NATIONAL BIOGRAPHY. A publication containing biographies of nationals of one country, usually in alphabetical order.

NATIONAL BOOK AWARDS. Bestowed in the U.S.A. to honour books worthy of a distinguished role in general and cultural life. They are not intended for outstanding research, scholarship or scientific achievement in themselves, or to recognize works written for professional or otherwise specialized audiences, but rather to recognize distinction of thought and spirit, and their creative, literary expression. The $1,000 awards are presented annually for books written by American citizens and published in the United States in the preceding two calendar years. The prizes are contributed by six American book industry associations. From 1960 onwards the awards have been administered by the National Book Committee, Inc., a non-profit and independent group of citizens. A twenty-member Awards Advisory Committee selects judges for each of the panels: arts and letters; children's literature; fiction; history and biography; poetry; translation; the sciences; philosophy and religion. *See also* NATIONAL BOOK COMMITTEE, NATIONAL MEDAL FOR LITERATURE.

NATIONAL BOOK CENTRE. *See* BRITISH NATIONAL BOOK CENTRE, NATIONAL CENTRAL LIBRARY.

NATIONAL BOOK COMMITTEE. An American non-profit, educational society of citizens devoted to the use of books. Founded in 1954, its purpose is 'to keep books free, make them widely available, and encourage people to read them'. The two principal continuing projects are the NATIONAL BOOK AWARDS (*q.v.*) and the National Library Week Program. On 4th May 1965 it instituted the annual presentation of the NATIONAL MEDAL FOR LITERATURE (*q.v.*).

NATIONAL BOOK LEAGUE. A non-commercial body the object of which is to provide certain services and facilities intended to foster and maintain an interest in books. It is supported largely by publishers and booksellers as well as by libraries of various kinds, authors and private individuals. A Book Information Bureau is maintained at the headquarters, 7 Albemarle St., London, W.1., where a restaurant, club and exhibition rooms are also provided. Lectures and exhibitions of books are held there, and some of the exhibitions are afterwards shown in other British towns and overseas countries. Book lists on a variety of subjects are published from time to time. The National Book League developed from the National Book Council which was formed in 1924, the change of name and a new constitution occurring in 1944. Abbreviated NBL. Publishes *Books* (bi-monthly).

NATIONAL BOOK SALE. A plan which was introduced in 1955 by the British book trade to sell new copies of fairly recent publications for which there was reduced demand, at considerably reduced prices.

The Sale is organized by a joint committee of the Publishers Association and of the Booksellers Association which fixes the date of the sale. No bookseller may sell at reduced prices before or after the agreed dates, and during the Sale may sell at any price but not higher than two-thirds of the published price.

NATIONAL BUREAU OF STANDARDS. This organization serves as the focal point in the American Federal Government for assuring maximum application of the physical and engineering sciences to the advancement of technology in industry and commerce. The work of the Bureau is organized into four institutes: the Institute for Basic Standards, the Institute for Materials Research, the Institute for Applied Technology and the Central Radio Propagation Laboratory. Abbreviated NBS. Publishes *Journal of the National Bureau of Standards* (in four sections *Physics and Chemistry* (6 p.a.), *Mathematics* and *Mathematical Physics* (q.), *Engineering and Instrumentation* (q.), *Radio Science* (m.), *Technical News Bulletin* (m.), *NBS Research Highlights* (a.).

NATIONAL CATALOGUE. A list of books in a number of libraries in a country. *See also* NATIONAL BIBLIOGRAPHY.

NATIONAL CENTRAL LIBRARY. Formerly the Central Library for Students; the national centre for lending books for study, and the clearing house for loans of books and periodicals between public, university and special libraries of all types, working in co-operation with Regional Library Bureaux, and with special libraries known in this connexion as OUTLIER LIBRARIES (*q.v.*). It is also the main centre for information about books, and the the re-distribution of 'unwanted' books, at home and abroad, the latter being carried out by the BRITISH NATIONAL BOOK CENTRE. Abbreviated NCL. *See also* REGIONAL BUREAUX.

NATIONAL COMMITTEE ON REGIONAL LIBRARY CO-OPERATION. *See* NCRLC.

NATIONAL DEFENSE EDUCATION ACT, TITLE III. This American Act of 1964 provides that the Federal government will pay 50 per cent of the cost of school books and audio-visual materials in science, mathematics, modern foreign languages, civics, English, geography, history, economics and reading; also the cost of full processing or for the cataloguing kits and minor re-modelling of existing facilities. The grants also apply to equipment in audio-visual libraries which are part of a school, an instructional materials centre, or a curriculum centre. Abbreviated NDEA.

NATIONAL FEDERATION OF SCIENCE ABSTRACTING AND

INDEXING SERVICES. A confederation of major abstracting and indexing service organizations. Founded in the U.S.A. in January 1958 to courage and improve the documentation (abstracting, indexing, and analysing) of the world's scientific and technological literature so as to make it readily available to all scientists and technologists by (a) encouraging the development of abstracting and indexing for the specialized subjects fields not covered by such services, and the further development of such services; (b) seeking greater uniformity in such matters as journal citations and abbreviations and transliteration of foreign titles; (c) co-operation, education, research, and the pursuit of mutually useful enterprises, to strive for the best possible research information services for science and technology in the U.S. and abroad. Abbreviated NFSAIS. Publishes *Proceedings* (a.).

NATIONAL HANDWRITING. *See* HANDWRITING.

NATIONAL LENDING LIBRARY FOR SCIENCE AND TECHNO-
LOGY. Founded (as a consequence of a recommendation in the *Eighth Annual Report* of the Advisory Council on Scientific Policy, 1955) in 1962 and based on the library of the Department of Scientific and Industrial Research with books and bound periodicals from the Science Museum Library and other sources. It aims to assemble a comprehensive collection of the world's literature (mainly periodicals and reports) of science and technology, including agriculture, and, to some extent, medicine, in all languages, and is strong in foreign, especially Russian, material in the original and in translation. The NLL took over the Book Loan Service from the Science Museum and lends material on request through university, technical, college, the larger public, and other libraries which have been appointed agents. Prepares and sells translations of technical articles and books in Russian. Answers enquiries about Russian technical literature, translations from the Russian, and the documents that were collected after World War II. Possesses 500,000 volumes. Subscribes to over 32,000 current serials of all kinds, including report literature, from all over the world. Situated at Boston Spa, Yorkshire, and is the responsibility of the Department of Education and Science through OSTI (*q.v.*). Abbreviated NLL and NLLST. Publishes *NLL Translations Bulletin* (m.).

NATIONAL LIBRARIES AUTHORITY. The name for the body which the *National Libraries Committee Report* recommended should be used for the administrative body responsible for the provision and administration of national libraries in the United Kingdom. *See also* DAINTON COMMITTEE.

NATIONAL LIBRARY. A library maintained out of government funds and serving the nation as a whole. Usually, books in such libraries are for reference only. They are usually copyright libraries. The function of such a library is to collect and preserve for posterity the books, periodicals and newspapers published in the country. This is best done by a law requiring publishers to deposit copies of all publications issued by them, and by purchasing books published in other countries. A copyright act normally has penalty clauses to enable the act to be enforced. *See also* COPYRIGHT, LEGAL DEPOSIT. The functions of national libraries vary considerably. They may compile union catalogues, produce a national bibliography, publish a retrospective national bibliography, or act as a national bibliographical centre. National libraries in the United Kingdom are: British Museum, Imperial War Museum Library, National Art Library (the library of the Victoria and Albert Museum), National Lending Library for Science and Technology, National Reference Library of Science and Invention (based on, and incorporating, the former Patent Office Library, now administered – in two buildings – by the Trustees of the British Museum of which it forms a part), Science Museum Library. These are in England. Additionally there are the National Library of Scotland and the National Library of Wales. For those which receive books under the Copyright Act, *see* COPYRIGHT LIBRARY. National libraries in the United States are: Library of Congress, National Agricultural Library (formerly the National Library for Agriculture) and National Library of Medicine.

NATIONAL LIBRARY FOR THE BLIND. The British library which makes books in raised characters available to blind persons, either directly through the post or through public libraries. It was founded in 1882 by Miss Arnold and Mrs. Dow and depends on subscriptions and legacies for most of its income. Abbreviated NLB.

NATIONAL LIBRARY OF IRELAND. Originally the library of the Royal Dublin Society, a semi-public, grant-aided institution; it became known as the National Library of Ireland in 1877. It benefits from Irish (but not English) legal deposit, and is controlled by the Irish government. It is the principal centre for research into Irish literature and history and contains 500,000 books, as well as collections of periodicals, newspapers, maps, prints, drawings, manuscripts, films and photographs, all relating to Ireland. It was the first library in the British Isles to adopt the Dewey classification.

NATIONAL LIBRARY OF MEDICINE. Founded in 1836 as the Library of the Surgeon General's Office, United States Army, re-named the Army Medical Library in 1922, again re-named the Armed Forces Medical Library in 1952 and finally re-named in 1956 when it became a part of the Public Health Service of the Department of Health, Education and Welfare. Situated in Washington, D.C., it assists the advancement of medical and related sciences, and aids the dissemination and exchange of scientific and other information important to the progress of medicine and public health. Abbreviated NLM. Publishes: *Index Medicus* (m.). *The National Library of Medicine Classification* has been published. *See also* MEDLARS.

NATIONAL LIBRARY OF SCOTLAND. The entire contents of the library of the Faculty of Advocates at Edinburgh, except the law books, legal manuscripts and papers. Faculty records, pictures and articles of furniture were transferred to the National Library of Scotland when it was formed in 1925. The Advocates' Library also transferred at the same time its privilege of receiving publications as a 'depository library' under the Copyright Act 1911. *See also* COPYRIGHT LIBRARY, DEPOSITORY LIBRARY.

NATIONAL LIBRARY OF WALES. A government-financed library which was founded in 1909 following the granting of a Royal Charter in 1907. It specializes in manuscripts and books relating to Wales and the Celtic peoples, and has a stock of nearly 2,000,000 printed books, 30,000 manuscripts, 3,500,000 deeds and documents, and numerous maps, prints and drawings. It is a Copyright Library in respect of books in the Welsh language or dealing with Wales.

NATIONAL MEDAL FOR LITERATURE. An award made annually to a living American author for the whole body of his or her work; it was first presented to Thornton Wilder on 4th May 1965. The award, of $5,000, is made possible by a grant from the Guinzburg Fund, honouring the late Harold K. Guinzburg, founder of the Viking Press, and was instituted by the NATIONAL BOOK COMMITTEE (*q.v.*). *See also* NATIONAL BOOK AWARDS.

NATIONAL MICROFILM ASSOCIATION. Founded in the United States in 1943 to 'promote the lawful interests of the micro-reproduction industry in the direction of good business ethics, the liberal discussion of subjects pertaining to the industry; technological improvement and research; standardization; the methods of manufacturing and marketing; the education of the consumer in the use of microfilm and related technique'. Abbreviated NMA.

NATIONAL PROGRAM FOR ACQUISITIONS AND CATALOGING. An acquisitions and cataloguing project initiated in the financial year 1966 and implemented in the following financial year, whereby the Library of Congress seeks to acquire abroad, catalogue immediately, and disseminate cataloguing data rapidly, all current monographs, as well as monographic series, of research value, in order to meet the current needs of American libraries through a national cataloguing effort. To avoid unnecessary duplication of cataloguing already accomplished in other countries, SHARED CATALOGUING (*q.v.*) techniques have been adopted wherever possible in co-operation with the producers of foreign national bibliographies. Abbreviated NPAC.

NATIONAL REFERENCE LIBRARY FOR SCIENCE AND INVENTION. Formed by amalgamating the Patent Office Library which was transferred to the British Museum in May 1966, with books on science in the British Museum in separate buildings apart from the British Museum, but under the control of the Trustees of the British Museum. A recommendation of this nature was made in the *Eighth Annual Report* of the Advisory Council on Scientific Policy, 1955. It possesses the largest and most comprehensive collection of the world's technical literature in the U.K., and is primarily intended to serve science graduates, qualified engineers and technologists, research workers and patent agents. Abbreviated NRLSI.

NATIONAL REFERRAL CENTER FOR SCIENCE AND TECHNOLOGY. Usually referred to as the National Referral Center. Formed in 1963, and functioning at the Library of Congress as a clearing house to provide comprehensive, co-ordinated access to the U.S.A.'s resources of scientific and technical information. It has as its four major areas of responsibility: (1) the identification of all significant information resources in the fields of science and technology; (2) the acquisition, cataloguing, and correlation of substantive and procedural data defining the nature, scope, and capabilities of these resources; (3) the provision of advice and guidance about these resources to any organization or individual requiring access to them by responding to requests for referral assistance, and by publishing directories and guides in selected subject fields; and (4) the exploration, through actual operating experience, of the roles and relationships that exist or should exist among the many elements of the scientific and technical information complex.

NATIONAL REGISTER OF ARCHIVES. Since 1945 the HISTORICAL MANUSCRIPTS COMMISSION (*q.v.*) has built up this collection of lists and related personal, subject and topographical indexes of non-official records in private custody and in libraries and record offices. The lists (in 1969 over 13,000), some summary, others detailed, cover a wide variety of accumulations from family and estate papers to the archives of institutions, political parties and businesses. The Register may be consulted without charge at the offices of the Historical Manuscripts Commission. The *Bulletin* (1–14, 1948–1967) is now discontinued; the *List of Accessions to Repositories* appears annually; and duplicated subject source lists are being issued.

NATIONAL REPROGRAPHIC CENTRE FOR DOCUMENTA-TION. Established January 1967 with a grant from OSTI (for three years initially). Runs in conjunction with HERTIS at the Hatfield Polytechnic. Offers members consultancy, testing and evaluation of equipment, seminars and courses, information service on reprography published in microform. Object: to advance the use of reprography, particularly microfilming. Abbreviated NRCD. Publishes *Bulletin* (q.), various symposia proceedings, evaluation reports, etc. Membership is open generally on subscription.

NATIONAL SCIENCE FOUNDATION. A United States federal agency established by Congress in 1950 'to promote the progress of science to advance the national health, prosperity and welfare; to secure the national defence; and for other purposes'. In carrying out these broad objectives, the Foundation supports research and education through grants and fellowships, fosters the exchange of scientific information among scientists in the U.S. and foreign countries, and surveys the nature and extent of scientific research and development activities in the U.S.

NATIONAL UNION CATALOG, THE. *The National Union Catalog, a cumulative author list* represents Library of Congress printed cards and titles reported by other American libraries. It commenced publication in 1948. The sequence of printed catalogues is as follows: *A catalog of books represented by Library of Congress printed cards issued to July 31, 1942* (167 vols.). *Supplement: cards issued August 1, 1942–December 31, 1947* (42 vols.), 1948. *Library of Congress author catalog; a cumulative list of works represented by Library of Congress printed cards, 1948–1952* (24 vols.), 1953. *Library of Congress catalog–books: authors, 1953–June 1956.* This was continued under the title *National union catalog: a cumulative author list representing Library of Congress printed cards and titles reported by other American libraries 1953–1957* (28 vols.), 1961. These volumes include one on music and phonorecords and one on motion pictures and film strips. This series was continued by one covering the years 1958–1962 and published in 1963; it comprised 54 volumes including two on music and two on motion pictures. This series is continuing with at least four volumes each year, being cumulations of monthly parts which are also cumulated quarterly. Meanwhile a series was published with the title *National union catalog, 1952–1955 imprints* (30 vols.), a similar author list, in 1961. The *National union catalog, pre-1956 imprints* began publication in 1968. The *Library of Congress catalog – books: subjects* began publication in 1950; 1950–1954 (20 vols., 1955); 1955–1959 (22 vols., 1960); 1960–1964 (25 vols., 1965); and then annually with a minimum of three volumes per annum. The publication of the *National union catalog of manuscript collections* was begun in 1959; these volumes contain descriptions of manuscript collections in over 660 archives, libraries and other institutions throughout the U.S.

NATIONAL UNION CATALOG OF MANUSCRIPT COLLECTIONS. A grant (the first of several) from the Council on Library Resources in 1959 enabled a commencement to be made on a large co-operative project to produce and bring together in a central file printed catalogue cards presenting uniform descriptions of some 24,000 manuscript collections in about ninety participating libraries and archives, and of some 3,000 collections in the Library of Congress. Cards are available for purchase. The first volume covering the years 1959–61 was published in 1961 and the second covering 1962, in 1964; these consist of reproductions of cards published in the years mentioned. A cumulated index volume to the first and second volumes was also published in 1964. Abbreviated NUCMC.

NATURAL CLASSIFICATION. One in which qualities which are essential to the existence of the thing or things to be divided is adopted as the 'difference' (*see* PREDICABLES, FIVE) or characteristic of arrangement. One which exhibits the inherent properties of the things classified, and which groups or separates them according to their likeness or unlikeness. *See also* ARTIFICIAL CLASSIFICATION, CHARACTERISTIC OF A CLASSIFICATION.

NATURAL ENVIRONMENT RESEARCH COUNCIL. Set up in June 1965, this Council is concerned with the earth sciences and ecology. It has brought together a number of activities which had previously been the responsibility of independent bodies or government departments, and is responsible for the Nature Conservancy including its nature reserves, the National Institute of Oceanography, the Hydrology Research Unit of the Hydraulics Research Station, the Geological Survey and Museum, and the Overseas Geological Surveys.

NAUTICAL ALMANAC. A publication which tabulates the position of the sun, moon, planets and navigational stars for each date at any time of day or night.

NEAR PRINT. A general term for substitute printing processes, the basic techniques being typewriter composition and offset printing. *See also* JUSTOWRITER which is an example of this method.

NEBITYPE. A slug-casting machine first made in 1958 in Italy for setting display matter. Linotype/Intertype and Ludlow matrices as well as Nebimats (the special Nebitype matrices) may be used to cast type from 6- to 72-point to a measure of 42 ems.

NECK. *Synonymous with* BEVEL (*q.v.*).

NEDERLANDS INSTITUUT VOOR DOCUMENTATIE EN REGISTRATUUR. *See* NIDER.

NEEDLEWORK BINDING. *Synonymous with* EMBROIDERED BINDING (*q.v.*).

NEGATIVE. 1. In photographing with a camera, a negative image normally results when a film is developed; in this the tones are reversed black being white and vice versa. A positive print, in which the tones are again reversed and then seen as with the naked eye, can be produced from the negative either by contact or by enlargement. By reversal developing, positive pictures can be obtained direct; this principle is commonly used in colour photography. 2. A transparent photographic film on which the image and the light values are reversed. 3. In some forms of documentary reproduction negatives are made on paper, and positives (prints with normal image and light values) are made from these. In some cases the light values, but not the image, are in reverse; these 'white on black' prints are called 'readable negatives'. 4. In printing, reversed image and light values appear on half-tone blocks of illustrations, and these stand in the same relationship to the resulting print as do negatives in the ordinary photographic or documentary reproduction process.

NEGATIVE PROCESS. The opposite of POSITIVE PROCESS (*q.v.*). *See also* NEGATIVE.

NEGATIVE SELECTION. *Synonymous with* WEEDING (*q.v.*).

NELL. Abbreviation for North East Lancashire Libraries. A co-operative organization formed in 1955 to encourage co-operation between the libraries of this area; *B.N.B.* is examined monthly with a view to co-operating in the purchase of books costing 40s. and over; matters of mutual interest affecting the library service in the area are discussed, as are means of co-operatively improving the efficiency of the library service in the area. About nine public libraries are members.

NELTAS. Abbreviation for North East Lancashire Technical Advisory Service, the formation of which was announced but never implemented.

NEO-CAROLINE. *Synonymous with* HUMANISTIC HAND (*q.v.*).

NEO-GROTESQUE. A group of LINEALE (*q.v.*) type faces derived from the GROTESQUE (*q.v.*) group compared with which they have less contrast in the thickness of the strokes, and are more regular in design. The ends of the curved strokes are usually oblique and the g often has an open tail. Of such are Edeh/Wotan, Helvetica and Univers.

NET BOOK. 1. One which, according to a national purchasing agreement, may be sold to a signatory to the agreement at an agreed discount. Books which are not subject to discount are known as 'non-net'. 2. One published at a price below which, subject to certain exceptions, it may not be resold to the public.

NET BOOK AGREEMENT. An agreement drawn up in 1929 (and revised in 1957) between the Publishers Association, the Booksellers Association, and the Library Association, enabling rate-supported libraries and other libraries admitting the public without charge throughout the usual opening hours to receive a discount of 10 per cent on all new books purchased, provided the library applies for a licence. In consequence of the Library Association becoming a professional association it has discontinued its functions under the Library Licence Agreement, and handed them over to the authorities responsible for public libraries and for libraries in universities and colleges.

NETWORK. A bookbinding design made of intersecting lines forming squares set lozengewise.

NEUTRALITY. In subject cataloguing, a situation in which user preference cannot influence one course over another because it is unascertainable or because it does not exist. Catalogues of general libraries are mostly neutral in this sense whereas those in special libraries may reflect the viewpoints of a homeogeneous clientele.

NEW-BOOK CARD. A temporary main entry catalogue card, made on a coloured card, and inserted in the catalogue until a permanent card is ready. This is often done when the regular entries are printed cards issued by a central cataloguing agency.

NEW-BOOK NUMBER. A temporary number assigned to a book which it is desired should be circulated before it is catalogued because it is in great demand or because of temporary shortage of staff. The number is from a special sequence, or preceded by some symbol, as: N.B., and the book is catalogued and finally processed subsequently. A temporary main entry is used in the catalogue.

NEW CLASSIFICATION SOCIETY. Formed in 1964 to study the principles of classification in its widest connotation, i.e. as applied to any subject, whether documentation, soil science, mathematics, etc.

NEW EDITION. An issue of a book in which misprints noticed in an earlier edition have been corrected. *See also* EDITION, FIRST EDITION, IMPRESSION, ISSUE, REPRINT, REVISED EDITION.

NEW ENGLAND DEPOSIT LIBRARY. A storage library (capacity 800,000 volumes) opened on 2 March 1942, housing books in three types of rental storage: (a) material classed as permanent with books available on request, the largest depositor being Harvard University Library which sends part of its current additions to store, (b) temporary and (c) 'dead' stock; (b) and (c) are not available for general use. A union catalogue is maintained, and the books stored are available for loan to member libraries, and, with the permission of the owning library, to the inter-lending system. The large windowless storage warehouse is owned and operated by eight libraries – Massachusetts State Library, Massachusetts Institute of Technology, Massachusetts Historical Society, Boston Public Library, Boston Athenaeum, Boston University and Harvard University Library – each paying rent for the space occupied in order to cover operating costs. The scheme was proposed in 1937. Abbreviated NEDL.

NEW IMPRESSION. *See* Impression.

NEW ZEALAND LIBRARY ASSOCIATION (INCORPORATED). A society incorporated by Act of Parliament in 1939 (The New Zealand Library Association Act 1939). Founded at a conference held in Dunedin in March 1910 as the Libraries Association of New Zealand. At a conference in 1935 the name was changed to New Zealand Library Association, and a new constitution adopted; this allowed among other things the formation of Branches and Sections. Abbreviated NZLA. Publishes *New Zealand Libraries* (11 p.a.), *Newsletter* (m. to membs.).

NEWARK CHARGING SYSTEM. An American method of recording book issues whereby the book cards are inscribed with the borrower's number and dated, so becoming the time record. The reader possesses a membership card which he retains whether he borrows books or not, and which enables him to borrow an unlimited number of books from any library in a system. *See also* DETROIT SELF-CHARGING SYSTEM.

NEWBERRY LIBRARY. A free reference library established in Chicago, Illinois, U.S.A., in 1887 and maintained by a moiety of the estate of Walter Loomis Newberry (1804–68), a Chicago merchant. This bequest is supplemented by subsequent gifts and by the continuing programme of the Newberry Library Associates. The stock totals 900,000 volumes on many subjects but mainly the humanities, certain subjects being relatively unrepresented by agreement with the Chicago Public Library and the John Crerar Library. The Library is particularly strong on Americana, American Indians, history of printing, Western Europe, Great Britain until the early twentieth century, Latin America, Portuguese discoveries and music, and there are treasures in each of the subject divisions.

NEWBERY MEDAL. An Award instituted by Frederic G. Melcher, administered by the Children's Services Division of the American Library Association, and awarded annually to the author of the most distinguished contribution to American literature for children, but may be by an author of any nationality or race. Named after John Newbery (1713–67) the famous British publisher of St. Paul's Churchyard who was the first to publish books for children; he was part-author of some of the best of those he published. The medal was first awarded (in 1922) to Hendrik Willem Van Loon for *The story of mankind*.

NEWS BULLETIN. An announcement, or statement, of news, relating to the health of an important person, or of general and miscellaneous items of news. In a bibliothecal context, a digest of current news concerning or relating to the work of members or users of a special library's organization. It is usually prepared daily and is issued to key personnel, or, more generally, widely distributed.

NEWSBOOK. A publication printed in a small 4to volume of up to twenty-four pages, and containing news. Newsbooks were first published in 1622, being dated and numbered, and although calling themselves 'weekly', were published at irregular intervals and never on a fixed day of the week. They contained all kinds of news from all over the world but were strictly forbidden to print home news. They were not numbered until 1641 and dealt almost exclusively with the *Thirty Years War*. Their publication was considerably diminished after the outbreak of the Great Rebellion towards the end of 1641, and ceased in 1642. At first they comprised one sheet of quarto, and later two. Variously called Diurnall, Mercurius Intelligence. *See also* CORANTO, RELATION.

NEWSLETTER. 1. A manuscript report of current happenings, written for special subscribers and issued irregularly or weekly in the sixteenth and seventeenth centuries. 2. A similar report published in the seventeenth century and sometimes set in scriptlike type and imitating the appearance of the earlier manuscript newsletter. 3. A brief publication conveying news. Frequently issued by societies or business organizations.

NEWSOM REPORT. *Half Our Future: a report of the Central Advisory Council for Education* 1963, so named after the Chairman, Mr. (later Sir) John Newsom. It was concerned with the education of children aged 13 to 16 years of age and of average, or less than average, ability.

NEWSPAPER. A publication issued periodically, usually daily or weekly, containing the most recent news. The word 'newspaper' was first used in 1670. Previously the word was CORANTO and later NEWSBOOK (*qq.v.*).

NEWSPAPER FILE. *See* STICK 2.

NEWSPAPER LIBRARY. A collection of reference books, pamphlets, reports, press cuttings and government publications provided to serve the needs of the staff of a daily newspaper.

NEWSPAPER RACK. A fitting for displaying newspapers. Also called 'Newspaper stand'.

NEWSPAPER ROD. *See* STICK 2.

NEWSPAPER STACK. Shelving designed to accommodate bound newspapers in which they lie flat.

NEWSPAPER STAND. A fitting on which one or more newspapers are displayed for consultation. Also called 'Newspaper rack'.

NEWSPAPER STICK. *See* STICK 2.

NEWSPRINT. The lowest grade of paper: it is made mostly from wood pulp and used for newspapers.

NEWSROOM. The department of a library in which current newspapers may be read. *See also* MAGAZINE ROOM.

NICK. The groove which is cut on the BELLY of a piece of movable type. Its purpose is to enable the compositor to set type the right way up without looking at the face of the type, and also (by reason of the position and number of nicks for each type size and face) to know immediately when a wrong SORT (*q.v.*) has come to hand. Also called 'Groove'. *See also* BODY.

NICKEL-FACED STEREO. A stereo which is given a facing of nickel in order to lengthen its effective life.

NICKELTYPE. An ELECTROTYPE (*q.v.*) which is faced with nickel instead of copper. (American.)

NICKNAME. A fanciful appellation given by others, in addition to, or in place of, a proper name, as, for example, Scaramouche to Tiberio Fiorella. Also called 'Byname,' 'Sobriquet'.

NICKNAME INDEX. A list of 'nicknames', or popular names, for places, persons, official reports, laws or organizations and giving the full, proper, or official names or titles. It is usually arranged alphabetically.

NIDER. Acronym for Nederlands Instituut voor Documentatie en Registratuur (Netherlands Institute for Documentation and Filing). Founded in the Netherlands in 1921 to promote documentation and co-operative action in its application, to disseminate knowledge about documentation, and to bring together all organizations and individuals concerned with this subject and to encourage their collaboration. It (a) works in close association with the Dutch Patent Office situated in the same building; (b) maintains a library covering documentation and related fields; (c) conducts an inter-library loan service; (d) provides a documentary reproduction service; and (e) gives advice on library administration. Publishes *Tidjdschrift voor Efficientie en Documentatie* (m.) in association with the Nederlands Instituut voor Efficientie and Nederlandse Vereniging van Bedÿfsarchivarissen.

NIGER MOROCCO. Leather produced on the banks of the River Niger from native-tanned goatskin. Often abbreviated to 'Niger'.

NIGERIAN LIBRARY ASSOCIATION. Founded as the West African Library Association in August 1953 as an outgrowth of the Unesco Seminar on the Development of Public Libraries in Africa; it was superseded by the Ghana Library Association, and the Nigeria Library Association in 1963. Abbreviated NLA. Publishes *Nigerian Libraries* (3 a year), *NLA Newsletter* (membs. only).

nihil obstat. (*Lat.* 'nothing hinders'). Sanction for publication given by a Roman Catholic censor and usually found on the verso of the title-page or the following leaf.

NINETY-ONE RULES. A cataloguing code comprising ninety-one rules which was compiled at the instigation, and with the guidance, of Sir Anthony Panizzi, as a guide to cataloguing the printed books in the British Museum. It was the first major code for the consistent cataloguing of books, and set the pattern for good cataloguing practice. It was approved by the Trustees of the British Museum in 1839 and was published in 1841.

NIPPER. *Synonymous with* BUMPER (*q.v.*).

No. Abbreviation for number (*It.* 'numero.'). *Pl.* Nos.

NO DATE. Abbreviation: n.d. Indicates that the date of publication is not known. If the book bears no indication of date of publication but this has been obtained from bibliographical or other sources, it is expressed in a bibliographical or catalogue entry within [ ]. The abbreviation 'n.p.' similarly indicates no place of publication, no printer's or publisher's name.

NO MORE PUBLISHED. A phrase used in a note to a catalogue entry for a work which was intended to be published in several volumes but the publication of which was not completed.

NO PLACE. *See* No Date.

NO PUBLISHER. *See* No Date.

NOC. Abbreviation for Notation of Content. *See* KWOC.

NODIS CASTER. A small, simple and versatile type-casting machine in which Monotype, Linotype and Intertype, as well as the Nodis, matrices may be used.

NOISE. 1. In information retrieval, items selected in a search which do not contain the information desired, or items delivered by a search through accidental code combinations (*Taube*). 2. An undesirable signal which disturbs the desired signal in a communication network (*IBM*). *See also* False Drop.

NOM DE PLUME. *Synonymous with* Pseudonym (*q.v.*).

NOMENCLATURE. A system of names for a system of classes, or classification; its terms.

NON-BOOK MATERIALS. Those library materials which do not come within the definition of a book, periodical or pamphlet and which require special handling, e.g. audio-visual materials, vertical file materials and similar items, and are not individually catalogued.

NON-COUNTY BOROUGH. Frequently used, when differentiating between the various forms of local government in England and Wales, to indicate boroughs which are not 'county boroughs'. In the Public Libraries and Museums Act, 1964 the councils of London boroughs are referred to but these have the same local government powers as boroughs in respect of libraries but not in respect of education; previously boroughs in the area of the London County Council were known as 'Metropolitan boroughs'. *See also* Borough Council, County Borough Council.

NON-DISTINCTIVE TITLE. One that is common to many serials, e.g. *Bulletin, Journal, Proceedings, Transactions*.

NON-EXPRESSIVE NOTATION. *See* Notation.

NON-FICTION. Books that are not prose fiction.

NON NET. Term indicating that a book is not sold by the publisher to the book trade at a discount; it must be sold at the full published price. This term is used almost exclusively to refer to reference books published at as low a price as possible for the benefit of the trade, and not normally re-sold by its members.

NON-PARLIAMENTARY PUBLICATIONS. Those published by HMSO but which are not Parliamentary Publications (*q.v.*). Prior

to about 1925 when this heading began to be used in HMSO catalogues, such publications were known as 'Official Publications' or
'Stationery Office Publications'. These can be roughly grouped into
(a) Statutory Instruments, (b) Reports, (c) other publications. Statutory Instruments are government orders or regulations made by a
Minister under the authority of a specific Act of Parliament. They are
numbered according to the calendar year in which they are made, a
new sequence beginning each year. Prior to 1948 they were known as
Statutory Rules and Orders. 'Reports' include a variety of departmental, committee and working party reports which are prepared for
submission to, or for the information of, Parliament. 'Other publications' include the immense range of publications which are issued
by HMSO and Departments which are authorized themselves to
publish, the Central Office of Information, government museums, the
Ordnance Survey and the Patent Office. It is the 'other publications'
group which has helped so much to make HMSO the United Kingdom's largest publisher.

NON-PERIODICAL. A publication which is published at one time,
or at intervals, in complete, usually numbered, volumes, the total
number of volumes being generally determined in advance.

NON-RELIEF TYPE. Engraved or incised type in which the printing
surface is not the character but the type-face around the incised
character. This results in a white letter on a printed background.

NON-RESIDENT MEMBER. A person who is permitted to use a
library in a district other than the one in which he resides, by paying a
subscription, or because he owns property in, is employed in, or
studies in, the district.

NON-SEMANTIC CODE. In information retrieval, one in which the
notation does not carry meaningful information beyond that which is
inherent in the spelling of the word in the source language for which
it stands as the equivalent. *See also* SEMANTIC CODE.

non. seq. Abbreviation for *non sequitur* (*Lat.* 'it does not follow logically').

NON-STRUCTURAL NOTATION. *See* STRUCTURAL NOTATION.

NON-THESIS EDITION. A work published commercially as well as
in thesis form. A catalogue entry has a note 'issued also as thesis'
followed by the name of the university concerned.

NONESUCH PRESS. A publishing house founded in 1923 in London
by Miss Vera Mendel with Francis Meynell to supervise book production and David Garnett to publish fine editions of scholarly works
to be sold at modest prices through normal trade channels. After a
period of inactivity during the Second World War production was

resumed in 1953 with the Nonesuch Shakespeare in four volumes. Nearly all the books were machine set by various printers but were designed by Meynell. Many 'Monotype' matrices were specially designed for this Press. The press publishes its own books but does not do the actual printing.

NONET. A combination of nine singers or musicians; the music for same.

NONPAREIL. 1. An out-of-date name for a type size of about 6 point. 2. A 6-point lead.

NORMAN TOMLINSON AWARD. *See* TOMLINSON AWARD, NORMAN.

NORTH EAST LANCASHIRE LIBRARIES. *See* NELL.

NORTH MIDLAND LIBRARY ASSOCIATION. Formed in March 1890, and covering the counties of Nottingham, Derby, Leicester, Northampton and Lincoln. It became a Branch of the Library Association in 1929 and is now known as the North Midland Branch of the Library Association.

NOT. A FINISH (*q.v.*) given to good quality rag papers – not glazed or hot pressed. Those with no finish are called 'rough'; 'not' is less rough but 'not-smooth'. *See also* HOT-PRESSED, MACHINE GLAZED, ROUGH.

NOTATION. 1. The symbols which stand for the divisions in a scheme of classification. The purposes of notation are (a) to mechanize the order of headings in a scheme of classification, (b) to serve as a short-hand sign for the easy arrangement of documents on shelves or in drawers or files, and also for entries in respect of them in catalogues and indexes (the alternative to which would possibly be cumbersome and not easy-to-remember sequences of words), and (c) to provide easily memorized links between catalogues and the storage position of documents. Symbols must be brief and easily extended. If the notation consists of two or more kinds of symbols it is called a 'mixed notation'; if of one kind only, a 'pure notation'. The notation may be expressive or non-expressive. Expressive notation reveals the hierarchical structure of the classification scheme, in addition to mechanizing the order of the headings. The notation must be (a) hospitable, i.e. enable symbols for additional subject to be added at any position, (b) easily comprehensible, i.e. consisting only of roman letters and/or arabic numbers, and (c) easily memorized, written and spoken. A 'flexible notation' is one which expands with the classification, and permits the insertion of new subjects without any dislocation. 2. In information retrieval, a symbolism which is not in natural language but humanly

15*

legible, as distinct from CODING (*q.v.*). 3. An arbitrary device to indicate the contents or location of a document (*IBM*). 4. In machine searching as part of information retrieval, the designation of a particular set of symbols used to represent a code; the physical representation of a code. *See Also* GRAPHIC LENGTH, HIERARCHICAL NOTATION, PHONIC LENGTH, STRUCTURAL NOTATION.

NOTCHED CARDS. *Synonymous with* MARGINAL-HOLE PUNCHED CARDS (*q.v.*).

NOTE. 1. An explanation of the text of a book or additional matter, appearing usually with other notes at the foot of a page, at the end of a chapter or at the end of the book. Where numbers are not used to separate and distinguish the notes, REFERENCE MARKS (*q.v.*) are used in a recognized sequence. Also called FOOTNOTE (*q.v.*). 2. A concise statement, following particulars of collation in a catalogue or bibliographical entry, giving added information such as the name of the series, contents, or bibliographical information. The term is sometimes limited to the information which appears below the collation and the main body of an entry. Notes should only be made to supply significant additional data in order to amplify a catalogue entry or be helpful to a reader. *See also* FACET INDICATOR, FACETED NOTATION, FENCE, HIERARCHICAL NOTATION, INTERCALATION DEVICE, RETRO-ACTIVE NOTATION.

NOTHING BEFORE SOMETHING. Alphabetizing 'word by word', counting the space between one word and the next as 'nothing'. *See also* ALPHABETIZATION. A word files before another word having the same letters plus additional ones, these additional ones being considered 'something'.

NOTION. In co-ordinate indexing, an ENTITY (*q.v.*) or an ATTRIBUTE (*q.v.*).

NOTTINGHAM AND NOTTINGHAMSHIRE TECHNICAL SERVICE. *See* NANTIS.

NOVEL. A long fictitious story of imaginary people and events.

NOVELA. A short prose narrative, generally with a structural centre represented by a surprising event. It requires a simple subject matter and disdains episodes.

NOVELETTE. A short novel.

NOVELIST. One who writes novels.

NOYES AWARD, MARCIA C. This Award consists of a silver tray, and is given, not necessarily every year, to a medical librarian, anywhere in the world, for outstanding achievement in his chosen field. It was first awarded in 1953, to Mary Louise Marshall.

NUFFIELD TALKING BOOK LIBRARY FOR THE BLIND. *See* NTBL.

NUMBER. 1. A single numbered or dated issue of a periodical or serial publication. 2. One of the numbered fascicules of a literary, artistic or musical work issued in instalments, ordinarily in paper wrappers, and called 'number' by the publisher. 3. In extended vocal works such as cantatas, oratorios and operas (especially the latter), one of the distinct and separate sections into which the composition is divided, each of which is complete in itself and in a specific form, such as aria, duet, chorus. 4. Any item in the programme of a concert or other entertainment. *See also* OPUS NUMBER.

NUMBERED AND SIGNED EDITION. An edition of a work the copies of which are numbered, and signed by the author. *See also* LIMITED EDITION.

NUMBERED COLUMN. Where the text of a book is printed in two or more columns to a page, and these instead of the pages are numbered consecutively. Where this is done a note to this effect normally appears at the head of the index.

NUMBERED COPY. A copy of a limited edition of a book which bears the copy number, usually on the page facing the title-page.

NUMBERED ENTRY. One of the entries in a printed bibliography or catalogue in which the entries are numbered consecutively.

NUMBERING. Placing (a) the call number on the spine of, or (b) the charging symbol in, a library book.

NUMERAL. A graphic symbol or character to represent a number or a group of numbers. A figure. *See also* ARABIC FIGURES, HANGING FIGURES, RANGING FIGURES, ROMAN NUMERALS.

NUMERALS. The correct printer's term for the figures and fractions.

NUT. *See* EN QUADRAT.

O.E. Abbreviation for OLD ENGLISH (*q.v.*).

OFR. Office for Recruitment. A department of the AMERICAN LIBRARY ASSOCIATION (*q.v.*).

O.P. Abbreviation for OUT OF PRINT (*q.v.*).

O.S. Abbreviation for OUT OF STOCK (*q.v.*).

O.S. Abbreviation for ORDNANCE SURVEY (*q.v.*).

OASIS. An area in a university or college library where selected students may read or undertake research. Less formal than a CARREL (*q.v.*) and more economic of space, it should be placed in a central and easily accessible position.

OBELISK. Alternative name for the dagger (†) reference mark. Similarly

a double dagger (‡) is also called a 'Double obelisk'. *See also* REFER-
ENCE MARKS.

OBERLY MEMORIAL AWARD, EUNICE ROCKWELL. Estab-
lished in 1923, this Award consists of a citation and the biennial
income (about $500) from the Eunice Rockwell Oberly Memorial
Fund. The selection is made by the Oberly Memorial Award Committee of the Reference Services Division of the American Library
Association every two years to the American citizen who compiles the
best bibliography in the field of agriculture or the related sciences in
the two-year period preceding the year in which the Award is made.
The Award was first made in 1925 to Max Meisel.

OBLONG. 1. A book that is wider than its height. Hence oblong folio,
oblong quarto. This is the result of folding a sheet of paper across the
long way (i.e. halving the short side). Also called 'Cabinet size',
'Landscape', 'Long'. The opposite of BROAD (*q.v.*). *See also* SIZE.
2. Applies to a BROAD (*q.v.*) sheet of paper halved lengthways. A
quarto size used with the longest dimension at the foot of the page, or
sheet, is termed 'oblong quarto' and is the reverse of 'upright'.

OBVERSE COVER. The upper cover of a book. Also called 'Front
cover'. 'Upper cover'. *See also* REVERSE COVER.

OCCUPATIONAL SAFETY AND HEALTH SCHEME. A scheme
of classification compiled by D. J. Foskett for the Division of Occupational Safety and Health of the International Labour Office in Geneva
and published in the *Proceedings of the International Study Conference
on Classification for Information Retrieval*, 1957.

OCE. *See* AZOFLEX.

OCTAVE DEVICE. In classification, the name given by Ranganathan
to a method of extending the decimal base of arabic numerals to
infinity, by setting aside the figure 9 as an extender to bring in a further eight figures at the end of the first eight. The series thus reads:
1, 2, 3, 4, 5, 6, 7, 8, 91, 92, 93, 94, 95, 96, 97, 98, 991, 992, and so on,
the figure 9 never being used unsupported. The figure 9 is known as
the Octavizing Digit. This device, which was first used by Ranganathan in his *Colon Classification*, and adopted by the UNIVERSAL DECI-
MAL CLASSIFICATION (*q.v.*) in 1948, can be extended to letters, z (or any
last letter of any other alphabet) being used in the same way. By this
means the octave device provides hospitality in array.

OCTAVIZING DIGIT. *See* OCTAVE DEVICE.

OCTAVO (8vo). 1. A sheet of paper folded three times to form a section
of eight leaves, or sixteen pages. The following size (in inches) of
printing papers are usually used to produce an octavo page:

		Double	*Quad*	*Size of 8vo*
Foolscap	$13\frac{1}{2} \times 17$	17×27	27×34	$6\frac{3}{4} \times 4\frac{1}{4}$
Crown	15×20	20×30	30×40	$7\frac{1}{2} \times 5$
Large Post	$16\frac{1}{2} \times 21$	21×33	33×42	$8\frac{1}{4} \times 5\frac{1}{4}$
Demy	$17\frac{1}{2} \times 22\frac{1}{2}$	$22\frac{1}{2} \times 35$	35×45	$8\frac{3}{4} \times 5\frac{5}{8}$
Medium	18×23	23×36	36×46	$9 \times 5\frac{3}{4}$
Royal	20×25	25×40	40×50	$10 \times 6\frac{1}{4}$
Super Royal	$20\frac{1}{2} \times 27\frac{1}{2}$	$27\frac{1}{2} \times 41$	41×55	$10\frac{1}{4} \times 6\frac{7}{8}$
Imperial	22×30	30×44	44×60	$11 \times 7\frac{1}{2}$

2. A book having sections of eight leaves, or sixteen pages. 3. Any book whose height is between $6\frac{1}{4}$ and 10 inches. *See also* BOOK SIZES, PAPER SIZES.

OCTAVO EDITION.   One issued in OCTAVO (*q.v.*) form.

OCTIFILM.   Trademark of the Ozalid Corporation for a sheet of diazo film.

OCTODECIMO (18mo).   *See* EIGHTEENMO.

ODD FOLIOS.   The page-numbers which come on the first, or recto, side of each leaf, the right-hand of each OPENING (*q.v.*), 1, 3, 5, 7, 9, 11, etc.

ODD PAGE.   The page of a publication bearing an odd number; the right-hand page of an OPENING (*q.v.*), and the recto of a LEAF (*q.v.*).

ODD PART.   One part of a serial publication, or of a work published in a number of parts, which is separately issued and isolated from the others.

ODD SORTS.   Characters not normally included in a standard fount of type. Also called 'Side sorts'. Such characters can be used on a machine which sets lines of type in SLUGS (*q.v.*) but the matrices from which they are cast must be inserted by hand in the correct position by the typesetter.

ODD VOLUME.   One volume of a work in several volumes which is the only one possessed.

ODDMENTS.   1. The items of a printed book which precede and follow the text. These are known as the PRELIMINARIES (*q.v.*) and the END-MATTER (*q.v.*). 2. When the pages of a book make an exact multiple of sixteen (or thirty-two if the sections are of 32 pages) it is said to make an even working. If an odd eight pages or so are needed to complete the printing it is termed 'uneven working' and the additional pages are said to be oddments.

OESTERREICHISCHE ZEITSCHRIFT FÜR BUCH– UND BIBLIOTHEKSWESEN, DOKUMENTATION UND BIBLIO-PHILIE (Austrian Society for Documentation and Bibliography).

Formed in 1951 to co-ordinate documentation services in Austria. Publishes *Biblos* (q.).

'OFF ITS FEET'.   Type which has been cast in such a way that its base is not true, with the result that it does not stand firm in the galley.

OFF-LINE EQUIPMENT.   (*Information retrieval*) The peripheral computer equipment, or devices, not in direct communication with a computer's central processing unit.

OFF-LINE OPERATION.   (*Information retrieval*) The accomplishment of functions which are not a part of the main processing operations, such as the conversion from punched cards to magnetic tape on equipment primarily used for main processing. *See also* ON-LINE OPERATION.

OFFCUT.   1. That part of a sheet which has to be cut off after 'imposition', as in the case of a 12mo., so that the sheet may be correctly folded, the cut off piece being folded and inserted in the larger piece after folding. The cut off piece is then called an 'inset' and usually bears a signature mark to indicate its proper place in the gathering. 2. A piece cut off a sheet of paper to reduce it to the size required for a particular job. 3. Remainders of reams which have been cut down to a smaller size.

OFFICE COLLECTION.   *Synonymous with* DEPARTMENTAL LIBRARY (*q.v.*).

OFFICE FOR RESEARCH AND DEVELOPMENT.   Became formally effective within the American Library Association on 1st September 1965, most of the cost of the Library Technology Project (which forms the nucleus of the Office) being provided by the Council on Library Resources, Inc. Abbreviated ORD.

OFFICE FOR SCIENTIFIC AND TECHNICAL INFORMATION. *See* OSTI.

OFFICE OF LIBRARY EDUCATION.   Set up within the American Library Association on 1st September 1966 to promote better co-ordination of the several programmes within the Association which are devoted to education for librarianship. The establishment of the Office was made possible by a grant of over $75,000 over six years (which will be matched by the ALA over the six years after which the ALA will assume complete support of the programme) from the H. W. Wilson Foundation, Inc., a charitable and educational foundation established by the late Mr. and Mrs. Halsey W. Wilson. Abbreviated OLE.

OFFICER.   *See* LIBRARY OFFICER.

OFFICIAL CATALOGUE. A union catalogue for the use of library staff only, and usually kept in the cataloguing department.

OFFICIAL GAZETTE. A periodical publication issued by, or on behalf of, a government or university to convey official news, statements or decisions.

OFFICIAL NAME. The legal name of a corporate body, office or government department.

OFFICIAL PUBLICATION. One issued by a government or government department, it may be in a series or isolated. The Unesco Convention Concerning the Exchange of Official Publications and Government Documents between States, 1958, considered the following, when they are executed by the order and at the expense of any national governmental authority, to be official publications: parliamentary documents, reports and journals and other legislative papers; administrative publications and reports from central, federal and regional governmental bodies; national bibliographies, State handbooks, bodies of law, decisions of the Courts of Justice; and other publications as may be agreed.

OFFICIAL TITLE. The title of a book appearing on the title-page, and which is accepted, either in whole or in part, by the cataloguer for purposes of cataloguing.

OFFPRINT. *Synonymous with* SEPARATE (*q.v.*).

OFFSET. 1. The printing process in which the impression is transferred from a litho stone or plate to a rubber-covered cylinder, and thence off-set by pressure on to the paper. *See also* OFFSET PRINTING. 2. Sometimes erroneously used to describe the unintentional transfer of ink from one sheet to another: this is correctly called 'set-off'. *See also* SLIP SHEET.

OFFSET FOIL. A printing plate used for making prints (copies of documents) by the offset process.

OFFSET LITHOGRAPHY. A method of printing in which a drawing is made on transfer paper the right way round, printed on to a rubber-covered cylinder and 'offset' on to paper. *See also* TRANSFER.

OFFSET PAPER. Paper especially made for use on an offset press. It should lie flat, be free from lint, and stretch as little as possible.

OFFSET-PHOTO-LITHOGRAPHY. *See* PHOTO-OFFSET.

OFFSET PRINTING. An adaptation of the principles of stone lithography, in which the design is drawn or reproduced upon a thin, flexible, metal plate which is curved to fit one of the revolving cylinders of the printing press; the design from this plate is transferred or 'offset' to the paper by means of a rubber blanket which runs over another cylinder and which has received its impression from the plate.

OGHAMIC CHARACTER.   *See* RUNIC LETTERS.

OGHAMIC SCRIPTS.   Inscriptions, peculiar to the Celtic population of the British Isles, usually found on wooden staves but sometimes also on shields or other hard material. They are also found on tombstones. Used for writing messages and letters. The alphabet consisted of twenty letters which were represented by straight or diagonal strokes varying from one to five in number and drawn, or cut, below, above or through, horizontal lines, or to the left, or right, of, or through, vertical lines.

OLA BOOKS.   Books made in Ceylon from olas, or strips of young leaves of the Talipat or Palmyra palm which are soaked in hot water and pressed smooth. They are cut into strips about 3 inches wide and from 1 to 3 feet long. A cord is passed through holes pierced at the ends of each so as to secure the leaves between two lacquered wooden boards. Writing is done with an iron stylus, and the incisions made more easily readable by rubbing in a mixture of charcoal and oil. The aromatic and preservative nature of the oil is believed to have enabled the books to survive from pre-Christian days. Buddhist monks still make ola books in Ceylon. Also called 'olla books'.

OLD ENGLISH.   An angular type of the black-letter group; abbreviated O.E. This is an example of Old English:

This is 12 point Old English

OLD FACE.   The majority of book types in England belong to this family of types. Its origin is generally attributed to Garamond (Paris, first half of sixteenth century) who modelled his design on the roman types of the Venetian printer Aldus Manutius which were actually cut in 1495 for Aldus by Francesco Griffo who also cut the famous Aldine italic. The Old Face group of letter is characterized by oblique emphasis, lightness of colour, comparatively small differences between thick and thin strokes and fairly substantial bracketed serifs. The capitals are slightly lower than the ascending lower case letters and the descenders are long. The modern versions of Old Face have a comparatively small X-HEIGHT (*q.v.*) and a narrow set. Examples are, Caslon Old Face (Stephenson Blake and others); Bembo, Fournier, Imprint, Plantin, Van Dijck (Monotype); Garamond (Monotype and Intertype). The figures of Old Face do not all stand on the line: 1234567890. The following is in 12-point Bembo:

This is BEMBO type face.

There is at present a revival of old faces, the most famous of recent years being Eric Gill's *Perpetua* which is effective and useful both as a book type, because it is narrow, (see example in TYPE FACE), and especially at titling. The term 'Garalde' has superseded 'Old face' for this category of type faces. *See also* ARABIC FIGURES, HANGING FIGURES, MODERN FACE, RANGING FIGURES, TRANSITIONAL.

OLD STYLE. A modification of OLD FACE (*q.v.*), the ascenders and descenders being shorter. Examples are: Old Style (Stephenson Blake); Old Style Antique (Miller & Richard); Bookprint (Linotype); Bookface (Intertype). This book is set in Plantin, an Old Face type. Old Style capitals, lower case letters and figures are as follows:

ABCDEFGHIJKLMNOPQRSTUVWXYZ
abcdefghijklmnopqrstuvwxyz   1234567890

OLD STYLE FIGURES. (*Printing*) Numerals, three of which are of x-height, the others having ascenders and descenders as in the specimen under OLD STYLE (*q.v.*).

OLEOGRAPH. A reproduction of an oil painting, printed by lithography, mounted on canvas, sized and varnished, the irregularities of the oil painting and canvas being reproduced by an embossing process.

OLEOGRAPHY. The lithographic process used to produce an OLEO-GRAPH (*q.v.*).

OLIN BOOK NUMBER. An author number from a scheme devised by Charles R. Olin. The use of Olin Numbers enables collective biography to be separated yet to be brought into close relation at the same class number. They convert all authors' or compilers' surnames into A followed by figures, thus enabling collective biographies to be arranged before the individual biographies bearing Cutter Author Marks. The following is section S from the Table:

| Sa | A77 | Scr | A79 | Sia | A82 | Sq | A84 |
| Sch | A78 | Sea | A81 | Sma | A83 | Sva | A85 |

Strickland's *Queens of England* would be A84 (Olin number) and be arranged before a life of Queen Anne, An 7 (Cutter Author Mark). The Olin Book Numbers and the Biscoe Time Numbers were printed in the 11th, 12th and 13th editions of the Dewey Classifications.

OMISSIBLE. Something which may be omitted if required, necessary or desirable.

OMISSION MARKS. Three dots, thus . . . , used on the BASE LINE (*q.v.*) in quoted text, or a catalogue entry, to indicate that something in the original has been omitted.

OMNIBUS BOOK. A volume containing reprints of short stories by various authors or of novels or other works by one or more authors.

OMNIBUS REVIEW. One which discusses a number of books of one type or field of literature.

ON APPROBATION. *Synonymous with* ON APPROVAL (*q.v.*).

ON APPROVAL. Applied to a transaction whereby a customer may have the opportunity of examining goods before deciding whether to purchase them, and to return same within a short specified time (for books usually three days) if he decides not to keep them. Abbreviated: on appro. 'On approbation' has the same meaning.

ON-LINE OPERATION. (*Information retrieval*) The accomplishment of functions as part of the main processing operations. *See also* OFF-LINE OPERATION.

ON-LINE EQUIPMENT. (*Information retrieval*) The peripheral computer equipment, or devices, in a system in which the operation of such equipment is under the control of the central processing unit, and in which information reflecting current activity is introduced into the data processing system as soon as it occurs; thus directly in line with the main flow of transaction processing, and receiving instructions from the computer.

ON SALE. Books supplied to a bookseller under an agreement that they may be returned if unsold. Also known as 'On sale or return'. *See also* HALF SEE SAFE, SEE SAFE.

ONE PLACE INDEX. *See* SPECIFIC INDEX.

ONE PLACE THEORY. The classifying of material on various aspects of a subject at one place only.

ONE SHEET ON. *Synonymous with* ALL ALONG (*q.v.*).

ONE SHOT. 1. The reprinting in one issue of a periodical of the full text, or an abridgement, of a book, as distinct from a serialized reprint. 2. A magazine of which only one issue has been published. 3. Single issue rights, where the whole of a literary work or an abridgement of it, appears in a periodical.

ONE SIDE COLOURED. Paper or board which has been intentionally coloured during manufacture.

ONION SKIN. A thin, glazed, transparent paper.

ONLAY. A decorative panel of paper or other material glued to the cover of a book without preparing the cover to receive it. *See also* INLAY.

ONLAYING. *See* INLAY, INLAYING.

ONULP. Acronym for Ontario New Universities Library Project. A pioneer venture, initiated by the University of Toronto Library to purchase and process books centrally for five participating academic institutions.

ONYMOUS. The exact opposite of ANONYMOUS (*q.v.*).

op. cit. (*Lat. Opere citato* 'in the work cited'). An abbreviation used in a footnote reference to avoid using the title or short title of the work referred to. It should not be used if there is more than one book by the author concerned, nor further than 1,000 words from the first citation, and preferably not if another book has been referred to since the first citation.

Op. no.   Abbreviation for OPUS NUMBER (*q.v.*).

OPACITY.   The quality of non-transparency in book papers. Creamy or off-white papers are more opaque than bright white ones, and a matt finish gives greater opacity than a glazed finish.

OPAQUE COPY.   A copy of a document on opaque, or non-transparent, material.

OPAQUE MICROCOPY.   A microcopy made on opaque, or non-transparent, material, usually paper or card. Also called 'Micro-opaque'.

OPAQUE PROJECTOR.   A projector which can project small opaque printed images such as maps, post-cards, illustrations, photographs, pages of books, etc., but much enlarged on to screens or walls. *See also* BALOPTICON.

OPAQUING.   Painting a negative with an opaque liquid to block out pin-holes and other defects, or render certain parts unprintable (*Verry*).

OPEN ACCESS.   Applied to a library where readers are admitted to the shelves.

OPEN BACK.   (*Binding*) *Synonymous with* HOLLOW BACK (*q.v.*).

OPEN-BACK CASE.   *Synonymous with* SLIP CASE (*q.v.*).

OPEN BACK FILE.   A box file for holding pamphlets and similar material, consisting of a five sided box the shape of a book. The sixth side (the back) is open to allow the easy insertion – and more easy removal – of material.

OPEN BAR SHELVING. Shelves consisting of a number of hollow steel bars about an inch square placed at intervals, one behind another, in place of a solid shelf. They are supported on cantilever type brackets fitting into slots, or are part of a rigid structure, and are suitable for very large and heavy volumes such as atlases and bound newspapers.

OPEN BIBLIOGRAPHY.   *Synonymous with* CURRENT BIBLIOGRAPHY (*q.v.*).

OPEN EDGE.   Any edge of a section of a book which is open and not enclosed by a BOLT (*q.v.*).

OPEN-ENDED.   Being possessed of the quality by which the addition of new terms, subject headings, or classifications does not disturb the pre-existing system (*IBM*).

OPEN ENTRY.   A catalogue entry which leaves room for the addition of information concerning a work which is in course of publication, or of which the library does not possess a complete copy or set, or concerning which complete information is lacking. Open entries usually occur in respect of serials still in course of publication, the date of the most recent issue and last volume number being omitted in the case of works in several volumes which are still in course of publication; or of living authors, in catalogues in which birth and death dates are given. Space may be left elsewhere than in the main part of the entry, e.g. in the notes, for particulars of publications or of the library's holdings. *See also* CLOSED ENTRY.

OPEN-LETTER PROOF. A proof of an engraving with the caption engraved in outline letters, whereas the finished engraving has solid letters.

OPEN LETTERS. Jobbing and display type which have the centres of the strokes of the characters incised, and so beyond the reach of the inkers; this gives the impression of white areas rather than black. Also called 'Outline letters'. *See also* INLINE LETTERS.

OPEN MATTER. Type which has been generously 'leaded'. *See also* LEADED MATTER.

OPEN ORDER. In book acquisition in North America, two types of order: (1) those made up of items listed individually, some or all of which have not been supplied, hence the orders are not closed or completed; (2) those which approximate to open requisitions, as they earmark sums of money with booksellers to be spent on a particular subject or category.

OPEN SCORE. The printed or written music for two or more voices or parts each of which is separately displayed one above another. Also called 'Extended score'. *See also* SCORE.

OPEN SHELF LIBRARY. *See* OPEN ACCESS.

OPENED. A book of which the top, fore, and sometimes bottom, edges have not been cut in manufacture but opened with a paper knife before being read.

OPENING. Two pages facing one another. *See also* CONJUGATE, DOUBLE-SPREAD.

OPERATION CODE. That part of an instruction in a computer programme designating the processing step to be performed (*IBM*).

OPERATORS. (*Classification*) Categories of relation, indicated by symbols, to mark steps of progression in analysing complex subjects. An analysis set down in this way is called an 'Analet'.

OPISTHOGRAPHIC. Applied to early-printed books printed on both sides of the paper and to manuscripts or parchments with writing on both sides. *See also* ANOPISTHOGRAPHIC PRINTING, BLOCK BOOK.

OPTICAL COINCIDENCE CARD. *Synonymous with* PEEPHOLE CARD (*q.v.*).

OPTICAL COPYING. 1. Making a copy of a document on photographic material in the same scale, or one different from the original. 2. A print made by such a means may be called an 'optical copy'. 3. A term used in REPROGRAPHY (*q.v.*) for a photograph. *See also* CONTACT COPYING.

OPTICAL PHOTOCOPYING DEVICE. A machine for making 'optical copies' of an original, i.e. copies on photographic material of the same, or a different, scale by means of an optical system.

OPTICAL PRINTER. A CONTINUOUS PRINTER (*q.v.*) for the production of copies (prints) by optical means.

OPTICAL STENCIL CARD. A card used in information retrieval in which holes are punched in certain positions to indicate files or documents containing particular information; a heading word is placed at the top of the card, and is chosen from a thesaurus which is specially compiled for the subject matter of the organization's material. Several cards are placed together so that light can shine through the punched holes and so indicate which files contain the information indicated by their heading words. These cards are used in Uniterm systems. *See also* PEEK-A-BOO, UNITERM CONCEPT CO-ORDINATION INDEXING.

OPTION. The privilege to buy rights in a manuscript or book if required.

OPUS ANGLICANUM. A form of split-stitch embroidery on satin; used as a decorative binding in the fifteenth century. *See also* FABRIC BINDING.

OPUS NUMBER. A number assigned to a musical work or collection of works, usually in the order of composition. The numbers are assigned by the composer or by the publisher. An opus number may refer to one work or to a group of works of similar form and for the same medium; each has a secondary number. Abbreviated Op. no.

OPUSCULE (*Pl.* Opuscula). 1. A lesser or minor literary or musical work or composition. 2. A small book or treatise.

OR. Abbreviation for ORIGINAL (*q.v.*).

ORCHESTRAL MUSIC. Music in which most, if not all, of each of the instrumental parts are played by more than one performer. *See also* CHAMBER MUSIC.

ORCHESTRAL SCORE. *See* SCORE.

ORDER BOOK OF THE HOUSE OF COMMONS. *See* PARLIAMENTARY PAPERS.

ORDER CARD. The card used for recording orders placed, and later, the delivery of the material and payment for it: the official record of each individual order.

ORDER DEPARTMENT.   The department of a library which deals with the ordering and sometimes processing of books and periodicals. *Also called* 'accession department', 'acquisition department'.

ORDER FILE.   The file containing records of the books on order from booksellers.

ORDER INFORMATION.   Data concerning the placing of orders for books and other library materials, and also of their receipt. It includes (1) entering an order, order number, date of order, name of supplier, and fund to which cost will be charged, and (2) after delivery of the goods, date of receipt, cost, and date of invoice.

ORDER LIBRARIAN.   Assistant in an order department or division of a library in North America.

ORDER SECTION.   *Synonymous with* ORDER DEPARTMENT (*q.v.*) except that it may be a section of another department, e.g. Cataloguing Department, rather than being an independent department.

ORDER SLIP.   *See* ORDER CARD.

ORDNANCE SURVEY.   A department of the British government, founded 1791, which exists to make an accurate map survey of the British Isles. Maps of various kinds are published in scales varying from $\frac{1}{4}$ to 50 inches to a mile. Maps of Ireland were issued until April 1922, since when the governments of Eire and Northern Ireland have issued their own. Abbreviated O.S.

ORGANIZATION FILE.   A file of written or published material by or about the organization of which a special library is a part. It may include official minutes, proceedings, records and other archive material, items prepared for the guidance or instruction of the staff, publicity material, information publications, etc. whether published for limited or for general distribution, periodical and newspaper articles about the organization, etc. Also called 'History file'.

ORIGINAL.   1. Finished art work (drawing, painting or photograph) as completed by the originator, and ready for reproduction. 2. In the author's own words or other original medium. 3. In the author's own language or as written by him. 4. A first copy. 5. A process block (halftone or line) as distinct from a duplicate block (stereotype or electrotype). Abbreviated: Or. or Orig. 6. In documentary reproduction, an object, or document, to be reproduced.

ORIGINAL BINDING.   The binding that was first put on a specific book.

ORIGINAL PARTS.   A first edition of a work which appeared serially in a number of parts, each provided with a paper wrapper, and numbered.

ORIGINAL SOURCES. *See* PRIMARY SOURCES.

ORIGINAL WRIT. One issuing from the Chancery.

ORIHON. 1. A book composed of a continuous, folded, uncut sheet or, of small single sheets, folded but uncut. It is held together by cords laced through holes stabbed down one side. This form is used in China and Japan where the paper is so thin that it can only be printed on one side. 2. A 'stabbed binding' of Oriental origin. 3. A manuscript roll on which the text was written in columns running the short way of the paper; the roll was not cut but folded down the margins between the columns of text. *See also* FRENCH FOLD.

ORNAMENTAL INITIAL. *See* INITIAL LETTER.

ORNAMENTAL INSIDE LINING. *Synonymous with* DOUBLURE 1 (*q.v.*).

ORNAMENTS. Printers' ornaments are little designs used to decorate printed matter. They are often arranged as borders, head-pieces, tail-pieces, etc. Also called 'Printer's ornament'.

ORTHOGRAPHY. Spelling correctly, or according to accepted usage.

OSMOSIS, METHOD OF. The classification by a newly adopted scheme, of all literature received after a given date, and the re-classification of the older literature in stock, as and when able to do so.

OSTEOPATHIC LIBRARIES ASSOCIATION. Founded in the U.S.A. in 1954 to promote osteopathic library services.

OSTI. The Office for Scientific and Technical Information was set up in April 1965 within the Department of Education and Science to promote more efficient handling and utilization of scientific and technical information. The broad function of the office is to advise the Secretary of State for Education and Science on the conduct of, and support for, United Kingdom activities in gathering and communicating scientific and technical information about the natural sciences and their related technologies and relevant aspects of the social sciences. The Office (a) stimulates research into scientific and technical information problems; (b) promotes and develops new documentation systems and techniques; (c) fosters the improvement and wider use of existing services, and experiments with new ones; (d) promotes the training of scientists for information work; (e) endeavours to ensure that British activities in this field are effectively co-ordinated and linked with those of other countries and international organizations. This Office is now responsible for the NATIONAL LENDING LIBRARY

FOR SCIENCE AND TECHNOLOGY and for grant aid to ASLIB (*q.v.*); it is also responsible for all support for research and development in this field which was previously administered by DSIR. *See also* DEPARTMENT OF SCIENTIFIC AND INDUSTRIAL RESEARCH.

OUSTINOFF SYSTEM. A method devised by Helen Oustinoff, Assistant Director of the University of Vermont Library, to reduce work and ensure accuracy in the ordering of books. By using a Polaroid CU–5 Close-up Land Camera, copies of bibliographical entries in books or catalogues, are made in 15 seconds; these are passed to ordering clerks for making up orders and subsequently filed with the orders. Such photographs of titles printed in characters which cannot be reproduced on a typewriter may be sent as orders to booksellers. Polaroid prints, after the addition of necessary 'local' information (headings, classification numbers, etc.) may be put through a copying machine to provide catalogue entries or other records.

OUT OF PRINT. A book is out of print when the publisher has no more copies for sale. Abbreviation: O.P.

OUT OF STOCK. Not available from the publisher (although in print) until his stock has been replenished. Abbreviated: O.S.

OUTER FORM. *See* FORM DIVISIONS.

OUTER FORME. The forme for the side to be printed first; it bears the SIGNATURE MARKS (*q.v.*). *See also* INNER FORME.

OUTER INDENTION. *Synonymous with* FIRST INDENTION (*q.v.*).

OUTGUIDE. A form card on which is recorded the loan of material from a file, or the file itself. It is substituted for the material lent, and being large enough to project above the folder, immediately indicates material on loan and possibly overdue.

OUTLIER LIBRARY. A library of a research institution, or one devoted to a particular subject, which does not generally participate in the work of a regional bureau, but whose stock is available to other libraries through the NATIONAL CENTRAL LIBRARY (*q.v.*). *See also* REGIONAL BUREAUX.

OUTLINE. 1. Usually a popular treatment of an extensive subject, e.g. H. G. Wells *The outline of history*. 2. (*Printing*) A type face in which the shape of the character is outlined in a continuous line of more or less consistent width. *See also* INLINE LETTERS.

OUTLINE LETTERS. *Synonymous with* OPEN LETTERS (*q.v.*).

OUTPUT. (*Information retrieval*) The product of a process – that is, the information transferred from the internal storage of a computer to output devices for external storage (*IBM*).

OUTSERT. An extra double leaf placed round the outside of a printed section of a book, and forming part of it. *See also* WRAP ROUNDS.

OUTSIDE MARGIN. *Synonymous with* FORE-EDGE MARGIN (*q.v.*).

OUTSIDE SOURCE. An idiom used, often by special librarians, to indicate a source of information outside their own organization which may be drawn upon when the resources of the library are inadequate to deal with enquiry needs. Such sources are often listed in the catalogue under appropriate subject headings or in a separate SOURCE INDEX (*q.v.*).

OVAL HALF-TONE. *See* HALF-TONE.

OVALS, IN. A binding with an oval arabesque centrepiece impressed in the centre of the top and lower covers. A common style in the late sixteenth and early seventeenth centuries, and found both in gold and blind.

OVER MATTER. Matter set ready for printing but held over through lack of space.

OVER-RUN. (*Printing*) 1. To turn over words from one line to the next for several successive lines as necessary after an insertion or a deletion. 2. Copies printed in excess of the number ordered.

OVER-RUNNING. Re-adjusting a paragraph of type which has been set up, due to corrections affecting the length of a line or poor make-up, or to avoid a RIVER (*q.v.*) or the unsatisfactory division of words. Words set in one line are carried forward or backward to adjacent lines as necessary.

OVERCASTING. *Synonymous with* OVERSEWING (*q.v.*).

OVERDUE. Colloquialism for an overdue book and also for an overdue notice.

OVERDUE BOOK. A library book which has been retained longer for home reading than the period allowed.

OVERDUE NOTICE. A request to a reader asking for the return of a book which has been kept out beyond the time allowed.

OVERLAY. 1. The placing of pieces of paper on the tympan or impression cylinder of a printing machine, by manipulation of which an even impression is obtained from the matter after it has been levelled as far as possible by UNDERLAY (*q.v.*). 2. A group of transparent or translucent prints or drawings which can be superimposed on one another to form a composite print or slide. This method is often used in overhead projectors. (*Information retrieval*) A technique for bringing routines into high-speed storage from some other form of storage during processing so that several routines will occupy the same storage locations at different times. Overlay functions when the total storage requirements for instructions are in excess of the main storage which is available. *See also* ROUTINE.

OVERPLUS. (*Printing*) Additional sheets printed in excess of the number actually ordered to allow for getting exact position, testing colour, determining register and for spoilt sheets so that on completion of a job the number ordered is available. These are usually known as 'overs'. Bibliophiles also apply the term to limited editions, copies of which are numbered serially.

OVERPRINT. 1. To revise printed matter by blocking out unwanted matter and printing a revision above it. 2. To print over matter which has already been printed whether blocked out or not. 3. To add information in a space, or in a Box (*q.v.*), on something which has already been printed. This frequently occurs with circulars, catalogues and advertising leaflets where a name and address are inserted to give the impression that the printed matter appears to originate from this source. *See also* SEPARATE. 4. More copies printed than needed, or ordered. 5. In colour printing, to obtain required colours by printing with one colour superimposed over another.

OVERPRINTING. 1. Printing in a primary colour over printing already carried out in a different colour in order to obtain a compound shade. 2. Application of a varnish or lacquer to matter printed from type or by a litho process, by means of a brush, spray or roller. 3. In blockmaking, superimposing one negative over another on the coated metal plate before developing. *See also* OVERPRINT. 4. The printing of additional material, as e.g. the name and address of a retailer's name and address, on to a sheet or page that has already been printed.

OVERS. 1. Extra sheets issued from the paper warehouse to the printing room, to allow for make-ready, testing colour, and for spoilt sheets, so that on completion of a job the number ordered is available. 2. Sheets or copies of a work printed in excess of the number ordered to make up spoiled copies, and to provide review and presentation copies. Also called 'Overplus'.

OVERSEWING. The act or process of sewing over and over the leaves of a book, usually done when it consists of single leaves or when the paper is too poor or too heavy for normal sewing to be satisfactory. Called 'whip-stitching' in America.

OVERSIZE BOOK. One which is too large to be shelved in normal sequence.

OWNERSHIP MARK. A rubber-stamp impression, perforation, embossment, or other mark of ownership in a book.

OXFORD BIBLE. *Synonymous with* VINEGAR BIBLE (*q.v.*).

OXFORD CORNERS. In book finishing, border rules that cross and project beyond each other.

OXFORD DECIMAL SYSTEMS. A scheme of classification based on the Universal Decimal Classification. It was worked out at the School of Forestry of Oxford University and is restricted to the field of forestry.

OXFORD FOLIO. *See* VINEGAR BIBLE.

OXFORD HOLLOW. A tube-like lining which is flattened, and one side stuck to the folded and sewn sections of the book and the other to the inside of the spine of the cover.

OXFORD INDIA PAPER. An INDIA PAPER (*q.v.*) about 8 lb demy (480) used by the Oxford University Press mainly for Bibles and prayer books, and made from selected rag stock according to a secret formula at their Wolvercote Mill since 1857. It is similar to an India paper first brought to Oxford in 1841, being very thin and opaque (one thousand sheets making less than an inch in thickness), and is a proprietary article. *See also* BIBLE PAPER, CAMBRIDGE INDIA PAPER.

OXFORD RULE. A rule with one thick and one thin line running parallel with each other.

OXFORD UNIVERSITY SCHOOL OF FORESTRY. Has an extremely valuable collection of material on forestry, the catalogue of which has been microfilmed with a grant from the Ford Foundation. Produces *Centralised Title Service*, a current bibliography of forestry, on cards which are despatched to subscribers every two weeks.

OXIDATION. The action which occurs when air contacts the unprotected areas of a lithographic plate which has been inadequately gummed. *See also* GUMMING UP.

OZALID. Trade name for a document copying process which uses the diazo technique. *See also* DIAZOTYPE PROCESS.

OZARAPID. Trade name for a machine made by the Ozalid Company for copying by the 'soft diffusion process'. *See also* TRANSFER PROCESS.

p. Abbreviation for page; pp., pages.

P-SLIP. A slip of paper 5 × 3 inches. P-slips are often made up into pads. (American).

PCMI SYSTEM. The Photo-Chromic-Micro-Image system, developed by the National Cash Register Company for data recording. It was demonstrated at the New York World's Fair in 1964, and enables 1,245 pages to be recorded on a 2 × 2 inches film.

P.E. NOTES. In an attempt to speed up decisions on extensions to the Universal Decimal Classification the International Commission sends out *P.E. notes* (Projets d'extensions) which invite criticisms to be submitted within four months, and *P.P.* *notes* (projets provisoires) which are intimations of provisional 'revolutionary suggestions.'

PMEST FORMULA. Ranganathan's five FUNDAMENTAL CATEGORIES (*q.v.*) – Personality, Matter, Energy, Space, Time – or facets, which, in this order, are arranged by decreasing concreteness.

p.p. Abbreviation for PRIVATELY PRINTED (*q.v.*).

PACIFIC NORTHWEST BIBLIOGRAPHIC CENTER. An independent co-operative, non-profit research organization sponsored by the Pacific Northwest Library Association. It is situated at the University of Washington at Seattle and is supported by the subscriptions of participating libraries. It is concerned with research into union cataloguing of book and other printed materials in forty libraries in the N.W. states of the U.S.A. and British Columbia.

PACK. A collection of cards, commonly a complete set of cards, which have been punched for a definite service (*IBM*). Called in America a 'Deck'.

PACKAGE LIBRARY. A feature of American practice, especially in society libraries, whereby 'packages' of publications consisting of anything from a few reprints or 'tear-sheets' to sufficient to fill a box file are sent to members. The material is arranged by subject or form and is sometimes published in microform, in which case it is called a 'Desk-top library'. The 'library' usually includes indexes, and the whole is regularly updated.

PACKET DEVICE. The symbol used in building classification numbers to connect class numbers from two parts of the classification schedules, the second one being used to show an aspect of the subject indicated by the first number.

PACKET NOTATION. The use of a connecting symbol, e.g. in the Colon Classification a bracket, or in the Universal Decimal Classification square brackets, to divide an isolate number by a number drawn from another schedule. Such a digit can be used as an OCTAVIZING DIGIT (*q.v.*) to extend the hospitality of an array.

PADDING. Blank leaves added at the back of a thin pamphlet when binding it to form a sizeable volume.

PADELOUP STYLE. A style of book decoration practised by the Padeloup family in France in the eighteenth century. It is mainly characterized by its inlays of coloured leathers of diapered simple geometrical form, devoid of any floreation.

PAGE. *See* LEAF.

PAGE BREAK. The point in the text of a book where one page ends and the next begins.

PAGE CATALOGUE. One in which only a few entries are made on a page at first, with spaces left for the insertion of subsequent entries in correct order. The catalogues in the Reading Room of the British Museum and in the Bodleian are of this variety. Also called 'Guard book catalogue', 'Ledger catalogue'.

PAGE CORD. A cord which withstands water, specially made for printers, and used to tie up pages of type prior to imposition or distribution.

PAGE HEADLINE. A summary of the contents of a page, or an OPENING (*q.v.*), or of the main topic of a page or opening, appearing on both left- and right-hand pages, or on one side only in conjunction with a section headline on the other page. Also called 'Page head'. *See also* HEADLINE, RUNNING TITLE, SECTION HEADLINE.

PAGE PROOF. *See* PROOF.

PAGE REFERENCE. In bibliographies, the number of the page on which the article, etc., indexed is to be found in a particular volume or volumes.

PAGINATION. 1. That part of a catalogue entry or bibliographical description specifying the number of pages in a book. 2. The system of numbers by which consecutive pages of a book or MS. are marked to indicate their order. Pagination is rare until 1500 and not really common until 1590.

PAINTED EDGES. *See* FORE-EDGE PAINTING.

PAISA LIBRARY SCHEME. A scheme which operated in Lahore in the early 1940s whereby children saved a paisa a day (less than a rupee, or ten U.S. cents, a month) and received a children's magazine and a children's book of from 72 to 112 pages each month. The scheme was discontinued, after more than fifty titles had been published, due to increasing costs caused by the war.

PAKISTAN ASSOCIATION OF SPECIAL LIBRARIES. Founded at Karachi in June 1968 and registered as the national organization of special libraries in the country. The main object of the Association is to promote the development of special libraries and information services.

PAKISTAN NATIONAL SCIENTIFIC AND TECHNICAL DOCUMENTATION CENTRE. This organization was established in Karachi in 1957, with the technical assistance of Unesco. Abbreviated PANSDOC.

PALAEOGRAPHY. The study and description of ancient and mediaeval manuscripts, documents and systems of writing, including the knowledge of the various characters used at different periods by the scribes of different nations and languages, their usual abbreviations, etc.

PALIMPSEST. Manuscript in which a second writing has been superimposed upon the original text, which has been wholly or partially obliterated.

PALLET. 1. A tool used to decorate the panels on the spine of a bound book. Pallets are usually used to make straight lines (sometimes decorative) but are also used to impress a whole word such as the author's name or a title. 2. A bookbinder's typeholder.

PALM LEAF BOOK. Manuscript books consisting of strips of Palmyra or Talipat palm leaf from 16 to 36 inches long and from 1½ to 3 inches broad. Writing was done by scratching with an iron stylus and ink prepared from oil and charcoal rubbed over the surface to fill the incisions. The strips were then bound by piercing a hole in the middle of each and stringing them on cords or a piece of twine, and attaching them to a board. They were made in India, Burma and Ceylon. The Palmyra and Talipat palm leaves which are thick but long and narrow, were the only writing material for books in ancient Odra and other parts of the Central Provinces of Southern India; they were also used to some extent in Ceylon, Burma, Thailand and Northern India. Sacred works were written on Talipat palm leaves in Thailand, the edges of the leaves being gilded, or painted with vermilion, and the leaves threaded on strings and folded like a fan.

PAMPHLET. A non-periodical publication of at least five but not more than 48 pages, exclusive of the cover pages. (General Conference of Unesco, 1964). *See also* BOOK. It usually has an independent entity, not being a SERIAL (*q.v.*), but it may be one of a series of publications having a similarity of format or subject matter.

PAMPHLET BINDING. 1. Binding done by, or for, a printer, in which the sheets as they come from the press, are wire-stitched. The term applies both to pamphlets and to magazines. 2. The manner in which such publications are bound when they come from the publisher, being WIRE-STITCHED, SIDE-STITCHED or SADDLE-STITCHED (*qq.v.*).

PAMPHLET BOX. A box, usually of cardboard covered with cloth, or of steel, for holding pamphlets and other unbound material. *See also* BOX FILE.

PAMPHLET-STYLE LIBRARY BINDING. A style of binding for a thin pamphlet or a group of thin pamphlets which are expected to be used infrequently. It is characterized by side stitching and a lightweight cover of plain boards, heavy paper, paper-covered boards or limp cloth, and an absence of gold lettering.

PAMPHLET VOLUME. A volume consisting of a number of pamphlets bound together with or without a title-page or table of contents.

PANEL. 1. A compartment of the external cover of a book enclosed in a BORDER 2 (*q.v.*) or FRAME 2 (*q.v.*). 2. The space between two bands on the back of a book. 3. The list of books 'by the same author' facing the title-page. This is more for bibliographical than for advertisting purposes and may therefore include out-of-print titles and those issued by other publishers.

PANEL BACK. In hand binding, a volume finished with panelled borders between the raised bands on the shelf-back.

PANEL STAMP. A large piece of metal, engraved intaglio, used for impressing a design on the sides of book covers. Some of the stamps used for the early leather bindings were of quarto and folio size, but often book covers of these sizes were impressed two, three, four or more times with small panel stamps. A popular form of ornamentation in the early sixteenth century.

PANIZZI CLUB. Founded in 1914 (first honorary secretary, E. W. Hulme, Librarian of the Patent Office Library) 'to provide opportunities for social intercourse between the Senior Officers of Reference and Research Libraries and to promote all measures tending to their higher efficiency'. Librarians of all kinds of library were admitted to membership. It is not known when the Club ceased to function, but it was the foundation on which the CIRCLE OF STATE LIBRARIANS (*q.v.*) was built.

PANORAMIC CATALOGUE. The endless chain principle adapted for displaying catalogue entries.

PANTOGRAPH. An instrument for copying a drawing to a premeditated scale.

PANTONE. A photo-engraving method of printing from a flat (planographic) plate with letterpress equipment, having the advantage over letterpress half-tone in that it can print from a screen up to 400 lines on antique paper and other rough surfaces. It is based on the principle that a printing plate bearing an image that is not in relief can be made to repel ink in the bare parts by treating them with mercury, while the printing parts will take up ink.

PAPER. 1. A fibrous material made by breaking down vegetable fibres, purifying them, interweaving them into a compact web and pressing them into thin sheets. Book papers are made from MECHANICAL WOOD (*q.v.*) pulp (used for the cheapest publications and newspapers), CHEMICAL WOOD (*q.v.*) pulp (for most books), ESPARTO (*q.v.*) or rags, which make the best quality hand-made papers (for fine books). 2. A brief, literary composition, especially one to be read at a public meeting. 3. Contraction for newspaper. 4. To insert the end papers and fly-leaves of a book before inserting in its cover.

PAPER-BACKED. *Synonymous with* PAPER-BOUND (*q.v.*).

PAPER BOARDS. *See* BOARDS.

PAPER-BOUND. Bound with a paper cover. Also called 'Paper backed'. A book so bound is called a PAPERBACK (*q.v.*).

PAPER COVERED. A pamphlet or small book which is not bound in boards, but covered with a stiff paper which is usually pasted on to the book or sewn through. If the paper covers are pasted down on to thin boards, cut flush at the head and tail, flaps turned over, the style is called 'Stiffened paper covers'.

PAPER FINISHES. *Antique:* a rough uneven surface. *Eggshell:* slightly finished surface, having the appearance of the shell of an egg. *Machine:* smoother than antique with a slight gloss, but not suitable for half-tone illustrations, excepting those of coarse-screen finish. *Smooth antique:* an antique slightly rolled. *Super-calendered:* smooth finish without lustre; this will print half-tone blocks up to 100-screen. *American:* a finish with medium gloss and suitable for half-tone illustrations up to 100-screen. *Enamel* or *coated:* has a very high gloss, being coated in the making with china-clay, satin white, and casein which fills in the pores. Takes illustrations of the finest screen. *Dull coated:* has the coating as on a coated paper, but is calendered for smoothness only, not for gloss. Thus it has a perfect surface of mellow softness for the finest cuts.

PAPER SIZES. The dimensions of a sheet of paper or board (generally rectangular shape) as supplied by the manufacturer, the width (the smaller dimension) being given first. The British Standards Specification for writing and printing paper is as follows:

Foolscap	$13\frac{1}{2} \times 17$
Foolscap, Double	17×27
Foolscap, Oblong Double	$13\frac{1}{2} \times 34$
Foolscap, Quad	27×34
Pinched Post	$14\frac{1}{2} \times 18\frac{1}{2}$
Post	$15\frac{1}{4} \times 19$
Post, Double	$19 \times 30\frac{1}{2}$
Large Post	$16\frac{1}{2} \times 21$
Large Post, Double	21×33

Demy	$17\frac{1}{2} \times 22\frac{1}{2}$
Demy, Double	$22\frac{1}{2} \times 35$
Demy, Quad	35×45
Medium	18×23
Medium, Double	23×36
Medium, Quad	36×46
Royal	20×25
Royal, Double	25×40
Crown	15×20
Crown, Double	20×30
Crown, Double Quad	40×60
Crown, Quad	30×40
Imperial	22×30
Imperial, Double	30×44

Other sizes are:

Pott	$12\frac{1}{2} \times 15\frac{1}{2}$
Pott, Double	$15\frac{1}{2} \times 25$
Post, Small	$15\frac{3}{4} \times 19\frac{1}{2}$
Royal, Large	20×27
Royal, Super	$20\frac{1}{2} \times 27\frac{1}{2}$

A sheet of 'quad' gives four times the number of sections as a sheet of ordinary size, a 'double' sheet twice the number. Papers for other purposes differ in size. *See also* BOOK SIZES, OCTAVO.

The American practice is not to use names but to specify the size of paper by inches and its weight per ream. The ordinary sizes of book papers in the U.S.A. are:

22×32	28×44	34×44	44×56
24×36	29×52	35×45	44×64
25×38	$30\frac{1}{2} \times 41$	36×48	
26×39	32×44	38×50	All the above
26×40	33×44	41×51	measurements
28×42	33×46	42×56	are in inches.

The German DIN A series of paper sizes is widely used in Europe,

DIN stands for Deutsche Industrie Normen, and indicates standards agreed by Deutscher Normenausschuss (Committee for Standards). a similar body to the British Standards Institution. The A is to distinguish this standard from others known as B and C which apply to related poster and envelope sizes. The chief features of the DIN A series are that they apply to all types of paper, and that the proportions of a sheet remain constant when it is cut or folded in half across the long side. The letters Ao indicate a basic size of 1 square metre. A sheet of paper half this size is indicated by A1, or half this size by A2 and so on. A larger sheet than Ao is indicated by a figure before the A; thus a sheet twice the size of Ao is indicated by 2A. The following table shows 7 trimmed sizes in the DIN A series which correspond to the British sizes from 8-demy to demy 8vo.

	Millimetres	*Inches (approx.)*	*Demy sizes*
2Ao	1189 × 1682	$46\frac{13}{16} \times 66\frac{3}{16}$	45 × 70
Ao	841 × 1189	$33\frac{1}{8} \times 46\frac{13}{16}$	35 × 45
A1	594 × 841	$23\frac{3}{8} \times 33\frac{1}{8}$	$22\frac{1}{2} \times 35$
A2	420 × 594	$16\frac{9}{16} \times 23\frac{3}{8}$	$17\frac{1}{2} \times 22\frac{1}{2}$
A3	297 × 420	$11\frac{11}{16} \times 16\frac{9}{16}$	$11\frac{1}{4} \times 17\frac{1}{2}$
A4	210 × 297	$8\frac{1}{4} \times 11\frac{11}{16}$	$8\frac{3}{4} \times 11\frac{1}{4}$
A5	148 × 210	$5\frac{7}{8} \times 8\frac{1}{4}$	$5\frac{5}{8} \times 8\frac{3}{4}$
A6	105 × 148	$4\frac{1}{8} \times 5\frac{7}{8}$	
A7	74 × 105	$2\frac{15}{16} \times 4\frac{1}{8}$	
A8	52 × 74	$2\frac{1}{16} \times 2\frac{15}{16}$	
A9	37 × 52	$1\frac{1}{2} \times 2\frac{1}{16}$	
A10	26 × 37	$1 \times 1\frac{1}{2}$	

There is also a 4Ao size: 1682 and 2378 mm.
(Continental practice is to state the smaller dimensions first.)

Series B is intended for posters, wall charts and other large items, and C for envelopes, particularly where it is necessary for an envelope in the C series to fit into another envelope. The International Organization for Standardization (ISO) adopted the A series for trimmed sizes for administrative, commercial and technical uses, and printed matter such as forms, professional periodicals and catalogues; the sizes do not necessarily apply to newspapers, published books, posters, continuous stationery or other specialized items. These sizes are sometimes referred to as 'ISO–A' sizes. The B sizes have also been adopted by ISO and are sometimes referred to as 'ISO–B' sizes, but, unlike the A series, have not been adopted by the British Standards Institution. The ISO recommends that these sizes are intended for use in exceptional circumstances, when sizes are needed intermediate between any two adjacent sizes of the A series. The C sizes have not been adopted by the ISO. *See also* PERIODICAL, UNTRIMMED SIZE.

PAPERBACK. A book bound in paper covers or covered with one piece of paper. A common term for novels of the late nineteenth century bound in this way and also for contemporary books similarly bound. A new type of publishing venture was begun in 1935 when Allen Lane founded Penguin Books in England and began publishing large editions of paperback books to sell at a very low price – sixpence, which was about a twentieth of the price of a hardback edition.

PAPYROLOGY. The study of ancient documents and literary manuscripts on papyrus.

PAPYRUS. 1. A giant water-reed from the stem of which the Egyptians made a writing material. 2. The material itself. 3. A manuscript written on papyrus.

PARAGRAPH INDENTION. (*Cataloguing*) *Synonymous with* SECOND INDENTION (*q.v.*). (*Printing*) Setting the first line of a paragraph one em or so in from the margin. Also called 'Paragraph indentation'. *See also* HANGING INDENTION.

PARAGRAPH MARK. 1. The reversed or 'blind' P sign (¶) used in a MS. or proof to indicate the commencement of a new paragraph. 2. The sixth reference mark for footnotes, coming after the parallel. *See also* REFERENCE MARKS.

PARALLEL. (*Information retrieval*) Pertaining to the simultaneous handling of all the elements in a group (*IBM*). *See also* SERIAL 3. (*Printing*) The printer's sign ‖; it is used as the fifth reference mark. *See also* REFERENCE MARKS.

PARALLEL ARRANGEMENT. Separating books of varying sizes to economize shelf space by arranging larger books by one of the following methods: (a) in a separate sequence on the bottom shelves of each tier; (b) in a separate sequence at the end of each class; (c) in a complete separate sequence of the whole classification.

PARALLEL CLASSIFICATION. Material classified by the same scheme is said to be placed in parallel classification when it is again divided by size, character, etc., e.g. there may be four perfectly classified sequences for octavos, folios, pamphlets and illustrations; thus giving four parallel classifications.

PARALLEL EDITION. A publication in which different texts of the same work are printed side by side, e.g. the Authorized and Revised versions of the Bible, or an original and a translation into another language, or two or more versions of a work.

PARALLEL MARK (∥). The fifth reference mark for footnotes, coming after the section mark. *See also* REFERENCE MARKS.

PARALLEL RULE. A RULE (*q.v.*) having two lines of the same thickness. *See also* DOUBLE RULE.

PARALLEL TEXT. *See* PARALLEL EDITION.

PARALLEL TRANSLATION. A text, with a translation into another language, both printed in parallel columns.

PARAPH. A mark or flourish after a signature, made often as a protection against forgery, and especially used by notaries. Also called a 'Flourish'.

PARAPHRASE. An arrangement, transcription or imitation of a vocal or instrumental work in a form for voices or instruments other than was originally intended.

PARCHMENT. 1. Sheepskin or goatskin dressed with alum and polished. It is not so strong as vellum (calfskin) which it resembles, and from which it can be distinguished by its grain. It is used for documents of a permanent nature and for binding large and heavy volumes. The term is now sometimes applied to fibrous imitations. 2. In the paper trade, wrapping paper with a high resistance to grease and atmospheric humidity. It is a tough, translucent, glossy paper resembling animal parchment and made by soaking ordinary unsized paper in cold dilute sulphuric acid, or in some instances zinc chloride. Such paper is impervious to air, water, moisture, fat or oil and is stronger wet than dry. It was first manufactured in France in 1846 by Poumarede and Le Figuier. This use of the word is an abbreviation for 'parchment-paper'. Also called 'Vegetable parchment', 'Imitation parchment', i.e. an imitation of parchment paper is made without treatment in sulphuric acid, the toughness being produced by long treatment in the beating engine. Such paper, although less impervious, is also suitable for wrapping greasy food, and similar products.

PARCHMENT-PAPER. *See* PARCHMENT 2.

PARENTHESES. Curved lines () used to include words inserted parenthetically. Used in cataloguing to enclose explanatory or qualifying words or phrases to set off some item in the entry, such as a series note. Also called 'Round brackets' or 'Curves'. *See also* SQUARE BRACKETS.

PARENTHESIS. A short explanatory clause inserted in a sentence, usually between parentheses.

PARISH LIBRARY.   One which was provided by a parish council.

PARISH MEETING.   Local government electors of a rural parish must meet annually on a day between 1st March and 1st April. It is not regarded as a local authority but has a number of miscellaneous powers. Under the Public Libraries Act, 1892 (until the Public Libraries Act, 1919 gave powers of adoption in respect of rural areas to county councils) it had powers to adopt the public libraries acts.

PARLIAMENTARY PAPERS.   A term which when used in the scholars' narrow sense means a particular group of Parliamentary Publications, e.g. (a) House of Lords Papers and Bills, (b) House of Commons Bills, (c) House of Commons Papers, (d) Command Papers, and not all the publications issued by Parliament and published by HMSO which alone has authority to publish on behalf of Parliament. *See also* PARLIAMENTARY PUBLICATIONS, SESSIONAL PAPERS.

PARLIAMENTARY PUBLICATIONS.

1. GENERAL DEFINITION. Papers printed for parliamentary purposes and placed on sale to the general public through HMSO. These comprise:

> House of Lords Papers
>   „   „   „   Bills
>   „   „   „   Journals
>   „   „   „   Debates
>   „   „   „   Minutes of Proceedings
> House of Commons Papers
>   „   „   „   Bills
>   „   „   „   Journals
>   „   „   „   Debates
>   „   „   „   Votes and Proceedings
> Command Papers
> Public General Acts
> Local and Private Acts
> Measures passed by the National Assembly of the Church
>   of England.

2. 'HOUSE' PAPERS. Documents presented either to the House of Lords or to the House of Commons under statute or by order of the House and 'ordered to be printed'. The sessional number appears at the bottom left hand corner of the title-page. House of Lords Paper and Bill numbers (in a common series) are printed in parentheses; House of Commons Bill numbers are in square brackets; House of Commons Paper numbers are not enclosed in brackets.

3. COMMAND PAPERS. Papers presented by a Minister to both Houses of Parliament by Command of Her Majesty. Occasionally, a Paper has been presented by Command to one House only, but with the exception of estimates (House of Commons Papers) the practice is now rare. The series is limited to documents relating to matters likely to be the subject of early legislation, or regarded as otherwise essential to Members of Parliament to enable them to discharge their responsibilities.

They were first published as Appendices to the House of Commons Journal but since 1836 have been numbered serially as follows:

1833–1869	[1]–[4222]
1870–1899	C.I.–C.9550
1900–1918	Cd.1–Cd.9239
1919–1956	Cmd.1–Cmd.9889
1956–	Cmnd.1–

4. 'HANSARD'. The official verbatim reports of the debates of both Houses of Parliament. The debates of the House of Commons and of the House of Lords (issued separately) are published daily while Parliament is sitting. They are named after Luke Hansard (1752–1828) and his descendants who printed these reports from 1811–1891. The issue of an officially authorized edition began in 1892, and in 1909 HMSO assumed the responsibility for printing and publication.

5. VOTES AND PROCEEDINGS OF THE HOUSE OF COMMONS. These are issued daily while the House is sitting and comprise six parts, each separately paged. They are:

Proceedings of the previous day;

Private business;

Questions, notices of Motions, Orders of the day;

Papers delivered to the House, notices of sittings of Public Committees;

Proposed amendments to Bills;

Proceedings in Standing Committees (each Committee's Proceedings are paged separately);

Divisions.

In addition, a list of the Public Bills which have been introduced during the Session, showing progress made, is circulated weekly with the Votes and Proceedings, and a similar list of Private Bills is included periodically in the private business section.

6. MINUTES OF PROCEEDINGS OF THE HOUSE OF LORDS. These, also, are issued daily while the House is sitting and contain:

The proceedings of the previous day;
Notices of judicial business;
Agenda for the day (including questions);
Notices of future questions and business;
Divisions;
A list of Bills showing the stages reached.

7. THE JOURNALS OF THE HOUSE OF COMMONS AND OF THE HOUSE OF LORDS, containing a complete record of Parliamentary proceedings, are published separately at the end of each Session.

8. THE ORDER BOOK OF THE HOUSE OF COMMONS is a consolidation of the business appearing in the Votes and Proceedings. It is issued daily for the convenience of Members and is not generally available to the public.

See also GREEN PAPER, NON-PARLIAMENTARY PUBLICATIONS, PARLIAMENTARY PAPERS, WHITE PAPER. All parliamentary publications are published by HMSO.

PARLIAMENTARY SESSION. A parliamentary year which begins with the opening of Parliament and normally ends with its prorogation. It usually begins in the first week of November, immediately after the old session, and does not correspond either with the calendar year or with the government's financial year. Also called a 'Session'. *See also* SESSIONAL PAPERS.

PARRY REPORT. The *Report of the Committee on Libraries* (HMSO 1967) which was set up in 1963 by the University Grants Committee; so named after Dr. Thomas Parry, Principal of the Universitv College of Wales, Aberystwyth, who was the chairman. It surveys libraries in British universities and makes recommendations on improving these and developing the British Museum Library as the chief functionary in the provision of library and bibliographical services.

PART. 1. A portion of a work in one or more volumes issued by a publisher as the work is completed for publication. Parts may be issued at frequent, regular intervals, as fortnightly, or at monthly, yearly, or irregular intervals, according to the nature of the work and its compilation. It usually has a separate title, half title, or cover title, and may have separate or continuous paging. It is distinguished from a FASCICLE (*q.v.*) by being a unit rather than a temporary portion of a unit. 2. A division of work (*see* WORK 1) according to its content (*IFLA*). 3. The music for any one of the participating voices or instruments of a musical composition. 4. The manuscript or printed copy of the music for such a participant. *See also* VOLUME. 5. A separately published number of a SERIAL (*q.v.*). Parts usually have paper covers bearing the title of the serial, the volume number (if any), issue number and date of issue. This information usually appears also on the first page of the text if the cover does not have textual matter on it, and nowadays often at the foot of each page in addition, the title usually being in an abbreviated form.

PART PUBLICATIONS. Long works which are issued in separate parts at regular intervals.

PART-TIME BRANCH. *See* BRANCH LIBRARY.

PART TITLE. *Synonymous with* DIVISIONAL TITLE (*q.v.*).

PARTIAL BIBLIOGRAPHY. One in which a mechanical limit has been put on the material included; e.g. periodicals only, books or articles of a certain period or in a certain country or library. *See also* SELECT BIBLIOGRAPHY.

PARTIAL CONTENTS NOTE. A note which gives only the more important items in the contents.

PARTIAL TITLE. One which consists of only a secondary part of the title as given in the title-page. It may be a CATCHWORD TITLE (*q.v.*), SUB-TITLE (*q.v.*) or ALTERNATIVE TITLE (*q.v.*).

PARTIAL TITLE ENTRY. A catalogue entry made under a PARTIAL TITLE (*q.v.*).

PASTE-DOWN. That part of an endpaper which is pasted down to the inner surface of the cover or boards of a book. Also called 'Board paper'. The free half of the endpaper forms a fly-leaf.

PASTE-DOWN ENDPAPER. *See* ENDPAPER.

PASTE-GRAIN. Split sheepskin hardened by coating with paste and given a highly polished surface.

PASTE-IN. 1. A correction or addition to the text supplied after the sheets have been printed, and tipped into the book opposite the place to which it refers. *See also* CORRIGENDA. 2. A separately printed illustration or map, cut to the size of the book, and the inner edge pasted into the text before gathering.

PASTE-UP. An arrangement on sheets of paper of proofs of a number of pages in order to plan the positioning of blocks, legends, illustrations and text. The use of a rubber adhesive simplifies re-arrangement.

PASTEBOARD. The material, made by pasting sheets of brown paper together, and lined on both sides with paper, which is used for printing and also for the covers of books. *See also* MILLBOARD, STRAWBOARD.

PASTICHE. A musical or artistic composition consisting of a medley of passages or parts from various sources, connected together.

PASTING DOWN. The action of attaching a sewn book to its case or cover.

PASTORAL. A book relating to the cure of souls.

PASTORAL LETTER. A letter from a spiritual pastor, especially from a bishop to the clergy or people of his diocese.

PATENT. 1. A specification concerning the design or manufacture of something which is protected by letters patent and secured for the exclusive profit of the designer or inventor for a limited number of years which varies in different countries from fifteen to twenty years. The department which controls the registration of patents is called a 'Patents office'. 2. A publication, issued by such an office, which gives details of the designs and processes.

PATENT BASE. A device for raising the level of the bed of a printing press so that the electrotypes or stereotypes need not be mounted on wood.

PATENT FILE. Patent specifications and drawings which may be arranged by country and number, name of patentee or subject, or an index of such material similarly arranged.

PATENT OFFICE LIBRARY. Founded in London in 1855 to stimulate developments in the field of invention by making relevant information on applied science freely and readily available to all. Since incorporation within the British Museum Library to form the NATIONAL REFERENCE LIBRARY OF SCIENCE AND INVENTION (*q.v.*), its scope has been widened to include developments and discoveries in any branch of the natural sciences and technology.

PATENT ROLL. A parchment roll upon which royal letters patent were enrolled at the Chancery.

PATRA. Abbreviation for the PRINTING, PACKAGING AND ALLIED TRADES RESEARCH ASSOCIATION (*q.v.*).

PATRISTICS. A publisher's series on the writings of the Fathers of the Christian Church, e.g. *The Library of Christian Classics* and *Ancient Christian Writers*.

PATTERN. A specimen volume, or rubbing, sent to a binder to indicate the style of lettering to be used.

PATTERN BOARD. A board maintained by a binder on which is mounted a specimen of the covering material to show titling lay-out, colour, size, etc., to ensure uniformity in the binding of a series.

PATTERN RUBBING. A rubbing made to ensure that subsequent volumes in a series are lettered in the same style. *See also* RUB.

PAY COLLECTION. *See* DUPLICATE PAY COLLECTION.

PAYNE STYLE. The style of book decoration practised by Roger Payne in England in the eighteenth century. It consisted of the repetition of small floral forms in borders or radiating corners, the background being formed with dots and circles.

PEACOCK ROLL. (*Binding*) A finisher's roll which includes a peacock in its ornamentation. It is characteristic of some English Restoration bindings, and also appears on eighteenth century Irish bindings.

PEARL. An out-of-date name for a size of type equivalent to 5 point.

PEAR TREE PRESS. A private printing press, begun in Essex in 1899 by James Guthrie. It moved to Flansham in 1907.

PEBBLING. *See* STIPPLING.

PEDESTRIAN WORK. (*Classification*) A work which is not a SACRED WORK (*q.v.*), a CLASSIC (*q.v.*) or a LITERARY WORK (*q.v.*), and is not treated as if it were a class or a subject in usage.

PEEK-A-BOO. A principle of punching ASPECT CARDS (*q.v.*) to record information which is represented by certain positions on the card. These positions may be numbered in columns (the punched cards which have been familiar in the U.K. for many years are of this kind), or, in the larger cards capable of having up to 10,000 positions on one side, be in numbered squares or grilles. Such cards are sorted by machine or are searched by placing several in front of the source of light, possibly in a light box. Wherever light shows through there is a coincidence of document-number punches and this identifies documents as possessing the aspects indicated by the position of the hole. The card represents an index unit and the holes stand for documents or parts of documents that have the particular index unit in common. The cards used in this system are also called 'Cordonnier cards' or 'Batten cards' after G. Cordonnier of France and W. E. Batten of Britain who were early exponents of the system. They are also called 'Optical coincidence cards'. *See also* BATTEN SYSTEM.

PEEPHOLE CARD. One with holes punched in it to represent information or characteristics possessed; it is used with a system of CO-ORDINATE INDEXING (*q.v.*). Also called 'Aperture card', 'Optical coincidence card'. It may also have an opening specifically prepared to mount one or more frames of a microfilm.

PELLET'S PROCESS. A blueprint process suitable only for the reproduction of line drawings whereby the prints have blue lines on an almost white background. It was introduced in 1877.

PEN-NAME. *Synonymous with* PSEUDONYM (*q.v.*).

PENCIL DATER. A combined rubber date stamp and pencil.

PENNY-DREADFUL. A thrilling story magazine for children sold at a very low price. A morbidly sensational story.

PERFECT. (*Binding*) A method of binding by which the folds of the sections forming the back of the book are cut away; the edges of the loose sheets so formed are then coated with a very flexible but strong adhesive and covered with paper, mull or other material. The book is then inserted into covers by ordinary methods employed when sections are not sewn on tapes. Also called 'Lumbecking'.

PERFECT COPY. A sheet of paper which has been printed on both sides from an 'inner forme' and also from an 'outer forme'.

PERFECTER. A printing machine which prints on both sides of the paper at the same time whereas stop-cylinder presses and two-revolution machines print on one side only. Also called a 'Perfecting machine' or 'Perfecting press'. The first machine of this kind was made in 1816 by Koenig and Bauer and was called by the maker a 'completing machine'.

PERFECTING. Printing the second side of a sheet. A perfecting press is one that prints both sides of a sheet in one operation. Also called 'Backing up'.

PERFECTING MACHINE. *See* PERFECTER.

PERFORATING STAMP. A punch or stamp which perforates a mark of ownership through the page of a book.

PERFORMANCE INDEX. A method of evaluating the service provided by a technical library; it is the ratio of (a) material supplied to (b) the material requested, the index being expressed as the percentage that (a) is of (b).

PERIOD BIBLIOGRAPHY. One limited to a certain period of time.

PERIOD DIVISION. 1. A division of a classification scheme for works covering a limited period of time. 2. A sub-division of a subject heading in a catalogue which indicates the period covered.

PERIOD PRINTING. Producing books in a style which is similar to that used when they were first published.

PERIODICAL. A publication with a distinctive title which appears at stated or regular intervals, generally oftener than once a year, without prior decision as to when the last issue shall appear. It contains articles, stories or other writings, by several contributors. *Newspapers*, whose chief function is to disseminate news, and the *memoirs, proceedings, journals*, etc. of societies are not considered periodicals under the cataloguing rules. *See also* SERIAL. At the General Conference of Unesco, held at Paris on 19th November 1964, it was agreed that a publication is a periodical 'if it constitutes one issue in a continuous series under the same title, published at regular or irregular intervals, over an indefinite period, individual issues in the series being numbered consecutively or each issue being dated'.

PERIODICAL BIBLIOGRAPHY. One which is published in parts and revised or extended by the cumulative method. *See also* CLOSED BIBLIOGRAPHY, CURRENT BIBLIOGRAPHY.

PERIODICAL CASE. *Synonymous with* MAGAZINE CASE (*q.v.*).

PERIODICAL INDEX. 1. An index to one or more volumes of a periodical. 2. A subject index to a group of periodicals; usually issued at short intervals and cumulated.

PERIODICAL RACK. A fitting for accommodating current and possibly a few recent issues of periodicals, either horizontally or perpendicularly without displaying the covers. Each compartment has a label bearing the title of the periodical. Sometimes illogically called a 'Periodical stack'. *See also* PERIODICAL STAND.

PERIODICAL STAND. A piece of furniture for displaying periodicals so that much of the cover is visible. Sometimes the display fitting on which current issues are placed is constructed at an angle of 15 to 30° and is hinged to accommodate back numbers on a shelf immediately behind the slope. If merely hinged, this is inconvenient to use, even if a supporting stay is provided; a design which permits the slope to be slid back horizontally immediately below the shelf above is much more satisfactory. Slopes on which the periodicals rest should be between 15 and 25° to the perpendicular to prevent their falling forwards when not in periodical cases. Periodical racks accommodate current issues (and sometimes one or two of the most recent issues) horizontally without displaying their covers.

PERIODICALS COLLECTION. A library collection of periodicals, newspapers, and other serials whether bound, unbound, or in microform, treated like periodicals; usually kept as a collection and separate from other library materials.

PERMANENT RECORD FILM. Photographic material made and treated in such a way that both the image and the base will have the maximum archival quality when stored in ordinary room conditions.

PERMISSION. Authority from the owner of copyright to quote passages or reproduce illustrations from a work.

PERMISSIVE COMMITTEES. Committees which a local authority may appoint 'for any such general or special purpose as in the opinion of the local authority would be better managed by means of a committee', to quote the Local Government Act, 1933. *See also* STATUTORY COMMITTEES.

PERMUTATION INDEX. *Synonymous with* KWIC index. *See* KWIC.

PERMUTATION INDEXING. Indexing by selecting as entry headings words, phrases or sentences which the author has emphasized as important by using them in the title, introduction, section headings, conclusion, summary, etc. This method has been developed to become a technique of machine indexing; each entry in the index being a cyclic permutation of all the words in the original titles, each term being brought to a predetermined position for alphabetizing. So far this method has been used only for indexing by machine titles of technical documents. *See also* KWIC.

PERMUTED TITLE INDEX. The result of a method of indexing, which can be carried out by a machine, whereby entries are made for every important word in a title. The alphabetizing position of each entry is just to the right of the page centre and an unprinted area of one or two ems (*see* EM) appears immediately before the alphabeting word to make this obvious. When the right-hand limit of the title printing area is reached, the title is continued at the beginning of the MEASURE (*q.v.*) on the same line. The document identification code follows each entry.

PERMUTED TITLE WORD INDEXING. Also called 'Keyword-in-Context (KWIC) Indexing', 'Permutation Indexing'. *See also* KWIC.

PERPETUA. Eric Gill's most popular roman typeface, named after St. Perpetua, a female saint who was martyred at Carthage in A.D. 203 with a companion named Felicity. Cut in 1929, it is one of the most distinguished types, being not only used effectively for books, where dignity, repose and stateliness are required, but also for book jackets where the related Bold, and Bold Titling, are specially useful. The serifs are small, firmly pointed, sharply cut and horizontal. For a specimen alphabet, *see* TYPE FACE.

PERSIAN MOROCCO. A badly-tanned leather derived from Indian goat and sheep. It is an inferior leather unsuitable for binding books, being fairly strong but not durable.

PERSONAL AUTHORSHIP. Authorship of a work in which its conception and execution is entirely the responsibility of an individual and carried out in his personal capacity, not by virtue of any paid or voluntary office held by him within a corporate body.

PERSONAL CATALOGUE. A catalogue in which entries are made under an individual's name for books both by him and about him. *See also* NAME CATALOGUE.

PERSONAL NAME. *Synonymous with* FORENAME (*q.v.*).

PERSONAL NAME ENTRY. An entry in a catalogue under the name of an individual.

PERSONAL SUBJECT. The name of an author who is well known in connexion with one particular branch of knowledge, and which is used as a subject heading in selective cataloguing.

pf. Abbreviation for portfolio.

pH VALUE.   Measurement of the acid and alkaline content of paper, as recorded on a scale. pH7 is neutral; a figure lower than 7 indicates acid quality, higher than 7 indicates alkaline quality, the strengths being indicated by the respective distances from 7 and extending from 1 to 14. The measurement is determined by an electrical apparatus called an Ionometer. pH is an abbreviation for 'hydrogen-ions concentration'.

PHASE.   In classification, that part of a complex subject (i.e. a sub-class representing the interaction of an original subject on another separate subject, e.g. the influence of the Bible on English literature) derived from any one main class of knowledge: that part of a complex subject derived from one distinct field of knowledge: any one of two or more classes brought into relation to one another in a document. The interaction of two normally distinct subjects is called a Phase Relation. So far five kinds of phase-relation have been isolated. (1) Form phase (the method of presentation); (2) Bias phase (one subject presented for the requirements of another): (3) Influencing phase (one subject influenced by another); (4) Comparison phase (one subject compared with another); (5) Tool phase (one subject used as a method of expounding another). Ranganathan suggests that Form is not a phase relation, that it is more closely allied to the individual book than to the subject, and that it should accordingly be shown as part of the book number, not the class number. *See also* CLASSIFYING, FACET, FOCUS. Where relations occur between foci in the same facet, these are called 'Intrafacet relations'.

PHASE RELATION.   *See* PHASE.

PHILOSOPHICAL CLASSIFICATION.   *See* KNOWLEDGE CLASSIFICATION.

PHLOROGLUCIN.   A chemical which is used in conjunction with hydrochloric acid and alcohol as a test solution to detect mechanical wood in paper, which it turns red.

PHONETIC WRITING.   A form of writing in which the signs or symbols represent sounds or groups of sounds, rather than objects or ideas as they did in earlier forms of writing such as ideography or pictography. Each element corresponds to a specific sound in the language represented. Phonetic writing may be syllabic or alphabetic, the latter being the more advanced of the two.

PHONIC LENGTH.   A characteristic of the length of a sequence of notation symbols in a scheme of classification, whereby there is ability to remember them easily by reason of their pronounceability. *See also* GRAPHIC LENGTH.

PHONOGRAM. 1. A symbol used to express a sound or idea; it can represent a complete word, a syllable, or the sound which a syllable represents. 2. A speech record made by a phonograph, i.e. a gramophone.

PHONOGRAPH. An obsolete instrument for recording sounds on cylindrical wax records and reproducing them.

PHONOGRAPH RECORD. *Synonymous with* GRAMOPHONE RECORD (*q.v.*).

PHONORECORD. Any object on which sound has been recorded.

PHONOROLL. A perforated roll, usually of paper, which is used to activate a player-piano, or player-organ.

PHOTOCHARGER. An electrical machine for recording the loan of books on microfilm.

PHOTOCHARGING. The recording of the loan of books by photographing on 35 mm film details of the book borrowed, the reader's identification card and a transaction card which is then placed in the book and taken by the reader.

PHOTOCHROMIC MICRO-IMAGE. *See* PCMI SYSTEM.

PHOTOCHROMIC SUBSTANCE. One which changes its colour when subjected to radiation from different light sources. Such substances are used in the PCMI SYSTEM (*q.v.*) of reprography.

PHOTOCLERK. The trade name for a well-known method of copying documents by a direct photocopying method; it employs an optical system for copying the original directly on to sensitized paper. On exposure, the camera lens with a mirror causes an image to be placed in readable form on the face of the sensitized paper. Chemical development, and drying, of the sensitized paper give a direct, negative copy of the original.

PHOTO-COMPOSING MACHINE. (*Printing*) A machine for setting solid text by photographic means, as distinct from metal-type composition. The following are makes of such machines: Fotosetter, Hadego, Highton, Huebner, Linofilm, Monophoto, Orotype, Photon, Rotofoto and Uhertype.

PHOTOCOMPOSITION. Setting type by means of a photo-composing machine, i.e. placing type images on photographic film or paper.

PHOTOCOPY. Strictly, a photographic copy made by a process which uses coatings of light-sensitive salts on the base material, but generally used to indicate any process, whether using light or other means of radiation, and with the aid of a camera or not. Dry-copying and all direct office copying methods are included. *See also* PHOTOSTAT, REFLEX COPYING.

PHOTO-ELECTROSTATIC REPRODUCTION. *Synonymous with* XEROGRAPHY (*q.v.*).

PHOTO-ENGRAVING. Any photo-mechanical process for reproducing pictures or the like in which the printing surface is in relief, as distinguished from photo-lithography and photo-gravure. It includes the half-tone process, zinc etching and other processes for making line cuts, the swelled-gelatine process, etc. *See also* ELECTRONIC PHOTO-ENGRAVING MACHINES.

PHOTO-GELATINE PROCESS. Any of the gelatine processes of photo-mechanical printing, as Collotype, Lichtdruck, Phototype, Albertype, Artotype, Heliotype, etc.

PHOTOGRAPHIC PAPERS. These are graded in thickness as follows:

Ultra thin (also called 'Extra lightweight')	between	0·0023	and	0·0031	inches inclusive
Extra thin	„	0·0032	„	0·0037	„	„
Thin	„	0·0038	„	0·0043	„	„
Lightweight	„	0·0044	„	0·0059	„	„
Single weight	„	0·0060	„	0·0083	„	„
Medium „	„	0·0084	„	0·0111	„	„
Double „	„	0·0112	„	0·0190	„	„

PHOTOGRAPHIC PHOTOCOPYING. A documentary reproduction process using a base material on which light-sensitive silver salts have been coated. A copy so produced is called a 'Photographic photocopy'. *See also* PHOTOCOPY.

PHOTOGRAPHY. 1. A basic printing process in which the normal principles of photography are used at some stage, e.g. photo-engraving, photo-offset, photo-lithography. 2. In REPROGRAPHY (*q.v.*), all the processes which use light-radiation and base materials with coatings of light-sensitive silver salts. *See also* ELECTROPHOTOGRAPHY.

PHOTOGRAVURE. 1. Any of the various processes for producing prints from a plate prepared by photographic methods. Also called 'Heliogravure'. 2. A print so produced. *See also* ROTOGRAVURE.

PHOTO-LITHOGRAPHY. The process of reproducing a picture or design photographically on to metal for lithographic printing.

PHOTO-LITHO-OFFSET. *Synonymous with* PHOTO-OFFSET (*q.v.*).

PHOTOMACROGRAPH. 1. A photograph of an object which is the same size as the original, or slightly magnified (the upper limit being about ten diameters). A macrograph made by photography. 2. A photomicrograph of very low magnification.

PHOTO-MECHANICAL PROCESS. *See* PROCESS ENGRAVING.

PHOTOMICROGRAPH. A photograph of a minute object, taken by means of a microscope in conjunction with a camera, i.e. by photomicrography which is not to be confused with microphotography – making minute photographs of large objects.

PHOTOMICROGRAPHY. Taking pictures by means of a microscope and a camera. The resulting photograph shows the original in greatly enlarged form. The opposite of MICROPHOTOGRAPHY (*q.v.*). *See also* PHOTOMACROGRAPH.

PHOTO-MONTAGE. A picture made by the combination of several photographs or portions of photographs with a related interest into one large composite photograph, or parts of photographs cut out and pasted together to achieve a particular effect. Other methods are to make a number of exposures on the same negative, or to project a number of negatives to make a composite print.

PHOTON. A photo-typesetting machine made in the U.S.A. by Photon Inc. and used since 1954. It consists of three major components, a standard Underwood electric typewriter, a telephone relay system, and a photographing unit. The operator using the keyboard selects the type style and type measure required to do a specific job and the machine automatically spaces and justifies the line. The mixing of styles and sizes is possible in the same line, thus allowing the operator greater flxibility. Photographic negatives or positives are produced and these may be used for lithography, gravure or to make letterpress blocks.

PHOTO-OFFSET. Offset printing in which the image is reproduced on a metal plate by photography. Also called 'Photo-litho-offset', and 'Offset-photo-lithography'.

PHOTOSETTING. (*Printing*) The setting of type by a photographic means. FOTOSETTER, LINOFILM, MONOPHOTO and PHOTON (*qq.v.*) are trade names of such methods and apparatus. *See also* FILMSETTING.

PHOTOSTAT. 1. A trade name of a machine for reproducing photographically pages of printed, drawn or written matter, either the same size, or larger or smaller than the original, on sensitized paper without films or plates. 2. A copy made by such a machine. *See also* CAMERA-GRAPH.

PHOTOTYPE. A form of collotype, being a plate with a printing surface usually in relief, obtained from a photograph.

PHOTO-TYPOGRAPHY. Any photo-mechanical process in which the printing surface is produced in relief so that it can be used with type.

PHOTO-ZINCOGRAPHY. A method of reproducing pictures, drawings, etc., by using a zinc plate on which the design has been produced by photographic means.

PHRASE PSEUDONYM. A pseudonym consisting of a phrase, as 'A Gentleman with a Duster'.

PHYLACTERY. A narrow band or scroll on which a name or a speech was inscribed. Sometimes seen in block books, illuminated manuscripts or incunabula where they are drawn as if issuing from the mouths of characters, or held in the hand. They also appear in contemporary comics and comic strips as 'balloons' coming from the mouths of characters.

pi. (*Bibliography*) The Greek letter π used to denote an unsigned gathering or leaf which precedes signed gatherings, and in respect of which no signature can be inferred. *See also* CHI. (*Printing*) (*Verb*) To mix up type. (*Noun*) Type which has been mixed up. (American.) *See also* PIE.

PIANO-CONDUCTOR SCORE. *See* SCORE.

PIANO REDUCTION. An arrangement for piano of the voice parts of a work for unaccompanied voices for use as an accompaniment during rehearsal, such accompaniment not being intended by the composer for performance. Such music may be indicated by some such designation at the head of the score as 'Piano, for rehearsal only'.

PIANO SCORE. *See* SCORE.

PIANO-VOCAL SCORE. *Synonymous with* VOCAL SCORE. *See* SCORE.

PICA. 1. A standard of measurement, approximately $\frac{1}{6}$ inch; in the Point System ·166 inch, equal to 12 point. *See also* EM. 2. Pica type, the largest size ordinarily used for books; 12 point, six lines to an inch, as this.

PICK UP. Type which has been kept standing since first used, ready to be 'picked up' for further use when required.

PICTOGRAM. *See* PICTOGRAPHY.

PICTOGRAPH. A pictorial sign or simple illustration which tells a story instantaneously by representing an object or an idea. A primitive form of writing consisting of pictographs.

PICTOGRAPHY. The most primitive stage of true writing, in which a picture or sketch represents a thing, or a sequence of pictures drawings or symbols (each of which is termed a 'pictogram') tells a narrative. Pictography is a semantic representation, not a phonetic one. *See also* ALPHABETIC WRITING.

PICTORIAL MAP. A map which contains pictures indicating the distribution of physical and biological features, and social and economic characteristics, etc.

PICTURE BOOK. A children's book consisting wholly or mostly of pictures.

PICTURE COLLECTION. A collection of pictures, or of reproductions of pictures. *See also* ILLUSTRATIONS COLLECTION, PICTURE FILE.

PICTURE FILE. A collection of illustrations, prints, reproductions of pictures, and possibly cuttings; small enough to be filed rather than needing to be displayed. They may be arranged by subject, artist, etc. This is American usage. *See also* ILLUSTRATIONS COLLECTION, PICTURE COLLECTION.

PICTURE-WRITING. *Synonymous with* PICTOGRAPHY (*q.v.*).

PIE. 1. A table, or collection, of ecclesiastical rules used before the Reformation in England to determine (from each of the 35 possible variations in the date of Easter) the proper service or office for the day. Also called 'Pye'. 2. An alphabetical index or catalogue, to count rolls and records (obsolete); usually called a 'pye book'.

PIE. (*Printing*) Type matter that has been mixed accidentally.

PIERCED. *See* MORTICE.

PIERCY AWARD, ESTHER J. Established by the Resources and Technical Services Division of the American Library Association to honour the late editor of *Library Resources & Technical Services*. The Award is given annually 'to recognize the contribution to librarianship in the field of technical services by younger members of the profession', and consequently it is restricted to those with not more than ten years of professional experience. First awarded to Richard M. Dougherty in 1969.

PIERPOINT MORGAN LIBRARY. Assembled by John Pierpoint Morgan (1837–1913), inherited by his son J. P. Morgan, Jr. (1867–1943), who expanded it and in February 1924 conveyed it to six trustees to administer as a public reference library for the use of scholars. Subsequently the State of New York incorporated the collection and dedicated it to 'the advancement of knowledge and for the use of learned men of all countries.' The collection comprises about 55,000 books and manuscripts, and in addition, cuneiform tablets, drawings, prints, Italian medals, and Greek and Roman coins. The collection of mediaeval illuminated manuscripts is unique for its geographical and linguistic coverage.

PIGEONHOLE CLASSIFICATION. *Synonymous with* RIGID CLASSIFICATION (*q.v.*).

PIGSKIN. A strong leather made from the skin of a pig; it has good lasting qualities and is used for covering large books..

PIN HOLES. 1. Minute and almost imperceptible pits in the surface of art papers, due to frothy coating material. 2. Minute holes in paper, caused by fine particles of sand, alum, etc., being crushed out during the calendering process, leaving a hole. 3. Tiny transparent dots which appear in a litho plate after development and which, unless covered with an opaque medium, will appear in resulting prints.

PIN-MARK. A small depression on one side of the body of a piece of movable type. It is made by the pin which ejects the types from the moulds of certain casting machines and sometimes bears the number of a body-size of the fount.

PIN SEAL. A binding leather from the skin of a very young, or baby, seal, having much finer grain and a more lustrous finish than ordinary SEALSKIN (q.v.). Used for expensive bindings.

PINEAPPLE. (*Binding*) An ornament bearing some likeness to a conventional pineapple, and used in the same position as a FLEURON (q.v.). *See also* TWISTED PINEAPPLES.

PIPE ROLL. A parchment roll upon which a record of the audit at the exchequer was kept.

PIRA. Abbreviation for Printing Industry Research Association. *See* PRINTING, PACKAGING AND ALLIED TRADES RESEARCH ASSOCIATION.

PIRACY. The publication in a foreign country of a literary work without the permission of, or payment to, the author.

PIRATED EDITION. *See* UNAUTHORIZED EDITION.

PIVOTED BOOKCASE. *Synonymous with* SWINGING BOOKCASE (q.v.).

PIVOTED SHELVING. *See* SWINGING BOOKCASE.

pl. (*Pl.* pls.). Abbreviation for PLATE (q.v.) (illustration), also place.

PLACARD. A large, single, sheet of paper, usually printed, but sometimes written, on one side with an announcement or advertisement, for display on a wall or notice board. Also called a 'Poster'.

PLACARD CATALOGUE. A list of books displayed on a large sheet, or sheets, and hung up for consultation.

PLACE OF PRINTING. A bibliographer's or cataloguer's term for the name of the town in which a book is printed.

PLACE OF PUBLICATION. A bibliographer's or cataloguer's term for the name of the town in which the office of a publisher who issues a book is situated.

PLAGIARISM. To copy the writings of another person and publish the same as original work.

PLAIN TEXT. An edition of a classic without notes, or possibly even an introduction, and intended for study in a class or with a tutor.

PLAN. The representation of anything drawn on a plane, as a map or chart; the representation of a building or other structure, landscape design, arrangement of streets or buildings, or arrangement of furniture in a room or building, in horizontal plane.

PLAN CABINET. A piece of furniture designed to accommodate plans, architectural drawings, or reproductions, either suspended or resting in a pocket vertically, or flat in shallow drawers. Also called 'Plan file'.

PLAN FILE. A container for filing plans and maps either vertically or horizontally. Also called 'Plan cabinet'.

PLAN PAPER. A thin, tough, paper which is made specially for printing maps, plans, etc. It is subject to much wear by constant handling and folding. Also called 'Map paper'. *See also* CHART PAPER.

PLANES. (*Classification*) In the Colon Classification these are three in number: Idea, Notation (or Notational) and Words (or Verbal); within which the designing or application of a scheme has to be done.

PLANETARY CAMERA. A camera used for photocopying in which the original being copied and the film are stationary during exposure. After each exposure the original is changed manually and the film is moved on one frame automatically. Also called a 'Flat-bed camera' or 'Stepwise operated camera'.

PLANOGRAPH. *Synonymous with* OFFSET PRINTING (*q.v.*).

PLANOGRAPHIC PRINTING. *See* PLANOGRAPHIC PROCESS.

PLANOGRAPHIC PROCESS. 1. A generic term for all printing which depends on chemical action, and in which the printing surface is a plane, merely transferring its image, as in lithography, collotype and offset. 2. The method of printing from flat surfaces, the parts to be printed accepting ink from the rollers while the non-printing areas reject it. The printing, or image, areas are greasy, the rest moist. Printing is by even pressure of a hand-roller or cylinder over the flat plate, or by offsetting the image from a curved plate on to a rubber roller and so to the paper. It is one of the six basic principles of printing, the others being relief, intaglio, stencil, photography and xerography. Also called 'Surface printing'.

PLANOGRAPHY. Printing processes which are dependent on the antipathy of oily ink and water, using methods of printing from flat surfaces other than stone. The term replaces 'zincography' and 'aluminography'. *See also* PLANOGRAPHIC PROCESS.

PLANTIN. A type face designed by Christopher Plantin (1514–89) one of the world's most distinguished printer-publishers, whose house and printing equipment now form the Plantin – Moretus Museum at Antwerp. This OLD FACE (*q.v.*) is characterized by the thickness, and consequent black appearance, of all the strokes. For a specimen alphabet, *see* TYPE FACE.

PLASTER OF PARIS MOULD. One made by placing a thin film of plaster of Paris mixed with water to a fluid consistency on a sheet of paper which is then transferred face downwards to the forme and subjected to moderate pressure after several sheets of an absorbent type of paper are placed on the paper-backed plaster of Paris. It is used for reproducing illustrations by half-tone and three- and four-colour half-tone processes.

PLASTIC BINDING. A type of binding used for pamphlets, commercial catalogues, etc. which are printed on unfolded leaves. These leaves and the separate front and back covers are kept together by means of a piece of curved synthetic plastic which has prongs, or combs, which pass through slots punched near the binding edge of the leaves and curled within the cylinder thus formed by the plastic. See also SPIRAL BINDING.

PLASTICISING. Putting a plastic cover or sleeve on to a book or BOOK JACKET (q.v.), either by securing a loose cover or by laminating the plastic by means of heat.

PLASTOCOWELL. A lithographic process introduced by W. S. Cowell, Ltd., of Ipswich, in which a plastic sheet is used as a substitute for stone or metal, and is easier and more convenient for the artist to work than the ordinary forms of auto-lithography.

PLAT. A map or chart, such as a precise and detailed plan, showing the actual or proposed divisions, special features, or uses of a piece of land, e.g. a town or town site (American).

PLATE. 1. An illustration, often an engraving taken from a metal plate, printed separately from the text of the book with one side of the leaf blank, and often on different paper. Plates may be bound into a book or they may be loose in a portfolio. They are not generally included in the pagination. See also FIGURE. 2. A flat block of wood or metal, usually of copper, nickel or zinc, on the surface of which there is a design or reproduction of a type forme, to be used for printing, engraving, embossing, etc. The method of printing may be relief, intaglio, or planographic. 3. To make an electrotype or stereotype from printed matter. 4. The Anglo-American cataloguing rules: British text considers a plate to be a page containing illustrative matter and that it may also contain some text; it does not form part of the sequence of pages either physically or in enumeration. Plates may be distributed throughout the publication or gathered together; they may, or may not, be numbered.

PLATE CYLINDER. The roller of an offset printing machine which bears the printing plate. See also OFFSET PRINTING PRESS.

PLATE GUARDED AND HOOKED. An illustration printed on a separate piece of paper and stuck to a narrow strip of paper or linen to form a guard which is then placed around, or hooked-in, a section before sewing. *See also* HOOKED ON OWN GUARD.

PLATE LINE. *Synonymous with* PLATE MARK (*q.v.*).

PLATE MARK. A line marking the boundary edge of a plate used in making an engraving; it is caused by the pressure used to make the impression on the sheet of paper. The part of the paper on which the plate rested is depressed and more smooth than the surrounding portion.

PLATE NUMBER. One or more figures, or a combination of letters and figures, assigned serially to each musical composition on preparation for printing, being copied by the engraver at the bottom of each page and sometimes on the title-page also. If on the title-page only, it is better designated as 'Publisher's number'.

PLATE PAPER. A superfine soft rag paper of good substance, made for steel-plate or photogravure printing. Of recent years cheaper esparto qualities have been introduced.

PLATEN. The flat part of a printing press which presses the paper on to the forme. *See also* PLATEN PRESS. (*Reprography*) A mechanical device which holds the film in position in a camera, or copying apparatus, in the focal plane during exposure.

PLATEN PRESS. A printing press which has a flat impression, not a cylindrical one. The type is normally fixed on the bed in a vertical or almost vertical position, and the platen bearing the paper is swung up and pressed against the type. Such machines are usually used for jobbing work. *See also* CYLINDER PRESS.

PLATES VOLUME. In a work of several volumes, the one which consists of illustrations to the text, and has no printed matter other than that relating specifically to the illustrations.

PLATING. The process of pasting book plates and other labels in library books.

PLAQUETTE. A small metal relief, like a classical cameo, which is inlaid into Italian book bindings of the sixteenth century.

PLAYERTYPE. The REFLEX COPYING (*q.v.*) method used by J. Hart Player in 1896.

PLEA ROLL. A parchment roll on which a record of cases heard in the King's Courts was entered.

PLOUGH. The tool used for cutting the edges of a book, the book being secured in the lying press.

PLOWDEN REPORT. The Central Advisory Council for Education

(England) was reconstituted in August 1963, under the chairman-ship of Lady Plowden 'to consider primary education in all its aspects and the transition to secondary education'. The Council's Report was published in two volumes in January 1967 under the title *Children and their primary schools* (H.M.S.O.). The principal recommendation was for special assistance for schools in slum areas – designated 'education priority' areas – in the form of more teachers, additional finance for school-building, and more generous supplies of equipment.

POCHOIR. French for 'stencil'. A hand-coloured illustration process which, although dating from the eighteenth century, is still used in France, and is similar to SILK SCREEN (*q.v.*) except that paper, cellu-loid or metal stencils are used and the colour is dabbed through, rather than drawn across, the stencil. It is an expensive method, and is used for editions de luxe. 2. A method of reproducing gauche paintings. The design, necessarily simplified is preprinted by collotype and the ink applied with stencil and brush.

POCKET. A wallet-like receptacle made from linen or stiff paper inside a cover of a book (usually the back cover) to hold loose music parts, diagrams, or maps. Also called 'Cover pocket'. *See also* BOOK POCKET.

POCKET CARD CHARGING. The recording of loans of books by using a card kept in a corner pocket stuck to the inside of the cover of a book. The best-known method is the BROWNE BOOK CHARGING SYSTEM (*q.v.*).

POCKET EDITION. A small edition of a book, already printed in an octavo edition, of $6\frac{3}{4} \times 4\frac{1}{4}$ inches or less. Sometimes these are paper-bound but they are then usually called 'paperbacks'.

POCKET PART. A separate publication which is issued to bring a book up-to-date, and is usually kept in a pocket on the inside of the back cover.

POINT. 1. The unit of measure for printer's type: approximately 1/72 (0·013837) of an inch. Thus 12 point type is 12/72 or 1/6 of an inch in the body. One inch equals 72·25433 points and 72 points equal 0·9962 of an inch. Each body size is an exact multiplication of the point size. Type bodies are measured in points. The width of a line of type (or ('measure') is determined in pica (12-pt.) ems – called 'picas' in America. The depth of a page of type is similarly measured in ems or picas. After a fire at the typefoundry of Marder, Luse & Co. in Chicago in 1872, this firm began to supply type the bodies of which were multiples of 1/12 part of a typical Pica measuring 0·166 inch. The United States Type Founders' Association recommended this system to its members in 1886, and British typefounders conformed to the American point-system in 1898. The standard measurements according to the British-American Point System are:

5-point	0·0692 in.	14-point	0·1937 in.
6-point	0·0830 in.	16-point	0·2213 in.
7-point	0·0968 in.	18-point	0·2490 in.
8-point	0·1107 in.	24-point	0·3320 in.
9-point	0·1245 in.	30-point	0·4150 in.
10-point	0·1383 in.	36-point	0·4980 in.
11-point	0·1522 in.	48-point	0·6640 in.
12-point	0·1660 in.		

2. Any mark of punctuation. A full point (full stop). *See also* DIDOT SYSTEM.

POINT SYSTEM. *See* POINT.

POINTILLÉ. A binding decoration in gold done with tools with a dotted surface.

POINTS. 1. Small holes made in the sheets during the printing process which serve as guides in registering when the sheets are folded by machinery. 2. The bibliographical peculiarities of a printed book, the absence or presence of which determine whether the book is a first or other edition, or a particular issue of an edition, or a variant, etc.

POLAIRE. The leather case or satchel in which the ancient monks placed their books. Polaires were usually made without decoration unless for a wealthy man in which case they bore a design stamped in relief.

POLISH LIBRARY ASSOCIATION. Founded in 1917 as the Alliance of Polish Librarians – 'and Archivists' being added after the end of the Second World War until the archivists formed a separate organization in 1953, when the present name was adopted.

POLONYM. A work by several authors.

POLYGLOT. A book giving versions of the same text in several languages, generally arranged in parallel columns. The first of the great Polyglot Bibles was the so-called COMPLUTENSIAN POLYGLOT (*q.v.*). The second of the famous polyglot Bibles was printed between 1569 and 1573 by Christopher Plantin, with the patronage of Philip II of Spain. It was in eight folio volumes, the text being in Hebrew, Greek, Latin, Chaldaic, and Syriac. The Paris polyglot Bible, 1654, in nine volumes edited by G. Michel Le Jay and others added Arabic, Syriac and Samaritan to Plantin's text. The *Biblia sacra polyglotta* published in six volumes in London between 1655–7 was in nine languages.

POLYGRAPHIC.   Written by several authors.

POLYGRAPHY.   Books consisting of several works or extracts from works by one or a number of authors.

POLYNOMIAL.   A work by several authors.

POLYONYMAL.   Having several, or different, names.

POLYONYMOUS.   Possessing many names.

POLYSEMIA.   The provision of instructions to an indexing machine as to how a significant word in a document is used in that document. Also called 'Multiple meaning'.

POLYTERMS.   An extension of UNITERM CO-ORDINATE INDEXING (*q.v.*) whereby a group heading, instead of one simple basic idea, is used on each uniterm card. Also called 'Unit concepts'.

POLYTOPICAL.   Treating of several subjects.

POLYTYCH.   *See* CODEX.

POMI.   A technique, developed by the National Cash Register Company's Electronic Division in California, U.S.A., for recording the contents of a 300-page book within one square-inch of film. The method is known as 'photochromic micro-images' and reduces printed material to microscopic size in a form that can be reproduced easily and inexpensively. It is not intended to replace conventional microfilm techniques; in fact the process consists of microfilming microfilm.

POPULAR COPYRIGHTS.   Used at the beginning of this century to denote books published by firms specializing in low-priced editions, who used, with the permission of the copyright owners, the plates made for the original editions.

POPULAR EDITION.   An edition of a book published on poorer paper, possibly without illustrations, and in a paper cover or a less substantial cloth binding than the normal edition, and sold at a cheaper price.

POPULAR LIBRARY.   In America, a department containing books of general interest for home-reading, those of special interest, or of an advanced character being placed in SUBJECT DEPARTMENTS (*q.v.*). *See also* BROWSING ROOM.

POPULAR NAME.   An abbreviated, shortened, or simplified form of the name of a government department, society or other corporate body, by which it is usually known, e.g. Stationery Office; British Association.

PORCELAIN.   A sheet of paper consisting of a sheet of blotting-paper pasted to one of coated stock. (American).

PORNOGRAPHY.   Writings of an obscene or licentious character:

originally applied only to treatises on prostitutes and prostitution. It comes from the Greek words meaning 'writing about harlots'. Many catalogues of old and rare books include such items under the term *Erotica*.

PORPHYRY, TREE OF. A device associated with the name of Porphyry, for abstracting the qualities of terms. It is, in a rough sense, a sub-dividing of the term Substance, by adding differences at different steps; thus Substance, by the addition of the difference Corporeality, divides into Corporeal and Incorporeal Substance; then (neglecting the Incorporeal), to corporeal is added the difference Body which results in Animate and Inanimate. This process is continued as the following Tree shows, until division reaches finality and a specific term (Plato) is reached.

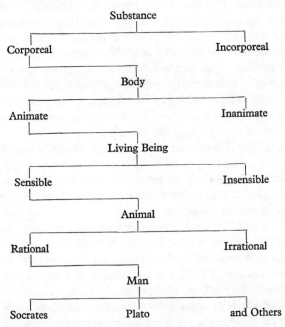

This method of division is known as bifurcate (or division in pairs, positive and negative). The Tree is used to illustrate the FIVE PREDICABLES.

port. (*Pl.* ports.). Abbreviation for PORTRAIT (*q.v.*).

PORTFOLIO. A case for holding loose paintings, drawings, illustrations, diagrams, papers or similar material. Usually made of two sheets of strawboard, covered with paper or cloth with a wide cloth joint to form the 'spine', often with cloth flaps attached at the edges of one board to turn in and so protect the papers, and with tapes at fore-edges to secure the contents. Abbreviated pf.

PORTOLAN. *Synonymous with* PORTOLAN CHART (*q.v.*).

PORTOLAN CHART. An early type of chart produced, often in MS., between the thirteenth and seventeenth centuries to guide mariners in coastwise sailing. Such charts were based on estimated bearings and distances between the principal ports or capes. They are believed to have been first produced by the admirals and captains of the Genoese fleet during the second half of the thirteenth century, and are some-times called 'Compass maps' or 'Loxo-dromes', but wrongly so, as they were used before compasses. Originally a harbour book or written sailing instructions, but the name has come to be used for a sea chart. In England a portolan became known as a 'ruttier' or 'rutter of the sea' (from 'route'). The portolan is much older than the sea-chart, and is known to have been made as early as the tenth and eleventh centuries. Also called 'Portolan', 'Portulan', 'Portolano'.

PORTOLANO. *Synonymous with* PORTOLAN CHART (*q.v.*).

PORTRAIT. 1. A representation of a person, made from life, especially a picture or representation of the face. 2. When portraits are a feature of a work they are indicated in the collation part of a catalogue entry as *ports*. Otherwise they are subsumed.

PORTULAN. *Synonymous with* PORTOLAN CHART (*q.v.*).

POSITIVE. In photography and documentary reproduction, the film or print which has the same tones as the original. It is sometimes made from a NEGATIVE (*q.v.*) in which the image and the tones are in reverse compared with the original.

POSITIVE COPY. In documentary reproduction, a copy prepared by a POSITIVE PROCESS (*q.v.*) and having the same tones and image as in the original. Also called 'Positive print'. *See also* NEGATIVE PROCESS.

POSITIVE MICROFILM. A film bearing microcopies with tone values corresponding to those of the originals (*Concepts . . .*).

POSITIVE PRINT. *Synonymous with* POSITIVE COPY (*q.v.*).

POSITIVE PROCESS. A documentary reproduction, or copying, pro-cess, in which the tones and the image are the same as in the original. *See also* POSITIVE. The opposite of NEGATIVE PROCESS. *See also* NEGATIVE.

POST. (*Information retrieval*) 1. To transfer an indicial notation from a parent or main entry to individual analytic entries – for example, to type the proper catalogue entry and number at the top of a group of catalogue cards. 2. In co-ordinate indexing, to put the accession number of a document under each entry representing a co-ordination term (*IBM*).

POST-DATED. A book which bears a date of publication which is later than the actual date. The opposite of 'Ante-dated'.

POST OCTAVO. A book size, 8 × 5 inches. *See also* BOOK SIZES.

POSTER. *Synonymous with* PLACARD (*q.v.*).

POSTHUMOUS WORK. One which is first published after the death of the author.

POT CASSÉ DEVICE. A device consisting of a broken jar, or urn, pierced by a wimble (Fr. *toret*) and usually accompanied by the motto 'non plus'. It was used by Geoffroy Tory the French printer on his title-pages. It was also used as part of the design for decorating book covers.

POTT. An obsolete name of a size of paper varying from 15 × 12½ inches to 17¼ × 14¼ inches, and being the smallest of the original (uncut) hand-made papers; the name is probably derived from a water-mark design of a pot. *See also* PAPER SIZES.

POUNCE. (*Binding*) An adhesive used under gold or colours.

POWDER or SEMÉ (SEMÉE, SEMIS). (*Binding*) An heraldic term signifying a diaper design of small figures (sprays, flowers, leaves, etc.) frequently repeated by the use of one to three small tools at regular intervals over the greater part of a binding, producing a powdered effect. Sometimes there is a coat of arms, or some other vignette, in the centre, or even at each corner; there may be a lightly tooled fillet around the side of the cover.

POWER PRESS. A printing press in which the operation of the machine was done by some form of power other than the human being. It was introduced in the nineteenth century and superseded the HAND PRESS (*q.v.*) for rapid operation.

PRACTICAL BIBLIOGRAPHY. *See* BIBLIOGRAPHY 2.

PRAESES. The person or persons who open an academical disputation by propounding objections to some tenet or proposition, usually moral or philosophical, as distinguished from the RESPONDENT (*q.v.*) who defends it.

PREBOUND. *Synonymous with* PRE-LIBRARY BOUND (*q.v.*).

PRECATALOGUED BOOK. One which is accompanied by catalogue cards when supplied, the cards being obtained by purchase, contract, or agreement from a commercial supplier.

PRE-CATALOGUING. The bibliographic searching, usually done before ordering a book, to establish the correct entry and Library of Congress card order information. (American.)

PRECEPT. A demand on a RATING AUTHORITY (*q.v.*) specifying the amount required in the £ of rateable value, made by a PRECEPTING AUTHORITY (*q.v.*) to meet its financial requirements for providing services such as police, education and libraries in the area of the authority on which the precept is levied.

PRECEPTING AUTHORITY. One which administers local government services on behalf of other authorities but does not itself raise rates. County councils and the Metropolitan Police Force are precepting authorities. The monies required by precepting authorities must be provided by the respective rate-raising authorities.

PREDICABLES, FIVE. A series of logical terms and notions, first explained by Porphyry in his treatise on Aristotle's *Topics*, and forming the basis of the science of classification. They are: 1. GENUS – a main class, or group of things, which may be divided into sub-groups called 2. SPECIES, the groups into which the genus is divided. 3. DIFFERENCE – a characteristic which enables a genus to be divided, e.g. add to the genus 'books' the difference 'method of production' and the species 'MS. books', and 'printed books' result. 4. PROPERTY – some quality of a thing or group of things which, although common, is not exclusive to them, e.g. 'jealousy' is common to 'human beings' and 'animals'. 5. ACCIDENT – a quality which is incidental to a class, which may or may not belong to it, and which has no effect on the other qualities of the class. *See also* PORPHYRY, TREE OF; BIFURCATION.

PREFACE. The author's reasons for writing, and his afterthoughts. It indicates the scope, history, and purpose of the book and the class of readers for whom it is intended, and expresses thanks to helpers. It is usually written by the author, follows the DEDICATION (*q.v.*), and precedes the INTRODUCTION (*q.v.*). It is usual to write a new preface to a new edition, outlining the extent of changes and additions. Sometimes called 'Foreword'.

PREFACE DATE. The date given at the beginning or end of the preface.

PREFERRED ORDER. The order in which the facets in a faceted classification schedule are arranged. Once this preferred order has been decided it is invariable. The purpose of preferred order is to display the relations between the terms to the best advantage.

PRE-LIBRARY BOUND. Books bound in a LIBRARY BINDING (*q.v.*) before being sold. Called 'prebound' for short.

PRELIMINARIES. Those parts of the book which precede the first page of the text. The order should be: half title, frontispiece, title, history of book (date of first publication, dates of subsequent reprints and revised editions) and imprint, dedication, acknowledgements, contents list, list of illustrations, list of abbreviations, foreword or preface, introduction, errata. All except the frontispiece, which faces the title-page, and the history and imprint which are on the verso of the title page, should begin on right-hand pages, but the errata may be placed on the left-hand or be printed on a separate slip and pasted in. They are usually printed last on a separate sheet or sheets, and paged separately, usually in Roman figures. Sometimes abbreviated to 'prelims'. When they are printed on leaves conjugate with leaves bearing part of the text, it is often an indication in very old books of an issue later than the first. Also called 'Front matter' in America, 'Preliminary matter'. *See also* SUBSIDIARIES.

PRELIMINARY CATALOGUING. The making of preliminary catalogue entries by typists utilizing data supplied by clerical officers or junior assistants who search the card catalogue for entries. These entries are examined with the books by the cataloguer, who is thus saved clerical work, being enabled to concentrate on professional work requiring judgment and decision. This system was devised by M. T. Franklin Currier, an American, in the 1920s. *See also* SEARCHING.

PRELIMINARY EDITION. An edition issued in advance of the ordinary edition. This is sometimes done in order to obtain criticisms of the text before the final edition is published. Also called 'Provisional edition'.

PRELIMINARY LEAF. One of the unnumbered leaves, printed on one or both sides, which appear before the numbered leaves at the beginning of a book.

PRELIMINARY PUFF. *See* PUFF.

PRELIMS. Abbreviation for PRELIMINARIES (*q.v.*).

PRE-NATAL CLASSIFICATION. Classifying material before it is published. This is usual in the U.S.A. where classification numbers (usually Dewey) are printed on the back of the title-pages of books.

PRE-PRINT. A portion of a work printed and issued before the publication of the complete work. A paper submitted at a conference which is published prior to the holding of the conference.

PRE-PROCESSED BOOK. One which is delivered by the book supplier with all the necessary processing completed. (American.)

PRE-PUBLICATION CATALOGUING. Cataloguing books at a national library or national bibliographic centre from gathered and folded sections or review copies of books which are submitted for the purpose by the publishers.

PRE-PUBLICATION PRICE. The price at which a book would be sold if ordered prior to a specified date (which is before the publication date) after which the book would cost substantially more.

PRESCRIBED BOOKS. Those which are prescribed for a course of reading.

PRESENTATION COPY. 1. A copy of a book bearing a presentation inscription, usually by the author. 2. A copy of a book presented by the publisher. Only a book that is spontaneously presented properly qualifies for this description; one that is merely autographed at the request of the owner should be called an 'inscribed copy'.

PRESS. 1. A double-sided bookcase of not less than four tiers (i.e. two each side), called in America, a 'Range'. In America a single-sided bookcase with more than two tiers placed end to end; formerly, a 'Bookcase'. *See also* BOOK PRESS, BOOK STACK, BOOKCASE, DOUBLE-FACED SHELF, DOUBLE-SIDED STACK, TIER. 2. The machine, or apparatus, used to press the paper on to the type, plate, engraving or block. In printing there are three methods of imparting this pressure: (a) by the PLATEN PRESS; (b) by the FLAT-BED CYLINDER PRESS; (c) by the ROTARY PRESS (*qq.v.*). *See also* PRINTING PRESS. 3. A simple piece of machinery, possibly a 'screw press', used to keep a book or books in position under pressure to effect adhesion of pasted or glued surfaces, or for some other purpose, during the binding process. 4. A popular name for the trade, and craft, of writing for, and publishing, newspapers and periodicals.

PRESS A UN COUP. A hand printing press on which the operator could lower the platen on to the type in a single movement. It was invented by François Ambroise Didot (1720–1804), the elder son of François Didot (1689–1759).

PRESS AGENT. One who arranges for editorial publicity in the press (*see* PRESS 4) for individuals, institutions, etc.

PRESS BOOK. One issued by a private press.

PRESS COPY. *Synonymous with* REVIEW COPY (*q.v.*).

PRESS CUTTING. A piece cut from a newspaper or periodical. Also called 'Clipping' (American), 'Cutting'.

PRESS ERRORS. Errors made by a compositor when setting type. These are corrected at the printer's cost. Also called 'Printer's errors'.

PRESS MARK. The symbol given to a book to indicate its location. Used in old libraries to indicate the *press* in which the book is shelved, not the book's specific place. This is not so precise as the CALL NUMBER (*q.v.*). Press marks are usually written on the spine of a book (often on a label or tag), on the endpaper, on the front or back of the title-page and against the entry in the catalogue. *See also* CLASS MARK, CLASS NUMBER, FIXED LOCATION.

PRESS NOTICE.   A short statement of specific information in a newspaper – including an 'obituary notice' – announcement of a death, notice of an engagement, birth or marriage, or a reference to, or a review of, a new book, or a criticism or commentary on an artistic performance of music, ballet, etc.

PRESS NUMBER.   A small figure which in books printed between 1680 and 1823 often appears at the foot of a page, sometimes twice in a gathering (once on a page of the outer forme and once on a page of the inner), the page on which it appears being apparently a matter of indifference, though there is some tendency to avoid a page bearing an ordinary signature. The press number is believed to have been used to indicate on which press the sheet was printed.

PRESS PHOTOGRAPHER.   One who takes and supplies photographs for publication in the press.

PRESS PROOF.   The final proof passed by the author, editor, or publisher for printing.

PRESS QUERIES.   Obscurities in a MS. referred to the author by the printer's proof reader.

PRESS-READY.   Sometimes used as a synonym for MAKE-READY (*q.v.*) but also to indicate other machine preparations than that of the forme, such as of the inking, paper-feed, and paper delivery mechanisms.

PRESS RELEASE.   An official statement giving information for publication in newspapers or periodicals.

PRESS REVISE.   An extra proof taken from type in which corrections marked on earlier proofs have been made, and when machining is about to take place. The press revise is submitted to the machine reviser who finally passes it for press. Also called 'Machine proof'.

PRESS RUN.   The number of copies to be printed rather than the number ordered: it is usually larger than the number ordered to allow for spoilage.

PRESSES.   1. In bookbinding, there are several kinds, namely, lying, cutting, standing, blocking and finishing. 2. In printing, the printing machines. In England, 'printing presses' refers to hand-operated apparatus, 'machines' to those operated by power. In America the term 'presses' refers to both. *See also* PRESS.

PRESSWORK.   Making an impression on paper from matter set up in type; in modern usage, the care and attention devoted to this as indicated by the quality of the result. It includes the preparation of the

17

printing surface for even printing and the control of inkflow during the running of the press. *See also* MACHINING.

PRESUMED AUTHOR. *Synonymous with* SUPPOSED AUTHOR (*q.v.*).

PRIMA. 1. The first word of the next page, sheet or slip being read, and printed (repeated) at the right hand of the measure immediately below the last line. 2. A mark made on copy where reading is to be resumed after interruption.

PRIMARY BIBLIOGRAPHY. 1. An original, 'extensive' or 'general' bibliography dealing with books unrelated in subject matter. 2. One which is the original record of the whole, or part of, a publication. *See also* SECONDARY BIBLIOGRAPHY. (American.)

PRIMARY BINDING. The style of binding used for a book when it is first published.

PRIMARY SOURCES. Original manuscripts, contemporary records, or documents which are used by an author in writing a book or other literary compilation. Also called 'Source material' and sometimes 'Original sources'. *See also* SECONDARY SOURCES.

PRIMER. A simple introduction, of an elementary nature, to a subject, possibly intended as a school class book. *See also* INTRODUCTION 2.

PRINCETON FILE. A free-standing box file which is open at the top and back, and which has a front securing the upper parts only of the sides of the file deep enough to take a large label. Such files are used for containing pamphlets on the shelves. *See also* CUT CORNER PAMPHLET FILE.

PRINCIPLES OF CLASSIFICATION. The rules formulated by logicians and classifiers by which a scheme of classification is made.

PRINT. (*Noun*) A reproduction of a picture or drawing by any printing process. Generally applied to etchings, engravings, mezzotints, etc. (*Verb*) To apply ink and then paper to blocks, plates or type to make an 'impression' or a 'print' of the image.

PRINT COLLECTION. A collection of prints such as engravings, etchings, etc.

PRINT FILM. A fine grain, high resolution film which is used primarily for making contact film copies.

PRINT ROOM. A room in a large library in which the collection of prints is kept.

PRINTED. Broadly, any representation of characters which are reproduced on any material by any method of mechanical impression, whatever it may be.

PRINTED AS MANUSCRIPT. *See* PRINTED BUT NOT PUBLISHED.

PRINTED BOOK. A book produced from type or by a similar process. (*IFLA*). *See also* BOOK, PUBLICATION.

PRINTED BUT NOT PUBLISHED.   Printed, but not put on sale, and therefore not published. This fact may be so noted on the title-page. Also called 'Printed as manuscript'.

PRINTED CATALOGUE.   A catalogue, printed and issued in book form as distinct from a card, or other, form of catalogue.

PRINTED EDGES.   Matter which is printed by means of rubber type on the cut edges of books. This is done on the fore-edge in order to aid speedy reference to the contents, but also here and on the top and bottom edges for the purposes of advertising.

PRINTED MATTER.   A literary composition in the sense of an intelligible, rather than a stylish, arrangement of words which has been set up in type and printed.

PRINTER.   The person or firm responsible for printing a book or other publication, as distinguished from the publisher or bookseller. Of considerable importance in old books. In cataloguing rare books, the printer statement, even when it includes a number of names, is given in the imprint. Added entries may be given under printers' names. When no publisher's name is given on the title page, the printer's may be given in the imprint.

PRINTER'S DEVICE.   *See* DEVICE.

PRINTER'S DEVIL.   An apprentice to the printing trade, especially to a compositor. The origin of the term is said to be that in 1561 a monk published a book called *The Anatomy of the Mass* (1561), and although it had only 172 pages, fifteen more were needed to correct the many typesetting mistakes. These were attributed to the special instigation of the devil, but they turned out to be the work of an apprentice learning the trade.

PRINTER'S ERRORS.   *Synonymous with* PRESS ERRORS (*q.v.*).

PRINTER'S FLOWER.   *See* FLOWER.

PRINTER'S IMPRINT.   *See* IMPRINT.

PRINTER'S KEEPSAKE.   *See* KEEPSAKE 3.

PRINTER'S MARK.   *See* DEVICE.

PRINTER'S ORNAMENT.   *See* ORNAMENT.

PRINTER'S PIE.   *See* PIE.

PRINTER'S READER.   *See* READER 1.

PRINTING.   *See* IMPRESSION.

PRINTING BLOCK.   A general term for any kind of BLOCK (*q.v.*) used in printing.

PRINTING HISTORICAL SOCIETY.   Founded in 1964 'to encourage the study of, and foster interest in, the history of printing; to encourage the preservation of historical equipment and printed matter; to promote meetings and exhibitions; to produce publications in connection with these aims'. Publishes *Journal* (a.).

PRINTING INDUSTRY RESEARCH ASSOCIATION. The name by which the PRINTING, PACKAGING AND ALLIED TRADES RESEARCH ASSOCIATION (*q.v.*) was known until 1930.

PRINTING, PACKAGING AND ALLIED TRADES RESEARCH ASSOCIATION. A research association which is grant-aided through the Ministry of Technology. Founded in 1930. It is concerned with printing (all printing processes, bookbinding, paper and ink, process control, machine operation, and adhesives) and packaging (protection of packaged goods against mechanical damage and attack by insects and moulds, effect of storage and climate, and transport hazards). Abbreviated PATRA. Publishes *PATRA News* (m.), *PATRA Journal* (4-m.), *Printing Abstracts* (m.), *Packaging Abstracts* (m.), *PATRA Memoirs, Laboratory Reports, Information Leaflets, PATRA Critical Appraisals Test Reports* to members. *Printing Abstracts* and *Packaging Abstracts* are available to non-members on a subscription basis. Has issued a number of other publications not in series. *See also* BRITISH PAPER AND BOARD INDUSTRY RESEARCH ASSOCIATION.

PRINTING PRESS. A machine for making impressions from a plate, block or type which has been inked, on paper or some other material. *See also* CYLINDER PRESS, FLAT-BED PRESS, INTAGLIO, LETTERPRESS, LITHOGRAPHY, OFFSET, PLATEN PRESS, ROTARY PRESS.

PRINTINGS. A general term for papers which are specially suitable for printing as distinct from other purposes.

PRISON LIBRARY. A library maintained in a prison for the use of prisoners. In many prisons in Great Britain the prison libraries are provided by the local authority, the Prison Commissioners contributing a fixed sum per prisoner towards the cost.

PRIVATE BILLS. Bills published by their promoters for submission in the House of Commons.

PRIVATE LIBRARIES ASSOCIATION. An international society of authors, publishers, booksellers, librarians and private book collectors – collectors of rare books, fine books, single authors, reference books on special subjects, and above all collectors of books generally for the simple pleasures of reading and ownership. Its functions include the organizing of lectures on subjects of bibliographical interest and visits to famous libraries, printing works, binderies, etc. running an Exchange Scheme enabling members to dispose of surplus material and advertise for desiderata; issuing publications of interest to members and running a Loans Library for members. An annual lecture is given. Publishes a Newsletter and Exchange List bi-monthly and *The Private Library* quarterly. Abbreviated PLA.

PRIVATE LIBRARY. One which is owned by a private individual.

PRIVATE MARK. Some indication of ownership, usually the name of the library impressed with a rubber stamp, which is always placed in a particular part of a library book.

PRIVATE PRESS. A printing establishment which undertakes only the work of the owner, or of publishing clubs who may be supporting it financially, or prints only those books (usually not first editions) which the proprietor fancies. Private presses are usually small establishments using hand presses or small letterpress machines, and producing well-printed books in limited editions on hand-made paper. Eric Gill, writing to the *Monotype Recorder* in 1933, said that such a press prints solely what it chooses and not what its customers demand of it, which is the case with a 'public' press, and that 'the distinction has nothing to do with the use of machinery or with questions of the artistic quality of the product'. Of such were the Kelmscott, Essex House, Doves, Vale, Gregynog, Ashendene, Cuala, Eragny, and Pear Tree.

PRIVATELY PRINTED. This term is given to books printed for the author or a private individual, usually for distribution gratis. It is also applied to books printed on a PRIVATE PRESS (*q.v.*). When printed on a public press it is often described as being printed at the author's expense, or by private subscription. Abbreviated p.p.

PRIVILEGE ISSUE. Books issued at the close of a lecture to persons who do not present a borrower's ticket.

pro tem. Abbreviation for *pro tempore* (*Lat.* 'for the time being').

PROBABLE ASSOCIATION, PRINCIPLE OF. The principle that the heading chosen for a catalogue entry (whether for a person, subject, place, organization, etc.) should be the one most users of the library are likely to look under. *See also* CATALOGUING, PRINCIPLES OF.

PROCEDURE MANUAL. *Synonymous with* STAFF MANUAL (*q.v.*) except that in an American special library it may be more detailed, and personnel matters are omitted if they are contained in, as is usual in the case of corporations, the employee handbook. Also called 'Work manual'.

PROCEEDINGS. The published record of meetings of a society or institution, frequently accompanied by abstracts or reports of papers read. *See also* TRANSACTIONS.

PROCESS BLOCK. A metal printing surface produced with the aid of photography and a chemical or mechanical process.

PROCESS CAMERA. One used for the production of a photographic intermediate (usually film – either negative or positive) necessary for making an image on a material from which prints can be made, e.g. an offset-litho plate.

PROCESS COLOUR PRINTING. *See* COLOUR WORK.

PROCESS EMBOSSING. *Synonymous with* EMBOSSING (*q.v.*).

PROCESS ENGRAVING. Any of the processes for reproducing pictures, print, etc. that uses plates or blocks prepared by photographic, mechanical or chemical action rather than by hand. Also called 'Photomechanical process', and 'Process work'.

PROCESS PHOTOGRAPHY. The reproduction of line copy as distinct from continuous tone copy, e.g. a line drawing compared with a photograph. Materials of great contrast are used with this method.

PROCESS RECORD. Usually a card record of a book or other item received at a library and in process of being added to library records.

PROCESS SLIP (ACCESSION SLIP, COPY SLIP, GUIDE SLIP, ROUTINE SLIP). A slip or card, usually the same size as a catalogue card, bearing author's name, title, imprint, collation, tracings, and allocations of copies to libraries or departments. It accompanies the book throughout the cataloguing department and is generally used as the copy for the typist or printer. Called also, in America, 'Rider slip'.

PROCESS STAMP. A rubber stamp impression on the back of the title-page of a book to give the library history of the book and to show which assistants were responsible for the various stages of its processing.

PROCESS WORK. *See* PROCESS ENGRAVING.

PROCESSES, DEPARTMENT OF TECHNICAL. *Synonymous with* PROCESSING DEPARTMENT (*q.v.*).

PROCESSING. 1. Strictly, the carrying out of the various routines such as stamping, labelling, numbering, etc., before a book is ready for the shelves, but it may include *all* the processes involved in so preparing a book. Also called 'Book preparation', 'Book processing'. In a technical information bureau or library, much more work may be done to enable information to be obtained readily ('retrieved') than is necessary in a general or public library. These processes may be grouped into three: library processing, bibliographic processing, and information processing. Library processing includes acquisition of materials; cataloguing; classification and filing of cards; physical processing as mentioned above, and the shelving of materials; notification of additions to stock. Bibliographic processing includes: bibliographic description; filing of cards in reference and bibliographic files; reproduction of cards; notification to individuals. Information processing includes: distribution of literature and documentation at the request of departments, members or others, or on standing order; notification of information, preparation of reference cards and filing in reference information file; preparation of abstracts; making of a translation; microfilming or photoreproduction; other forms of reproduction of materials; ordering of materials needed; assembling selections on particular topics. 2. In photography and documentary reproduction, the carrying out of such processes as are necessary after the projection of the image to be copied on to the sensitized material. *See also* MECHANICAL PREPARATION.

PROCESSING CENTER. In America, a building in which the processing of books for a number of libraries is carried out, thus releasing trained personnel for other work and reducing costs by various means. Such centers have developed by co-operation of librarians in adjoining areas, often being initiated under the provisions of the Library Services Act. Sometimes they operate from an existing public library, from a state library agency, as an entirely separate enterprise on a contract or other co-operative basis among a group of libraries, or as a commercial project.

PROCESSING DEPARTMENT. 1. A combined book-ordering (or acquisition) and cataloguing department. 2. In some libraries, a department in which the work of preparing books for circulation, other than cataloguing and classification, is carried out. *See also* CATALOGUING DEPARTMENT, TECHNICAL SERVICES DEPARTMENT.

PROCESSOR-CAMERA. A device which functions as a camera and film processor. *See also* CAMERA CARD.

PROCTOR ORDER. The system of classification of incunabula named after the order used by R. G. C. Proctor in his *Index of Early Printed Books in the British Museum*, 1897–1903.

PROFESSIONAL ASSISTANT. In American libraries, a member of the professional staff performing work of a nature requiring training and skill in the theoretical or scientific parts of library work as distinct from its merely mechanical parts.

PROFESSIONAL AUDITOR. A person who is a member of an appropriate recognized body may be appointed as a professional auditor to audit the accounts of a borough or non-county borough council which are not subject to district audit. Professional auditors have no power of disallowance. In most county boroughs, accounts which are not required to be audited by the district auditor are audited by professional auditors. *See also* BOROUGH AUDITOR.

PROFILE. A biographical account combined with a description and assessment of the subject's achievements.

PRO-FORMA INVOICE. An invoice received for checking and approval prior to receiving the formal invoice. It is used as a check list for periodical renewals and then returned for authorization for placing renewal orders, or as a request for confirmation of an order for an unexpectedly expensive item. It is never approved and forwarded for payment. (American.)

PROGRAM DISSERTATION. A dissertation accompanying a 'program' (i.e. announcement of a memorial exercise, lecture, etc.) published by a university or school, especially in Germany, Austria, Switzerland or one of the Scandinavian countries. (American.)

PROGRAMME. (*Information retrieval*) (*Noun*) An outline giving the schedule of actions to be followed or the order and arrangement of such a schedule. A series of instructions expressed in symbols which a machine system can accept and understand (*IBM*). A sequence of steps or coded instructions to be executed by the computer to solve a given problem. (*Verb*) To determine the steps and plan the procedures necessary for the computer to solve the problem.

PROGRESS, IN. *See* IN PROGRESS.

PROGRESSIVE PROOF. A proof showing the sequences and effect at each stage of a colour-printing process as each colour is added. *See also* FLAT PROOF.

PROJECT INTREX. A long range programme, established in January 1964 by the Massachusetts Institute of Technology, for the application of the principles and methods of information processing to library operation, with the specific object of establishing the bases upon which the technical library of the future may be modelled. Intrex stands for Information Transfer Exchange.

PROJECT LEER. A joint undertaking by the Books for the People Fund, Inc. and the Bro-Dart Foundation for the compilation and publication of annual lists of children's books and elementary reading materials for adults which are available in the Spanish language, and for the encouragement of the production and use of such reading materials. The project is being directed from the offices of the Organization of American States in Washington, D.C.

PROJECTED BOOKS. Microfilmed books intended for projecting on to a ceiling, wall or screen for the benefit of physically-handicapped people.

PROJECTION. The method used by a cartographer for representing on a plane the whole, or part, of the earth's surface, as Mercator's Projection.

PROJECTION PRINT. In documentary reproduction, a copy having a larger scale than the original: an enlargement. Also called a 'Blow-up'.

PROJECTION PRINTING. A method of obtaining a photographic copy by exposing a photosensitive surface by projecting an image through an optical system.

PROMPT BOOK. *Synonymous with* PROMPT COPY (*q.v.*).

PROMPT COPY. The copy of a play used by a prompter, showing action of a play, cues, movements of actors, properties, costumes, and scene and light plots.

PROOF. 1. In bookbinding: the rough edges of certain leaves left uncut by the plough are proof that the book is not cut down. 2. An impression made from type before being finally prepared for printing. Proofs are made on long sheets of normal page width (GALLEY or SLIP PROOF) for the author's inspection and correction but not until after a FIRST PROOF has been made, corrected by the printer's reader and returned to the compositor. When the printer has made the corrections the type is divided up into pages, the page numbers inserted, and a further proof submitted to the author. This third proof is called the PAGE PROOF. A MARKED PROOF is one marked by the printer's reader, corrected by the author and again read by the printer's reader, and a REVISE or REVISED PROOF is a further one embodying corrections made by the author/or reader to the first proof. *See also* AUTHOR'S PROOF, CLEAN PROOF. 3. A preliminary impression taken from an engraved plate or block, or a lithographic stone. Usually called 'Trial proof'. 4. An impression taken from a finished plate or block before the regular impression is published and usually before the title or other inscription is added. Also called 'Proof print' or 'Proof impression'.

PROOF BEFORE LETTERS. A proof of an engraving, etching or other illustration process made before the addition of title, artist's and engraver's name, date, dedication or other matter.

PROOF CORRECTIONS. Signs used by proof readers on printers' proofs to indicate corrections to be made in the typesetting. These have become established over the centuries and the British code is published in the *British Standard* 1219: 1958.

PROOF PRESS. A small or medium-sized press operated electrically or by hand on which proofs from type or other relief surfaces are made.

PROOF READER. A person who reads printers' proofs to discover errors in type, punctuation, statement and so forth.

PROOF READER'S MARKS. *Synonymous with* PROOF CORRECTIONS (*q.v.*).

PROOF READING. The process of reading a printer's proof and comparing it with the MS. or COPY (*q.v.*) in order to detect errors in typesetting. Errors are marked on the proof in accordance with generally accepted signs and the resulting 'corrected proof' is returned to the printer so that the necessary corrections may be carried out. *See also* PROOF, PROOF CORRECTIONS.

PROOF SHEET. A sheet of paper on which a proof of type-matter, plate, or block, is made by a printer. *See also* PROOF.

PROPER NAME. A name used as the designation of a single person, place or thing, e.g. Leonard, Wimbledon, Festival Hall, Loch Ness Monster.

PROPERTY. *See* PREDICABLES, FIVE.

PROSPECTUS. 1. A leaflet or pamphlet issued by a publisher and describing a new publication. 2. A publication written to inform, arouse interest in, and encourage the reader to take some action concerning, a book about to be published, a school or other education institution, or the issue of stock or shares of a company, etc.

PROVENANCE. A record or indication of previous ownership of a book or manuscript. A special binding, book plate, or inscription may indicate previous owners, collections or libraries through which a particular book has passed.

PROVINCIAL JOINT FICTION RESERVE. A national scheme for the co-operative preservation of books, similar to the scheme initiated by the former Association of Metropolitan Chief Librarians. It commenced to operate on 1st January 1962; each Regional Bureau outside London and the South East, which already had schemes, is responsible for a part of the alphabet. The scheme provides only for the purchase and retention of new publications and is not retrospective, although offers of older novels are sometimes made to the responsible library. Allocation by author amongst the regions is as follows:

A–C	North-Western	K–M	West Midlands
D–F	Northern	N–S	Yorkshire
G–J	East Midlands	T–Z	South-Western

PROVISIONAL EDITION. A book which is published in a small edition, possibly by some near-print process, and circulated to selected individuals or sold in the ordinary way, so that observations, criticisms and suggestions may be submitted and considered before a final edition is published. Also called 'Preliminary edition'.

PRUDENTIAL COMMITTEE. *Synonymous with* ADMINISTRATIVE COUNCIL (*q.v.*).

PRUSSIAN INSTRUCTIONS. The German cataloguing code; an

English translation was published by the University of Michigan Press in 1938.

PSALM-BOOK. A PSALTER (*q.v.*).

PSALTER. The Book of Psalms in which the Psalms are arranged as in the Book of Common Prayer for use in a religious service, whether to be spoken or sung; in the latter case they may be in a metrical version.

PSEUDANDRY. The use by a woman author of a masculine name as a pseudonym. *See also* PSEUDONYM.

PSEUDEPIGRAPHY. The attributing of false names to the authors of books.

PSEUDOGRAPH. A literary composition falsely attributed to a particular writer.

PSEUDOJYN. A man writing under a feminine pseudonym.

PSEUDONYM. A name used by an author, which is not his real name. Also called a 'Pen name' or 'Nom de plume'. *See also* SYNCOPISM, TELONISM, TITLONYM.

PSEUDONYMOUS WORKS. Those written by persons who have used a name other than their real name on the title-page in order to conceal their identity. *See also* PSEUDONYM.

PSEUDO-PHOTOGRAPHIC PHOTOCOPYING. Copying processes which are not photographic. Of such are THERMOFAX and XEROGRAPHY (*qq.v.*).

PSEUDO-WEEDING. *See* WEEDING.

PUBLIC CATALOGUE. A catalogue issued for the use of the public as distinct from one issued for use by officials.

PUBLIC DOCUMENTS. The regular official publications of a government, containing reports, statistics, etc.

PUBLIC LENDING RIGHT. A subsidy paid to authors in respect of books issued from public libraries. It has been in operation in Denmark, Sweden and Norway for many years and in Finland since 1961. Suggestions were made in 1951 that such a scheme should be adopted in Great Britain and in 1960 an 'Authors' and Publishers' Lending Right Association Committee' was formed to negotiate with the Library Association; no positive results were achieved. In the Scandinavian countries the subsidies are paid from government funds, either according to the books stocked in public libraries or according to the number of times copyright books are borrowed. Abbreviated PLR.

PUBLIC LIBRARIES ACTS. The 'adoptive' acts (i.e. those which apply only where they have been adopted by the appropriate authority) which govern the provision and management of libraries are: the

Public Libraries Act, 1892; the Public Libraries (Amendment) Act, 1893; the Public Libraries Act, 1901; and the Public Libraries Act, 1919. Some provisions of the Local Government Act, 1933, also affect public libraries. *See also* LOCAL GOVERNMENT (RECORDS) ACT, 1962, PUBLIC LIBRARIES AND MUSEUMS BILL, APPENDIX 3.

PUBLIC LIBRARIES AND MUSEUMS ACT 1964. *See* APPENDIX 3.

PUBLIC LIBRARIES AND MUSEUMS BILL. Introduced to the House of Commons on 24 January 1964, this bill provided a completely new legal basis for the public service, would repeal all existing library legislation by one comprehensive law for public library services in England and Wales. It would impose a statutory duty on local library authorities to provide a 'comprehensive and efficient public library service'. It would also give to the Minister of Education, for the first time, the responsibility 'to superintend and promote the development of the service and to secure the proper discharge by local authorities of their library functions, England and Wales would have their own National Advisory Councils to advise the Minister on library matters, and Regional Councils would be set up to make and supervise arrangements for co-operation within the region and with other bodies concerned with libraries. The Bill would take effect not earlier than 1 April 1965. It was based on the report of the two working parties set up in 1961 which resulted from the Roberts Committee Report of 1958. The resulting act was passed on 31 July 1964. *See* PUBLIC LIBRARIES AND MUSEUMS ACT 1964, Appendix 3. *See also* BAKER REPORT, BOURDILLON REPORT, ROBERTS REPORT.

PUBLIC LIBRARY. A library provided wholly or partly from public funds, and the use of which is not restricted to any class of persons in the community but is freely available to all. A major agency of enlightenment for adults, providing also for children the recorded experiences of others which will help them to grow into adulthood.

PUBLIC LIBRARY ASSOCIATION. A Division of the American Library Association under this name since 1958; it was originally organized in 1951 to provide for the exchange of ideas and experience, and to stimulate continued professional growth, to improve and extend public library services, to raise library standards, to secure adequate support for libraries and to co-operate in the promotion of library service generally. Abbreviated PLA. Publishes *Just Between Ourselves* (3 a. to membs.).

PUBLIC RECORD OFFICE. The depository for British Official documents; it is situated in Chancery Lane, London, W.C.2., and contains documents from the twelfth century to date. The Public Records Act

1958, much of which was based on the report of the Committee on Departmental Records (the 'Grigg Report') transferred the direction of the PRO from the Master of the Rolls to a Minister of the Crown, the Lord Chancellor, who now has a general responsibility for public records; he is authorized to appoint an Advisory Council on Public Records, of which the Master of the Rolls is the Statutory Chairman; this Council is particularly concerned with those aspects of the work of the PRO which affects members of the public making use of the facilities provided. The Act places on government departments a duty to select records for permanent preservation and to pass them to the PRO within thirty years of their creation. They were open to public inspection when they were fifty years old until 1 January 1968 when the period was reduced to thirty years. The Lord Chancellor has power to appoint for any class of records a special place of deposit; this enables public records accruing in local courts and offices to be kept in local repositories, and those of a technical character to be kept in appropriate specialist institutions. The 1958 Act declares that 'records' includes not only written records but those conveying information by any other means whatsoever.

PUBLIC RECORDS. Records made in the process of government and including those made by any means whatsoever, not only those which are written.

PUBLIC RECORDS ACT 1958. *See* PUBLIC RECORD OFFICE.

PUBLIC (SERVICE) AREA. That portion of the area of a library to which the public are admitted but which is occupied by fixed furniture used by both staff and public (staff enclosure, circulation desk, information, enquiries or registration desks, etc.), catalogues, exhibits and displays.

PUBLICATION. 1. A work (*see* WORK 1) issued to the public in the form of a document (*see* DOCUMENT 2) or book (*see* BOOK 4) (IFLA). 2. The act of issuing a book to the public (IFLA).

PUBLICATION DATE. *Synonymous with* DATE OF PUBLICATION (*q.v.*).

PUBLICATION DAY. 1. The day of the week or month on which a periodical is issued. 2. The first day on which a book may be sold to the public.

PUBLISH. 1. The action of a publisher in issuing and offering for sale to the public, a book or print produced on some kind of printing, copying or photographic reproducing machine. 2. The action of an author, artist, or composer of music, in creating something, and arranging for it to be reproduced in quantity and offered for sale.

PUBLISHED. A document which has been reproduced in a number of copies and made available to the public to whom it may be sold or distributed free of charge and whether or not it is intended to have a restricted readership such as to members of parliament, of a learned, professional or political organization.

PUBLISHED PRICE.   The price at which a book is published.

PUBLISHER.   A person, firm, or corporate body responsible for placing a book on the market, as distinguished from the printer. Publisher and printer may be the same, but in modern books usually is not. Relates also to publication of music, reproduction of works of art and of maps and photographs. A firm which undertakes publishing is sometimes referred to as a 'Publishing house' or 'Publishing firm'.

PUBLISHERS ASSOCIATION.   A trade association which was founded in Britain in 1896. Membership is open to any publisher in the United Kingdom whose business, or an appreciable part of it, is publishing books. The original object of the Association was to maintain the prices of net books, and while this is still a matter of considerable interest, the Association is largely engaged in assisting its members to secure a greater, and more efficient, distribution of books, and in the education of publishers' staffs. It deals with problems which face publishers as a whole, regulates conditions of employment within the trade, supplies its members with information and advice on all matters of technical, economic and legal aspects of publishing, and represents publishers in discussions or negotiations with the government, local authorities, and public and trade bodies.

PUBLISHER'S BINDING.   The binding in which a publisher issues a book.

PUBLISHER'S CASE.   *Synonymous with* PUBLISHER'S COVER (*q.v.*).

PUBLISHER'S CATALOGUE.   A list of books issued for sale by a publisher.

PUBLISHER'S CLOTH.   Used to indicate a book as issued by the publisher in a cloth binding.

PUBLISHER'S COVER.   The cover for a book that is provided by a publisher for the normal trade edition of a book. Also called 'Publisher's case'. *See also* CASE, EDITION BINDING.

PUBLISHER'S DEVICE.   *See* DEVICE.

PUBLISHER'S DUMMY.   A dummy book made up of the right number of sections of plain paper, and sometimes cased, to indicate the size of a proposed book.

PUBLISHER'S IMPRINT.   *See* IMPRINT.

PUBLISHER'S LIST.   A list of books published by one publisher and still in print.

PUBLISHER'S MARK. *See* DEVICE.

PUBLISHER'S NUMBER. *See* PLATE NUMBER.

PUBLISHER'S READER. One whose calling is the reading, judging and criticizing of manuscripts offered for publication.

PUBLISHER'S SERIES. The name given to a series of books which usually have been published previously, and comprising standard or current books on related or unrelated subjects, issued in a uniform style and at the same price, and bearing a series title such as *World's Classics*, or *Everyman's Library*. Each volume contains one or more distinct works, and some series include books published for the first time. Also called 'Trade series'. Series which comprise only books previously published are sometimes called 'Reprint series'.

PUBLISHING. The trade of publishing books; this includes negotiations with authors or their agents, design of books in conjunction with printers, book production, publicity and sales through book wholesalers and retailers. In addition to books it relates to music, reproduction of works of art and of photographs and maps.

PUFF. A term, in use since the seventeenth century, for exaggerated praise for a book, usually written by the author or publisher for use in advertisements and on the book's jacket. A 'Preliminary puff' is supplied to the publisher's travellers as pre-publication publicity. *See also* BLURB.

PUGILLARES. From two to eight small wooden writing tablets of ivory, wood, or metal and covered with wax on one side upon which writing could be scratched with a stylus. Sometimes the tablets were hinged together with rings or leather cords down one side to form a tablet book. Notebooks of this sort were known as *pugillaria*. *See also* CODEX.

PULL. A trial print taken from type or a block before an edition is printed.

PULLED. In bookbinding, a book the cover of which has been removed and all the sheets separated. *See also* TAKE DOWN.

PULLED TYPE. Type letters which have been pulled out of the forme by ink-balls.

PULLING. (*Binding*) Stripping the old covers off a book, separating the sections and removing any old glue prior to rebinding.

PULP. The mechanically or chemically prepared mixture made from vegetable fibres which becomes paper when passed over the wire and dried. *See also* CHEMICAL WOOD, HAND-MADE PAPER, MECHANICAL WOOD. 2. A cheap magazine printed on newsprint.

PULP BOARD. Board manufactured in one thickness, or by bringing two or more thicknesses of board or paper together into a single structure on a multiple-wire machine, as distinct from boards made by laminations of paper pasted together and called 'Pasteboard'. Sizes:

	inches
Imperial	22 × 30
Postal	$22\frac{1}{2}$ × $28\frac{1}{2}$
Pulp Royal	$20\frac{1}{2}$ × 25

PULP MAGAZINE.   A cheap magazine printed on newsprint and containing stories of adventure, mystery or love, usually of poor quality.

PUNCH.   A piece of steel on which a type character is engraved. After hardening it is used as a die to strike the matrices from which type is cast.

PUNCH ENGRAVING.   A method of book illustration which had previously been used by goldsmiths and ornament engravers. The tools used consisted of a dotting punch, a small pointed punch set in a wooden handle and used by hand pressure, and larger punches with either grained or plain striking surfaces intended for use with a hammer.

PUNCHED CARD.   A lightweight card which has holes punched in certain positions either round the edges (edge-punched) or in the body of the card (body-punched) to represent specific pieces of information. Edge-punched cards are sorted manually with the aid of a 'needle' and body-punched cards usually by machine. They are used to record particulars of membership, book stock or classified material or information. Extensive use of them is made in connexion with information retrieval or document systems. Also called an 'EAM [electronic accounting machine] card'. *See also* DEQUEKER SYSTEM, EDGE-NOTCHED CARDS, MARGINAL-HOLE PUNCHED CARDS. Punched cards are also used in BOOKAMATIC, PHOTO-CHARGING and PUNCHED CARD CHARGING (*qq.v.*) methods of recording the loan of books to avoid the manual sorting of, and searching for, transaction cards.

PUNCHED CARD CHARGING.   A TRANSACTION CARD CHARGING (*q.v.*) system whereby a punching machine is used to punch two transaction cards simultaneously, to record book number, reader's number, main class number and date due for return. One card is placed in the book and is taken away by the reader; it has a readable date due for return stamped on it. The other is retained. *See also* CHARGING METHODS.

PUNCTUATION.   *See also* LINKS, QUOTES.

PUNCTUATION SYMBOLS. A device used in co-ordinate indexing to associate terms or symbols in order to indicate relationship. For example, a double dot (..) may be used before each associated set of words to indicate that they are to be considered together.

PURE BIBLIOGRAPHY. The type of bibliography which treats of the value of the contents of books, including textual criticism (*Maire*).

PURE NOTATION. *See* NOTATION.

PUSTAKA. A book consisting of long strips of the thin bark of trees or of a kind of paper made from tree bark; it may deal with magic medicine, domestic remedies, or 'the art' of destroying life. The Sanskrit word "pustaka" is used for this kind of book in North Sumatra, Java and other countries, but in South Sumatra 'pustaha' is used; here such books were used as divination texts, for codes of law and for legends. Pustakas were written in a brilliant ink on long strips of writing material, folded concertina-fashion and tied together with a string of woven rushes.

PUT TO BED. *See* BED.

'PUTTING KNOWLEDGE TO WORK'. The slogan of the (American) SPECIAL LIBRARIES ASSOCIATION (*q.v.*).

PUTWITHS. Acknowledgements and other consequential papers such as corrigenda and addenda relating to documents already filed in a correspondence or similar file, and which in themselves are of no significance from a filing or indexing point of view.

PYE. An alternative spelling of PIE (*q.v.*).

PYE BOOK. *See* PIE 2.

PYES. A kind of ecclesiastical calendar.

q.v. Abbreviation for *quod vide* (*Lat.* 'which see'); *Pl. qq.v.* (*quae vide*). Also for *quantum vis* (*Lat.* 'as much as you will').

QUAD. Abbreviation for QUADRAT. 1. A piece of metal, lower in height than type, and used for spacing.

An em quad (mutton), the square of the body.

An en quad (nut), $\frac{1}{2}$ the body or 2 to an em.

A thick space, $\frac{1}{3}$ the body or 3 to an em.

A middle space, $\frac{1}{4}$ the body or 4 to an em.

A thin space, $\frac{1}{5}$ the body or 5 to an em.

A hair space, $\frac{1}{12}$ the body approximately.

See also EM QUADRATS, EN QUADRATS, PAPER SIZES. 2. Prefix to standard paper-size names to indicate a sheet four times the size of a single and twice the size of a double, sheet. *See also* OCTAVO, PAPER SIZES.

QUAD MARK.   *Synonymous with* BACK MARK, BLACK STEP, COLLATING MARK (*q.v.*).

QUADRAT.   A term which is never used in its full form, but in the abbreviated version QUAD (*q.v.*).

QUADRATA.   An early style of Latin manuscript writing; it was practised from the second to the fifth century A.D. and was characterized by a square capital letter based on formal inscriptions cut with a chisel in stone. Also called 'Square capital' hand.

QUADRIGESIMO-OCTAVO.   *See* FORTY-EIGHTMO.

QUADRILLE.   Paper ruled so as to form a very large number of small squares; it is used for graphs, etc.

QUALIFICATION.   The addition of one or more words in parentheses to a subject heading, usually in dictionary catalogues, indicating the sense in which the heading is being used. Also used in indexes to the scheme of classification. Chiefly used to distinguish homonyms.

QUALIFIED HEADING.   A heading followed by a qualifying term which is usually enclosed in parentheses, e.g. Composition (Art), Composition (Law) (*IBM*).

QUALIFIED LIST.   Produced by deleting False and Unsought links of the chain (when using the chain procedure to produce subject index entries) and adding qualifiers to the remaining terms. It is the second stage of the conversion of a classification symbol to a verbal subject heading, the first being BASIC ANALYSIS (*q.v.*).

QUALIFIER.   A sub-heading in a subject index which has been constructed by CHAIN PROCEDURE (*q.v.*).

QUARTER BINDING.   A binding in which the spine and a very small part of the sides is covered with a stronger material than the rest of the sides. 'Half binding' has the corners covered with the same material as the spine. In 'three-quarter binding' the material used on the spine extends up to three-quarters of the width of the sides.

QUARTER BOUND.   *Synonymous with* QUARTER LEATHER (*q.v.*).

QUARTER LEATHER.   A term used to describe a book with a leather spine and cloth sides. *See also* HALF LEATHER, LEATHER BOUND, THREE-QUARTER LEATHER.

QUARTERLY.   A periodical published once every quarter.

QUARTERNION.   Paper or vellum folded into a section of four leaves.

QUARTO.   1. A sheet of paper folded twice to form a section of four leaves. The sheets given under the definition OCTAVO are folded twice to give the following quarto book sizes in inches. Double size sheets folded three times would give the same size sections but would be described bibliographically as octavos, not quartos.

Foolscap	$8\frac{1}{2} \times 6\frac{3}{4}$
Crown	$10 \times 7\frac{1}{2}$
Large Post	$10\frac{1}{2} \times 8\frac{1}{4}$
Demy	$11\frac{1}{4} \times 8\frac{3}{4}$
Medium	$11\frac{1}{2} \times 9$
Royal	$12\frac{1}{2} \times 10$
Large Royal	$13\frac{1}{2} \times 10$
Super Royal	$13\frac{1}{2} \times 10\frac{1}{4}$
Imperial	15×11

Abbreviated 4°, 4to. 2. A book having sections of four leaves, or eight pages. 3. A book over 10 and under 13 inches high. This is the popular, or book trade, definition.

QUARTO EDITION. One issued in QUARTO (*q.v.*) form.

QUARTO SHELVING. Shelves to accommodate quarto books.

QUASI-FACSIMILE BIBLIOGRAPHY. One which attempts to reproduce the kind of type used in the original—roman, italic or gothic, etc.

QUERY. The symbol ? written in the margin of a proof by the printer's reader to indicate to the author that he is required to check some detail. Sometimes 'Qv' is used.

QUESTION MARK. *Synonymous with* INTERROGATION POINT (*q.v.*).

QUICK-REFERENCE BOOKS. Books which are essentially of a reference character, such as directories, dictionaries and gazetteers.

QUINTERNION. A GATHERING (*q.v.*) of five sheets folded once to form ten leaves or twenty pages.

QUIRE. 1. 24 sheets of paper and one 'outside', making 25; the twentieth of a ream; 25 copies of a newspaper or periodical. 2. A gathering, section or signature, especially when unfolded. Books in sheets, unbound, are said to be 'in quires'. *See also* SECTION. For 'Cording quires', *see* CASSIE.

QUOINS. Wedges of metal or wood, used to lock the matter in the CHASE (*q.v.*).

QUOTATION MARKS. *See* QUOTES.

QUOTATIONS. (*Printing*) Very large quads, used for filling up large areas of space in printed matter: they are usually hollow, simply four walls, sometimes strengthened by one or more internal girders. Also called 'Quotes'.

QUOTES. The inverted commas " " placed at the beginning and end of quotations. *See also* QUOTATIONS. Sometimes called 'Double quotes' to distinguish them from 'Single quotes': '. . .'. *See also* DOUBLE QUOTES, DUCK-FOOT QUOTES, SINGLE QUOTES, TURNED COMMA. In

Germany and Austria they are printed thus „ . . .". although some German printers now prefer the French guillemets but pointing inwards (» . . . «). Spanish printers prefer the guillemets (« . . . ») pointing outwards.

RCA 'VIDEO FILE'. A filing system, based on the manufacturer's video magnetic tape recording methods, employing television recording techniques to store pictorial data whether consisting of maps, charts, typewritten or handwritten matter, coloured or black and white. Coloured material is reproduced in black and white without half tones.

R.P. Indicates that a book is not available from the publisher but is 'reprinting'. If R.P. is followed by a date as 'R.P. Jan.' it indicates when a reprint will be ready.

RACK. A shelf, or group of shelves, or a case, usually built on to a wall or into a piece of furniture, for displaying books, magazines or periodicals, and distinguished as Book Rack, Magazine Rack, according to the special use of the fitting. The term is becoming out of fashion, 'case' or 'stand', being used now. *See also* BUTTERFLY PLAN.

RADIAL ROUTING. *See* ROUTING. Also called 'controlled circulation'.

RADIATING STACKS. Island stacks arranged like a fan, the point being towards the staff enclosure thus enabling all readers on both sides of every stack to be visible from the enclosure.

RADIO SCRIPT. The text of an item for broadcasting.

RADIX NOTATION. The significance of digits in the representation of numeric data which is governed by their relative position with respect to 'period' (.).

RAG PAPER. Paper made from rags, especially cotton rags.

RAISED BANDS. When the cords, on which the sections of a book are sewed, are not embedded in their backs and consequently show as ridges, they are called raised bands. The opposite of SUNK BANDS (*q.v.*).

RAISED-LETTER PRINTING. *Synonymous with* THERMOGRAPHY (*q.v.*).

RAMEAN TREE. *Synonymous with* the Tree of Porphyry. *See* PORPHYRY, TREE OF (*q.v.*).

RAMIE. China (Chinese) grass which has been used for paper making in China since the third century A.D. In Europe it is normally used only for textiles and banknotes.

RAMIFYING CLASSIFICATION. *Synonymous with* BRANCHING CLASSIFICATION (*q.v.*).

RANDOLPH J. CALDECOTT MEDAL. *See* CALDECOTT MEDAL, RANDOLPH J.

RANDOM ACCESS STORAGE. A storage technique in which the time required to obtain information is independent of the location of the information – that is, items do not have to be processed in sequence (*IBM*).

RANFURLY LIBRARIES. A scheme started by the Countess of Ranfurly and sponsored by the English-Speaking Union for collecting books from individuals and institutions and sending them to Commonwealth countries where there is an urgent need for books in English. Books are sent to a central point in each country whence they are sent to libraries of all kinds and institutions where they might be useful. In addition to the head depot and branches in the United Kingdom, there are donor libraries in Canada, Australia and New Zealand, and books are despatched regularly to thirty-seven countries in the Commonwealth.

RANGE. An American term for a bookcase, equivalent to the English PRESS (*q.v.*).

RANGING FIGURES. The numerals of modern type-faces which do not have ascenders or descenders but extend from the base line to the cap line, e.g. the Times New Roman figures 1234567890. Also called 'Lining figures'. *See also* HANGING FIGURES.

RANK. (*Information retrieval*) A measure of the relative position in a series, group, classification or array (*IBM*).

RAPID COPYING. A speedy method of making copies of documents inexpensively. Used mainly in offices.

RAPID SELECTOR. A machine for document storage and retrieval. Documents are photographed on to 35 mm microfilm and alongside are placed digital dot codes indexing each frame. In searching, a reel of film is run past an optical scanner which reads the optical dot pattern. Documents selected are copied automatically from the reel of film (*IBM*). The original model was first conceived in 1939 by Vannevar Bush and developed by Ralph Shaw; it is one of the earliest retrieval systems and is of the roll film type. It has limited facilities for indexing the document content, and access to the material is by description rather than by address.

RARE BOOKS GROUP. A Group of the Library Association. It was formed (on the initiative of the then University and Research Section) in October 1967 'to unite librarians, who are concerned with the custody of collections of rare books and similar materials, and other members of the Library Association who are interested in rare books, and to promote the study and discussion of questions relating to the acquisition, maintenance and use of such collections'.

RATE, LIBRARY. *See* LIBRARY RATE.

RATING AUTHORITY. The local authority responsible for levying and collecting rates; it is the council of a county borough, London borough, or county district, or the Common Council of the City of London.

RATTLE. The sound produced by shaking or snapping a sheet of paper; it is indicative of hardness (due to the degree of wetness or hydration) and, generally speaking, of quality. Called 'crackle' in the U.S.A. Linen rags will give a toughness and rattle to papers which is distinctive from those made from cotton.

RAW PAPER. *Synonymous with* BODY PAPER (*q.v.*).

READABLE NEGATIVE. *See* NEGATIVE 3.

READER. 1. A person employed by a printer to read through proofs with the 'copy' to make sure that corrections have been properly made. 2. A person who makes use of literary material in a library; a member of a lending library is frequently called a Borrower. *See also* PUBLISHER'S READER. 3. In an American special library or information department, the member of staff who scans current publications to select articles, news items, etc., pertinent to the work of individuals and departments of the organization of which the library is a part, for subsequent dissemination. 4. In a newspaper library, the member of the library staff who scans the several editions of the paper and marks articles for cutting and filing. *See also* DISSEMINATION OF INFORMATION. 5. In reprography, a device for projecting a readable image of a microcopy on to a screen within the device or on to a separate portable screen or suitable surface which may be opaque or translucent.

READER AREA. That portion of the total floor space of a library which is allocated for use by readers.

READER FOR THE PRESS. A printer's reader. *See* READER 1.

READER-INTEREST CLASSIFICATION. A very simple and broad classification, intended to reflect the special interests of readers rather than the subject contents of books as such. It was developed in the Detroit Public Library.

READER-PRINTER. In documentary reproduction, a reading machine which can also be used to make enlargements automatically.

READERS' ADVISER. An experienced, cultured and tactful member of the staff who is detailed for advising readers on their choice of books, interesting casual readers in more systematic reading, recording results of interviews, maintaining a close touch with local educational agencies and generally furthering the use of books.

READER'S CARD. The card issued to a reader when registering to use a library.

READER'S PROOF. The first proof which is made from composed type; it is read by the printer's reader and sent to the compositor who makes any necessary alterations before the second proof is pulled and which is the first one sent to the author.

READERS' REGISTER. A register, on cards or in a handwritten volume (usually the former) giving details of the members of a library.

READER'S SET. A set of proofs on which corrections are to be made, usually so marked on the proofs by the printer's reader.

READER'S TICKET. The ticket issued to a reader on joining a library.

READING CASE. *Synonymous with* MAGAZINE CASE (*q.v.*).

READING CIRCLE. A group of people who meet regularly in the library to read or study books.

READING COPY. A copy of a book offered for sale in poor condition but the text of which is complete and legible. Also called 'Binding copy'.

READING LIST. A list of recommended books and/or periodical articles in some special order and on a particular subject, often with guidance as to their purpose and features.

READING MACHINE. Apparatus made for enlarging the image of microphotographic records (whether on film or paper) so that they can be read.

READING ROOM. A room set aside for the reading of periodicals or books.

READING SHELVES. Examining books to see that they are in correct order on the shelves. Also known as 'Shelf tidying', and in American practice as 'Shelf reading' and 'Revising shelves'.

READY REFERENCE. Reference work concerned with questions of a factual nature which can be answered readily, often from QUICK-REFERENCE BOOKS (*q.v.*) which in many libraries are shelved together with standard reference books, sometimes in a separate area reserved for dealing with questions of this nature.

REAL TIME. (*Information retrieval*) The technique of co-ordinating data processing with external related physical events on a time basis, thereby making possible the prompt reporting of conditions, such as the airline reservations system which can report reservation openings almost instantly.

REALIA. Three-dimensional objects such as museum materials, dioramas, models and samples which may be borrowed or purchased by a school library and used in connexion with class lessons.

REAM. A pack of 500 identical sheets of paper. A ream contains twenty quires. In the U.K., packs of 480 sheets for special classes of papers, such as wrapping papers and blotting paper, are recognized. A ream of hand-made and drawing papers may contain 472, 480 or 500 sheets. Originally a ream contained 516 sheets. A 'short ream' has 480 sheets, a 'long ream' 500 or 516 sheets.

REAR PROJECTION. The projection of an image on a transparent or opaque material through an appropriate type of projector on to a translucent screen from the side opposite to that from which the image is viewed.

RE-BACK. To repair a book by providing a new spine without re-covering the sides or re-sewing. See also BACKED.

RE-BOUND. Said of a book which has been stripped of its original binding and replaced with another, usually after resewing the sections.

REBUS. 1. A form of riddle, in which words or their syllables, names, mottoes, etc., are represented by objects or by a combination of objects, letters or words. 2. An enigmatical representation of a name, word or phrase by figures, pictures, arrangement of letters, etc., which resemble the intended words or syllables in sound.

RECALL. (Verb) To request the return to the library of a book or other item which is on loan.

RECALL NOTICE. A notice sent to a reader requesting the return of a book or other item which is overdue or required for use by some-one else. See also OVERDUE NOTICE.

RECALL RATIO. In information retrieval, the number of documents actually recalled from an index in response to a question on a given theme, in proportion to the number of documents on that theme which are known to be indexed. See also RELEVANCE RATIO.

RE-CASING. The re-insertion of a book into its original cover, with or without re-sewing.

RECEIVING DESK. See CIRCULATION DESK.

RECENSION. A revision. Used to indicate a scholarly edition of a work, for instance of a classic, in which the existing text is thoroughly re-edited, revised and re-examined by collation with all known sources of textual emendation. See also REDACTION.

RECESS PRINTING. Intaglio, photogravure and other processes whereby the ink is obtained from cavities or recesses in the printing plate or cylinder.

RECOMMENDATION CARD. Synonymous with SUGGESTION CARD.

RECOMMENDER. A ratepayer who recommends an applicant for

membership of a lending library as being a fit and proper person to borrow books.

RECOMMENDING COMMITTEE. A (library) committee which recommends its proposals to the local council for approval.

RECORD. A document preserving an account of fact in permanent form.

RECORD OFFICE. An office in which contemporary official records concerning local government and also earlier records relating to the respective area which have been obtained by purchase, gift, or on deposit, are preserved and made available to persons desiring to consult them. *See also* COUNTY RECORD OFFICE.

RECORDACALL. A proprietary installation for automatically receiving on a tape machine telephoned messages, for example the renewal of library books. Similar machines are ANSAPHONE and TEL-STOR (*qq.v.*).

RECORDS. Materials in written or other form setting out facts or events, or otherwise recording information. *See also* ARCHIVES.

RE-COVERING. The process of making a new book cover and affixing it to a volume without re-sewing the sections.

RECTANGULAR STYLE. Bindings executed for Charles II while Samuel Mearne was the Royal Bookbinder. Their design consists of a simple three-line gilt rectangular panel with a crown or similar emblem at each corner. Crimson morocco was mostly used.

RECTO. 1. The right-hand page of an open book or manuscript, usually bearing an odd page number. Sometimes called an uneven page. 2. The first side of a printed or ruled sheet of paper as distinct from the 'verso' which is the reverse side. *See also* VERSO.

RED EDGES. The edges of a book cut, coloured red, and burnished.

RED OCHRE. A powder used by type casters to coat the inner surface of their moulds when casting very small sorts to make the metal flow more easily.

RED PRINTING. Printing in a second colour (usually red) for headings, capitals, etc. This is usually performed on a separate machine after the text has been printed.

RED UNDER GOLD EDGES. The three edges of a book cut, coloured red, and then gilt. *See also* EDGES.

REDACTION. 1. The editing, arranging, or revision for publication of a literary work which was left by the author incomplete or in a state unsuitable for publication. *See also* RECENSION. 2. A new, or revised, edition of a work.

REDCLIFFE–MAUD REPORT. The Report *Management of local government,* named after Committee Chairman Sir John Maud, later Baron Redcliffe-Maud. *See also* MAUD REPORT.

REDUCING. In documentary reproduction, the decrease of the DENSITY or CONTRAST of a negative or print (*Concepts* . . .).

REDUCTION. In documentary reproduction, a copy the scale of which is reduced compared with the ORIGINAL (*q.v.*).

RE-EDITION. A publication which is distinguished from previous editions by changes made in contents (revised edition) or layout (new edition). (*Unesco.*)

REEL FED. A printing press which prints on paper in a reel instead of single sheets.

RE-ENLARGEMENT. An enlarged reproduction from a MICROCOPY (*q.v.*).

'REFER FROM' REFERENCE. An indication, in a list of subject headings, of the headings from which references should be made to the given heading; it is the reverse of the indication of a 'See' or 'See also' reference (*IBM*).

REFERENCE. (*Cataloguing*) 1. A direction from one heading to another. References may be *general* to indicate a class, giving an individual heading only as an example, as

ANIMALS, *see also under the names of animals as* LION.

or *specific* by stating the exact heading to which reference must be made, as,

ANIMALS, *see* LION.

CLEMENS, S. L., *see* TWAIN, MARK.

They may be made between (a) synonymous headings – *see* references, and (b) related headings – *see also* references. 2. A partial registry of a book, omitting the imprint and collation, under subject or title, but referring to the main entry. 3. (*Information retrieval*) An indication referring to a document or passage (*IBM*). *See also* COLLATERAL REFERENCE, DOWNWARD REFERENCE, UPWARD REFERENCE.

REFERENCE ASSISTANT. An assistant librarian, working in a reference library.

REFERENCE BOOKS. 1. Books such as dictionaries, encyclopaedias, gazetteers, year books, directories, concordances, indexes, bibliographies and atlases, which are compiled to supply definite pieces of information of varying extent, and intended to be referred to rather than read through. 2. Books which are kept for reference only and are not allowed to be used outside the building.

REFERENCE CARD. A catalogue card bearing a cross reference. *See also* CROSS REFERENCE.

REFERENCE CENTRE. In the U.S.A., a scheme, which is stimulated through Library Service Act funds, whereby a number of small public libraries in a given geographical area contribute funds to a large library in the area having a good reference library which is willing to expand its resources and services to meet the reference and information needs of enquirers throughout the whole area. 'Information services' and 'bibliographic centres' undertake similar functions.

REFERENCE COLLECTION. A collection of books which may not be borrowed for use outside the library.

REFERENCE CORNER. The junction of the REFERENCE EDGES (*q.v.*), i.e. the bottom left-hand corner of a microcard or microfiche grid.

REFERENCE DEPARTMENT. The department of a library containing books which may not be taken away but are for consultation in the library only.

REFERENCE EDGES. The left-hand and bottom limits of a microfiche or microcard grid.

REFERENCE LIBRARIAN. A librarian in charge of, or undertaking the work of, a reference library.

REFERENCE LIBRARY. A library or department containing books which may not normally be used elsewhere than on the premises.

REFERENCE MARKS. Printers' marks used to indicate references to other books or passages or to footnotes on the page. Where more than one reference is given on a page the order of the marks is as follows: * (asterisk or star), † (dagger or obelisk), ‡ (double dagger or double obelisk), § (section mark), ‖ (parallel mark), ¶ (paragraph mark). If more than six notes are required to a page, these signs are given first in single, then double and afterwards in treble sequence. Letter and figures in alphabetical or numerical order are more often used for the same purpose.

REFERENCE MATERIAL. Books and other library materials which may not be borrowed for use out of the library, either because their nature is such that they are prepared for brief consulation rather than for continuous reading, or because they belong to a reference collection.

REFERENCE MATTER. *See* SUBSIDIARIES.

REFERENCE RETRIEVAL SYSTEM. One which provides a complete reference to a document in response to a general research request. A card catalogue or other index is such a system. An aspect of INFORMATION RETRIEVAL (*q.v.*).

REFERENCE ROOM. *Synonymous with* REFERENCE DEPARTMENT (*q.v.*).

REFERENCE SERVICE. The provision and organization by a library of REFERENCE WORK (*q.v.*).

REFERENCE SERVICES DIVISION. A Division of the ALA since

1956; it is concerned with the improvement and extension of informational, bibliographical and research activities in all types of library, at all levels, and in every subject field: reference materials, enquiries and enquirers, indexes and indexing, bibliographies and bibliographic method. Abbreviated RSD. Publishes *RQ* (q., free to membs.).

REFERENCE SOURCE. Any publication which is used to obtain authoritative information.

REFERENCE, SPECIAL AND INFORMATION SECTION. A Group of the Library Association. It was formed on 6th October 1950 and has as its objects 'to unite members engaged or interested in the work of reference and special libraries and information departments, to foster their interests within the Library Association, and to increase the usefulness of all reference and special libraries and information departments'. There are seven Regional Groups of the Section, formed on a geographical basis.

REFERENCE WORK. 1. That branch of the library's services which includes the assistance given to readers in their search for information on various subjects. 2. The work of the Reference Library. 3. A book, or work, compiled to be referred to rather than for continued reading. 4. Personal assistance given by the librarian to individual readers needing information.

REFLECTOGRAPHY. *Synonymous with* REFLEX COPYING (*q.v.*).

REFLEX COPY. In documentary reproduction, a reproduction of an ORIGINAL (*q.v.*), prepared by the reflection principle of exposure, using 'reflex' materials. (*Concepts . . .*). Also called 'Reflex print'. *See also* REFLEX COPYING.

REFLEX COPYING. A process for reproducing photographically copies of documents which are opaque or printed on both sides. The light-sensitive emulsion on the paper is placed against the document: light is passed through the sensitized paper and reflected back from the light parts of the document – not from the dark or printed parts. The reversed negative which results may then be used to print a positive by transmitted light on the same kind of paper. The apparatus used does not include either a camera or lenses. Many modern methods of documentary reproduction use the reflex principle of exposure but the term 'reflex' is reserved for the negative-positive method described. Stabilized machines which do away with the usual photographic washing and drying routines enable a copy to be produced in about ten seconds but the keeping qualities of such prints are doubtful. Makes of apparatus which enable documents to be copied by this method are Contoura, Copycat and Rutherstat. A print, or copy, made by this method may be called a 'Reflex copy'. Also called 'Reflectography', 'Reflex printing'. *See also* CONTACT PHOTOGRAPHY, PHOTOSTAT.

REFLEX PRINT. *Synonymous with* REFLEX COPY (*q.v.*).

REFLEX PRINTING. *Synonymous with* REFLEX COPYING (*q.v.*).

REGINA MEDAL. Established in 1959 by the (American) Catholic Library Association 'to dramatize its standards for the writing of good literature for children'. The award has been made possible through the generosity of an anonymous donor, and is given without regard to the recipient's religion, country, or birth, or the nature of the contribution (author, publisher, editor, illustrator, etc.) and in recognition of a lifetime contribution to the field of children's literature, which has been most representative of Walter de la Mare's philosophy 'Only the rarest kind of best in anything can be good enough for the young'. It was established in 1959 and was first awarded to Eleanor Farjeon.

REGION. (*County Libraries*) A part of the County Library area including branch libraries, centres, travelling libraries and other facilities administered from a REGIONAL HEADQUARTERS or REGIONAL BRANCH (*qq.v.*). as a library unit within the county library system.

REGIONAL BIBLIOGRAPHIC CENTRE. A clearing house for regional co-operation among library groups in the U.S.A., locating books required and facilitating their loan between libraries, directing research workers and students requiring materials on particular subjects and possibly compiling complete or partial union catalogues.

REGIONAL BIBLIOGRAPHY. *Synonymous with* NATIONAL BIBLIOGRAPHY (*q.v.*).

REGIONAL BRANCH. A library which, because of its larger size and greater resources, answers reference enquiries, supplies bibliographical information, display material, and books in bulk or individually, for a group of smaller libraries in a large county or urban system, as well as serving the public. Sometimes also called a 'Regional library'.

REGIONAL BUREAUX. The offices which act as clearing-houses for requests for particular books which are not in stock where asked for, and pass on the requests to other libraries in their own regional areas. If the books cannot be provided from within these areas, the bureaux forward the requests to the NATIONAL CENTRAL LIBRARY (*q.v.*). Each bureau usually compiles and maintains a catalogue of all the non-fiction books in the libraries within the region and forwards copies of the entries to the National Central Library where they are incorporated in the national union catalogue. The libraries in each bureau area, between them buy all new books appearing in *BNB*, and also as a whole undertake subject specialization in an agreed area of knowledge; since these arrangements became operative nationally, books appearing in *BNB* have not been included in union catalogues.

REGIONAL CATALOGUE. 1. A catalogue of the books in libraries situated in a given geographical region. 2. A catalogue of books relating to, or written by, people living in a given geographical region.

REGIONAL CLASSIFICATION. Classification by place rather than by subject.

REGIONAL HEADQUARTERS. Premises from which, in a county library system, are administered the library service points in its region but at which the public may or may not be served directly. It provides the control, bookstock, postal services and other facilities which are normally available from a county headquarters in a centralized system. *See also* AREA HEADQUARTERS.

REGIONAL LIBRARIAN. One who is responsible for the administration of a REGIONAL BRANCH library, and also the distribution of books to service points in a REGION (*q.v.*) centred on that branch.

REGIONAL LIBRARY. *Synonymous with* REGIONAL BRANCH (*q.v.*).

REGIONAL LIBRARY SYSTEM. *See* REGIONAL BUREAUX.

REGIONAL OFFICER. A librarian who is responsible for the development and administration of all aspects of a county library service throughout a REGION (*q.v.*), but not combining with this the functions of a Branch Librarian. *See also* REGIONAL LIBRARIAN.

REGISTER. 1. The ribbon attached to a volume to serve as a bookmarker. 2. A list of signatures attached to the end of early printed books, or printed above the colophon or on a separate leaf, for the guidance of the folder or binder. A 'registrum'. 3. In printing, a term used when the type area on the recto coincides exactly with that on the back of the verso. The adjustment of colour blocks so that the colours are superimposed with absolute accuracy. Register is of tremendous importance in multi-colour process work. When properly adjusted the work is said to be 'in register', when not, 'out of register'. 4. A catalogue or bibliography; particularly, an official list or enumeration.

REGISTER OF ELECTORS. A printed list of persons who are entitled to vote at a local government or parliamentary election. A new register is prepared each year and comes into force on 16th February. Also called 'Voter's list' and 'Electors' roll'.

REGISTER TABLE. A table with an opaque-glass top and a box-like interior fitted with lights and painted white. It is used to position negatives on positives together with any accompanying type matter, on a layout sheet. It is also used for other purposes, e.g. register work in colour printing. Also called a 'Lining-up Table', 'Shining-up Table'.

REGISTRATION. 1. The process of filing readers' application forms and making out membership tickets. This may be done at one library in a system (centralized registration) or at each library. 2. The entering of particulars of books added to a library in the ACCESSIONS REGISTER.

REGISTRATION CARD. A membership, or identity, card which is issued to members entitling them to use, or borrow books from, a library.

REGISTRATION DEPARTMENT. The unit which is concerned with maintaining records of membership and issuing membership tickets.

REGISTRATION PERIOD. The period during which a REGISTERED READER (*q.v.*) is entitled to use library services before being required to re-register.

REGISTRUM. *See* REGISTER 2.

REGLET. A strip of wood, about the height of leads, used to separate lines of type, thus saving leads, lightening the forme and making it easier to handle. They are chiefly used in poster work. *See also* LEADS.

REGNAL NUMBERS. In Brown's classification, the first divisions of each block of numbers devoted to a country relate to the country's historical development, by reigning monarch or other ruler. These numbers provide for all royal biographies, State papers, histories and special monographs, or any event of a historical nature.

REGULAR FOLIO. *See* FOLIO.

REIMPOSITION. The rearrangement of pages of type matter in a forme, consequent upon the addition of new matter to type already arranged in pages, or to the use of a different type of folding machine.

REINFORCED BINDING. Publisher's binding strengthened by a library bookbinder.

REINFORCED UNION PAPER. UNION PAPER (*q.v.*) which has a lining between the two sheets of which it is made, in order to increase its mechanical strength.

REINFORCING-PIECE. (*Binding*) The paper or parchment, on which for greater strength, the backs of some or all of the sections are sewn, and part of which shows under the paste-downs. *See also* PASTE-DOWN.

RE-ISSUE. A re-publication at a different price, or in a different form, of an impression, or edition, which has already been issued, usually from standing type or plates.

REJECTION SLIP. A printed acknowledgement sent out by a publisher, or magazine editor, when returning a MS. to an author informing him that the MS. has not been accepted for publication.

REJECTS. Copies of printed matter which are rejected by publisher or customer because of inferiorities.

RELATED TITLE. A title which has a relationship to another by being a subsequent book in a series, or a commentary on, or a 'reply to' an earlier work. In the eighteenth century many anonymous pamphlets of this kind were published. Such books are catalogued under their title with an added entry under the title of another book included therein.

RELATED WORK. (*Cataloguing*) A work which has some relationship to another. It may be a continuation, supplement, index, concordance, manual, sequel, scenario, choreography, libretto, special number of a serial, collection of extracts from serials, a work produced by the editorial staff of a serial, or a work in a subseries.

RELATION. A non-periodical pamphlet published in England and describing a battle or some other event. A forerunner of the newspaper. Also called a 'Discourse' or a 'Narration'. *See also* CORANTO, NEWSBOOK.

RELATION MARKS. Symbols used in an agreed order when building up the classification numbers of the UNIVERSAL DECIMAL CLASSIFICATION (*q.v.*) in order to separate the various parts and also to indicate their meaning.

RELATIVE CLASSIFICATION. Classification which shows, as most modern schemes purport to do, the relationships between subjects.

RELATIVE INDEX. An alphabetic index to a classification scheme in which all relationships and aspects of the subject are brought together under each index entry (*IBM*). An index to a scheme of classification also translates a natural language term into a class number; this it does by putting the class number after the natural language term. Such an index is provided for the Dewey Decimal Classification. The indexes to the classification of Cutter and the Library of Congress, and to the *Encyclopaedia Britannica* are relative. *See also* SPECIFIC INDEX.

RELATIVE LOCATION. An arrangement of books according to their relation to each other and regardless of the shelves or rooms in which they are placed and allowing the insertion of new material in its proper relation to that already on the shelves. Also called 'Movable Location'. The opposite of FIXED LOCATION (*q.v.*).

RELATIVE RELIEF MAP. One which shows the relative height of land areas by colour or shading, but not the steepness of slope: this is shown by an AVERAGE SLOPE MAP (*q.v.*).

RELEVANCE RATIO. In information retrieval, the number of documents which are actually wanted in proportion to the number of documents retrieved in response to a question on a given theme. *See also* RECALL RATIO.

RELEVANT CHARACTERISTIC. *Synonymous with* 'essential characteristic'. *See* CHARACTERISTIC OF A CLASSIFICATION.

RELIEF. (*Binding*) Said of a finisher's tool which is made in such a way that the design, when impressed on the leather, appears in relief.

RELIEF MAP. One which represents elevations of the earth's surface by various methods.

RELIEF PRINTING. Printing from characters or designs that are raised above their surrounding surface, such as type, plates, etc., as distinguished from INTAGLIO PRINTING (*q.v.*). It includes woodcuts, wood engravings, zinc etchings, and half-tones.

REMAINDERS. When books have ceased to sell well, the publisher's stock remaining is sold off by auction or at a price, to a bookseller. Such books are then known as remainders.

REMAKE. To re-page a book, either partly or completely. To re-arrange typographic elements in a page or publication.

REMARQUE PROOF. *See* ARTIST'S PROOF.

REMFLEX. A copying unit made by Remington Rand; it incorporates both the processing equipment and the light box in which the exposure is made.

REMOVAL SLIP. A card inserted in a catalogue to indicate that an entry has been removed for alteration. It bears sufficient information for the book to be identified, and indicates the whereabouts of the permanent card.

REMOVES. Quotations, passages or notes set, usually at the foot of a page, and in smaller type than that of the text.

RENAISSANCE ORNAMENT. (*Binding*) Conventional decorative ornament, apparently suggested by columns, urns, vases, beasts, birds, garlands and foliage which appear in Renaissance architecture.

RENEW. To extend the period (a) for which a book or other item is on loan; (b) during which a library membership ticket is valid; (c) for supplying a periodical on subscription.

RENEWAL. 1. The extension of the time allowed to the same borrower for reading a book. 2. The re-registration of a reader at the expiry of a period of library membership.

RENEWAL SLIP. A form on which is recorded information necessary to renew a loan or a membership ticket.

RENTAL BOOK. A book which is in the stock of a DUPLICATE PAY COLLECTION (*q.v.*).

RENTAL CARD. 1. A membership card on which loans from a DUPLI-CATE PAY COLLECTION (*q.v.*) are issued. 2. A book card for a book in such a collection.

RENTAL COLLECTION. *Synonymous with* DUPLICATE PAY COLLEC-TION (*q.v.*).

RENTAL FEE. A payment made to borrow a book from a DUPLICATE PAY COLLECTION (*q.v.*).

REPAIRING. The repair of a worn binding including restoring the cover and reinforcing the joints. Not to be confused with MENDING (*q.v.*).

REPERTORY CATALOGUE. A catalogue of books in more than one library.

REPLACEMENT. 1. A book bought to take the place of a worn out copy of the same title. 2. The routine involved in substituting a volume for one which has been withdrawn.

REPLICA. A copy or reproduction of a work of art, especially one made by the artist himself, and assumed to be of equal quality to the original. A doublette. A facsimile or nearly exact copy.

REPLIKA. The trade name of a particular firm's photo-lithographic process.

REPORT. A publication giving a formal or official record, as of the activities of a committee or corporate body, or of some special investigation, or the proceedings of a governmental body. *See also* TECHNICAL REPORT.

REPORTING COMMITTEE. A (library) committee which reports its actions (within the limit of the powers delegated to it – *see* DELEGATION OF POWERS) to the local council.

REPRESENTATIVE FRACTION. The ratio between distance measured on a map and the corresponding distance on the ground. Thus a map on the scale 1 inch to 1 mile has a representative fraction of 1 : 63,360 there being 63,360 inches in a mile.

REPRINT. 1. A copy of a book, made from the same type or stereotype as the original, with which it is identical except for possibly a new title-page and a note on the verso of the title-page of the number and date of reprinting and the correction of minor errors. *See also* EDITION, FACSIMILE REPRINT, FIRST EDITION, IMPRESSION, ISSUE, NEW EDITION, REVISED EDITION, SEPARATE. 2. Setting up type and printing again, using a previous printing as 'copy' as distinct from manuscript 'copy'. 3. A contribution to a periodical, afterwards issued separately, though not necessarily from the same type as the original. Sometimes called a SEPARATE (*q.v.*).

REPRINT SERIES. A series of books, which have been published previously by one or more publishers, in the same format by one publisher and bearing a series name. The books need not be related in either subject matter or treatment. *See also* PUBLISHER'S SERIES.

REPRINTED ARTICLE. One which has been reprinted, but with its own pagination. *See also* SEPARATE.

REPROGRAPHIC MARKING. The reprographic transfer of workshop drawings directly on to the materials, e.g. sheets of metal, to be fashioned (*Concepts* . . .).

REPROGRAPHY. The reproduction in facsimile of documents of all kinds by any process using light, heat or electric radiation – photocopies, micro-copies, blueprints, electro-copies, thermo-copies, etc.; also reproduction by methods of duplicating and office printing.

REPUBLICATION. 1. The re-issuing of a publication by a publisher other than the original, without changes in the text. Sometimes used of reprints made in another country. 2. Broadly, re-issuing a work, with or without textual changes, or as a new edition.

REQUEST CARD. *Synonymous with* SUGGESTION CARD (*q.v.*).

REQUEST FORM. A form, or card distributed to the users of a special library to request information or material from the library. It can be so designed as to show the progress of steps taken to meet the request, record the borrowing of material from another library and record the loan of material to the user.

REQUISITION CARD. *Synonymous with* SUGGESTION CARD (*q.v.*).

REQUISITION FORM. *Synonymous with* CALL SLIP (*q.v.*).

RE-REGISTRATION. The re-registering (automatic or otherwise) of persons whose library tickets have expired.

RESEARCH BOOK. In film studio research libraries, a scrapbook made up of sketches, abstracts, and other information relating to the settings, architecture, costumes, etc., which are gathered in advance of the production of a particular picture in order to ensure that the presentation is historically and artistically accurate.

RESEARCH CARREL. *Synonymous with* CARREL (*q.v.*).

RESEARCH LIBRARIAN. A title often used in respect of the librarian in a special library who undertakes the work of a RESEARCH SERVICE (*q.v.*) as distinct from one who undertakes the work normally carried out in a reference library. *See also* INFORMATION OFFICER.

RESEARCH SERVICE. A service rendered by special librarians by examining, appraising and summarizing information obtained from written sources and from individuals and organizations considered to be authorities in the appropriate fields. This implies giving the solutions to problems, providing statistics and other information as distinct from supplying publications from which the information may be obtained. The information assembled is usually presented in tabular, report or memorandum form. Also called 'Search service'. *See also* LITERATURE SEARCH.

RESEARCH STALL. *Synonymous with* CARREL (*q.v.*).

RESEARCH TICKET. *Synonymous with* SUPPLEMENTARY TICKET (*q.v.*).

RESERVATION. A request for a specific book or other item to be reserved for a reader as soon as it becomes available on completion of processing, or on its return from the binder or another reader.

RESERVE CARD (FORM, SLIP). A card on which borrowers enter particulars of books to be retained for them when available for borrowing.

RESERVE COLLECTION. 1. Library materials for which there is infrequent demand and which consequently is not kept on open shelves, but individual items of which are obtained on request. 2. In academic libraries, material which is in great demand because of being placed on reading lists and set on one side for very short limited periods, or for an academic term, and then only for use on the premises or overnight.

RESERVED BOOK. One which after having been returned by another reader is held on payment of any necessary fee for a certain length of time at a reader's request and until he can call and collect it for home reading. S.8 (2) of the Public Libraries and Museums Act, 1964 provides for the making of a charge for notifying readers that books and other articles reserved are available for borrowing.

RESERVOIR LIBRARY. *Synonymous with* STORAGE CENTRE (*q.v.*).

RE-SET EDITION. One printed from newly set type but without revision of the text.

RE-SETTING. Setting type again, because of corrections, additions, changes of layout, etc.

RESIST. A coating of glue, enamel or shellac used to protect a plate from acid corrosion during the etching process.

RESKA SHELVING. Trade name for a design of Danish bracket type shelving. Shelves are supported on brackets which fit into slots in wall uprights or the central pillars of island stacks. The brackets serve as book ends; book supports fit into the under sides of shelves and slide easily from one end to the other. Fittings are available to display periodicals, with or without storage for back numbers behind the current numbers.

RESOLUTION. In documentary reproduction, the measure of the ability of an emulsion to record fine line detail or of a lens to record minute lines or points clearly, distinctly and separately (*Concepts*). Also called 'Resolving power'.

RESOLVING POWER. *Synonymous with* RESOLUTION (*q.v.*).

RESOURCES AND TECHNICAL SERVICES DIVISION. A Division of the American Library Association since 1957; it is responsible for these activities: acquisition, identification, cataloguing, classification and preservation of library materials, development and co-ordination of America's library resources; those areas of selection and evaluation involved in the acquisition of library materials and pertinent to the development of library resources. Has several sections and groups. Abbreviated RTSD. Publishes *Library Resources and Technical Services* (q., free to membs.).

RESPONDENT. The candidate for a degree who, in an academical disputation, defends a tenet or thesis against the objections proposed by the PRAESES (*q.v.*). The respondent is also called the defendant.

REPRODUCTION PROOFS. Proofs of exceptional cleanliness and sharpness to be used as copy for reproduction.

RESTORATION STYLE. *Synonymous with* MEARNE STYLE (*q.v.*).

RESTRICTED LOAN. A loan of library material with some form of limitation, as on period of loan, or number of volumes allowed at one time.

RET. The second side of a sheet of paper.

RETOUCHING. 1. Hand etching or improvements carried out to a photographic print or negative used in PROCESS ENGRAVING (*q.v.*). 2. The hand-correcting of colour separations used in the photo-engraving and photo-lithographic processes. Called 'Dot-etching' in America.

RETREE. Slightly defective sheets of paper. Derived from the French *retiré*, 'withdrawn'.

RETRIEVAL. 1. The act of finding again, recovery, retrospective searching and securing of documents. The act of going to a specific location or area and returning therefrom with an object or document (*IBM*). 2. The act and means of obtaining (a) facts and other information which is recorded and indexed in some way by subject, or (b) the documents containing the required facts. *See also* RETRIEVAL DEVICE.

RETRIEVAL DEVICE. A record of documents or information which is consulted in order to obtain what is needed and recorded as being in the STORE (*q.v.*). An abstracts journal, a text-book, a library catalogue, a mechanical selector or an electronic data processor used to select documentary information, are all retrieval devices.

RETRIEVAL SYSTEM. A sequence of actions which result in obtaining (retrieving) required information. The system requires such components as a SELECTOR (*q.v.*) which enables the information to be identified in the STORE (*q.v.*).

RETRO-ACTIVE NOTATION. (*Classification*) 1. A NOTATION (*q.v.*) in which FACET INDICATORS (*q.v.*) and intra-facet connectors are eliminated by using one species of characters indicating the construction of the notation (and thereby the subject matter of the material) in reverse order to the schedules. 2. A notation in which compounds are specified merely by adding earlier numbers to later ones. The notation to Dewey's Decimal Classification is of this kind, where, e.g. the form number 08 is used as a facet indicator to indicate the literary form in which a work is presented.

RETROSPECTIVE BIBLIOGRAPHY. A bibliography which lists books published in previous years as distinct from a 'current' bibliography which records books recently published. Also called a 'Closed bibliography'. *See also* BIBLIOGRAPHY.

RETURN DESK. *See* CIRCULATION DESK.

RETURNS. Unsold publications which are returned by a bookseller to the publisher. Also called 'Crabs'.

rev. Abbreviation for revise, revised, revision. *See also* REVISED EDITION.

REVENUE STAMPS. Stamps which were stuck on English newspapers in accordance with the Stamp Act, 1712. The paper had to be stamped before printing. The duty was the same irrespective of the size of the newspaper, and the Act, which was repealed in 1855, consequently had the effect of increasing the size of newspapers.

REVERSAL MICROFILM. In documentary reproduction, sensitized material which gives by a reversal process a POSITIVE COPY (*q.v.*) only from a positive ORIGINAL (*q.v.*).

REVERSAL PROCESS. Developing in such a manner that the material exposed in the camera shows a positive instead of a negative image. Developing is carried out in the ordinary way until a negative silver image appears but instead of fixing this, the developed material is put into a bleaching bath which dissolves the silver reduced by the developer but leaves the silver bromide unchanged. The whole is then exposed to the light and again developed, only the silver bromide left after the first development being blackened. In this way a positive image is obtained. The reversal process is used extensively in colour photography, in amateur film photography, and for producing duplicate negatives.

REVERSE BROWNE. A method of issuing books which is similar to the BROWNE BOOK CHARGING SYSTEM (*q.v.*) but which uses a pocket book-card and a card ticket.

REVERSE COVER.   The lower cover of a book, i.e. that nearest to the last leaf. Also called 'Back cover', 'Lower cover'. *See also* OBVERSE COVER.

REVIEW.   1. A periodical publication which is devoted largely to critical articles and reviews of new books. 2. An evaluation of a literary work published in a periodical or newspaper. *See also* OMNIBUS REVIEW.

REVIEW COPY.   A copy of a book sent by the publisher to a newspaper or magazine for the favour of a review. Sometimes called 'Press copy'.

REVIEW DATE.   The date of commencement of the Public Libraries and Museums Act 1964, i.e. 1 April 1965. This date, or a date falling within ten years thereof, or any subsequent review date regulates the period on or during which the Secretary of State may, under s. 6 of the Public Libraries and Museums Act 1964, provide by order that a non-county borough or an urban district with a population of less than 40,000, shall cease to be a library authority. *See also* APPENDIX 3.

REVISE.   *See* PROOF.

REVISED EDITION.   A new edition of a book in which errors have been corrected, and possibly new material added. Sometimes wrongly called 'Enlarged edition'. *See also* EDITION, FIRST EDITION, IMPRESSION, ISSUE, NEW EDITION, REPRINT.

REVISED PROOF.   *See* PROOF.

REVISING SHELVES.   *Synonymous with* READING SHELVES (*q.v.*).

REVOLVING BOOKCASE.   One having shelves on four sides; built around a central cylinder it rotates in either direction on a spindle.

RIBBON ARRANGEMENT.   A method of arranging books in a public library with non-fiction on upper shelves and novels on lower shelves, or vice versa, or novels on middle shelves and non-fiction above and below, the object being to disperse the readers around the library and avoid congestion at the fiction shelves.

RICE PAPER.   Paper made from the pith of a small tree, *Aralia* (also *Fatsia*) *papyrifera*, grown in Formosa.

RIDER.   An additional MS. added to a proof.

RIDER SLIP.   *Synonymous with* PROCESS SLIP (*q.v.*).

RIDGE.   One of the two projections along the sides of a rounded and backed volume against which the board is fitted. Also called 'Flange' or 'Shoulder'. (American.) *See also* BINDING EDGE.

RIGHT.   The printer often needs to know which is the right side of a sheet of paper owing to differences in surface, and the undesirable effect of using sheets laid one way mixed with those laid another way in the same publication. Flat papers are usually packed with the right side uppermost; if folded, the right side is outside. In hand-made papers, the right side touches the wire cover of the mould; the 'wire' side is therefore known as the right side. In blue and azure papers the right side is usually darker than the other. In machine-made papers, it is the upper side which is the right side, i.e. the one on which the couch roll acts and not the wire. A WATERMARK (*q.v.*), in both hand-made and machine-made paper is read from the right side. Thus, it can be taken that in hand-made papers, the 'wire' side is the right side, but in machine-made papers this is the wrong side.

RIGHT READING. (*Reprography*). An image which is legible in a normal reading position as opposed to being LATERALLY REVERSED (*q.v.*).

RIGHTS. The privileges of entitlement to permit the publication, performance, or adaptation of authorship and receive payment for same. *Volume rights* give the publisher 'the exclusive rights to publish a work in volume form' within the territorial area for which he makes himself responsible. These include the right to reprint in paperback form, in book club or school editions, or to negotiate these on behalf of the author. Digest rights, ONE SHOT (*q.v.*) rights and anthology rights – are also included. *Subsidiary rights* include foreign publication, and film, TV, translation, serial, dramatic and mechanical reproduction rights; these may or may not be handled by the original publisher of the work.

RIGID CLASSIFICATION. 1. The classification of books relative to their positions on shelves rather than according to a scheme of book classification. Such methods of classification were used before the formation of modern schemes of bibliographical classification, and resulted in the allocation of numbers to books according to the shelf, in a given tier of a particular press, or alcove, in a specific room. Another form of rigid classification is the arrangement of books in broad subjects according to size and accession number. 2. The characterization of each document from a single point of view and thereby the allocation of only one classification symbol to it. When a document is shelved or stored, and only one copy is available, one single physical location must be provided: this is indicated by a symbol representing one point of view, usually the most important, or major, one. Sometimes called a 'Pigeonhole classification'. *See also* MULTI-DIMENSIONAL CLASSIFICATION.

RINCO PROCESS. Trade name of a gravure printing process.

RISING SPACE. *Synonymous with* WORK UP (*q.v.*).

RISING TYPE. Type which rises up in the forme, usually in the centre, when locked up too tightly. Spaces and quads rise and print through poor justification or loose lock-up.

RIVER. What appears to be a streak of white running vertically or diagonally through printed matter. It is caused by spaces between words occurring almost one below the other in several lines of type. Rivers are avoided by re-setting the type and varying the spacing or placing a very short word on a line above or below.

ROAN. A thin sheepskin used for binding books.

ROBERTS COMMITTEE. *See* ROBERTS REPORT.

ROBERTS REPORT. Popular name for the Report of the 'Roberts Committee' which was set up by the Minister of Education in September 1957 under the chairmanship of Sir Sydney Roberts, 'to consider the structure of the Public Library Service in England and Wales, and to advise what changes, if any, should be made in the administrative arrangements, regard being had to the relation of public libraries to other libraries'. The Report is entitled *The Structure of the Public Library Service in England and Wales*, 1959. Cmnd. 660. This Report resulted in the setting up of working parties by the Minister of Education in 1961. *See also* BAKER REPORT, BOURDILLON REPORT, PUBLIC LIBRARIES AND MUSEUMS BILL, PUBLIC LIBRARIES AND MUSEUMS ACT 1964.

ROBINSON MEDAL. Awarded to firms and individuals – librarians or not – for originality shown in devising new and improved methods in library technology and any aspect of library administration. Funds for the award come from a bequest by the late Mr. Frederick Robinson, formerly Deputy Librarian at Colchester who left to the Library Association a trust fund from the proceeds of which a Medal and one hundred guineas are awarded at intervals. The Award was first made in 1969 to Mansell Information/Publishing Ltd. who have been responsible for the development of an automatic camera and associated techniques for use in producing book catalogues from library cards or other sequential material. The unique camera used was built to Mansell's specification by the Williamson Manufacturing Company Ltd. of Willesden, who had previously been responsible for the special cameras which had enabled Balding and Mansell to produce the 263-volume *British Museum general catalogue of printed books*. The experience gained with this publication and also with the *Union list of serials* was applied to the related problems of the Library of Congress *National union catalog: pre-1956 imprints* which forms a

18*

series of some 610 large volumes each of over 700 pages recording details that had previously existed only on 12¾ million cards.

ROLE DIRECTORS. *See* ROLES.

ROLE FACTORS. *See* ROLES.

ROLE INDICATORS. *See* ROLES.

ROLES. In CO-ORDINATE INDEXING (*q.v.*), generally but not necessarily, symbols appended to terms or term numbers and thereby narrowing the definition of the terms by designating the role of a word in its context. They describe the use of a term in its context, not how terms are related. Also called 'Modifiers', 'Modulants', 'Role factors', 'Role directors', 'Role indicators', 'Scope notes'.

ROLL. 1. A bookbinder's tool consisting of a brass wheel about 3 inches in diameter secured in a long handle which rests against the shoulder when being used. The edge of the wheel is engraved so as to impress a continuous line or repeating pattern as it revolves under pressure. Also called 'Fillet'. 2. The design impressed by the tool referred to. *See also* SCROLL, TOOLING.

ROLL CASSETTE. A light-proof container for roll film on a spool. Also called a 'Roll magazine'.

ROLL MAGAZINE. *Synonymous with* 'ROLL CASSETTE' (*q.v.*).

ROLL MICROFILM. Microcopies on roll film as distinct from those on sheet microfilm, as MICROFICHE (*q.v.*).

ROLLED EDGES. Edges of book covers decorated with a roll, or 'roulette', a finishing tool having a brass wheel with a design on its rim.

ROLLER SHELVES. Deep shelves which rest on a series of rollers or ball bearings and are drawn out so that folio volumes such as bound volumes of newspapers can be lifted off instead of being dragged off with possible damage to the binding. Also a series of rollers placed horizontally behind one another and which support large books; they revolve on their spindles as the volumes are pushed on and off.

ROLLING BOOKCASE. A metal bookcase secured to a framework on wheels, which runs on metal rails or wheels, and placed as close as possible to others side by side, so as to permit maximum storage in a book stack. The bookcases are rolled from one position to another to permit access to the books. *See also* COMPACT STORAGE, COMPACTUS.

ROLLING PRESS. 1. A bookcase suspended from overhead tracks or running on rails let into the floor enabling cases to be placed very close together and pulled out to permit consultation of the books. 2. A hand press, for printing from incised or etched plates. Power is applied by passing the plate and paper, covered by thick blankets, between oak rollers held in a rigid frame. The upper roller which is turned by a capstan, carries the plate through the press.

ROLSON. *See* ROTARY CARD FILE.

ROL-STAR. *See* ROTARY CARD FILE.

Rom. Abbreviation for ROMAN (*q.v.*).

ROMAINS DU ROI. A series of roman and italic types made for use in the Royal Printing Office of Louis XIV in the Palace of the Louvre, Paris, between 1694 and 1745. They were based on drawings which accompanied a report made to Louis XIV, and are characterized by being condensed letters with thin, flat, unbracketed serifs. Designed by Philippe Grandjean, they were first used in 1742 for *Médailles sur la événements du règne de Louis-le-Grand*.

ROMAN. Ordinary type as distinct from italic, being vertical instead of sloping and having graduated thick and thin strokes and serifs. It is based on the Italian Humanistic or Neo-Caroline hand of the fifteenth century and was first used by Adolf Rusch in Strasbourg in 1464, and perfected by Johannes da Spira, a German who used roman type for the first book to be printed in Venice, in 1469, and by Nicholas Jenson, a Frenchman, also in Venice, 1470. The use of roman types was greatly expanded in Italy in the last quarter of the fifteenth century; they may be divided into three main groups, VENETIAN TYPE, OLD FACE and MODERN FACE (*qq.v.*). Written in full, or in its abbreviated form 'Rom', the word 'Roman' is used on printer's copy or on a proof to indicate that the matter is to be set up in Roman type. This book is set in Roman. *See also* ANTIQUA, EGYPTIAN, ITALIC, ROMAN NUMERALS, TRANSITIONAL, TYPE FACE.

ROMAN À CLEF. A novel in which one or more characters are based on real people but are given fictitious names.

ROMAN INDEX. *See* INDEX LIBRORUM PROHIBITORUM.

ROMAN NUMERALS. Capital letters which are used as numbers in books for chapter headings and for the designation of part numbers, appendixes, on title-pages for date of publication, etc., and in lower-case italic form for the pagination of preliminary pages. The roman capitals most commonly in use as numerals are:

1	5	10	50	100	500	1000
I	V	X	L	C	D	M

A complete sequence to 20 in small capitals is: I, II, III, IV, V, VI, VII, VIII, IX, X, XI, XII, XIII, XIV, XV, XVI, XVII, XVIII, XIX, XX, and in tens from 30 to 100: XXX, XL, L, LX, LXX, LXXX, XC, C. The numerals from x to xx indicate the method of building numbers. Italic figures 1 to 20 are: *i, ii, iii, iv, v, vi, vii, viii, ix, x, xi, xii, xiii, xiv, xv, xvi, xvii, xviii, xix, xx*. Combinations of numbers are made up by addition and subtraction, e.g. XX = 20; XIX = 19; XXIV = 24; MCMLVII = 1957. 1000 was first represented by the Greek letter, *phi* Φ, which in lettering and in architectural inscription became CIƆ; this soon became M. 500 was half a *phi*, a IƆ, and soon became D. 100 was represented by the symbol θ *(theta)* which became Ϛ then C, and 50 by the Chalcidian form of the letter *chi* Ѱ which became ⊥ and later L. The following table includes most of the known numerals.

B	300	CCƆ	5000
C	100	L	50
CIƆ	1000	M	1000
CIƆCIƆ	2000	N	900
D	500	Q	500
E	250	R	80
F	40	T	160
G	400	V	5
H	200	X	10
I	1	Ҳ	1000
IƆ	500	∞	1000

A bar or dash placed over a letter increases its value a thousand times. Roman numerals were used by the earliest fifteenth-century printers because they had no arabic figures, and were normally used in early printed books. *See also* CHRONOGRAM.

ROMANIZATION. The representation of 'picture writing' characters, such as Chinese, Japanese and Korean in the Roman alphabet. *See also* TRANSLITERATION.

ROMANTIC STYLE. A bookbinding decoration with an informal, non-classical style in which fancy predominates.

RONDE. An upright angular form of script type. Being based on a French manuscript it has the appearance of upright handwriting.

RONEO, to. To duplicate, using a wax stencil on a machine with a rotating cylinder to which the stencil is attached. So named after the proprietary make of machine, RONEO.

ROTAPRINT. An offset lithographic printing and duplicating machine made by the Rotaprint Co.

ROTARY CAMERA. *Synonymous with* CONTINUOUS FLOW CAMERA *(q.v.)*.

ROTARY CARD FILE. A filing cabinet in which cards are placed on their edges in a wheel- or drum-like container. The container revolves on an axle in the side of the drum in such a way that the cards are always on their edges, those in the lower half being prevented from falling out by a fixed retaining strap of webbing or other material. Up to four containers may be placed side by side in a cabinet. 'Rolson' and 'Rol-star' are trade names for files of this kind. Another type consists of large round trays which revolve on a pivot, each tray being divided up so as to provide several rows of cards side by side. Each fitting or cabinet will hold up to five such trays one above another. 'Kraft Rotacol' and 'Cardmaster' are trade names of units employing this principle.

ROTARY GRAVURE. *Synonymous with* ROTOGRAVURE (*q.v.*).

ROTARY PRESS. A style of press that prints from curved electrotype or stereotype plates held on a cylinder, the paper being fed from a continuous roll and passing between this cylinder and another one which makes the impression. It is used for printing newspapers, periodicals or large editions and occasionally for books of a large run. There are also 'sheet-fed rotary presses'. All printing presses are rotary in principle except the flat-bed press and the platen press which are largely used in letterpress work. Where printing is done from the original flat forme on an endless web of paper, this is called a 'flat-bed web press'. Also called a 'Web press' when the paper is fed from a continuous reel. *See also* CYLINDER PRESS, FLAT-BED PRESS, PLATEN PRESS.

ROTATED CATALOGUE. A classified catalogue in which entries are made under each integral part of the classification symbol, instead of making an entry under the class number with merely references from headings or parts comprising the composite symbol. Also called 'Cyclic classified catalogue'.

ROTATED ENTRY. An entry in an index to documents, or a classified catalogue, where full information and not merely a reference is given under each heading.

ROTATED INDEX. An index to a catalogue of documents classified by a faceted classification whereby entries are made under every heading and inverted heading which comprises part of the classification symbol. Also called 'Cyclic index'.

ROTATED INDEXING. The indexing of documents classified by a faceted classification whereby a full entry, and not a reference, is made under each heading representing, or being, a part of the classification symbol. Also called 'Cyclic indexing'.

ROTATIONAL INDEXING. The making of a CORRELATIVE INDEX

(*q.v.*) wherein each term is 'rotated' so as to file in the first position (*IBM*).

ROTOFOTO PHOTO-TYPESETTING MACHINE.   A British mach-ine incorporating a standard Monotype keyboard. It was invented by George Westover of London and announced in 1948.

ROTOGRAVURE.   1. An intaglio or photogravure printing process for rotary presses, in which the impression is obtained from an etching made on a copper cylinder revolving in ink. 2. An illustration produced by this process.

ROTUNDA.   *See* GOTHIC, TYPE.

ROUGH.   Rag paper that has not been given a finish. *See also* FINISH, HOT-PRESSED, NOT.

ROUGH CALF.   A calf skin prepared with a nap similar to suede leather; used for bookbinding from the seventeenth century.

ROUGH EDGES.   A widely used term to indicate paper with rough edges whether because they are UNCUT (*q.v.*) or a result of the way the paper was made. *See also* DECKLE EDGES.

ROUGH GILT EDGES.   A book which has been 'cut rough' and the edges gilded, or which has been cut solid and gilded before sewing so that when the book is later sewn the edges are slightly uneven. This method has been widely used by English binders, specially by non-trade binders who dislike the solid-block-of-metal appearance of solid gilding. *See also* GILT ON THE ROUGH, MARBLING UNDER GILT, SOLID GILT.

ROUGH PULL.   *Synonymous with* FLAT PULL (*q.v.*).

ROULETTE.   *Synonymous with* FILLET (*q.v.*).

ROUND BACK.   1. The back of a thin booklet of which the folded sheets have been inserted inside each other and wire-stitched, sewn, or corded to the cover from the centre. 2. A book which has been rounded during the binding process and so given the familiar round back. The opposite of 'Flat back'. *See also* BACKING, FLAT BACK, ROUNDING.

ROUND BRACKETS.   *Synonymous with* PARENTHESES (*q.v.*).

ROUND LETTER.   *See* ANTIQUA.

ROUNDED CORNERS.   In library bookbinding the sharp corners of the boards are sometimes cut and slightly rounded as a preventative against wear.

ROUNDEL.   (*Binding*) A decoration consisting of a double ring, usually with a centre dot.

ROUNDING.   The bookbinding process which gives the book a convex spine – and consequently concave fore-edges. It is achieved by a for-warder hammering the spine of a book, after it has been sewn and had its first coat of glue, with a round-headed hammer while gripped between backing boards at the same time as the book is backed. This operation can be done by machine. In Britain and America books are backed (to provide joints) as well as rounded. In most European countries backing is seldom done, with the result that there are no joints. *See also* BACKING, FLAT BACK, ROUND BACK.

ROUNDLET. A small circle in gold used by bookbinders' finishers as part of a book's decoration.

ROUTINE. (*Information retrieval*) A set of coded instructions arranged in proper sequence in order to direct the computer to perform a desired operation or sequence of operations. A subdivision of a programme consisting of two or more instructions that are related functionally – for this reason, a PROGRAMME (*q.v.*).

ROUTINE SLIP. *Synonymous with* PROCESS SLIP (*q.v.*).

ROUTING. (*Printing*) Cutting away mechanically the non-printing areas of a half-tone or line block.

ROUTING. The systematic circulation of periodicals or other printed material among the staff or officers of a library or organization in accordance with their interests in order to keep them informed of new developments. *Automatic routing* is the sending of each issue as soon as it is received to a pre-arranged list of persons. *Selective routing*, or *selective circulation*, is sending articles and publications individually selected by a reader (*see* READER 3) on the basis of an individual's known interests to the individual, usually with an ATTENTION NOTE (*q.v.*). *Circular routing* is the sending of a periodical to all who need it before it is returned to the library: this is achieved by sticking to the cover a slip with the names of persons and/or departments for rapid perusal; such slips may bear a space for the insertion of the date of onward transmission. *Radial routing* (also called *controlled circulation*) ensures that the periodical is returned to the library by each reader before it is passed on to another reader. This method enables the librarian to keep better control of loans. *See also* ROUTING SLIP, SELECTIVE ROUTING.

ROUTING SLIP. A slip pasted on to the cover of a periodical and bearing the names of the persons (possibly with space for dates of sending) to whom it is to go. *See also* ATTENTION NOTE, ROUTING.

ROXBURGHE BINDING. A book with plain black leather back, without raised bands, lettered in gold near the top within a border, having cloth or paper sides, and leaves gilt at top otherwise untrimmed. So named after the third Duke of Roxburghe (Scotland), a famous book collector who adopted this style for the books in his library.

ROYAL. A sheet of printing paper measuring 20 × 25 inches.

ROYAL COMMISSION ON HISTORICAL MANUSCRIPTS. *See* HISTORICAL MANUSCRIPTS COMMISSION.

ROYALTY. Payment made to an author by the publisher of a book, the basis being calculated as an agreed percentage of the retail price of the book, and paid half-yearly in respect of every copy of the book sold.

RUB. A representation of the back or sides of a book showing the lettering, bands, decoration, etc. It is done by firmly holding a piece of paper or tracing linen over the part of the binding of which an impression is to be made, and rubbing with a cobbler's heel-ball, lead pencil or soft crayon all over it until a recognizable copy of all details of the back or sides of the volume is obtained.

RUB-OFF. Printing ink which has rubbed on to the fingers from a printed sheet which has not dried sufficiently.

RUBBER BACK BINDING. A binding in which the folds of the sections are cut off and the spine dipped in rubber solution before insertion in the cover.

RUBBING. *See* RUB.

RUBRIC. 1. The heading of a chapter, section or other division of a book, and catchwords or marginal index words printed or written in red (the remainder of the text being in black), or otherwise distinguished in lettering, as a guide to the contents of pages. 2. A particular passage so marked.

RUBRICATED. A book in which rubrics have been used.

RUBRICATION. 1. Underlining in red the filing entries on the tracings on standard printed catalogue cards or slips. Sometimes a red diagonal line leads from the upper left-hand corner to lead the eye to the underlining. 2. The carrying out of rubrics.

RUBRISHER. One who carried out rubrication, or the plain painting of the large initial letters at the commencement of chapters of MSS. or early printed books, in red and blue. *See also* RUBRIC.

RUBY ENGLISH. English in which every word has one, and only one, conceptual meaning, and each concept has only a single word to describe it. Terms proposed by S. Newman of the U.S. Patent Office to develop certain index codes (*IBM*). *See also* MODULANT.

RULE. A strip of metal used to print lines; it is of type height of varying thickness (hair, fine, medium, 1½, 3, 4, 6, 12 point) with a face finished to a continuous line or lines. Rules which are placed at right angles to form frames or borders are said to be abutted or mitred according to whether the ends of the rules are square or mitred at an angle of 45°. A rule may also be designed to print dots or patterns. A SWELLED RULE is a line which is wide in the middle and tapers to a fine point at each end. *See also* DOTTED RULE, DOUBLE RULE.

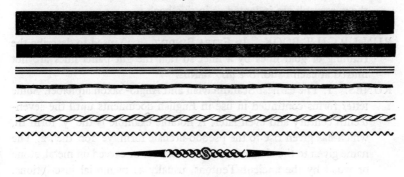

RULE BORDER. (*Printing*) A frame, made up of rules, fitted around a page of type. Also called 'Rule frame'. *See also* BOX.

RULE FRAME. *Synonymous with* RULE BORDER (*q.v.*).

RULES AND REGULATIONS. Regulations are made by a local authority for the admission of the public to, and for the safety and use of, every library, museum and art gallery under its control. Regulations do not require confirmation by the Secretary of State for Education as do bye-laws, or by any other authority.

RUN. A machinist's term for a number of impressions taken from a forme, or plate, at one time. On completion, the job is said to be 'run-off'.

RUN-AROUND. Variation of length of lines of type to fit around blocks.

RUN ON. 1. A term, used in manuscripts and proof reading, to indicate to the printer that printed matter must be continuous and not broken up into paragraphs. This indication is marked by a line joining the end of one piece of matter to the beginning of the next and the writing of 'run on' in the margin. 2. To let a printing press continue to print sheets after the printing order has been completed. Sheets so printed 'run on cost' and involve little more than charges for paper and machine time.

RUN-ON CARD. A catalogue card which bears the continuation of an entry on the previous card. The heading is usually repeated on successive cards which are numbered 'Card 1', 'Card 2', etc. Also called 'Extension card'.

RUN-ON CHAPTERS. Chapters which do not start on a new page but run on at the end of the previous chapter. This is a style used in cheap bookwork.

RUN OUT AND INDENTED. A style of typesetting where the first line is set to the full measure and the second and subsequent lines of the paragraph are indented as in this book.

RUN OVER. The continuation of matter on to another page.

RUN-UP GILT BOOK. In EXTRA BINDING (*q.v.*), used to describe the running of gold lines by a fillet so that the gilt panel lines are not mitred at each band. *See also* BANDS.

RUNES. 1. The earliest Scandinavian and Anglo-Saxon alphabet. Some letter forms continued in use in English documents until the seventeenth century and even later. A notable example is the 'y' form th, which has given rise to the pseudo-archaic form 'ye' for 'the'. 2. The name given to the characters which were cut or carved on metal, stone or wood by the ancient Teutons, usually as memorial inscriptions, but also for divination and for messages, and for carving the name of the artist or for the owner of weapons or ornaments. Runic characters were used for secular documents; amongst the more important runic manuscripts are: the old Danish legal MS., *Codex Runicus* (end 13th century), *Fasti Danici* (*c.* 1348), *Codex Leidensis* at Leyden, the *Codex Sangallensis* (878) at St. Gallen, and the *Codex Salisburgensis* (140). The old name of the Runic alphabet was 'futhark' or 'futhorc'.

RUNIC LETTERS. The 'national' writing of the ancient Germanic peoples; the characters have thorny, elongated and angular shapes.

RUNNERS. Figures or letters printed for reference purposes at regular intervals down the margins of a book and against lines of type to indicate the particular number or position of any given line. This is usually done in long poems or in school texts of plays or of texts in foreign languages.

RUNNING HEADLINE (RUNNING HEAD). *Synonymous with* RUNNING TITLE (*q.v.*).

RUNNING NUMBER. One, such as an accession number, which is given from a consecutive sequence to a book or other object.

RUNNING TITLE. The title that runs through a book or section of a book, repeated at the head of each page or at the top of the left-hand pages, with the chapter heading or the subject contents of both open pages on the right-hand page. Also called a 'Running head'. *See also* DROP-DOWN TITLE, HEADLINE, PAGE HEADLINE, SECTION HEADLINE.

RURAL DISTRICT COUNCIL. A statutory local authority which provides a limited number of local government services within its geographical area. Abbreviated RDC.

RUSSIA. A variety of calf leather used for bookbinding. It is specially tanned, and finished with birch oil which gives it a characteristic spicy odour. 'American Russia' is cowhide.

RUSTIC CAPITAL. 1. An upper case letter with a design engraved on the face, or an ornamentally designed letter. 2. The form of roman capital letters used by early scribes as a book hand between the second and sixth centuries A.D. The letters were less formal and not so heavy as the QUADRATA or SQUARE CAPITALS (*q.v.*) from which they were derived, giving a thinner, and more condensed appearance to the page. Also called 'Scriptura actuaria'.

RUSTICA. A freely-written, rather elegant fourth- and fifth-century writing used in Roman manuscripts. This style seems to have been influenced by Greek artistry and craftsmanship; it was displaced as a manuscript letter by the UNCIAL (*q.v.*), but used as initials or for emphasis in the line, in the same way that italics or small capitals are used by modern printers, in manuscripts until the eleventh century.

RUTHERSTAT. A trade name for a particular make of machine by means of which documents can be copied by reflex photography using silver halide paper. *See also* REFLEX COPYING.

RUTHVEN PRESS. An iron printing press, patented in 1813 by John Ruthven, an Edinburgh printer. In this, the bed which carried the type remained stationary while the platen was moved over it on a wheeled carriage. Springs kept the platen raised until the moment of impression, when power was applied through a series of levers which were worked by depressing a bar at the side of the press. It was not popular with the trade.

RUTLAND. Trade name for a fine-quality sheepskin used for bookbinding.

RUTTIER. *See* PORTOLAN.

SBN. Acronym for STANDARD BOOK NUMBER (*q.v.*).

s.c. 1. Abbreviation for (1) small capitals; (2) super-calendered paper.

SD CLASSIFICATION. The scheme of classification, used by the U.S. government's Superintendent of Documents who is responsible for the centralized control and distribution of U.S. government documents. It is not a systematic scheme in that there is no visible subject relationship between the various parts. The notation consists of a combination of letters and numbers.

SDI. Abbreviation for Selective Dissemination of Information system which is an automated system of information retrieval utilizing a computer for disseminating relevant information to users. An interest profile depicting and defining each area of interest is compiled for each user; it consists of terms which are likely to appear in relevant documents. These profiles are stored on magnetic tape for computer processing. Key words representing documents are matched with these interest profiles. If, for any given document and user, the terms match, its abstract is sent to the user.

s.f. Abbreviation for *sub finem* (*Lat.* 'towards the end').

SfB. A classification system for trade literature, periodicals, and information concerning the building industry. The letters stand for the initials of the Swedish committee which originated it, Sanarbetskommittèn för Byttnadsfrågor.

S.R. Abbreviation for the Register of the STATIONERS' COMPANY (*q.v.*).

S/S. Abbreviation for same size; an instruction, written on the illustration, to the blockmaker to make a block the same size as the copy, and neither larger nor smaller.

STC. Abbreviation for *A short-title catalogue of books printed in England, Scotland, and Ireland, and of English books printed abroad, 1475–1640,* by A. W. Pollard and G. R. Redgrave, London, Bibliographical Society, 1926.

SVD. Schweizerische Vereinigung für Dokumentation/Association Suisse de Documentation. *See* ASD.

SAALIC. Abbreviation for Swindon Area Association of Libraries for Industry and Commerce, formed in 1961 and based on the Central Library, Regent Circus, Swindon, Wilts. The scheme arranges the inter-loan of books and periodicals, and the co-operative filing of periodicals, and deals with requests for information. There are no membership limitations.

SACRED WORK. A basic writing of a religion, such as the *Bible, Koran, Talmud, Upanishads,* etc., which is generally accepted as such by those who follow that religion. In classification, it is often treated as if it were a class or a subject.

SADDLE STITCHING. Binding a pamphlet by placing it on the saddle-shaped support of a stitching machine where it is automatically stitched with wire or thread through the centre of the fold. *See also* FLAT STITCHING, SIDE-STITCH.

SADSACT. Abbreviation for Self-Assigned Descriptors from Self and Cited Titles; statistical association techniques which have been used in the U.S.A. for small-scale experiments in machine indexing by members of the Information Technology Division (formerly Data Processing Systems Division) of the National Bureau of Standards.

SALALM. Acronym for Seminars on the Acquisition of Latin American Library Materials. The first Seminar was held in 1956 'to consider the problems involved in finding, buying and controlling library materials relating to Latin America'. A Seminar has been held each year since. *See also* LACAP.

SALLE. A well-lighted room in a paper-mill where the paper is examined sheet by sheet, sorted, counted and arranged in reams. Also called 'Finishing house' or 'Finishing room' in a machine paper mill.

SAMPLE BACK. A strip of leather, cloth or other material made up to represent the back of a book and used as a sample for matching colour, material, lettering, etc.

SAMPLE PAGES. Selected pages of a proposed book, set by the printer as a specimen and model for the whole book.

SANDING. Rubbing down the edges of a book with sand-paper, or a sand-wheel machine, so as to remove as small an amount of paper as possible.

SANS SERIF. A type face without SERIFS (*q.v.*). The best known is 'Gill Sans' designed by Eric Gill; other well-known sans serif types are Futura and Vogue. The first sans serif type, designed by William Caslon, was named Egyptian; it was afterwards re-named Sanserif.

SARAH JOSEPHA HALE AWARD. *See* HALE AWARD, SARAH JOSEPHA.

SARUM USE. In the fifteenth century, certain Parisian presses specialized in books of Hours of the Virgin (the layman's prayer book) which were similar in format but differed slightly according to the locality in which they were to be used. To prevent the printer and binder mixing the various editions, abbreviations such as 'Sar' for 'secundum usum Sarum' or 'Par' for 'secundum usum ecclesie Parisiensis' were placed after the signature letter. The version used mostly in England, particularly in the southern part, and in Scotland, was that of Salisbury or 'Sarum', the York use being confined to the north. Their use was discontinued after the Reformation. Sarum books were largely produced in Paris and Rouen.

SAW CUTS. Grooves made in the back of a book with a saw to take the cords used in sewing.

SAWING-IN. Sawing grooves in the back of a book for the reception of the cord in sewing.

SAYERS MEMORIAL PRIZE. This Prize takes the form of professional books, and was created from the royalties of the *Sayers memorial volume*, and donated by the editors D. J. Foskett and B. I. Palmer. The volume was produced as a tribute to the late W. C. Berwick Sayers, Chief Librarian of the Croydon Public Libraries for many years, a former President of the Library Association, and particularly noted for his teaching and writing on classification. The Prize is awarded to the candidate gaining the highest mark in classification in the Final Examination of the Library Association. It was first awarded in 1965 to Henry Gilby.

sc. Abbreviation for *scilicat* (*Lat.* 'namely').

SCALING. The process of calculating the area by which an illustration block must be altered to fit a given layout.

SCAN. To examine every reference or every entry in a file routinely as part of a retrieval scheme (*IBM*). To examine periodicals and other materials to determine the usefulness of the information contained to the library's users, especially to the interests and work of individuals served by a special library. This enables decisions to be made as to ROUTING (*q.v.*), the preparation of ABSTRACTS and ATTENTION NOTES (*qq.v.*), and how cataloguing and classifying should be carried out.

SCAN-COLUMN INDEX. A co-ordinate book-form index developed by J. O'Connor which provides for manual serial searching of terms arranged in columns (*IBM*). *See also* CO-ORDINATE INDEXING.

SCAN PLATES. A generic term for plates made by an electronic photo-engraving machine.

SCANDIA PLAN, THE. A system of voluntary co-operation between public, special and research libraries in Denmark, Finland, Norway and Sweden (where it originated) in the systematic acquisition of literature, implying a rational distribution of the obligation to purchase, exchange and store old and new materials in each subject in the broad field of the humanities which has been allocated, acts as a bibliographical centre, and lends freely. The initiative for the scheme was taken by the inter-Scandinavian federation, the Nordisk Vitenskapeliget Bibliotekarforbund; the expenses entailed by the numerous planning conferences are defrayed by the Nordic Cultural Commission, an inter-Scandinavian governmental organization for cultural affairs. None of the co-operating libraries receives any extra financial support to fulfil its special acquisitional commitments; each acts independently on its purchase and exchange policies; the allocation of special subject fields is made on the basis of the existing library collections and fields of interest. It is the only international scheme of its kind and has been operated since 1957. The practical development of the plan is promoted by the Federation of Nordic Research Librarians. It is hoped that the Plan will be extended to more countries, reduce duplication, and move into the fields of science and social science.

SCANDINAVIAN FEDERATION OF RESEARCH LIBRARIANS. Founded 1947 in Copenhagen to promote and facilitate contacts and co-operation between Scandinavian assistant librarians and their libraries. Associations in Denmark, Finland, Norway and Sweden are members. Abbreviated NVBF (Nordisk Videnskabeligt Bibliotekarieforbund).

SCANDOC. The Scandinavian Documentation Center, set up in Washington, D.C., by Nordforsk (a co-operative institution for research in the technical and natural sciences in Scandinavia). It aims to acquire materials, watch the literature, carry out research, and send out inventories of publications which might be of interest to Scandinavian countries. It also acts as a centre for Scandinavian research and industry in the U.S.A.

SCANNING. In information retrieval, the examination of tallies (records). This may be done (a) *sequentially*, in sequence one after another right through a file, (b) *simultaneously*, e.g. as a batch of edge-notched cards is needled, (c) *fractionally*, in a series of separate and intermittent consultations, e.g. as a catalogue is searched.

SCARECROW PRESS AWARD FOR LIBRARY LITERATURE. Presented annually by the Scarecrow Press, this Award is $500 cash and a citation; it is administered by the ALA Awards Committee, the selection being made by a jury composed of one representative of each type-of-library division of the American Library Association. The first recipient (in 1960) was Mrs. Marjorie Fiske Lowenthal for *Book selection and censorship*.

SCATTERING. *See* LAW OF SCATTERING.

SCENARIO. 1. The outline of a film plot. 2. Any abbreviated presentation of the personages, plot, and outline of a dramatic work, such as a play, dramatic oratorio, cantata or opera. In cataloguing music, the term is also used for a ballet plot, directions for a dance composition, etc.

SCHEDULE. 1. A statement of the sub-divisions of a classification as set out on paper so as to show hierarchical relationship. *See also* SUMMUM GENUS. 2. A series of serial classifications, arranged in one series of co-ordinate classes, with sub-classes, if there are any, arranged in secondary series, or columns, indented to show the subordination. These secondary series may be sub-divided successively, resulting in tertiary and quaternary series. These forms are equivalent to TABULAR CLASSIFICATION (*q.v.*) of three or more dimensions. 3. In information retrieval, any list of terms used in constructing a file. *See also* FILE 3.

SCHEDULED MNEMONICS. *See* MNEMONICS.

SCHEME. Provisions for inter-library co-operation in library regions in England and Wales and for the setting up of library councils in connexion therewith. *See also* LIBRARY COUNCIL.

SCHEME. *See* BILL OF TYPE.

SCHEME OF CLASSIFICATION. The schedules, index, and apparatus of a classification; the complete classification tables.

SCHOLISM. (*Pl.* Scholia.) An explanatory marginal note or comment, or interpretative remark, especially an annotation on a classical text by an ancient grammarian.

SCHOOL DISTRICT LIBRARY. A free public library established and financially supported by action of a school district for the use of residents of the district. Such a library is supervised by a local board of education or by a separate library board appointed by a board of education. (American.)

SCHOOL EDITION. An edition of a book especially prepared for use in school. It usually has no answers, or is in some other way less complete than the ordinary edition, it may be printed on poorer paper, or bound less substantially, and sold at a cheaper price.

SCHOOL LIBRARIES DEPARTMENT. A section of a public library service, or local education service, which administers a system of 'school libraries', comprising collections of books for home reading. Each collection, which varies in size according to the number of children to be served, and is made up from a large reservoir stock, is sent to each school at regular intervals, the exchange usually being made during school holidays.

SCHOOL LIBRARIES SECTION. A Section of the Library Association, the formation of which was agreed by the Council of the Association on 4th December 1936. It became a constituent part of the School Library Association when this was formed in 1937.

SCHOOL LIBRARY. An organized collection of books placed in a school for the use of teachers or pupils, but usually for pupils. It may comprise books of reference and/or books for home reading, and be in the care of a professional librarian, teacher, or teacher-librarian. Variously called in America in the later 1960s an *Instructional Materials Center*, a *Learning Resources Centre* or a *Media Centre*, due to the role of the centre being the housing and distributing of visual aids materials to teachers throughout a school.

SCHOOL LIBRARY ASSOCIATION. Formally constituted on 23 January 1937, strengthened in 1945 by the adhesion of the former School Libraries Section of the Library Association, and incorporated in 1955. This Association aims to promote development of the school library as an instrument of education in schools of all kinds; to encourage efficient methods of administration and routine; and to provide opportunities for interchange of experience among school librarians and others interested in the aims of the Association. Corporate membership is open to any school, college, institute of education, or library; Personal membership is available to individuals, and Associate membership to students. Abbreviated SLA. Publishes *The School Librarian and School Library Review* (3 p.a.).

SCHOOL LIBRARY SUPERVISOR. The American term for a librarian who supervises and co-ordinates the work of several other school librarians. The American Association of School Librarians recommends one for every system having five or more schools. Duties and responsibilities vary but usually include: consulting with school administrators, providing leadership, guidance and knowledge in school librarianship to stimulate improvement in the service. Also called 'Adviser', 'Consultant', 'Co-ordinator', 'Director', 'District-Librarian', 'Head Librarian', 'Specialist'.

SCHOOL OF LIBRARIANSHIP. *Synonymous with* LIBRARY SCHOOL (*q.v.*).

SCHOOL SYSTEM MATERIALS CENTER. A library located in the central office of a system of school libraries from which are circulated films, filmstrips, records, tapes and other audio-visual materials and equipment to the schools in the system.

SCHROTHLATT. *Synonymous with* MANIÈRE CRIBLÉE (*q.v.*).

SCHWABACHER. 1. An early variety of Gothic type used in Germany. 2. A type used in Germany today, based on early Gothic designs.

SCHWEIZERISCHE GESAMTKATALOG. The Swiss National Catalogue, which is housed at the National Library in Berne, lists all books published in Switzerland, and foreign books. Over 2,000,000 titles are entered on cards, and these are the basis of inter-library loans.

SCHWEIZERISCHE VEREINIGUNG FÜR DOKUMENTATION. The Association Suisse de Documentation. *See* ASD.

SCIENCE CITATION INDEX. A printed index of books and periodical articles and all kinds of references to them in subsequent publications. Compiled and published by the Institute for Scientific Information, of Philadelphia, Pa., U.S.A., it is published quarterly, the fourth issue being a cumulation of the previous three issues.

SCIENCE FICTION. Imaginative fiction describing life and adventure in the future, life on other worlds, interplanetary travel, etc. It usually has a scientific or prophetic background.

SCIENCE RESEARCH COUNCIL. Established by Royal Charter following the passing of the Science and Technology Act 1965, this Council, which came into formal existence in April 1965, covers the whole field of fundamental science other than those parts which are the responsibility of the AGRICULTURAL RESEARCH COUNCIL, the MEDICAL RESEARCH COUNCIL and the NATURAL ENVIRONMENT RESEARCH COUNCIL (*qq.v.*). It took over the functions of the DEPARTMENT OF SCIENTIFIC AND INDUSTRIAL RESEARCH (*q.v.*) in respect of research grants and post-graduate training awards. The Council is authorized by its charter to carry out research and development through its own establishments, encourage and support research by any other person or body, and provide and operate equipment for common use by universities, technical colleges and like institutions.

SCIENCE-TECHNOLOGY DIVISION. A division of the (American) Special Libraries Association. Often abbreviated Sci-Tech.

SCIENTIFIC RESEARCH. Following the passing of the Science and Technology Act 1965, the responsibility of various scientific organizations was placed under different bodies, and new councils and committees were set up to enable the government to develop scientific research. *See also* ADVISORY COUNCIL ON TECHNOLOGY, AGRICULTURAL RESEARCH COUNCIL, COMMITTEE ON MANPOWER RESOURCES FOR SCIENCE AND TECHNOLOGY, COMMONWEALTH AGRICULTURAL BUREAUX, COUNCIL FOR SCIENTIFIC POLICY, DEFENCE RESEARCH COMMITTEE, DEPARTMENT OF INDUSTRIAL AND SCIENTIFIC RESEARCH, MEDICAL RESEARCH COUNCIL, MINISTRY OF TECHNOLOGY, NATURAL ENVIRONMENT RESEARCH COUNCIL, SCIENCE RESEARCH COUNCIL.

SCI-TECH. Abbreviation for the SCIENCE-TECHNOLOGY DIVISION (*q.v.*) of the Special Libraries Association.

SCOGGIN SCHOLARSHIP, MARGARET. Offered by the Young Adult Services Division of the American Library Association to a librarian or prospective librarian working with youth. The Scholarship is offered to honour Margaret Clara Scoggin (1905–1968) who was Co-ordinator of Young Adult Services in the New York Public Library from 1952 until the end of 1967.

SCOLLUL. Acronym for Standing Conference of Librarians of the Libraries of the University of London which holds periodic meetings to consider aspects of co-operation between the libraries of the University.

SCOLMA. Acronym for Standing Conference on Library Materials on Africa. This organization was set up at a meeting held in Chatham House on 2 April 1962. Its aims are: to facilitate the acquisition and preservation of library materials needed for African studies; to assist in the recording and use of such materials. Membership is by invitation of the committee and is of two kinds, full membership which is limited to institutions in the United Kingdom actively acquiring materials on Africa and co-operating in the schemes promoted by the Conference, and supporting membership which is open to other bodies interested in the aims of the organization. Publications: The SCOLMA newsletter *Library Materials on Africa* (3 p.a.), *The SCOLMA Directory of Libraries and Special Collections on Africa, U.K. Publications and theses on Africa* (a.).

SCONUL. Abbreviation for the Standing Conference of National and University Libraries; a British organization which is primarily concerned with co-operation. Founded in September 1950 'to promote the work of national and university libraries'. The main body of the organization meets twice a year, but much of its work is done by subcommittees which are formed as necessary to deal with specific matters; courses of instruction are arranged for members of library staffs, and exhibitions of foreign books are arranged. It is the equivalent of the (American) ASSOCIATION OF RESEARCH LIBRARIES (*q.v.*).

SCOPE CARD. A comprehensive catalogue card indicating the extent of musical or other works possessed in one form or medium, or of an identical title by one author or composer.

SCOPE NOTE. 1. In information retrieval, a statement giving the range of meaning and scope of a subject heading or descriptor and usually referring to related or overlapping headings (*IBM*). 2. In co-ordinate indexing, a symbol appended to a term or term number to narrow the definition of the term rather than designate the role of a word in its context. *See also* ROLES.

SCORE. A printed or written version of a musical work which shows the whole of the music for the participating voices or instruments on two or more staves ('staffs' in America), one above the other. The term is not usually applied to music for one performer. A *Full Score* shows the music for each participating voice or instrument on separate staves one above the other, with the music for each solo voice, each choral part and each instrument being set out on a separate stave one above another. The customary order in Europe is (reading from the top to the bottom) woodwind, brass, timpani, percussion, strings, solo instrumental parts (for concertos); additional orchestral parts such as harp(s) and organ, and choral parts, are normally placed between the percussion and strings. American scores usually place solo voices and chorus parts between the upper and lower strings, with organ at the bottom. A *Miniature Score* has the same music as a full score but is reduced considerably in size by photographic reproduction. Miniature scores are usually so described on the title-page, but if not, can be considered to be such if the music is smaller than normal and the page size is less than 21 ems. An *Orchestral Score* is the full score of an orchestral work. A *Piano Score* is an orchestral or vocal work reduced to a piano version. A *Piano-Conductor Score* (violin-conductor score, etc.) is a piano (or violin etc.) part in a concerted work, with cues to indicate when vocal or instrumental performers 'come in', i.e. begin to perform. The pianist (or violinist etc.) performs and conducts (or attempts to) at the same time. A *Vocal Score* shows the music for voices on separate staves but the orchestral parts reduced to a piano version. This is the common version for members of choirs, of the music of cantatas, operas, and oratorios. Also called 'Piano-vocal score'. A *Close Score* has the music for more than one part or instrument on one stave. Also called 'Compressed score', 'Short score'. An *Open Score* has the music for each voice or part on a separate stave, each being placed above one another, as in a full score. Also called 'Extended score'.

SCORING.   Compressing the fibres of heavy paper along a line, to facilitate either folding or tearing. Scoring with a dull rule increases folding endurance. The use of a sharp rule however partially breaks the paper fibres and has a similar effect to perforating.

SCOTAPLL.   The Standing Conference of Theological and Philosophical Libraries in London. This Association was founded in 1948 to improve facilities for research in these subjects, and to interchange books between constituent libraries. It was merged with the Association of British Theological and Philosophical Libraries in 1964. *See also* ABTAPL.

SCOTTISH CENTRAL LIBRARY.   The Scottish counterpart to the National Central Library; formed on 1 July 1952. It is situated in Edinburgh where it was founded in 1921 as the Scottish Central Library for Students. As from 1 October 1953 it absorbed the Regional Library Bureau of Scotland (founded in 1945) and became responsible for the Scottish Union Catalogue from the same date. Abbreviated SCL.

SCOTTISH LIBRARY ASSOCIATION.   A Group of the Library Association. It was an independent association, having been formed in October 1908 at Edinburgh, until January 1931 when it was affiliated with the LA and incorporated as a Branch, its terminology being changed to Group on the revision of the constitution of the Library Association in 1963. There are four regional branches each of which is represented on the SLA Council. Abbreviated SLA. Publishes *SLA News* (q.), *Proceedings* of the annual conferences

(1950–), Annual Report of the Council (1909–), *Scottish Libraries*, a report on libraries in Scotland, 1960, 1961, 1962 and triennially for 1963–5 onwards, and miscellaneous reports.

SCOTTISH STYLE. An eighteenth-century style of book decoration resembling the HARLEIAN STYLE (*q.v.*), but which has for a centre-piece a straight stem from which short sprays branch at regular intervals on either side, or else consists mainly of a large wheel pattern.

SCRAPERBOARD. 1. A method of drawing for reproduction. It utilizes a 'board' coated with a chalk surface and covered with a black wash which the artist scrapes away to reveal the white lines and areas of his drawing. Black lines may be drawn in afterwards if desired. 2. A drawing made by this method. It is similar in appearance to a wood engraving.

SCRATCHBOARD. American term for paper coated with black ink which is scratched away to show the white paper underneath. The picture drawing so produced. A scraperboard.

SCREAMER. The printer's term for exclamation marks used for display purposes.

SCREEN. A grid of opaque lines cut in glass (used in making half-tone blocks) crossing at right angles, and producing transparent square apertures between the intersections which split up the image into dots; these dots are distinctive of the half-tone process. The number of lines to the inch varies from forty-five for a coarse screen for use with rough or poor quality paper to 175 for a fine screen for use with art paper. *See also* HALF-TONE.

SCREEN. (*Reprography*) A surface of any material on to which, or if translucent, through which, an image is projected.

SCREW PRESS. A press used by bookbinders to flatten paper or books in process of binding, especially after pasting or glueing. It is operated by turning a wheel or lever attached to the upper end of a large-dimension screw placed perpendicularly which has at its lower end a heavy iron plate below which, and on the bed of the press, are placed the papers or books to be pressed. *See also* PRESS.

SCRINIUM. A cylinder-shaped container with movable lid used by the Romans to hold a number of scrolls.

SCRIPT. 1. A form of printer's cursive type resembling handwriting. 2. Any type face which is cut to resemble handwriting. 3. Handwriting, as opposed to printed characters. 4. A typescript, specially of a play, film scenario, or text of spoken matter for broadcasting.

This, Trafton Script, is an example of 1.

SCRIPT WRITING. *Synonymous with* DISJOINED HAND (*q.v.*).

SCRIPTORES. Writers who copied books by hand in Roman times.

SCRIPTORIUM. The room in a mediaeval monastery or abbey which was set aside for the copying of manuscripts, and for writing and studying generally.

SCRIPTURA ACTUARIA. *Synonymous with* RUSTIC CAPITALS (*q.v.*).

SCROLL. 1. A roll of paper or parchment, usually containing writing and rolled onto rollers. This was an early form of manuscript, called by the Romans *volumen* (roll) from which the word *volume* is derived. The scroll (or 'roll') comprised a number of sheets of papyrus or parchment glued together to form a 20- or 30-feet long strip which was wound on a cylinder with projecting ornaments or knobs in ivory or colours, and was finished with a coloured parchment cover, fastened with laces and identified with a 'sittybus', or title label. The text was written in rather narrow columns on the recto of the material, where, if papyrus, the fibres run horizontally. 2. (*Binding*) A scroll-shaped stamp used for bearing an inscription, or an ornament of similar shape, and generally used between Flowers on a roll.

sculpt. Abbreviation for *sculpsit* (*Lat.*). Indicates on an engraving the name of the engraver, and on sculpture the name of the sculptor.

SEAL PRINT. A woodcut with blind embossing around the picture, the embossing being done after the printing. Practised in the fifteenth century. Also called 'Gypsographic print.'

SEALSKIN. Binding leather made from the skin of the seal; it has a coarse grain, but is soft to the touch. *See also* PIN SEAL.

SEARCH RECORD. A record which shows the publications, organizations, and individuals consulted in answering an enquiry or obtaining information. The completed memorandum, information statement, or report, may be inserted on the form or attached to it, or it may form a separate record kept in a JOB FILE (*q.v.*).

SEARCH ROOM. 1. A room associated with an archive, in which members of the public may carry out their searches in the documents. 2. A room in which volumes of indexes to periodicals, volumes of abstracts, and similar bibliographical and search tools are provided for users to conduct literature searches.

SEARCH SERVICE. *Synonymous with* RESEARCH SERVICE (*q.v.*).

SEARCHER. A member of a library's staff who verifies the information available concerning a book it is proposed to purchase and then makes certain that the book is not already in stock.

SEARCHING. The act of checking a book against the catalogue to determine whether it is a duplicate, another edition of a book already in stock, or a new title (to be) added to the library. In PRELIMINARY CATALOGUING (*q.v.*), the searcher notes such descriptive and subject cataloguing details as may be helpful to the cataloguer. Often, searching slips are provided to standardize the operation. The term is also applied to the checking of titles for acquisition purposes.

SECOND GENERATION MICROFILM. *Synonymous with* FIRST REPRODUCTION MICROFILM (*q.v.*). *See also* GENERATION.

SECOND HALF-TITLE. A repetition of the title of a book between the preliminaries and the text.

SECOND INDENTION. The tenth typewriter space from the left edge of a catalogue card; the second, or inner, vertical line on a catalogue card ruled for handwriting. It is at this position that the title normally begins; if it runs over the line, it continues at the 'First indention', and is followed by particulars of edition and imprint. The *collation* also begins at the second indention, but without spacing between these two parts of the description. The collation is followed by a series note. The *notes* and the *contents* also begin at the second indention, but a 'blank line' is left between these and the previous parts of the description. Should either collation, notes or contents over-run the first line, subsequent lines begin at the first indention. Also called 'Title indention', 'Inner indention' and 'Paragraph indention'. *See also* FIRST INDENTION, INDENTION, SECOND VERTICAL, THIRD INDENTION.

SECOND LINING. A strip of brown paper the full size of the back of a book which is glued into position after the FIRST LINING (*q.v.*) has been affixed.

SECOND REPRODUCTION MICROFILM. A microfilm copy made from the FIRST REPRODUCTION MICROFILM (*q.v.*). Also called 'Third generation microfilm'. *See also* GENERATION.

SECOND VERTICAL. The second vertical line printed on a standard ruled catalogue card and serving as a guide to where the title should begin – at the SECOND INDENTION (*q.v.*). *See also* FIRST VERTICAL.

SECONDARY BIBLIOGRAPHY. 1. An 'intensive' or special bibliography dealing with books relating to one subject for the compilation of which primary bibliographies have been used. 2. A bibliography in which material is rearranged for convenience of research. (American.) *See also* BIBLIOGRAPHY, PRIMARY BIBLIOGRAPHY.

SECONDARY ENTRY. An entry in a catalogue other than the MAIN ENTRY (*q.v.*): an ADDED ENTRY (*q.v.*). *See also* GENERAL SECONDARY.

SECONDARY FULLNESS. The detail with which, in full cataloguing, an author's name is given in all secondary entries, e.g. the Christian name is given in full if there is only one, but initials if there are more than one. Also called 'Subject fullness'.

SECONDARY SOURCES. Books or unpublished literary material in the compilation of which PRIMARY SOURCES (*q.v.*) have been used.

SECOND-HAND BOOK. One which has previously been owned by another person. A bookseller who deals in such books is called a 'Second-hand bookseller'. Librarians refer to such books when purchased for a library as 'Second-hand copies'.

SECOND-HAND CATALOGUE. A list of second-hand books offered for sale.

SECRET LITERATURE. *Synonymous with* CLANDESTINE LITERATURE (*q.v.*).

SECRET PRESS. *See* CLANDESTINE PRESS.

SECTION. 1. The unit of paper which is printed, folded and sewn, and which, together with other sections, goes to make up a printed book. It usually consists of one sheet of paper, but may be one and a half or two sheets, or even one sheet and an extra leaf pasted in. Also called 'Signature', 'Gathering', 'Quire', 'Stave'. Each section of a book bears a different SIGNATURE (*q.v.*). *See also* FOLDINGS. 2. All the shelves arranged between two uprights. *Synonymous with* TIER (*q.v.*). 3. A sub-division of an administrative unit or department of a library, e.g. 'Processing section'. Sometimes called a 'Division' or 'Department'. 4. In the Dewey Classification a sub-division of a 'division'. 5. One of the separately folded parts of an American newspaper, such as the 'Home section'. 6. A portion of a text of a book which can logically be divided into separate parts or sections. 7. A portion of the membership of the Library Association who were interested in a particular aspect of librarianship. Under the present bye-laws of the Association these are now mostly known as Groups although some still bear the former name of Section.

SECTION HEADLINE. One which consists of whatever subdivisions (chapters, books, parts, etc.) the book may have. *See also* HEADLINE, PAGE HEADLINE, RUNNING TITLE.

SECTION MARK. 1. The sign § used before a numeral thus: §6, to refer to a section. 2. The fourth reference mark for footnotes, coming after the double dagger. *See also* REFERENCE MARKS. It is sometimes also used in quantity for borders.

SECTION TITLE. A half title which introduces a section of a book.

SECTIONAL BRACE. *See* BRACE.

SECTIONALIZED INDEX. An index to a periodical split into sections such as (a) long articles of importance, (b) short paragraphs and brief news items, (c) literature abstracts, and similar well-defined groups.

SECTIONING. Microfilming a very large document in two or more parts in such a way as to permit mounting the film in the same number of aperture cards.

SECTIONS. *See* SECTION. For use in classification, *see* MAIN CLASS.

SECTOR DEVICE. The device of using a sectorizing digit, i.e. to form another sector or stretch of co-ordinate digits by adding to it the successive digits of the species and deeming the resulting double-digited numbers as if fused into a single digit, and repeating this process to form successive sectors. *See also* GROUP NOTATION DEVICE.

SEDANOISE. The smallest size type of the early seventeenth century, designed by Jannon at Sedan. *See also* JANNON, JEAN.

See. (*Cataloguing*) A reference from a heading under which no entries are placed, to one or more which contain them.

See also. (*Cataloguing*) A reference often found in dictionary catalogues – and sometimes in classified ones – from one heading with entries under it, to related ones.

SEE COPY. An instruction written on a proof to a printer to refer to the 'copy' in order to correct a typesetting error.

SEE SAFE. Said of books bought from a publisher by a bookseller, and paid for, but with the understanding that at some future date the publisher may be asked to exchange unsold copies for copies of another title. *See also* HALF SEE SAFE, ON SALE.

SELECT BIBLIOGRAPHY. One which gives only a selection of the literature of a subject, the selection having been made with a view to excluding worthless material or to meeting the needs of a special class of people. Also called 'Selective bibliography'. *See also* BIBLIOGRAPHY I, CURRENT SELECTIVE BIBLIOGRAPHY, PARTIAL BIBLIOGRAPHY.

SELECT LIST. A reading list which includes a selection only of the books in the library on the subject of the list.

SELECT LIST OF REFERENCES. A partial list of references for material for further reading, the selection having eliminated items which for one reason or another are not particularly appropriate in the circumstances. The details included in the entries may be similar to those provided in a bibliography, although some items of a bibliographical nature may not be included, and the subject coverage would not be so great.

SELECTASINE. A process in silk screen printing; the term implies that one screen only is used for all the colours of a design.

SELECTION SECTION. The division of a cataloguing, accessions, or order department, which deals with the selection of books.

SELECTIVE ABSTRACT. *See* ABSTRACT.

SELECTIVE BIBLIOGRAPHY. *Synonymous with* SELECT BIBLIOGRAPHY (*q.v.*).

SELECTIVE CATALOGUING. The omission of certain types of entry, or of entries for little-used books, or of parts of an entry (as for example some items of collations), in order to reduce the bulk and cost of a catalogue without impairing its efficiency.

SELECTIVE CHARGING. The practice of recording the loan of certain classes of books, usually non-fiction or particularly expensive books, while others are issued by a TOKEN CHARGING (*q.v.*) system.

SELECTIVE CIRCULATION. *See* ROUTING.

SELECTIVE CLASSIFICATION. The arrangement of large groups of little-used books either alphabetically or chronologically rather than by specific subject in order to save the expense of cataloguing and classifying.

SELECTIVE DISSEMINATION OF INFORMATION SYSTEM. *See* SDI.

SELECTIVE ROUTING. ROUTING (*q.v.*) to only a selection of the officers of a library or organization.

SELECTOR. The component in a RETRIEVAL SYSTEM (*q.v.*) which enables the information required to be identified in a STORE (*q.v.*). It may consist of, or comprise, recording media, code symbols or reading devices.

SELECTOR CODE. *See* MARGINAL-HOLE PUNCHED CARDS.

SELF-CHARGING SYSTEM. Any system for recording book loans in which the borrower makes part or all of the record.

SELF-COVER. A pamphlet in which the same paper is used for cover and text.

SELF-ENDS. Endpapers which are leaves forming part of the end sections of a book.

SELF POSITIVE. In documentary reproduction, a positive print which is prepared without the use of an intermediate negative. Also called 'Direct positive'.

SELF-WRAPPER. The paper cover of a pamphlet or book which is an integral part of the sheet or sheets comprising the publication. It may or may not be printed.

SEMANTEME. The ultimate, smallest irreducible element or unit of meaning, such as a base or root which contains and represents the general meaning of a word or group of derivatives (*Pei*).

SEMANTIC CODE. 1. A linguistic system developed for use on machines designed to detect logically defined combinations; a symbol representing the concept of a word (*IBM*). 2. In information retrieval, one in which the notation carries meaningful information in addition to that which is carried by the source word. *See also* NON-SEMANTIC CODE.

SEMANTIC FACTOR. 1. In co-ordinate indexing, the separate unit of a code entry, representing one of a number of highly generic concepts. The semantic factors forming a code are arranged in alphabetical order. *See also* DESCRIPTOR. 2. A generalized concept used, with others, to construct a SEMANTIC CODE (*q.v.*).

SEMANTIC FACTORING. American term for FACET ANALYSIS (*q.v.*).

SEMANTICS. The study of the relations between linguistic symbols (words, expressions, phrases) and the objects or concepts to which they refer (*Pei*). Semantics relates a symbol to its meaning. *See also* SYNTAX.

SEMÉ, SEMIS. *Synonymous with* POWDER (*q.v.*).

SEMI-ANNUAL. A periodical which is issued at six-monthly intervals. Also called 'Half yearly'.

SEMI-CHEMICAL PULP. The product of an intermediate process between Mechanical Wood Pulp (merely ground wood without the addition of chemicals or heat) and Chemical Wood Pulp which is obtained by the action of chemicals on wood chips. Also called 'Mechanical Wood pulp'.

SEMI-DRY PROCESS. A method of documentary reproduction in which copies are developed by a liquid but are nearly dry when they emerge from the copying machine. This method is used in some diazo processes and in ELECTROPHOTOGRAPHY (*q.v.*). The diazo compound is contained in the base and the coupler in a separate liquid developer. *See also* AMMONIA PROCESS, DIAZOTYPE PROCESS, DRY PROCESS.

SEMI-INDEXING. Listing a number of items to be indexed on one sheet of squared paper, either separate or bound into an exercise book, bearing the letters of the alphabet at the top to serve as guide-line headings. The entries commence on the lines having the corresponding initial letters entered at the top.

SEMI-MONTHLY. *Synonymous with* FORTNIGHTLY (*q.v.*).

SEMIOTICS. The science of signs; it is divided into three main subdivisions: semantics, syntatics, and pragmatics, each of which (as can semiotics as a whole) can be pure, descriptive or applied. *Pure semiotic* elaborates a language to talk about signs, *descriptive semiotic* studies actual signs, *applied semiotic* utilizes knowledge about signs to accomplish various purposes.

SEMI-PULP. A term applied to the product of the grinding process in paper making, the ground wood still containing impurities and large fragments of wood.

SEMI-RAG.   Paper made partly of rags.

SEMI-WEEKLY.   A serial publication issued twice a week. Also called 'Twice weekly'. *See also* FORTNIGHTLY.

SEMINAR COLLECTION.   *Synonymous with* DEPARTMENTAL LIBRARY (*q.v.*).

SENIOR ASSISTANT.   An assistant librarian who has the supervision of the work of junior assistants but does not have the responsibility for a department.

SENSING MARK.   (*Reprography*) A mark on film or paper which activates an electrical device to carry out automatically a function such as cutting paper.

SENSITIZED PAPER.   Paper used in documentary reproduction which is coated with an emulsion sensitive to light or heat as used in a thermographic process. *See also* SENSITIVE PAPER, THERMOGRAPHY.

SENSITIVE PAPER.   A paper which has been treated with light-sensitive chemicals for photographic purposes. *See also* SENSITIZED PAPER.

SEPARATE.   A copy of an article published in a periodical, specially reprinted for the author's use, but retaining the numbering of the issue from which it was taken. It may or may not have a title-page. Sometimes called 'Extracted article', 'Off-print', 'Overprint' or 'Reprint'. *See also* REPRINTED ARTICLE.

SEPARATION NEGATIVES.   Individual negatives for each colour used in colour reproductions. *See also* COLOUR SEPARATION.

SEPARATRIX.   The diagonal stroke / , used in proof correction to mark and separate alterations.

SEPARATUM (*Pl.* Separata). A reprint of one of a series of papers. An offprint or SEPARATE (*q.v.*).

seq. (*Pl. Seqq.*).   Abbreviation (in singular) of Latin *sequens* 'the following', *sequente* 'and in what follows', *sequitur* 'it follows' and (in plural) of *sequentes, -tia* 'the following', *sequentibus* 'in the following places'. *See also et seq.*

SEQUEL.   A literary work, usually a novel, which is complete in itself, but continues an earlier work.

SEQUENCE OF SIGNS.   The use of recognized signs in notes (*see* REFERENCE MARKS) and especially of 'Relation marks' in the UNIVERSAL DECIMAL CLASSIFICATION (*q.v.*) to separate the different components of a classification number and at the same time indicate their meaning.

SEQUENTIAL CAMERA.   One which produces a sequence of images in column form on one film of suitable width from cards which are fed into the camera in a pre-determined sequence.

SERIAL. 1. Any publication issued in successive parts, appearing at intervals, usually regular ones, and, as a rule, intended to be continued indefinitely. The term includes periodicals, newspapers, annuals, numbered monographic series and the proceedings, transactions and memoirs of societies. Not to be confused with SERIES (*q.v.*). 2. A book consisting of parts or volumes published successively with a common title and intended to be continued indefinitely, not necessarily at regular intervals. (In the United States of America the term 'serial' is used to mean a periodical, regular or irregular) (*IFLA*). 3. (*Adj.*) The handling of data in a sequential fashion (*IBM*). *See also* PARALLEL. 4. A long story published in instalments.

SERIAL SERVICE. A serial publication which is revised, accumulated or indexed by means of new or replacement pages. *See also* LOOSE-LEAF SERVICE.

SERIAL CATALOGUE. An official, or a public, catalogue of serials in a library.

SERIAL CLASSIFICATION. A classification, the classes of which are in a series, or in an order of gradation.

SERIAL NUMBER. 1. The number indicating the order of publication in a series. 2. One of the consecutive numbers appearing in front of an entry in a bibliography or catalogue.

SERIAL PUBLICATION. *Synonymous with* SERIAL (*q.v.*).

SERIAL RECORD. A record of a library's holdings of serials.

SERIAL RIGHTS. An author's rights in the publication of his work by instalments.

SERIAL SECTION. A division of an order, or an acquisition, department that has charge of the acquisition of serials; or a subdivision of a preparation division where responsibility is taken for the cataloguing of serials.

SERIALS DEPARTMENT. The administrative unit in charge of handling serials; this may include ordering, checking, cataloguing, preparation for binding, etc.

SERIES. 1. Volumes usually related to each other in subject matter, issued successively, sometimes at the same price, and generally by the same publisher, in a uniform style, and usually bearing a collective 'series title' on the HALF TITLE (*q.v.*) or the cover, or at the head of the TITLE-PAGE (*q.v.*). 2. Succeeding volumes of essays, etc., issued at intervals or in sequence. 3. Successive volumes of a serial publication numbered separately to distinguish them from other sequences of the same serial. *See also* SERIAL. 4. A number of articles or stories of a similar nature or by the same author published in succession. *See also* PUBLISHER'S SERIES, REPRINT SERIES. 5. (*Classification*) A succession of classes, or terms, in some relation.

SERIES CARD. A catalogue card on which the SERIES ENTRY (*q.v.*) appears.

SERIES ENTRY. In a catalogue or bibliography, a brief entry under the name of the series for such volumes as the library may possess. *See also* SERIES.

SERIES NOTE. In a catalogue or bibliography, a note following the collation, and giving, in parentheses, the name of the series to which a book belongs.

SERIES NUMBER. The number assigned by a publisher to an individual book or piece of music published in a series. The series may contain titles which are unrelated, or they may be related to one another by subject, musical form, medium of performance (musical), or the titles may be unrelated. *See also* PUBLISHER'S SERIES.

SERIES STATEMENT. The information on a publication which names the series to which it belongs and gives the number of the publication in the series.

SERIES TITLE. The title of a series to which a book belongs. It may appear on the half-title page, title-page, or a page following the title-page.

SERIF. A fine finishing stroke or grace, drawn at right angles to, or obliquely across, the ends of stems or arms of a letter. Letters without serifs are usually described as 'sans serif'.

SERIGRAPHY. *Synonymous with* SILK SCREEN PROCESS (*q.v.*).

SERIM. *Synonymous with* MULL (*q.v.*).

SERRATED SQUARE. (*Binding*) A stamp, more or less square with concave serrated sides, and usually a cruciform centre; often used in a group and giving the effect of a number of circles with serrated inner edges.

SERTAFILM. Trade name for a catalogue-card size device for holding short pieces of microfilm; the top third is of plain card stock on which identifying information is entered and to which a clear plastic sleeve for holding the microfilm is attached.

SERVICE AREA. *See* PUBLIC (SERVICE) AREA.

SERVICE BASIS. A method of determining prices for a publication or series of publications issued periodically and cumulated at regular intervals. The prices are scaled for individual libraries according to book expenditure, circulation and anticipated potential use to the subscriber. For periodical indexes, it is based on the number of indexed periodicals taken in a library.

SERVICE POINT. A place at which a library service is provided for all members of the public, including a major service such as a large branch, or a small service such as that at a training college or lighthouse, but excludes collections of books provided for limited periods for such groups as an adult class or a dramatic society.

SERVICE POINTS. (*County libraries*) Places at which the public are served. Include branches (inclusive of mobile branches and travelling libraries, each halt to count as a separate service point), centres, school libraries, hospital libraries, youth clubs, prisons, lighthouses, training colleges, military camps, etc. The characteristic denoting a Service Point is that provision is intended to be permanent and/or continuous, is of a relatively wide subject range, and is located at a definite place. Does not include the supply of collections of books to adult classes, choral and dramatic societies, and for other similar purposes where the use of the collection is intended to be limited in duration and where the books cover a relatively narrow subject range.

SESSION. *See* PARLIAMENTARY SESSION.

SESSIONAL PAPERS. Two series (*House of Commons Sessional Papers* and *House of Lords Sessional Papers*) of Parliamentary Papers arranged (and probably bound) in sessional sets. The *House of Commons Sessional Papers* consist of the *House of Commons Bills*, the *House of Commons Papers* and the *Command Papers*. The *House of Lords Sessional Papers* consist of the series called the *House of Lords Papers and Bills*.

SET. 1. series of publications associated by common publication or authorship, and which form one unit, being issued in a uniform style. They may be by one author, or on one subject, or they may be a file of periodicals or be unrelated but printed and bound uniformly. 2. (*Printing*) The distance between the left- and right-hand sides of a piece of movable type. Type is said to have a wide or narrow set according to the width of the BODY (*q.v.*); a figure is used to indicate the comparative width of a Monotype design, e.g. 12-point 10½ set, is narrower than 12-point 12 set. 3. To compose type.

SET FLUSH. 1. An instruction to the typesetter to set the type right up to the left-hand margin, avoiding indentions at the beginning of paragraphs. 2. Matter so composed.

SET HAND. Writing which conforms to definite rules, such as set abbreviations. Not generally applied to hands later than the seventeenth century.

SET OF DOCUMENTS. Any collection of documents, large or small, restricted to an organization's research papers, or a collection of miscellaneous material, in many different languages, but homogeneous in that they will be indexed by one index. *See also* FEATURE CARD.

SET OF QUESTIONS. (*Information retrieval*) A number of questions that will be put to a single subject index.

SET-OFF. 1. The accidental transfer of ink from one printed sheet to another. 2. Any kind of paper placed between a sheet after printing to prevent the ink from one sheet soiling another. Also called 'Slip sheet'. *See also* OFFSET.

SET SOLID. Type matter with no leads between the lines.

SETTING RULE. *Synonymous with* COMPOSING RULE (*q.v.*).

SETTING TYPE. Composing type either by hand or by machine so that it is ready for printing.

SEVENSMA PRIZE, THE. A money prize awarded for an essay written on a prescribed subject to a member, under forty years of age, of any member-association of IFLA (*q.v.*). The Prize has a double purpose: honouring T. P. Sevensma, the Dutch librarian who was successively Director of the Public Library of Amsterdam, of the League of Nations Library, and of the University Library in Leyden. In 1929 he became Secretary of IFLA, and in 1939, on the occasion of his completing ten years in this honorary office, also on the occasion of his sixtieth birthday, the President of IFLA announced the establishment of the prize bearing Dr. Sevensma's name. The subject of the essay is set every two years and is on some aspect of libraries in their relation to practical life. The awards have been made as follows: 1948 to Mr. Valter Ahlstadt of Stockholm City Library 'Unit cataloguing', 1950 to Miss Olga S. Newman of Northallerton, England, 'A study in the field of rural library services'; 1952 to Mr. W. D. Richardson of Leeds, England, 'A study in the field of photographic reproduction in libraries'; 1955 Dr. E. Egger of the Swiss National Library, Berne, 'Der Schweizerische Gesamtkatalog'; 1959 shared by Mr. H. Fairhurst of Salisbury, Southern Rhodesia, 'The information service in the library' and Miss Wanda Polaszewska of Poznan, Poland, 'The reference service in the library'; 1964 to Mr. P. W. Plumb, Lecturer at the School of Librarianship, North-Western Polytechnic, London, 'Central library storage of books'; 1968 to Miss M. J. Lewis, Lecturer at the same School, for 'Libraries for the handicapped'.

SEVENTY-TWOMO (72mo). A sheet of paper folded into seventy-two leaves, making 144 pages.

SEWED. In cataloguing a pamphlet stitched without covers.

SEWING. When the sections of a book have been gathered and collated, they are sewed together, one by one, with thread, usually by machinery. In job binding they are usually sewed by hand. As the art of sewing the sections and of attaching the covers to them was never reduced to a skilful practice until well on in the sixteenth century, books could not be stood on their bottom edges as they are now, but were laid flat on shelves or lecterns. This is why it was customary to decorate the top and back covers. *See also* ALL ALONG, STABBING, STITCHING, THREAD STITCHED, WIRE STITCHED.

SEWING FRAME. The frame on which cords or tapes are attached and stretched taut, and to which the sections of a book are sewn by hand.

SEWING ON TAPES. When the sections of a book are sewn together and two or more tapes are used to secure the book to the covers, some of the loops pass over the tapes thus also securing the sections to them. In LIBRARY BINDING (*q.v.*) and hand-sewing, each section is sewn to every tape.

SEWN. A book is said to be sewn when the sections are fastened together with linen threads passing round tapes or cords.

SEXAGESIMO-QUARTO. *Synonymous with* SIXTY-FOURMO (*q.v.*).

SEXTO (6to). A sheet of paper folded three times to form a section of six leaves or twelve pages; a half-sheet of twelves.

SEXTODECIMO (16mo). A sheet of paper folded four times to form a section of sixteen leaves (thirty-two pages); a half-sheet of thirty-two. Now called foolscap 8vo. Also called 'Sixteenmo'.

SHADED TOOLS. (*Binding*) Finisher's tools partly in outline and partly solid.

SHADOW. A type face which gives a three-dimensional effect.

SHAGREEN. A type of leather with a rough, granular surface. When used for bookbinding it is usually prepared from sharkskin.

SHAKEN. A cataloguing term used in the U.S.A. to describe copies of books which have loose leaves and/or binding.

SHANK. The rectangular body of a type letter, on which are the NICK, or nicks, PINMARK, BELLY and BACK (*qq.v.*). Also called BODY (*q.v.*) and STEM (*q.v.*). The piece of metal on which the shoulder bearing the FACE (*q.v.*) or printing surface of a type-letter is supported. *See also* SHOULDER.

SHAPE. Books which are not of normal proportions are described as 'oblong' or 'landscape' when the width of the page exceeds its height, 'narrow' when the width is less than $\frac{3}{5}$ of the height, and 'square' if more than $\frac{3}{4}$. *See also* SIZE.

SHARED CATALOGUING. A form of cataloguing being undertaken

19*

by the Library of Congress and other agencies responsible for national bibliography. The L. of C., under the United States Higher Education Act, 1965 is charged with '(a) acquiring so far as possible, all library materials of value to scholarship currently published throughout the world; and (b) providing catalogue information, for such materials promptly after receipt . . .' and in order to achieve these objects has arranged with other national agencies to send catalogue entries for all works published in their country to the L. of C. Blanket-order suppliers acquire the works represented by the catalogue entries and send them together with the catalogue entries, to the L. of C. On their receipt, the L. of C. prints catalogue cards for each title and publishes entries in the *National Union Catalog*.

SHAVED. A book which has been trimmed by the binder so closely that the lines of print have been grazed, without actually being cut into. *See also* CROPPED.

SHEAF BINDER. A case or binder to hold a sheaf of papers to form a loose-leaf catalogue or other record. The sheets of paper are punched with holes to go over posts which keep the sheets in position, and there is some form of locking device to keep the covers and the sheets securely in position.

SHEAF CATALOGUE. A catalogue made on slips of paper, as distinct from one made on cards, and fastened into a sheaf binder which permits the insertion of new material in correct order.

SHEAF HOLDER. *Synonymous with* SHEAF BINDER (*q.v.*).

SHEEPSKIN. The skin of a sheep prepared as a bookbinding material. Such skins have been used for bookbinding in the United Kingdom since about 1400. The boards they covered were usually of oak. *See also* ALASKA SEAL, LAW CALF, ROAN, RUTLAND, SKIVER, SMYRNA MOROCCO.

SHEET. A large piece of paper as manufactured. Also used of the sheet after it has been printed and folded to form a section of a book or pamphlet; to avoid confusion this is best called a section. Sheets of paper bearing the same size name can be had in double ('double') or quadruple ('quad') size. *See also* OCTAVO, PAPER SIZES.

SHEET-FEED. Said of a printing press which takes paper cut into sheets instead of paper in a continuous roll.

SHEET MUSIC. Printed music which a musician would use in learning a musical composition from memory, or in performance, which has not be bound into stiff covers. There is no limit on the number of pages. *See also* MINIATURE SCORE, SCORE.

SHEET STOCK. A stock of unbound printed sheets of a book which are kept in stock by the printer until the publisher orders them to be bound up. This method of binding books as required to meet orders, is done to spread the cost of production.

SHEET WORK. Printing one side of a sheet of paper from an 'inner forme' and the other from an 'outer forme'. Also called 'Work and back'. When both sides have been printed, the sheet is known as a 'Perfect copy'. By this method, one sheet is used to print one copy using two formes. *See also* HALF-SHEET WORK.

SHEETS. The printed pages of a book, either flat or folded, but unbound. *See also* IN SHEETS.

SHEETWISE. A method of printing in which a separate forme is used for printing each side of a sheet of paper. *See also* WORK AND TURN.

SHEFFIELD SCHEME. *See* SINTO.

SHELF. A flat piece of wood, steel or other material, which is placed horizontally between two uprights, or supported on brackets, to hold books. Metal shelves are usually turned down along back and front to form a flange and give strength. Shelves may be constructed of rollers to save wear on the binding of very heavy and large books. The normal length of shelves is 3 feet from centre to centre of the uprights supporting them.

SHELF-BACK. *Synonymous with* SPINE (*q.v.*).

SHELF CAPACITY. The capacity of a library for storing books on shelves; it is generally expressed by the total number of books which can be so accommodated or by the number of linear feet or metres available for housing books or other library materials.

SHELF DEPARTMENT. The administrative unit of a library responsible for the care of books on the shelves, and sometimes for other work such as classification and shelf-listing.

SHELF DUMMY. A piece of wood or cardboard placed on a shelf to indicate a specific book which is shelved out of sequence.

SHELF GUIDE. A guide placed on the edge of a shelf to indicate its contents. Also called 'Shelf label'.

SHELF HEIGHT. The distance between two shelves.

SHELF LIFE. The length of time which sensitized materials used in photocopying or documentary reproduction may be kept before exposure without loss of efficiency.

SHELF LIST. A list of the books in a library, the entries being brief and arranged on cards or sheets in the order of the books on the shelves, and forming, in effect, in a classified library, a subject catalogue without added entries, analytics and cross-references.

SHELF MARK. *Synonymous with* SHELF NUMBER (*q.v.*).

SHELF NUMBER. With FIXED LOCATION (*q.v.*) a number given to a shelf to assist in the finding of books by indicating the one on which any individual book will be found. This number is incorporated in the BOOK NUMBER (*q.v.*). *See also* CALL NUMBER.

SHELF READING. *Synonymous with* READING SHELVES (*q.v.*).

SHELF REGISTER. *Synonymous with* SHELF LIST (*q.v.*).

SHELF SUPPORT. 1. The upright part of a book stack which holds the shelves, either directly or by means of a bracket. 2. The small fittings which fit into slots in the uprights and actually support the shelves. These may be pins, studs or brackets.

SHELF TIDYING. *Synonymous with* READING SHELVES (*q.v.*).

SHELL. (*Printing*) The electro plate before it is backed with metal.

SHELVING. 1. All the shelves in a library. For different kinds of shelving *see* ADJUSTABLE SHELVING, BRACKET SHELVING, CANTI-LEVER SHELVING, COMPACT STORAGE, 'LUNDIA' SHELVING, MULTI-TIER STACK, OPEN BAR SHELVING, 'RESKA' SHELVING, ROLLER SHELVES, ROLLING BOOKCASE, ROLLING PRESS, SLOTTED SHELVING, 'SPUR' SHELVING, STORAGE SHELVING, 'STOR-MOR' SHELVING. 2. The act of putting books away in their proper places on the shelves of a library.

SHINER. A mineral impurity in paper seen as a shining speck on the surface of the paper; sometimes it is due to mica in the china clay which is used as LOADING (*q.v.*) being compressed into a translucent spot during passage through the calenders. Hard, brittle materials fall out and leave 'pinholes'.

SHINING-UP TABLE. *Synonymous with* REGISTER TABLE (*q.v.*).

SHIPPING ROOM. The room of a library where parcels of books, etc., are unpacked and distributed to the various departments, and from which the outgoing material is despatched. (American.)

SHOES. (*Binding*) Metal attached to the edges only at the corners of the covers of books, and sometimes at the base of the spine, to protect the leather binding.

SHOOTING STICK. A tool of metal or hardened wood used to hammer wooden quoins into position against the side of a chase when locking up a forme.

SHOP LIBRARY. A library opened in a former shop, usually as a temporary measure and until permanent premises can be built. Sometimes such accommodation is taken for a short time to test the best site for a permanent library.

SHORT AND. *See* AMPERSAND.

SHORT CATALOGUING. The style of cataloguing in which the entries give author, main title, and date only. *See also* FULL CATA-LOGUING.

SHORT DESCENDERS. Lower case letters with descenders (g, j, p, etc.) which are shorter than usual; these can be obtained with certain founts of type.

SHORT FORM CATALOGUING. *See* SHORT CATALOGUING.

SHORT GRAIN. Paper in which the fibres lie in the shorter direction of the sheet. *See also* GRAIN DIRECTION, LONG GRAIN.

SHORT LETTER. A character, such as a, o, s, which has neither ascender nor descender. *See also* LONG LETTER.

SHORT PAGE. A page of type matter with fewer lines of type than there is room for, or than has been specified. In bookwork the space at the foot is left blank or it may be filled with a decorative piece. *See also* LONG PAGE, TYPE PAGE.

SHORT REAM. 480 sheets of paper. *See also* LONG REAM, REAM.

SHORT SCORE. *Synonymous with* CLOSE SCORE (*q.v.*). *See also* SCORE.

SHORT STORY. A complete story of from 1,000 to 8,000 words in length.

SHORT-TITLE. 1. The abbreviated title by which an Act of Parliament is known and officially designated. 2. Enough of the title of a book to enable it to be identified in a catalogue or bibliography.

SHORTS. 1. The copies of different sheets needed to complete an imperfect edition. 2. Books ordered from, but not delivered by, a bookseller owing to their not being in stock.

SHOULDER. The top of the shank of a piece of movable type. Its parts are the BEVEL (or neck), BEARD, LINE and SIDE BEARING (*q.v.*). The FACE (*q.v.*) is above the bevel.

SHOULDER-HEAD. A short descriptive heading, which precedes a paragraph; it is set in large or small capitals, or in italics, flush to the left-hand margin occupying a separate line and with a line of leading between it and the following paragraph. It marks the second division of text within the chapter, subsidiary to the CROSS HEAD (*q.v.*) and superior to the SIDE HEAD (*q.v.*). *See also* HEADING 4.

SHOULDER-NOTE. A note or sub-heading in the margin at the top outer, or fore-edge, corner of a page. *See also* MARGINAL NOTES.

SHOW THROUGH. Printed matter which shows through from the other side of a printed leaf, due to ink penetration because of the paper being insufficiently opaque or to improper pressure during machining. *See also* STRIKE THROUGH.

sic. (*Lat.* 'so, thus, in this manner') Usually printed in [ ] to indicate that an exact reproduction of the original is being made.

SIDE. 1. The right hand or left hand of a piece of type when the printing surface is uppermost and facing the viewer. The front is called the 'belly' and the back the 'back'. 2. The front or back cover of a bound book.

SIDE BEARING. The amount of 'shoulder' on either side of a piece of movable type; it controls the amount of white space left between characters when composed into lines.

SIDE HEAD (SIDE HEADING). A short descriptive sub-heading dividing sections of a chapter, indented one em and usually printed in italics (but maybe in caps, large and small, or in bold), not occupying a separate line, and placed at the beginning of a paragraph with the matter running on. It is the third division of text within a chapter, subsidiary to the SHOULDER HEAD (q.v.). See also CROSS-HEAD, HEADING 4.

SIDE LETTERING. Synonymous with SIDE TITLE (q.v.).

SIDE NOTE. A marginal note outside the type page, and usually set in narrow measure in type several sizes smaller than the text of the page. Synonymous with MARGINAL NOTE (q.v.). Also called 'Hanging shoulder note'. Sometimes it is a substitute for a CROSS-HEAD (q.v.), but more usually provides a gloss on the text, or running commentary, which does not interrupt the argument; if read with continuity, side notes give an abstract of the whole book.

SIDE SEWING. See SIDE-STITCH.

SIDE SORTS. Synonymous with ODD SORTS (q.v.).

SIDE STICK. See CHASE.

SIDE-STITCH. (Binding) To stitch a booklet or pamphlet of two or more folded signatures from back to front through the leaves or sections (not through their folds), and near their binding edges, using thread or wire. Also called 'Flat stitching', 'Side sewing', 'Stab-stitch'. When wire is used the process is called 'Wire-stabbing'. See also SADDLE STITCHING, SINGER SEWING.

SIDE TITLE. A title impressed on the front cover, or side, of a bound book.

SIDE-WIRE. To side-stitch a pamphlet with wire staples.

SIGIL. A chronological CODEN (q.v.) in which the first characters would represent the date of publication followed by those representing the title.

SIGILLOGRAPHY. The science or study of seals, being a branch of diplomatics. Also called 'SPHRAGISTICS'.

SIGLA. Symbols; it is sometimes printed at the head of a table of these.

SIGN MANUAL. A signature written with the person's own hand, especially the signature of a sovereign or head of state, to give authority to a state document.

SIGNATURE. 1. A folded printed sheet, forming part of a book; a section. 2. The letter or number, or combination of letters and numbers, printed at the foot of the first page, and sometimes on subsequent leaves of a section, as a guide to the binder in arranging them in their correct order. These were written or stamped in until 1472 when Johann Koelhoff of Cologne, printed a signature as the last line of a text page. The binders of MSS. usually cut off the signature letters. Each section has a different signature and when letters are used, as is usual, they progress in alphabetical order, J, V and W usually being omitted to avoid confusion. There is also a historical reason for the omission of these letters: MSS. and early printed books were usually written in Latin, in which alphabet I stands for both I and J, and V for both U and V, and there is no W. When the alphabet has been used up a lower case sequence or a new sequence of double letters followed by one of treble letters, or sequences combining capital and lower case letters are used. If the same sequence is used again it is known as a duplicated or triplicated signature. Signatures are usually omitted in American books. Also called 'Signature mark'. *See also* COLLATION, COLLATING MARK, DESIGNATION MARK, DIRECTION LINE, SECTION, TITLE SIGNATURE, VOLUME SIGNATURE. 3. The name or initials, written in a person's own hand to authenticate a document.

SIGNATURE AND CATCHWORD LINE. The line of type which in an old book bears both the signature and the catchword. It is usually below the lowest line of text. Also called 'Direction line'; should the signature and catchword be on separate lines, the lower is called the direction line.

SIGNATURE MARK. The letter or number, or a combination of both, placed at the left of the tail margin of the first page of each section of a book. *See also* SIGNATURE 2.

SIGNATURE TITLE. *Synonymous with* TITLE SIGNATURE (*q.v.*).

SIGNATURES, LIST OF. *See* REGISTER 2.

SIGNED EDITION. *Synonymous with* AUTOGRAPHED EDITION (*q.v.*). *See also* LIMITED EDITION.

SIGNED PAGE. The first page of a section – the one bearing the SIGNATURE (*q.v.*).

SILHOUETTE. 1. To remove non-essential background from a half-tone block to produce an outline effect. 2. A print, illustration, drawing, or other form of artistic reproduction from which background has been removed.

SILK PAPER. Produced at Baghdad in the Middle Ages and famous throughout Persia. It was prepared from linen. The term is also used for papers containing a quantity of short, coloured silk fibres, or even one or more strands of silk or metal running through the sheet; this is used for bank notes, and is difficult to counterfeit.

SILK SCREEN. A stencil process for multiplying an original design and for lettering in colours which is used for posters and other jobs requiring short runs and for which lithography would be too expensive. Bolting silk, organdie, phosphor bronze or steel gauze are tightly stretched over a wooden frame. A stencil bearing the design is fixed to the underside of the silk or other material and paint is forced through the silk at the open parts of the stencil with a rubber squeegee on to the paper, silk, metal, glass, wood or other material to be printed.

SILKED. A leaf of a book which has been repaired by backing it on both sides with transparent silk.

SILKING. The application of silk chiffon to one or both sides of a sheet of paper as a means of repairing or preserving it. *See also* LAMINATION.

SILVER BOOK AWARD. A little silver book mounted on a plaque; it is awarded by the (American) Library Binding Institute on the nomination of a Certified Library Binder to people who have made some significant or outstanding contribution to the field of library science.

SILVER HALIDE PAPER. A paper used in lensless copying machines. It is necessary to use the traditional photographic developing processes of making negatives (i.e. developing, rinsing, fixing, washing, drying) before making positive copies.

SILVER PROCESSES. A group of processes using silver halide sensitized materials for document copying. These include DIFFUSION TRANSFER (*q.v.*), Direct Positive (*see* LENSLESS COPYING), PHOTOSTAT, REFLEX (*qq.v.*). *See also* DRY SILVER HALIDE, TRANSFER PROCESS.

SILVERED. The edges of a book which are treated with silver instead of gold.

SILVERFISH. A small, quick-moving hexapod resembling a centipede. It flourishes in damp conditions, feeds on the glazed surface of photographs, the starchy content of paper, cardboard and paste, sometimes leaving narrow trenches where it has been feeding. D.D.T. or gammezane can be used as an exterminant.

SIMPLE HEADING. *See* MAIN HEADING.

SIMPLEX. A microcopying method using the width of the film for one set of pictures only (*Concepts . . .*).

SIMPLIFIED CATALOGUING. The elimination of some of the information normally given in full catalogue entries to reduce the work involved in cataloguing and thereby the cost, or to make the catalogue simpler to use. *See also* FULL CATALOGUING, LIMITED CATALOGUING, SHORT CATALOGUING.

SINGER SEWING. Side-stitching with thread, the sewing extending the full length of the volume. *See also* SEWING, STABBING, THREAD STITCHED.

SINGLE QUOTES. Superior commas used to indicate quoted matter already within quoted matter: '. . .'. So named to distinguish them from double quotes ". . .", the more common form of quotation mark. *See also* DOUBLE QUOTES.

SINGLE-REVOLUTION MACHINE. A letterpress printing machine in which the continuously running cylinder, having a diameter twice that of the TWO-REVOLUTION MACHINE (*q.v.*), runs at a constant speed. During the first half-rotation the bed moves forward and the impression is made; during the second half-rotation the bed returns. Some makes of this type of machine have varying speeds for the bed and/or cylinder.

SINGLE WEIGHT PAPER. Sensitized photographic paper between 0·0060 and 0·0083 inches inclusive. *See also* PHOTOGRAPHIC PAPERS.

SINKAGE. Space left at the top of a printed page in excess of the normal margin, as e.g. at the beginning of a new chapter.

SINTO. Abbreviation for Sheffield Interchange Organization. This is the earliest British scheme of local library co-operation, having been commenced in 1932. Membership is open to organizations with a library of over fifty books and subscriptions to ten appropriate periodicals. Its objects are 'to make known and to secure the greatest possible use of the contents of member libraries by means of an organized system of interlending and to provide a means of co-operation in solving problems of common interest'. The Department of Commerce, Science and Technology of the Sheffield City Libraries is the Headquarters of SINTO, and houses the union catalogue of books and periodicals of members excluding those of the City Libraries and of the Sheffield University and its Applied Science Libraries. The Headquarters acts as the liaison agent between members who make their own contacts for borrowing material; it acts as a steel information centre, has conducted research into the holdings of foreign patents in Great Britain, pressed the Patent Office to improve its publications, urged Aslib to produce a central Translations Index, compiled an extensive index of foreign standard specifications, and co-operated with the Sheffield Education Authority in providing courses of training for special librarianship.

SISO. A Dutch 'scheme for the classification of the subject catalogues in

public libraries' which was published in 1958 by the Central Association of Public Libraries of Holland. It is basically Dr. Greve's 'Hague
Scheme' first published in 1931; it has a decimal notation, and the
schedules resemble the Universal Decimal Classification and Dewey,
compared with which the arrangement of subjects shows improvements.

SITTYBUS.   A title label which identified papyrus rolls. *See also* SCROLL 1.

SIXTEENMO.   *See* SEXTODECIMO.

SIXTY-FOURMO (64mo).   A sheet of paper folded six times to form a
section of sixty-four leaves, making 128 pages. Also called 'Sexagesimo-
quarto'.

SIZE.   1. (*Cataloguing*) The size of a book is measured by its height; a book
is called 'narrow' if the width of the cover is less than $\frac{3}{5}$ of the height;
'square' if more than $\frac{3}{4}$; and 'oblong' or 'landscape' if the width of the
cover is greater than the height. Width is usually given only when unusual, or for old books. When both height and width are given, the
height is given first. Measurements are usually given in centimetres in
bibliographies and catalogues, although often in inches in the latter.
The *Anglo-American Code* requires that size be given in centimetres to
the nearest half centimetre. The fold symbol (e.g. f°, 4°, 8°, 12°) is
often used as an indication of approximate size. *See also* BOOK SIZES,
FOLD SYMBOL, FOLDINGS, TYPE SIZES. 2. (*Paper*) A mixture of gelatine, alum and formaldehyde through which paper is passed, after
coming from the paper-making machine, in order to produce a better
surface and to repel water. 3. (*Binding*) A bonding material placed
between binding material and lettering.

SIZE COPY.   A thickness or dummy copy. *See also* DUMMY 1.

SIZE LETTERS.   The symbols (F, Q, O, D, etc.) used to indicate the
size of books. *See also* FOLD SYMBOL, FOLDINGS.

SIZE NOTATION.   The method of indicating the size of a book: it may
be by measurement in centimetres or inches, by FOLD SYMBOLS (*q.v.*)
or by SIZE LETTERS (*q.v.*).

SIZE RULE.   A rule graduated in inches and/or centimetres with fold
symbols and corresponding size letters marked at the proper places;
it is used for measuring books.

SIZED PAPER.   Paper which has been treated to make it less receptive
to water. Blotting paper is unsized: writing paper is hard-sized. The
treatment consists of adding resin to the stuff in the beater or to the
surface of the paper or board (surface sizing) so that the finished paper
will be non-absorbent. The suitability of resin for this purpose is said
to have been discovered by Moritz Friedrich Illig of Darmstadt in

1806. Animal glue, starch or casein may be used as alternatives. *See also* SIZE (*Paper*).

SIZING. The act of applying size. *See* SIZE 2, 3.

SKANDIA PLAN. *See* SCANDIA PLAN.

SKELETON. The cross-bars which separate the pages of type in a forme, the 'furniture' (pieces of wood or metal) which form the page margins, and the running titles, which are left in position when the pages of type have been removed after printing for breaking up, ready for the emplacement of the next pages of the same volume.

SKELETON CATALOGUE CARD. An outline catalogue card bearing the names of the parts of an entry to show a student of cataloguing the proper placing of the various parts.

SKETCH. 1. A drawing. 2. A brief description of a person or event. 3. A short musical or dramatic play.

SKINNER DEVICE. Any of a number of devices in mechanical teaching by teaching machines which provide a small space for the presentation of information, a small space for the student to write his response, and a mechanism to reveal the correct answer after he has responded.

SKIVER. A leather made from the hair or grain side of split sheepskin; it is often embossed and finished in imitation of various leather grains.

SKIVER LABEL. A paper-thin skiver used for a label on the spine of a book.

SLAB SERIF. (*Printing*) A serif consisting of a plain horizontal stroke which is not bracketed to the upright stroke of a letter. **Rockwell, Clarendon and Playbill are faces of this kind.**

SLANTED ABSTRACT. An abstract giving emphasis to a particular aspect of the contents of a document so as to cater for the interests of a particular group of readers.

SLIC INDEX. An index compiled on the principle of Selective Listing In Combination. It consists of deriving every combination of terms from the set of alphabetically ordered terms assigned by the indexer, selecting from these combinations only those which do not form the beginnings of longer combinations, and listing these selected groups in alphabetical order. Not more than five terms are assigned as a set, but these can be re-arranged so as to give a total of sixteen entries, or each can be transferred to a punched card.

SLICK. A large-circulation consumer magazine printed on coated stock and usually characterized by articles chosen for popular appeal and fiction limited to formulized stories with happy endings. (Webster's *Third New International Dictionary*). The authors of the material published receive a higher rate than for the 'pulps'. Also called 'Slick paper'. *See also* PULP 2.

SLIDE BOX.   *Synonymous with* SLIP CASE (*q.v.*).

SLIDE CASE.   *Synonymous with* SLIP CASE (*q.v.*).

SLIDING SHELVES.   Large shelves for the flat storage of folios; designed so that they may be pulled out to facilitate handling and save wear and tear on the bindings.

SLIP.   (*Verb*) 1. To discharge a book. *See* BOOK CARD, DISCHARGING BOOKS.   2. To list books on separate slips of paper, one for each book. (*Noun*) A small piece of paper, usually of standard 5×3 inches size, used to record briefly author and title, etc., as part of the book-preparation processes, or for some temporary recording purpose. The master catalogue entry or the catalogue entry for a typist to copy, may be written on such a slip. *See also* P-SLIP, SLIPS.

SLIP CANCEL.   A small piece of paper bearing a printed correction and pasted over the incorrect matter in a printed book.

SLIP CASE.   A cardboard box made to fit one or more volumes published together, and open at the front to show the titles. Also called 'Open-back case', 'Slide box', 'Slide case', 'Slip-in case'.

SLIP CATALOGUE.   *Synonymous with* PAGE CATALOGUE (*q.v.*).

SLIP-IN CASE.   *Synonymous with* SLIP CASE (*q.v.*).

SLIP PROOF.   *See* PROOF.

SLIP SHEET.   A sheet of paper which is placed between sheets as they come from the printing machine to prevent offset. *See also* SET-OFF.

SLIPPING BOOKS.   The American term for DISCHARGING BOOKS (*q.v.*).

SLIPPING DESK.   *See* CIRCULATION DESK.

SLIPS.   1. The pieces of sewing cord or tape which project beyond the back of the book after it is sewn, and which are afterwards attached to the boards. Also called 'Tabs'. 2. The paper slips on which are written the instructions to the binder. 3. Applied to matter not set up into pages, but pulled as proofs, on long slips of paper called galley proofs. *See also* PROOF.

SLOPING SHELVES.   *Synonymous with* TILTED SHELVES (*q.v.*).

SLOTTED CARDS.   Cards which have had slots punched in them in rows. Information is recorded by punching out the space between two or three holes. The cards are kept in a cradle, and when cards recording particular information are required, needles are inserted through the holes which represent the wanted features and the cradle inverted. This causes the cards to fall out of position for examination, but not out of sequence. *See also* DEQUEKER SYSTEM, EDGE-NOTCHED CARDS, MARGINAL-HOLE PUNCHED CARDS.

SLOTTED SHELVING. A form of adjustable steel shelving whereby the shelves slide into slots running through the uprights from back to front.

SLUG. 1. A line of type set solid on a composing machine. 2. A metal bar the length of a line of type characters, to print an entire line, having the appearance of a solid line of type and serving the same purpose.

SLUG-CASTING MACHINE. A machine for setting up type in the form of cast lines or slugs. These include INTERTYPE, ITALTYPE, LINOTYPE, LUDLOW and TYPOGRAPH (qq.v.).

SLUR. A letterpress machine printing fault caused by an irregular movement of the paper while the impression is being taken, and resulting in the distortion of dots in a half-tone or a double impression of the type characters.

SMALL CAPITALS. The smaller capital letters (as distinct from the full capitals) of which they are about $\frac{2}{3}$ the size, thus: A, B, C; the same size as the X-HEIGHT (q.v.) of a letter. Indicated in a MS. or proof by two strokes underneath. Abbreviated s.c., s.cap., sm.cap., s.caps, small caps (pl.). See also CAPITALS, LOWER CASE LETTERS, UPPER CASE LETTERS.

SMALL DEMY. See DEMY.

SMALL PAPER COPY. A copy, or an edition, of a book which is printed on paper of a smaller size than a LARGE PAPER COPY (q.v.) or large paper edition. Also called 'Small paper edition'.

SMALL PICA. An obsolete size of type, about 11 point.

SMALLER PUBLIC LIBRARIES GROUP. An association of the smaller public library authorities (in towns with a population of up to 50,000) which was formed in 1956 to (a) influence opinion and combat the views of individuals and organizations who considered that public library services could be provided more efficiently if such small libraries were incorporated into larger units and to maintain the right of efficient library authorities to continue to enjoy the powers they have under the Public Libraries Acts; and (b) to raise the standards of efficiency in the smaller library authorities. This controversy developed at the time the 'Roberts Committee' was collecting evidence on public library services for the guidance of the British Government. See also ROBERTS REPORT.

SMALT. A species of glass, usually deep blue through the use of oxide of cobalt, and finely pulverized for use as a colouring medium in paper making. It is usually used as a 'loading', and as it is resistant to acids alkalis, heat and moisture, it is a very permanent colouring material.

As it has a low colouring power it is expensive, and is used mainly for hand-made and the better machine-made azures for writings. Having a high specific gravity, it usually sinks through the pulp and colours one side more than the other.

SMASHER.   *Synonymous with* BUMPER (*q.v.*).

SMASHING MACHINE.   A machine used in binderies for compressing folded signatures to render them more compact for binding by expelling the air from between the pages.

W. H. SMITH & SON LITERARY AWARD.   A cash award of £1,000 which has been offered by W. H. Smith & Son Ltd. annually since 1959 when Patrick White received it for *Voss*. The Award is made to the Commonwealth author whose book (originally written in English and published in the United Kingdom within the twenty-four months ending on 31st December preceding the year of the award) makes, in the opinion of the judges, the most outstanding contribution to literature. The composition of the panel of judges is at the discretion of W. H. Smith & Son Ltd. who submit a list of published books, for the information of the judges and also supply any books required, but are in no way consulted by the judges. The making of an award does not create any contractual or other rights.

SMOOTH ANTIQUE.   *See* PAPER FINISHES.

SMYRNA MOROCCO.   A sheepskin finished with a grain to imitate MOROCCO (*q.v.*). *See also* SHEEPSKIN.

SMYTH SEWING.   Sewing through the sections of a book; done by a Smyth sewing machine. The usual kind of sewing in Edition binding (*q.v.*), usually without tapes. (American.) *See also* CASE.

SNAG.   A book for which no record of loan can be found. (American.)

SNAG FILE.   A file into which are placed items that will not fit into the organization of a main file, either because of certain weaknesses or deficiencies in the main file organization, or because the file system must perform a function which is not part of the original design.

SOBRIQUET.   A nickname: a fanciful appellation. As these names are usually better known than the real names, books by or about them are often entered in catalogues under the sobriquet. *See also* NICKNAME.

SOCIETY.   A group or association of persons united under a set of regulations, conditions of membership, etc., for the promotion of common purposes or objects, such as politics, research, business, recreation, etc. For its distinction from an institution for purposes of cataloguing, see INSTITUTION.

SOCIETY OF AMERICAN ARCHIVISTS.   Founded in 1936 to promote sound principles of archival economy, and to facilitate co-operation among archivists and archival agencies. Is concerned with the management of current records, archival administration, and the custody of historical manuscripts in government, business and semi-public institutions. Abbreviated SAA. Publishes *The American Archivist* (q.).

SOCIETY OF ARCHIVISTS. Founded in 1947 to foster the care and preservation of archives and to enable archivists to discuss common problems and interchange technical knowledge in Great Britiain and the Commonwealth. Publishes *Journal* . . . (two p.a.).

SOCIETY OF COUNTY LIBRARIANS, THE. First formed in 1954. It was re-formed in January 1966 by county librarians in England and Wales and has for its objects: 'to promote and facilitate discussion and exchange of views on matters affecting county libraries in England and Wales; to promote and safeguard the interests of county libraries in England and Wales'. Before the Society was re-formed, the second object was to safeguard the interests of county *librarians,* whereas now it is the interests of the county *libraries* which are safeguarded. The Society operates on a wider basis than formerly; it advises the County Councils' Association on library matters, collects information, and has its own officially appointed advisers. Membership is open to persons designated as County Librarians, directors of county library services, chief librarians in charge of county library systems, or any variant terminology denoting similar responsibilities. Abbreviated SCL.

SOCIETY OF INDEXERS. Founded in London on 30th March 1957 with the aim of improving standards of book indexing and securing some measure of uniformity in its technique, advising publishers and editors on the qualification and remuneration of indexers, and safeguarding their interests. Publishes *The Indexer* (2 p.a.).

SOCIETY PUBLICATION. An official publication issued by, or under the auspices of, a society, institution or association.

SODA PULP. (*Papermaking*) Chemical wood pulp which is prepared by digesting the wood fibres under pressure with a solution of caustic soda. This process is usually applied to straw and soft or deciduous trees such as aspen, poplar, etc. which cannot be treated by the sulphite process (*see* SULPHITE PULP) usually confined to coniferous woods.

SOFT COVER. *Synonymous with* PAPERBACK and PAPER-BOUND (*qq.v.*).

SOFT GELATINE TRANSFER PROCESS. *See* TRANSFER PROCESS.

SOFT-GROUND ETCHING. One in which the ground commonly used is softened by mixing with tallow, the design being made with a pencil on a piece of fine-grained paper stretched over the ground. This, when etched with acid gives the effect of pencil or chalk lines in the printed impression. (*United Typothetæ*.)

SOLANDER CASE. A book-shaped box for holding a book, prints, pamphlets or other material, named after its inventor, Daniel Charles Solander (1736–82). It may open at the side or front with hinges, or have two separate parts, one fitting over the other. Its most developed form has a rounded back, projecting SQUARES (*q.v.*) like a book, and possibly one or more spring catches. Also called 'Solander', 'Solander box', 'Solander cover'.

SOLID GILT. A book the edges of which have been gilded 'in the round', i.e. after the book has been ROUNDED (*q.v.*). *See also* GILT ON THE ROUGH, MARBLING UNDER GILT, ROUGH GILT.

SOLID MATTER. Type which has been set without 'leads'. Matter so set is said to be 'Set solid'. *See also* LEADED MATTER, LEADS.

SOLIDUS. An oblique stroke used for various purposes, e.g. to indicate two or more adjoining premises in one occupancy, as: 14/18 Essex Road; to indicate line endings in a bibliographical description of a title-page, as: An/address/to the/ . . .

SORORITY LIBRARY. A library in a sorority on an American college or university campus. It may be a circulating collection from the main library, or owned by the sorority, a girls' or women's club.

SORT. A single type-letter. The complete muster of sorts, made up in the correct proportion of characters, is called a 'fount'. Also called 'Character'. *See also* CODE, DIGIT, SPECIAL SORTS.

SORTER. A machine which arranges punched cards in a pre-determined sequence according to the holes punched in the cards.

SOUND LIBRARY. A collection of audio records such as gramophone records, magnetic or other tape and sound film.

SOUND RECORDINGS GROUP. A Group of the Library Association which was formed in 1964.

SOUNDEX. A coding system for names which groups together those which sound the same or tend to be confused when communication is blurred. Each name is represented by the first letter followed by three decimal digits. The latter are chosen according to the following rules: (1) double letters are treated as single letters, (2) A, E, I, O, U, W, H, Y are always ignored, (3) letters with similar sounds are then identified by the appropriate code number:

BFPV	1	L	4
CGJKQSXZ	2	MN	5
DT	3	R	6

(4) If there are less than three such consonants after the initial letter, zeros are added to produce the three-digit code.

Examples:	*Name*	*Soundex code*
	Kuckuck	K220
	Swinhart	S563
	Whiffen	W150
	Wullerwaber	W451

This system, perhaps the most popular of codes used in conjunction with large name files, permits filing and searching of large groups of names phonetically as well as alphabetically. It was developed by Remington Rand, and, as with other such systems, can be used as an important element of a mechanized system.

SOURCE INDEX. A card, or other, index to sources of unusual and elusive information. This is usually built up in the process of dealing with enquiries.

SOURCE LANGUAGE. The natural language in which a document is written. *See also* CODE LANGUAGE.

SOURCE MATERIAL. *See* PRIMARY SOURCES.

SOUTH AFRICAN LIBRARY ASSOCIATION. Founded on 5th July 1930 as a result of a conference held at Bloemfontein in 1928. Among its aims are: to unite all persons engaged in, or interested in, library work; to promote the better administration of libraries; to promote whatever may tend to the improvement of the position and qualifications of librarians; to promote the establishment of libraries for the use of the public; to watch any legislation affecting public libraries; to hold examinations in librarianship and to issue certificates of efficiency; to promote the fullest co-operation between libraries, public, governmental, institutional and private. Membership is open to libraries and other institutions and to librarians, bibliographers, members of library committees and other persons connected with the administration of libraries, or interested in the objects of the Association. Abbreviated SALA. Publishes *South African Libraries* (q.) and *Newsletter* (m). A number of branches have been formed to function in geographical areas.

SPACE. (*Printing*) A small rectangular block of metal not bearing a character, which is used between letters or words to provide spacing. Spaces are less than type height, cast in point sizes and smaller than an em quad (mutton), the square of the body. The usual sizes are:
en quad (nut), $\frac{1}{2}$ body or two to the em;
thick space ($\frac{1}{3}$-em space), $\frac{1}{3}$ body or three to the em;
middle space ($\frac{1}{4}$-em space), $\frac{1}{4}$ body or four to the em;

thin space ($\frac{1}{5}$-em space), $\frac{1}{5}$ body or five to the em;

hair space ($\frac{1}{12}$-em space), $\frac{1}{12}$ body or twelve to the em.

SPACE DOT. *Synonymous with* CENTRED DOT (*q.v.*).

SPACES LINES. Strips of brass which are often used in place of LEADS (*q.v.*).

SPACE TO FILL. Space left in a printing layout through insufficient COPY (*q.v.*) being provided.

SPACEBANDS. Wedge-shaped pieces of metal used in line-casting machines such as LINOTYPE and INTERTYPE (*qq.v.*) to separate words and at the same time automatically justify lines of type.

SPACING. The distribution of printed matter on a printed page or pair of pages so that it is aesthetically satisfactory. It relates to the space between letters, words, lines, and any decorative or illustrative matter.

SPANISH. The best grade of esparto grass. Cheaper grades grown in N. Africa are known as Tripoli.

SPANISH CALF. A light-coloured calf on which brilliant effects can be obtained by staining.

SPECIAL BIBLIOGRAPHY. *See* BIBLIOGRAPHY 1.

SPECIAL CLASSIFICATION. A classification which is applied to a section of knowledge; for example:

Barnard's *Classification for medical and veterinary libraries,*

Cutter's *Labor classification for the Baker Library, Harvard School of Business Administration,*

Dabagh's *Mnemonic classification for law libraries,*

Smith's *Classification of London literature,*

Classification scheme of agricultural science,

British catalogue of music classification

Schwerin, Kurt. *Classification for international law.*

Stein, Jay W. *A classification for communications materials.*

World Health Organization. *Manual of the international statistical classification of diseases, injuries, and causes of death.*

ASM-SLA. *Metallurgical literature classification.*

Commonwealth Agricultural Bureau. *The Oxford system of decimal classification for forestry.*

SPECIAL COLLECTION. A collection of books connected with local history, celebrities, industries, etc., or on a certain subject or period, or gathered for some particular reason, in a library which is general in character.

SPECIAL EDITION. 1. An edition of a work or works, re-issued in a new format, sometimes with an introduction, appendix, or illustrations, and having a distinctive name. 2. An edition which differs from the normal edition by some distinctive feature, such as better paper and binding or the addition of illustrations. 3. An extra or enlarged number of a newspaper or periodical, such as an anniversary, Christmas, or souvenir number.

SPECIAL ESTIMATE. *See* ESTIMATES.

SPECIAL ISSUE. 1. *Synonymous with* SPECIAL NUMBER (*q.v.*). 2. The loan of a book to a person who does not possess a membership ticket, or a loan for an unusual period.

SPECIAL LIBRARIAN. One who is in charge of, or is employed in, a special library; he should have a knowledge of the literature of the field covered by the library (not necessarily a special knowledge of the field itself) and also of the means of organizing it for use.

SPECIAL LIBRARIANSHIP. The branch of librarianship which is concerned with selecting, administering, and evaluating books and non-book materials in specific and limited fields of knowledge, and disseminating the information contained therein to meet the needs of the particular institution or its clientele.

SPECIAL LIBRARIES ASSOCIATION. Founded in the U.S.A. in 1909 to encourage and promote the utilization of knowledge through the collection, organization, and dissemination of information, to develop the usefulness and efficiency of special libraries or information centres, to stimulate research in the field of information services, to promote high professional standards, to facilitate communication among its members, to co-operate with organizations that have similar or allied interests. It has as its slogan 'Putting knowledge to work'. The work of the Association is carried out through many subject divisions. Abbreviated SLA. Publishes *Scientific Meetings* (3 a year), *Special Libraries* (10 issues a year), *Technical Book Review Index* (10 issues a year), *Unlisted Drugs* (m.). *See also* DIVISION.

SPECIAL LIBRARY. 1. A library maintained by an individual, corporation, association, government agency or any other group for the collection, organization, and dissemination of information and primarily devoted to a special subject and offering specialized service to a specialized clientele (*Special Libraries Association*). 2. A collection of books and other printed, graphic or record material dealing with a limited field of knowledge, and provided by a learned society, research organization, industrial or commercial undertaking, government department or educational institution. It may also be a special branch of a public library serving certain interests or occupational groups, such as a technical library; or a special subject library meeting the needs of all enquirers on a given subject, such as a music library. A special library is broadly one which is neither academic, commercial, national nor public. It is intended to serve the needs of a portion of the community requiring detailed information respecting a limited subject field. Users of such libraries often require up-to-date information promptly and their requests may be for information rather than for a book or periodical known by the enquirer to contain the information required.

SPECIAL NUMBER. A special issue (usually enlarged in size) of a periodical devoted to a special subject or occasion. More routine occasions to which issues of periodicals are wholly or partly devoted are: (a) directory issue containing a directory of the trade or group served by the periodical; (b) membership list containing a list of members; (c) proceedings issue containing papers read at a conference, or a summary of the same; (d) an annual review, or annual report, issue surveying the past year and giving tables of statistics, possibly with forecasts relating to the following year; (e) yearbook (handbook, or almanac) issue combining any or all of the foregoing types, together with general data kept up to date by annual revisions. *See also* SPECIAL EDITION.

SPECIAL SORTS. Type characters which are not usually included in a FOUNT (*q.v.*), and are supplied on request, such as fractions, musical signs, superior and inferior letters and figures, etc.

SPECIAL TITLE-PAGE. A title-page, usually with imprint, preceding a single part of a larger work. Also one preceding the normal title-page of a complete work which is issued or re-issued as part of a collection, series, or serial publication.

SPECIES. 1. In classification, the groups into which a genus is divided. *See also* PREDICABLES, FIVE. 2. In computer coding, each conventional set of 'sorts' comprising a symbol. *See also* DIGIT.

SPECIFIC CLASSING. Allocating a book to the most specific or detailed place in a scheme of classification.

SPECIFIC CROSS REFERENCE. A reference in a catalogue to a specific heading or headings.

SPECIFIC DIFFERENCES. (*Classification*) Differences which characterize some individuals as a *specific* sub-class within a more comprehensive *generic* class.

SPECIFIC ENTRY. An entry in a catalogue under the actual subject, as distinct from one under some broader heading embracing that subject. It should be as specific as, but not more specific than, the content of the book. This is the principle for entry of subjects in a dictionary catalogue. *See also* CATALOGUING, PRINCIPLES OF.

SPECIFIC INDEX. An index such as that to Brown's *Subject Classification*, which has one entry only to each subject. Also called 'One-place index'. *See also* RELATIVE INDEX.

SPECIFIC REFERENCE. (*Cataloguing*) One which states the exact heading to which reference must be made as (in a dictionary catalogue): AUTOMOBILES *see* MOTOR CARS, whereas a general reference would be: ANIMALS see also under the names of individual animals, as ANTELOPE. In the subject index to a classified catalogue references are usually specific as: RELIGION 200, METHODISTS 287. *See also* GENERAL REFERENCES.

SPECIFICATION. 1. Instructions prepared for a binder, printer or builder setting out the details of work to be carried out. 2. (*Information retrieval*) The cataloguing, bibliographical, or similar description, of a document. *See also* UNIT RECORD. 3. (*Classification*) Definition by SPECIFIC DIFFERENCES (*q.v.*) in characters.

SPECIMEN PAGES. Printed pages which are submitted by the printer to show the proposed style of setting. They usually number four and include a chapter opening with any sub-headings.

SPECKLED SAND EDGE. A bound book the top-, fore-, and bottom-edges of which have been rubbed down with sandpaper and sprinkled or sprayed with colour.

SPECTRUM. Trade name for a make of periodical display rack which has sloping pieces of 'Perspex' projecting at an angle to a wall or backboard on which periodicals rest so as to display the whole of the front cover.

SPECULUM HUMANAE SALVATIONIS. *See* BLOCK BOOKS.

SPHRAGISTICS. *Synonymous with* SIGILLOGRAPHY (*q.v.*).

SPINE. The part of the cover of a book which conceals the folds of the sections. It normally bears the title, author and (when in a publisher's case) the publisher's name. Also called 'Back', 'Backbone', 'Shelfback', 'Backstrip'.

SPINE TITLE. The title which appears on the spine of a book. It is often shorter than the title as given on the title-page.

SPIRAL BINDING. A type of binding used for pamphlets, art reproductions, commercial catalogues, and occasionally books, printed on separate leaves, usually of art paper. These leaves are drilled near the binding edge to take a spiral-twisted wire which is drawn through the holes. A tendency for the wire to be torn through the holes makes this style unsuitable for publications likely to be subject to much, or to careless, handling. Also called 'Coil binding', 'Spirex binding'. *See also* PLASTIC BINDING.

SPIREX BINDING.   *See* SPIRAL BINDING.

SPIRIT DUPLICATOR.   A machine for duplicating copies of typed, written or drawn matter. A master copy is made by typing, writing or drawing on a piece of art paper which has a sheet of coloured hectograph carbon paper (black, purple, blue, green or red) underneath it. The carbon then adheres to the art paper where pressure has taken place and appears in reverse. Master copies may also be made by a thermal process. This is then placed on the drum of the duplicating machine and some of the carbon is transferred to the paper on which a copy is required as this passes into contact with the master copy and after having passed over a spirit-impregnated pad. *See also* HECTOGRAPH PROCESS.

SPLICE.   A join made by cementing or welding together two pieces of film or paper so that they will function as one when passing through a camera, processing machine, projector or other apparatus. Lap splices are those in which the two pieces overlap and are cemented together. Butt splices are those in which the two pieces are placed together without overlapping and welded.

SPLIT BOARDS.   The boards forming the covers of a book which are split to receive the ends of the tapes on to which the sections are sewn.

SPLIT CATALOGUE.   A library catalogue in which the different varieties of entry – e.g. subject, author, title – are filed in separate alphabets (*IBM*).

SPLIT FRACTIONS.   Type for setting fractions cast in two parts which when combined make the complete fraction. The upper half contains the upper figure and the lower half the dividing line and the lower figure. Fractions may be set horizontally, e.g. $\frac{3}{8}$ or diagonally, e.g. 3/8 or 3/8.

SPLIT LEATHER.   Leather which has been divided into two or more thicknesses.

SPOILED LETTER.   *Synonymous with* DAMAGED LETTER (*q.v.*).

SPOILED SHEETS.   Printed sheets which bear imperfections; it is to allow for such that additional sheets, called 'overs', are issued to the printer. Often called 'Spoils'.

SPOILS.   *See* SPOILED SHEETS.

SPONGY PAPER.   *Synonymous with* FEATHERWEIGHT PAPER (*q.v.*).

SPONSOR.   A person or corporate body subsidizing or otherwise encouraging the production of a book (*IFLA*).

SPREAD.   A pair of facing pages.

SPRINKLED EDGES.   The three cut edges of a book which have been finely sprinkled with colour to prevent them becoming, or appearing to be, soiled. *See also* EDGES.

SPUR SHELVING. Trade name for particular designs of suspension and cantilever shelving.

SQUABBLE. A printing fault caused by one or more letters being pushed into an adjacent line.

SQUARE. Said of a book the width of the cover of which is more than three-quarters its height.

SQUARE. (*Binding*). The boards of a book are cut slightly larger than the bound sections after trimming so as to leave an even projection over the HEAD, TAIL and FORE-EDGE (*qq.v.*). This projection of the boards is called the 'square'.

SQUARE BACK. *Synonymous with* FLAT BACK (*q.v.*).

SQUARE BRACKETS. Signs [ ] used in a catalogue or bibliographical entry to indicate that whatever appears within them does not appear in the original, but has been supplied by the copier. Not to be confused with PARENTHESES (*q.v.*).

SQUARE CAPITALS. The alphabet used as a book hand from the third to the fifth centuries, being adapted from the Roman lapidary capitals. The letters had square serifs instead of being sharply pointed as were those cut in stone. Also called 'Capitales quadrata' and 'Quadrata'. *See also* LAPIDARY TYPE, RUSTIC CAPITALS.

SQUARE CORNER. (*Binding*) Folding the covering material over the boards in such a way that after cutting a wedge-shaped piece at the corner, one turn-in may neatly overlap the other. *See also* LIBRARY CORNER, MITRED CORNER.

SQUARE UP. To trim, or adjust, illustrations so that all corners are right angles.

SQUARED-UP HALF-TONE. *See* HALF-TONE.

SQUARES. The portions of the boards of a bound book which project beyond the paper on which it is printed.

STAB MARKS. Punctures made in folded sheets of printed paper preparatory to sewing.

STAB-STITCH. *See* SIDE-STITCH.

STABBED. *See* STABBING.

STABBING. Binding together one or more sections of a book with wire or thread passed through holes stabbed through the back edge of the folded sheet. This method prevents the book from lying flat when open. A book so bound is said to be 'stabbed'. Piercing the boards with a bodkin for the slips to pass through is sometimes termed 'stabbing'. *See also* STITCHING.

STABILIZATION. A process which renders a photocopy on silver halide paper relatively stable to light, the stabilizer being used instead of the usual fixative and having the effect of rendering the unexposed and undeveloped silver salts colourless when applied to a print after development. A print made in this way will last several years if not exposed to light but is not considered to possess ARCHIVAL QUALITY (*q.v.*). *See also* TWIN-BATH STABILIZATION.

STACK. 1. A piece of furniture containing at least four tiers of shelves back to back. 2. The space equipped for the storage of books on one or more floors; more properly, the self-supporting structure of steel book cases, often extending for several floors, or decks, and independent of the walls of the building. For American terms used in connexion with book stack equipment, *see* COMPARTMENT, DECK, PRESS, RANGE, SECTION. 3. A stack room usually adjoining a public department, containing lesser-used books, and to which only the staff have access.

STACK ROOM. *See* STACK.

STAFF. American spelling for a STAVE (*q.v.*) in music. *Pl.* Staffs.

STAFF ENCLOSURE. That part of a public department of a library such as a junior, lending, or reference library, which is restricted to the use of the staff. Also called a 'Charging desk', 'Counter', or 'Desk'.

STAFF MANUAL. A guide book indicating the correct procedures and processes to be followed by the staff in the various departments or branches of a library system. Called in the U.S.A. a PROCEDURE MANUAL (*q.v.*).

STAFF ROOM. A room reserved for the use of the staff for purposes of rest, refreshment and recreation.

STAINED EDGES. The edges of a book which have been stained with colour. Where only the top edges have been stained the term 'stained top' is used. *See also* EDGES.

STAINED LABEL. A coloured panel painted or printed on the spine of a book as a background for lettering, and to simulate a leather label.

STAINED TOP. *See* STAINED EDGES.

STALLS. In old libraries, combined book shelves and reading desk, or LECTERN (*q.v.*), the books being stood upright on shelves (of which there were three) above the reading desk. The fore-edges of the books faced outwards, and the books were chained. This type of shelving was first used by Sir Thomas Bodley at the Bodleian Library, Oxford, and replaced the mediaeval lectern.

STAMP. *See* PANEL STAMP, TOOLING.

STAMP ACTS. Towards the end of the seventeenth century duties were imposed on certain legal documents, and paper, vellum and parchment. The Stamp Act of 1712 added to the list of dutiable articles, e.g. essay periodicals like the *Spectator*, and from time to time the list increased. The notorious Stamp Act of 1765 ordered a stamp to be applied to all legal documents in the colonies; it met with great opposition in N. America, and was repealed the following year. The subsequent history of the duties is of innumerable variations, generally increasing in the eighteenth, and declining in the nineteenth and twentieth centuries.

STANDARD AUTHOR. An author whose writings have sufficient literary merit to justify a place in the literature of the country, and which, it is hoped, will not become out of print.

STANDARD BOOK NUMBER. The use of a sequence of nine numbers to individualize books, or volumes, in a series. The numbers comprising the first group are allocated to U.K. and Northern Ireland publishers, the remainder – except the last which is a check number to guard against mistakes when feeding a computer – are allocated by the publishers to individual titles published by them. The system was prepared by the Publishers Association of Great Britain and the Booksellers Association so that identification and recording can be done by computers if desired, and came into operation on 1st January 1968. The numbers appear against entries in *The Bookseller*, in the *British National Bibliography* and in publishers' catalogues. The American Book Publishers Council and the American Educational Publishers Institute have approved U.S.A. adherence to the SBN Scheme and authorized the R. R. Bowker Company to administer it in America. Abbreviated SBN or sbn. Early in 1969, at a meeting sponsored by ISO, the following countries agreed in principle to adopt the scheme internationally but using ten digits to identify the books: Denmark, France, Federal Republic of Germany, Netherlands, Norway, Switzerland, the United Kingdom and the United States. The number is being referred to as an INTERNATIONAL STANDARD BOOK NUMBER (ISBN).

STANDARD EDITION. The edition of an author's books, so called by the publisher, to suggest a good quality of book production which is better than that used for a cheaper edition. It may contain notes and an introduction but need not be a CRITICAL EDITION nor a DEFINITIVE EDITION (*qq.v.*).

STANDARD SIZE CARD. A card used for cataloguing and other purposes, of the internationally agreed size of 5 × 3 inches (7·5 × 12·5 centimetres in Continental countries). This is the size which is almost

20

universally used for catalogues, although other standard sizes, particularly 6 × 8 inch cards are sometimes used. Tear-resistant card (weight 160–180 grammes per square metre) should be used. *See also* A7 LIBRARY CARDS.

STANDARD STACK. Name sometimes given to a steel bookcase made by manufacturers of high quality library shelving where good design and fine finish are of importance. Such shelving incorporates a continuous shelf-base supporting double sheet-steel uprights and a corniced cover plate.

STANDARD TITLE. The title under which copies of a work, or musical composition, appearing under different titles, is entered in a catalogue. Also called 'Conventional title', 'Uniform title'.

STANDARD WORK. A book recognized as of permanent value.

STANDARDS. 1. Objective, observable, and usually quantitative, measures of library service; these are usually drawn up by a body of practising librarians, bibliographers and information scientists, as being within the achievement of the average library or other service, and below which an individual service should not be allowed to fall. 2. In all countries, standards are drawn up for the manufacture of goods and provision of services with the object of trying to ensure the provision and maintenance of high qualities. These standards are produced by committees of representatives of professional and trade organizations working under the impetus and supervision of national standards organizations, each of which produces standards concerned with libraries and the materials libraries contain. They are affiliated with the INTERNATIONAL STANDARDS ORGANIZATION (*q.v.*). *See also* AMERICAN NATIONAL STANDARDS INSTITUTE, INC., BRITISH STANDARDS INSTITUTION, INTERNATIONAL STANDARDS, NATIONAL BUREAU OF STANDARDS, PERIODICAL.

STANDING COMMITTEES. Committees which local authorities may set up to carry out particular and continuing functions, or manage departments, or provide services. The following are examples of standing committees: County Roads and Bridges: Public Libraries; Public Baths; General Purposes; Civil Defence; Weights and Measures; Parliamentary. They are also known as 'Permissive' committees and some, according to their purpose, may be called 'Departmental' or 'Service'. *See also* STATUTORY COMMITTEES.

STANDING CONFERENCE OF COMMERCIAL AND TECHNICAL LIBRARY CO-OPERATIVE SERVICES. Formed in 1964 to further co-operation between schemes of local library co-operation, to investigate the possibilities of procuring government grant-in-aid for the work of the schemes, and to further the dissemination of commercial and technical information by joint action where necessary.

STANDING CONFERENCE OF LIBRARIANS OF LIBRARIES OF THE UNIVERSITY OF LONDON. *See* SCOLLUL.

STANDING CONFERENCE OF NATIONAL AND UNIVERSITY LIBRARIES *See* SCONUL.

STANDING CONFERENCE ON LIBRARY MATERIALS IN AFRICA. *See* SCOLMA.

STANDING CONFERENCE ON THEOLOGICAL AND PHILOSOPHICAL LIBRARIES IN LONDON. *See* SCOTAPLL.

STANDING FORMES. *See* Standing Type.

STANDING ORDER. 1. An order to supply each succeeding issue of a serial, periodical or annual publication, or subsequent volumes of a work published in a number of volumes issued intermittently. 2. One which is to be acted upon until countermanded. Also called (in America) a 'Till-forbid order'.

STANDING PRESS. A larger press than a BENCH PRESS (*q.v.*). It stands on the floor and is used to press cased books. Pressure is applied by a platen which is screwed down with a crow bar. *See also* BUILDING-IN MACHINE which dries and presses books in a few seconds.

STANDING TYPE. The type from which a book has been printed and is kept 'standing' exactly as it came from the machine, to be used again if further copies are to be made. Also called 'Live matter', 'Standing formes'.

STANHOPE PRESS. The first all-iron printing press introduced in 1800 by Charles Mahon, 3rd Earl Stanhope (1753–1816). The platen, which covered the whole forme, was operated by a screw which had several levers thus enabling a satisfactory impression to be obtained with less physical effort than with previous machines.

STAPLED. A book or pamphlet the leaves or sections of which are held together by wire staples.

STAR. *Synonymous with* ASTERISK (*q.v.*). *See also* REFERENCE MARKS.

STAR MAP. A map of the heavens. Also called an 'Astronomical map'.

STAR SIGNATURE. A signature indicating an off-cut (part of a sheet) and distinguished by an asterisk placed with the signature letter or figure of the main part of the sheet. This part of a section is usually placed inside the part bearing the plain signature.

STARCH. The original material for sizing paper. It is now used in addition to other sizing agents as a loading agent in order to give a hard 'rattle' and an improved 'finish' to paper.

STARR. A Hebrew deed, covenant, contract, or obligation, anciently required to be filed in the royal exchequer, and invalid unless so deposited. The name was applied to all agreements between Jews and Christians and, occasionally, to other Jewish documents before the expulsion of the Jews from England in 1290. Starrs were written in two languages, Latin or Norman-French, with an acknowledgement in Hebrew at the foot.

START. Leaves of a book are said to 'start' when the sewing is defective, causing the leaves to become loose.

STARTER. (*Classification*) The first curve, used in the Colon Classification to enclose the Subject Device Number. The second, or closing, curve is called the 'Arrester'. *See also* BRACKETS, CIRCULAR BRACKETS, CURVES.

STATE. An impression of an engraving taken from a plate at any stage in the perfecting process. Various states include *open letter proof* and *publication state*. An *early impression* is one of the first copies to be taken; it is consequently sought after by collectors as representing a print taken when the plate is in its best condition.

STATE DOCUMENT CENTRE. A library that has the responsibility of collecting, preserving and organizing as complete a file as possible of the public documents of the state in which it is situated. (American.)

STATE LIBRARY. In America, a library maintained by state funds, which preserves the state records and provides books for the use of state officials, books relating to the history of the state, books published by authors living in the state, and newspapers published in the state. In many states, all classes of books are purchased in order to supply any resident's needs for books or information. Books are sent by post or express to residents. *See also* NATIONAL LIBRARY.

STATE LIBRARY ADMINISTRATIVE AGENCY. A term used in the (American) Library Services Act, 1961, to mean the official State agency charged by State law with the extension and development of public library services throughout the State.

STATE LIBRARY AGENCY. An American state organization existing to extend and improve library services in the state. It should be free from partisan politics and political interference of all kinds, led by professional librarians, supported by law, and adequately financed. Amongst its functions are the planning of a state-wide public library service, promotion of the development of these libraries, supervising library provision with a view to improving services by formulating and enforcing minimum standards; providing a consulting and advisory service to librarians, boards of library trustees and citizen groups;

administering a state system of grants-in-aid as well as federal grants-in-aid to libraries; providing supplementary services such as inter-library loans of books and non-book materials; travelling libraries; providing a centralized information and bibliographic service; centralized cataloguing; providing library services to schools, clubs and individuals where no public library services exist.

STATIONARII. Men commissioned by universities in mediaeval times to attend to the production and distribution of books.

STATIONER. From *Lat. stationarius* 'one who stands' (i.e. at a stall). One who sells stationery. Originally used to mean a bookseller.

STATIONERS' COMPANY. The authority which regulated and organized printing and the book trade in England. It was established by a Royal Charter from Queen Mary in 1557, created a livery company in 1560, and until the passing of the Copyright Act in 1842 had an absolute monopoly, as all apprentices to the printing trade were obliged to serve a member of the Company, and every publication was required to be 'Entered at Stationers' Hall' as proof of registration. The *Registers* which commenced in 1554 are of great value in the history of English literature.

STATUTORY COMMITTEES. Committees which local authorities are required by law to set up in order to carry out certain functions. Finance, health, fire brigade and education committees, and library committees of Scottish burghs, are included amongst statutory committees. *See also* STANDING COMMITTEES.

STATUTORY INSTRUMENTS. Documents by which the power to make, confirm, or approve Orders, Regulations, or other subordinate legislation, conferred by an Act of Parliament on Her Majesty in Council or on a Minister of the Crown, is exercised. Prior to 1 January 1948, when the Statutory Instruments Act, 1946, came into operation, they were known as *Statutory Rules and Orders*. Although Statutory Instruments are frequently required to be laid before Parliament, they rank as Non-Parliamentary Publications.

STAVE. The five horizontal lines on which musical notation is written or printed. Spelt 'staff' in America.

STAVE. *Synonymous with* SECTION (*q.v.*).

STEEL ENGRAVING. *See* ENGRAVING.

STEM. 1. The outline of the design of a type letter; the bare lines apart from the serifs, which indicate most clearly the character and height of the letter. The main stroke of a letter. 2. The body of a type letter between the face and the foot. Also called the SHANK (*q.v.*) or BODY (*q.v.*).

STENCIL. 1. The basic principle of printing, in which a wax, silk or other stencil is used. The ink is applied to the back of the printing image carrier (i.e. the stencil) and reaches the front through the image areas which are porous and open. *See also* SILK SCREEN. 2. The 'master' or image area which carries the image, and by means of which the printing is done. 3. A thin cut metal plate which allows the transfer of a design, etc., to paper when an ink roller or brush is passed over its surface.

STENCIL DUPLICATING. A method of producing multiple copies from a specially prepared wax master. A particular kind of ink is forced through the cuts made by a typewriter in the stencil and transferred to the paper.

STEP-AND-REPEAT CAMERA. A microfilm camera which provides a series of latent image frames in a predetermined pattern on a single sheet of film.

STEP-AND-REPEAT MACHINE. A machine for multiple copying (on offset plates, etc.), with devices for the adjustment of each copy. Intended specially for reproduction in colour in which the printing plates for each colour must be superimposed precisely when printing.

STEPWISE OPERATED CAMERA. *Synonymous with* PLANETARY CAMERA (*q.v.*).

STEREO. *See* STEREOTYPE.

STEREOSCOPIC SLIDE. A pair of positive photographic prints made from negatives taken from two slightly different viewpoints to give a 3-D effect when viewed through a specially made viewer. They have become familiar through the 'Viewmaster', a cheap viewer the slides for which can be purchased in many shops.

STEREOTOME. Trade name for a special container resembling a book, which can be stood upright on a shelf, and holds a set of stereo slides.

STEREOTYPE (STEREO). A metal printing plate carrying a printing surface in relief, made by pouring stereotype metal into a papiermâché (called 'flong'), or plaster of paris, mould of the original type, line block or very coarse half-tone. Future printings are made from the resulting 'stereos'. The whole process is known as stereotyping. Curved stereos are used on rotary presses for high-speed work, particularly newspaper printing. The process was patented in 1725 by William Ged, a Scottish printer, who was commissioned by Cambridge University to stereotype prayer-books and bibles. *See also* MATRIX.

STEREOTYPE METAL. An alloy of tin, antimony, and lead; used for casting stereos.

stet. (*Lat.* 'let the matter stand'.) Written in the margin of printer's copy or proof to denote the cancelling of any correction marked thereon. Dots under the words indicate the correction to which the 'stet' refers.

STEWARD. Agent and representative of the lord of a manor.

STICK. 1. The tool used by the compositor for setting or forming into lines the types as he picks them out of the CASE (*q.v.*). It usually contains about twenty lines of 8 point type. 2. A device like a small-diameter walking stick divided down its length, used for holding from one to about six copies of a newspaper. Also called 'Newspaper file', 'Newspaper rod', and 'Newspaper stick'.

STIFF BACK. *See* TIGHT BACK.

STIFFENED AND CUT FLUSH. *See* CUT FLUSH.

STIFFENED PAPER COVERS. *See* PAPER COVERED.

STIGMATYPY. The use of small type-units to design and print a picture or portrait.

STIGMONYM. Dots instead of the name of the author. Used on the title-page and elsewhere in a book. Where the authorship of such books cannot be traced, they are catalogued under their titles.

STIPPLE. A printing surface of a copper plate used for making illustrations; it consists of dots, instead of lines. The process is to cover the plate with ordinary etching ground, and through this to sketch the contours and lightly indicate the main shadows with dots by means of the etching needles and a roulette. The portions of the plate thus uncovered are bitten with acid, after which the drawing is completed and given brilliance by flicking or dotting directly on to the surface of the plate with a specially curved graver or roulette. The dots may be fine or coarse, to give effects of light and dark. Although this method was used by W. W. Ryland (1732–83) the Royal engraver, it was first made popular in the eighteenth century by Francesco Bartolozzi, an Italian painter and engraver who came to London in 1764 from Venice and worked for the publisher John Boydell. Half-tones are a kind of stipple engraving.

STIPPLED EDGES. The edges of a book which have been spotted irregularly with colour to prevent them appearing to be soiled. *See also* EDGES, MARBLED EDGES, SPRINKLED EDGES, STAINED EDGES.

STIPPLING. 1. (*Paper*) A roughened finish, also called 'Pebbling'. 2. (*Printing* and *art*) A gradation of light and shade produced by dots.

STITCHING. The operation of fastening a pamphlet consisting of a single section, with wire or thread passed through the centre of the fold. *See also* SEWING, STABBING, THREAD STITCHED.

STOCHASTIC PROCESS. A system which produces a sequence of discrete symbols according to certain probabilities, as for example the sequence of letters which makes up a passage of printed English. If the probabilities depend on previous events in the series this is called a 'Markov process' after the Russian mathematician.

STOCK. 1. (*Printing*) Paper or other material for printing upon. 2. (*Paper*) The material (rags, waste-paper, esparto, ropes, etc.) used for making paper; the term is applied at any stage of manufacture, whether to untreated materials or the finished paper. *See also* HALF-STUFF, PULP, STUFF, WHOLE-STUFF. Also, the printing trade term for paper. 3. All the books and other items in a library. 4. All the books available for sale by a bookseller or publisher.

STOCK BOOK. *Synonymous with* ACCESSIONS REGISTER (*q.v.*).

STOCK EDITOR. A member of the staff of a library who is responsible for maintaining the book stock in good physical condition and up-to-date as well as for ensuring that the latest and most useful titles are available in adequate quantities.

STOCKHOLDING BOOKSELLER. A retail bookseller who keeps a varied and large stock of books on his shelves.

STOCKTAKING. The process of taking stock by checking records of books possessed with copies on the shelves or records of books on loan.

STONE. Usually a steel-top table (originally it was stone) on which the imposing work – that is, the assembling of the various parts of a printing job – is done. It is on the stone that the type, blocks, etc., are locked in the chase and levelled with mallet and planer. *See also* IMPOSITION.

STONE ENGRAVING. Engraving on blue or grey lithographic stone (fine-grained, compact limestone); a hand process which is used chiefly for script and line drawings in which sharpness and precision of line are more important than artistic expression. The outline is traced and then deeply scored with a steel or diamond pen. The process is used chiefly for script and line drawings of which relatively few copies are required. As the number of copies which can be made on a hand press is small, it is usual for a stone engraving to be made as an original for transferring to a plate for use on a printing press. Also used to indicate a print made from an engraved stone.

STONE PROOF. One made after the forme has been locked up for press, but before it has been put on the press.

STOP-CYLINDER PRESS. A type of printing machine in which a cylinder (which is placed over a reciprocating bed on which rests the forme) revolves once during which the impression is made on paper fed underneath the cylinder, and stops until the forme is again in position for printing the next sheet. Often called a 'Wharfedale' press. *See also* MIEHLE, PERFECTER, SINGLE-REVOLUTION MACHINE, TWO-REVOLUTION MACHINE.

STOPPING OUT. Painting with varnish such parts of an etching plate as are not to be further etched by acid during repeated dipping in the acid bath. In blockmaking, painting out of the screen or the negative, parts of the subject which are not required to be printed.

STORAGE. A source from which documents or information of specified descriptions may be supplied. A receptacle for information (*IBM*).

STORAGE AND RETRIEVAL. The recording of the holdings of library material of various kinds and of information recorded in such material, and the means of ascertaining the whereabouts of the material or information by means of catalogue cards, indexes, and particularly punched cards or other kinds of record which are used in high-speed sorting machines.

STORAGE AREA. That portion of the total floor area of a building which is allocated to the storage of materials, furniture, equipment and supplies not in current use. (American.)

STORAGE CENTRE. A library or library agency in which co-operating libraries store little-used library materials, and which are readily available on request. Also called 'Deposit library', 'Reservoir Library'. (American.)

STORAGE SHELVING. Shelving which is intended for accommodating little-used books or stores. It may consist of wooden slats or fixed steel shelves. If made of steel and the shelves are adjustable they are an integral part of the structure and can only be moved by unscrewing nuts and bolts; for this reason this kind of shelving is seldom used in libraries. *See also* ADJUSTABLE SHELVING, LIBRARY SHELVING.

STORE. 1. In information retrieval, the set of all codes which have been physically recorded in some medium (*Taube*). 2. A collection of books or other documentary information which are the subject of records: it may be a library but it may well be a single publication such as a textbook or abstracts journal. An index, or catalogue to a store, can be called a 'Retrieval device'.

STOR-MOR SHELVING. Trade name for a variety of compact book storage invented by Ingold, a Swiss engineer.

STORY HOUR. A definite period (which is usually about half an hour) set aside for telling stories to the youngest members of a junior library. The stories are told by members of the staff, particularly the children's librarians, and their friends.

20*

STRAIGHT-GRAIN LEATHER. A leather that has been dampened and rolled, or 'boarded', to make the grain run in straight lines. An innovation credited to Roger Paine.

STRAIGHT-GRAIN MOROCCO. Morocco leather in which the natural grain has been distorted by elongated lines or ridges all running in the same direction.

STRAIGHT MATTER. Text uninterrupted by illustrations, tables or any special settings.

STRAIGHTENING. The task (usually performed daily in a busy library) of arranging tidily books in correct classified order.

STRAP BINDER. A binder fitted with thin steel strips which pass through the staples of the periodicals.

STRAPWORK. (*Binding*) Interlaced double lines, usually forming a geometrical pattern.

STRAWBERRY HILL PRESS. The private press on which Sir Horace Walpole, fourth Earl of Orford, printed his own and other books. The Press functioned between 1757 and 1789, and the printers included successively William Robinson, Thomas Kirgate, Benjamin Williams, and others. The Press was situated at Walpole's estate at Strawberry Hill, Twickenham, Middlesex.

STRAWBOARD. A coarse yellow board, made from straw and used for the covers of books.

STREAMER. A printed poster used in shop or window advertising.

STREET INDEX. An index of streets in a town showing the number of houses and the number of persons therein who hold membership tickets for a public library. Also, an alphabetical list of streets in any given area.

STRESS. The thickened part of a curved stroke or letter.

STRIKE. *See* MATRIX 3.

STRIKE THROUGH. A fault in printing when ink printed on one side of a sheet penetrates to the other. *See also* SHOW THROUGH.

STRIP CARTOON. Small drawings, fewer than about eight or ten in number, about 2 inches square, appearing side by side in a row in a newspaper or periodical. They are usually serials and tell a continuing story or relate the adventures and experience of the characters.

STRIP IN. To combine one photographic record with another, or others, or a photograph and lettering, preparatory to using all in making a printing plate. In lithography the operation of stripping is analogous to the operation of imposing in letterpress.

STRIP INDEX. A form of visible index in which entries are made on strips of card shallow enough to take only one line of typewriting.

These strips are placed in a metal frame and the surface of the whole of each strip is visible and may be typed or written on.

STRUCTERM. A term or descriptor having an appended role code indicating context in which the term is used (*IBM*).

STRUCTURAL NOTATION. A notation to a classification which indicates the hierarchy or structure of the scheme. A non-structural notation does not do this. *See also* HIERARCHICAL NOTATION.

STUB. 1. The part of an original leaf which is left after most of it has been cut away to insert a CANCELLING LEAF (*q.v.*). 2. A narrow strip of paper or linen sewn between sections of a book for attaching folded maps or other bulky items. *See also* COMPENSATION GUARD, GUARD.

STUDENTS' LIBRARY. A collection of books provided for the use of a particular group or category of students.

STUDENTS' SECTION. The department of a county library which sends (usually by post) non-fiction books specially requested by readers. It is usually accommodated at the County Library Headquarters.

STUDENT'S TICKET. *Synonymous with* SUPPLEMENTARY TICKET (*q.v.*).

STUDY ISSUE. Books issued to students in excess of the usual number and for a longer period than usual.

STUDY SCORE. A musical score, similar to a MINIATURE SCORE (*q.v.*) but of a somewhat larger size due to the work being fully scored, i.e. having music for so many instruments that it would be difficult to read if reduced to the normal miniature score size.

STUFF. The pulp in the paper-maker's vat prior to its being removed to the mould. *See also* HALF-STUFF, PULP, STOCK 2, WATER-LEAF, WHOLE-STUFF.

STYLE BOOK. *Synonymous with* STYLE MANUAL (*q.v.*).

STYLE MANUAL. A set of rules drawn up by a printing establishment for the guidance of its staff to ensure that details of typography, spelling, capitalization, punctuation and other matters about which opinions and customs differ, are in accordance with the prevailing practice of that establishment. Such rules are known as the 'style of the house'. *Rules for Compositors and Readers of the Oxford University Press* are a standard set followed by many printers and authors.

STYLE OF THE HOUSE. (*Printing*) The practice of a printing establishment with regard to capitals, italics, spelling, punctuation, etc. It is called a 'Style manual' or 'Style book' when printed as a guide for use.

STYLE SHEET. 1. A guide to a printer's HOUSE STYLE. 2. A list of types and their sizes, style of setting, etc., proposed for a given publication. *See also* STYLE MANUAL, STYLE OF THE HOUSE.

STYLUS, STYLE. A writing instrument, pointed at one end, which was used in ancient and mediaeval times for writing on wax or clay. *See also* ELECTRIC STYLUS.

SUBALTERN GENERA. The intermediate classes of a classification between the SUMMUM GENUS (*q.v.*) and the INFIMA SPECIES (*q.v.*).

SUB-BRANCH. A small branch library open a few hours each day. A part-time library. *See also* BRANCH LIBRARY. In America, a smaller book-circulating agency than a COMMUNITY LIBRARY (*q.v.*), having a minimum book collection with emphasis on popular reading. The population served would be not less than 10,000, and the library open on some part of five days a week.

SUB-COMMITTEE. A committee formed from members of a larger committee to consider one or more matters on behalf of the larger committee to which it reports its deliberations.

SUBDIVISION. 1. The word commonly used to denote the process of dividing a scheme of classification into its parts. 2. The result of such subdivision.

SUB-ENTRY. In indexing, the part of the entry following the entry-word or heading which is used to subdivide a large number of references into a group of related items, i.e. the whole entry minus the entry-word or heading.

SUB-HEAD. *See* SUB-HEADING.

SUB-HEADING. 1. A secondary heading, used in the subdivision of a subject. In a verbal heading it is the second or subsequent word, separated from the preceding by punctuation. 2. A word or group of words added to a heading and designed to delimit a particular group of entries under the heading, or to designate a part of the entity named in the heading (*IFLA*). Sub-headings may be subjected to modification, and if there is more than one modification of a sub-heading, each of the modifications is then known as a sub-sub-heading. Each group of sub- and sub-sub-headings is indented in printing to make the meaning clear. The terms sub- and sub-sub-headings are often abbreviated to 'sub-head' and 'sub-sub-head'.

SUB-INDEX. An index within an index.

SUBINFEUDATION. The granting or sub-letting of lands by a feudal vassal to an undertenant on the same terms as he held them from his overlord. Abolished in England in 1290, but the principle still survives in Scotland.

SUBJECT. 1. The theme or themes of a book, whether stated in the title or not. 2. (*Indexing*) A unit concept found in, or derived from, manuscript or published literary material. It may be found, or expressed, as a theme, name, date, first line of a poem, title of a book, or be an expression coined to convey the gist of the material indexed, etc.

SUBJECT ANALYTIC. *See* ANALYTICAL ENTRY.

SUBJECT ARRANGEMENT. Books arranged in order of subject, either alphabetically or according to some scheme of classification.

SUBJECT AUTHORITY CARD. A card which, in addition to citing the authorities consulted in determining the choice of a given heading, also indicates the references made to and from related headings and synonymous terms (*IBM*).

SUBJECT AUTHORITY FILE. The list in a book, or on cards, of subject headings used in a given catalogue, and the references made to them. Also the entries made for the classified list of class symbols or numbers and the appropriate subject index entries made when first allocating a book to a particular position in the classification. An entry is made for each step taken when indexing by the chain indexing method. *See also* AUTHORITY CARD, AUTHORITY LIST, CHAIN INDEXING, NAME AUTHORITY FILE.

SUBJECT BIBLIOGRAPHY. A list of material about a particular subject or individual.

SUBJECT CARD. A catalogue card bearing a subject entry.

SUBJECT CATALOGUE. Any catalogue arranged by subjects, whether in alphabetical or classified order, which directs users to the documents dealing with them. *See also* ALPHABETICO-SPECIFIC SUBJECT CATALOGUE, ALPHABETICO-CLASSED CATALOGUE.

SUBJECT CATALOGUING. 1. That part of cataloguing which involves the allocation of subject headings to entries for specific books or other documents. 2. The branch of cataloguing which is not concerned with DESCRIPTIVE CATALOGUING (*q.v.*) but with the provision of subject headings. In 1940 the Library of Congress adopted this term to cover both classification and subject heading; previously, subject headings had been assigned by the descriptive cataloguers, not the classifiers.

SUBJECT CLASSIFICATION. The scheme devised by J. D. Brown in 1906, in which the main classes are Matter and Force, Life, Mind, and Record. The notation is mixed (letter and figure) and does not permit of easy extension (as does Dewey's Decimal Classification by the use of decimal figures) although the CATEGORICAL TABLES (*q.v.*) enable a certain amount of subdivision. It is the best-known general scheme of British origin.

SUBJECT CONCEPTS. (*Classification*) The terms which result when a subject is divided by a single characteristic. The group of terms which so results is called a 'Facet'.

SUBJECT DEPARTMENT. A department in a large general library in which are shelved all the books on a particular subject, e.g. science, whether intended for reference or for home-reading. Where such departmentalization exists there is usually a POPULAR LIBRARY (*q.v.*) containing a selection of books of interest to the 'general reader'. Also called 'Departmentalized library'.

SUBJECT DEVICE. Ranganathan's term for the process of dividing by the whole classification. It is one of the distinctive principles of the Colon Classification for determining the sequence of subjects and is used in the Dewey Classification when a subject such as 016 Subject Bibliography is divided by the whole classification.

SUBJECT DEVICE NUMBER. In the Colon Classification, that part of an Isolate Number which is contributed by the SUBJECT DEVICE (*q.v.*).

SUBJECT ENTRY. 1. In a catalogue, an entry under the heading adopted to indicate a book's subject. In a subject catalogue it is the basic unit, and includes the description of the document, and its location. In the classified file of the CLASSIFIED CATALOGUE (*q.v.*) the heading may also be the LOCATION MARK (*q.v.*). Subject entries for music are entered under the medium of performance (*see* MEDIUM) or the form (*see* FORM 2) in which the music is written. They may also be given under the subject described in the music. 2. In an index, an entry relating to a subject as distinguished from one beginning with the name of a person.

SUBJECT FULLNESS. *See* SECONDARY FULLNESS.

SUBJECT GUIDE. A guide to the shelves of a library, showing where books on particular subjects may be found. Also called 'Topic guide'.

SUBJECT HEADING. The word or group of words under which books and other material on a subject are entered in a catalogue in which the entries are arranged in alphabetical order. The heading may include punctuation to which an arranging significance may be assigned. In a classified catalogue the subject heading consists of a classification symbol with or without its verbal meaning. It may also include entries for all material on the same subject in an index or bibliography, or arranged in a file.

SUBJECT HEADING LANGUAGE. The terms used as subject headings and under which entries are made, as well as those from which references are merely made to other subject terms.

SUBJECT INDEX ENTRY. An entry in the subject index of a classified catalogue which directs to the class number under which entries for books on the required subject will be found.

SUBJECT INDEX ILLUSION. The term used by H. E. Bliss for the alphabetical arrangement of subjects in a scheme of classification according to the first letter of the subject name, etc., e.g. Q Quartos, R Roman Antiquities, S Science, T Technology, U Unclassified. As subjects are subdivided similarly, an alphabetical index is essential to determine the position of any subject in the sequence, and Bliss wrote 'no index, however convenient or necessary, can convert an arbitrary or disordered arrangement into a systematic classification'.

SUBJECT LIBRARIES. *See* SUBJECT DEPARTMENT.

SUBJECT REFERENCE. A reference from one subject to another whether a synonym or a related heading.

SUBJECT SERIES. A number of books published in a named series by one publisher and dealing with different phases of a single subject or with a particular field of knowledge. The books are usually written by different authors, are not usually reprints, and are uniform in textual and physical characteristics. Similarly, a number of musical compositions dealing with different phases of music, media of performance, form, etc.

SUBJECT SPECIALIZATION. A scheme of co-operation whereby public libraries in a restricted geographical area purchase books on a specific subject. In some schemes the libraries act as depositories for preserving little-used books on their particular subject which might otherwise be discarded. *See also* JOINT FICTION RESERVE.

SUBJECT STYLE. The use of red for headings in catalogue entries to indicate subjects. As an alternative (owing to the tendency of red ink or red typescript to fade) black capitals are sometimes used. *See also* AUTHOR STYLE.

SUBJECT-WORD ENTRY. Entry in a catalogue under a word of the title of a book indicative of its subject matter.

SUB-LIBRARIAN. *See* DEPUTY LIBRARIAN.

SUBORDINATION. The allocation of a subject term to its right place in the classification schedules; its order of precedence in the HIERARCHY (*q.v.*).

SUB-PROFESSIONAL ASSISTANT. In American libraries, one who undertakes, under the immediate supervision of professional staff members, work largely concerned with the lighter routine processes which are peculiar to library work and which require some knowledge of library procedure.

SUBSCRIBER. 1. A person who lives outside the municipal or county or other local authority boundary but who is permitted to use the public library on payment of an annual subscription. 2. A person who pays a subscription to receive a periodical as published, or to a society.

SUBSCRIBERS' EDITION. An edition prepared for circulation only to persons who have agreed to purchase on announcement and before publication. It may differ from the ordinary 'trade edition' by the inclusion of a list of subscribers, by being printed on hand-made or other special paper and having larger margins, or by being sumptuously bound.

SUBSCRIPTION AGENT. A firm or organization which arranges, usually for a consideration, at the order of an individual or library, for the regular delivery of serials as published.

SUBSCRIPTION BOOKS. 1. Those published at intervals by societies and issued to subscribing members. 2. Individual books of limited appeal, the publication of which depends to some extent on subscriptions promised prior to publication, and the price of which is raised after publication.

SUBSCRIPTION EDITION. One which is published after enough subscriptions have been received to ensure financial success.

SUBSCRIPTION LIBRARY. A commercial lending library the members of which pay subscriptions entitling them to borrow books during the period of the validity of their subscription. They were first formed in England in the late seventeenth and early eighteenth centuries. *See also* CIRCULATING LIBRARY.

SUBSCRIPTION PRICE. The price at which books are sometimes offered for sale before they are published. The price is usually lower than the after-publication price. This is done to give the publisher some guidance as to the potential sales of the book and therefore of the number to be printed.

SUBSIDIARIES. The parts of a book in addition to the text and including notes (whether placed in the pages or massed at the end of a book), bibliographies, appendices, glossaries, plates, indexes, imprint, colophon, blank leaves, end-papers and book jackets. Sometimes called 'Reference matter'. Also called 'End-matter', 'Back matter'. *See also* PRELIMINARIES.

SUBSIDIARY RIGHTS. An author's rights to literary property other than the original one of first publication. These include dramatic, film, translation and serial rights.

SUBSIDY PUBLISHERS. *Synonymous with* VANITY PUBLISHERS (*q.v.*).

SUBSTANCE. The weight of paper expressed in terms of weight per ream of sheets of a given size; the weight of a ream of a particular size and number of sheets is known as the 'substance number'. The 'substance' of the paper is the product of the density, i.e. the degree of dilution of the stuff flowing on to the machine wire, and the speed at which it is permitted to flow, plus the speed of the machine wire.

SUBSTITUTION GENERIC. In a HIERARCHICAL SEARCH (*q.v.*), a situation in which two headings in the alphabetico-specific subject catalogue, each with the same number of sub-headings, represent concepts in hierarchical relationship, i.e. the heading and the first sub-heading are identical, the second sub-heading being different. *See also* ALPHABETICAL COLLATERAL SEARCH, SYSTEMATIC COLLATERAL SEARCH.

SUB-SUB-HEADING. *See* SUB-HEADING.

SUB-TITLE. A secondary or subordinate title, usually explanatory, and often following a semicolon, 'or', 'an', or 'a'.

SUGGESTION CARD. A printed card which is filled in by a reader with particulars of a book suggested for addition to a library. All appropriate bibliographical information is entered, and in some libraries it subsequently serves as an ORDER CARD (*q.v.*). Also called 'Recommendation card', 'Request card', 'Requisition card', 'Suggestion slip'.

SULPHATE PULP. (*Papermaking*) Chemical wood pulp which has been prepared by cooking wood chips under pressure and high temperature in a solution consisting mainly of sulphate of soda (Glauber's salt). The resulting paper is strong, and is often used unbleached, but it can be bleached white. The process was introduced by Dahl in 1883–4. *See also* SODA PULP.

SULPHITE PULP. (*Papermaking*) Chemical wood pulp which has been prepared by submitting the wood fibres to the action of sulphurous acid and its acid salts (bisulphite of lime, magnesia, or soda) at high pressure and in closed vessels. The process was invented by B. C. and R. Tilghmann in 1863–6 and is usually used with coniferous woods. *See also* SODA PULP.

SUMMUM GENUS. The first, comprehensive class from which the division of a classification commences. The terminology of schedule construction, as used by Ranganathan is: *universe* (=*summum genus*) an aggregate of *entities* (things or ideas) under consideration which is *divided* by a succession or *train* of *characteristics* each of which gives rise to an *array* of classes. The *order* of a class is the number of characteristics used to divide it out of the universe; the *rank* of a class is its position in its array. A *chain* is a series of classes in successive subordination, each one being subordinate to the preceding one. *See also* INFIMA SPECIES, SUBALTERN GENERA.

SUNK BANDS. (*Binding*) Cords or bands (in old books, often of leather) which are placed in grooves sawn into the backs of sections of a book to give a smooth back or spine. The sewing of the sections passes round the bands. The opposite of RAISED BANDS (*q.v.*). Also called 'Sunk cords'.

SUPER. *See* MULL.

SUPER ROYAL. A sheet of printing paper measuring $20\frac{1}{2} \times 27\frac{1}{2}$ inches.

SUPER-CALENDER. A machine, separate from the paper-making machines, which consists of a stack of from five to sixteen rolls. Paper is passed through under pressure to be given a highly glazed finish; it is then known as 'Super-calendered'. *See also* CALENDERED.

SUPER-CALENDERED PAPER. Paper which is given an extra smooth, glossy surface by rolling between 'calenders' (metal rollers) in a super-calender machine.

SUPER-CASTER. An instrument for casting large sizes of type for hand-composition.

SUPERINTENDENT OF BRANCHES. The liaison officer between the branch librarians of a large system and the chief librarian or his deputy. His duty is to make the units of the system smooth-working parts of a homogeneous whole.

SUPERINTENDENT OF THE READING ROOM. The librarian responsible for the service to readers in the reading room of a national, university or research library.

SUPERIOR FIGURES (LETTERS). Very small characters aligning with the top of the text type, usually as reference marks to footnotes or notes at the end of the chapter or text, or in a margin. They are cast on the mean line, and often on the same body as the type with which they appear. Also called 'Superiors'. *See also* INFERIOR LETTERS (FIGURES), MEAN LINE, REFERENCE MARKS.

SUPERORDINATE CLASS. (*Classification*) A class which is of more general extension or higher grade, or rank: a more general class. *See also* CO-ORDINATE CLASSES.

SUPPLEMENT. 1. Additional matter continuing, or adding new matter to that already published. It is usually issued separately. 2. An extra sheet, section, or number accompanying a normal issue of a newspaper or periodical. *See also* ADDENDUM.

SUPPLEMENTAL ESTIMATE. *See* ESTIMATES.

SUPPLEMENTARY TABLES. Additional tables, provided in the fourteenth edition of Dewey's *Decimal Classification*, for extending the 'common subdivisions', of Viewpoints, and of Miscellaneous Signs of Relation.

SUPPLEMENTARY TICKET. A non-fiction ticket which is issued to students, teachers, the clergy and others in addition to the number usually allowed.

SUPPLIED TITLE. The title composed by the cataloguer to indicate the nature and scope of the monographic work under study (*IBM*).

SUPPOSED AUTHOR. One to whom is attributed by some authoritative source the authorship of a work published anonymously or of which the stated authorship is doubted. Also called 'Attributed author', 'Presumed author'. Such a book is catalogued under the name of the supposed author which phrase appears after the name to qualify it. The authority for the supposition is given in a note.

SUPPOSITITIOUS AUTHOR. One who is substituted for the genuine author with intent to defraud.

SUPPRESSED. 1. Withheld from publication or circulation by author, publisher, government, or ecclesiastical authority because of unreliability, inaccuracy or moral tone. 2. (*Bibliography*) Of a leaf which has been cancelled because of some inaccurate, imperfect, or objectionable feature.

supra (*Lat.* 'above'). Used in footnotes and sometimes in the text to refer to an item previously mentioned.

SURFACE PAPER. *Synonymous with* COATED PAPER (*q.v.*).

SURFACE PRINTING. *Synonymous with* PLANOGRAPHIC PROCESS (*q.v.*).

SURFACE SIZING. The addition or resin or other materials to the surface of a sheet of paper or board to render it more resistant to liquids, especially writing ink. *See also* ENGINE-SIZING.

SURNAME. A family name which a person uses in conjunction with his personal names. He bears it in common with other members of a group who are related to him. It is used, often without his personal names, and sometimes in conjunction with a title of address, when referring to him outside the circle of his personal acquaintances. It is the name used as a heading for entries in a catalogue or bibliography.

SURNAME INDEXING. The allocation of symbols to surnames so that they may be arranged in order other than by strict alphabetization. *See also* SOUNDEX.

SURVEY. An account of some research, examination, or enquiry which has been done by a scientific or organized method.

SUSPENSION FILE. Loops of tough manila, the full width of a filing cabinet drawer, which are attached to, and suspended from, rigid metal or plastic bars which at their extreme ends rest on a cradle, or framework, contained in the drawer. Into these loops are placed files or wallets containing documents, papers, photographs, etc.

SUSPENSION SHELVING.   Shelves affixed to, or between, shelf-ends having lugs which engage in slots in uprights fixed to the wall. No support other than the shelf end is provided at the front of the shelves. The shelf-ends are the full depth of the shelf and serve as book supports. Also called 'Bracket shelving'.

SWASH LETTERS. Italic capitals and lower-case letters with tails and flourishes, as

B G N F A W P T R₀ N_i

SWEDISH BINDING.   *Synonymous with* CUT FLUSH (*q.v.*).

SWELLED RULE.   *See* RULE.

SWINDON AREA ASSOCIATION OF LIBRARIES FOR INDUSTRY AND COMMERCE.   *See* SAALIC.

SWINGING BOOKCASE.   A form of compact book storage whereby two presses consisting of hinged three-foot tiers are placed one on each side of one fixed press. When the books on either side of the fixed press or on the inner sides of the two outside presses are to be consulted, the hinged tiers are swung out into the gangways. Also called 'Pivoted bookcase'.

SWUNG DASH.   A curved dash ∼ similar to a TILDE (*q.v.*).

SYLLABIC WRITING.   The middle stage in picture writing in which a symbol was used to represent each syllable or vowel when this constitutes a syllable in the spoken language; thus, a combination of signs representing a group of syllables conveys a spoken word. A syllabic form of writing is known as a syllabary. *See also* PHONETIC WRITING.

SYLLABICATION.   *Synonymous with* SYLLABIFICATION (*q.v.*).

SYLLABIFICATION.   The action or method of dividing words into syllables. Also called 'Syllabication'.

SYMBOL.   A substitute or representation of characteristics, relationships, or transformations of ideas or things (*IBM*).

SYNCOPISM.   Applied to a pseudonym where dots take the place of certain letters. Such books are catalogued under their titles when the author's full name cannot be ascertained, with added entries under the leading initials of the syncopism. *See also* PSEUDONYM.

SYNDETIC.   Having entries connected by cross references. In information retrieval, co-ordination of two or more related documents.

SYNDETIC CATALOGUE. A dictionary catalogue that connects entries by a scheme of cross-references to form a co-ordinated whole. References are made from broad subjects to those that are less broad, and from these to still more subordinate subjects, and sometimes *vice versa*.

SYNECDOCHE. A figure of speech in which a species is used for the whole genus (e.g. 'bread' for food in general) or the genus for a species. As applied by C. L. Bernier to information retrieval, the use of a GENERIC DESCRIPTOR (*q.v.*) to represent a set of included words.

SYNOPSIS. 1. A brief outline of the plot, setting, or important points of a play, book or serial. 2. A factual summary of an article or paper contributed to a learned journal, suitable for use as an abstract, published in accompaniment with the article, presumed to be prepared by the author of the article but in any case subjected to the same editorial scrutiny and correction which is given to the full article.

SYNTAX. Concerned with the relations between symbols without reference to their meanings. *See also* SEMANTICS.

SYNTHETIC CLASSIFICATION. *See* FACETED CLASSIFICATION.

SYNTHETIC INDEXING. *Synonymous with* CO-ORDINATE INDEXING (*q.v.*).

SYNTOL. Abbreviation for Syntagmatic Organization Language, an artificial indexing and classification language adequate to represent written information and intended for manipulation by computing devices. It was devised by J. C. Gardin.

SYSTEM MEDIA CENTRE. A centre provided by a school libraries system to provide supporting and supplementary services in individual schools in the system.

SYSTEMATIC AUXILIARY SCHEDULES. Twenty schedules provided in Bliss' *Bibliographic Classification* to serve as tables of common subdivision. Only the first three – form divisions (*see* ANTERIOR NUMERICAL CLASSES), geographical subdivision, subdivision by language – are of general application throughout the scheme, the remainder being applicable to groups of classes, to single classes, or to sub-classes. Symbols from these schedules are added to those from the main tables of the classification which indicate subject matter. Auxiliary tables are also provided in the UNIVERSAL DECIMAL CLASSIFICATION (*q.v.*).

SYSTEMATIC BIBLIOGRAPHY. The enumeration and classification of books (*Besterman*). The assembling of bibliographical entries into logical and useful arrangements for study and reference.

SYSTEMATIC CATALOGUE. A classified catalogue. One in which the classes and subjects are arranged in a logical order according to some scheme of book classification.

SYSTEMATIC COLLATERAL SEARCH.   An examination of entries under headings which, in a scheme of classification, would be co-ordinate with, and stand next to, each of the headings covered in the HIERARCHICAL SEARCH (*q.v.*). *See also* ALPHABETIC COLLATERAL SEARCH, SUBSTITUTION GENERIC.

SYSTEMATIC FILE.   *Synonymous with* CLASSIFIED FILE (*q.v.*).

SYSTEMATIC MNEMONICS.   *See* MNEMONICS.

SYSTEMATIC SCHEDULES.   *See* SYSTEMATIC AUXILIARY SCHEDULES.

T-CARD CHARGING.   Abbreviation for TRANSACTION CARD CHARGING (*q.v.*).

t.e.g.   Abbreviation for top edge gilt. *See* GILT TOP.

T.L.S.   *See* A.L.S.

TPI.   Abbreviation for Title-page, Index. Used to refer to the separately published title-page and index to a volume of a serial which may often have to be separately ordered for insertion in a bound volume.

T.S.   Abbreviation for typescript and tub-sized. *See also* TUB-SIZING.

TTS.   Abbreviation for TELETYPESETTING (*q.v.*).

TAB.   (*Binding*) A small piece of paper, card, plastic or fabric attached to the outer edge of a card, or leaf of a book, and bearing one or more characters to serve as a guide or index.

TABBED.   A GUIDE CARD (*q.v.*) which has tabs projecting from the upper edge. They are called 'three-, four- or five-tabbed' according to the portion of the card which projects. A 'three-tabbed' card is one, the tab of which is a third the length of the card.

TABLE.   1. An arrangement of written words, numbers or signs, or of combinations of them, in a series of separate lines or columns. 2. A synoptical statement or series of statements; a concise presentation of the details of a subject; a list of items. *Synonymous with* FILE 3 (*q.v.*).

TABLE BOOK.   1. An ancient writing book comprised of wax-covered tablets of metal, ivory or wood and fastened together at the back by rings or thongs of leather. The writing was done with a stylus. 2. An obsolete name for a note-book. 3. An elaborately decorated edition of a book, often covered in velvet or silk, for display on a drawing-room table. Popular in the nineteenth century.

TABLE OF CONTENTS.   *See* CONTENTS.

TABLEDEX INDEX.   A co-ordinate book-form index developed by R. S. Ledley. Terms are arranged in tables with document numbers and associated term numbers in ascending number sequence (*IBM*). *See also* CO-ORDINATE INDEXING.

TABLET. An ancient writing material made of clay (used when moist and afterwards baked), stone, lead, wood or ivory and covered with wax. Also called 'Tabula'.

TABULA. *Synonymous with* TABLET (*q.v.*).

TABULAR CLASSIFICATION. A classification or table consisting of several columns and several horizontal series, some of which may not be of equal numbers of terms. The terms need not recur as in cross-classifications. A tabular classification may be less regular and less complete than a cross-classification (*Bliss*). *See also* COLUMNAR, HORIZONTAL.

TABULAR WORK. (*Printing*) Figures and other matter arranged vertically in columns, with or without rules.

TABULATED CODE. In machine sorting as part of information retrieval, one that requires a code book or dictionary to provide code equivalents for source words and vice versa. Also called an 'Arbitrary code'. *See also* CODE.

TACK MARKS. Small dots incorporated in imposing schemes for sheets printed by the WORK AND TURN (*q.v.*) method. One dot is used for the first side printed and two for the second.

TAIL. The bottom or lower edge of a book. The term is applied both to the margin below the text and to the cover of the book.

TAIL. In typography, the lower portion of letter *g* and the projection on the *Q*.

TAIL EDGE. *Synonymous with* LOWER EDGE (*q.v.*).

TAIL FOLD. *See* BOLT.

TAIL MARGIN. The space below the bottom line of a page of type matter. Also called 'Lower margin'. *See also* MARGIN.

TAIL ORNAMENT. An ornament appearing at the foot of a page or the end of the matter occurring on it, especially at the end of a section, chapter or book. It is sometimes called a 'Tail piece'. *See also* HEAD ORNAMENT.

TAIL PIECE. *Synonymous with* TAIL ORNAMENT.

TAILBAND. A decorative band similar to a HEADBAND (*q.v.*) but placed at the tail of a book.

TAILCAP. The fold of leather at the foot of the spine of a book to protect the TAILBAND (*q.v.*).

TAILED LETTER. One which, appearing to be a digraph consisting of a letter and a full stop, gives the impression of being a letter with a horizontally tailed last stroke. *See also* SWASH LETTERS.

TAKE. The amount of copy taken at one time by a compositor to set up in type. *See also* BREAK LINE, END A BREAK, END EVEN.

TAKE DOWN. (*Binding*) To take a book to pieces and reduce it to its original sections. *See also* PULLED.

TAKING OUT TURNS. Inserting the correct type character where the twin black footmarks (as ▮ ▮) on a galley proof indicate that the correct one was not available. *See also* TURNED SORT.

TALBOTYPE. *Synonymous with* CALOTYPE (*q.v.*).

TALIC. Abbreviation for Tyneside Association of Libraries for Industry and Commerce which was inaugurated in 1958; it is based on the Newcastle-on-Tyne Public Libraries' Commercial and Technical Library. Its purpose is to co-ordinate library facilities on Tyneside in order to make information more readily available to industry and commerce, and especially to assist the smaller firms which have not the facilities to set up their own libraries. A union list of periodicals totalling 2,500 titles is maintained at Headquarters. No subscription is charged to members, and non-members may use the service.

TALKING BOOK. A book for the blind in the form of gramophone records, and played on a slowly revolving turntable. *See also* NTBL.

TALL COPY. A book that has lost nothing of its original height in binding.

TALLY. 1. The physical record, or unit, on which may be made one or more entries in connection with information retrieval. *See also* ENTRY, FILE 3. 2. Notched piece of wood used as a receipt for money or goods, both public and private, from the early Middle Ages until about the third decade of the nineteenth century.

TANN COLLECTION. A representative collection of children's books which is maintained by the Department of Education and Science, and is exhibited at teachers' courses and conferences.

TAPE. (*Data processing*) 1. A plastic strip coated or impregnated with magnetic or optically sensitive substances, used for data input, memory or output. 2. A paper or plastic strip with punches or other arbitrary signs representing alphabetic or numerical data and operations (*IBM*).

TAPES. The pieces of tape to which the sections of a book are sewn, the ends being pasted to the boards or between the split boards which form the covers.

TARRED BROWN PAPER. Wrapping paper consisting of one or more sheets of paper coated or impregnated with coal- or wood-tar or bitumen and so given some degree of waterproofing. *See also* UNION PAPER.

TAUBER REPORT. A report, *Resources in Australian Libraries*, written by Maurice F. Tauber, Melvil Dewey Professor of Library Service at Columbia University, New York, of a systematic survey of the total library resources of Australia. It was published in 1963.

TAXONOMY. The science of classification. Also, the study of the names and naming of items in generic assemblies (*IBM*).

TAYLORISM. The study of management and administration and the application of the results to the increase of production and economy. Named after Frederick W. Taylor who pioneered this field in the U.S.A.

TEACHER-LIBRARIAN. A teacher who is also a school librarian. The Library Association, jointly with the School Library Association, sponsors examinations each year and awards a Certificate for Teacher-Librarians to successful candidates.

TEACHER'S BOOK. An explanatory handbook issued with a series of textbooks or a single textbook for the use of teachers. It sometimes has a 'key' or answers to questions and problems.

TEAR SHEET. A sheet of paper torn from a publication; when the item consists of more than one sheet, it is called a 'clipped article' or 'clipping'. *See also* CUTTING.

TECHNICAL JOURNAL. A journal which is devoted to a particular branch of technology. Also called a 'Technical periodical'.

TECHNICAL LIBRARY. A library containing mostly books of a technical nature. When connected with a public library, it may be a section of the reference library, a separate department in the central building, or a separate building.

TECHNICAL PERIODICAL. *Synonymous with* TECHNICAL JOURNAL (*q.v.*).

TECHNICAL PROCESSES, DEPARTMENT OF. *Synonymous with* PROCESSING DEPARTMENT (*q.v.*).

TECHNICAL REPORT. A scientific paper, article, translation, probably recording the current position of scientific research and development, etc., whether security classified, unclassified or declassified.

TECHNICAL SERVICES. All the activities and processes concerned with obtaining, organizing and processing library material for use. (American.)

TECHNICAL SERVICES DEPARTMENT. A department of a library where the functions of book acquisition, cataloguing, classification and processing are carried out. Also called 'Technical services division'.

TEES-SIDE, LIBRARY INFORMATION SERVICE FOR. *See* LIST.

TELEGRAPHIC ABSTRACT. 1. A special abbreviated style of abstract commonly considered suitable for machine input (*IBM*). *See also* ABSTRACT. 2. An essential part of the American Society of Metals (ASM) Documentation Service; it is made up of (1) significant words selected from the articles, (2) code symbols, called 'role indicators' which fit the selected words into context, and (3) punctuation symbols which separate and group the words and role indicators into various units in a somewhat similar way to conventional punctuation. A telegraphic abstract is prepared in addition to a conventional abstract and is an 'index' to be read, ultimately, by a machine.

TELETYPESETTING. The process of setting type with a teletypesetter apparatus, which automatically operates a keyboard slugcasting machine consisting essentially of a separate keyboard that perforates a tape which is fed into an attachment to the slug-casting machine, or into a sender that transmits electrical impulses telegraphically to any number of re-perforators, with the perforated tape causing the slug-casting machine to set type by automatic operation of the keyboard. Abbreviated TTS.

TELONISM. Terminal letters of an author's name used as a pseudonym, as N.S. (John Austis). *See also* TITLONYM.

TEL-STOR. Trade name for a telephone answering machine which records telephone conversations on tape, recording a conversation after the telephone has been replaced (if desirable), or acting as a separate dictating machine. Somewhat similar machines are ANSAPHONE and RECORDACALL (*qq.v.*).

TEMPORARY BRANCH. A service of books for home-reading provided in temporary quarters until it is determined whether there is sufficient demand to justify the erection of a permanent building, until the best site for a permanent building has been determined, or until authorization or finances permit the erection of a permanent building.

TEMPORARY CARD. A card, bearing brief particulars of a book, which is inserted in a catalogue in place of the usual card during its temporary removal for emendation. Also called 'Temporary slip'.

TEMPORARY SLIP. *Synonymous with* TEMPORARY CARD (*q.v.*).

TERM. (*Information retrieval*) In an index, the subject heading or DESCRIPTOR (*q.v.*) (*IBM*). *See also* FEATURE CARD, ITEM.

TERM CARD. *Synonymous with* ASPECT CARD, FEATURE CARD (*qq.v.*).

TERM ENTRY. In information retrieval, the 'inverted' form of entry used by UNITERM (*q.v.*), peephole card, and other co-ordinate indexes, in which a TALLY (*q.v.*) is made and filed under a term chosen to describe a characteristic of information kept by the library or information centre, and on which are recorded symbols representing all the documents possessing this characteristic. Also called 'Aspect system'. *See also* ITEM ENTRY.

TERM PAPER. An undergraduate-level research paper. It may be a report (a) which relates facts for the purpose of informing the reader or of showing progress over a period of time, or (b) based on the student's investigations, which analyses an event, a situation, or a period. It may also be a thesis (i.e. a dissertation presented by a candidate for an academic degree, usually the M.A. or M.S. degree) (a) which states and maintains by argument a position or a proposition, or (b) which presents and evaluates facts for the purpose of persuading or recommending (American).

TERMATREX SYSTEM. A DATA PROCESSING (*q.v.*) system which uses the inverted mode, information retrieval being achieved by placing characteristic cards over a light source to reveal light spots which indicate the characteristics possessed. This is a commercial form of PEEK-A-BOO (*q.v.*) cards: each card represents an index unit (a piece of information) and has room for 10,000 punches, the position of each indicating a document number that has as one of its assigned index units the concept represented by the card. The Termatrex cards can be used with the 'Minimatrix' system; each of the record cards is photographed on film strip, the size of the record being reduced to $\frac{1}{2} \times \frac{1}{2}$ inch, and consulted in the Visual Minimatrex Recorder.

TERMINAL DIGIT POSTING. Arranging and recording serial numbers of documents on the basis of the last digit of the serial number.

TERMS. The headings – words or combinations of words – used in a scheme of classification for classes, divisions, subdivisions, or sections. The *names* of any subjects that may be included in the classification.

TERNION. Three sheets folded together in folio.

TETRAEVANGELIUM. A book containing the four Gospels.

TETRALOGY. A set of four related dramatic or literary compositions, said especially of three Greek tragedies and a satyric comedy.

TEXT. 1. The body of a work following the PRELIMINARIES (*q.v.*). 2. The type matter on a page as distinct from the illustrations.

TEXT HAND. A style of writing employed for books, treatises and the headings of business documents from about 1100 to the sixteenth century.

TEXT TITLE. *Synonymous with* CAPTION TITLE (*q.v.*).

TEXT TYPE. Type used for setting the text of a book or periodical, or other large amounts of copy. It is seldom larger than 14 point.

TEXTBOOK. A book written specifically for use by those studying for an examination in any particular subject.

TEXTILE BINDING. An ornate style of binding using fabrics. It was popular in France and England during the Renaissance. Coloured satin and velvet, often embellished with many-coloured silk embroidery and gold and silver threads, was frequently used.

TEXTURA. See GOTHIC, or BLACK LETTER, TYPE.

TEXTUAL MANUSCRIPT. See LITERARY MANUSCRIPT.

THAMES BOARD. A British-made board much used in EDITION BINDING (*q.v.*). Each side is covered with brown kraft paper to give equal tension, and thus rigidity.

THEATRE LIBRARY ASSOCIATION. Founded in the U.S.A. in 1937 to further the interests of collecting, preserving and using theatre material (books, photographs, playbills, etc.) in libraries, museums and private collections. Publishes *Broadside* (irreg. to membs.).

THEMATIC CATALOGUE. One containing a list of a composer's works and the opening themes or passages of each composition, or for each section of lengthy musical compositions. Entries are usually arranged in chronological order, or by categories.

THEME. *Synonymous with* TOPIC (*q.v.*).

THERMAL DIAZO PROCESS. A DIAZOTYPE PROCESS (*q.v.*) in which heat is used to release the neutralizing alkaline chemicals contained in the base with the acidic stabilizers.

THERMAL PROCESS. A process for copying documents without the use of liquid chemicals. Heat sensitive paper is used to make copies from an original having carbon or metallic writing or printing inks; some materials will not reproduce vegetable inks. THERMOFAX (*q.v.*) and Eichner Dry Copy are both thermal processes. Also called 'Heat copying', 'Thermography'. *See also* DIRECT CONTACT COPYING.

THERMIC COPYING. A documentary reproduction process which uses thermo-sensitive coatings on the base material. A copy made by this method may be called a 'Thermic copy'. *Synonymous with* THERMOGRAPHY. *See also* THERMAL PROCESS.

THERMOFAX. Trade name for a machine and method of copying documents; it is manufactured by the Minnesota Mining and Manufacturing Company. The method consists of passing a controlled beam of infra-red light across a sheet of heat-sensitive paper which is in contact with the document to be copied. The heat-sensitive material on the Thermofax paper is a non-transparent material which melts between 60° and 115°C. and then becomes transparent, revealing the colour of an infra-red transmitting material underneath. The print or other matter which is being copied converts the rays into heat, burns through the non-transparent material, exposes the colour of the material underneath and so produces a copy of the original.

THERMOGRAPHIC COPY. · A copy of a document made by a THERMAL PROCESS (*q.v.*), or thermography. Also called 'Thermic copy'.

THERMOGRAPHY. 1. Any printing process which involves the use of heat; specifically that method of printing from ordinary type or plates on an ordinary press and in which a special ink is used, the type impression being sprinkled while still wet with a special powder and then subjected to a heating process which causes the particles to adhere to the printed surface and fuse together to give the printing a raised effect. Also called 'Raised-letter printing', 'Imitation embossing' and 'Virkotype process'. 2. The THERMAL PROCESS (*q.v.*) of document copying. *See also* DIRECT CONTACT COPYING.

THERMOPLASTIC BINDING. A method of binding a book without sewing. The folds are cut off, the edges roughened and glued and the covers stuck on.

THERMOPLASTIC PROCESS. A microfilming process whereby an electrostatic image is made to produce a permanent deformation of a plastic film layer. Recording can be made by optical projection, electron beams, or computer print-out devices. Thermoplastic systems also have a higher capacity than magnetic tape for carrying coded information for use with computers.

THESAURI (*Pl.*). *See* THESAURUS.

THESAURUS. 1. Literally, a storehouse, or treasury, of knowledge. A term which is best known through its use in the title *Thesaurus of English words and phrases* by P. M. Roget, first published in 1852 and frequently revised. 2. A lexicon, more especially where words are grouped by ideas; a grouping or classification of synonyms or near synonyms; a set of equivalence classes of terminology (*IBM*). 3. A compilation of groups of words, consisting of the links between words used in documents and words used as DESCRIPTORS (*q.v.*), prepared for consultation by a machine used in information retrieval. They display relations within the vocabulary based on semantics, not on orthography. The (American) Engineers Joint Council has prepared a thesaurus of the most commonly used terms to achieve a unity of indexing terminology within the entire field of engineering. Also called 'Dictionary' or 'Words authority file'.

THESIS. *Synonymous with* DISSERTATION (*q.v.*).

THICK SPACE. (*Printing*) A space whose width is one-third of its own body.

THICKNESS COPY. *Synonymous with* DUMMY (*q.v.*).

THIN PAPER. Sensitized photographic paper between 0·0038 and 0·0043 inches inclusive. *See also* PHOTOGRAPHIC PAPERS.

THIN SPACE. (*Printing*) A space whose width is one-fifth of its own body.

THIRD GENERATION MICROFILM. *Synonymous with* SECOND REPRODUCTION MICROFILM (*q.v.*). *See also* GENERATION.

THIRD INDENTION. The twelfth typewriter space from the left edge of a card, and the second space from the second or inner vertical line on a ruled card. The distance from the left-hand edge of a catalogue card at which certain parts of the description begin or continue. It is generally as far to the right of the SECOND INDENTION (*q.v.*) as this is from the FIRST INDENTION (*q.v.*). *See also* INDENTION.

THIRTY-SIXMO (36mo). A sheet of paper folded to form thirty-six leaves, making seventy-two pages. Also called 'Trigesimo-sexto'.

THIRTY-TWOMO (32mo). A sheet of paper folded five times to form a section of thirty-two leaves (sixty-four pages) each leaf being one thirty-second of the sheet. Also called 'Trigesimo-secundo'.

THOROUGH-BASS. *Synonymous with* FIGURED-BASS (*q.v.*).

THREAD STITCHED. A booklet that is fastened with thread through the section fold. *See also* SEWING, SIDE-STITCH, WIRE STITCHED.

THREE-COLOUR PROCESS. Printing by photo-mechanical colour separation in half-tone, which will reproduce colour in the copy in three printings of yellow, red and blue. *See also* TWO-COLOUR PROCESS, TWO-COLOUR REPRODUCTION.

THREE-DECKER. A novel published in three volumes during the latter half of the nineteenth century and sold at $1\frac{1}{2}$ guineas.

THREE DOTS. Used on the type BASE LINE (*q.v.*) thus . . . in quoted text, or a catalogue entry, to indicate that some part of the original has been omitted. Called 'Omission marks'.

THREE-LAYER PAPER. *See* FURNISH LAYER.

THREE-QUARTER BINDING. *See* QUARTER BINDING.

THREE-QUARTER LEATHER. A book bound similarly to one in HALF LEATHER (*q.v.*), but with the leather of the spine projecting across a third of the sides. *See also* LEATHER BOUND, QUARTER LEATHER.

THRILLER. A novel of a sensational character, usually dealing with crime and criminals.

THROW OUT. Maps, tables, or diagrams likely to be much consulted during the reading of a book, are sometimes 'thrown out' by the binder. This is done by making the 'guard' the size of the page, or printing the map on extra large paper, and pasting it at the end of a book or beyond the text which refers to it, so that the whole of the map, etc., when opened out, may remain in view during reading.

THUMB BOOK. *Synonymous with* BIBELOT (*q.v.*).

THUMB INDEX. A series of rounded notches cut into the fore-edges of a book, with or without tabs let in and bearing in progressive order from top to bottom the letters or words showing the arrangement. Usually provided for Bibles and dictionaries.

TICKLER SYSTEM. Any method of recording or filing notes, enquiries, loans, material, publications 'in progress', etc., to ensure follow-up on a particular future date.

TIDU. The Technical Information and Documents Unit formerly a unit of the Board of Trade, but later a part of the Department of Scientific and Industrial Research: it was the U.K. clearing house for the deposition of Government-sponsored scientific and technical literature under a scheme initiated by the Organization for European Co-operation (OEEC). The Unit dealt with the administration and dissemination of the valuable material of a scientific, economic and technical nature which was discovered in Germany, Italy and Japan by the Allied forces as they advanced into these countries during the 1939–45 war. Reports were published and sold under the series names CIOS (Combined Intelligence Objective Sub-Committee) and BIOS (British Intelligence Objectives Sub-Committee). BIOS succeeded CIOS when the Supreme Headquarters Allied Expeditionary Force was dissolved in 1945 and the main interest of the investigations and reports shifted from the military to the industrial sphere.

TIED DOWN. (*Binding*) Where the fillets which flank the bands of the spine are carried on to meet at a point near the hinge.

TIED LETTER. *Synonymous with* LIGATURE (*q.v.*).

TIED UP. Said of type-matter that has been made up into pages and tied up with page-cord to secure it until imposition.

TIER. A set of shelves one above another between two uprights and reaching from the floor to the top of the shelving: a section of a PRESS (*q.v.*). *See also* BOOK PRESS, BOOK STACK, BOOKCASE, DOUBLE-FACED SHELF, DOUBLE-SIDED STACK, PRESS.

TIER GUIDE. A guide to the contents of a TIER (*q.v.*).

TIES. 1. Silk, leather, cord, tape, ribbon or other slips attached, usually in pairs, to the outer edges of boards of books for a decorative purpose, or to prevent sagging by holding the covers together. 2. Terminations to tooled lines on each side of projecting bands on the spine of a bound book and carried over on to the covers to form ornamental features.

TIGHE REPORT. A report, prepared largely by the late Mr. F. C. Tighe and based on a national survey of the conditions of service of assistant librarians in British public libraries. The *Recommendations on welfare and working conditions of public library staffs*, based on this report, were approved by the Council of the Association of Assistant Librarians and adopted by the Council of the Library Association in May 1953.

TIGHT BACK. A binding in which the cover of leather or other material is pasted or glued to the spine of the book, so that it does not become hollow when open. The pages do not lie flat when the book is open unless the paper used is thin and not stiff, as e.g. India paper. This is therefore a less satisfactory form of binding than either Flexible or Hollow. Also called 'Fast back', 'Stiff back'. *See also* FLEXIBLE SEWING, HOLLOW BACK.

TIGHT JOINT. *Synonymous with* CLOSED JOINT (*q.v.*).

TILDE. (*Printing*) An accent in the form of a wavy line as used over letters in Spanish and Portuguese: ñ; õ.

TILL-FORBID ORDER. *Synonymous with* STANDING ORDER (*q.v.*).

TILTED SHELVES. The bottom or lower two or three shelves of a bookcase which are arranged in a sloping position to render the examination of titles easier.

TIME NUMBERS. A series of numbers or letters designed to facilitate the arrangement of books in chronological instead of author or alphabetical order. *See also* BISCOE TIME NUMBERS, MERRILL ALPHABETING NUMBERS.

TIME-SCHEDULE. *See* TIME-SHEET.

TIME-SHARING. (*Information retrieval*) Being able to use a device for more than one purpose in the same time period. This process may be accomplished by interspersing different operations.

TIME-SHEET. A schedule showing the exact hours each day that each assistant is scheduled to be on duty. Also called 'Time-schedule'.

TIMES NEW ROMAN. A type face designed under the direction of Stanley Morison by the Monotype Corporation for the *Times* newspaper in 1932 and later extensively used in book work. Usually called 'Times Roman'. For a specimen alphabet, *see* TYPE FACE.

TIPPED IN. A single leaf, errata slip or illustration, inserted in a book at the inner edge with a narrow edge of paste against the following page.

TIPPING MACHINE. A bookbinding machine for the gluing of single plates and end-papers on to folded sheets or sewn sections. Some models also glue paper covers on to the folded and sewn sections.

TIPS. Very thin millboards used for book-binding.

TISSUE-PAPERS. Sheets of superfine thin paper placed in front of illustrations to protect them from set-off while the ink is fresh. These are often removed after the ink has dried, but sometimes they are to be found tipped-in, and they frequently bear a typographical description of the illustration.

TISSUED PLATE. An illustration in a book which has a thin tissue placed between it (either loose or pasted to the inner margin) and the text page to protect it from SET-OFF (*q.v.*). Sometimes the tissue bears the caption relating to the illustration or an appropriate quotation. *See also* INTERLEAF.

TITHE DOCUMENTS. Documents relating to tithes. The Tithe Act, 1936, as amended, provides that the Master of the Rolls may direct that sealed copies of tithe documents shall be transferred to the Public Record Office or to any public library or museum or historical or antiquarian society willing to receive them. On the transfer of such documents the governing body of the library, museum or society assumes responsibility for their proper preservation. The Tithe (Copies of Instruments of Apportionment) Rules were made in 1946 (S.R. & O., 1946, No. 2091) to implement the provisions of the Act.

TITLE. Ordinarily, the name by which a work is designated on its title-page, and – usually – distinguished from any other work. In its fuller sense, it includes any sub-title, alternative title, or associated descriptive matter, but excludes the name of the author and/or editor, translator, etc. (unless the name forms a grammatically inseparable part of the title) and the edition, but not the imprint. *See also* BACK TITLE, BINDER'S TITLE, COLLECTIVE TITLE, COVER TITLE, SPINE TITLE.

TITLE-A-LINE CATALOGUE. A catalogue in which the entries occupy only a single line of type.

TITLE ANALYTIC. *See* ANALYTICAL ENTRY.

TITLE BACKING. The material, or treatment, applied to the back of the title area (i.e. the area extending the full width of the film and above the micro-images) of a microfiche so that the title can be more easily read by reflected light. It is usually applied to a distribution MICROFICHE (*q.v.*) not intended to be used for the reproduction of additional microfiches.

TITLE CARD. A catalogue card bearing an entry under the title of a work.

TITLE CATALOGUE. A catalogue consisting only of title entries.

TITLE-CUT. *Synonymous with* FRAMED-CUT (*q.v.*).

21

TITLE ENTRY.   A record in a catalogue for a book, generally beginning with the first word of the title not an article. In practice such entries are limited to unusual or striking titles which are likely to be remembered, and are added entries, unless the authorship is unknown in which case the title entry may be the main entry.

TITLE INDENTION.   *Synonymous with* SECOND INDENTION (*q.v.*).

TITLE INDEX.   *Synonymous with* Key-word-in-context, or KWIC (*q.v.*) index.

TITLE LEAF.   The leaf at the beginning of a book, the recto of which is the title-page. The verso usually bears bibliographical details of printer, copyright date and any earlier editions.

TITLE OF HONOUR.   A title which denotes superior rank or station, or special distinction of any kind.

TITLE-PAGE.   Usually the recto of the second leaf which gives the title in full, sub-title (if any), author's name in full together with particulars of qualifications, degrees, etc., edition, publisher's name and address, and date of publication. The verso may give particulars of edition, printer's name and sometimes his address, binder's name, details of type and paper used in making the book, owner of copyright, and in the case of American books the Library of Congress catalogue card number. If there is more than one page giving particulars of the title, the title-page is that which gives the fullest information. *See also* DOUBLE TITLE-PAGE, ENGRAVED TITLE-PAGE, SECOND HALF-TITLE, SECTION TITLE.

TITLE-PAGE BORDER.   A frame, at first a woodcut, and later made of heavy type ornaments, surrounding the matter on the title-page.

TITLE-PAGE TITLE.   The title of a book as it appears on the title-page. It is the authority for the correct reference to the book; other versions of the title as given on the spine, cover, half-title, top of the pages or jacket may vary slightly.

TITLE PIECE.   A leather label, sometimes coloured, pasted on the back of a binding, and bearing the title of the book.

TITLE SHEET.   The first printed sheet of a book containing the title-page and other preliminary matter.

TITLE SIGNATURE.   The title (often abbreviated to initial letters) placed on the signature line of signed pages to prevent the binder mixing up the sheets of various books. Also called 'Direction line'. *See also* SIGNATURE AND CATCHWORD LINE.

TITLE SPACE.   The area specifically allotted on a microfiche or microcard for title information. *See also* TITLE BACKING.

TITLE STRIP.   Wording at the beginning of a FILM STRIP (*q.v.*) or other sequence of microcopy frames giving the title or indicating their contents.

TITLING. Capital letters of modern Roman type which are cast 'full face' on the BODY (*q.v.*); there are thus no BEARD (*q.v.*) or LOWER CASE (*q.v.*) letters. They are used for headlines, titles, jackets, or posters.

TITLONYM. A quality or title used as a pseudonym, as 'A Barrister'. If the author's name cannot be determined, such books are catalogued as if they were anonymous, entry being made under the title. An added entry is made under the titlonym. *See also* TELONISM.

TOGGLE PRESS. The Albion press which was introduced in 1823 and allowed the platen to be lowered and given great pressure by means of a toggle-jointed lever instead of the screw method. A toggle-jointed lever is one with an elbow-shaped joint with two arms known as the chill and the wedge. When the joint is straightened so that chill and wedge form a straight line, great endwise pressure is produced.

TOKEN CHARGING. A system of issuing books whereby the borrower on entering the lending department of a library is given a token which he exchanges for a book as he leaves. It was first introduced at the Westminster Public Libraries in 1954.

TOME. A volume, or book, especially a heavy one.

TOMLINSON AWARD, NORMAN. Made first in 1969, in recognition of the work Mr. Tomlinson has done for the London and Home Counties Branch of the Library Association in connection with the Portway Reprints since 1963. It is intended to help personal research into practical problems which are likely to result in improved library services, over a wide area, either for readers or for staffs. Chartered librarians who have had a minimum of seven years' experience after their election to the Register are eligible, and the Award is confined to those thus qualified who are, or who have been previously personal members of the London and Home Counties Branch.

TONKS FITTINGS. The most generally used form of adjustable shelving fittings. They consist of slotted strips of metal into which small studs are placed to support book shelves (four for each shelf). Two strips are placed on one side of each upright, towards the back and front edges, so that each shelf rests on the four studs placed at the same level, one in each strip. These fittings are made by Tonks (Birmingham) Ltd.

TOOL PHASE. In classification, where one discipline is used to assist the investigation of another, the document is classified under the thing investigated, not under the tool of investigation. It is one of

Ranganathan's three main 'phase relations', the other two are BIAS PHASE and INFLUENCE PHASE (*qq.v.*).

TOOLED EDGES. The edges of a book which have been impressed with designs. *See also* EDGES.

TOOLING. The impressing of designs – by means of finishing tools such as rolls – into a leather or cloth binding. The tools used may be 'embossed' in which case there is modelling on the top surface (i.e. the bottom of its impression), 'outline', 'shaded' or 'azured'. When this is done through gold leaf it is called 'gold tooling', when neither leaf nor pigment is used it is called 'blind tooling'. When the entire cover design is a single piece, it is called a 'stamp'. Gold tooling is believed to have been introduced by Thomas Berthelet, royal binder to Henry VIII. The tools used may be 'embossed' in which case there is modelling on the top surface, 'outline', 'shaded' or 'azured'. *See also* AZURE TOOLING, BLOCK 3, EDGE-ROLLED.

TOP EDGES GILT. The top edges of a book cut smooth and gilded. Abbreviated 't.e.g.' Also called 'Gilt top'.

TOP MARGIN. The space between the top line of type of a book or periodical, and the edge of the page. *See also* MARGIN.

TOP SIDE. *Synonymous with* FELT SIDE (*q.v.*).

TOPIC. In co-ordinate indexing, a group of terms describing a given subject. Also called 'Information item' and 'Theme'.

TOPIC GUIDE. A guide to a specific subject; it is usually a narrow block of wood or piece of cardboard bearing the subject and class number, placed on the shelf at the beginning of the books on the subject. Also called 'Subject guide'.

TOPICAL BIBLIOGRAPHY. A subject bibliography, consisting of short lists of books or references placed at the ends of chapters.

TOPOGRAPHICAL CATALOGUE. A catalogue of books relating to places.

TOPOGRAPHICAL INDEX. An index of places arranged in alphabetical order.

TOPOGRAPHICAL MAP. One which shows physical or natural features of an area.

TORY STYLE. A style of binding executed in the sixteenth century for Geoffroy Tory the famous French printer, wood-engraver and designer. Distinguished by arabesque panels, borders and ornaments.

TOWN PLAN. A map of a town showing the organized arrangement of streets, open spaces, etc. *See also* PLAT.

Tr. (trans.). Abbreviation for Transactions (*q.v.*), translated, TRANSLATION (*q.v.*), TRANSLATOR (*q.v.*).

TRACING. An indication on the front or back of a main entry catalogue card showing under what additional headings added entries appear. Also, the record (on the main entry card, or on an authority card) of all the related references made. Specially important in a dictionary catalogue in order to ensure that in case of change, correction or removal, all the cards referring to a given book may be traced and the change applied to all of them. In co-ordinate indexing, a list of the descriptors, Uniterms, etc., applied to a specific document.

TRACING PAPER. Paper treated with a coating of Canada balsam in turpentine, or a solution of castor oil or linseed oil in alcohol. The papers chosen for this treatment must have excellent transparency, high tearing strength, and be resistant to erasure; they must contain no loading and be engine-sized. Tracing papers cockle readily on absorbing moisture from the atmosphere and must therefore be wrapped in waxed or other waterproof paper.

TRACT. 1. A pamphlet containing a short propagandist discourse, especially on a religious, political or social subject. 2. A pamphlet printed on a single sheet and imposed in pages.

TRADE BIBLIOGRAPHY. *See* BIBLIOGRAPHY 1, TRADE CATALOGUE 1.

TRADE BINDING. 1. The binding in which a publisher issues a book. Also called 'Publisher's binding'. 2. Plain calf or sheep bindings which were used in England by publishers from the fifteenth–eighteenth centuries; only rarely did they carry lettering on the spines. Until the nineteenth century, purchasers usually bought books unbound or enclosed in wrappers, and had them bound to order.

TRADE BOOK. A common U.S. publishing term for a book intended for general readership. It is neither a children's book, a textbook, nor a technical treatise, but a book which would interest anybody, and be published by a commercial publisher as distinct from one published by a society, institution, governmental agency or other non-commercial group.

TRADE CATALOGUE. 1. A list of the books in print published in a country, and frequently of books published abroad, for which the home publishers are agents. 2. A publication containing particulars of goods manufactured by, or sold by, a firm; frequently illustrated and containing prices.

TRADE EDITION. Copies of a book which are regularly printed and supplied to booksellers by publishers at the appropriate wholesale rates. *See also* LARGE PAPER EDITION, SUBSCRIBERS' EDITION, especially such an edition contrasted with a de luxe, paperback, library-bound, or book club edition.

TRADE INFORMATION. *Synonymous with* BIBLIOGRAPHIC INFORMATION (*q.v.*).

TRADE JOURNAL. A periodical restricted to the interests of a trade or industry and including all or some of the following: news items, articles and descriptions of goods, products and manufactured articles, lists of new publications, statistical data, patents, personal notes, legislative activities, etc. Also called 'Trade paper'.

TRADE LIST. A list of publications in print, which is issued by a publisher for the information of the bookselling trade, often providing space for ordering the various titles and giving particulars of the terms under which the books are sold to booksellers.

TRADE PAPER. *Synonymous with* TRADE JOURNAL (*q.v.*).

TRADE SERIES. *See* PUBLISHER'S SERIES.

TRADE TERMS. The provision of facilities for retailers to obtain goods at a discount for re-sale to the public. In the book trade, the discounts may vary according to the kind of book (general, children's, educational, technical, etc.) but they are fairly standard. Export terms are usually different from those for the home market.

TRADITIONAL ABSTRACT. *See* ABSTRACT.

TRADITIONAL FORMAT. The format of oriental books, consisting of double leaves with folds at the fore-edge and with free edges sewn together to make a fascicle. Usually several fascicles are contained in a cloth-covered case.

TRAILER. A portion of developed but unexposed copying material, such as film strip, at the end of a sequence of exposures, which is not cut off; it serves to protect the exposed portion and assists projection.

TRAILER MICROFILM. *See* MICROFICHE.

TRAINING COLLEGES AND INSTITUTE OF EDUCATION, SUB-SECTION. Subsequently the Colleges, Institutes and Schools of Education Sub-Section of the UNIVERSITY, COLLEGE AND RESEARCH SECTION (*q.v.*), but now an independent Group, of the Library Association.

TRANSACTION CARD. A card which is inserted in a book, the loan of which is recorded by a TRANSACTION CARD CHARGING (*q.v.*) method.

TRANSACTION CARD CHARGING. Book issue methods in which the records of loans are kept in the order in which they are made, transactions being given numbers in consecutive order. At the time of recording the loan a numbered 'transaction card' is inserted in the book and remains there until the book is returned to the library when it is withdrawn. Transaction cards for all returned books are then put into number order, any missing ones indicating overdue books. The transaction cards usually have the date the books are due for return stamped on them. Photo-charging, AUDIO-CHARGING (*q.v.*) and PUNCHED CARD CHARGING (*q.v.*) and the BOOKAMATIC (*q.v.*) systems are transaction card charging methods. Abbreviated T-card charging.

TRANSACTION ROOM. A room to which books issued by a method using transaction cards are taken on their return by readers, for examination, checking with lists of reserved books, or sorting for shelving. The manual sorting of transaction cards may also be done here, punched transaction cards being sent to the machine sorter.

TRANSACTIONS. The published papers read at meetings of a society or institution, or abstracts of the same. *Also sometimes synonymous with* PROCEEDINGS (*q.v.*). A general distinction made between Transactions and Proceedings is that the Transactions are the papers presented and the Proceedings the records of meetings.

TRANSCRIPT. A copy made from an original, particularly of a legal document.

TRANSCRIPTION. 1. The act or process of transcribing a document; the result of this process. 2. In music, the arrangement for one musical medium of music originally composed for another, e.g. an organ piece from an orchestral overture. 3. An arrangement in which some liberty is taken by way of modification or embellishment. *See also* VERSION.

TRANSFER. A chemically prepared paper for transferring drawings direct on to lithographic stone or a rubber-covered cylinder used in offset lithography.

TRANSFER BOX. A box, somewhat similar to a PAMPHLET BOX (*q.v.*) but of less durable construction and serving to store lesser used pamphlet material which is transferred from the current sequence.

TRANSFER FILE. 1. A container of some kind (box-like or folder) of a less sturdy type and cheaper, to contain older material which must be filed but which is seldom referred to and encumbers current files. 2. The material itself which is removed from current files.

TRANSFER PRINTING. *See* DECALCOMANIA.

TRANSFER PROCESS. A method of making copies of documents. The 'soft gelatine transfer process' involves the mechanical transference of the image; in this the negative material consists of paper coated with a gelatine emulsion containing silver halide – a light-sensitive compound, a tanning, or non-diffusing, developer, and a dye-forming agent. After exposure the paper is put in an alkali solution known as an activator, in which the dye is formed and the exposed portions of the image hardened, leaving the unexposed portions soft. A sheet of plain white paper is placed in contact with the negative and the two sheets pressed firmly together by a roller; this transfers the dye from the negative to the white paper. The two are peeled apart, the image having been transferred to the white paper which is almost dry. Up to three copies can usually be made from the same negative which is placed in the activator for each printing: if the negative is contrasty and the correct exposure made, it might be possible to make six copies. The other transfer process, called the 'diffusion transfer process', involves a chemical transference of the image. This process requires two gelatine emulsion-coated papers, the negative one being coated with a silver halide emulsion which is sensitive to light, the positive one being coated with a non-light-sensitive layer containing colloidal silver. After exposure the negative paper is placed in contact with the positive (emulsion side to emulsion side) and they are inserted in adjacent slots in a developing machine where they pass through a weak alkaline developing solution and are then pressed firmly together by a pair of rollers. Soon after they emerge from the machine they are peeled apart. Only one positive can be made from each negative unless a multi-copy paper is used for the master, but a transfer can be made on to translucent paper and this can be used for printing diazo copies.

TRANSFORMER.   In information retrieval, the selector which searches the DESCRIPTOR FILE (q.v.).

TRANSITIONAL.   A name sometimes given to the type face designed about 1760 by John Baskerville, and those based on it. Transitional types retain the bracketed serifs of old face and suggest by their precision the engraved quality of modern face types. The faces are more angular, with sharper contrast between the thick and thin strokes. *See also* EGYPTIAN, MODERN FACE, OLD FACE, TYPE FACE.

The following is in 12 point BASKERVILLE:

ABCDEFGHIJKLMNOPQRSTUVWXYZ

abcdefghijklmnopqrstuvwxyz   1234567890

This sentence is set in Bell which is a 'transitional' type face, as are also Fournier, Caledonia and Columbia.

TRANSITIONAL FACE.   *See* TRANSITIONAL.

TRANSLATED TITLE LIST.   A periodically issued bulletin which lists, usually in a systematic order, the translated titles of periodical articles and documents which are likely to be of interest to its readers.

TRANSLATION.   1. The act of turning a literary composition from one language into another. 2. The work so produced.

TRANSLATION POOL.   A centrally held collection of translations acquired from a variety of sources, and available for use on a co-operative basis.

TRANSLATION RIGHTS. The right to allow or refuse the publication of any literary production in another language is a part of COPYRIGHT (*q.v.*).

TRANSLATOR. One who translates from one language into another.

TRANSLITERATION. The representation of the ordinary characters of a language by those of another, as from Russian, Arabic, Cyrillic, Irish or Greek into Roman, each digit or letter being transcribed independently of the others. *See also* ROMANIZATION.

TRANSLUCENT COPY. In documentary reproduction, a copy on translucent material.

TRANSLUCENT SCREEN. A sheet of glass treated in some way (ground, opal, coated, etc.), or of plastic, on to which an image is projected in a microfilm reader.

TRANSMISSION COPYING. In documentary reproduction, making a photocopy by passing light through a one-sided original which is in contact with sensitized paper. Included in this method are blue-print and Diazo or dyeline processes and the use of silver halide paper in contact with a single-sided document which is thin enough to permit light to pass through it.

TRANSMISSION PRINT. A copy of a document made by TRANSMISSION PRINTING (*q.v.*).

TRANSMISSION PRINTING. The making of contact prints by passing light through the original and on to the material of reproduction. *See also* CONTACT COPYING, TRANSMISSION COPYING.

TRANSPARENCY. An image, in black and white or colour, on transparent base-stock, usually film, which may be viewed by transmitted light.

TRANSPARENT VELLUM. A method (patented in 1785) used by Edwards of Halifax which rendered the vellum to be used in bookbinding transparent. A painting or drawing was done on the underside and the whole then lined with white paper.

TRANSPOSE. To change over the positions of letters, words or lines of type. This is marked on a proof by putting a loop round the characters to be changed and writing 'trs.' in the margin.

TRANSPOSING INSTRUMENT. A musical instrument for which the music is written in a key or in an octave other than its actual sound, but which (mechanically and without thought on the part of the player) transposes the music to a higher or lower pitch.

TRAVELLING CARD. A catalogue card on which subsequent issues

21*

of annuals or other serial publications (*see* CONTINUATION 3) are entered and which is passed to each department or library in turn for the appropriate addition to be made to the catalogue entry. On completion of the addition to all the catalogues, this card is filed in the official catalogue, or in a special sequence, to await subsequent publications when the process is repeated.

TRAVELLING LIBRARY. A large motor vehicle equipped with shelves and a staff enclosure, which visits districts where there is no other library service at specified times on a certain day or days of the week. The public may choose their books from the shelves. In British county libraries there is a tendency to describe such a vehicle as a 'Mobile Branch Library' or 'Mobile Library' and to use the term 'Travelling Library' for a small vehicle which is shelved or otherwise equipped to provide a service to villages, and isolated farms and houses, with short stops for issuing books. *See also* DELIVERY VAN, EXHIBITION VAN, MOBILE LIBRARY. In America, the term also refers to a small collection of selected books sent by a central library agency for the use of a branch, group or community, during a limited period.

TRAVELLING MOULD. *See* WIRE.

TRAY LABEL. A label inserted in the holder provided on the front of a catalogue drawer to indicate its contents.

TREADLE LATCHES. Latches to release wickets which are worked with the foot.

TREE CALF. A calf binding which has had acid poured on it in such a way as to form stains resembling a tree-like pattern.

TREE OF PORPHYRY. *See* PORPHYRY, TREE OF.

TREND REPORT. *Committee of enquiry into the organization of Civil Science* (Cmnd. 2171), the report of the committee appointed by the Prime Minister (then Mr. Harold Macmillian) in March 1962 and under the chairmanship of Sir Burke Trend, to consider whether any changes were desirable in the existing functions of the various scientific agencies and research organizations. The report was published on 30th October 1963 and led to the dissolution of the Department of Scientific and Industrial Research and the formation of a system of independent research councils.

TRIAL BINDING. A sample of the proposed cover for a book submitted by the binder or casemaker to the publisher.

TRIAL ISSUE. A few copies of a book printed for circulation to critical friends prior to the printing of the edition for publication which was printed without re-setting of the type. If re-setting occurred then the preliminary edition was known as a 'trial edition'.

TRIAL PROOF. *See* PROOF.

TRIGESIMO-SECUNDO (32mo). A sheet of paper folded five times to form a section of thirty-two leaves (sixty-four pages). Also called 'Thirty-twomo'.

TRIGESIMO-SEXTO. *Synonymous with* THIRTY-SIXMO (*q.v.*).

TRILOGY. A set of three related dramatic or literary compositions.

TRIMMED. 1. Paper which has been trimmed on one or more sides to ensure exactness of corner angles and to reduce to the size required. 2. (*Binding*) The top edge untouched, and only the inequalities removed from the others, the folds not being opened. *See also* EDGES.

TRIMMED PAGE SIZE. The size of a sheet after folding and trimming.

TRIMMED SIZE. The final dimensions of a sheet of paper. British papermakers may interpret this term as 'guillotine trimmed'. *See also* PAPER SIZES, UNTRIMMED SIZE.

TRINITY COLLEGE LIBRARY, DUBLIN. The oldest library in Ireland; it was established by Royal Charter in 1592 and in 1801 was granted the right to receive a copy of every publication issued in the United Kingdom. It is rich in manuscripts, its best-known treasure being the *Book of Kells*.

TRIPLE LINING. A method of LINING (*q.v.*) used to give added strength. It is used in better-quality cased books and consists of providing a strip of crêpe manila lining, with head-and-tailbands if desired. All the lining processes used in this instance number seven and can be carried out mechanically.

TRIPLEX PAPER. *See* DUPLEX PAPER.

TRIPOLI. The cheaper grades of esparto grass, grown in N. Africa. *See also* ESPARTO.

TRIPPER. (*Reprography*) A device, operated mechanically or electronically, to control lights, film advance, or the beginning or end of the operation.

TRIPTYCH. *See* CODEX.

TROY TYPE. A type cut by William Morris in 1892; it was an 18-point Gothic type based on the early types of Schoeffer, Mentelin and Zainer. *See also* CHAUCER TYPE, GOLDEN TYPE.

trs. Abbreviation for transpose; in proof correcting it is written in the margin to indicate that the position of the words, letters or lines around which a loop is drawn are to be exchanged.

TRUE ANONYMA. Books which would be catalogued as Type A, i.e. under the author's name if their authors were known. These are catalogued in the Library of Congress and some other libraries with the author line left blank so that it can be entered without re-typing the whole entry should the authorship be discovered. This method is known as 'hanging indention'. *See also* FORMAL ANONYMA.

TRUE SIDED.   Reflecting a document or object to be reproduced without the aid of a mirror.

TUB-SIZING.   Dipping sheets of WATERLEAF (*q.v.*) into a tub of animal glue, gelatine, a prepared starch, or a combination of these, drying on cow-hair ropes or hessian, and then glazing them. Tub-sized paper (abbreviated 'T.S.') is strong and has a high resistance to moisture. Also called 'Animal Tub-sized' (abbreviated 'A.T.S.'). *See also* ENGINE-SIZING.

TUMBLER SCHEME.   The method of perfecting sheets to be printed from a form imposed in the oblong, or landscape, manner. In order to obtain correct page sequence, the sheet must be turned or tumbled, in its short direction. *See also* WORK AND TURN.

TURN-IN.   1. That portion of the material covering the boards of a book which overlaps the head, tail and fore-edges of the boards and is turned-in over these edges of the boards. 2. To make use of type matter which is already set. 3. The turned-over end of a book jacket which is folded around the cover.

TURN OVER.   1. An extension of printed matter, beyond the space allotted. 2. The part of an article continued from a preceding page. Also called RUN OVER (*q.v.*).

TURNED COMMA.   A comma which is used upside down and in a superior position, i.e. on the MEAN LINE (*q.v.*); it is used at the beginning of quoted matter '. . .' and in the abbreviation of the Scottish 'Mac', as in M'Gregor.

TURNED LETTER.   A letter used upside down such as a 'u' for an 'n'.

TURNED SORT.   A type letter used foot uppermost for one not known or not available, thus: ▉. This is very conspicuous in galley proof. When turned sorts are replaced with the correct letters, the process is called 'taking out turns'.

TURNS.   *See* TAKING OUT TURNS.

TUTOR LIBRARIAN.   A librarian of an adult education institution who gives lectures to students on the library and how to make the best use of it, and sometimes on academic subjects, as well as having some responsibility for the administration or functioning of the library.

TWELVEMO.   *See* DUODECIMO.

TWENTY-FOURMO (24mo).   A sheet of paper folded to form a section of twenty-four leaves (forty-eight pages). Also called 'Vicesimo-quarto'.

TWENTYMO (20mo). A sheet of paper folded into twenty leaves, making 40 pages.

TWICE WEEKLY. A periodical which is published twice a week. Also called 'Semi-weekly'. *See also* SEMI-MONTHLY.

TWIN-BATH STABILIZATION. A reprography process which employs two solutions for processing – a developer or activator and a stabilizer. Transfer of the exposed material from one solution to the other is usually automatic. *See also* STABILIZATION.

TWIN WIRE PAPER. A DUPLEX PAPER (*q.v.*) made by bringing the two wet webs together, WIRE SIDES (*q.v.*) innermost, to form a single sheet with two top or FELT SIDES (*q.v.*) and no wire side or 'underside'. Such paper is particularly suitable for offset printing. *See also* RIGHT.

TWISTED PINEAPPLES. (*Binding*) The form of ornament used on a number of English and French finishers' rolls, and consisting of twisted stems with conventional pineapples at intervals. *See also* PINE-APPLE.

TWO-COLOUR HALF-TONES. Two half-tone plates in which one of the plates is made with the line of the screen as in a one-colour half-tone, and the other with lines at a different angle, usually about 30°. The colours tend to blend into one another in different tones.

TWO-COLOUR PRESS. A machine which prints in two colours at one operation. The principle is applicable to letterpress, lithographies and offset machines. Most offset printing is carried out on two-colour presses.

TWO-COLOUR PROCESS. A photo-mechanical process in which the printing is done in two colours.

TWO-COLOUR REPRODUCTION. Printing in two colours instead of the more usual three. The colours used are normally green or blue, and orange; subjects have to be carefully chosen or the resulting prints may be not true to the original, or they may be crude.

TWO-COMPONENT DIAZOTYPE MATERIALS. Diazotype materials having in the layer, the diazo compounds as well as the coupling components (two component paper) (*Concepts . . .*). *See also* DIAZO-TYPE PROCESS.

TWO-LAYER PAPER. *See* FURNISH LAYER.

TWO-LINE LETTER. (*Printing*) A capital letter having a depth of body (or height of letter on the printed page) equal to double that of the size specified, as 'two-line pica'. Three- and four-line letters are used similarly. They are often used as the initial letter for the first word of a chapter.

TWO ON. Printing two sheets, jobs, page, etc., at the same time. The printing of small jobs in duplicate is done to facilitate the work and economize in time and costs.

TWO-REVOLUTION MACHINE. A printing machine in which the cylinder, over which the paper is fed, does not stop after traversing the forme but continues to revolve, rising slightly during its second revolution so that it cannot come into contact with the type, and descending when the form is again in position for printing. During its second revolution, the bed with the forme returns and the sheet is delivered. The earliest machine of this kind was made by Koenig in 1814. *See also* MIEHLE, PERFECTER, SINGLE-REVOLUTION MACHINE, STANHOPE PRESS, STOP-CYLINDER PRESS.

TWO SHEETS (SECTIONS) ON. The method of sewing books when two sections are treated as one. In hand-sewing two sheets at a time are placed on the sewing-frame; the thread is passed from the kettle stitch of the lower section, and brought out at the first tape or cord, when it is inserted in the upper section, and so on. Thus, two sections receive only the same number of stitches one would do by the ALL ALONG method (*q.v.*). This is a less strong method than the 'all along' but it helps to reduce the swelling in the back in the case of very thin books.

TWO SIDES COLOURED. Paper or board both sides of which have been coloured intentionally during manufacture.

TWO-UP. 1. Printing two texts, or duplicate stereos made from the same forme, side by side on the same sheet of paper. It is an economical way of machining short runs. 2. The processing of two books as a single unit from the forme through all the binding processes until they are separated by the trimmer. A method which is sometimes used for mass-producing PAPERBACKS (*q.v.*).

TWO-WAY PAGING. The system of page numbering used for a book with the texts in two languages, one of which reads from left to right (as English) and the other from right to left (as Hebrew or Arabic); the texts being in two sections with page sequences from opposite ends of the book.

TWOPENNY LIBRARY. A circulating library, usually in shop premises, for which the charge for borrowing a book was twopence a week. The charge became much greater but the name persisted.

TYING-UP. The tying of a volume after the cover has been drawn on, so as to make the leather adhere better to the sides of the bands; also for setting the headband.

TYMPAN. A kind of leaf consisting of a thin frame of metal over which is stretched parchment or cambric, and which is hinged to the carriage bearing the forme of a printing press in such a way that it places the paper resting on it in the exact position for printing.

TYNESIDE ASSOCIATION OF LIBRARIES FOR INDUSTRY AND COMMERCE. *See* TALIC.

TYPE. (*Classification*) *See* CHARACTERISTIC. (*Printing*) A small rectangular block of metal or wood, having on its upper end a raised letter, figure, or other character, for use in letterpress printing. Also, a number of such characters. *See also* TYPE FACE, TYPE SIZES. For purposes of nomenclature, a single movable type character has always been considered as a human being standing erect, and having a BODY (but no head), a FACE, BEARD, NECK, SHOULDER, BACK, BELLY, FEET. Type letters are formed within three imaginary lines: the 'base line' on which the bases of capitals rest, the 'mean line' running along the top of the lower-case letters which are without ascenders, the 'cap line' which runs across the top of the capital letters. *See also* BODY, X-HEIGHT.

TYPE A CATALOGUE ENTRY. An entry, being the main entry, made under the personal name of the author, even if there is an editor, translator or subordinate editor.

TYPE AREA. The area, or part, of a page of a book, periodical or other publication which will be, or has been, filled with printed matter.

TYPE C CATALOGUE ENTRY. An entry which is used for a book which, because a corporate body is responsible for its existence, has its main entry under the name of the corporate body. A *Type CG entry* is one in which the corporate name, or a formalized version of it, is added to a geographic base, e.g. Manchester, Chamber of Commerce. A *Type CGG entry* is one in which the name of a government body, or office, is added to a geographic base, e.g. Great Britain, War Office.

TYPE-CASTING MACHINE. Originally, one which cast single type units which were then set up in a stick by hand. Modern machines such as *Monotype*, *Linotype* and *Intertype* both set and cast.

TYPE CG CATALOGUE ENTRY. *See* TYPE C CATALOGUE ENTRY.

TYPE CGG CATALOGUE ENTRY. *See* TYPE C CATALOGUE ENTRY.

TYPE F CATALOGUE ENTRY. An entry, being the main entry, for six classes of work, which, although usually treated by the codes with corporate entries, are virtually in the same category as conventional title entries. The six classes are: charters; constitutions; constitutional conventions; laws, statutes, etc.; ordinances, etc.; treaties, etc.

TYPE FACE. 1. The printing surface of the upper end of a piece of type which bears the character to be printed. 2. The style, or design, of characters on a set of pieces of type, comprising all the sizes in which the particular design is made. There are four classes of type face: ABSTRACT, CURSIVE, DECORATIVE, ROMAN (*qq.v.*), and they may also be divided in the following nine categories: HUMANIST, GARALDE, TRANSITIONAL, DIDONE, SLAB-SERIF, LINEALE, GLYPHIC, SCRIPT and GRAPHIC. The following is a selection of type faces (nearly all in 12-point):

12 pt Antique
ABCDEFGHIJKLMNOPQRSTUVWXYZ -
abcdefghijklmnopqrstuvwxyz - 1234567890

12 pt. Baskerville
ABCDEFGHIJKLMNOPQRSTUVWXYZ–abcd
efghijklmnopqrstuvwxyz–1234567890 –1234567890
*ABCDEFGHIJKLMNOPQRSTUVWXYZ – abcdefg
hijklmnopqrstuvwxyz–*

12 pt. Bell
ABCDEFGHIJKLMNOPQRSTUVWXYZ–abcdefg
hijklmnopqrstuvwxyz – 1234567890 – *ABCDEFGHI
JKLMNOPQRSTUVWXYZ – abcdefghijklmnopqrst
uvwxyz*

12 pt. Bembo
ABCDEFGHIJKLMNOPQRSTUV WXYZ – abcdefghijk
lmnopqrstuvwxyz – 1234567890–*ABCDEFGHIJKLMNO
PQRSTUVWXYZ – abcdefghijklmnopqrstuvwxyz*

12 pt. Poliphilus & Blado
ABCDEFGHIJKLMNOPQRSTUVWXYZ – abcde
fghijklmnopqrstuvwxyz– 1234567890–*ABCDEFGHIJK
LMNOPQRSTUVWXYZ – abcdefghijklmnopqrstuvwxyz*

12 pt. Bodoni
ABCDEFGHIJKLMNOPQRSTUVWXYZ – abcde
fghijklmnopqrstuvwxyz – 1234567890 –*ABCDEFG
HIJKLMNOPQRSTUVWXYZ – abcdefghijklmno
pqrstuvwxyz*

12 pt. Bookprint
ABCDEFGHIJKLMNOPQRSTUVWXYZ– abc
defghijklmnopqrstuvwxyz– 1234567890- 1234567
890 – *ABCDEFGHIJKLMNOPQRSTUVWXYZ
– abcdefghijklmnopqrstuvwxyz*

12 pt. Caslon
ABCDEFGHIJKLMNOPQRSTUVWXYZ - abcde
fghijklmnopqrstuvwxyz - 1234567890 - *ABCDEFGH*
IJKLMNOPQRSTUVWXYZ - *abcdefghijklmnopqrstu*
vwxyz

12 pt. Centaur
ABCDEFGHIJKLMNOPQRSTUVWXYZ - abcdefghijkl
mnopqrstuvwxyz - 1234567890 - *ABCDEFGHIJKLMNOPQ*
RSTUVWXYZ - abcdefghijklmnopqrstuvwxyz - 1234567890

12 pt. Clarendon
ABCDEFGHIJKLMNOPQRSTUVWXYZ - ab
cdefghijklmnopqrstuvwxyz - 1234567890

12 pt. Cochin
ABCDEFGHIJKLMNOPQRSTUVWXYZ -
abcdefghijklmnopqrstuvwxyz - 1234567890 - *ABCD*
EFGHIJKLMNOPQRSTUVWXYZ - abcdefghijk
lmnopqrstuvwxyz

10 pt. Cornell
ABCDEFGHIJKLMNOPQRSTUVWXYZ - abcdefghijklmn
opqrstuvwxyz - 1234567890 - *ABCDEFGHIJKLMNOPQR*
STUVWXYZ - abcdefghijklmnopqrstuvwxyz

12 pt Egmont
ABCDEFGHIJKLMNOPQRSTUVWXYZ—abc
defghijklmnopqrstuvwxyz—1234567890
ABCDEFGHIJKLMNOPQRSTUVWXYZ—abc
defghijklmnopqrstuvwxyz—

12 pt. Ehrhardt
ABCDEFGHIJKLMNOPQRSTUVWXYX - abcdefg
hijklmnopqrstuvwxyz-1234567890 - 1234567890 - *ABCD*
EFGHIJKLMNOPQRSTUVWXYZ - abcdefghijklmno
pqrstuvwxyz

12 pt. Fournier
ABCDEFGHIJKLMNOPQRSTUVWXYZ - abcdefghijk
lmnopqrstuvwxyz - 1234567890 - *ABCDEFGHIJKLMN*
OPQRSTUVWXYZ - abcdefghijklmnopqrstuvwxyz

12 pt. Garamond
ABCDEFGHIJKLMNOPQRSTUVWXYZ – abcdef
ghijklmnopqrstuvwxyz–1234567890–*ABCDEFGHI*
JKLMNOPQRSTUVWXYZ – *abcdefghijklmnopqrstuw*
wxyz

12 pt. Georgian
ABCDEFGHIJKLMNOPQRSTUVWXYZ – abcdefg
hijklmnopqrstuvwxyz – 1234567890 – 1234567890 – *A*
BCDEFGHIJKLMNOPQRSTUVWXYZ – *abcdefghi*
jklmnopqrstuvwxyz

12 pt. Gill
ABCDEFGHIJKLMNOPQRSTUVWXYZ – abcdefghij
klmnopqrstuvwxyz – 1234567890 – *ABCDEFGHIJKLM*
NOPQRSTUVWXYZ – *abcdefghijklmnopqrstuvwxyz*

12 pt. Goudy
ABCDEFGHIJKLMNOPQRSTUVWXYZ - abcde
fghijklmnopqrstuvwxyz - 1234567890 - ABCDEF
GHIJKLMNOPQRSTUVWXYZ - *abcdefghijklmn*
opqrstuvwxyz

12 pt. Granjon
ABCDEFGHIJKLMNOPQRSTUVWXYZ – abcdefghi
jklmnopqrstuvwxyz – 1234567890 – *ABCDEFGHIJKL*
MNOPQRSTUVWXYZ – *abcdefghijklmnopqrstuvwxyz*

11 pt. Grotesque 215   (12 pt. not cut)
ABCDEFGHIJKLMNOPQRSTUVWXYZ – abcdefghij
klmnopqrstuvwxyz – 1234567890 – *ABCDEFGHIJKLMN*
OPQRSTUVWXYZ – *abcdefghijklmnopqrstuvwxyz*

12 pt. Imprint
ABCDEFGHIJKLMNOPQRSTUVWXYZ – abcd
efghijklmnopqrstuvwxyz – 1234567890–*ABCDEFG*
HIJKLMNOPQRSTUVWXYZ – *abcdefghijklmnop*
qrstuvwxyz

12 pt. Juliana
ABCDEFGHIJKLMNOPQRSTUVWXYZ – abcdefghij
klmnopqrstuvwxyz–1234567890 – ABCDEFGHIJKLM
NOPQRSTUVWXYZ–*abcdefghijklmnopqrstuvwxyz*

12 pt. Modern
ABCDEFGHIJKLMNOPQRSTUVWXYZ – abcd
efghijklmnopqrstuvwxyz–1234567890–*ABCDEF*
GHIJKLMNOPQRSTUVWXYZ – abcdefghijklm
nopqrstuvwxyz

11pt Pastonchi
ABCDEFGHIJKLMNOPQRSTUVWXYZ ∮ abcdefghijklmno
pqrstuvwxyz ∮ 1234567890 ∮ *ABCDEFGHIJKLMNOPQRST*
UVWXYZ ∮ abcdefghijklmnopqrstuvwxyz

12 pt. Perpetua
ABCDEFGHIJKLMNOPQRSTUVWXYZ – abcdefghijklmn
opqrstuvwxyz–1234567890 – *ABCDEFGHIJKLMNOPQRST*
UVWXYZ–abcdefghijklmnopqrstvwxyz–

12 pt. Pilgrim
ABCDEFGHIJKLMNOPQRSTUVWXYZ – abcdefghijkl
mnopqrstuvwxyz – 1234567890 – *ABCDEFGHIJKLM*
NOPQRSTUVWXYZ – abcdefghijklmnopqrstuvwxyz

12 pt. Plantin
ABCDEFGHIJKLMNOPQRSTUVWXYZ – abcd
efghijklmnopqrstuvwxyz–1234567890–*ABCDEFGH*
IJKLMNOPQRSTUVWXYZ – abcdefghijklmnopqrs
tuvwxyz

12 pt. Rockwell
ABCDEFGHIJKLMNOPQRSTUVWXYZ – abcdef
ghijklmnopqrstuvwxyz – 1234567890 – *ABCDEF*
GHIJKLMNOPQRSTUVWXYZ–abcdefghijklmno
pqrstuvwxyz

12 pt. Scotch
ABCDEFGHIJKLMNOPQRSTUVWXYZ–abcd
efghijklmnopqrstuvwxyz– 1234567890 – *ABCDE*
FGHIJKLMNOPQRSTUVWXYZ–abcdefghijk
lmnopqrstuvwxyz

12 pt. Times
ABCDEFGHIJKLMNOPQRSTUVWXYZ–abcd
efghijklmnopqrstuvwxyz–1234567890–*ABCDEFG*
HIJKLMNOPQRSTUVWXYZ–abcdefghijklmnop
qrstuvwxyz

12pt. Van Dijck
ABCDEFGHIJKLMNOPQRSTUVWXYZ– abcdefghijklmno
pqrstuvwxyz–1234567890–*ABCDEFGHIJKLMNOPQRSTU*
VWXYZ – abcdefghijklmnopqrstuvwxyz

11D on 12 pt. Walbaum
ABCDEFGHIJKLMNOPQRSTUVWXYZ – abcdefghijklm
nopqrstuvwxyz – 1234567890 – *ABCDEFGHIJKLMNOP*
QRSTUVWXYZ – abcdefghijklmnopqrstuvwxyz

The type suppliers providing the above faces are as follows:

INTERTYPE:
- Cornell
- Egmont

LINOTYPE:
- Bookprint
- Georgian
- Granjon
- Pilgrim

MONOTYPE:
- Baskerville
- Bell
- Bembo
- Blado
- Bodoni
- Caslon
- Centaur
- Cochin
- Ehrhardt
- Fournier
- Garamond
- Gill Sans Serif
- Goudy
- Grotesque
- Imprint
- Juliana
- Modern
- Pastonchi
- Perpetua
- Plantin
- Poliphilus
- Rockwell

    Scotch
    Times New Roman
    Van Dijck
    Walbaum
  TYPE FOUNDERS:
    Antique
    Clarendon

TYPE FACSIMILE. A reprint in which a printed original is copied exactly.

TYPE FLOWERS. Conventional designs cast in type metal of type height and used to decorate a book as an alternative to using blocks. *See also* FLOWERS.

TYPE GAUGE. A rule marked off in ems, points and inches and used for measuring width of type, page depths, etc.

TYPE HEIGHT. 1. The standard height to which type bodies are cast. In the U.K. and the U.S.A. this is 0·918 of an inch from the feet, on which the type rests, to the printing surface, except for the Oxford University Press which works to 0·9395 inches. On the continent of Europe the standard height is 'Didot Normal' (0·9278 inches). 2. The height to which a printing plate is mounted for use in letterpress work; it must be the same height as the letterpress.

TYPE-HIGH. A printing block or plate which has been mounted on wood or metal to the same height as type for use on a printing machine.

TYPE M CATALOGUE ENTRY. An entry for a work of joint authorship where one of several alternative headings (for individuals, a corporate body, or a form) can be chosen with equal correctness and clarity.

TYPE METAL. (*Printing*) An alloy of tin, lead, antimony and sometimes copper which is used for casting type.

TYPE ORNAMENTS. Conventional designs cast in type metal, being larger than TYPE FLOWERS (*q.v.*) and used to ornament chapter heads and tails, and title-pages.

TYPE PAGE. The part of a page that is printed upon; i.e. the type area, the margins being excluded.

TYPE SIZE. The measure of the dimensions of type, taken from the body of the individual type rather than the actual printing area. Also called 'Body size'. The following are the type sizes normally used in book-work:

	Old name:
5 point	Pearl
6 point	Nonpareil

	Old name:
7 point	Minion
8 point	Brevier
9 point	Bourgeois
10 point	Long Primer
11 point	Small Pica
12 point	Pica
14 point	English
16 point	Columbian
18 point	Great Primer
22 point	Double Pica

Larger sizes exist, but these are used for display and not book work. Other, mostly discarded, sizes with their names, are:

$3\frac{1}{2}$ point	Minikin (or Brilliant)
4 point	Brilliant
4 point	Gem
$4\frac{1}{2}$ point	Diamond
$5\frac{1}{2}$ point	Ruby (or Agate)
$6\frac{1}{2}$ point	Emerald
16 point	Two-line Brevier
20 point	Paragon
24 point	Two-line Pica
28 point	Two-line English
36 point	Two-line Great Primer
40 point	Two-line Paragon
44 point	Two line Double Pica
48 point	Four-line Pica (or Canon)
60 point	Five-line Pica
72 point	Six-line Pica.

TYPE T CATALOGUE ENTRY. A main catalogue entry, made under the title of the work. There are four main classes of Type T main entry: (1) for a strictly anonymous book; (2) where the cataloguing code prefers to put the entry under the title on technical grounds, e.g. (a) for a work of joint authorship where four or more authors are involved, (b) for a work normally cited under its title, (c) for a work whose only clue to authorship consists of initials, a non-descriptive phrase as 'A Lady of Leisure', a typographical device, (d) for a work the authorship of which is indicated by a statement 'By the Author of' another anonymous work; (3) for certain anonymous works which are frequently reprinted and the wording of the titles of which can vary from one edition to another so that the entries would be scattered in the catalogue unless brought together under a common entry; (4) periodicals other than serials, e.g. annual reports, which go under a corporate name.

TYPESCRIPT. Typewritten matter; a typed manuscript. Abbreviated T.S.

TYPESETTER. One who sets type; a compositor.

TYPESETTING. The arrangement of printing types in order for printing, including the operation of Intertype, Linotype, Ludlow or Monotype machines.

TYPE-SETTING MACHINE. A machine for selecting, assembling and spacing typefounders' letterpress printing types which are stored and arranged in channels instead of cases. *See also* Type-casting Machine.

TYPICAL CHARACTERISTIC. *See* Characteristic.

TYPICAL CLASS. *See* Characteristic.

TYPOGRAPH. Trade name for a typecasting, setting and distributing machine which casts a slug or line of type, similar to the Linotype (*q.v.*) machine.

TYPOGRAPHER. One who is responsible for the lay-out and appearance of printed matter.

TYPOGRAPHICAL ERROR. A mistake made by the typesetter.

TYPOGRAPHY. 1. Printing, or taking impressions from movable letter-units or 'types'. The art of printing. The opposite of Xylography (*q.v.*). 2. The character and appearance of printed matter.

TYPOMETER. A gauge for measuring the body and thickness of type and comparing them with a standard.

USA STANDARDS INSTITUTE. *See* American National Standards Institute, Inc.

USASI. Abbreviation for United States of America Standards Institute, now the American National Standards Institute, Inc.

UFOD. Acronym for Union Française des Organismes de Documentation (French Union of Documentary Organizations). Provides professional training for assistants in documentation services. Publishes *Informations UFOD* (irr.), *Documentation en France* (6 p.a.), *l'Aide-Mémoire du Documentaliste*.

ÜHERTYPE. A photo-composing machine built in 1928 by Edmund Üher, a Hungarian. It was first called Luminotype.

ult. Abbreviation for *ultimo* (*Lat.* 'last'). Used for 'last month'. *See also* inst.

ULTIMATE CLASS. The class of the smallest extension admitted by the scheme of classification, into which a document can be placed. *See also* ASSOCIATED CLASS.

ULTIMATE STORE. *See* MARLIS.

ULTRA-MICROFICHE. A MICROFICHE (*q.v.*) with such small images that 3,000 page-images can be accommodated on one 4×6 inch fiche.

ULTRA THIN PAPER. Sensitized photographic paper between 0·0023 and 0·0031 inches inclusive. Also called 'Extra lightweight'. *See also* PHOTOGRAPHIC PAPERS.

ULVERSCROFT SERIES. A series of books printed in large type (18 pt.) and published by Mr. F. A. Thorpe, of Ulverscroft, with whom the Library Association has cooperated in the selection of titles for this venture which has proved very successful. The volumes are available to public libraries, welfare organizations and blind agencies direct, and not through the book trade.

UNAUTHORIZED EDITION. An edition issued without the consent of the author, his representative or the original publisher. The responsibility to the author would be moral, not legal. A *pirated edition* is an unauthorized reprint involving an infringement of copyright.

UNBLEACHED PAPER. Special paper made from unbleached STUFF (*q.v.*). Such papers do not usually have a good colour; they retain the colour of the original white rags, no bleaching during the process of manufacture having taken place. The paper is consequently stronger, as bleaching weakens the pulp.

UNBOUND. A publication the leaves or sections of which have not been fastened together.

UNCIAL. Style of majuscule writing, resembling capitals in some letter forms, but with rounder curves. This was a more flowing, cursive form of Latin manuscript handwriting and was used for commercial and everyday writing. In use generally from the fourth to the eighth centuries.

UNCUT. A book is described as being 'uncut' when the edges have not been trimmed or cut by a guillotine, thus leaving 'bolts' which have to be opened with a paper knife. Until this has been done the book is described as being unopened. *See also* EDGES.

UNDERGROUND LITERATURE. *Synonymous with* CLANDESTINE LITERATURE (*q.v.*).

UNDERGROUND PRESS. A printing press which secretly prints leaflets, pamphlets, periodicals or books which have as their object the overthrow of the government, or of authority, or the propagation of subversive or generally unacceptable political views.

UNDERLAY. Work done on the printing machine by placing paper, thin card, etc., under the matter in the forme so as to level it up as much as possible for printing, before the final touches are put on by means of OVERLAY (*q.v.*).

UNDERLINE. A line or series of lines placed under parts of 'copy' or proof to indicate style of type to be used: a single line indicates italic; a double line, small capitals; a treble line, capitals; a wavy line (which can be placed under any of the forementioned) bold face. Called 'Underscore' in America.

UNDERRUN. A shortage in the number of copies printed.

UNDERSCORE. *Synonymous with* UNDERLINE (*q.v.*).

UNESCO. Abbreviation for United Nations Educational, Scientific and Cultural Organization, an international body which exists to further the development of emerging nations in the fields mentioned. Constituted 16th November 1945 in London by representatives of forty-four governments; an agreement between the United Nations and Unesco was approved by the General Assembly of the U.N. in New York at its October-December 1946 session. It is financed by Member States of the U.N. who are all eligible for membership. There is a division of libraries, documentation and archives which operates as part of the cultural programme. Many books and periodicals have been published; among the latter are the *Bulletin on bibliography, documentation and terminology* (bi-monthly), *Museum* (q.) and *Unesco bulletin for libraries* (bi-monthly).

UNESCO COUPONS. A form of international currency enabling foreign payments to be made for education, scientific and cultural materials without the tedious and time-consuming procedures of making payments through the normal machinery of banks, and the involvement of currency control regulations. The government of a country wishing to use Unesco coupons nominates a body to distribute the coupons against local currency payment to organizations or individuals who send them to suppliers of goods who then obtain cash for them. The denominations of the coupons, in equivalents of U.S. dollars, are $1, $3, $10, $30, $100, $1,000. They are used extensively for purchasing books.

UNEVEN PAGES. Those which bear the odd page-numbers. The right-hand, or recto, pages.

UNEVEN WORKING. *See* EVEN WORKING.

UNEXPURGATED EDITION. An edition of a work in which the full text is given, including any objectionable material which normally would be omitted.

UNGATHERED. The printed sheets of a book which have not been gathered, or collected, into order.

UNIFORM HEADING. The form of a heading adopted for use in the catalogue for an author (personal or corporate), title, or for any other heading (IFLA).

UNIFORM TITLE. The distinctive title by which a work, which has appeared under varying titles and in various versions, is most generally known, and under which catalogue entries are made. Also called 'Conventional title', 'Filing title', 'Standard title'.

UNION CATALOGUE. A catalogue of the various departments of a library, or of a number of libraries. It may be an author or a subject catalogue of all the books, or of a selection of them, and may be limited by subject or type of material. *See also* CENTRALIZED CATALOGUING, CO-OPERATIVE CATALOGUING.

UNION FINDING LIST. American term for a complete record of the holdings of a given group of libraries. It may be of materials of a given type, in a particular field, or on a particular subject.

UNION FRANÇAISE DES ORGANISMES DE DOCUMENTATION. *See* UFOD.

UNION LIST. A complete record of holdings of material in a certain field, on a particular subject, or of a given type such as of periodicals or annuals, for a group of libraries.

UNION OF INTERNATIONAL ASSOCIATIONS. Founded in Brussels in 1907 as the Central Office of International Associations and became a federation under its present name at the first World Congress of International Organizations in 1910. Serves as a documentation centre on international governmental and non-governmental organizations, their activities and meetings; undertakes and promotes research on legal, administrative and technical problems common to international non-governmental organizations, publicizes their work and encourages their mutual contacts, and secures understanding of the necessity for maintaining a balance at the international level between the governmental and the private non-governmental sectors.

UNION PAPER. Two sheets of wrapping paper stuck together with tar, bitumen, or some similar material with a waterproofing property. *See also* REINFORCED UNION PAPER, TARRED BROWN PAPER.

UNIQUE ENTRY, PRINCIPLE OF. (*Cataloguing*) The entry for a book under a heading chosen (from more than one alternative) for person, subject, organization, place, etc., cross-references being provided from the other words which might have been used as alternatives. *See also* CATALOGUING, PRINCIPLES OF.

UNIT ABSTRACT CARD. A card, or other record, bearing an abstract prepared for use in a selective dissemination of information, or other current awareness, system. *See also* SDI.

UNIT BIBLIOGRAPHY. A bibliography of different editions of a book with the same title.

UNIT CARD. A basic catalogue card, in the form of a main entry, a duplicate of which may be used as a unit wherever an entry for that particular book is required in any catalogue, after the addition of any heading which may be necessary. The Library of Congress catalogue cards are the most-used form of unit cards, although several American organizations are now issuing printed cards, usually for subject groups or form groups of literature. Entries which appear in the *British National Bibliography* (*q.v.*) are issued on cards and on sheaf paper. *See also* LOCAL UNIT CARD, WILSON CARDS.

UNIT CONCEPTS. *Synonymous with* POLYTERMS (*q.v.*).

UNIT CONSTRUCTION. *See* MODULAR PLANNING.

UNIT ENTRY. A basic catalogue entry which gives the fullest information – a MAIN ENTRY (*q.v.*) – and which, being reproduced by printing or other duplication method, is used for all ADDED ENTRIES (*q.v.*), usually with the addition above the entry of appropriate headings (subject, author, title, series, editor, illustrator, translator, etc.).

UNIT RECORD. The records comprising a descriptor file. Each consists of (a) descriptors (e.g. subject headings or class numbers) appropriate to the subject of the documents, (b) specifications of the documents (e.g. author, title, publisher, date, pagination, etc., plus possibly an annotation or abstract), (c) a document address, i.e. class number, call number, shelf number, file number, accession number or other indication of its whereabouts in the STORE (*q.v.*).

UNIT SYSTEM. *See* MICROFILM.

L'UNITÉ. A system for analysing abstracts and coding them without using human agency. 'L'Unité-cards' are finally punched and these are machine sorted to retrieve the information required.

UNITED STATES BOOK EXCHANGE. *See* USBE.

UNITED STATES GOVERNMENT PRINTING OFFICE. Created by a Congressional Joint Resolution on 23rd June 1860, the Government Printing Office executes orders for printing and binding placed by Congress and the departments, independent establishments, and agencies of the federal government; it distributes government publications as required by law, and maintains necessary catalogues and a library of these publications; it also prints for sale to the public, documents which are of a non-controversial nature. It has the largest printing plant in the world.

UNITED STATES INFORMATION AGENCY. Abbreviated USIA. An arm of U.S. foreign policy which receives its foreign policy guidance from the President of the U.S. and the Department of State. It has public information missions in 106 countries, libraries or information centres in eighty-six, and seventy reading rooms in thirty-four countries. The responsibilities of USIA include explaining those activities of American domestic agencies which have significance in the foreign field. The functions of USIA are (a) to explain abroad U.S. foreign policies and programmes; (b) to disseminate accurate information about the U.S.; (c) to counter and correct Communist propaganda distortions and lies about U.S. policies and intentions; (d) to administer cultural and educational exchanges and programmes as the cultural and educational arm of the Department of State. Gives financial assistance in the publishing of American books in foreign languages, arranges for such translation to be undertaken; publishes books in English overseas; arranges with U.S. publishers to publish books in paperback and simplified editions for distribution overseas; supplies books to USIS libraries, to foreign libraries, bi-national centres, schools and other institutions.

UNITED STATES INFORMATION SERVICE. *See* USIS, UNITED STATES INFORMATION AGENCY.

UNITED STATES OF AMERICA STANDARDS INSTITUTE. *See* AMERICAN NATIONAL STANDARDS INSTITUTE, INC.

UNITERM CONCEPT CO-ORDINATION INDEXING. With this system, invented by Mortimer Taube in 1953, periodical articles or other documents to be indexed are scanned to see their subject contents. Aspects of the subject, called 'concepts', are expressed in one or two simple basic words called 'keywords' (which are to be found in the *Thesaurus* (q.v.) containing all the keywords likely to be used in the literature of the subject) and the accession number of the document recorded (by punching holes in numbered squares) on cards on which are entered as headings the 'keywords' or 'uniterms', sometimes called 'descriptors'. The cards are arranged in alphabetical order of uniterms, and the information is retrieved by placing the cards several at a time (for a separate card is punched for each aspect of the document's subject) over an illuminated glazed frame so that the light shines through the holes; alternatively the numbers may be written in columns according to the last digit and the numbers on each card visually examined to discover identical numbers. Sometimes instead of punching holes the 'accession' number is written in the appropriate column (each column being reserved in numerical sequence for the last unit figure) of each selected keyword card. This involves reading the numbers and comparing them on each card to discover which documents are entered on *each* of the chosen cards and therefore which document has all the qualities needed. Light shining through holes on the punched card reveals the same information. The use of a uniterm system is an attempt to replace traditional schemes of classification by a method based on an alphabetical arrangement of 'aspects' of the subject-matter covered by the material to be indexed. It also has the merit of being a method which can be carried out by persons untrained in classifying. 'Uniterm' is a trademark of the developer of the system, Documentation, Inc., Washington, D.C., and is the abbreviation for Uniterm Concept Co-ordination System. *See also* COMAC, CO-ORDINATE INDEXING.

UNITERM INDEX. A method of indexing which involves the selection of 'key words' from graphic records. Keywords represent the content of the record or document that is being indexed. It is not necessary to create or maintain a list of approved headings since a list is compiled as the work proceeds. The keywords must be predicted when analysing a question in order to provide searching clues.

UNITIZE. The separation of a roll of microfilm into separate frames for use individually.

UNITYPER. A modified Remington Electric typewriter which is equipped with electronic circuits and will record pulse patterns on magnetic tape.

UNIVERSAL BIBLIOGRAPHY. A bibliography of the world's books. None exists at present, but an attempt has been made by the Fédération Internationale de Documentation (formerly the Institut International de Documentation and the Institut International de Bibliographie). *See also* INTERNATIONAL FEDERATION FOR DOCUMENTATION.

UNIVERSAL COPYRIGHT CONVENTION. *See* COPYRIGHT, INTERNATIONAL.

UNIVERSAL DECIMAL CLASSIFICATION (UDC). French abbreviation: CDU; German: DK. A general scheme of classification covering the whole field of knowledge. It is an elaborate expansion of the Dewey Decimal Classification which was first suggested by Senator Henri La Fontaine and Paul Otlet at the first International Conference of Librarians held at Brussels in 1895, and carried out by the Institut International de Bibliographie, now called the Fédération (formerly

(Institut) Internationale de Documentation. It has been called the International Classification, is constantly under revision, and is extremely flexible. In application, the three-figure notation of Dewey is simplified where possible (usually by the omission of 'unit') and, when both occur, 'tens' (noughts), and auxiliary signs or Relation Marks sometimes called 'Common auxiliaries' which are recommended to be filed in the following 'Standard' order:

SYNOPSIS OF AUXILIARIES (IN ORDER OF FILING)

a. Aggregation signs + and / (*preceding the simple class number*)
b. Relation signs: and [ ]
c. Language auxiliaries = . . .
d. Form and presentation auxiliaries (o . . .)
e. Place, region, country auxiliaries (1/9)
f. Race, people, nationality auxiliaries (= . . .)
g. Time, date, period auxiliaries '. . .' (alternatively before e.)
h. Alphabetical and numerical (non-UDC) auxiliaries A/Z, No. 1 to . . .
i. Point of view subdivisions .oo. . .
k. Special auxiliaries –. . . and .o. . .

These are called 'Common auxiliaries'.

The object of the scheme is to arrange and individualize, by the use of the subdivisions tabulated above, the entries in a great general catalogue or bibliography, or the written or printed material, however detailed, in a specialized library, in order that users may, to some extent, judge the material without actually handling it. The U.D.C. is used by several hundred libraries, abstracting services and individuals in Great Britain. It has been adopted by the International Organization for Standardization (ISO) which has recommended it for adoption by the national standards bodies which are members of ISO for the classification of their published standards. It has therefore become the most widely used of all classification systems. Full editions of the whole, or of sections, have been published in French, English, German, Japanese, Spanish, Polish and Portuguese; abridged editions have been published in seven languages and a three-language (German-English-French) one in 1958 – BS. 1080B: 1958. The English translation is published complete (BS. 1000), abridged (BS. 1000A), and also in sections each of which incorporates all authorized extensions and modifications up to the date of publication. The third English abridged edition was published in 1961 (BS. 1000A), (F.I.D. No. 289) and is the shortest abridgement suitable for practical classification. It contains some new sections, and some thoroughly revised ones; the detailed alphabetical index has been extended accordingly. A *Guide to the Universal Decimal Classification (UDC)* was published in 1963 – BS. 1000C: 1963. The first section of this publication, by Mr. J. Mills, outlines the modern theory of classification and examines the practical problems of classifying by means of the U.D.C. This is followed by an outline of the U.D.C. tables. *See also* INTERNATIONAL COUNCIL FOR BUILDING RESEARCH STUDIES AND DOCUMENTATION.

UNIVERSITY AND RESEARCH SECTION. Former name for the UNIVERSITY, COLLEGE AND RESEARCH SECTION (*q.v.*) of the Library Association.

UNIVERSITY, COLLEGE AND RESEARCH SECTION. A section of the Library Association; formerly the University and Research Section. It was the first 'section' of the Library Association to be formed (in 1927). The objects of the Section are to increase the usefulness of national, university, and other academic libraries serving research. There are several regional groups and sub-sections. Abbreviated UCR.

UNIVERSITY LIBRARY. A library or group of libraries established, maintained, and administered by a university to meet the needs of its students and members of the academic staff.

UNLETTERED. A book without the title or the author's name on the spine.

UNOPENED. When the 'bolts' or folded edges of the sections of a book, have not been opened with a paper-knife. Not to be confused with UNCUT (*q.v.*).

UNPAGED. Pages of a book which do not bear page numbers. These usually occur amongst the PRELIMINARIES (*q.v.*), if referred to in a catalogue or bibliography, the total number, or the page numbers which the individual pages would have been given, are entered within [ ].

UNPROCESSED PAPER (OR BOARD). Paper or board in sheets or reels as supplied to the printer or stationer.

UNSCHEDULED MNEMONICS. *See* MNEMONICS.

UNSEWN BINDING. *Synonymous with* PERFECT (*q.v.*).

UNSIGNED. A book, the sections of which bear no signature letters or figures, and are therefore 'unsigned'.

UNSOUGHT LINK. (*Classification*) In chain indexing, a step in a notational hierarchy which is unwanted for indexing purposes, either because no enquirer is likely to search under the appropriate verbal term, or because of faulty subordination in the classification scheme itself. *See also* CHAIN INDEX, FALSE LINK, SUBORDINATION.

UNTRIMMED PAGE SIZE. The size of a sheet after folding and before trimming – BS. 1413: 1966.

UNTRIMMED SIZE. The dimensions of a sheet of paper, untrimmed and not specially squared, sufficiently large to allow a trimmed size to be obtained from it as required. British papermakers may interpret this term as 'not guillotine trimmed'. *See also* PAPER SIZES, PERIODICAL, TRIMMED SIZE.

UPPER CASE LETTERS. Capital letters, i.e. those contained in the upper of the two cases of printer's type. The 'terms' in this glossary are printed in capitals. Their use is indicated in a MS. or proof by underlining with three lines. Abbreviation: u.c. *See also* CAPITALS, LOWER CASE LETTERS, SMALL CAPITALS.

UPPER COVER. *Synonymous with* OBVERSE COVER (*q.v.*).

UPRIGHT. 1. A book that is taller than its width. 2. Printing, or a printing job, that is set to an upright size. *See also* BROAD, UPRIGHT.

UPWARD REFERENCE. A direction from a less to a more comprehensive subject heading in an alphabetico-specific subject catalogue. The reverse of DOWNWARD REFERENCE (*q.v.*).

URBAN DISTRICT COUNCIL. A statutory local authority which provides local government services within its geographical area. It is entitled to provide public library services under the Public Libraries Act 1892. Councils which had not adopted this act by the time the Act of 1919 became operative lost their power to become library authorities. Abbreviated UDC.

URBAN LIBRARY. A public library provided by a local authority other than a county council, to serve an urban area.

URBANDOC. An American project to control the vast literature of urban planning and renewal by developing a computerized system for the retrieval of information. The name URBANDOC was first used in 1964 although the scheme had its origins at a Special Library Association Convention at Denver in 1963.

USBE. The UNITED STATES BOOK EXCHANGE, INC. (*q.v.*). A private, non-profit making, self-supporting library service organization centred at Washington, D.C., and consisting of scholars and representatives appointed by eleven (American) national library associations, five learned and professional councils, the Smithsonian Institution, the Library of Congress, the National Library of Medicine, and the National Agricultural Library, which took over the stock of the American Book Center for War Devastated Libraries and began its present activities on 1 January 1949. Its function is to transfer publications obtained on exchange from libraries in the United

States and the countries, and as gifts from professional organizations, individuals and publishers in the United States, to libraries where they will be useful. These materials are stored in a depository until needed. United States libraries and libraries all over the world are thus able to complete runs of periodicals which are not readily available through commercial channels. About 85 per cent of the exchange members are U.S. and Canadian institutions. Its activities extend to providing books for libraries in developing countries with financial assistance from the Agency for International Co-operation. A reservoir of four million periodical items and 50,000 books in research fields received from libraries and other agencies as gifts is maintained: items are donated to libraries on request at a fee of 35 cents for the single issue of a periodical and $1.10 for a book. In recent years it has endeavoured to simplify communication between U.S. libraries and the six other national book exchange agencies. Abbreviated USBE. Publishes *USBE Newsletter* (irreg.).

USER-PROFILE.   *Synonymous with* INTEREST-PROFILE (*q.v.*).

USER RELEVANCE.   The appropriateness of information retrieved for a user even if it is not exactly what was requested.

USIS.   Abbreviation for the United States Information Service which provides libraries in overseas countries as part of the work of the UNITED STATES INFORMATION AGENCY (*q.v.*).

ut infra.   (*Lat.* 'as below'.)

ut sup.   Abbreviation for *ut supra* (*Lat.* 'as above').

v.   Abbreviation for verse, *versus* (against), *vide* (see), *vice* (in place of), *violino* (violin), *voce* (voice) and VOLUME (*q.v.*).

v.d.   Abbreviation for VARIOUS DATES (*q.v.*).

v.p.   Abbreviation for 'various places' or 'various publishers'.

VSC FORMULA.   A method of calculating the total desirable floor space for public libraries. It was enunciated by Wheeler and Githens in *The American Public Library Building* and is as follows:

V = number of volumes the building is to contain,

S = number of seats for readers,

C = circulation (loans) per annum (for central libraries the figure for the whole system, for a branch library the figure for the branch only).

Average relations of the above to square footage of area, based on a study of American buildings, gives 10 volumes per square foot, 40 square feet per seat, one square foot of space for loans of 40 volumes per annum; these convert into the formula $\dfrac{V}{10} + 40\,S + \dfrac{C}{40}$ to give the required area of a library in square feet. This formula is affected by the type of plan and particularly by the relative extent of the basement. Wheeler records that this formula applied to his own library at Baltimore approximates to the actual size of the library, but Anthony Thompson in *Library Buildings of Britain and Europe* records that when it was tested out on two branch libraries it gave an area two or three times greater than the buildings actually occupy.

VADE-MECUM. A guide, handbook, or manual which can be conveniently carried for reference.

VAN GELDER PAPER. A brand of good-quality paper which is produced in Holland and used mainly for fine paper copies. A variety with an ANTIQUE FINISH (*q.v.*) is used by artists for drawings, sketches and water-colour paintings. Also called 'Dutch paper'.

VANITY PUBLISHERS. Firms who publish and market books at authors' risk and expense. Also called 'Subsidy' or 'Co-operative' Publishers.

VARIABLE MNEMONICS. *See* MNEMONICS.

VARIANT. A term given to corrections inserted in later printings of a book. These are frequent in hand-printed books and are accounted for by the fact that mistakes were noticed and the type altered during printing, the sheets already printed remaining untouched.

VARIANT EDITION. The edition of a work which gives the author's variations, textual changes and alterations in the text of his work possibly from their first composition to their final appearance in a DEFINITIVE EDITION (*q.v.*).

VARIORUM. Abbreviation of the Latin *cum notis variorum* 'with notes by various editors'.

VARIORUM EDITION. An edition of a work composed from a comparison of various texts which have been published previously, variations being given in footnotes, and including the notes of various commentators. In the U.S.A., publishers tend to use this term for Definitive Edition, Textual Variant or Variant Edition.

VARIOUS DATES. Used to describe a volume containing several works of different date or a work consisting of several volumes published at different dates. Abbreviated v.d.

VARITYPER. An electric typewriter (formerly the Hammond) which enables characters additional to normal roman ones to be typed. This is possible by the use of shuttles, of which there are several hundred different ones, bearing the particular type face required. The shuttles, which are semi-circular bands of metal, can be exchanged quickly; an alternative set of type can be brought into action without stopping the machine.

VARNISHING. A process applied to book jackets to give them a shiny appearance.

VAT. The tank containing beaten pulp from which hand-made sheets of paper are made.

VAT PAPER. Another name for HAND-MADE PAPER (*q.v.*).

VAT-SIZED. Said of paper when the size is added to the pulp before the pulp is used to form a sheet.

VATICAN CODE. The Vatican Library's *Rules for the Catalog of Printed Books* (A.L.A. 1931. 2nd ed., 1948, tr. from the 2nd Italian ed. publ. in 1938) were drawn up to provide a new general catalogue of the Library.

VEGETABLE PARCHMENT. A partially transparent wrapping paper. *See* PARCHMENT 2.

VELLUM. Calf skin dressed with alum and polished, and not tanned like leather. A smooth, fine parchment.

VELLUM PARCHMENT. A very strong hand-made vellum paper, similar in appearance to animal parchment, but almost indestructible and not as easily affected by heat, mildew and insects as are skins. Called 'art parchment' in the U.S.A.

'VENDOR-SPECS-MICROFILE'. A service, designated V-S-V-F, which offers, on microfilm, vendors' catalogues and manufacturers' specifications by industry groups. A Recordak Reader-Printer enables immediate enlargements of selected pages to be made.

VENETIAN TYPE. A roman type which is characterized by heavy slab serifs, thick main strokes, and a slightly oblique calligraphic emphasis in the round forms. The bar of the small 'e' is tilted. The roman types of Nicholas Jenson (for specimen, *see* TYPE FACE) are the finest examples of this kind of type. *See also* HUMANISTIC HAND.

VERAC. A matrix microfilm storage system (*see* MICROFILM) which was originally known as 'The Mechanized Library'. Information is stored on sheets of film approximately 8×8 inches in size. Reduction is between seventy and 140 times. This system has an impressive retrieval speed whereby any one of a million pages can be produced in approximately one second.

verbatim et literatum. (*Lat.* 'word for word' or 'letter for letter'). A literal translation or transcription.

VERBATIM REPORT. A word for word version of a speech, lecture, or debate.

VERIFAX. Trade name for a Kodak copying machine using the soft gelatine transfer process. After the negative sheet (matrix) is made it can be used to transfer six or more images to uncoated paper, each copy becoming progressively fainter. A RAPID COPYING (*q.v.*) process. *See also* TRANSFER PROCESS.

VERNACULAR. The language of a country. When it is directed that a name shall be given in the vernacular, it means the form which is customary in the country concerned.

VERSION. 1. A rendering in graphic art form, or sequence of words, of a record, publication, or document, especially a translation of the Bible. 2. One of several intellectual forms taken by the same work. (These may be an original text and its translation, or various texts in one language based on the same original work) (IFLA). 3. In music, a TRANSCRIPTION (*q.v.*) in which the original work is so changed as to be virtually a new work, either in the same or in a different medium.

VERSO. The left-hand page of an open book or manuscript, usually bearing an even page number. The reverse, or second, side of a sheet of paper to be printed. *See also* RECTO.

VERTICAL FILE. 1. A drawer, or number of drawers, in a case, in which papers or similar material may be filed on their edges. 2. A collection of pamphlets, cuttings, correspondence, or similar material arranged on their edges in a drawer or box.

VERTICAL FILING CABINET. A cabinet of two, three or four drawers, each of which is wide enough to take quarto or foolscap files resting on their spines.

VERTICAL INTEGRATION. The opening of a library for use after all chairs and tables had been removed and serving patrons only on a stand-up check-out basis. This occurred in the Southern States of the U.S.A. during the period, in the early 1960's, of developing racial equality, and followed a few months when some all-white or all-Negro libraries were closed for a period and subsequently opened upon court orders.

VERTICAL PRESS. A printing press in which the flat forme moves up and down instead of to and fro horizontally.

VESICULAR FILM. Film which has the light-sensitive element suspended in a plastic layer and which, upon exposure, creates strains within the layer in the form of a latent image. Heating the plastic layer releases the strains and the image becomes visible; it becomes permanent when the layer cools and the film has received a second exposure which acts as a fixation process.

VICESIMO-QUARTO (24mo). *Synonymous with* TWENTY-FOURMO (*q.v.*).

vid.   Abbreviation for *vide* (*Lat.* 'see').

vide ante.   (*Lat.* 'see before'.)

vide infra.   (*Lat.* 'see below'.)

vide post.   (*Lat.* 'see below'.)

vide supra.   (*Lat.* 'see above'). Used in footnotes to refer to an item previously mentioned.

VIGNETTE.   A small illustration or ornament used principally in book production at the beginning and ends of chapters, not having a definite border but the edges shading off gradually.

VIGNETTED HALF-TONE.   *See* HALF-TONE.

VINCULUM.   In mathematics a straight, horizontal line placed over two or more numbers of a compound quality to join them. An old name for a BRACE (*q.v.*).

VINEGAR BIBLE.   A Bible printed in two volumes at Oxford by John Baskett, the King's Printer, in 1716–17; so-called from one of its misprints, the 'Parable of the vineyard' in Luke XX being rendered the 'Parable of the vinegar'. Although the production was excellent, it was so full of errors that it became known as a 'Basket(t) full of Printers' Errors'. It was also known as the 'Oxford Folio'.

VINITI.   Vsesoyuznyi Institut Nauchnoi i Tekhnicheskoi Informatsii. (All-Union Institute of Scientific and Technical Information). Viniti is subordinate to the U.S.S.R. State Committee for the Co-ordination of Scientific Research, Moscow and to the U.S.S.R. Academy of Sciences, Moscow. It was established in 1952 and is the most important of the organizations concerned with scientific information in the Soviet Union, and has as its main tasks: (a) the preparation of abstracts in the natural and applied sciences, excluding architecture, building, medicine and agriculture; (b) the organization of instruction in scientific information in universities and institutes at undergraduate and postgraduate levels; (c) the organization and co-ordination of research into the rational organization of information activities, and the mechanical and automatic means of processing and retrieving scientific information. Publishes *Referativnyi Zhurnal* (the basic Viniti publication; it is issued in twenty-four series representing various individual branches of the natural and technical sciences excluding building and architecture; over a third of the world's output of scientific and technical periodicals and a great quantity of other literature being processed, and providing the most comprehensive abstracting service in the world), *Scientific and Technical Information* (m.), *Achievements of Science* (a.), *World Scientific and Technical Periodicals*, an annotated index is in process of being published in ten to twelve volumes.

VIRKOTYPE PROCESS. *Synonymous with* THERMOGRAPHY (*q.v.*).

VISIBLE CLOTH JOINT. A cloth joint used to fasten the sections of a sewn book to its covers, and visible when the book is bound.

VISIBLE INDEX. 1. A frame, or series of frames, usually of metal, for holding cards or strips of card, on which records are entered. They are made so that all the headings contained in the frame are visible at the same time. *See also* BLIND INDEX. 2. A record, as of periodicals or a list of subjects, contained in such a device.

VISIGOTHIC HANDWRITING. A Spanish form of handwriting, being a national adaptation of the Latin cursive after the dissolution of the Roman Empire. It was used in Spain in the eighth and ninth centuries, and also spread to Italy. *See also* CURSIVE, HANDWRITING.

*VISI*SCAN. *See* BRISCH-VISTEM SYSTEM.

VISUAL AIDS. Film strips, films, lantern slides and other illustrative material used as an adjunct to teaching or lecturing.

VISUAL PUNCHED CARD. Cards which are punched in positions to represent specifically numbered documents, each card being named according to a list of keywords, or thesaurus, and so reserved to represent a particular aspect of information. *See also* UNITERM CONCEPT CO-ORDINATION INDEXING. A card punched to record specific information.

viz. Abbreviation for *videlicet* (*Lat.* 'namely').

VOCABULARY. *See* INDEX LANGUAGE.

VOCAL MUSIC. Music written to be sung by one or more persons: if for many people, it is known as choral music, and in its larger concerted forms of cantata, oratorio, or opera is accompanied by an orchestra, otherwise it may be unaccompanied, or a piano or organ used.

VOCAL SCORE. *See* SCORE.

VOCATIONAL EDUCATION ACT. Passed in 1963, this Act provides for the payment of librarians' salaries, books and other materials for libraries in American vocational and technical high schools.

vol. (*Pl.* vols.). Abbreviation for VOLUME (*q.v.*).

VOLLANS REPORT. *Library Co-operation in Great Britain*, 1952, the report on the working of the National inter-lending system which R. F. Vollans wrote at the request of the joint working party set up by the National Central Library in 1949. The recommendations, together with other proposals were incorporated in a joint memorandum, *Recommendations on library co-operation*, was issued by the joint working party in 1954, and measures to implement them were taken by the National Committee on Regional Library Co-operation.

VOLUME. 1. A book distinguished from other books or from other volumes of the same work by having its own title-page, half-title, cover title or portfolio title, and usually independent pagination, foliation, or register. It may be designated 'part' by the publisher, and it may have various title-pages, paginations, or include separate works or portfolios, etc. The volume may be as originally issued or as bound subsequently; in this sense 'volume' as a physical, or material, unit, may not be the same as 'volume' as a bibliographical unit. A volume of music may consist of a score, of loose parts, or of a score with loose parts in pockets. 2. Whatever is contained in one binding. 3. A document (*see* DOCUMENT 2) or part of a document bound or intended to be bound in one cover and, normally, having its own title-page (IFLA). 4. For library statistical purposes, any book, pamphlet, or document, in whatever form it exists which has been separately catalogued and accessioned. 5. A collection of items forming part of the Ultimate Store of information recorded as part of the information retrieval system known as MARLIS (*q.v.*). In a catalogue entry the statement of the number of volumes relates to the physical, not the bibliographical, number, e.g. 1 *vol in* 2; 2 *v. in* 1; 8 *vols. in* 6. The abbreviation for volume is optional.

VOLUME CAPACITY. *Synonymous with* SHELF CAPACITY (*q.v.*).

VOLUME NUMBER. A number used to distinguish certain volumes of a work, set or series.

VOLUME RIGHTS. *See* RIGHTS.

VOLUME SIGNATURE. The number of the volume, as 'Vol. I,' or simply 'I,' or a letter, placed on the same line as the signature (*see* SIGNATURE 2) to prevent the binder mixing the sections of various volumes.

VOLUMEN (*Lat.* 'a thing rolled up'). The papyrus roll used in ancient Egypt, Greece and Rome, which was written on one side in ink with a reed pen, the text being in columns, the lines of which ran parallel with the length of the roll. The last sheet of the papyrus was rolled round a stick which had knobbed ends and served as a handle. The rolls were kept in boxes or on shelves, and for purposes of distinction when placed in this position had a vellum label attached to the end of the roll. This label bore the title of the work, and was sometimes coloured. A wooden case (*Manuale*) was sometimes used to protect the edges of the roll from being frayed by the owner's toga or cloak.

VOLUMINOUS AUTHOR. An author under whose name many titles are entered in a catalogue, whether for different books or for books the various editions of which have different titles. (American.)

VOLUNTARY CENTRE.   A library service point which is staffed by unpaid workers – usually in a county library system.

VOLUNTARY OVERSEAS LIBRARIES SERVICE.   Formed in conjunction with the Voluntary Overseas Service Association, the organization aims to create libraries in communities that have no official assistance for the buying of books, hoping to supply a need where no other grant is available. British volunteers working in developing countries are asked to gauge demand and to advise on the subject matters of the books required, to ensure that all books are housed safely and accessibly, and that libraries will be maintained after their departure. Abbreviated VOLS.

VOLUTE.   (*Binding*) An ornament consisting of a large curl in the form of a Corinthian volute, and at the opposite end a small curl turning the other way. Found in pairs in sixteenth-century finishers' rolls of the heads-in-medallions type.

VOTERS' LIST.   *Synonymous with* REGISTER OF ELECTORS (*q.v.*).

VOTES AND PROCEEDINGS OF THE HOUSE OF COMMONS.   *See* PARLIAMENTARY PAPERS.

VOUCHER.   *See* APPLICATION FORM.

VOWEL-LIGATURES.   The ligatures æ or œ are used in Old English and French words (Ælfric, Cædmon, hors d'œuvre, etc.), but the combinations *ae* and *oe* are printed as two letters in Latin, Greek and English words (Aetua, Boeotia, larvae, etc.).

VULGATE.   The Latin Bible translated by St. Jerome in the fourth century and authorized by the Roman Catholic Church.

w.a.f.   With all faults. An abbreviation used in booksellers' and auctioneers' catalogues to indicate that a book is, or may be, faulty and is offered for sale in this condition and therefore not subject to return because of defects.

w.f.   *See* WRONG FOUNT.

WADEX.   Abbreviation for Word and Author Index. A computerized indexing system which uses authors' names as well as titles, printing authors and significant words from titles on the left-hand margin, using them as headings and following them with the full author and title. *See also* KWIC, KWOC.

WALIC.   Abbreviation for Wiltshire Association of Libraries of Industry and Commerce which was founded in 1961 to develop co-operation between the colleges of further education and the County Library in the matter of improving the supply of, and facilities for access to, technical literature. Lending between libraries is on a voluntary basis; a location list of publications is maintained centrally; the librarians meet regularly to confer about the purchase of books and effect co-operation. The organization is based on the Headquarters of the Wiltshire County Libraries which provides administrative facilities and maintains the union catalogue of the libraries' holdings and the Association's holdings of abstracts.

WALL SHELVING. Shelving placed against walls.

WALNUT. Trade name for a mechanized storage and retrieval system which uses photographic and computer techniques. Made by the I.B.M. Corporation.

WALTER PRESS. A rotary press which was first used in 1866 for printing *The Times*. It was constructed by J. C. MacDonald and J. Calverlye for J. Walter, owner of *The Times*. By 1880 this kind of press was in use throughout Europe.

WANDPETLS. Wandsworth Public, Educational and Technical Library Services; a co-operative organization formed as a result of librarians meeting over National Library Week, 1966. Most of the members are attached to educational institutions in Wandsworth. Aims are to provide better facilities for students by exchanging bibliographies, pooling information, co-operatively purchasing special periodicals and books, and making known the resources of individual libraries by means of visits and talks.

WANDSWORTH PUBLIC, EDUCATIONAL AND TECHNICAL LIBRARY SERVICES. *See* WANDPETLS.

WANTING. This word when followed by details of parts or volumes of a publication in a catalogue entry, indicates that those items are not possessed.

WANTS LIST. A list of books wanted, which is issued by a librarian or second-hand bookseller.

WASH DRAWING. An illustration, usually in sepia or black and white, done with a brush.

WASHING. When developing photographic negatives, or making prints on sensitized paper, the materials are thoroughly washed in clean running water after they have been in the fixing solution so as to remove all traces of the developing or fixing solutions.

WASHINGTON PRESS. The American counterpart of the ALBION PRESS (*q.v.*). It was invented in 1827.

WATERLEAF. Hand-made paper in its initial stage of manufacture, consisting of pulp spread and evened by shaking in the hand mould, and pressed between felts. It is semi-absorbent, being unsized, and

22*

must be sized before it is suitable for use as writing paper. *See also* ENGINE-SIZING, TUB-SIZING.

WATERLEAF PAPER. BODY PAPER (*q.v.*) which has been prepared for surface sizing or impregnation.

WATERMARK. A paper-maker's device which can be seen on any sheet of good paper when held up to the light. In handmade paper this is caused by twisting or soldering wire into the mould on which the paper is made; in machine-made paper, by a special roller called a 'dandy', which revolves over the moving pulp on the mould, impressing the mark at every revolution. The watermark is usually placed in the centre of one-half of the sheet. *See also* COUNTER MARK, IMPRESSED WATERMARK.

WATERMARKED PAPER. Paper containing a watermark.

WATTS-VERNON TEST. A test devised by Dr. A. F. Watts and Professor P. E. Vernon for determining a person's reading ability. It consists of thirty-five questions of increasing difficulty and has a time limit of ten minutes. For each question the examinee has to select the right answer from five given words. The range varies from the average reading and comprehension ability of an eleven-year-old to that of a grammar school fifteen-year-old.

WAVE-BORDER. (*Binding*) An eighteenth-century finisher's roll border incorporating an undulating line with other conventional ornament. Found in both English and Irish bindings.

WAVY LINE. A line placed underneath words in 'copy' or proof to indicate that bold-faced type is to be used.

WAX ENGRAVING. A method of making electros from which to print maps in letterpress work. The outline is drawn on a wax mould and the lettering impressed by hand. On this a copper shell is then deposited.

WEB. A large roll of paper which is fed into a printing machine.

WEB FED. A printing machine which receives paper from a reel instead of loose sheets.

WEB PERFECTING PRESS. A rotary press which prints consecutively on both sides of a reel of paper.

WEB PRESS. A printing machine on which the paper is fed from a continuous reel. A 'web perfecting press' prints consecutively on both sides of a continuous reel of paper. Also called 'Web machine'.

WEEDING. Discarding from stock books which it is considered are of no further use in the library. PSEUDO-WEEDING is transferring from one department to another, from stack to shelf and *vice versa*, or from files to bound form.

WEEKLY. A newspaper or periodical published once a week.

WEIGHT. 'The degree of blackness of a typeface'. (BS. 2961: 1958.) The types in a FAMILY (*q.v.*) vary in weight from extra-light to ultra bold.

WEIGHT OF FACE. Comparative colour value of type faces when printed, as light, medium, bold.

WEIGHT OF TYPE. Four square inches of solid type weigh approximately one pound.

WEST AFRICAN LIBRARY ASSOCIATION. *See* NIGERIAN LIBRARY ASSOCIATION.

WEST GERMAN SCHEME. A scheme for the co-operative acquisition of foreign books and periodicals which has operated since 1949 and benefits from a state subsidy from the Deutsche Forschungs- gemeinschaft (German Research Association). Thirty-six participating research libraries have been given assistance in purchasing foreign books of a scholarly standard in their allotted subject fields, and over 7,000 foreign periodicals have been distributed. All such materials are available to German researchers.

WEST LONDON COMMERCIAL AND TECHNICAL LIBRARY SERVICE. *See* CICRIS.

WESTERN. An adventure story set in the 'Wild West' of America.

WET END. The part of the paper-making machine where the wet pulp is formed into a web of paper, up to the first drier. The other end is known as the 'Dry end'.

WET FLONG. *See* FLONG.

WHARFEDALE. *See* STOP-CYLINDER PRESS.

WHATMAN PAPER. A brand of fine grade English hand-made wove drawing paper which was originally made by James Whatman from *c.* 1770 at Turkey Mill near Maidstone, Kent. Sometimes used for limited editions and privately-printed books.

WHEATLEY MEDAL. An award made to a British person who compiles an index to a book published by a British publisher. The index must set an outstandingly high standard. The award, which is named after Henry B. Wheatley (author of *How to Make an Index*, 1902), is made annually by a joint committee of the Library Association and of the Society of Indexers. The first award was made in respect of a book published in 1962. A list of books awarded the medal is published in the Library Association *Year Book*.

WHIP-STITCHING. The American term for OVERSEWING (*q.v.*).

WHITE BOOK. An official report published by the German government, so-called because issued in a white paper cover. *See also* BLUE BOOK.

WHITE EDGES. Edges of books which have been cut but not coloured or gilded. *See also* EDGES.

WHITE LETTER. 'Roman' type as opposed to BLACK LETTER or GOTHIC TYPE (*qq.v.*). This book is printed in roman type.

WHITE-LINE METHOD. *See* WOOD ENGRAVING.

WHITE-OUT. To space out composed matter, as in displayed or advertisement work.

WHITE PAPER. A term often used to denote a Report, Account or other Paper ordered by the House of Commons to be printed, or prepared primarily for debate in the House, and printed in the parliamentary series of official publications. There is a growing tendency, however, to apply the term to similar official publications not required by Parliament and published accordingly in the non-parliamentary series. *See also* BLUE BOOK, PARLIAMENTARY PUBLICATIONS.

WHITE PRINT. A print made by the DIAZOTYPE PROCESS (*q.v.*).

WHOLE BOUND. Books bound entirely in leather.

WHOLE NUMBER. The number given by a publisher to an issue of a periodical or serial publication, and continuing from the first issue. It is distinguished from the numbers assigned for volume and part of volume, and from those assigned for series and volume.

WHOLE-STUFF. The pulp used in making paper after it has been thoroughly beaten and bleached, and is ready for the VAT (*q.v.*) or the paper machine. *See also* HALF-STUFF.

WHO'S WHO FILE. *Synonymous with* BIOGRAPHY FILE (*q.v.*).

WICKERSHAM QUOINS. Expanding steel QUOINS (*q.v.*) which are inserted with FURNITURE (*q.v.*) at the side and foot of a CHASE (*q.v.*). They are adjusted with a key to lock and unlock pages of type in the chase.

WICKETS. The hinged gates fixed at both sides of the staff enclosure to control the entrance and exit of readers.

WIDE. Any material, such as a map or illustration that is wider than the type pages.

WIDE LINES. *Synonymous with* CHAIN-LINES. *See* LAID PAPER.

WIDENER LIBRARY. Collected by Harry Elkins Widener (1885–1912) who lost his life in the steamship *Titanic* in 1912. The books, which are all 'rare', are placed in a special room in the building which was given to Harvard University in 1913 by his mother as a memorial to her son; the building, known as the Harry Elkins Widener Memorial Library, also houses the college library.

WIDOW. An incomplete line of type at the top of a column or page, usually the last line of a paragraph, and avoided in good typography because of its unsightliness.

WIDTH. Type faces are of varying widths in the same FAMILY (*q.v.*), and are distinguished by the following (in progressive order): ultra-condensed, extra-condensed, condensed, semi-condensed, medium, semi-expanded, expanded, extra-expanded, ultra-expanded. 'Medium' is the width usually used and indicates the width which the manufacturer determines is the one representing the design and from which variants in the family have been, or may be, derived. *See also* FOUNT, TYPE FACE 2, WEIGHT.

WILD LOOK-THROUGH. LOOK-THROUGH (*q.v.*) which is irregular and cloudy.

WILDER MEDAL, LAURA INGALLS. A bronze medal designed by Garth Williams, awarded by the Children's Services Division of the American Library Association, to an author or illustrator whose books, published in the U.S., have over a period of years made a substantial and lasting contribution to children's literature. It was first awarded (to Laura Ingalls Wilder) in 1954, and beginning in 1960 was awarded every five years. The selection is made by a special committee of The Children's Services Division.

WILLIAM L. CLEMENTS LIBRARY. *See* CLEMENTS LIBRARY, WILLIAM L.

WILLOW. A machine consisting mainly of two rotating drums inside which spikes are fixed to tear out the raw material (rags, esparto, waste paper, etc.) for paper-making. Also called a 'Devil'. Often combined with a 'duster' which removes unwanted dust from the material.

WILSON CARDS. Catalogue cards printed by the H. W. Wilson Company which can be purchased for use in library catalogues. They are specially useful for school or 'popular' libraries, using a simpler form of cataloguing than the Library of Congress. Entries have annotations, and the cards may, if desired, be purchased with class marks, subject headings and added entry headings printed on the top of the cards ready for filing.

H. W. WILSON COMPANY LIBRARY PERIODICAL AWARD. A cash award of $100 and a certificate offered annually by the H. W. Wilson Company in respect of a periodical published by a local, state, or regional library, library group, or library association in the United States or Canada which has made an outstanding contribution to librarianship. Publications of the ALA, CLA, and their divisions are excluded. The Award is administered by the ALA Awards Committee, the selection being made by a jury of 3, including an editor of a national library periodical and a member of the Library Periodicals Round Table. The first periodical to receive the Award (in 1961) was *The California Librarian*, the journal of the California Library Association which was then edited by William R. Eshelman. All issues for the calendar year prior to the presentation of the Award are judged on the basis of sustained excellence in both format and content, with consideration being given to purpose and budget.

WILSON LIBRARY RECRUITMENT AWARD, HALSEY W.   A cash award of $1000 made by the H. W. Wilson Company annually, and administered by the ALA Awards Committee. It is given to any local, state, or regional library association, any library school, or any other appropriate group concerned with recruitment to the profession. The Award is made for the development of a sustained programme of recruitment for librarianship based on a total continuing programme, not limited to one year's activity. The money comprising the Award is to be used for the continuation and further development of a recruitment programme. The first recipient (in 1966) was the Pennsylvania State Library, Harrisburg.

WILTSHIRE ASSOCIATION OF LIBRARIES OF INDUSTRY AND COMMERCE.   *See* WALIC.

'WINDOW' COPY.   Printed pages pasted up on sheets of paper cut to expose the type area so that both sides of each printed page are visible.

WIRE.   The endless band of plain brass or bronze, tinned or leaded, or of nickel or stainless steel wires, which forms the moulding unit of a paper-making machine and carries the pulp from the breast box to the couching rolls and so felting it into a sheet, or web of paper. The mesh of the wire varies from fifty to ninety wires per inch according to the quality of paper made. Also called 'Machine wire', 'Wire-cloth', 'Wire-gauze' or 'Travelling mould'.

WIRE-CLOTH.   *See* WIRE.

WIRE-GAUGE.   *See* WIRE.

WIRE LINES.   *See* LAID PAPER.

WIRE MARK.   *See* LAID PAPER.

WIRE SEWING.   Sewing the sections of a book with wire staples driven through the folds of the sections and through tapes, canvas or muslin to which the staples are clinched. Also called 'Wire stitching'. *See also* SADDLE STITCHING, SEWING, STITCHING, THREAD STITCHED.

WIRE SIDE.   The side of a sheet of paper which has come in contact with the WIRE of the paper-making machine during the course of manufacture. *See also* FELT SIDE, RIGHT SIDE, TWIN WIRE PAPER.

WIRE STABBING.   Securing a number of leaves or sections by inserting one or more wire staples, usually from back to front (i.e. not through the fold of sections). This work is done on a stapling machine. Also called 'Side-stitching'. *See also* SADDLE STITCHING.

WIRE STITCHED. The fastening of a single section with wire driven through the centre of the fold and clinched (saddle stitched) or through the inner margin of the section (side stitched).

WIRED. *Synonymous with* WIRE STITCHED (*q.v.*).

WITH THE GRAIN. Said of paper which has been folded in the direction in which the fibres tend to lie. *See also* AGAINST THE GRAIN.

WITHDRAWAL. The process of altering or cancelling records in respect of books which have been withdrawn from the stock of a library.

WITHDRAWALS REGISTER. A record (in book form or on cards) which gives particulars of all books withdrawn from the stock of a library.

WOOD BLOCK. A block of wood, usually box, on which a design for printing from has been cut in relief.

WOOD ENGRAVING. 1. The art or process of cutting designs with a graver or burin upon the end-grain of a block of box-wood, leaving the designs in intaglio for printing. The resulting print appears as white lines or masses on a dark background; this has caused the process to be known as the 'white-line' method. This technique was introduced by Thomas Bewick. 2. A print from a wood engraving.

WOOD LETTER. A large type-letter of wood; used in poster printing.

WOOD PULP. Wood reduced to a pulp by mechanical or chemical means for subsequent paper-making.

WOOD TYPE. Wood letters above 72-point used in poster work, because they are lighter and cheaper than metal.

WOODCUT. An illustration made by pressing a sheet of dampened paper on a block of soft wood such as beech or sycamore which has been cut away to leave a design at the surface, so that when the block is inked an impression will be left on the paper, the cut-away parts showing white. The side-grain of a block of softer wood such as pear or sycamore, is used for woodcuts than for wood engravings, and the design is executed with a knife whereas a variety of gravers are used for wood engravings. The design of a woodcut is of black lines or masses on a white background whereas that of a wood engraving is the reverse; woodcutting is therefore known as a *black-line* method whereas wood engraving is a *white-line* method. Before the invention of movable type, books (text and illustrations) were printed in this way; these are called BLOCK BOOKS (*q.v.*). When movable type came into use, only borders, capitals and illustrations were printed from wooden blocks. *See also* FLORENTINE WOODCUTS.

WOODCUT TITLE-PAGE WITH PANEL. *Synonymous with* FRAMED CUT (*q.v.*).

WOODEN BOARDS. Said of books made before the sixteenth century which had covers made of thick wooden boards. By 1550 they had been replaced almost completely by pasteboards in England, although these had been used in the East for centuries. Leather was stretched over the boards and secured.

WORD. In information retrieval, a spoken or written symbol of an idea (*Pei*). In computer terminology, the contents of a storage location.

WORD-BOOK. A lexicon, or dictionary.

'WORD BY WORD'. *See* ALPHABETIZATION.

WORD INDEXING. A form of indexing which is the simplest to apply as it assumes on the part of the indexer a minimum knowledge of the subject-matter background and the least amount of technical skill. Such a type of indexing can be performed with precision by machines. *See also* CONCORDANCE, KWIC, PERMUTATION INDEXING and UNITERM INDEX which are of this kind, and CONTROLLED INDEXING, INDEX, UNITERM CONCEPT CO-ORDINATION INDEXING.

WORDS AUTHORITY FILE. *Synonymous with* THESAURUS (*q.v.*).

WORK. 1. Any expression of thought in language or symbols or other medium for record and communication [i.e. a work before printing or other publication] (IFLA).

WORK AND BACK. *See* SHEET WORK.

WORK AND TUMBLE. The method of printing the second side of a sheet of paper by turning it over in its narrow direction and feeding it into a printing machine to print the reverse side.

WORK AND TURN. To print from a forme in which the pages have been so imposed that when a sheet has been printed on both sides and cut in half it will provide two copies. *See also* SHEETWISE, TUMBLER SCHEME.

WORK AREA. That portion of a library's total floor space which is allocated for use as working space for the staff. It includes space for desks, furniture and equipment as well as rooms set aside for the exclusive use of staff members.

WORK BOOK. A departmental log book which sets out the duties for the staff each day.

WORK CARD. A card used to record the results of bibliographical searching and checking prior to ordering a book. The SUGGESTION CARD (*q.v.*) sometimes serves for this purpose.

WORK MANUAL. *Synonymous with* PROCEDURE MANUAL (*q.v.*).

WORK MARK. A letter indicating the title, edition, etc., of a work.

This is added to the normal author mark to distinguish several books by one author on the same subject, and to give each a definite location. It usually consists of the letter of the first word not an article of the title, plus, in the case of later editions, the edition number, and/or in the case of other titles beginning with the same letter and having the same class number, a figure (consecutively for each title). *See also* AUTHOR MARK, BOOK NUMBER, CALL NUMBER, VOLUME NUMBER.

WORK OFF. To print the paper; to finish printing.

WORK RESPONSIBILITY SCHEDULE. A schedule concerned with the special work assigned to each member of the staff as his own individual responsibility. (American.)

WORK ROOM. A room not open to the public in which any of the technical library routines or manual processes are carried out.

WORK SPACE. The part of a book stack which is allotted to assistants to carry out routine duties, including the space for necessary furniture or apparatus. This space is included in calculations of floor areas and cubic capacity.

WORK UP. A smudge or mark on a printed page caused by a letter or piece of spacing material in an improperly locked forme working up into a printing position during a press run. Also called 'Black', 'Rising space'.

WORKARD. Trade name for the microfilm card made by the Microseal Corporation.

'WORKING WITH FIGURES'. *See* PRESS NUMBER.

WORLD BIBLIOGRAPHY. *Synonymous with* UNIVERSAL BIBLIOGRAPHY (*q.v.*).

WORM-BORE (WORMHOLE). A hole or series of holes bored into, or through, a book by a book worm. A book containing such holes is said to be 'wormed'.

WOVE PAPER. Paper which, when held up to the light, shows a faint network of diamonds. This is caused by the weave of an ordinary DANDY ROLL (*q.v.*) (machine-made paper) or mould (hand-made paper). James Whatman was probably the first manufacturer of wove paper, and it was first used by John Baskerville in 1757 when he printed his Virgil on it. Not to be confused with LAID PAPER (*q.v.*).

WRAP. Writing and Reading Aids for the Paralysed. This is a sub-committee of the Polio Research Fund; it was responsible for the Samaritan Microfilm Reader which is used by those unable to hold a book or to turn its pages.

WRAP-AROUND GATHERING. A book in which one or more leaves at one end are printed on paper forming part of a section at the other end. This practice was used most in the late seventeenth and eighteenth centuries.

WRAP ROUNDS. Units of four pages of illustrations, or multiples of four, wrapped around a section of a book and sewn with it. Also called 'Outserts'.

WRAPPER. *Synonymous with* BOOK JACKET (*q.v.*).

WRIT. King's precept in writing under seal commanding an official to perform or abstain from some action.

WRITING MASTERS. In the fifteenth century professional writers, no longer needed for literary works because of the invention of printing, became writing masters. The increase of reading led to a general demand to learn the art of writing, and these masters found employment in the universities, schools, Courts, and houses of the wealthy. 'Writing Masters' Books' giving examples of the various hands, appeared in the sixteenth century.

WRONG. *See* RIGHT.

WRONG FOUNT. A letter of a different face or size from the rest of the text. This is caused in hand-set printing by placing type in a wrong case of type when 'distributing' after a printing job. Abbreviated w.f.

X-HEIGHT. The height of that part of a lower case letter between the ASCENDER (*q.v.*) and the DESCENDER (*q.v.*), i.e. the height of a lower case x. Used to describe the apparent height of a type which may vary within the same point size according to the design of the type face, e.g. in 12-point type from 0·056 to 0·08 inches. Centaur, Egmont, Perpetua and Walbaum have small x-heights, Plantin and Times Old Roman have big.

XEROCOPIES. Books reproduced by XEROGRAPHY (*q.v.*).

XERODUPLICATING. The taking of duplicate copies of a document by the Xerox process.

XEROGRAPHY. A method of making copies by the use of light and an electrostatically charged plate. It was invented by Chester F. Carlson, patented by him in 1937 and developed in the Graphic Arts Research Laboratory at the Battelle Memorial Institute. Rank-Xerox Limited., a joint company formed by the Haloid Company and Rank Organization (Rank-Xerox), exploits this process throughout the world. It is used for 5% of the reprographic market and 30% of the office copying market in the United States. Smaller and larger copies than the original can be made, as also can offset plates on a paper base. This is a dry method of positive reproduction of drawn or written material (whether in ink, pencil or colour) and of printed or typewritten matter, or the representation of objects, directly on to ordinary paper which does not need a coated or emulsified surface. The process depends on the ability of static electricity to attract particles of black powder to un-exposed areas of the image. A selenium-coated surface is given a positive electrostatic charge and the image is then exposed to it through a camera. Where light is reflected, the charge will be dissi-pated, leaving a positive charge in the image areas. When a negatively-charged black resinous powder is cascaded over the selenium it is attracted to the charged area. Paper which is then placed over the selenium and charged positively will have the powder image trans-ferred to it, and the image is fused permanently to the paper by the application of heat. The process is automatic and speedy. Books can be copied by using the Copyflo machine. Microfilm can be copied on to rolls of paper or card (giving a normal-sized image) which can be cut to a standard size afterwards. The machines doing this work operate automatically at great speeds.

XERORADIOGRAPHY. The xerographic process used with X-rays. *See also* XEROGRAPHY.

XEROX. Trade name for machines produced by the Haloid Company, Rochester, New York, and available in the U.K. from Rank-Xerox, Ltd., which use the xerographic method of copying. They are being used extensively for copying records, catalogue cards and books. *See also* XEROGRAPHY.

XEROXED BOOK. A copy of a book made by a XEROGRAPHY (*q.v.*) method.

XYLOGRAPH. 1. A block book. 2. A wood engraving.

XYLOGRAPHIC BOOK. *See* BLOCK BOOKS.

XYLOGRAPHICA. Block books.

XYLOGRAPHY. The art or process of engraving on wood. (*United Typothetae*). *See also* WOODCUT, WOOD ENGRAVING.

XYLOTYPE. Wood engraving, or a print from a wood engraving.

YANKEE MACHINE. A machine on which machine-glazed papers are made. Its chief characteristic is one large steam-heated cylinder with a highly polished surface in place of the usual drying rolls. Machine-glazed papers are glazed on only one (the under) side, the other being in the (rough) condition in which it comes from the WET END (*q.v.*) of the machine.

YAPP EDGES. *Synonymous with* CIRCUIT EDGES (*q.v.*).

YEAR BOOK. A volume often called an annual, containing current in-formation of a variable nature, in brief descriptive and/or statistical form, which is published once every year. Often year books review the events of a year.

YEAR NUMBER. A symbol used to represent the year in which a book was published. This may form part of the BOOK NUMBER (*q.v.*), as used with the Colon Classification, and is obtained by translating the year of publication into the appropriate symbols in accordance with the Scheme's Time Schedule.

YELLOW BOOK. An official report published by the French government, so called because issued in a yellow paper cover. *See also* BLUE BOOK.

YELLOW PRESS. A popular name for sensational newspapers and periodicals.

YELLOWBACK. A cheap popular novel, usually not of the first quality. So named from the fact that such books were published in shiny yellow paper covers with a picture on the front.

YEWTIC. Abbreviation for Yorkshire (East and West Ridings) Technical Information Centre. Established in November 1963 and sponsored by the Department of Scientific and Industrial Research, this organization is based on the Leeds Chamber of Commerce and has the object of helping industry, particularly the smaller firms, to make better use of existing technical information. This is done by solving technical enquiries, developing liaison between industrial firms and research associations, universities, technical colleges, etc., and through co-operation with other formalized co-operative library schemes.

YORKSHIRE COBOOK GROUP OF LIBRARIES. This organization commenced to function in 1955 as a scheme of voluntary co-operation among eight small and adjoining public library authorities in the West Riding of Yorkshire. Now there are fourteen, with populations ranging from 13,000 to 56,800. The Scheme's principal object is to provide in the area covered by these libraries an adequate coverage of the more expensive books. An inter-lending service for books operates between member libraries by means of the Cobook Slip Circulating System which involves the postal circulation of slips for books requested. Libraries making requests pay all postal charges. The Group supplements the work of the Yorkshire Regional Library System and renders the member libraries less dependent on the large libraries in the Region. It also provides a means of supplying books which cannot be obtained through the Yorkshire Regional Library System.

YORKSHIRE (EAST AND WEST RIDINGS) TECHNICAL INFORMATION CENTRE. *See* YEWTIC.

YOUNG ADULT BOOK. One intended for adults but suitable for adolescents.

YOUNG ADULT SERVICES DIVISION. Established as a Division of the American Library Association on 1st January 1957. It is interested in the improvement and extension of services to young people in all types of library, and has specific responsibility for the evaluation and selection of books and non-book materials and the interpretation and use of materials for young adults, except when such materials are designed for only one type of library. Abbreviated YASD. Publishes *Top of the News*, jointly with the Children's Services Division.

YOUNG PEOPLE'S DEPARTMENT. *Synonymous with* CHILDREN'S LIBRARY (*q.v.*).

YOUNG READER'S CHOICE. An award bestowed on the author of a children's book. It takes the form of a parchment presented by Harry Hartman, a Seattle bookseller, and was first awarded in 1940 to Dell McCormick for *Paul Bunyan swings his axe*. Except for three years, it has been awarded annually; the Work with Children & Young People Division of the Pacific Northwest Library Association makes the award.

YOUTH LIBRARIES GROUP. A Group of the Library Association; it exists to bring together all those interested in encouraging children and young people to use and enjoy books. There are five Branches of the Group. It was founded as the Work with Young People Section in 1946 and changed its name when the present constitution of the Library Association came into operation in 1963. Publishes *Newsletter* (3 p.a.).

Z–39. Abbreviation for Sectional Committee Z–39, a committee of the American National Standards Institute, which represents, in an organized and official channel, the progress of the library profession towards 'standards for concepts, definitions, terminology, letters and signs, practices, methods, supplies, and equipment used in the field of library work, and the preparation and utilization of documents'. It has been sponsored and administered by the Council of National Library Associations since 1951.

ZATOCODING. A punched card system for the mechanical selection of information. It uses cards with marginal perforations for notching and was invented by Calvin N. Mooers. A card is used for each document and its subject content is indicated by the notches in the edges of the cards; these permit a mechanical sorter (a Zator '800' Selector) to scan the cards and select those required.

ZATOR. Trade name for a notched-card system of recording information in connexion with information retrieval. A list of subjects must be developed for a specific application, then the coding is done; this consists of a pattern of notches for each subject, all of them overlapping one another. The system can only be used under contract with the Zator Co.

ZIG-ZAG FOLD. *Synonymous with* CONCERTINA FOLD (*q.v.*).

ZINC ETCHING. *Synonymous with* ZINCOGRAPHY (*q.v.*).

ZINCO. 1. Abbreviation for ZINCOGRAPH (*q.v.*). 2. A block made of zinc and used as an alternative to a BINDER'S BRASS (*q.v.*). It is less durable, and the impression made with it lacks sharpness.

ZINCOGRAPH. 1. A zinc plate which is etched and mounted for use as a line block for printing book illustrations and diagrams in black and white. The printing method is known as Zincography. 2. A print or design made from such a block. Abbreviated 'zinco'.

ZINCOGRAPHY. A photo-mechanical method of printing whereby designs or line drawings are produced in black and white. It is a relief method, zinc being used for the blocks, although copper is used for specially fine work.

ZINCPLATE LITHO. *See* LITHOGRAPHY.

ZOOMORPHIC INITIAL. In a mediaeval illuminated manuscript, an initial letter formed by the bodies of beasts.

ZURICH INDEX. *See* CONCILIUM BIBLIOGRAPHICUM.

Appendix 1

*Some Latin place names, which are used bibliographically,
with their English equivalents*

Aarhusium = Arhisium, Arhusen, Aarhusi, or Aarhus, Denmark.

Abbamico Villa, or Abbatis Villa = Abbeville, France.

Abbatia Sorethana = Schussenried, Germany.

Abbatisvilla = Abbeville, France.

Aberdonia, Abredea, or Abredonia = Aberdeen, Scotland.

Abredonia = Aberdeen, Scotland.

Albani (St.) Villa = St. Albans, England.

Ambrianum = Amiens, France.

Amstelodamum, or Amstelredamum = **Amsterdam, Netherlands.**

Andegavensis Ager = Anjou, France.

Andegavum = Angers, France.

Andgolismum = Angoulême, France.

Andreapolis = St. Andrews, Scotland.

Aneda = Edinburgh, Scotland.

Antverpia = Antwerp, Belgium.

Aquae = Aqui, Italy.

Aquae Bonae = Bonn, Germany.

Aquae-Grani = Aix-la-Chapelle, Germany.

Aquae Sextiae = Aix-en-Provence, France.

Aquae Statiellae = Acqui, Italy.

Aquilia = Aquila, Italy.

Aquincum = Buda, Hungary.

Aquisgranum = Aachen, or Aix-la-Chapelle, **Germany.**

Araugia = Aarau, Switzerland.

Arelas, Arelate or Arelatum = Arles, France.

Argentina, or Argentoratum = Strasbourg, **France.**

Arhusium = Arhusen, or Aarhus, Denmark.

Arosia = Västerås, Sweden.

Asculum Piocinum = Ascoli Picen, Italy.

Asturica Augusta = Astorga, Spain.

Athenae Rauracae = Basle, Switzerland.

Atrebatum = Arras, France.

Audomaropolis, or Audomarum = St. Omer, France.
Augusta = Augsburg, Germany; sometimes London.
Augusta Nemetum = Spires, or Speyer, Germany.
Augusta Perusia, or Perusia = Perugia, Italy.
Augusta Rauracorum = Augst, Switzerland.
Augusta Taurinorum, or Taurinum = Turin, Italy.
Augusta Tiberii = Ratisbon, or Regensburg, Germany.
Augusta Trebocorum = Strassburg, Austria.
Augusta Trevirorum = Treves, Germany.
Augusta Trimobantum = London, England.
Augusta Vangionum = Worms, Germany.
Augusta Vindelicorum = Augsburg, Germany.
Augustoritum Lemavicensium, Augustoritum Pictonum = Limoges,
    France.
Auracum = Aurach, or Urach, a small town in Würtemberg, Germany.
Aurelia, Aureliacum, Aureliani or Aurelianum = Orleans, France.
Aurelia Allobrogum = Geneva, Switzerland.
Austriae Civitas = Cividad di Friuli (Cividale del Friuli), Italy.
Avaricum = Bourges, France.
Avenio = Avignon, France.
Babenburga, or Bamberga = Bamberg, Germany.
Bacodurum, or Batava Castra = Passau, Germany.
Bancona = Oppenheim, Germany.
Barchino, Barcino, or Barxino = Barcelona, Spain.
Barcum = Barco, Spain.
Barxino = Barcelona, Spain.
Basilia = Basle, Switzerland.
Bellovacum = Beauvais, France.
Bellovisum = Bellevue (part of Paris), France.
Bergomum = Bergamo, Italy.
Berma = Bremen, Germany.
Berna = Berne, Switzerland.
Berolinum = Berlin, Germany.
Berona = Münster, Germany.
Bisuntia, Bisuntium, Vesontio, or Vesuntio = Besançon, France.
Biturigae = Bourges, France.
Blabyria = Blaubeuen, Germany.
Bonna = Bonn, Germany.
Bononia = Bologna, Italy.
Borbetomagus = Worms, Germany.
Brachara, or Braclara = Braga, Portugal.

Brangonia = Worcester, England.

Bransberga, or Braunsberga = formerly Braunsberg, Germany; now Braniewo, Poland.

Bravum Burgi, or Burgi = Burgos, Spain.

Bresla, or Bresoavia = formerly Breslau, Germany; now Wroclaw, Poland.

Brixia = Brescia, Italy.

Brugae, or Brugae Bearniae = Bruges, Belgium.

Brunna = Brünn, now Brno, Czechoslovakia.

Brunonia, or Brunsviga = Brunswick, Germany.

Brunopolis = Braunsberg, Poland.

Brunsviga = Brunswick, Germany.

Bruxellae = Brussels, Belgium.

Buda = Buda (part of Budapest), Hungary.

Burgdorfium = Burgdorf, Germany.

Burgi = Burgos, Spain.

Burgum Auraceuse = Aurach, or Urach, Germany.

Byzantium = Istanbul, formerly Constantinople, Turkey.

Cabelia, or Cabelium = Chablis, France.

Cadomum = Caen, France.

Caesar Augusta = Saragossa, Spain.

Caesarodonum Turonum = Tours, France.

Cale = Oporto, Portugal.

Caletum = Calais, France.

Calium, or Callium = Cagli, Italy.

Camberiacum, or Chamberium = Chambery, France.

Camboricum, Cantabrigia, or Capitabrigia = Cambridge, England.

Camulodunum = Colchester, England.

Cantabrigia = Cambridge, England.

Cantuaria = Canterbury, England.

Capitabuga = Cambridge, England.

Carmanola = Carmagnola, Italy.

Carnutum = Chartres, France.

Caroli Hesychium, or Carobruha = Karlsruhe, Germany.

Casale Majus = Casalmaggiori, Italy.

Caselae, Casella = Casale, Italy.

Casseletum, Cassella, or Castellum Cattorum = Cassel, Germany.

Casulae = Casoli, Italy.

Casurgis = Prague, Czechoslovakia.

Cenabum = Orleans, France.

Chalybon = Aleppo, Syria.

Chamberium, or Camberiacum = Chambery, France.

Christiana = Oslo, formerly Christiana, Norway.
Chrysii Auraria = Altenburg, Germany.
Cibinium = Sibiu, or Hermannstadt, Rumania.
Civitas Austriae = Civiad di Friuli (Cividale del Friuli), Italy.
Civitas Nemetum = Spires, or Speyer, Germany.
Clavasium = Chivasso, Italy.
Cliniacum, or Cluniacum = Cluny, France.
Coburgum = Coburg, Germany.
Codania = Copenhagen, Denmark.
Colla, or Collis = Colle, Italy.
Colonia, Colonia Agrippina, Colonia Claudia, or Colonia Ubiorum =
    Cologne, Germany.
Colonia Allobrogum = Geneva, Switzerland.
Colonia Claudia = Cologne, Germany.
Colonia Julia Romana = Seville, Spain.
Colonia Munatiana = Basle, Switzerland.
Colonia Ubiorum = Cologne, Germany.
Colonia Viriata = Madrid, Spain.
Complutum = Alcalá de Henares, Spain. Famous for the 'Complutensian'
    polyglot Bible, printed there in 1514-17.
Comum = Como, Italy.
Condivincum Nannetum = Nantes, France.
Conimbria, or Conimbrica = Coimbra, Portugal.
Consentia = Cosenza, Italy.
Constantinople = almost always a fictitious imprint.
Constantinopolis = Istanbul, formerly Constantinople, Turkey.
Corduba = Cordova, Spain.
Coria = Coria, Spain.
Corona = Kronstadt (Brasov), Rumania.
Cosmopolis = always a fictitious imprint.
Cracovia = Cracow, Poland.
Cremona = Cremona, Italy.
Crisopolis = Parma, Italy.
Culenburgum = Culemborg, Netherlands.
Cusentia = Cosenza, Italy.
Cutna = Kuttenberg, or Kutná Hora, Czechoslovakia.
Damaspo = Damascus, Syria.
Dantiscum = Danzig, Poland.
Darmstadium = Darmstadt, Germany.
Daventria = Deventer, Netherlands.
Debrecinum = Debrecen, Hungary.

Delfi, or Delphi = Delft, Netherlands.

Derbatum, or Derpatum = Dorpat or Tartu, Esthonia, U.S.S.R.

Deva = Chester, England.

Divio = Dijon, France.

Divodurum = Metz, France.

Dola Sequanorum = Dôle, France.

Dordracum, Dordrechtum, or Dorteracum = Dordrecht, or Dort, Netherlands.

Dresda = Dresden, Germany.

Duacum = Douai, France.

Dublinum, Eblana = Dublin, Eire.

Dunelmia = Durham, England.

Durobrivae = Rochester, England.

Durocortorum = Rheims, France.

Durovernum = Canterbury, England.

Eblana = Dublin, Eire.

Eboracum = York, England.

Edinbruchium, Edinburgum, or Edinum = Edinburgh, Scotland.

Einsilda = Einsiedeln, Switzerland.

Eleutheropolio = literally 'free city', a fictitious imprint found on 'free' books.

Elna = Perpignan, France.

Elvetiorurn Argentina = Strasbourg, France.

Emmerani Coenobium = Ratisbon, or Regensburg, Germany.

Engolismum = Angoulême, France.

Ergovia = Münster, Germany.

Erfordia, or Erfurtum = Erfurt, Germany.

Eridanium = Milan, Italy.

Eslinga, or Ezelinga = Esslingen, Germany.

Essium = Jesi, Italy.

Etona = Eton, England.

Eustadium = Aichstadt, or Eichstätt, Germany.

Ezelinga = Esslingen, Germany.

Fanum, or Fanum Fortunae = Fano, Italy.

Fanum S. Galli = St. Gall, Switzerland.

Felsina = Bologna, Italy.

Ferraria = Ferrara, Italy.

Firenze, or Florentia = Florence, Italy.

Fivizanum = Fivizzano, Italy.

Florentia = Florence, Italy.

Forum Julium = Cividad di Friuli, Italy.

Forum Livii = Forli, Italy.

Francofurtum ad Moenum = Frankfurt am Main, Germany.

Francofurtum ad Oderam = Frankfurt-an-der-Oder, Germany.

Freiberga in Misnia = Freiberg, Germany.

Friburgum Brisgoviae = Freiburg in Brisgau, Germany.

Friburgum Helvetiorum = Fribourg, or Freiburg, Switzerland.

Frisia = Friesland, Netherlands.

Frisinga, or Fruxinum = Freysingen, Freisgenn, or Freising, Bavaria, Germany.

Fulgentium = Foligno, Italy.

Fulginia, or Fulginium = Foligno, Italy.

Gaietta, or Gaietto = Gaeta, Italy.

Galgocinum = Galgoc, Czechoslovakia.

Galli Fanum = St. Gall, Switzerland.

Ganabum, or Genabum = Orleans, France.

Ganda, or Gandavum = Ghent, Belgium.

Gauda = Gouda, Netherlands.

Gebenna, Genava, Geneva, or Gobenna = Geneva, Switzerland.

Genabum = Orleans, France.

Genua = Genoa, Italy.

Gerunda = Gerona, Spain.

Giennium = Jaen, Spain.

Gippesvicum = Ipswich, England.

Glascovia, or Glascua = Glasgow, Scotland.

Goslaria = Goslar, Germany.

Gothoburgum = Gothenburg, Sweden.

Gotorum = Lund, Sweden.

Granata = Granada, Spain.

Gratianopolis = Grenoble, France.

Gravionarium, or Gravionatium = Bamberg, Germany.

Gronaicum, or Gronvicum = Greenwich, England.

Hadrianapolis = Adrianople, Turkey.

Hafnia = Copenhagen, Denmark.

Haga, Haga Comitis, or Hage Comitum = The Hague, Netherlands.

Hagenoa = Haguenau, France.

Hala, Hala Magdeburgica, Hala Saxonum, or Hala Suevorum = Halle, Germany.

Halebum = Aleppo, Syria.

Hammona = Hamburg, Germany.

Harlemum = Haarlem, Netherlands.

Hasseletum = Hasselt, Belgium.

Havnia = Copenhagen, Denmark.
Heiddelburga, or Heidelberga = Heidelberg, Germany.
Helenopolis = Frankfurt am Main, Germany.
Herbipolis = Würzburg, Germany.
Hermanopolis = Sibiu, formerly Hermannstadt, Rumania.
Hesychia Carolina = Karlsruhe, Germany.
Hierosolyma = Jerusalem, Palestine.
Hispalis, or Ispalis = Seville, Spain.
Holmia = Stockholm, Sweden.
Hyctopolis ad Istrum = Ratisbon, or Regensburg, Germany.
Ianua = Genoa, Italy.
Ilarda, or Ilerda = Lerida, Spain.
Ingoldstadium = Ingoldstadt, Germany.
Insula, or Insulae = Lille, France.
Isca = Exeter, England.
Ispalis = Seville, Spain.
Juliomagum = Angers, France.
Koburgum = Coburg, Germany.
Kralia = Kralitz, Czeckoslovakia.
Krettemberga, Kuttenberga, or Cutna = Kuttenberg, or Kutna Hora,
    Czechoslovakia.
Lautreguerum = Tréguier, France.
Lauginga = Lauingen, Germany.
Lausanna = Lausanne, Switzerland.
Laus Pompeia = Lodi, Italy.
Lavinga = Lauingen, Germany.
Leida = Leyden, Netherlands.
Leiria = Leiria, Portugal.
Lemovicense Castrum = Limoges, France.
Leodicum Eburonum, or Leodium = Liège, Belgium.
Leovardia = Leeuwarden, Netherlands.
Leucorea = Wittenberg, Germany.
Leuphana = Lüneburg, Germany.
Lignicium = Legnica, Poland (formerly Liegnitz, Germany).
Limonum = Poitiers, France.
Lingonensis, Civitas = Langres, France.
Lipsia = Leipzig, Germany.
Lobavia = Löbau, Germany.
Lodecum, or Loudeacum = Loudéac, France.
Londinium, Londinum, Londinia, or Londonia = London, England.
Londinum Gothorum = Lund, Sweden.

Lovanium = Louvain, Belgium.

Lubeca, or Lubicensis = Lübeck, Germany.

Luca = Lucca, Italy.

Lucerna Helvetiorum = Lucerne, Switzerland.

Lugdunum = Lyons, France.

Lugdunum Batavorum, or Lugd. Bat. = Leyden, or Leiden, Netherlands.

Lunda, or Lundinum Scanorum = Lund, Sweden.

Luneburgum = Luneburg, Germany.

Lutetia Parisiorum = Paris, France.

Madritum = Madrid, Spain.

Magdeburgum = Magdeburg, Germany.

Maguntia = Mainz, Germany.

Malborow ('in the land of Hessen') = Marburg, Germany. English books
    with this imprint were, however, probably printed at Cologne.

Mancunium = Manchester, England.

Mantoa, or Mantua = Mantua, Italy.

Mantua Carpetanorum = Madrid, Spain.

Marionis = Hamburg, Germany.

Marionis Altera = Lubeck, Germany.

Marsiburgam, or Marsipolis = Merseburg, Germany.

Massilia = Marseilles, France.

Matisco = Mâcon, France.

Matritum = Madrid, Spain.

Mechlinia, or Mechlinium = Malines, Belgium.

Mediolanum = Milan, Italy.

Melita = Malta.

Memminga = Memmingen, Germany.

Mesnium = Brunswick, Germany.

Messana = Messina, Italy.

Misena, or Misna = Meissen, Germany.

Moguntia, or Moguntiacum = Mainz, Germany.

Mohilavia = Mohilev (Mogilev), U.S.S.R.

Monachium, or Monacum = Munich, Germany.

Monasterium, or Monasterium Ergoviae = Münster, Germany.

Monasterium Tavestok = Tavistock, England.

Monasterium Wadstenense = Vadstena, Sweden.

Mons Regalis, or Mons Regius = Monreale, Sicily, Italy.

Mons Serratus, on Montis Serrati Monasterium = Monserrat, Spain.

Monyorokerekinum = Eberau, Austria.

Moscovia, or Moscua = Moscow, U.S.S.R.

Mounts = Mons, France.

Murcia = Murcia, Spain.

Mussipontum = Pont-à-Mousson, France.

Mutina = Modena, Italy.

Namnetum, or Namnetus Portus = Nantes, France.

Nanceium, or Nancum = Nancy, France.

Nannetae, Nannetes, or Nannetum = Nantes, France.

Neapolis = Naples, Italy.

Neapolis Casimiriana, Neapolis Nemetum, or Neapolis Palatinorum = Neustadt, Germany.

Neoburgum Cattorum = Neuburg, Germany.

Neocomum = Neufchâtel, Switzerland.

Neostadium ad Hartam = Neustadt, Germany.

Nicaea = Nice, France.

Nonantula = Nonantola, Italy.

Nordovicum = Norwich, England.

Norica, Norimburga, or Noriberga = Nuremberg (Nürnberg), Germany.

Nova Pelsna, or Nova Plzna = Pilsen, Czeckoslovakia.

Novi = Novi, Yugoslavia.

Noviomagus Rhenanus, or Noviomagium = Nijmegan, or Nimeguen, Netherlands.

Novum Eboracum = New York, U.S.A.

Nozanum = Nozzano, Italy.

Ocellodurum = Zamora, Spain.

Oenipous = Innsbruck, Austria.

Offenburgam = Offenburg, Germany.

Olomucum, or Olomutium = Olmutz, Czeckoslavakia.

Olyssipo = Lisbon, Spain.

Oppenhemium = Oppenheim, Germany.

Othonia, or Othinium = Odense, Denmark.

Oxonia, or Oxonium = Oxford, England.

Palaeopragu, or Praga = Prague, Czeckoslovakia.

Palma Balearia = Majorca, Spain.

Pampalona = Pampeluna, or Pamplona, Spain.

Panormum = Polermo, Sicily, Italy.

Papia = Pavia, Italy.

Parisü, or Parisius = Paris, France.

   Parisius is a peculiar locative plural found regularly in the fifteenth century where Parisüs would be expected.

Parthenopa, or Parthenope (rarer than Neapolis) = Naples, Italy.

Parthenopolis = Magdeburg, Germany.

Passavium, or Patavia = Passau, Germany.

Patavium = Padua, Italy.
Pelsna = Pilsen, Czeckoslovakia.
Perpinianum = Perpignan, France.
Perusia, or Augusta Perusia = Perugia, Italy.
Petriburgum = Peterborough, England.
Petropolis = Leningrad, formerly St. Petersburg, U.S.S.R.
Philadelphia = Philadelphia (Asia Minor), Turkey.
Phorca = Pforzheim, Germany.
Pictavia, or -ium (*loc.* Pictavis) = Poitiers, France.
Pinarolium = Pinerolo, Italy.
Pincia = Valladolid, Spain.
Pisae = Pisa, Italy.
Piscia = Pescia, Italy.
Placentia = Piacenza, Italy.
Plebisacium = Piove di Sacco, Italy.
Pompeiopolis = Pampeluna, Spain.
Pons ad Monticulum, or Pons Moncionis = Pont à-Mousson, France.
Pons Neviae = Puebla de Naira, Spain.
Pons Oeni = Innsbruck, Austria.
Pontimussum = Pont-à Mousson, France.
Portesium = Porto (Oporto), Portugal.
Posnania = Posen, Poland.
Praetorium = Kingston, England.
Praga = Prague, Czeckoslovakia.
Probatopolis = Schaffhausen, Switzerland.
Promontorium = Promenthoux (Cape St. Vincent), Portugal.
Provincum, or Prunvinum = Provins, France.
Ratiastum Lemovicum = Limoges, France.
Ratisbona, Reginum Augusta Tiberii, or Castra Regina = Ratisbon, or
     Regensburg, Germany.
Regiomontium Borussiae = Konigsberg, Germany.
Regiopolis = Kingston, England.
Regium = Reggio, Italy.
Regum = Chichester, England.
Reutlinga = Reutlingen, Germany.
Rhedones = Rennes, France.
Rhegium = Reggio, Italy.
Richensteinum = Reichenstein, Poland.
Rhodopolis, or Rostochium = Rostock, Germany.
Richensteinium = Reichenstein, Poland.
Ripa = Ribe, Denmark.

Roë Fontes, or Roeskildia = Roskilde, Denmark.

Roma = Rome, Italy.

Romanovia = Romanov, U.S.S.R.

Rostochium = Rostock, Germany.

Rothomagum, or Rotomagus = Rouen, France.

Rubens Mons = Rougemont (a Benedictine Abbey in Burgundy), France.

Ruotlinga = Reutlingen, Germany.

Sabate, or Sabatis = Savona, Italy.

S. Albani Villa, or Villa Sancta Albani = St. Albans, England.

Saena = Siena, Italy.

Salisburia = Salzburg, Austria.

Salmantica = Salamanca, Spain.

Salutive = Saluzzo, Italy.

Sarum = Salisbury, England.

Savillianum = Savigliano, Italy.

Savona = Savona, Italy.

Scandianum = Scandiano, Italy.

Schedamum = Schiedam, Netherlands.

Senae, or Saena = Siena, Italy.

Soncinum = Soncino, Italy.

Sora, or Soria = Soria, Spain.

Sorethum, or Sorteuse Monasterium = Schussenried, Germany.

Spira = Spires, Speyer, Germany.

Stockholmia = Stockholm, Sweden.

Sublacense Monasterium = Subiaco, Italy.

Stutgardia = Stuttgart, Germany.

Sylvia-Ducalis, or Sylvia Ducis = Bois le Duc, or 's Hertogenbosch, Netherlands.

Szegedinum = Szegedin, or Szeged, Hungary.

Taraco = Tarragona, Spain.

Tarrazona, Tirasso, or Turiaso = Tarragona, Spain.

Tarvisium = Treviso, Italy.

Taurinum = Turin, Italy.

Ternavia or Ternobum = Trnava, or Tyrnau, Czeckoslovakia.

Theatrum (Sheldonianum) = Oxford (1st) University Press, England.

Thessalonica = Salonika, Greece.

Tholosa = Toulouse, France.

Ticinum = Parvia, Italy.

Tigurum = Zurich, Switzerland.

Toletum = Toledo, Spain.

Tolosa Tectosagum, or Tolosia Pallidea = Toulouse, France.

Tornacum Neviorum = Tournai, Belgium.

Trajectum ad Rhenum, Trajectum Inferius, or Ultrajectum = Utrecht, Netherlands.

Trajectum Mosae, or Trajectum Superius = Maastricht or Maestricht, Netherlands.

Trajectum ad Viadrum = Frankfurt an der Oder, Germany.

Trebia, or Trevium = Trebbia, Italy.

Trecae, or Tricasses = Troyes, France.

Trecora, or Trecorium = Trêguier, France.

Treviri, or Trevium = Trebbia, Italy.

Triboccorum = Strasburg, Germany.

Troyga = Trogen, Switzerland.

Tubinga = Tubingen, Germany.

Turiaso = Tarragona, Spain.

Turicum Helvetiorum, Turigum, or Turingum = Zurich, Switzerland.

Turones, or Turonis = Tours, France.

Tyrnovia = Tyrnau, Czeckoslovakia.

Tzernogavia = Tschernigov, or Chernigov, U.S.S.R.

Ubu = Cologne, Germany.

Ulma = Ulm, Germany.

Ultinum = Udine, Italy.

Ultrajectum = Utrecht, Netherlands.

Ulyssipo, or Ulyssipolis = Lisbon, Spain.

Upsalia = Upsala, Sweden.

Urbinum = Urbino, Italy.

Utinum = Udine, Italy.

Valentia = Valence, France.

Valentia, or Valentia Edetanorum = Valencia, Spain.

Vallisoletum, or Pincia = Valladolid, Spain.

Varadinum = Crosswardein, Rumania.

Varsavia = Warsaw, Poland.

Venetiae = Venice, Italy.

Venta Belgarum = Winchester, England.

Vercellae = Vercelli, Italy.

Verona = Verona, Italy.

Vesontio, Vesuntio, Bisuntia, or Bisuntium = Besançon, France.

Viburgum = Viborg, Denmark.

Vicentia = Vicenza, Italy.

Vienna Austriae, Vindabona, or Vindoliona = Vienna, Austria.

Vienna in Delphinatu, or Vienne = Vienna, Austria.

Vigornia = Worcester, England.

Villa Sancta Albani = St. Albans, England.

Vilna = Vilnyus, Vilnius, Vilna, Vilno, or Wilno, Lithuania.

Vindalona = Vienna, Austria.

Vindoliona = Vienna, Austria.

Vinterberga = Winterberg, now Vimperk, Czechoslovakia.

Virceburgum = Würtzburg, Germany.

Viriathica = Madrid, Spain.

Viterbium = Viterbo, Italy.

Vratislavia = Breslau, now Wroclaw, Poland.

Westmonasterium = Westminster, England.

Wigornum = Worcester, England.

Wintonia = Winchester, England.

Wirceburgum = Würzburg, Germany.

Zamora = Zamora, Spain.

Zamoscium = Zamosc, Poland.

Zwolla = Zwolle, Netherlands.

Appendix 2

Subject Lists of Terms Defined

BIBLIOGRAPHY

36-line Bible
42-line Bible
48-line Bible
A.D.S.
A.L.S.
Aberrant copy
Abridged edition
Abstract
Added title-page
All published
Alphabetic writing
Alphabetology
Analects
Analytical bibliography
Anepigraphon
Annalistic arrangement
Anopisthographic block book
Anopisthographic printing
Ante-dated
Antiphonary
Apocalypse
Apocryphal
Apograph
Apostil
Armorial binding
Ars moriendi
Artistic manuscript
Arundel Psalter
Ashendene Press
Association book
Asterism
Atlas folio
Attributed author
Author bibliography
Autographed edition
Back page
Bay Psalm Book
Beneventuan handwriting
Bibelot

Bibliogenesis
Bibliognost
Bibliograph
Bibliographee
Bibliographer
Bibliographic centre
Bibliographic index
Bibliographic Index
Bibliographic item
Bibliographic volume
Bibliographical description
Bibliographical index
Bibliographical note
Bibliographical service
Bibliographical tool
Bibliographical unit
Bibliographing
Bibliographize
Bibliography
Bibliography of bibliographies
Bibliological
Bibliologist
Bibliomania
Bibliomaniac
Bibliophile edition
Bibliotheca
Biobibliography
Bishop's Bible
Blank
Blank book
Blank leaves
Blind reference
Block book
Boar's Head Press
Bolt
Book form
Book hand
Book of Armagh
Book of hours

Current bibliography
Current complete national
  bibliography
Current comprehensive
  bibliography
Current selective bibliography
Cursive
Cut to register
D.S.
Daniel Press
Date line
Date of issue
Dedication
Dedication copy
del., delt.
Demonym
Demy
Descriptive bibliography
Device
Direction line
Direction number
Disjunct leaf
Distinctive title
Divinity calf
Documentography
Dos-a-dos binding
Double-book
Double columned
Double dagger
Double plate
Doves Press
Duodecimo
Duplicate title
Duplicated signatures
Editio princeps
Edition
Elephant folio
Elzevier
Emblem book
Enchiridion
End matter

Endnotes
English stock
Engraved title-page
Enumerative bibliography
Epistolaria
Erotica
Essay periodical
Etruscan alphabet
Etruscan style
Even page
Explicit
Expurgated edition
Extra-illustrated
Fabric binding
fac.
Faceted initial
Facetiae
Facsimile
Facsimile edition
Facsimile reprint
'False first' edition
Family name
Fanfare style
Fasciculus
Fell types
Fictitious imprint
Figure initial
Filing title
Finding list
Fine copy
Fine paper copy
First edition
First English edition
First impression
First-line index
First printing
First published edition
First separate edition
Firsts
Florentine woodcuts
Fly sheet

23*

Line division mark
Line-ending
Literary manuscript
Local bibliography
Location mark
Logographic writing
Lombardic handwriting
Long
Loose leaf service
Lower edge
Luttrell Psalter
Made-up copy
Mainz Psalter
Majuscule
Map
Masthead
Mazarin Bible
Memorial volume
Merovingian handwriting
Metabolic map
Microbibliography
Miniature book
Mint
Minuscule
Missal
Modelled initial
Mottled calf
Multi-volume book
Narrow
National bibliography
News letter
Newsbook
No date
Non-distinctive title
Note
Numbered and signed edition
Numbered copy
Numbered entry
Oblong
Obverse cover
Octavo

Octodecimo
Ola books
Old English
Omission marks
One shot
op. cit.
open edge
Opened
Opisthographic
Opuscule
Original binding
Original parts
Orihon
Ornaments
Outsert
Page reference
Palimpsest
Palm leaf book
Pamphlet
Pamphlet volume
Paper covered
Paperback
Parallel edition
Part
Partial bibliography
Pear Tree Press
Penny-dreadful
Period bibliography
Periodical bibliography
Phonetic writing
Phylactery
Pi
Pictography
Plates volume
Pocket edition
Pointillé
Polaire
Popular copyrights
Portolan
Post-dated
Preliminaries

Stationarii
Strawberry Hill Press
Stub
Study score
Stylus, style
Subject bibliography
Subject series
Supposed author
Suppressed
Surname
Syllabic writing
Syncopism
Systematic bibliography
Table book
Tablet
Tally
Telonism
Tetraevangelium
Title leaf
Title-page title
Titlonym
Topical bibliography
Trade binding
Trade catalogue
Traditional format
Type facsimile

Type flowers
Type ornaments
Unbound
Uncial
Unexpurgated edition
Uniform title
Unit bibliography
Universal bibliography
Unlettered
Unopened
Unpaged
Unsigned
V.P.
Variant
Verso
Vinegar bible
Volume
Volumen
Vulgate
Walter Press
Wrap-around gathering
Xeroxed book
Xylograph
Xylographica
Yellowback
Zoomorphic initial

BOOK ACQUISITION AND PROCESSING

Accession
Accession date
Accession number
Accession order
Accession stamp
Accessions
Accessions register
Accessions section
Acquisition
Acquisition department

Acquisition record
Acquisition work
Acquisitions officer
Added copies
Added edition
Addition
Agent
Alphabet mark
Antiquarian bookseller
As issued

As new
Author mark
Autograph
Auxiliary number
Back order
Bibliographic information
Bill book
Biscoe time numbers
Board label
Book card
Book coupon
Book number
Book plate
Book pocket
Book processing center
Book selection
Book stamp
Call number
Carding
Cataloguing department
Central shelf list
Certificate of issue
Check list
Claim
Class mark
Code mark
Consideration file
Continuation list
Continuation order
Continuation record
Continuous processing
Co-operative purchasing
Copy number
Cutter author marks
Cutter-Sanborn three-figure table
Dead file
Desiderata
Destination slips
Discard
Donation record
Donor's list

Drop ship
Duplicate
Editions file
Ex-library copy
Ex libris
Firm order
Follow-up file
Gift card
Invoice
Jobber
Kirkus Service
Laminated
Lettering
Library stamp
List, Publisher's
Loose leaf service
Markers
Marking
Merrill alphabeting numbers
Olin book number
On approval
Order card
Order department
Order information
Order librarian
Order section
Out of print
Out of stock
Perforating stamp
Plasticising
Plating
Pocket
Pre-library bound
Press mark
Process record
Process slip
Process stamp
Processing
Processing department
Pro-forma invoice
Project LEER

Replacement
Review copy
Running number
Scandia Plan
Searching
Second-hand book
Selection section
Serial record
Serial section
Serial service
Shelf number
Shorts

Size letters
Standard book number
Standing order
Stock editor
Technical services
Technical services department
Time numbers
Trade list
Unesco coupons
Wants list
Work card
Work mark

BOOK PRODUCTION

Abridged edition
Addendum
Advanced copy
All rights reserved
Analytical index
Antonymous catchwords
Apparatus criticus
Appendix
Art work
Author-publisher
Authorized edition
Author's copies
Author's edition
Author's rights
Auxiliary publication
Back list
Back matter
Back page
Backlining
Backlist
Backs
Berne Convention
Berne Copyright Union
Bi-annual

Bibliogenesis
Bibliogony
Bibliopoesy
Bi-monthly
Blind page
Blurb
Body of the book
Bom proof
Book band
Book club
Book crafts
Book jacket
Book production
Book sizes
Book trade
Booklet
Bottom edge
Boxed
Broad
Building-in machine
Bulk
Butting
Cameragraph
Caption title

Fly leaf
Fly-sheet
Fold symbol
Folded leaf
Folding plate
Foldings
Foliated
Folio
Folio edition
Foot
Footnote
Format
Fortnightly
Forty-eightmo
Free sheet
French fold
Frontispiece
Gatefold
General title
Guard sheet
Gutter
Habitationsschriften
Half monthly
Half see safe
Half-title
Handbook
Hardback
Head and tail
Hinged
Hinged and jointed plates
Home library
Hooked on own guard
Hors texte
Import
Impression
Imprimatur
Imprint
In quires
In sheets
In the press
In the trade

Index
Index tab
Indian Bible
Instalment
Interleaving
Introduction
Issue
Jacket band
Keepsake
Label title-page
Large paper copy
Layout
Leaderette
Leaders
Leaflet
Legal deposit
Legend
Lettering on the spine
Library
Library edition
Limitation notice
Limited edition
Limp cloth
Limp covers
Linked books
Linson
List of contents
List of illustrations
List price
List, Publisher's
Livres vignettes
Long
Long page
Lower edge
Magazine
Make-up copy
Map endpapers
Margin
Marking
Master card
Masthead

Publisher's catalogue
Publisher's cloth
Publisher's cover
Publisher's list
Publisher's reader
Publisher's series
Puff
Pull-case
Quarterly
Quire
Recension
Recto
Reference marks
Register
Re-issue
Remainders
Reprint
Reprint series
Reprinted article
Republication
Re-set edition
Reverse cover
Review
Review copy
Revised edition
Rights
Rough edges
Rounding
Royalty
Run-on chapters
Runners
Sample book
Sample pages
School edition
Second half-title
Section
See safe
Select list of references
Self-cover
Self-ends
Self-wrapper

Semi-annual
Semi-weekly
Separate
Separation negatives
Sequel
Sequence of signs
Serial
Serial number
Serial rights
Serial service
Series
Series number
Series statement
Service basis
Set
Shape
Shaved
Sheet stock
Short page
Side
Sigla
Signature mark
Sinkage
Size copy
Slick
Slip case
Small paper copy
Smashing machine
Smyrna morocco
Spacing
Special edition
Special number
Spine
Spine title
Sponsor
Spread
Square
Square up
Stab marks
Standard edition
Standard work

Star signature
Stationarii
Stationers' Company
Stockholding bookseller
Strap binder
Stubb
Subject series
Subscribers' edition
Subscription edition
Subscription price
Subsidiaries
Subsidiary rights
Sub-title
Supplement
Suppressed
Syndics
Tail
Tail ornament
Tall copy
Teacher's book
Technical journal
Text
Thirty-twomo
Three-decker
Throw out
Tipped in
Tissue papers
Tissued plate
Title leaf
Title sheet
Top margin
Trade binding
Trade book
Trade list
Trade paper
Trade terms

Translation rights
Trial binding
Trial issue
Trilogy
Turn-in
Two-up
Two-way paging
Type area
Type ornaments
Type page
Typescript
Ulverscroft Series
Unauthorised edition
Uncut
Uneven pages
Unexpurgated edition
Ungathered
Uniform title
Unopened
Untrimmed page size
Van Gelder paper
Vanity publishers
Variorum edition
Varnishing
Verso
Volume
Whole number
Wide
Wire stabbing
With the grain
Wooden boards
Xerography
Xeroradiography
Xeroxed book
Zincograph

BOOKBINDING

Acanthus
Agate
Ajouré binding
Alaska seal
Aldine leaves
Aldine style
All along
All-over style
'All through'
American Russia
Animals in foliage panel
Antique
Antique tooling
Arabesque
Armarian
Armenian bole
Armorial binding
Arms block
Art vellum
Assembling
Attaching
Author's binding
Azure tooling
Azured tool
Back board
Back cornering
Back lining
Back mark
Back title
Backed
Backing
Backing boards
Backing machine
Backless binding
Bands
Basil
Bedford bindings
Bench press
Bevelled boards

Bibliopegic
Bibliopegy
Bibliophegus
Bibliophile binding
Bibliophile edition
Bind in
Binder
Binder's brass
Binder's dies
Binder's ticket
Binder's title
Binder's waste
Bindery
Binding
Binding edge
Binding from sheets
Binding record
Binding variations
Black step
Blank book
Blank cover
Blank leaves
Blanking
Bled
Bleed
Blind
Blind-blocked
Blind stamping
Blinded-in
Block
Blocking
Blocking foil
Blocking press
Boards
Bolt
Book cloth
Book decoration
Book press
Bookbinder

Diaper
Diced
Divinity calf
Divinity circuit
Doublure
Drawer handle
Ducali bindings
Dummy bands
Dutch leaf
Ecrasé leather
Edge decoration
Edge-rolled
Edges
Edition bindery
Edition binding
Electric stylus
Elephant folio
Embossed
Embossing press
Embroidered binding
End leaf
Endpaper
Established
Etruscan style
Even page
Extra binder
Extra binding
Fabric binding
Fabrikoid
Fabrolee
Facsimile binding
Fan
Fanfare style
Feather ornament
Feathering
Featherwork
Fern-tip
Fillet
Fine paper copy
Finish
Finisher

Finishing
First lining
Flat back
Flat stitched
Flat stitching
Fleur-de-lis lozenge
Fleuron
Flexible binding
Flexible sewing
Floret
Flower-headed rivet
Flush binding
Flush boards
Flush trim
Fly sheet
Foil
Folded leaf
Folding machine
Foldings
Foliaged staff
Fore-edge
Fore-edge title
Forel binding
Format
Forwarding
Frame
Free
Free endpaper
French joint
French sewing
Fret
Fringed foliage ornament
Front board
Full binding
Full bound
Full-gilt
Gascon
Gatefold
Gathering
Gauffered edges
Gauffering

Gift binding
Giggering
Gilt edges
Gilt extra
Gilt in the round
Gilt in the square
Gilt on the rough
Gilt top
Girdle book
Glaire
Glazed morocco
Glueing off
Goatskin
Gold
Gold cushion
Gold knife
Gold stamped
Gouge
Grained leather
Graining
Greek fashion
Grid
Grolieresque
Grooves
Growing flower
Guard
Guarding
Guillotine
Gutter
Half bands
Half cloth
Half leather
Half-stamp
Hand sewing
Hand stamp
Hard bound
Harleian style
Hatching
Head
Head title
Headband

Headcap
Heraldic cresting
Hinge
Hinged
Hinged and jointed plates
Holing
Hollow
Hollow back
Hooked on own guard
Hotmelt
Illuminated binding
Imbrication
Imitation binding
Imitation leather
Imperfections
Impression
Imprint
In boards
Independents
Inlaid
Inlay
Inlaying
Inset
Integration
Interlacing
Intersecting frame
Irish style
Jaconet
Jansenist style
Joint
Jute boards
Kerfs
Kettle stitch
Knotwork
Label
Lacing-in
Lambskin
Laminated
Lamination
Landscape binding
Lattice stamp

Law calf
Le Gascon style
Leaf
Leather
Leather bound
Leather joints
Leathercloth
Leatherette
Lemonnier style
Lettering on the spine
Lettering piece
Levant
Library binding
Library corner
Limp binding
Limp cloth
Limp leather
Lined
Linen
Linen-grained
Lining
Lining paper
Linson
Loose
Loose leaf binding
Lozenge
Lumbecking
Lyonese (Lyonnaise) style
Maioli style
Manière criblée
Marbled edges
Marbling
Marbling under gilt
Marking up
Mearne style
Mechanical binding
Merrythought
Michel style
Millboard
Misbound
Misleading title

Mistletoe tool
Mitred
Mitred corner
Morocco
Mosaic
Mottled calf
Mudejar bindings
Mull
Network
Niger morocco
Onlay
Original binding
Outsert
Ovals, In
Oversewing
Oxford corners
Oxford hollow
P-slip
Padding
Padeloup style
Pallet
Pamphlet binding
Pamphlet volume
Pamphlet-style library binding
Panel
Panel back
Paper-bound
Paper covered
Paste-down
Paste-grain
Pasteboard
Pasting down
Pattern board
Pattern rubbing
Payne style
Peacock role
Perfect
Persian morocco
Pigskin
Pin seal
Plaquette

Singer sewing
Sittibus
Skiver
Skiver label
Slip case
Slips
Smashing machine
Smyth sewing
Solid gilt
Spanish calf
Speckled sand edge
Spine
Spiral binding
Split boards
Split leather
Sprinkled edges
Square
Square corner
Squares
Stab marks
Stabbing
Stained edges
Stained label
Standing press
Stapled
Stippled edges
Stitching
Straight-grain leather
Straight-grain morocco
Strapwork
Strawboard
Style sheet
Sunk bands
t.e.g.
Tail cap
Tailband
Take down
Tapes
Ternion
Textile binding

Thames board
Thermoplastic binding
Thread stitched
Three-quarter leather
Thumb index
Tied down
Ties
Tight back
Tipping machine
Title piece
Title sheet
Tooled edges
Tooling
Top edges gilt
Tory style
Trade binding
Transparent vellum
Tree calf
Trimmed
Triple lining
True anonyma
Turn-in
Twisted pineapples
Two sheets on
Tying-up
Uncut
Unopened
Vellum
Visible cloth joint
Volute
Wave border
Whip-stitching
White edges
Whole bound
Wire sewing
Wire stabbing
Wire stitched
Wooden boards
Zinco

CATALOGUING AND INDEXING

A5 size
A7 library cards
Abbreviated card
Abbreviated catalogue entry
Abridged edition
Acting edition
Adaptation
Adapter
Add-to-cards work
Added edition
Added entry
Added title entry
Adequate description, Principle of
Aerial map
All published
Allonym
Allusion book
Almanac
Alphabetic subject catalogue
Alphabetical arrangement
Alphabetical catalogue
Alphabetico-classed catalogue
Alphabetico-direct catalogue
Alphabetico-specific subject cata-
logue
Alphabetization
Alpha-numerico indexing
Alternative title
Ambiguous title
Analects
Analysis
Analytical cataloguing
Analytical entry
And others
Anepigraphon
Anglo-American code
Annal
Annotate
Annotation

Annotating
Annual
Anonym
Anonymous
Anonymous classic
Anonymous entry
Ante-dated
Anthology
Apostil
Apocryphal
Apograph
Appraisal
Approach term
Aristronym
Arranger
Artistic manuscript
Artistic map
Ascetonym
Association book
Asterism
Astronomical map
Asyndetic
Atlas
Atlas folio
Attributed author
Author
Author affiliation
Author card
Author catalogue
Author entry
Author heading
Author index
Author mark
Author order
Author statement
Author style
Author table
Author-title added entry
Author-title index

Authority card
Authority entry
Authority list
Autograph
Autographed edition
Automatic indexing
Autonym
Auxiliary number
Auxiliary publication
Average slope map
Back
Back page
Backslide
Berghoeffer system
Bias phase
Bibliographical description
Bibliographical note
Bibliographical unit
Bibliotheca
Biographee entry
Birth and death date
Biscoe time numbers
Bishop's rules
'Black' headings
Blind index
Blind reference
Block book
Body of the entry
Bonnange card catalogue tray
Book catalogue
Book number
Book of hours
Book sizes
Bound with
Boxed
Brackets
Brief cataloguing
Broadsheet
Broadside
Brochure
Cadastral map

Cadenza
Call number
Capitalization
Card
Card cabinet
Card catalogue
Card drawer
Card index
Card number
Card tray
Cardmaster
Cartogram
Cartographer entry
Cartouche
Cartouche title
Catalogue
Catalogue card
Catalogue code
Catalogue drawer
Catalogue raisonné
Cataloguer
Cataloguing
Cataloguing department
Cataloguing in source
Cataloguing, Principles of
Catchword entry
Catchword title
Catena
Ceased publication
Central catalogue
Centralized cataloguing
Chain indexing
Chain procedure
Changed name
Changed title
Chapbook
Chart
Check marks
Chorochromatic map
Chorographic map
Choropleth map

Curves
Cutter author marks
Cutter-Sanborn three-figure table
D.S.
Dash entry
Date of issue
Date of publication
Decet
Dedication copy
Dedication date
Definitive edition
Demonym
Demopleth map
Departmental catalogue
Dependent work
Depository catalogue
Descriptive cataloguing
Diagram
Dictionary catalogue
Disc number
Dissertation, Academic
Divided catalogue
Document
Document catalogue
Dot map
Double authorship
Double entry
Double faced catalogue cabinet
Double leaves
Double titlepage
Downward reference
Duplicate paging
Duplicate title
Dynamic map
Edited
Edition
Edition statement
Editor
Editor reference
Engraved title-page
Entry

Entry-a-line index
Entry word
Epithet
Epitome
Essay periodical
Evaluation
Even page
Exact size
Explanatory guide cards
Expurgated edition
Extension card
Extra-illustrated
Facsimile
Facsimile catalogue
False date
Fasciculus
Featuring
Festschrift
Fictitious imprint
Figured bass
Filing
Filing-cars
Filing chair
Filing code
Filing medium
Filing title
First edition
First impression
First indention
First name
First printing
First vertical
First word entry
Floruit
Flow-line map
Folded leaf
Folding plate
Foliated
Foliation
Folio
Folio edition

Main subject
Main title
Main title-page
Manuscript catalogue
Map
Map projection
Master card
Mechanized indexing
Medium
Medium catalogue
Memorial volume
Merrill alphabeting numbers
Modification
Monograph
Multiple approach, Principle of
Multiple entry
Musical description
Musical work
Name authority file
Name catalogue
Name entry
Name index
Name reference
Narrow
National catalogue
Neutrality
New-book card
New-book number
New edition
Nickname
Nickname index
Ninety-one rules
No date
No more published
Nonet
Non-thesis edition
Note
Nothing before something
Number
Numbered entry
Oblong

Official catalogue
Official gazette
Official name
Official publication
Official title
Olin book number
Omission marks
One shot
Open entry
Open score
Orchestral music
Original binding
Oustinoff system
P.
Page catalogue
Pagination
Pamphlet
Panoramic catalogue
Paragraph indention
Parallel translation
Paraphrase
Parentheses
Part
Partial contents note
Partial title
Partial title entry
Period division
Personal catalogue
Personal name entry
Personal subject
Phonograph
Phonorecord
Phonoroll
Phrase pseudonym
Piano reduction
Placard catalogue
Place of printing
Place of publication
Plan
Plate
Polygraphic

24

Single entry
Size
Size letters
Size notation
Size rule
Skeleton catalogue card
SLIC index
Slip
Sobriquet
Society
Society publication
Special edition
Special number
Special title-page
Specific cross reference
Specific entry, Principle of
Specific reference
Spine title
Split catalogue
Sponsor
Square brackets
Standard size card
Standard title
Star map
Strip cartoon
Study score
Sub-entry
Sub-heading
Subject authority card
Subject authority file
Subject card
Subject catalogue
Subject cataloguing
Subject entry
Subject heading
Subject heading language
Subject index entry
Subject reference
Subject series
Subject-style
Subject-word entry

Subsidiaries
Substitution generic
Sub-title
Supplement
Supplied title
Supposed author
Supposititious author
Surname
Syncopism
Syndetic
Syndetic catalogue
Systematic auxiliary schedules
Systematic catalogue
Systematic collateral research
Systematic file
Tabbed
Technical report
Telonism
Telereference
Tellers
Temporary card
Term paper
Thematic catalogue
Third indention
Three dots
Throw out
Time numbers
Title
Title-a-line-catalogue
Title card
Title catalogue
Title entry
Title leaf
Title of honour
Title-page
Title-page title
Titlonym
Topographical catalogue
Town plan
Tracing
Transactions

Translation
Transliteration
Transposing instrument
Travelling card
Tray label
Trilogy
Type A catalogue entry
Type C catalogue entry
Type F catalogue entry
Type facsimile
Type M catalogue entry
Type T catalogue entry
Uniform heading
Uniform title
Union catalogue
Union finding list
Union list

Unique entry, Principle of
Unit card
Unit entry
Unlettered
Unpaged
Upward reference
v.p.
Variorum
Various dates
Vatican code
Version
Verso
Vocal music
Volume
Volume number
Wanting
Work
Wrap-around-gathering

CLASSIFICATION

Abridged Decimal Classification
Abstraction
Addition
Adjustable classification
Alphabetical collateral search
Alphabetical device
Alternative locations
Analet
Analysis
Analytical method
Analytico-synthetic classification
Anterior numerical classes
Anteriorizing value
Array
Arrester
Artificial classification
Associated book

Auto-bias device
Auxiliary schedules and tables
Auxiliary tables
Baconian classification
Base of a notation
Basic analysis
Bias phase
Bibliographic Classification
Bibliographical classification
Bibliographing
Bibliography
Bibliology
Bibliothecal classification
Bifurcate classification
Bifurcation
Binomial
Book classification

Book number
Branching classification
Broad classification
Brown Classification
British Catalogue of Music Classification
Brussels Expansion
C.D. System
Casual mnemonics
Categorical tables
Category
Centesimal device
Chain
Chain index
Chain indexing
Chain procedure
Characteristic
Characteristic of a classification
Cheltenham Classification
Chronological device
Circular brackets
Citation order
Class
Class letter
Class list
Class mark
Class number
Classer
Classic device
Classical author
Classification code
Classification Decimale Universelle
Classification for Social Sciences
Classification of library science
Classification Research Group
Classification Research Study Group
Classification schedule
Classification scheme
Classification Scheme of Agricultural Science

Classification system
Classificationist
Classified catalogue
Classified library
Classified order
Classifier
Classify
Classifying
Classing
Close classification
Cock
Coding
Cole size card
Collection number
Collocation
Colon
Colon Classification
Columnar
Common isolates
Common subdivisions
Connotation
Complex subject
Compound class
Compound subject
Co-extensiveness
Co-ordinate classes
Co-ordination of terms
Correlation of properties
Cranfield Classification for Aeronautics and Allied Subjects
Critical classification
Cross classification
Decimal Classification
Decimal division
Decimal number
Decimal notation
Decreasing concreteness, Principle of
Definition
Denudation
Depth classification

Knowledge classification
Language number
Language subdivision
Library of Congress Classification
Likeness
Literary warrent
Literature review
Local list
Logical notation
Macro-thought
Main class
Main subject
Mechanization
Micro-thought
Mixed notation
Mnemonic characteristic
Mnemonics
Modification
Modulation of terms
Multi-dimensional classification
Natural classification
Nomenclature
Notation
Occupational Safety and Health Scheme
Octave device
One place theory
Operators
Osmosis, Method of
Oxford Decimal System
P.E. notes
PMEST Formula
Packet device
Packet notation
Parallel classification
Pedestrian work
Period division
Phase
Phonic length
Planes
Porphyry, Tree of

Predicables, Five
Preferred order
Pre-natal classification
Principles of classification
Qualification
Qualified list
Qualifier
Ramean Tree
Reader-interest classification
Regnal numbers
Relation marks
Relative classification
Relative index
Relative location
Retro-active notation
Rigid classification
Rotated entry
Rotated index
Rotational indexing
S.D. Classification
SfB
Sacred work
Schedule
Scheme of classification
Section
Sector device
Selective classification
Sequence of signs
Serial classification
Siso
Special auxiliary schedules of limited applicability
Special classification
Species
Specific classing
Specific differences
Specific index
Starter
Structural notation
Subaltern genera
Sub-division

ILLUSTRATIONS

Credit line
Cut
Cut line
Daguerrotype
Dampers
Deep etching
Del., delt.
Desensitization
Direct half-tone
Direct-image plate
Dotting wheels
Double plate
Dragon's blood
Drypoint etching
Duotype
Duplex half-tone
Electronic photo-engraving
Engraver's proofs
Engraving
Enlargement
Etching
fecit
Ferrotype
Figure
Flat copy
Flat proof
Florentine woodcuts
Gelatine print
Glossy print
Graver
Gravure
Ground
Gumming up
Half-tone
Half-tone paper
Half-tone screens
Heliograph
Heliography
Heliogravure
Highlight
Iconography

Image
India proof
Intaglio
Japanese paper
Klischograph
Legend
Lettered proof
Levigation
Levigator
Lichtdruck
Line
Line block
Line drawing
Line engraving
Linocut
Linoleum block
Linoleum drypoint
Litho crayon
Lithograph
Lithography
Lithogravure
Lithotint
Metallography
Mezzotint
Miniature
Monochrome
Mordant
Mounted plate
Offset lithography
Oleograph
Oleography
Open-letter proof
Original
Pellet's process
Photo-engraving
Photogelatine process
Photogravure
Photo-lithography
Photomontage
Phototype
Photo-zincography

Planographic process
Plastocowell
Plate mark
Pochoir
Powder
Print
Print state
Process engraving
Proof before letters
Punch engraving
Relief printing
Reproduction proofs
Resist
Retouching
Rotogravure
Scraperboard
Screen
sculpt
Separation negatives

Silhouette
Soft-ground etching
State
Stigmatypy
Stipple
Stone engraving
Stopping out
Two-colour half-tones
Van Gelder paper
Vignette
Wash drawing
Whatman paper
Wood block
Wood engraving
Woodcut
Wrap arounds
Xylography
Xylotype
Zincograph

INFORMATION RETRIEVAL

Abstract
Abstracting service
Access
Address
Algorithmic code
Alphabetical collateral search
Alphanumeric
Alphanumerical indexing
Annotated
Aperture
Aperture card
Arbitrary code
Area search
Array
Aspect card
Aspect system
Association

Attribute
Auto-abstract
Auto-abstracting
Auto-encode
Auto-encoding
Automatic abstracting
Automatic indexing
Auxiliary publication
Auxiliary syndesis
BASIC
Batch processing
Batten cards
Batten system
Bibliography
Binary
Binary number system
BIOSIS

24*

Bit
Block indexing
Bound
Brisch-Vistem System
Browsability
Browse
Bricket
Byte
Camera card
Card stock
Cardatype
Catchword index
Centre for Documentation and
  Communication
Chain index
Character recognition
Checkout routine
Chip
Cipher
Code
Code language
Coded tape
Codeless scanning
Coding
Collate
COMAC
Combination coding
Command Retrieval Information
  System
Composite subject
Compresence
Concept
Concept co-ordination
Concept indexing
Concordance
Conjunctive
Controlled indexing
Conversion
Co-ordinate
Co-ordinate indexing
Correlation

Correlative index
CRAM
CRIS
CROSS
Data
Data processing
Data storage and retrieval system
Deck
Decklet
Decoder
Decorative
Dequeker system
Descriptor
Descriptor file
Descriptor language
Dictionary
Digit
Direct coding
Discrete record
Dissemination of information
DOCA
Document
Document address
Document card
Document retrieval
Document retrieval system
Document store
Document system
Documentary information
Documentation
Documentation centre
Dyadic alphabet
EAM
Edge-notched cards
Edge-punched cards
EDIAC
Encode
Encoding
Enriched co-ordinate indexing
Entity
Entropy

Magnaprint
Magnavue
Magnetic tape
Manipulable text
Manipulative index
Marginal-hole punched cards
Mark-sense
MARLIS
'Master' hole
Master microfilm card
Matching
Matrix
Mechanized library
Media
Merge
Metonomy
Metron
Microcard
Microcite
Microcopy
Microfilm flow camera
Microsecond
Minicard
Minimatrix system
Minitext edition
Modifiers
Modulant
Mooers' Law
Multi-aspect indexing
Multi-dimensional classification
Multiple meaning
NLL cards
Nanosecond
Noise
Non-semantic code
Notation
Notched cards
Notion
Off-line equipment
Off-line operation
On-line equipment

On-line operation
Opaque projector
Open-ended
Operation code
Optical coincidence card
Optical stencil cards
Output
Overlay
PCMI
Pack
Parallel
Peek-a-boo
Peephole card
Permutation index
Permutation indexing
Permuted title index
Permuted title word indexing
Polysemia
Polyterms
Post
Processing
Programme
Project Intrex
Punched card
Punctuation
Punctuation symbols
Qualified heading
Radix notation
Random access storage
Rank
Rapid selector
Real time
Recall ratio
'Refer from' reference
Reference retrieval system
Relevance ratio
Retrieval
Retrieval device
Retrieval system
Role indicator
Roles

Rotated entry
Rotated index
Rotational indexing
Routine
Ruby English
SDI
SADSACT
Scan
Scan-column index
Scanning
Schedule
Scope note
Sectionalized index
Selector
Selector code
Semanteme
Semantic code
Semantic factor
Semantics
Semiotics
Serial
Serta film
Set of documents
Set of questions
Sigil
Slanted abstract
Slotted cards
Sort
Sorter
Soundex
Source language
Species
Specification
Stochastic process
Storage
Storage and retrieval
Store
Structerm
Sub-entry
Sub-index
Surname indexing

Symbol
Syndetic
Synecdoche
Syntactic indexing
Table
Tabledex index
Tabulated code
Tally
Tape
Telegraphic abstract
Term
Term card
Term entry
Termatrex system
Theme
Thesauri
Thesaurus
Time sharing
Title index
Title strip
Topic
Transformer
Unit abstract card
Unit concepts
Unit record
L'Unité
Uniterm concept co-ordination
  indexing
Uniterm index
Unitize
Unityper
Urbandoc
User relevance
Verac
*VISI*scan
Visual punched card
Vocabulary
WADEX
Walnut
Word
Word indexing

Words authority file
Zatocoding

Zator

LIBRARIES AND LIBRARY WORK IN GENERAL

Adapter
Administrative office assistant
Adolescent library
Affiliated library
Alcove mark
American Library Association
Aperture card
Armaria
Armarian
Armed Services Technical Information Agency
Associate librarian
Association library
Association of Jewish Libraries
Association of London Chief Librarians
Attention
Audit
Author order
Autograph
Back file
Back number
Basic stock
Best books
Berkshire Libraries Group
Bibliographic centre
Bibliotheca
Bibliopsychology
Bibliotherapist
Bibliotherapy
Binding book
Binding copy
Binding record
Binding slip

Birmingham and District Periodicals Interchange Scheme
Birmingham Public Libraries Works Libraries Loan Scheme
Board of library trustees
Book boxes
Book display
Book drive
Book list
Book mark
Book number
Book stock
Book talk
Book van
Bookmark list
Books, USA, Inc.
Borough auditors
Borough council
Bound volume
Box file
Bradford Scientific Technical and Commercial Services
Branch librarian
Branch library
Broken order
Bulletin
Bulletin board
Bye-laws
C-library
CADIG
Call slip
Canadian Library Association
Cancel a loan
Center for Research Libraries

Central library
Chained books
Chained library
Charge a book
Chartulary
Chief assistant
Children's Book Circle
Children's library
Chronological order
CICRIS
Circle of State Librarians
Circulating library
Clapp-Jordan formula
Class guide
Classified arrangement
Classified library
Clerical assistant
Clinical librarian
Clipping
Clippings file
Coden
Coding
Collator
College library
Commercial section
Commissioners
Committee on Library
    Co-operation
Conservative Library Association
Consolidated system
Co-operation, local
Co-opted member
Co-ordinated decentralization
Copyright library
Counter duty
County library
Curator
Current number
Currently received
Custodian
Cutting

Date label
Date stamp
Delegation of powers
Delivery station
Delivery van
Department
Department head
Departmental library
Departmentalized library
Deposit library
Depository library
Deputy librarian
Desk schedule
Differential rating
Display van
District audit
Division head
Documents depository
Duplicate
Duplicate entry
Estimates
Exchange
Exchange centre
Extension centre library
Extension work
External reader
Federal Library Committee
Field visit
Film library
Five laws of library science
Fixed location
Flat rate
Folger Shakespeare Library
Fugitive facts file
Gaylord electric automatic charging
    machine
General library
Gramophone library
HALDIS
HATRICS
Hawnt Report

HILC
Holdings
Home bindery
Hospital library
Huntington Library
Information clearing house
Information centre
Information desk
Information file
Information officer
Information retrieval
Information scientist
Information service
Information work
Institute for Library Research
Instituto Brasileño de Bibliografía
  e Documentaçao
Interavailability of tickets
Interests record
Interlending
Inter-library loan
Intermediate library
Intern
Interne
International Copyright Act 1886
International Documentation
  Centre
Inter-Regional Subject Coverage
  Scheme
Joint board
Joint committee
Joint Fiction Reserve
Junior assistant
Junior librarian
LADSIRLAC
Laminated
Lamination
Ledger charging
Legal deposit
Lending department
Liability slip

Liaison officer
Librarian-in-charge
Library administration
Library authority
Library binding
Library commission
Library committee
Library consultant
Library council
Library economy
Library extension
Library hand
Library materials
Library organisation
Library practice
Library rate
Library Research Center
Library school
Library science
Library sign
Library ticket
Limited Editions Club
LINOSCO
Loan
Loan collection
Loan fee
Loan period
Loan sanction
Local collection
London Boroughs Committee
Loose
LULOP
Manuscript librarian
Map file
MARLF
Mending
METRO
MISLIC
Mobile librarian
Multicounty library
Municipal audit

Municipal library
NTBL
NANTIS
National library
NELL
NELTAS
Newberry Library
Non-fiction
Outguide
Outlier library
Outside source
Oversize book
Ownership mark
Panizzi Club
Parallel arrangement
Parry Report
Patent file
Pattern
Pencil dater
Picture file
Pierpoint Morgan Library
Pocket
Press cutting
Press mark
Print room
Prison library
Private mark
Procedure manual
Process assistant
Processing department
Provincial Joint Fiction Reserve
Public library
Quick-reference books
Ranfurly Libraries
Rate, Library
Rating authority
Reader
Readers' adviser
Reader's card
Reader's register
Reader's ticket

Reading circle
Reading list
Reading shelves
Recommending committee
Reference assistant
Reference books
Reference centre
Reference collection
Reference department
Reference librarian
Reference library
Reference material
Reference work
Regional bibliographic centre
Regional bureaux
Regional catalogue
Registration card
Registration department
Relative location
Rental fee
Replacement
Reporting committee
Routing
Routing slip
Rub
Rules and regulations
SAALIC
Scandia Plan
SCANDOC
Scheme
School district library
School library
School library supervisor
SCOLLUL
SCOLMA
SCONUL
SCOTAPLL
Scriptorium
Section
Selection section
Selective charging

Selective routing
Senior assistant
Shelving
SINTO
Slips
Snag file
Sorority library
Source index
Special collection
Special librarianship
Staff manual
Standards
Standing committees
Standing Conference of Commercial and Technical Library Co-operation Services
State document centre
State library
State Library Administrative Agency
State library agency
Statutory committees
Stocktaking
Storage centre
Story hour
Straightening
Sub-professional assistant
Subject arrangement
Subject department
Subject specialization
Subscriber
Subscription library
Suggestion card
Superintendent of branches
Superintendent of the reading room
Suspension file
Suspension shelving

Swinging bookcase
Tear sheet
Telereference
Tickler system
TIDU
Time numbers
Time-sheet
Topic guide
Transaction card
Transaction card charging
Transaction room
Transfer box
Transfer file
Travelling library
Tutor librarian
Union finding list
University library
Urban district council
USBE
Vertical file
Visible index
Vollans Report
Volume
WALIC
WANDPETLS
Weeding
West German scheme
Widener Library
Wilson cards
Withdrawal
Withdrawals register
Work book
Work responsibility schedule
YEWTIC
Yorkshire Cobook Group of Libraries
Z-39

LIBRARY SERVICES, BUILDINGS, AND EQUIPMENT

Adjustable periodicals list
Adjustable shelf
Adjustable shelving
Adult department
Aisle
Album
Album letter (number)
Album title
Alcove
Analytical booklet
Ansaphone
Application form
Area
Area headquarters
Area librarian
Area of service
Arrangement
Armaria
Audio charging
Audio visual area
Audio visual materials
Barrier
Bay
Bay guide
Bibliographic centre
Bibliotekstjänst
Biblio-train
Binding department
Black list
Book barrow
Book bin
Book boat
Book card
Book conveyor
Book fund
Book lift
Book rack
Book railbus
Book rest

Book shrine
Book slide
Book stack
Book stand
Book store
Book support
Book tray
Book trough
Book truck
Book van
Bookamatic
Bookcase
Booketeria
Bookmobile
Borrower's number
Borrowers' register
Borrower's ticket
Box file
Box library
Bracket shelf
Bracket shelving
Branch
Branch library
Browne book charging system
Browsing room
Bulletin board
Butterfly plan
Cantilever shelving
Caravan libraries
Card charging
Card-operated typewriter
Carrel
Cart
Cataloguing department
Catchment area
Cell
Cello-clips
Central library
Centralized registration

Centre
Charge
Charging machine
Charging methods
Charging tray
Chartulary
Cheque book charging method
Children's library
Circulating library
Circulation
Circulation department
Circulation desk
Circulation record
Circulation statistics
Circulation work
Class library
Classroom Collection
Closed access
College library
Commercial library
Commercial section
Community library
Compact storage
Compactus
Compartment
Continuous-form loan records
Contract services
Conveyor belt
Co-operative system
Copycat
County district
County library
County regional branch
County schools library
Cross reference sheet
Cubook
Curriculum materials center
Cut corner pamphlet file
D-library
Date due
Date guide

Date label
Deck
Defaulter
Delayed discharging
Delivery hall
Delivery room
Delivery station
Demco self-charging system
Department
Departmental library
Deposit library
Depositors
Depository library
Detroit self-charging system
Dickman charging system
Discharging books
Discharging counter
Discobus
Display stand
Display van
District
District central library
District librarian
District library
Division library
Double-faced shelf
Double-sided stack
Draw-out shelves
Duplicate pay collection
Entrance counter
Exhibition case
Exhibition van
Exit counter
Extension agencies
Extension centre library
Face
Feltboard
Field work
File
Fine
Fine computor

Fixed-function planning
Fixed shelf
Floating library
Floor duty
Folder
Follow-up notices
Full-time branch library
Gramophone library
Gross square footage
Guarantee
Guarantor
Holiday issue
Home bindery
Identification card
Illustrations collection
Indicator
Infectious diseases
Instructional materials centre
Interlibrary reference service
Intermediate library
Island stack
Islington charging system
Issue guides
Joint report
Kinderbox
Knapp foundation
Knapp School Libraries Project
Kodagraph
Laid in
Lateral filing
Learning resources center
Lectern
Lending department
Library
Library area
Library officer
Library service
Library shelving
Library ticket
Loan department
Loan period

Local authority
Local librarian
Location index
Lundia shelving
Magazine case
Magazine rack
Magazine room
Map room
Media
Media aide
Media center
Media programme
Media specialist
Media staff
Media technician
Medical Library Assistance Act
Membership voucher
METRO
Minafile
Mobile librarian
Mobile library
Modular construction
Modular planning
Mothers' room
Motorised shelves
Multi-tier stack
Muniment room
Music library
Musikriter
NCR
Newark charging system
Newspaper rack
Newspaper stack
Newsroom
Non-resident member
Open access
Open back file
Open bar shelving
Order department
Overdue book
Overdue notice

Paisa Library Scheme
Pamphlet box
Parish library
Periodical rack
Periodical stand
Permissive committees
Photo-charger
Photo-charging
Plan cabinet
Plan file
Plowden report
Pocket card charging
Popular library
Precept
Precepting authority
Press
Princeton file
Privilege issue
Public (service) area
Punched card
Punched card charging
Quarto shelving
Rack
Radiating stacks
Range
Reading machine
Reading room
Ready reference
Realia
Recommender
Recordacall
Reference department
Reference service
Region
Regional branch
Regional headquarters
Regional librarian
Regional officer
Registration
Renewal
Renewal slip

Rental book
Re-registration
Reska shelving
Reserve card (form, slip)
Reserved book
Restricted loan
Reverse Browne
Review date
Revolving bookcase
Ribbon arrangement
Roller shelves
Rolling bookcase
Rolling press
Rotary card file
Rural district council
School libraries department
School library
School library supervisor
Scriptorium
Search room
Searcher
Section
Self-charging system
Serials department
Service point
Shelf
Shelf capacity
Shelf department
Shelf dummy
Shelf guide
Shelf height
Shelf list
Shelf support
Shelving
Shipping room
Shop library
Skandex shelving
Sliding shelves
Slip
Slipping books
Slotted shelving

Snag
Special collection
Special issue
Special library
Specification
Spectrum
Spirit duplicator
Spur shelving
Stack
Staff enclosure
Staff room
Stalls
Standard stack
Start
State document centre
Storage area
Storage shelving
Stor-mor shelving
Street index
Strip index
Students' library
Students' section
Study issue
Sub-branch
Subject department
Subject guide
Subscription library

Supplementary ticket
System media centre
Teacher-librarian
Technical library
Tel-stor
Temporary branch
Tier
Tier guide
Tilted shelves
Token charging
Tonks fittings
Transaction room
Transfer box
Transfer file
Travelling library
Treadle latches
Union finding list
University library
Urban library
VSC formula
Vertical filing cabinet
Vertical integration
Voluntary centre
Wall shelving
Wicket
Work room
Work space

PALAEOGRAPHY AND ARCHIVES

Acrophony
Archive
Archivist
Artistic manuscript
Autography
Bailiff
Beneventan handwriting
Bill
Bill of Middlesex

Bolognese letter
Brief
Bull
Calendar
Calligraphy
Catchword
Chancery
Charter
Charter Roll

Chartulary
Close roll
Colophon
Court baron
Court hand
Court leet
Court roll
Curia Regis
Cursive
Diplomatic
Documents
Dorse
Enrolled account
Enrolment
Explicit
Feet of fine
Flourish
Fonds
Frankpledge
Free hand
Germanic handwriting
Glosses
Gothic minuscule
Grigg Committee
Half uncial
Historiated initial
Hundred rolls
Illuminated initial
Incipit
Indenture
Joined hand
Judicial writ
Later cursive
Lemma
Letters close
Letters patent
Liberate roll
Librarii
Literary manuscript
Locus sigilli
Majuscule

Manorial courts
Marginalia
Membrane
Miniature
Minim
Ministers' accounts
Minuscule
Oghamic script
Original writ
Palimpsest
Papyrology
Papyrus
Paraph
Parchment
Patent roll
Pipe roll
Plea roll
Public records
Public Records Act 1958
Quadrata
Record
Record Office
Records
Recto
Runes
Runic letters
Rustic capital
Rustica
Search room
Serif
Set hand
Sign manual
Signature
Square capitals
Stamp Acts
Starr
Steward
Storage area
Storage centre
Subinfudation
Tally

Text hand
Tithe documents
Uncial
Vellum
Verso

Visigothic handwriting
Vowel ligatures
Work area
Writ
Writing masters

PAPER AND PAPER MAKING

A4 size
A5 size
A7 library cards
Absorbency
Absorbent paper
Acid-free paper
Against the grain
Air-dried
Alfa
Antique
Antique finish
Antique laid
Art
Baryta paper
Basic weight
Bible paper
Bleach
Bleached kraft
Body paper
Boiling
Book paper
Bookbinding board
Breaker
Bristol board
Brown mechanical woodpulp
Brush coated
Bulk
Bursting strain
Cabinet
Calendar
Calendered paper

Cambridge India paper
Cameo-coated
Carbonized forms
Card stock
Cartridge paper
Cassie
Cast coated paper
Cater cornered
Cellulose
Charcoal paper
Chart paper
Chemical wood
China clay
China paper
Cloth-centred
Coated paper
Cockle
Collecting drum
Colombier
Coloured printings
Comb pattern
Conditioning
Contraries
Cotton linters
Couch roll
Countermark
Court
Cover paper
Creasing
Cross direction
Crown

Curl
Cut to register
Cylinder dried
d.c.
Dandy roll
Deckle
Deckle edge
Demy
Digester
Double
Double Crown
Dry end
Drying end
Dull-coated
Duodecimo
Duplex paper
Eggshell
Elephant
Enamel paper
Engine-sizing
English finish paper
Esparto
Extra thin paper
Fabriano paper
Featherweight paper
Felt mark
Felt side
Festoon drying
Fibres
Finish
Flatness
Flong
Fold symbol
Folio
Foolscap
Forty-eightmo
Fourdrinier machine
Furnish
Furnish layer
Glassine
Grain

Grain direction
Guillotine
Half stuff
Half-tone paper
Hand made paper
Hemi-cellulose
Hemp
Hollander
Hot-pressed
Imitation parchment
Imperial
Impressed watermark
Index board
India paper
Ingrain
Ivory board
Japanese paper
Japanese vellum
Japon vellum
Jute
Kier
Kraft paper
L sheet
Label title-page
Laid paper
Laminated
Lamination
Large post
Large royal
Leatherette
Linen faced
Linen finish
Linen paper
Lining paper
Lint
Litho papers
Loading
Loft-dried
Long
Long grain
Look-through

M.F.

M.G.

Machine coated

Machine finish

Machine glazed

Machine-made paper

Manilla paper

Marbled paper

Marbling

Mechanical wood

Medium

Mottled finish

Mould

Mould-made paper

Not

Oblong

Octavo

Octodecimo

Offset paper

One side coloured

Onion skin

Opacity

Open edge

Oxford India paper

pH value

Paper

Paper finishes

Paper sizes

Phloroglucin

Pinholes

Plan paper

Plate paper

Pott

Printings

Pulp

Pulp board

Quadrille

Quarto

Quire

Rag paper

Ramie

Rattle

Ream

Reinforced union paper

Ret

Retree

Rice paper

Right

Rough

Rough edges

Royal

Salle

Semi-chemical pulp

Semi-pulp

Seventy-twomo

Sexto

Sexto-decimo

Sheet

Shiner

Short grain

Silk paper

Sixty-fourmo

Sized paper

Sizing

Smalt

Soda pulp

Spanish

Standards

Stippling

Stock

Stuff

Substance

Sulphate pulp

Sulphite pulp

Super-calender

Super-calendered paper

Super royal

Surface sizing

T.S.

Tarred brown paper

Thirty-sixmo

Thirty-twomo

Tracing paper
Tricesimo-secundo
Trimmed
Trimmed page size
Trimmed size
Tub sizing
Twenty-mo
Twin wire paper
Two sides coloured
Unbleached paper
Union paper
Unprocessed paper
Untrimmed size
Van Gelder paper
Varnishing
Vat
Vat-sized
Vellum parchment
Verso
Vicesimo-quarto
Waterleaf
Waterleaf paper
Watermark
Watermarked paper
Web
Whatman paper
Whole stuff
Wild look-through
Willow
Wire
Wire side
With the grain
Wood pulp
Wove paper
Wrap rounds
Yankee machine

PRINTING

48-line Bible
Acrography
Addendum
Against the grain
Agate
Agate line
Albion press
Albumen process
Alcophoto
Aldine Press
Aldus
Algraphy
Alignment
All-purpose linotype
Alphabet length
Alterations
Aluminium plates
Ambrogal printing
Anopisthographic printing
Antiqua
Apostil
Arm
Arming press
Art canvas
Art work
Artype
Ascender
Ascender line
Ashendene Press
Assembling
Asterisk
Asterism
Atlas folio
Author's proof
Author's revise
Autography

Auto-lithography
b.f.
Back
Back margin
Back mark
Back up
Backs
Bad copy
Bar
Base line
Base of the type
Baskerville
Bastard type
Battered
Beard
Bearers
Bed
Bellows press
Belly
Bembo
Bevel
Biblio
Bibliographical note
Bill of type
Black
Black letter
Black step
Blind embossing
Blind P
Blind page
Block
Block printing
Block pull
Blocking out
Blueprint
Bodoni
Body
Body matter
Body type
Bold face
Bole

Bolognese letter
BOM proof
Bourgeois
Bowl
Box
Box-in
Boxhead
Boxhead ruling
Brace
Brayer
Break
Break-line
Brevier
Brilliant
Bring-up
Broad
Broken letter
Bronzing size
Buckle-folder
Butted
Butted slugs
Cameo
Canon
Cap
Cap line
Capitals
Caption
Caption title
Card front
Caret
Carriage
Case
Caslon
Cast coated paper
Cast-up
Casting box
Casting off
Catch letters
Catchline
Catchword
Centre note

Centred dot
Cerography
Cerotype
Chalk overlay
Chapel
Chapter
Chapter heading
Character
Character count
Chase
Chaucer type
Cheltenham
Chiaroscuro
Chiswick Press
Cicero
Clarendon
Clarendon Press
Clean proof
Cliché
Clogged
Close
Close matter
Close up
Closed up
Clump
Cock-up initial
Coffin
Cold composition
Cold type
Collation mark
Collecting drum
Colloplas
Colour gravure
Coloured printings
Columbian
Columbian press
Column
Combination plate
Common ruling
Compose
Composing rule

Composition
Composition fount
Compositor
Concertina fold
Condensed type
Continuous feed
Copal
Copy
Copy edit
Copy fitting
Copy holder
Copy preparation
Copy reader
Corrected proof
Correction marks
Corrigenda
Counter
Creasing
Credit line
Criblé initial
Cropper
Cross-bars
Cross direction
Cross head
Crotch
Cul de lampe
Cum privilegio
Curves
Cut
Cut-in heading
Cut-in letter
Cut line
Cut to register
Cylinder press
d.c.
Dagger
Damaged letter
Dampers
Daniel Press
Dash
Date line

Factotum
False hyphen
Falstaff
Family
Fancy type
Fat faces
Fat matter
Faulty margin
Feathering
Feed board
Feeder
Feet
Feint ruling
Fell types
Figure
Filigree
Filigree initial
Filigree letter
Filling in
Filmset
Filmsetting
Final proof
Fine-face rule
Fine screen
Finish
Flange
Flat
Flat-bed cylinder press
Flat-bed press
Flat-bed web press
Flat proof
Flat pull
Florentine woodcuts
Floret
Flourish
Flowers
Flush
Flush paragraph
Fold to paper
Fold to print
Folding guides

Folding stick
Follow copy
Footline
Footnote
Fore-edge margin
Forme
Forty-eightmo
Fotosetter
Foul case
Foul proof
Founders' type
Foundry
Foundry proof
Fount
Four-colour process
Fournier
Fournier point
Fraktur
Frame
Framed-cut
French fold
French rule
Fret
Friar
Frisket
Frontispiece
Fugitive colours
Full colour
Full measure
Full on the body
Full out
Full point
Furniture
Galley
Galley press
Garalde
Garamond
Gatefold
Gauge
Geneva Bible
Geometric

25

Interlay
Interlinear
Interlinear matter
Interlinear space
Interlinear translation
Interrogation point
Intertype
Inverted commas
Isobath
Italic
Italtype
Ivory board
Japanese paper
Jeté en moule
Joanna
Job printer
Joiner's press
Justifying
Justowriter
Keep down
Keep in
Keep out
Keep standing
Keep up
Kelmscott Press
Kern
Kerned
Kettle stitch
Key
Key plate
Keyboarding
Kill
Killing
Klischograph
Knife-folder
Lampblack
Lapidary type
Large face
Large folio
Lay edges
Layout

Laystool
Lead, To
Lead moulding
Leaded matter
Leader
Leaders
Leads
Lean-face type
Legend
Letter spacing
Letterpress
Lever press
Levigation
Levigator
Lifted matter
Ligature
Light face
Line
Line block
Line-casting machine
Lineale
Lining figures
Linofilm
Linotype
Literal
Litho papers
Lithographic press
Lithographic printing
Lithographic ribbon
Lithography
Lithogravure
Lithotint
Live matter
Locking up
Logography
Logotype
Long-bodied type
Long descender
Long page
Long primer
Lower case letters

Parallel
Parallel mark
Parallel rule
Parentheses
Patent base
Pearl
Perfect copy
Perfecter
Perfecting
Period printing
Perpetua
Photocomposition
Photogravure
Photo-lithography
Photon
Photo-offset
Photo-setting
Photo-typography
Pica
Pick up
Pie
Pin holes
Pin mark
Placard
Planography
Plantin
Plaster of Paris mould
Plate
Plate cylinder
Platen
Platen press
Pochoir
Point
Points
Power press
Press
Press à un coup
Press book
Press errors
Press number
Press proof

Press queries
Press-ready
Press-revise
Press run
Presses
Presswork
Prima
Print page
Print state
Printed
Printed as manuscript
Printed but not published
Printed matter
Printer
Printer's devil
Printing block
Printing press
Private press
Privately printed
Process block
Progressive proof
Proof
Proof corrections
Proof press
Proof reader
Proof reading
Proof sheet
Pull
Pull-case
Pulled type
Punch
Quad
Query
Quoins
Quotations
Quotes
Ranging figures
Reader
Reader for the press
Reader's proof
Reader's set

Ream
Recess printing
Recto
Red ochre
Red printing
Re-edition
Reel fed
Reference marks
Register table
Reglet
Reimposition
Reinforcing-piece
Rejects
Relief printing
Remake
Removes
Replika
Reprint
Reset
Resetting
Resist
Ret
Retouching
Rider
Rinco process
Rising type
River
Romains du roi
Roman
Roman numerals
Ronde
Rotaprint
Rotary press
Rotofoto
Rotogravure
Rub-off
Rubric
Rule
Rule border
Run
Run-around

Run on
Run out and indented
Run over
Runners
Running title
Rustic capital
Ruthven Press
S/S
Sample pages
Sans serif
Scaling
Scan plates
Schwabacher
Screamer
Screen
Screw press
Script
Second half-title
Section headline
Section mark
Section title
Sedanoise
See copy
Select list of references
Selectasine
Separation negatives
Serif
Set
Set flush
Set off
Set solid
Setting type
Shadow
Shank
Sheet-feed
Sheet work
Sheets
Sheetwise
Shell
Shooting stick
Short descender

Short page
Shorts
Shoulder
Shoulder head
Shoulder note
Show through
Side
Side bearing
Side head
Side note
Sigla
Signature
Signature and catchword line
Signature mark
Signed page
Silhouette
Silk screen
Single quotes
Sinkage
Skeleton
Slab serif
Slip sheet
Slips
Slug
Slug-casting machine
Slur
Small capitals
Small pica
Solid matter
Sort
Space
Space bands
Space lines
Space to fill
Spacing
Special sorts
Specimen pages
Split fractions
Spoiled sheets
Square capitals
Square up

Stab marks
Standing type
Stanhope press
Star signature
Starch
Stem
Stencil
Stenotype
Step and repeat machine
Stereotype
Stereotype metal
Stet
Stick
Stigmatypy
Stippling
Stock
Stone engraving
Stone proof
Stop-cylinder press
Stopping out
Store
Straight matter
Strawberry Hill Press
Streamer
Stress
Strike through
Strip in
Style manual
Style of the house
Style sheet
Super-caster
Superior figures (letters)
Swash letters
Swung dash
Tab
Table
Tabular work
Tack marks
Tail
Tail ornament
Tailed letter

Take
Taking out turns
Teletypesetting
Tellers
Text type
Thermography
Thick space
Thin space
Thirty-twomo
Three-colour process
Tied up
Tilde
Times New Roman
Tint blocks
Title-page border
Title signature
Titling
Toggle press
Top margin
Transfer
Transitional
Transitional face
Troy type
Tumbler scheme
Turned comma
Turned letter
Turned sort
Turnover
Two-colour half-tones
Two-colour process
Two-colour reproduction
Two-line
Two-revolution machine
Two-up
Tympan
Type
Type area
Type-casting machine
Type face
Type facsimile
Type flowers

Type gauge
Type height
Type-high
Type metal
Type ornaments
Type page
Type size
Typescript
Typesetter
Typesetting
Typesetting machine
Typograph
Typographer
Typographical error
Typography
Typometer
Uhertype
Underlay
Underline
Underrun
Unit spacing
Upper case letters
Upright
Variant
Venetian type
Verso
Vertical press
Vinculum
Volume signature
Walter press
Washington
Wavy line
Wax engraving
Web
Web fed
Web machine
Web perfecting press
Web press
Weight
Weight of face
Weight of type

White letter
White out
Wickersham quoins
Widow
Width
With the grain
Wood letter
Wood type
Work and tumble
Work and turn

Work off
Work up
Workard
Wrap-around gathering
Wrap rounds
Wrong fount
X-height
Xylography
Zincograph
Zincography

REPROGRAPHY

Achromatic lens
Acid resist
Aiglonne
Ammonia process
Angstrom
Aperture
Arc lamp
Archival quality
Aristo paper
Artype
Autopositive
Autopositive paper
Autotype
Autotypy
Azoflex
Back-projection reader
Balopticon
Base stock
Blocking out
Blow up
Blue-line print
Book holder
Burn-in
Burn-out
Camera microfilm
Carbro

Card to card printer
Centreing arrows
Chloride paper
Cloth print
Coating
Colour filter
Colour separation negative
Colour transparency
Contact
Contact copying
Contact photography
Contact printer
Contact printing
Continuous flow camera
Continuous printer
Continuous processing
Contrast
Convenience copy
Copier-duplicator
Copy-board
Copy-flo
Copy holder
Copying process
Copytron
Cyanography
Cybernetics

Deliquescence
Densitometer
Density
Depth of field
Desensitization
Diaphragm control
Diapositive
Diapositive stencils
Diazo
Diazotype process
Diffusion transfer
Direct coding
Direct contact copying
Direct-image film
Direct-image plate
Direct positive
Documentary reproduction
Double document
Double weight paper
Dry process
Dry silver
Dual spectrum
Duo
Duostat
Duplex
Duplicate
Dust development
Dye-line film copy
Dyflex
Edge fog
Eichner dry copy
Electrofax
Electrophotographic processes
Electrophotography
Emulsion
Enlarger-printer
Extra lightweight paper
Facsimile
Fair copying declaration
'Fair dealing'
Facsimile edition

Facsimile transmission
Ferrotype process
Film base
Film jacket
Filmac
Filmstrip
Filter
Final title strip
First reproduction microfilm
Fixing
Flat copy
Frame
Frame margin
Frame size
Front-projection reader
Generation
Glossy print
Gum arabic
Half frame
Heat copying
Hectograph process
Hectography
Heliograph
Heliographic materials
Holograph
Holography
Hypo
Identification caption
Illustrations collection
Image
Indian ink
Information area
Intermediate copy
Inverpos paper
Jacketed film.
Kalvar
Kard-a-film
Kodagraph
Laterally reversed
Leader
Ledger weight

Lensless copying
Lexicon
Line original
Lithographic ribbon
Macroform
Macrograph
Master
Master film
Medium weight paper
Microcard
Microcopy
Microdesensitometer
Microfiche
Microfilm
Microfilm flow camera
Microfilm print
Microfilm reading glass
Microfilm strip
Microform
Microlex
Micro-opaque
Micro-opaque reader
Micro-opaque type
Microphotography
Microprint
Microrecord
Microrecording
Microreproduction
Microseal
Micro-Skaner
Microslide
Microstrip
Micro-transparency
Microxerography
Miracode
Negative
Offset foil
Opaque copy
Opaque microcopy
Opaqueing
Optical copying

Optical photo-copying device
Optical printer
Original
Ozalid
Ozarapid
PCMI system
Pellets process
Permanent record film
Photochromic substance
Photoclerk
Photo-composing machine
Photocopy
Photographic papers
Photography
Photomicrograph
Photomontage
Photostat
Pin holes
Planetary camera
Player type
Pomi
Positive
Positive copy
Positive microfilm
Positive process
Print film
Process camera
Process photography
Processing
Processor-camera
Projection print
Projection printing
Pseudo-photographic photocopying
RCA 'Video File'
Rapid copying
Reader printer
Rear projection
Reducing
Reduction
Re-enlargement
Reference corner

Reference edges
Reflex copy
Remflex
Reprographic marking
Reprography
Resolution
Reversal microfilm
Reversal process
Right reading
Roll cassette
Roll microfilm
Rutherstat
S/S
Second reproduction microfilm
Sectioning
Security collection
Self positive
Semi-dry process
Sensing mark
Sensitized paper
Sequential camera
Shelf life
Short letter
Silver halide paper
Silver processes
Simplex
Single weight paper
Splice
Squabble
Stabilization
Step-and-repeat camera
Stereoscopic slide
Stereotome
Tack marks

Thermal diazo process
Thermal process
Thermic copying
Thermofax
Thermographic copy
Thermoplastic process
Thin paper
Title backing
Title space
Trailer
Transfer process
Translucent copy
Translucent screen
Transmission copying
Transmission print
Transmission printing
Transparency
Transpose
Tripper
True sided
Twin bath stabilization
Two-component diazotype
    materials
Ultra-microfiche
Ultra thin paper
Vendor-Specs-Microfile
Verifax
Vesicular film
Washing
White print
Xeroduplicating
Xerox
Xeroxed book

SPECIAL LIBRARIANSHIP

Academic libraries
Administrative council

Advertisement file
Alphabetical collateral search

Attention

Author affiliation

Bank letter

Clearing house of information

Company file

Competitor file

Confidential file

Data compilation

Dormitory library

Facsimile catalogue

Finding unit

Fraternity library

Government library

In-Service training

Industrial libraries

Information bureau

Information centre

Information department

Information desk

Information librarian

Information library

Information officer

Information resource

Information retrieval

Information scientist

Information service

Information work

Interests record

Job press

Jobfile

Kalvar

Kard-a-film

Law of scattering

Library keys

Literature search

Literature survey

Map file

Market letter

Media file

Neutrality

News bulletin

Newspaper library

Nickname index

Oasis

Official gazette

Organization file

Outguide

Outside source

Performance index

Procedure manual

Processing

Request form

Research book

Research librarian

Research service

Scan

SCONUL

Search record

Source index

Special librarian

Special library

Tickler System

Trade journal

Appendix 3

Summary of the Public Libraries and Museums Act 1964

THIS Act (in full – An Act to place the public library service provided by local authorities in England and Wales under the superintendance of the Secretary of State, to make new provision for regulating and improving that service and as to the provision and maintenance of museums and art galleries by such authorities, and for purposes connected with the matters aforesaid) repeals all previous library acts, the Museums and Gymnasiums Act 1891, and sections of certain other acts, relating to England and Wales.

It came into force on 1 April 1965, and gives the Secretary of State the duty to superintend, and promote the improvement of, the public library service, and to secure the proper discharge by local authorities of the functions in relation to libraries conferred on them (Section 1).

The Act authorises the Secretary of State to appoint two Library Advisory Councils, one for England and one for Wales, to advise him on the provision or use of library facilities (Section 2).

England and Wales are divided into regions and a scheme made in respect of each region for the setting up of a library council for each, for facilitating co-operation between library authorities and other bodies having functions in relation to libraries, and for supervising the carrying out of requirements of the council including contributing towards its expenses (Section 3).

Councils of counties, county boroughs, London boroughs, the City of London, non-county boroughs and urban districts are library authorities providing (a) the council was a library authority before the commencement of the Act, or (b) the council has been approved by the Secretary of State under section 6(3) of this Act, which provides for the granting of library powers to non-county boroughs and urban districts with populations of not less than 40,000. Any other local authority being a library authority before 1 April 1965 ceases to be a library authority (Section 4).

Joint boards may be set up by two or more library authorities and they become the library authority in lieu of those authorities. Such boards may subsequently be dissolved under certain conditions (Section 5).

Where (a) the council of a non-county borough or an urban district was a library authority immediately before 1 April 1965 (referred to as a 'review date'), or falling ten years after that date, or any subsequent review date, and (b) the population of the borough or urban district is less than 40,000 at the review date, the Secretary of State may, after consulting the local authorities concerned, order the council to cease to be a library authority if he considers that to do so would lead to an improvement in library facilities. The power to make such an order is exercisable by statutory instrument which is subject to annulment in either House of Parliament (Section 6).

Where the council of a non-county borough or urban district was *not* a library authority immediately before the review date but the population was over 40,000, the Secretary of State may, within six months of an application by the council, and after consulting the county council (or where the county council is comprised in a joint board, the joint board), approve the council as a library authority.

The council of a non-county borough or urban district may at any time relinquish its functions as a library authority to another library authority with confirmation of the Secretary of State (Section 6).

'It shall be the duty of every library authority to provide a comprehensive and efficient library service for all persons desiring to make use thereof . . . provided that although a library authority shall have power to make facilities for the borrowing of books and other materials to any persons it shall not . . . be under a duty to make such facilities available to persons' other than residents or non-resident students or employees. A library authority shall in particular have regard to the desirability of (a) securing (by keeping adequate stocks, by arrangements with other library authorities, and by any other appropriate means) that facilities are available for borrowing, or referring to, books and other printed matter, pictures, gramophone records, films and other materials, sufficient in number, range and quality to meet the general and any special requirements of both adults and children; (b) encouraging adults and children to make full use of the library service; and (c) securing full co-operation between the persons engaged in carrying out the functions of a library authority as such and those engaged in carrying out other functions in the library area (Section 7).

No charge shall be made (other than to another library authority) for library facilities, except such an amount as may be specified by the Secretary of State, for (a) notifying a person that a reserved book or other article has become available for borrowing, or (b) in respect of failure to return a book or other article before the end of the period allowed. A charge may be made for the borrowing of any article, except that residents, non-resident employees or students shall not be charged for borrowing (a) a book, pamphlet or similar article, or (b) a reproduction made by photographic or other means of the whole or a part of any such article. A charge may be made for book catalogues or indexes, or any similar articles, where they become the property of the purchaser. A charge may be made for facilities which go beyond those ordinarily provided as part of the library service (Section 8).

A library may contribute towards the expenses of another library authority or any other person providing library facilities for the general public. The Secretary of State may make grants to any body which maintains book catalogues or indexes to which all library authorities are permitted to refer, or otherwise makes available to all library authorities facilities likely to assist them in discharging their duty to provide library services under the Act (Section 9).

If a complaint is made to the Secretary of State that any library authority has failed to carry out duties imposed on it under this Act, or the Secretary of State is of opinion that an investigation should be made as to whether any such failure has occurred, and after a local enquiry has been held into the matter he is satisfied that there has been such a failure, he may make an order directing the authority to carry out specific duties. Should a library authority fail to comply with such a direction the Secretary of State may make an order specifying the date on which the council shall cease to be a library authority, if it is a council of a non-county borough or urban district; or if the authority is a joint board, the date on which it shall be dissolved and to what authorities the library powers shall be transferred; in any other case the powers shall be transferred to the Secretary of State (Section 10).

A local authority may provide and maintain museums and art galleries providing that a local authority not being a library authority and not already maintaining a museum or art gallery shall not do so without the consent of the Secretary of State. A local authority maintaining a museum or art gallery may, with the consent of the Secretary of State, transfer same to another local authority (Section 12).

A charge may be made for admission to a museum or art gallery. A local authority being a library authority, or maintaining a museum or art gallery, may make contributions towards expenses incurred by any person (a) in providing or maintaining a museum or art gallery in any place within England and Wales, or (b) in providing advisory or other services or financial assistance for the benefit of a museum or art gallery in any such place. A local authority, other than the council of a parish or of a borough included in a rural district, maintaining a museum or art gallery, may establish a fund for the purchase of any objects for exhibition in any museum or art gallery it maintains (Sections 13 to 15).

The Secretary of State may hold an enquiry into any matter relating to the functions of a local authority under this Act (Section 16), and he may authorise any local authority being a library authority to purchase compulsorily any land which it requires for the purposes of its functions under this Act (Section 18).

A local authority may make byelaws regulating the use of facilities provided by the authority under this Act, and for the conduct of persons in premises where those facilities are provided, and the Secretary of State shall confirm them. Byelaws may include provisions enabling officers of the local authority to exclude, or remove, from premises maintained under this act, any person who contravenes the byelaws, and a copy of the byelaws must be displayed in such premises to which the public have access (Section 19).

A local authority may use premises maintained under the Act, or allow them to be used (whether in return for payment or not), for the holding of meetings and exhibitions, for the showing of films and slides, the giving of musical performances, and the holding of other events of an educational or cultural nature, and may make or authorise the making of a charge for admission (Section 20).

Expenses of a county council in respect of the public library service shall not be charged on any non-county borough or urban district outside the library area of the county council (Section 21).

The Secretary of State may, after consulting with the Council of the Isles of Scilly, make an order to provide that this Act shall apply to those Isles (Section 24).

There are three schedules for (1) superannuation and other benefits in cases of transfer, etc., (2) management of funds for purchase of exhibits, and (3) repeals.